Baseball's Pivotal Era, 1945-1951

Baseball's
Pivotal Era
1945–1951

William Marshall

THE UNIVERSITY PRESS OF KENTUCKY

Copyright © 1999 by William Marshall

Published by The University Press of Kentucky

Scholarly publisher for the Commonwealth,
serving Bellarmine College, Berea College, Centre
College of Kentucky, Eastern Kentucky University,
The Filson Club, Georgetown College, Kentucky
Historical Society, Kentucky State University,
Morehead State University, Murray State University,
Northern Kentucky University, Transylvania University,
University of Kentucky, University of Louisville,
and Western Kentucky University.

Editorial and Sales Offices: The University Press of Kentucky
663 South Limestone Street, Lexington, Kentucky 40508-4008

03 02 01 00 99   5 4 3 2

Frontispiece: Nothing symbolized the end of World War II more than
the return of Hank Greenberg from the service in July of 1945. Greenberg
rewarded his fans by leading the Detroit Tigers to the American League
pennant with a dramatic home run in the team's final game of the season.
(The Sporting News)

Library of Congress Cataloging-in-Publication Data

Marshall, William, 1944–
        Baseball's pivotal era, 1945-1951 / William Marshall.
            p.   cm.
        Includes bibliographical references (p.   ) and index.
        ISBN 0-8131-2041-1 (cloth : alk. paper)
            1. Baseball—United States—History—20th century.   I. Title.
        GV863.A1M353   1999   98-36951
        796.357'0973'09045—dc21

This book is printed on acid-free recycled paper meeting
the requirements of the American National Standard
for Permanence of Paper for Printed Library Materials.

Manufactured in the United States of America

In memory of my father, who transferred his love of baseball to each of his sons, and for Jan, Anne, and Jennifer, whose love and patience have sustained me through this project.

Contents

Acknowledgments

When I sat down to conduct my first oral history interview on A.B. Happy Chandler with sportswriter Shirley Povich at the *Washington Post* in 1976, I had no idea that I would someday author a full-blown history of the game during the commissioner's tenure. While the Commissioner of Baseball series in the Chandler Papers housed at the University of Kentucky contained significant material from Chandler's Versailles, Kentucky, office files, we have been unable to locate the files initially maintained in the commissioner's Carew Tower office in Cincinnati. As both an archivist who firmly believes in using oral history as a methodological tool to fill in history's gaps and a lifelong baseball fan, I needed no other excuse to begin interviewing four or five persons each year who had worked with commissioner Chandler or who were affiliated with the game during his era. By 1980, with more than twenty interviews behind me, it was obvious that I was beginning to gather enough material for a book on Chandler's commissionership. When Jules Tygiel visited the university that year to conduct research for his book *Baseball's Great Experiment,* his willingness to share his own work and his enthusiasm inspired me to proceed.

With a book in mind, I broadened the scope of my research to include events that occurred during the seasons served by commissioner Chandler, such as Bobby Thomson's famous playoff home run in 1951. Thus, this book is not a biographical account of Chandler. Although he is one of the work's most important figures, his commissionership serves to define the book's framework. The volume is divided into seven sections, each containing a chapter about a season in the period and additional chapters that address related topics. The season chapters treat the game on the field and chronicle several exciting pennant races during a time when baseball's popularity reached all-time highs. The topical chapters document and interpret baseball as social history. Baseball during the Pivotal Era was inseparable from the effects of World War II and the resulting economic, labor, political, technological, and social forces at work. I call the era "pivotal" because, for the first time, a sports institution, through Jackie Robinson's entry into the game, took the lead in reshaping American society. The period was also a watershed because other opportunities and potential reforms presented themselves, in the form of labor relations, altered business conditions, the introduction of television, and changing demographic patterns brought about by America's love affair with the automobile. The Pivotal Era is the story of how the game battled to protect its legal monopoly over its players at the expense of other potential gains. It is the tale of a group of owners whose status as competitors prevented them from working in concert to provide the game with a vision. Finally, the Pivotal Era is the period during which many of the seeds of baseball's current problems took root.

I am indebted to numerous persons for the opportunity to create this book. Without the support of Paul Willis, Director of Libraries at the University of Kentucky, who not only approved my sabbatical leave in 1989 but also allowed me the freedom of action to pursue this quest, this book might never have been written. I am also grateful to colleagues Terry Birdwhistell and Claire McCann, who, in addition to offering their encouragement, cheerfully supervised Special Collections and Archives during my absences. Moreover, Terry was responsible for providing support from the Library's Oral History Program. I would also like to thank Jim Birchfield, through whose generosity I was able to gain access to the *Sporting News*--a tremendous resource that is almost essential to any serious study of baseball in the twentieth century.

I owe a debt of gratitude to the interlibrary-loan staffs at the University of Missouri at Columbia and at the University of Kentucky and to the reference staffs at the Cincinnati Historical Society, the Cleveland Public Library, the Manuscript Division of the Library of Congress, the Philadelphia Public Library, and the Seattle Public Library. I also wish to thank archival and library colleagues Steve Gietscher of the *Sporting News*, Tom Heitz, formerly of the National Baseball Library at Cooperstown, New York, John Vernon of the National Archives, and Andy Anderson at the University of Louisville Photographic Archives, for their encouragement, good will, and continued support on my trips to their institutions. Others who deserve recognition for their interest and assistance include Tom Appleton, Martha Birchfield, Janet Cabaniss, Britt Davis, Charles Faber, Joseph Famularo, William Hannegan, Jim Klotter, Bill LaRose, Art Lawson, Terry Lehmann, Larry Lester, Paul LeVeque, Lee Lowenfish, Stephen Milner, Dick and Christie Robinson, Charles Roland, Roger Sheffer, Steve White, and Gene Williams.

I am particularly appreciative to the more than seventy individuals who agreed to participate in oral history interviews with me. For those who are deceased, I would like to thank their families. This is their era, and they were kind to share their recollections for posterity. The interviews are part of the University of Kentucky Library's Oral History Program and most are open for use by researchers. Interviews were conducted with Red Barber, Lon C. Barton, Frank Baumholtz, Bobby Brown, Willard Brown, Lou Boudreau, Bob Broeg, Richard Butler, Bob Cain, Pete Castiglione, A.B. "Happy" Chandler, W. Graham Claytor, Barry Craig, DeLores and Ray Dandridge, Leon Day, Bill DeWitt, Larry Doby, Augie Donatelli, Jim Enright, Bob Feller, John Galbreath, Danny Gardella, Ned Garver, Mel Harder, Ernie Harwell, Jim Hegan, Robert Holbrook, Monte Irvin, George Jefferson, Sam Jethroe, Frederick Johnson, George Kell, Ralph Kiner, Bowie Kuhn, Max Lanier, Hal Lebovitz, Eddie Lopat, Bob Lemon, Al Lopez, Barney McCosky, Lee MacPhail, Sal Maglie, Effa Manley, Marty Marion, Willard Marshall, Charley Metro, Edgar Munzel, Stan Musial, Don Newcombe, Mickey Owen, Joseph Paparella, Max Patkin, Gabe Paul, Shirley Povich, Al Rosen, Fred Saigh, Red Schoendienst, Hal Schumacher, Andy Seminick, Rip Sewell, Red Smith, Bobby Thomson, Bill Toomey, Virgil Trucks, Bill Veeck, Harry Walker, Ted Williams, Gene Woodling, and Adrian and Mary Zabala. I am also indebted to colleague Bill Cooper, who interviewed Carl Erskine and Calvin Griffith.

As the book developed, I began to farm out early draft chapters to several persons. I would like to thank Bill Cooper, Jeremy Popkin, and Rose Shrimpton for their comments and suggestions. I am also indebted to Tom Parrish for his advice and remarks regarding the preparation of my book proposal. Finally, I am most grateful to the four individuals who agreed to read the entire manuscript—Tom Blues, Brent Kelley, Jan Marshall, and Jeff Suchanek. All offered constructive criticism and helpful suggestions. Finally, Jan Marshall served as a constant confidant, personal reference librarian, and critic. Her sacrifices and burdens because of this project were borne with good humor and stoicism. Jan's unwavering support and love often provided me with the impetus to continue.

In many respects the ability to research and write this book has been a dream come true. Having grown up in Cleveland in the 1950s, I was able to watch many of the players I interviewed—Ned Garver, Al Rosen, George Kell, Larry Doby, Ted Williams, and Eddie Lopat, to name only a few. Not unlike other children of my era, the game was a bond between parent and child—a time spent playing catch with a busy father or frequent trips to watch major-league games. In the summer, an entire neighborhood of children played baseball daily with nailed bats, worn gloves, and balls held together with electrician's tape. At night, there was always the game, played low on a hidden radio, long past official bedtimes. In the fall, the World Series represented not just the opportunity to see baseball's best teams compete but the chance to view portions of an entire series of games. My first World Series recollections date to the early 1950s, when I took it for granted that Mel Allen was the permanent Series announcer. I can recall racing home from school to catch the final innings on our small-screen, black-and-white television and praying that some of the games would go into extra innings.

Not unlike the four seasons, the game has always been there—with its heroes, its colorful characters, and its statistics that begged comparisons between players and eras. For many of us, the game served as a constant reminder of a carefree and happy youth. Even when our continuum was broken by the loss of the 1994 World Series during baseball's most recent strike (1994-1995), my anger was tempered by the ability to research and write in a period whose issues were far less complicated and certainly more hopeful than those facing the game today. As one Pivotal Era player wrote in a recent note, "It's unbelievable how much the youngsters make and how little we made, yet, we had more fun."

1945

Phil Cavarretta, Hank Borowy, Charlie Grimm, and Bill
Nicholson of the National League Champion Chicago Cubs
meet with Commissioner Chandler. (Special Collections and
Archives, University of Kentucky)

1

Winds of Change

Coverage in America's major newspapers of the death of commissioner of baseball Judge Kenesaw Mountain Landis on November 25, 1944, was subdued. Throughout 1944, almost all events of major interest were eclipsed by news of a war that had reached its apex. German armies were reeling, following the Allied D day invasion in June, and Japanese strength in the Pacific continued to wane under the onslaught of increased American military pressure.

Although the passing of Judge Landis did not go unnoticed, the implications of his death and the effects of the war itself on the game were not readily apparent to those who ran organized baseball. Whereas the game would assume its familiar trappings once the war ended, baseball, not unlike American society, would never be the same. The winds of change were already carrying the seeds that would alter baseball's physical, economic, and social makeup. Landis's death was the beginning of a new era.

This new era witnessed the return of hundreds of veterans hungry to recoup lost time and income. The period was marked by labor unrest and a serious challenge to the game's reserve system. Even more significant, black athletes were unshackled and allowed to compete in America's most visible arena, its national pastime. The era also ushered in a growth and prosperity never before equaled. Attendance records were shattered, and minor-league growth, for a few fleeting years, was unparalleled. For the first time, players began to assert some control over their own destinies. New minimum-salary guidelines were implemented, uniform contracts were created, a pension plan was initiated, and player representation was established. Moreover, the presence of television, a technology that forever changed American leisure-time habits, began to make itself felt. Finally, following World War II, baseball experienced one of the most

3

colorful, exciting, and eventful periods in its history. The postwar era was nothing less than a watershed between the game we know today and the game as it had existed since the 1903 National Agreement was reached between the American and National Leagues.

The foundation of baseball's renaissance can be traced to Babe Ruth's popularization of the game in the 1920s and to Landis, whose twenty-four-year reign stabilized baseball. Hired by the owners in 1920 to sanitize baseball's tarnished image following the Black Sox scandal, Landis was the epitome of political and social conservatism. Appointed to the federal bench by Theodore Roosevelt, Landis became famous for trying communists, socialists, and "Wobblies" and for his attempt to extradite the Kaiser to the United States for having sunk the *Lusitania*.[1] Landis was best known as the judge who fined the Standard Oil Company of Indiana more than $29 million for accepting rebates from the Chicago and Alton Railroad.[2]

Landis first came to the owners' attention with his handling of the Federal League case in 1915. The case, which threatened baseball's reserve system, was settled out of court, in large part because of Landis's delay in issuing a decision. Had Landis ruled that baseball was akin to a trust, it would have thrown the game's structure into chaos. At the trial, it became obvious to the owners that the Judge was an ardent baseball fan.

By 1920, the three-man National Commission, which had supervised the game since 1903, was in disarray. Dissension among the owners prevented the reelection of chairman Garry Herrmann, and an impasse on the choice of his successor between American League and National League presidents Ban Johnson and Joseph Heydler could not be resolved. When the Black Sox scandal broke in the last week of the 1920 season, there was a public outcry that the game needed to appoint someone from outside its ranks who could run the game and restore its lost integrity. The desperate owners met on November 12 and, fearing for their investments, agreed to offer Judge Kenesaw Landis the post of High Commissioner of Baseball. They also decided that the commissioner should be the titular head of the game, stipulated that Landis's successor should be elected in the same manner, and determined that a new National Agreement should be drafted.[3] After accepting the owners' offer of an annual salary of $50,000 for seven years, Landis told them that he would subtract his $7,500 federal salary from that figure each year. Seeing him as baseball's savior, the owners granted Landis great powers and thus set the tone of their relationship for the next twenty-five years.

Three major themes emerged from Judge Landis's commissionership—his aversion to gambling, his hatred of the farm system, and his desire to keep baseball out of the courts. First, he was determined to rid the game of any connection with gambling. When the trial of the eight Chicago White Sox players charged with throwing the 1919 World Series ended in acquittals for each, Landis quickly and arbitrarily banned the players from the game. No pardons were ever granted. Thus, baseball, in violation of the players' right to due process, prevented them from pursuing their livelihood. As baseball historian David Voight wrote, "Today, such a sentence would be preposterous."[4] Landis, however, was consistent in his treatment of gambling associations throughout his tenure. He banished both player and owner alike for wagering on contests. A case in point was William Cox, owner of the Philadelphia Phillies, who was charged with betting on his team and was forced by Landis to sell the franchise in 1943. Landis also prevented Bing Crosby and Alfred Gwynne Vanderbilt and other celebrities from buying into teams, because they owned race horses or were affiliated with racing.[5] In addition, in 1921 he told John McGraw and Charles Stoneham to rid themselves of their investments in a Cuban racetrack and casino venture, and in 1937 Landis banished future Hall of Famer Rogers Hornsby from any affiliation with the game because of his well-known predilection for wagering on horses.

Judge Landis's support of independent ownership of minor-league teams and his hatred of the farm system led to several clashes with the creator of the farm system, St. Louis Cardinal general manager Branch Rickey. In 1938, Landis freed ninety-one players from the Cardinals system, charging the club with hiding players and preventing them from playing at higher classifications. Those released included Pete Reiser, who became the 1941 National League batting champion with the Brooklyn Dodgers. Similarly, he freed 106 Detroit Tiger farmhands in 1940. Landis was also hard on Cleveland. In 1936, he freed Tommy Henrich from the Cleveland organization after uncovering a series of agreements that allowed the team to circumvent the option system. In 1940, Henrich hit .307 for the Yankees, and Cleveland lost the American League pennant by one game. Cleveland was also fined $500 by Landis in 1944 for tampering with then-high-school player Richie Ashburn, another player destined for the Hall of Fame.

In direct contrast was overnight sensation Bob Feller—an eighteen-year-old pitcher put on the Cleveland roster in 1936 in violation of the major-minor–league agreement that prevented major-league teams from directly signing amateur players. Had Landis ruled that Feller was a free agent, a huge bidding war would have ensued.[6] Instead, Cleveland was fined $7,500 and was allowed to retain a player who would become one of the greatest pitchers in the game's history. The real reason behind

Landis's decision in the Feller case involved the Landis principle of keeping baseball out of the courts. Both Feller and his father, through whom he had signed originally, wanted the pitcher to remain with the Indians. According to Feller, it was his father's threat to sue Landis in civil court if the Judge nullified his contract with Cleveland that affected the commissioner's decision. "The Judge was no dummy," recalled Feller. "He let me play with Cleveland."[7]

Finally, Landis was protected from court action by U.S. Supreme Court Justice Oliver Wendell Holmes's decision in the 1922 Federal League suit, in which the court ruled that baseball's involvement in interstate commerce was incidental and thus that the game was not subject to antitrust regulation. In addition, the Holmes decision buttressed baseball's claim that it was more a sport than a business.[8] The major court test to Landis's authority came in 1931 when St. Louis Browns' owner Phil Ball challenged the commissioner in federal court over a decision that freed one of his players. When the lower court ruled in favor of Landis, Ball threatened to take the case to the Supreme Court. Repeating a tactic he had used against the owners in his 1927 dispute with Ban Johnson, Landis threatened to resign unless the owners stopped Ball from pursuing further legal action. True to form, the ploy worked, as the owners derailed Ball's efforts.

World War II also posed a major threat to baseball. Landis, who referred to Franklin Roosevelt as "that bastard in the White House," swallowed his pride and sent a note to the president following the Japanese attack on Pearl Harbor.[9] In it he requested guidance on whether baseball should be suspended or whether the nation would be best served by the game's continuation. Clark Griffith, owner of the Washington Senators, was called to the White House, where he argued persuasively for maintaining the game on the assumption that it would provide a much-needed diversion for war-weary workers.[10] Convinced by Griffith's words, Roosevelt sent his so-called Green Light letter in reply. Although he disclaimed that the letter contained an official point of view, the president noted that he honestly felt "that it would be best for the country to keep baseball going."[11]

In spite of the fact that Landis, Griffith, and Roosevelt preserved baseball during World War II, the game struggled to maintain any semblance of its former identity. One after another, some of its best-known players were inducted into the armed services. Hank Greenberg, at age thirty, was the first player called by the newly instituted draft, in October 1940. On December 6, 1941, Congress passed a law exempting all men over twenty-eight from the draft, and Greenberg appeared in newspaper photographs the next day "tying a civilian tie, turning in his equipment, shaking hands with his barracks buddies, [and] tossing a final salute to the guard at the gate."[12] The next day, December 7, Japanese forces attacked Pearl Harbor, and Greenberg, determined to forget baseball for the duration, reenlisted to become the first player to enter the war. He was followed by Bob Feller, who joined the Naval Physical Training Division two days later as a chief petty officer.

Other ballplayers soon followed—even such stars as Joe DiMaggio and Ted Williams enlisted after the 1942 season. More than a thousand men who played major-league baseball during the period 1931-46 served in the armed forces during the war.[13] By the spring of 1945, only 18 percent (26/144) of those major leaguers who were in their team's starting lineups in 1941 were still there, and no team possessed more than four of its 1941 starters.[14] In 1944, Landis's last year as commissioner, most teams competed with a motley group of old veterans, 4-F players, and youngsters. The war also prolonged the careers of several major-league veterans, as a total of sixty-one players aged thirty-five years or older appeared on team rosters. Many players represented household names out of the 1930s, including Paul and Lloyd Waner, Stan Hack, Jimmy Foxx, Thornton Lee, Paul Derringer, Ernie Lombardi, Jim Turner, Claude Passeau, Chuck Klein, Mel Ott, Joe Kuhel, Whitlow Wyatt, Al Lopez, Rip Sewell, Billy Jurges, and Joe Cronin. At the other end of the spectrum was a group of predraft youngsters—men who would someday make their own mark on the game—including Art Houtteman, Billy Pierce, Carl Scheib, Cass Michaels, Ed Yost, Herm Wehmeier, Ralph Branca, Tommy Brown, Granny Hamner, and the youngest player to play major-league baseball in the twentieth century, Cincinnati's fifteen-year-old Joe Nuxhall.

Baseball's 4-F classification players, those exempted from the draft, in large measure carried the game during the war. They were players whose physical disabilities made them unacceptable for military service. Any number of maladies would suffice. The Dodger's Curt Davis suffered from an ulcer and often pitched in pain. Catcher Paul Richards, shortstop Marty Marion, and outfielder Danny Litwhiler had trick knees. Relief pitcher Ted Wilks suffered from a chronic stomach disorder, and the ace of the Giants' pitching staff, Bill Voiselle, was hard of hearing. Pitchers Hal Newhouser and Russ Christopher both had heart ailments that kept them out of the service. Newhouser's faulty heart certainly did not prevent him from dominating the American League in 1944 with a 29 and 9 record. Other 4-F players returned from the service before their normal tours of duty were completed. Red Schoendienst was discharged because of a vision problem, and St. Louis Browns' catcher Frank Mancuso ended his military career as a paratrooper when he was badly injured during a jump.

Many of the athletes were recruited by the services themselves. As William Meade wrote in *Even the Browns*, "America's best baseball teams during the war may not have been in the major leagues at all, but rather in the Army or Navy."[15] Even before the war began, the Navy had signed up boxer Gene Tunney to organize a physical fitness program. After the outbreak of hostilities, he assisted the Navy in forming a baseball team at its base in Norfolk, Virginia, that included such players as Phil Rizzuto, Pee Wee Reese, Dom DiMaggio, Bob Feller, Fred Hutchinson, and Eddie Robinson. The Navy also commissioned catcher Mickey Cochrane to coach its Great Lakes team. With stars such as Billy Herman, Johnny Mize, Gene Woodling, Walker Cooper, and Schoolboy Rowe, the team was 163 and 26 in the period 1942-44. Conversely, the Army dispersed the athletes it signed up and did not begin to bring them together until 1944, when an Army-Navy series was initiated in Honolulu. In both services, most of the men put in full days, supervising calisthenics and other recreation programs.[16]

Although many major-league baseball players received special treatment in the service, none of the game's major stars requested special consideration. Joe DiMaggio, the darling of New York, was originally placed in the class C section of the draft—a classification reserved for married men with children—and did not enlist in the Army until February 1943. Initially assigned to a Special Services unit in California, he was sent to Hawaii to play with the Seventh Army Air Force team, which hoped to contend for the Far Eastern Service title. Plagued by marital problems and a duodenal ulcer, DiMaggio was reassigned in September 1944 to an air transport command responsible for ferrying wounded soldiers between Hawaii and the mainland. Late in 1944, DiMaggio was reassigned again—this time to a physical training section at Atlantic City, New Jersey, where he spent the remainder of the war.

For Ted Williams, the war provided another quest—the art of flying. Not unlike hitting or fishing, flying was an activity that took concentration, could be analyzed and dissected, required excellent eye-to-hand coordination, and still retained enough unknown variables to make it a constant challenge. Classified III-A in 1943 because he was supporting his divorced mother, Williams soon tired of a negative press questioning his patriotism and signed up for Naval Aviation School with Johnny Pesky and Johnny Sain. Williams took to flying quite easily and eventually became a flight instructor, flying Navy SNJs (North American Texan Trainers) out of Pensacola, Florida. In 1945, when the war ended, his combat orders were canceled as he was en route to the Pacific theater. The bulk of his ball playing in the service came after the conflict had ended.

After initially receiving choice assignments, Hank Greenberg and Bob Feller both requested combat duty. In 1943 Captain Greenberg was assigned to the first group of B-29s sent overseas, where he spent time in India and China. In one incident, Greenberg was blown off his feet by a bomb explosion as he raced along a runway to assist the crew of a stricken B-29. "Some of them were pretty banged up but no one was killed," Greenberg told reporter Arthur Daley of the *New York Times*. "That was one occasion," he continued, "when I didn't wonder whether or not I'd be able to return to baseball. I was quite satisfied to be alive."[17]

After six months working with the physical fitness program, Bob Feller attended gunnery school and was then put in charge of an antiaircraft battery on the USS *Alabama,* a 35,000-ton battleship. While aboard ship, Feller usually worked out below decks to keep in shape and was occasionally able to do some throwing and running when he could get to an aircraft hangar ashore. While the *Alabama* was based in the Pacific on the New Hebrides, Feller formed a team on the ship, outfitted it with equipment sent by the Indians, and supervised the building of a couple of ballfields. In 1944, the *Alabama* provided support for Allied landings on several island chains. The most intense activity experienced by Feller's battery came during the battle for Saipan on the day called "the Great Marianas Turkey Shoot"—a period that saw Japanese forces lose more than a hundred aircraft. Although the *Alabama* dodged several near misses from torpedoes, bombs, and Kamikaze pilots, whom Feller likened to "blind maddened bulls," the ship came through unscathed.[18] On January 14, 1945, a war-weary but pleased Bob Feller returned home.

St. Louis star Stan Musial escaped being drafted until late 1944 and as a result was able to lead the Cardinals to two straight National League pennants in 1943 and 1944. Musial's deferment was based on his need to support both his parents and his immediate family. Moreover, he was fortunate to be in a local Pennsylvania draft pool that was well stocked with men of draft age. Beginning in 1945, he served a fourteen-month hitch in the Navy and was assigned to a ship repair unit in Hawaii, where he played three or four times a week with players such as Billy Herman, Bob Lemon, and Cookie Lavagetto. Musial was pleased that he joined the navy instead of heeding Pete Reiser's advice to join the army's great Fort Riley, Kansas, team. Not long after, recalled Musial, many of the army players "like Harry Walker, Murry Dickson, Al Brazle, and Peter Reiser . . . ended up in the Battle of the Bulge."[19]

In 1943, St. Louis Cardinal outfielder Harry Walker played in the All-Star game and the World Series. Exactly one year later, he and teammate Al Brazle were with General George Patton's Third Army in Europe. Although stricken with spinal meningitis while at Fort Riley, a disease that sent most GIs home, Walker was retained by the Army because he was a ballplayer and his discharge might cause the Army bad publicity. After seeing action during the Battle of the Bulge, Private First Class Walker's reconnaissance unit plunged deep into Bavaria and found itself in combat, defending a bridge. "I shot maybe about fifteen before we got out of that thing—with a machine gun. They thought we were Germans at first . . . then I saw the gun. [When] I asked him to drop his gun, he threw it up in my face." Walker also recalled the internment camps. "We saw people slaughtered like animals. We buried them by the hundreds. . . . We do not know what suffering is like."[20] Even in the field, Walker could not escape his baseball past. General Emil Reinhardt asked him to form a baseball team to compete on weekends for the entertainment of the troops. Arguing that the team would have to travel over torn-up bridges and roads with the possibility of snipers still in the woods, Walker demanded air travel. When "I told him that," remembered Walker, "it like to have floored him." The Cardinal outfielder got his aircraft—first a B-25 and then a B-17 named *Bottoms Up.* He put together a very competitive team that included teammate Al Brazle, Ken Heintzelman of the Phillies, and the Dodgers' Rex Barney.[21]

The vast majority of professional ballplayers who saw action were minor leaguers—several of whom were destined to become major-league players. For instance, eighteen-year-old Yogi Berra, property of the New York Yankees, served on a converted LCT (landing craft, tank) fitted with rocket launchers and participated in both the D day and Mediterranean landings in southern France. He was sent home with a hand wound. Another future Yankee catcher, Ralph Houk, was wounded during the Battle of the Bulge.[22] One of the most courageous actions of the war involved Bill Reeder, a young Shreveport, Louisiana, pitcher who had a trial with the St. Louis Cardinals in 1949. When Reeder's infantry unit was pinned down by mortar attacks on the island of Okinawa, Reeder heaved several grenades toward the mortar position while under constant fire from the enemy. After several tosses, the position was silenced. When the distance was paced off between Reeder's "pitching mound" and the mortar position, much to everyone's amazement it was discovered to be more than 300 feet. Asked about his exploit, Reeder replied, "Way I look at it, it is better to have a dead arm on a live body than the other way around."[23]

Another unsung baseball campaigner was southpaw pitcher Warren Spahn of the Boston Braves. Up for only a few games with the Braves in 1942, Staff Sergeant Spahn saw action with the 276th Engineer Combat Battalion in the Ardennes, Alsace, the Rhineland, and in Central Europe. The future Hall-of-Fame star was also at the Remagen bridgehead, where his unit worked feverishly for six days under constant fire to keep this key entrance into Germany under repair. On March 17, 1945, Spahn went to the center of the bridge to confer with some officers. Only moments after he walked off the span, the bridge took a direct hit at the exact spot where the conference had taken place. Spahn and his men turned around just in time to see the men with whom he had been speaking, along with a section of the bridge, plunge into the swiftly flowing Rhine River. A few months later Spahn became one of the few professional baseball players to receive a battlefield commission as a second lieutenant.[24]

Minor-league player and former college basketball star Frank Baumholtz almost spurned baseball to become a physician when he returned from the service in 1945. As a child, Baumholtz often buried himself in medical books. While serving as a gunnery officer aboard a series of naval vessels in the Atlantic and Pacific theaters, Baumholtz carried a medical kit with him and was often called on to attend injured sailors. In one instance, while aboard a cargo ship in the Atlantic, the outfielder was asked to stitch up a sailor who had been badly cut in a fight. When the sailor returned to New York, physicians were amazed by Baumholtz's handiwork. In another instance, while his ship was under attack from Kamikazes off Okinawa, Baumholtz was asked to assist the ship's doctor in reconstructing a sailor's hand injured by a twenty-millimeter gun fragment. The fear generated by the Kamikaze attacks remained with Baumholtz long after the war. He witnessed a Kamikaze as it plunged through the smokestack of a big battleship anchored off Okinawa. "It was a horrible, horrible thing," he recalled.[25]

Baseball executives also were not exempt from the war. Private First Class Bill Veeck, the owner of the Milwaukee Brewers, ran his team in absentia while serving with an antiaircraft outfit on Bougainville in the South Pacific. Veeck was trained as an ammunition passer, gunner, and searchlight operator. He noted, "Our battery did get a couple of Jap bombers. They provided the most thrilling moments I can remember. Whenever our lights would catch one of them in the sky at night, the boys would all gather around and cheer themselves hoarse . . . yelling, 'Get that Imperial son of a so-and-so.'"[26] In November 1944 Veeck returned to the States, suffering from an ankle that collapsed because of an old football injury and from jungle rot—conditions that eventually resulted in the loss of both legs.

For some minor-league ballplayers, the war permanently changed their careers. August Donatelli was a shortstop who played at Penn State and in the Class D Kitty League before the war. During March of 1944 he was a tail gunner on a B-17 that was shot down during the first daylight raid over Berlin. Suffering from a broken leg as the result of his fall, Donatelli

Judge Landis's death left baseball leaderless in 1945. (George Brace Photo)

was interned in two different prisoner of war camps. He was beaten, suffered a broken toe, and was taken on a forced march to evade the oncoming Russian Army. He escaped and spent several days hiding in hay lofts before he was recaptured. At his last prison camp, Donatelli was forced to bury Russian dead and was present when Russian tanks came and "crushed the camp all to hell." When liberated, the once-healthy ballplayer weighed only 130 pounds. With all aspirations of a baseball career gone, Donatelli used his entitlements under the GI Bill to become an umpire—a profession that later allowed him to reach the National League.[27]

By the beginning of 1945, with many of its young men at war, the game's status was cloudy at best. As if the world was not already turned upside down, the St. Louis Browns appeared in the World Series—the franchise's first and only time. Most of the game's identifiable stars were in uniform, as were hundreds of minor leaguers. Others, such as pitcher Mel Harder of the Cleveland Indians, who also worked at the Ohio Rubber Company, were forced to split their time between baseball and laboring in war plants. The game, which was now being played by youngsters, old-timers, and 4-F players, had slipped badly in quality. Permission to continue play hinged largely on an informal letter from a sympathetic president. Finally, baseball's savior and spiritual leader, Judge Kenesaw Mountain Landis was dead. At a critical time, baseball was leaderless.

2

"No One Is Qualified"

In the midst of the heaviest fighting along the Bastogne front in Belgium, in December 1944, a girl drove her jeep into the American front lines. She wore a GI helmet and overcoat but carried no identification. After lengthy questioning by those who suspected her of being an infiltrator, she was released and sent on her way. "I finally convinced the major that I was an American," explained Virginia Von Lampe of Yonkers, New York, "when I rattled off the Brooklyn Dodgers' lineup for the 1941 World Series."[1] Not unlike this Red Cross girl, baseball, by the beginning of 1945, was undergoing an identity crisis.

With the onset of spring training in March 1945, organized baseball found itself leaderless and unprotected. The game, which was now headed by a three-man advisory council (National League president Ford Frick, American League president Will Harridge, and assistant to the late Judge Landis Leslie O'Connor), could ill afford to wait until the war was over to select a new commissioner. Although President Roosevelt's "Green Light" letter allowed baseball to continue, it did little to protect playing conditions or the quality of play. The owners were sensitive to any criticism and made every effort show their patriotism. "The Star-Spangled Banner" was played before every game, ticket prices were reduced, free tickets were given to wounded veterans, and more night games were played, permitting warplant workers to attend.

In 1943, when the nation's Office of Defense Transportation asked baseball clubs to reduce travel mileage and schedules, Judge Landis, in his enthusiasm to cooperate, did even more. He banned the use of spring training sites in California and Florida and ordered teams, with the exception of the Cardinals and Browns, to restrict their spring training activities to sites above the Ohio and Potomac Rivers. As a consequence, teams trained in such exotic locations as French Lick, Indiana, Bear Mountain, New York, and Cape Girardeau, Missouri. Many teams were forced to play on substandard fields in the wind, snow, cold, rain, and spring floods, while others located at West Point, New York, and Purdue University, in Indiana, vied with already scheduled activities for access to huge indoor fieldhouses. "We played inside all the time," recalled pitcher Mel Harder, who trained at Purdue. "It was different, but it was a fact of life then. . . . You just took it—no crabbing or anything like that."[2] There were some amenities, however, including those at the Giants' beautiful site on the former Lakewood, New Jersey, estate of John D. Rockefeller and the sumptuous quarters enjoyed by the Dodgers at an inn on Bear Mountain. None, however, could top the hospitality at the French Lick Springs Hotel, where the owner supplied Cubs and White Sox players with two quarts of goat milk a day from his pedigreed herd—a ration that he claimed was also guaranteed to turn out pedigreed players.[3]

By 1945, travel restrictions made traveling secretaries' jobs a nightmare. Before the war, teams made their reservations months in advance. During wartime, however, they could make plans only five days ahead of time. Moreover, clubs used to traveling in special sleeping cars were fortunate to find accommodations for most of their players. Sometimes two or more trains on different railroads were used to get teams to their destination. Some teams were even forced to make entire trips on day coaches.

As wartime travel became increasingly disrupted, players took out their frustrations on the traveling secretary. Cardinals players retaliated against traveling secretary Leo Ward in 1943 by not voting him a World Series share, because of his inability or unwillingness to secure satisfactory accommodations. While his brother Dixie and the Brooklyn Dodgers still traveled on fine Pullmans, Harry Walker recalled that the Cardinals players were often covered with soot because their hot cars forced them to travel with open windows. When the players complained, Walker remembered Ward replying, "'Well, the war's on. You can't do any better.' But you had to sneak a little money under the table to get better cars," added Walker. "You know, it's like everybody else—they took advantage of it."[4]

Baseball and enterprises affiliated with the game attempted to enhance its public image by assisting the war effort in a number of ways. During the off-season, small groups of players were sent overseas on USO tours to entertain the troops or on stateside trips to sell war bonds. Professional baseball also sent thousands of bats, balls, and gloves overseas. In addition, Hillerich and Bradsby, the maker of the Louisville Slugger, sent hundreds of prints of the 1944 World Series film worldwide, and the *Sporting News* prepared an overseas edition that often appeared in war zones long before any other American newspaper. Finally, as one of his last official acts, Judge Landis decreed that half of the 1944 World Series receipts were to be donated to war-relief agencies and that 10 percent of the players' shares were to be placed in war bonds. For once, the St. Louis Browns shared in a World Series, only to have much-needed capital slip away. As general manager William O. DeWitt said, "Landis's decision really was a jolt to us financially, because we really needed that money.[5]

In spite of these efforts baseball's existence was in doubt as the 1945 season dawned. War mobilization chief James F. Byrnes ordered all horse and dog racing tracks to cease operation, and he asked the chief of the Selective Service, General Lewis B. Hershey, to reexamine the draft status of all athletes. Byrnes openly questioned how men with major disabilities could perform so ably as athletes and yet be unfit for military service. He noted that, if these players were indeed unfit, it would not be unreasonable to expect them to perform light military service or to find employment in war factories.[6] With 260 of baseball's 400 players in the 4-F classification, the owner's worst fears were on the verge of being realized. A powerful figure in the Roosevelt administration was questioning the credibility of the patchwork 4-F system that had allowed the game to continue with some semblance of integrity. By banning dog and horse racing, Byrnes was sending the message that baseball might be next.

The Selective Service was also singling out professional athletes for scrutiny. Players could no longer receive medical discharges or be classified 4-F without having their cases reviewed in Washington. In addition, players who held 2A or 2B occupational deferments were warned to stay in their off-season jobs or risk being drafted. The Selective Service's action placed 4-F players in a quandary. Major leaguers previously classified as 4-F, including Howie Schultz, Hugh Poland, brothers Walker and Mort Cooper, Danny Litwhiler, and Ron Northey, were reexamined. Shultz was rejected again because of his height (6'7"), as was Mort Cooper because of a twisted spine, cracked kneecap, and damaged hip, but the rest were drafted. Others, like player-manager Lou Boudreau of the Indians, who was classified as 4-F because of a rheumatic ankle, felt trapped in their factory jobs; Boudreau's was in an airplane factory in Harvey, Illinois. "The players won't leave their war jobs unless they have specific assurance that they will be allowed to play ball," said Boudreau. "So long as this uncertainty continues to exist, we won't have many ballplayers."[7]

Voices on Capitol Hill were also heard on the issue. Foremost was Kentucky Congressman Andrew May, an ardent supporter of the horse industry, who cosponsored a fight-or-work bill that, had it passed, would have brought baseball to its knees. May reportedly stated, "They closed down the Kentucky Derby and they ought to close down baseball also."[8]

On the other side was fellow Kentuckian Albert Benjamin "Happy" Chandler, who proclaimed that Army rejects would be more useful playing than "fiddling around at something else." Citing morale as a reason for continuing the game, the Kentucky senator pledged to fight May's legislation.[9]

Recognizing the danger to baseball, J.G. Taylor Spink, editor and publisher of the *Sporting News*, urged the owners to act immediately to appoint a new commissioner instead of waiting until the war was over.[10] The owners, who were also moving slowly in this direction, selected a four-member committee at the beginning of February to choose a new commissioner "as soon as possible." In the meantime, there was speculation in Washington that baseball's two leagues would be asked to combine and that intersectional play would be banned. Several owners commented favorably on the proposal, without checking on the authenticity of the rumor. Using their statements to fuel his assertion that baseball needed a commissioner at once, Spink wrote, "Had the game had a commissioner, any discussion would have been referred to him, and the major leagues would have been spared the embarrassment of approving a ridiculous scheme which nobody in authority had suggested."[11]

Fortunately, Clark Griffith, along with league presidents Ford Frick and Will Harridge, had been working behind the scenes with the Office of Defense Transportation and had successfully persuaded the government to agree to a plan that called for twenty-two-man squads, a 25 percent cut in travel, and the cancellation of the annual Cooperstown and All-Star games. Furthermore, baseball agreed to cancel the World Series, although it could be reinstated by the government if war conditions permitted. On March 13, when Clark Griffith visited the president to deliver some passes, Roosevelt issued his second "Green Light," when he publicly told Griffith that the game should continue as long as it did not use perfectly healthy men who could be doing more useful war work. Finally, in late March, the War Manpower Commission declared that players working in war plants were free to leave those jobs to play baseball until the following October. This ruling, which had the blessing of James F. Byrnes, guaranteed that the game would continue at almost the 1944 level.[12]

By March 1945, the uncertainties caused by decisions in Washington, baseball's lack of representation there, and the game's inability to exercise control over its own destiny, convinced most owners that they needed a new commissioner immediately. Finally, on March 31, baseball's search committee announced that they had a "recommendation" and called for a joint meeting of both leagues on April 24 in Cleveland. Many candidates were suggested for the post, including Ford Frick, former Postmaster General James A. Farley, FBI chief J. Edgar Hoover, Coast Guard Admiral Robert Donohue, James F. Byrnes, chairman of the National

Democratic Committee Robert Hannegan, Supreme Court Justice William O. Douglas, Happy Chandler, former federal judge Fred Vinson, and John Bricker, former Governor of Ohio. The early favorite of several owners and the media was Frick. The National League president's activities in Washington, his newspaper background, his easygoing temperament, and his inside knowledge of the game all worked in his favor.

Nevertheless, it appeared that no candidate had enough support to be elected. Several days before the conference, Larry MacPhail, one of the Yankees' three new owners, told journalist Dan Daniel that the committee had sent out a list of candidates that "might have been clipped from the sports pages." According to MacPhail, no recommendations accompanied the list—just names and biographies that could have been taken from *Who's Who*. Indicating that several names stood out, MacPhail announced that he would go to the meeting and demand that the doors be locked and that no one be allowed to leave until a new commissioner was chosen.[13] Nevertheless, on the eve of the meeting, the great number of candidates and the owners' seeming inability to identify the type of person needed for the job convinced the other owners that baseball should delay action until after the war.[14]

Even though major-league baseball meetings, and especially those at which commissioners are to be elected, are closed to the public, a record of the Cleveland meeting exists in the form of a memorandum written by Branch Rickey on April 25, 1945. According to Rickey, the search committee came up with a list of six persons they thought would be qualified for the post, but because these individuals had not been approached, the committee recommended that a temporary commissioner be appointed until a permanent one could be found. Indeed, Donald Barnes, owner of the St. Louis Browns, announced that American League attorney Joseph Hostetler had tentatively agreed to serve in that capacity. Pittsburgh owner William Benswanger declared his opposition to electing a temporary commissioner and argued that the reasons used in favor of having the post filled on a temporary basis were the same as those for appointing a permanent commissioner. At that point, Warren Giles of the Cincinnati club announced, "with a great deal of vehemence, that he did not know of anyone who was both qualified and available" and explained that more candidates would be available after the war.[15]

Tom Yawkey, the dark-haired millionaire owner of the Boston Red Sox, countered with the argument that most industries and businesses looked inward for leadership and that "it would seem to be a [poor] reflection if baseball could not produce somebody to handle its own jobs." After perusing the committee's report, Rickey noted that it was gratifying to him that the committee was able to locate "about six" candidates, and questioned why their names had not been included in the report. "It seems that four owners feel that one or more of the other twelve cannot be trusted," said MacPhail. Benswanger agreed, as did two or three others. Responding to this surge of sentiment, committee chair Alva Bradley of the Indians agreed to produce a list. Cubs owner Philip K. Wrigley revealed the committee's real problem when he admitted that its members could not agree on the six names and that the list would actually contain more candidates. The committee returned with a list of eleven names that included such personages as Fred Vinson, Paul McNutt, J. Edgar Hoover, Frank Lausche, James A. Farley, Robert Hannegan, Thomas Dewey, and John Bricker. After a discussion of each man on the list, MacPhail took the floor and stated that he thought a name not mentioned by the committee might be given consideration—a man both qualified and available. "I refer to Senator Chandler of Kentucky," MacPhail stated, as he produced a brief biographical sketch of Chandler.[16]

Resuming the initiative, Rickey urged that the owners vote on the names suggested, including Chandler's. Noting that he would gladly cast the first vote for a number of men on the list, Rickey said, "If there are eleven men in this room who can make a similar statement, then we can elect a man from that list today, and I don't know of anything I would rather not do than leave this room without the election of a Commissioner."[17] At this point, MacPhail produced a letter written by Robert Carpenter, in which the owner of the Phillies argued that the failure of the owners to elect a commissioner at the meeting would be bad for public relations and a silly position for baseball to take. "It seemed to me," wrote Rickey, "that it [the letter] had a special effect on the mental processes of Sam Breadon, who among others, spoke right away upon the advisability of our voting for a limited number of those twelve names, just to see how we stood."[18]

Agreeing to reduce the list to not more than five names on a vote that would not be final, the owners proceeded to discuss the candidates. A biography of Justice William O. Douglas, described by Rickey as being "very carefully and skillfully prepared," was read and was followed by another that was highly complimentary of Ohio's governor Frank Lausche. Robert Hannegan of St. Louis was discussed, and favorable comments on his candidacy were made by Barnes, Breadon, and Rickey. Phil Wrigley questioned Hannegan's political activities and connection with the recent presidential election. "By this time," wrote Rickey, "Mr. MacPhail had corralled a biography of Chandler, who, someone stated, had probably prepared his own biography, and indeed, that was not disputed by anyone." At this juncture, Clark Griffith discussed the other Washington candidates, including Justice Douglas, and through his remarks succeeded in eliminating most of them, at least from Rickey's consideration.[19]

Griffith then addressed the merits of Ford Frick and, much to Rickey's astonishment, came out in opposition to Frick's candidacy. Observing that Frick had recently done an excellent job in Washington, the Senators' owner argued that both leagues needed to be served. In reaction, Rickey wrote, "I was so upset by what I regarded at the time as this change of attitude on the part of Mr. Griffith toward Mr. Frick's candidacy that I took particular note of the effect of his remarks upon the gentlemen at the table. It was obvious to me that several clubs agreed with Mr. Griffith and I knew Mr. Frick had no chance for election."[20]

James A. Farley's name was then brought to the fore by Rickey, who praised his "ability, industry" and public-relations skills. Lou Perini of the Braves also argued vigorously on his behalf. Alva Bradley then produced a biography of Farley that Rickey asserted "proved to be the most scurrilous attack I have ever heard read on any man." Rickey questioned the authorship of the biography, and Perini added, "that is not the Farley I know." Obviously dismayed, Rickey wrote, "I then felt, of course, that Mr. Farley could not be elected." As a result of this discussion, Rickey ascertained that Lausche was favored by Wrigley and Bradley and that Hannegan had the support of the St. Louis owners Breadon and Barnes and that this split was behind the screening committee's inability to come forward with a recommendation.[21] The group then proceeded to narrow their list to five candidates: Lausche, Frick, Farley, Chandler, and Hannegan.

A proposal, opposed by Donald Barnes and Warren Giles, was made by Sam Breadon, suggesting that the owners narrow the field to three candidates—Hannegan, Chandler, and Lausche. Seeing that there was significant support for such a vote, Alva Bradley proposed that a nonbinding test ballot be taken to see whether a commissioner could be elected at this meeting. Further, the teams were instructed to vote for only two of the candidates. The results of the first and second ballots are given in tables 1 and 2.

The trend was clear. Chandler gained three first-place votes, and Hannegan added one. Following this vote, the discussion became very heated. Barnes vehemently opposed taking additional ballots and stressed the importance of what the owners were about to do and asked them to think about the consequences if they made a mistake. Giles spoke disparagingly of Chandler and, according to Rickey, referred "to his singing proclivities and the fact that in his political campaigns he had his children singing from the platform and some reference was made to some kind of scandal that had something or other to do with a swimming pool."

Table 1. Results of First Ballot for Commissioner

Candidate	Place Votes				
	First	Second	Third	Fourth	Fifth
Frick	2	1	...	2	...
Lausche	3	3	7	1	1
Farley	2	1	2	3	1
Chandler	5	6	1	3	1
Hannegan	4	3	5	1	1

SOURCE: *Branch Rickey, Memorandum, April 25, 1945, Branch Rickey Papers, Library of Congress, Box 27.*

Breadon laughed off Giles's criticism and satisfactorily rebutted the issue of Chandler's "political cleanliness."[22]

Giles argued further that he did not know enough about Chandler, but Rickey countered that it would be impossible to know much more about Chandler than they already did. MacPhail then made several effective points on behalf of Chandler. Hannegan received support, but none was forthcoming for Lausche. Rickey observed that Breadon was exercised over the entire process, and he made a strong plea for another vote, insisting that this vote should be between Hannegan and Chandler. At this point, Rickey was sure that Breadon was going to switch his support to Chandler and that the Kentuckian would receive all the votes, except for those of Giles and Barnes. Phil Wrigley suggested that, if either person were to receive twelve of the sixteen votes, the vote should be final. Agreement was reached that the vote would be final and that those in opposition to the winning candidate would change their votes to make the election unanimous.[23]

White Sox executive Harry Grabiner called out the votes. The first five went to Chandler; the next two to Hannegan; the next three for Chandler; the next for Hannegan; the following three for Chandler; and then the next to Hannegan. With one vote remaining, and with the tally 11-4 in favor of Chandler, the final vote was announced—it was for Chandler.[24]

Though Chandler was thrilled to be offered the commissionership and its accompanying $50,000 salary, he initially refused the post because of the war and the importance of his Senate seat. When assured that he could temporarily keep both positions, Chandler readily accepted. A former semi-pro and minor-league ballplayer himself, Chandler viewed the post as the best job in the country. Although Chandler joked that "Senators get

Table 2. Results of Second Ballot for Commissioner

Candidate	Place Votes	
	First	Second
Chandler	8	5
Lausche	3	5
Hannegan	5	6

SOURCE: *Branch Rickey, Memorandum, April 25, 1945, Branch Rickey Papers, Library of Congress, Box 27.*

beat or die, they don't leave," his love of the game and the position's $50,000 salary made his decision easy. (In 1945, United States senators received an annual salary of $10,000).[25]

Warren Giles, who had serious misgivings about Chandler, must have been in wonderment at the results of the election. His closeness in Cincinnati to Kentucky politics and his opinion should have carried some weight. Instead, internal baseball politics carried the day. Each of the significant candidates had an opponent. Griffith torpedoed Frick, Wrigley or someone else on the screening committee harbored disdain for the politics of both Farley and Hannegan, and Lausche had no powerful supporters.

Giles was simply no match for Breadon, Rickey, and MacPhail. They were the power brokers among the league's representatives—the men who represented baseball's strongest teams and who had shown the most progressive leadership during their careers. Nor was Giles likely aware of the rump meeting at the Commodore Hotel, at which five of the clubs had gathered and had determined to support Chandler if their first two candidates, Frick and Farley, proved unacceptable. Finally, the appearance of the imaginative and persuasive MacPhail as one of the three new owners of the Yankees and the fact that Chandler was his candidate were the major keys to the Kentuckian's election.

Other factors played a role in Chandler's selection. Although he may not have been acceptable to Giles, he was certainly available. Only two months before, Chandler had openly admitted that he coveted the baseball commissionership. "If the war were over, and baseball wanted me and the job were clothed with all the authority enjoyed by the late Judge Landis," he confessed. "I would take it in a minute." In his next breath, however, he insisted that he was not a candidate for anything, when he said, "I could not accept the post now. I could not resign from the Senate while the war yet was on, as that would make me a slacker. My term

Following his election, A.B. "Happy" Chandler posed with Horace Stoneham, Larry MacPhail, and Branch Rickey. (Special Collections and Archives, University of Kentucky.)

expires in 1949. I have certain obligations to fulfill."[26] These were the words of a man running for office.

Second, Chandler clearly had helped baseball in its efforts to survive. In 1943, he arranged a meeting between President Roosevelt and baseball officials to discuss the status of the game, and in 1945, when baseball's existence was threatened, Chandler became Washington's most visible spokesman on the game's behalf. Here was a defender who had strong Washington ties at a time when the owners feared they might not be able to keep the game going. A third rationale was Chandler's obvious love for the game. Chandler had played baseball in high school and college and had also played semiprofessional ball in South Dakota and with the Lexington Reos (the same team with which Yankee great Earle Combs had gotten his professional start). Chandler had experience coaching and umpiring and was a frequent visitor at Cincinnati's Crosley Field throughout his political career. He was a fan, and baseball players and figures within the game were still his heroes.

A fourth factor was Chandler's legal background. As an attorney, the owners expected him to keep the game out of the courts and away from gambling influences just as Judge Landis had done. A fifth rationale was Chandler's personality and his experience on the political stump. A natural promoter, the Senator was comfortable meeting people and made an effort to remember everyone he met by first name—a skill that established a kinship with his electorate and won him many votes. In addition, he could kiss babies or use his powerful grip when shaking hands to impress his sincerity on a prospective voter. Chandler was extroverted and impulsive, and his desire to be respected and liked was unfeigned. This was in sharp contrast to Landis, whose idea of promotion was a baseball player on a field.

It was Chandler's promotional potential that most likely drew him to Larry MacPhail. MacPhail had known Chandler since the 1930s, when the former was an executive with the Cincinnati Reds. A promoter himself, MacPhail was on record as wanting a commissioner who would travel around the country selling baseball. He wanted someone who could devise ways of strengthening the game at all levels: schools, colleges and universities, and in the American Legion junior program. Moreover, he also desired to see the minor leagues strengthened and even envisioned centralizing professional baseball so the game could begin planning in a coordinated fashion.[27]

Finally, Chandler was an outsider. He had no apparent allegiances to a particular league, team, or owner. As such, his credibility would lend baseball some of the integrity it badly needed. The owners obviously did not want another Landis—or any man who would run the game in such an autocratic manner. In Chandler, whose personality was in direct contrast to Landis's, they thought they had their man.

Warren Giles's criticism of the election process was well founded. The manner in which Chandler was elected did not allow the owners to obtain a good picture of the man. No interviews were conducted, and no questions were asked of the nominee. The screening committee was made up of four persons who lived in three cities—logistics alone made their job difficult. This factor, coupled with the split in their ranks, made them unsuited to carry out their mission. Only the seriousness of the times and the actions of the rump committee forced their hand and prompted the election of Chandler.

Chandler himself was driven by motives far more complex than most owners realized. A brief examination of his background yields some insights into the man. He was born in 1898 in Corydon, a little town in western Kentucky, southwest of Henderson, Kentucky, and Evansville, Indiana. His childhood was marred by the separation of his parents and the tragic loss of a brother. Raised by his father, a farmer who was barely able to provide support, Chandler was forced to work at an early age. He was a regular churchgoer and was most influenced by his grandfather, a Confederate veteran whom Chandler described as "one of the most wonderful human beings that he had ever known." The grandfather's only flaw was intemperance—a vice that led Chandler to abstain from alcoholic beverages. A fine athlete and better-than-average student, Chandler finished school in spite of his father's opposition. He was always a class leader, and on the athletic field he excelled.[28] As one noted historian suggested, Chandler mastered the hardships before him "with flair. Instead of turning inward, souring on life, wallowing in self-pity, he grew up cheerful, buoyant, self-assured."[29]

In 1917, he packed his possessions in a single cardboard box and traveled to Lexington, Kentucky, to attend Transylvania University. Although he worked his way through college, Chandler somehow found time for athletics and other extracurricular activities. He had an excellent tenor voice, sang in the college glee club, and was involved in theatrical productions. In addition, he was the star of the university's baseball team and was one of the better football players at the school.[30] While at Transylvania, Chandler acquired the nickname "Happy"—a title he later admitted was "worth tens of thousands of votes."[31]

Although his grades were not exceptional, they were still good enough to get him into law school, first at Harvard and then the University of Kentucky, where he graduated in 1924. He established a law office in Versailles, Kentucky, where, to make ends meet, he also coached high school football teams and acted as a scout and assistant coach for the famed Praying Colonels football team of Centre College.[32] In 1925, Chandler married Mildred Watkins, a Versailles schoolteacher, to begin what was a lifelong love affair. She was intelligent, attractive, and ambitious and later proved to be an invaluable political advisor and campaigner on behalf of her husband.

By 1929 Chandler's connections, legal reputation, and local political activities allowed him to capture a seat in the Kentucky State Senate, and within two years he was elected Lieutenant Governor of Kentucky. Soon thereafter, he split with Governor Ruby Laffoon over the state sales tax. Laffoon forces in the legislature retaliated by having the lieutenant governor stripped of most of his senatorial responsibilities. The next time Laffoon left the state, Chandler used his power as acting governor to call the state legislature into special session for the purpose of enacting a primary law that would replace the existing system of nominations through party boss–dominated caucuses. As historian Charles Roland noted, the move "led him directly into the Governor's Mansion."[33]

In 1935, after finishing second in the Democratic primary, but then winning a run-off, the popular Chandler defeated his Republican opponent for governor by a landslide. At age thirty-seven, the youngest governor in the United States wasted little time in making his mark. Through governmental reform, he sought to create his own New Deal for Kentucky. Chandler accomplished this by surrounding himself with young, bright, self-motivated advisors and administrators and by selecting men such as economist James W. Martin to create an entirely new structure for Kentucky government. It was a New Deal, however, that differed markedly from Roosevelt's, in that Chandler's aim was to streamline government and to relieve the people's tax burden rather than to provide relief to the state's citizens through direct aid. Legislation drafted by Chandler repealed the hated sales tax and replaced it with a modest income tax, increased inheritance taxes, and taxes on whiskey and tobacco. State government was reorganized, and a balanced-budget policy instituted. Other reforms were made in the areas of state roads, the penal system and correctional facilities, and the state's health and welfare programs. As Terry Birdwhistell has indicated, "Chandler's social philosophy, neither elaborate nor consistent, most closely resembled conservatism. As a politician he combined populist rhetoric and some progressive programs with fiscal conservatism."[34]

Chandler could also be politically ruthless and vindictive. Within a month of taking office in 1935 and immediately before Christmas, thousands of state employees were laid off. When Chandler located political enemies in governmental office, he fired them.[35] Moreover, he demanded absolute loyalty within his own ranks. In Chandler's mind, people were either for him or against him, and to be for him they had to support all of his policies and all those he supported.[36]

In 1938 Chandler's political ambition consumed him, as he decided to take on U.S. Senate majority leader Alben Barkley in the Democratic primary. The young governor conducted a whirlwind tour of the state and, accompanied by his wife Mildred, entertained crowds with a rendition of the song "Gold Mine in the Sky."[37] Concern for his majority leader brought President Roosevelt to Kentucky to campaign for Barkley. Not to be outdone, the irrepressible and opportunistic Chandler met Roosevelt's special train and attempted to appear wherever the president appeared. At one point during the campaign, Chandler had the audacity to seat himself between Roosevelt and Barkley in their motorcade limousine. Chandler's presence, an embarrassment to some of his followers, failed to deter the president from strongly endorsing Barkley's candidacy. Chandler was defeated by the largest margin in any Democratic primary in state history.[38]

Chandler's ambition to reach the U.S. Senate, however, was realized when he resigned as governor of Kentucky and had himself appointed to fill the unexpired term of M.M. Logan, who died in office in 1939. During World War II, Chandler served on the Military Affairs Committee and traveled to the Aleutian Islands and around the world to tour the various war theaters. An ardent proponent of America's war effort against Japan, Chandler was most famous for his support of General Douglas MacArthur and belief that the Pacific theater should be won first. Moreover, Chandler often exhibited a mistrust of the British and their motives in his speeches on the floor of the Senate.

This was the man elected as baseball's second commissioner: an ambitious and determined politician from a poor border state, with a Southern accent, an infectious laugh, and a desire to be liked. He loved athletics and the game of baseball most of all, but knew little of its inner workings. Himself an emotional man, he knew how to play on the emotions of others. To take Chandler lightly, particularly in view of his political record, would prove to be a mistake.

3

1945: Season of Hope

The death of President Franklin Delano Roosevelt on April 12, 1945, cast a pall over the nation and further dampened the spirits of those faced with a cold and rainy month. The pennant races in both leagues were largely determined by the manpower shortage caused by the war and by the recent decimation of baseball's 4-F ranks. When President Harry S Truman declared victory in Europe on May 8, 1945, however, the reviews of 4-F players were suspended, and baseball began a slow climb to regain its prewar strength.

In spite of the reversal of the government's policy, however, baseball's manpower shortage remained acute. The player who best symbolized baseball's plight was Pete Gray, the one-armed outfielder of the St. Louis Browns. After hitting .333 in the Southern Association in 1944, Gray became a starter with the Browns in 1945. At the plate he "choked up" about four inches on a thirty-five-ounce bat and generated power by taking a lengthy stride toward first base. In the field, he was adept at catching fly balls, tucking his glove away, and throwing almost in the same motion. An inspiration to the handicapped and disabled veterans, Gray noted, "They seem to feel encouraged over what I am doing, and think that if a one-armed man can get by in the big leagues, they can learn to do things with one arm."[1]

Another inspirational figure was Air Force lieutenant Bert Shepard, who lost a leg when his Thunderbolt fighter was shot down over Europe. An excellent minor-league pitcher, Shepard became the Senators' batting practice pitcher and even got into a major-league game, allowing three hits and a run in five innings. Manpower shortage or not, baseball persevered and the game continued.

Pete Gray, St. Louis Browns
outfielder. (George Brace Photo)

The National League Pennant Race

In the National League race, the Philadelphia Phillies were no factor, finishing fifty-two games out of first place and with only one player, Andy Seminick, who would appear on their roster two years later. The Cincinnati Reds simply had a weak team. Star pitcher Bucky Walters, still ill from a European USO Tour, could fashion only a 10-10 win-loss record. The pitching staff of the sixth-place Braves also faltered. Outfielder Tommy Holmes (.352 batting average, 28 home runs, and 117 runs batted in) broke the National League Record set by Rogers Hornsby in 1922 with a thirty-seven game hitting streak, but could not carry the Braves by himself. Poor pitching also hobbled the fifth-place New York Giants, who were led by player-manager Mel Ott, a veteran of twenty seasons. Ott established a new career record for total bases in the National League with 1,856, surpassing Honus Wagner's mark of 4,862.

The fourth-place Pittsburgh Pirates were in second place as late as June, but untimely hitting slumps by hitters Bob Elliott (.290-8-108), Bill Russell (.284-12-77), and Babe Dahlgren (.250-5-75) sabotaged their season. The sale of the Ebbets's family stock holdings to Branch Rickey, Walter O'Malley,

Table 3. Final Major-League Regular-Season Standings, 1945

American League					National League			
	W	L	%	G.B.		W	L	%	G.B.
Detroit	88	65	.575	–	Chicago	98	56	.636	–
Washington	87	67	.565	1 1/2	St. Louis	95	59	.617	3
St. Louis	81	70	.536	6	Brooklyn	87	67	.565	11
New York	81	71	.533	6 1/2	Pittsburgh	82	72	.532	16
Cleveland	73	72	.503	11	New York	78	74	.513	19
Chicago	71	78	.477	15	Boston	67	85	.441	30
Boston	71	83	.461	17 1/2	Cincinnati	61	93	.396	37
Philadelphia	52	98	.347	34 1/2	Philadelphia	46	108	.299	52

and John Smith seemed to have a salubrious effect on the Dodgers' fortunes, as the team rose to third place. Brooklyn star Dixie Walker (.300-8-124) led the National League in runs-batted-in.

Though the Chicago Cubs failed to relinquish first place after July 8, the St. Louis Cardinals provided a serious challenge. St. Louis practically owned Chicago, taking sixteen of twenty-two games from the Cubs—one of the largest margins ever held by a second-place team over a league champion. The debut of outfielder Al "Red" Schoendienst was not enough to offset the loss of star Stan Musial to the Navy in late 1944. The Cardinals also lost Max Lanier, Danny Litwhiler, and catcher Walker Cooper. A salary dispute between the Cooper brothers (Mort and Walker) and Cardinal owner Sam Breadon caused the latter to trade both players. Mort Cooper was traded to the Braves for pitcher Red Barrett who won twenty-one games for the Cardinals in 1945. Walker Cooper was sent to the Giants for $175,000, an astronomical figure for the time, in a transaction that would come back to haunt the Cardinals.[2]

Another deal, the Hank Borowy sale, shook baseball and provided the Cubs with the edge they needed to win the National League pennant. Borowy, the Yankees' top pitcher, was a ten-game winner at the time of the sale and winner of forty-six more during the previous three seasons for New York. In spite of his record, the talented right-hander worked his way into New York general manager Larry MacPhail's "doghouse" by failing to finish five consecutive starts. MacPhail figured Borowy was expendable and decided to send him to a National League club by putting him on the waiver list after the June 15 trade deadline. The trade deadline and waiver rule were instituted twenty years earlier to keep good ballplayers from being sent to the minor leagues. The list also was

The Cubs' trade for twenty-game winner Hank Borowy helped them to the 1945 National League pennant. (George Brace Photo)

used as a subterfuge to hide a name or as a means of letting other clubs know that a club would like to deal certain players.[3]

When MacPhail placed Borowy's name on the waiver list, he caught all the American League teams napping. Indeed, he even had a difficult time convincing Chicago general manager Jim Gallagher that he was

serious.[4] When the sale was consummated for $97,000, it produced a fu-
ror among the other owners. Clark Griffith, whose Senators were in a
rare race for the pennant, complained, "Had I got a crack at Borowy, I
would have gone to $100,000 for him." MacPhail in rejoinder, stated, "Griff
would not have paid a hundred grand for the pitcher if I had thrown in
the Queen Mary."[5]

A quiet and introspective Fordham graduate, Borowy (2.65, 21-7), went
on to win eleven games for the Cubs, including three important decisions over the Cardinals. Before acquiring Borowy, the Cubs already had
a good staff in Hank Wyse (2.68, 22-10), Ray Prim (2.40, 13-8), Claude
Passeau (2.46, 17-9), and Paul Derringer (3.45, 16-11). Wyse was considered the ace of the staff. A half-Cherokee Indian whose nickname was
"Hooks," Wyse was a control pitcher who relied heavily on his sinker.
Thirty-nine-year-old Ray Prim, called "Pop" by the younger players because of his silver-gray hair, was a spot starter. Another ancient pitcher,
also thirty-nine, was Kentuckian Paul Derringer. Renowned for his fine
wardrobe and culinary habits, Derringer carried the club early in the year
in what was the last season of an outstanding career. The fourth pitcher
in the rotation, Mississippian Claude Passeau, was a tung-nut farmer and
a farm implement dealer with a degree from Millsaps College. Passeau
was easily the wealthiest member of the team. A gunshot wound suffered when he was a teenager closed half his hand, but it did not keep
him from becoming a superb pitcher at age thirty-four.

The Cubs infield was anchored at third base by thirty-five-year-old
Stan Hack (.323-2-43). Famous for his perpetual smile, Hack was talked
out of retirement in 1944 because of the manpower shortage and continued his productive career through 1947. The big gun in the lineup was
first baseman Phil Cavarretta (.355-6-97). Though shy in public, the Chicago native's hustle and hard play easily made him the team leader.
Cavarretta, who was the first Cub to win the batting title since Heinie
Zimmerman did it in 1912, also captured the National League's Most
Valuable Player award for 1945. The Cubs' keystone combination consisted of Don Johnson (.302-2-58) at second base and Len Merullo (.239-2-
37) at shortstop. Johnson was a quiet, unassuming person and a steady
fielder who enjoyed a career year at the plate. Shortstop Len Merullo was
an intelligent, scrappy player from Boston who had a gun for an arm.

The Cubs' catching corps was unspectacular. Mickey Livingston (.254-
2-23), released from the service because an old head injury prevented
him from wearing a steel helmet, was as close to a regular as the Cubs
had. Three other catchers shared the job during the season. In the outfield, the Cubs had three solid players in Andy Pafko (.298-12-110), Bill
Nicholson (.243-13-88), and Harry "Peanuts" Lowrey (.283-7-89). Pafko,

the pride of immigrant parents from Czechoslovakia, grew up on a Wisconsin dairy farm. Andy was an excellent fielder, possessed a strong arm, and in 1945 provided much of the team's firepower. Just twenty-three, Pafko was to border on stardom through a long and distinguished career. Bill Nicholson, nicknamed "Swish" because of his powerful swing, found himself in a yearlong slump. Lowrey, at 5'8", made up for what he lacked in stature with hustle and desire. Equipped with fine defensive skills, he was also the team's best clutch hitter. The Cubs were led by popular manager "Jolly" Charlie Grimm. The former slick-fielding Cubs first baseman was a master of mimicry and humor. Although he ran a loose ship, he was a sound baseball man and was in his second tour with the team. Grimm had left in the middle of the 1938 season because of poor health.

The American League Pennant Race

The American League race was tight to the end, with the Tigers, Senators, Yankees, and defending champion Browns all having a shot at first place. In late May the Philadelphia Athletics, under the guidance of the venerable Connie Mack, replaced Boston in last place and never relinquished that position. The highlight of their season was the no-hitter thrown by Dick Fowler against the Browns, the only one in the major leagues in 1945. Seventh-place Boston, decimated by the war, lost their first eight games and never recovered. Rookie pitcher Dave "Boo" Ferris (2.96, 21-10) used a tricky sidearm curveball to give Boston fans something to cheer about. The Chicago White Sox led the league through mid-May. Excellent pitching and the timely hitting of thirty-seven-year-old Tony Cuccinello (.308-2-49) allowed them to sweep eight consecutive doubleheaders, but the Sox soon faded to sixth place. The fifth-place Cleveland Indians were paced by right-hander Steve Gromek (2.55, 19-9) and buoyed by the return from the Navy of pitching great Bob Feller (2.50, 5-3). The latter's triumphal debut, a victory over Hal Newhouser on August 24, sparked a brief wave of pennant fever in Cleveland. Their fervor, however, was short-lived when player-manager Lou Boudreau broke his ankle only a few days later.

The New York Yankees' fourth-place finish was their worst since 1925. The team's fortunes improved in August with the return of the team's manager Joe McCarthy, who had been sent home because of ill health, and servicemen Red Ruffing, Spud Chandler, and Charlie Keller. The Yankees were led by American League batting champion George Snuffy Stirnweiss (.309-10-64). The defending American League champion St. Louis Browns also challenged for the lead in August not long after St.

Louis ice executive Richard Muckerman purchased the team from Donald Barnes. Led by American League home-run hitter Vern Stephens (.289-24-89) and pitcher Nelson Potter (2.47, 15-11), the team faltered late in the season when they lost eight of ten games to the Senators and Athletics.

The surprising Washington Senators went from the basement in 1944 to second place in 1945 behind the great pitching of diminutive Marino Pieretti (3.32, 14-13) and four knuckleball specialists, Johnny Niggeling (3.16, 7-12), Roger Wolff (2.12, 20-10), Emil "Dutch" Leonard (2.13, 17-7), and Mickey Haefner (3.47, 16-14). The Senators' hitting was just the opposite. Only one of the team's twenty-seven home runs was hit at home and that was an inside-the-park homer by Joe Kuhel. With distances of more than 400 feet to left and center fields at Griffith Stadium, the team had to rely on the speed of outfielders George Myatt and George Case, each of whom had thirty steals.

Although always close, the Senators could not quite catch the Tigers. To make matters worse, Clark Griffith arranged the team's schedule so that it finished the season a week early in order to clear the stadium for professional football. Thus, the Senators were helpless bystanders during the season's final week. With two contests to go for the Tigers, the Senators were trailing Detroit in the loss column by two games, at 87-67 and 87-65, respectively. The Tigers were scheduled to play a double-header with the Browns in St. Louis on the last day of the season. If they lost two, they would be tied with the Senators. As dawn appeared on September 30, 1945, rain was falling for the tenth straight day in the city, and the field at Sportsman's Park was a virtual swamp. When the rain turned to a foggy mist, the umpires decided that the first game would be played. The Tigers, who trailed the Browns 3-2 going into the ninth inning, loaded the bases with one out against pitching ace Nelson Potter. The next batter was army veteran slugger Hank Greenberg, who returned to the Tigers in July. With the count at one ball and no strikes, Greenberg explained what happened next: "As he wound up on the next pitch, I could read his grip on the ball and I could tell he was going to throw a screwball."[6] Greenberg lined the pitch into the corner of the left-field bleachers, and pandemonium broke out on the Detroit bench. Greenberg became the toast of Detroit.

As Fred Lieb wrote, the home run "electrified fans sitting in front of radios. . . . It was fitting indeed that a returned serviceman should decide a pennant race with his bat, on the final day of the season. Military men around the world will glory in his feat."[7] Although Greenberg (.311-13-60) made obvious contributions, the Tigers' success rested on the arms of Hal Newhouser (1.81, 25-9) and Paul "Dizzy" Trout (3.14, 18-15). Newhouser, the only pitcher in baseball history to win the Most Valuable Player award in consecutive years (1944 and 1945), was undeniably the best left-handed pitcher in the game during the Pivotal Era. His physical abilities, fierce desire to win, and tenacity made him a formidable competitor. Other Tiger pitchers making contributions included returned servicemen Al Benton (2.02, 13-8), Les Mueller (3.68, 6-8), and 4-F hurler Frank "Stubby" Overmire (3.88, 9-9).

Prior to Greenberg's return, the Tigers' only true power hitter was first baseman Rudy York (.264-18-87). Nicknamed the "Big Indian" because of his native American heritage, York was a gentle, easygoing fellow who, in 1945, was one of only three active players to have hit more than 200 career home runs. Two other players, second baseman Eddie Mayo (.285-10-54) and catcher Paul Richards (.256-3-32), were also important influences on the team. Mayo, described by one writer as "a brilliant fielder and a consistent hitter," was a hustler who insured that his teammates followed suit.[8] Richards, who shared catching duties with Bob Swift (.233-0-24), was a natural teacher and was credited with helping Hal Newhouser become a more effective pitcher. Other regulars included outfielders Roy Cullenbine (.277-18-93) and Roger "Doc" Cramer (.275-6-58). The team's manager was former Cleveland catcher Steve O'Neill. Kind and well respected, O'Neill specialized in developing young players and rehabilitating "washed-up" pitchers.

Merely conducting the 1945 season proved a challenge to most clubs. As agreed, the All-Star game was replaced by seven interleague games between natural rivals (the eighth between Detroit and Pittsburgh was canceled because of its distance). Held on July 9 and 10, the contests generated $245,000 for the War Service Relief Fund. Other exhibitions were suggested. Theatrical producer Michael Todd, future husband of actress Elizabeth Taylor, proposed sending two All-Star teams to play before convalescing soldiers at Hitler's huge stadium in Nuremberg. Not to be outdone, the Navy suggested sending the World Series teams on a Pacific theater tour. Both ideas failed to materialize because of the danger of plane crashes and the potential loss of entire teams or star players. Nevertheless, the entertainment value of those ballplayers still in uniform was not lost on the services, which staged an Army-Navy series in Honolulu before thousands of servicemen.

A sure sign that the war was over was the appearance of several well-known soldiers at September games, including Generals Dwight Eisenhower, George C. Marshall, and Jonathan Wainright, the gaunt hero of Bataan and Corregidor. With the defeat of the Japanese in August, fears that a World Series would not be played disappeared. Travel restrictions were still in force, however, and the first three games of the Series were to be played in Detroit and the remaining games, if all were needed, in Chicago.

Hal Newhouser won his second straight American League Most Valuable Player award in 1945. (George Brace Photo)

The 1945 World Series

Although the 1945 World Series was exciting and went the entire seven games, the affair was not an artistic success. One writer complained that "there was too much loose play, too many mental lapses, [and] too many run-of-the-mine players involved."[9] The Cubs, led by Hank Borowy and Claude Passeau's 9-0 and 3-0 shutouts, came out of Detroit with a 2-1 lead in the series. In the first game, the Cubs were led by Phil Cavarretta, who homered, singled twice, and walked. The Tigers evened the series with a 4-1 win in the second game behind ex-servicemen Virgil Trucks, who threw a complete game, and Hank Greenberg, who homered. Claude Passeau threw a masterful one-hitter in the third game.

After switching venues to Wrigley Field, the Tigers evened the series behind the five-hit pitching of Dizzy Trout, who recovered from a bad back to defeat the Cubs 4-1 with a combination of excellent control and a booming fastball. In the fifth game, Hank Greenberg wielded a hot bat for three hits, and Hal Newhouser allowed just two hits through seven innings, as the Tigers triumphed 8-4. The series was knotted at three games apiece on the following day, when the Cubs beat Detroit 8-7 in a crazy twelve-inning contest. Cubs pitcher Claude Passeau again pitched brilliantly, until the sixth, when a torn fingernail forced him to leave the game. The floodgates opened for both teams, as relief pitchers failed to hold leads, causing a 7-7 tie through seven innings. Hank Greenberg's gigantic home run over the left-field wall capped a four-run Detroit rally in the seventh. In the twelfth inning, Stan Hack hit a double that eluded Hank Greenberg to score Frank Secory with the winning run.

The outcome of the seventh game, played on October 10, was almost a foregone conclusion after the first inning, when the Tigers ripped starting pitcher Hank Borowy and reliever Paul Derringer for five runs on their way to a 9-3 victory. Hal Newhouser scattered ten hits to earn his second World Series victory. Twenty-one World Series records were set, including total attendance (333,457), batting average for a losing team (Cubs—.263), players used in one game by both clubs (thirty-eight in game six), strikeouts by a pitcher over a seven-game series (Newhouser—22), and most decisions by one pitcher (Borowy—2-2). So ended the final wartime World Series.[10]

The 1945 season was also a season of hope for Happy Chandler. Becoming commissioner of baseball was an impossible dream come true. Chandler's Senate colleagues seemed to agree. On the day following his election, speeches in his honor were delivered by Senators Lister Hill, Kenneth McKellar, and Hiram Johnson. The move even pleased the senator's seventy-four-year-old father, who said, "I would rather that my boy be baseball commissioner than hold all the political jobs in the world. I love baseball, but I don't have much love for politics."[11]

While the owners and writers knew little about the new commissioner-elect, Chandler knew even less about the internal workings of professional baseball. Much of 1945 was spent in mutual self-discovery. In seeking guidance, Chandler naturally turned to his sponsor and friend, Larry MacPhail. At Chandler's request, MacPhail outlined baseball's predicament in a confidential letter written on April 27, 1945. Demonstrating a keen insight into the game's problems, the Yankees executive discussed the commissioner's authority and the role of the office, in addition to his own ideas on promoting the game as well as the dangers posed by gambling interests. MacPhail began the letter by explaining that "baseball faced serious problems. It has been going backward—not forward. In a great degree, responsibility for solving the problems, and reversing the trend, is squarely on your shoulders," he counseled.[12]

Belying his own emphasis on promotion, MacPhail told Chandler that the commissioner should be involved in "all phases of the game's operation and that there had been 16 votes in Cleveland behind a promotional department in the commissioner's office—an idea that would have been impossible to sell to Judge Landis." MacPhail also stressed the importance of closer ties to the minor leagues. Many executives in both camps, he noted, felt that baseball should be administratively "under one big tent." He further explained that, in promotional matters, "the Majors will not appropriate money for promotional or development work to be spent by an organization in which they have only indirect voice." Warning that promotion was essential because baseball was in danger of losing its hold as America's preeminent sport, MacPhail emphasized that baseball was no longer played in every school or college and that the minor leagues were being kept alive through direct subsidies provided by the major leagues.[13]

Gambling was another of MacPhail's major concerns, as he cautioned Chandler that "gamblers damned near ruined the game once and if they bore in again, they will finish it." Praising Landis, he noted that the Judge "had the idea that it was his job to keep the game clean—to preserve its high standards—to keep undesirable elements away—to protect the interest of the public and the players." MacPhail also argued that, with the tracks closed, the gambling situation was particularly "critical." Pointing to recent scandals in basketball, he indicated that few people realized how entrenched gamblers were in intercollegiate sports.[14]

Although noting that Landis had "functioned as a combined states attorney, one man grand jury, and trial judge and jury," MacPhail allowed that there was a difference of opinion among the owners regarding the basic mission and objectives of the commissioner's office. Nevertheless, he seemed to downplay the revisions to the Major-League Agreement made by the owners in early 1945. "There has been no limitation of authority of the Commissioner," he stated flatly. "The Commissioner has had, and still has absolute authority in all matters pertaining to 'conduct detrimental to baseball,'" MacPhail added. Where Landis erred, however, was in his attempt to seize both "legislative and judicial authority" in his application of the concept. "There was nothing in the rules or his contract to justify such interpretation," MacPhail maintained.[15]

Contrary to MacPhail's interpretation, the changes to the Major-League Agreement were significant and soon formed the basis of disagreement between Chandler and the owners. Indeed, the changes provided a clear message that the owners were not looking for and would not accept another tyrannical commissioner in the mold of Landis. Alterations in the agreement included the creation of an advisory council to the commissioner for the purpose of submitting rules or amendments to existing regulations, the restoration of an owner's right to challenge a commissioner's ruling in a court of law, and the elimination of a provision under which the commissioner could act on his own authority in any matter he considered "detrimental to baseball." In addition, the owners increased the vote required to elect a new commissioner from a simple majority to three-fourths of the clubs.[16]

Chandler's honeymoon with baseball owners, officials, and writers was short lived. Although Chandler was attuned to the controversies surrounding Kentucky politics, he was not accustomed to the sudden deluge of microscopic attention he received from sportswriters who represented every metropolis in the nation. In sharp contrast to Landis, who discussed nothing but golf in great detail, Chandler was candid almost to a fault with the press. Another potential source of amusement for some writers was the new commissioner's penchant for singing in public. He ended a dinner in his honor for New York writers by singing "My Old Kentucky Home" and "Take Me Out to the Ball Game." One writer who admired Chandler's tenor voice commented that "if Landis could play Hamlet roles for years, why shouldn't Chandler cut loose in song?"[17] Others, particularly New York writers, had difficulty with the image Chandler projected. A man who sang "My Old Kentucky Home" at the slightest urging was not considered dignified enough to be taken seriously.[18]

Chandler's first crisis occurred when he "innocently" told a reporter that he did not feel that ballplayers ought to bet on horses. Having been shut down during the war, when almost every other sport was allowed to continue, racing interests in Kentucky were extremely upset with their native son. In *The Blood-Horse*, Joe Estes criticized baseball for assuming a "somewhat holy attitude" that it was beneficial and that somehow racing was "a special contaminating influence on ballplayers."[19] Chandler held firm, and eventually the furor died down. Nevertheless, he learned very quickly what effect his remarks could have when they reached the media.

In another incident, which he eventually admitted was "a horrible thing," Chandler's good intentions succeeded in getting an umpire fired and in alienating Will Harridge.[20] Deeply concerned over their poor salaries and working conditions, one of the new commissioner's pet interests was the welfare of umpires. During a chance meeting on a rainy summer night in Washington, Chandler chatted with a group of umpires and told them that they should have a minimum salary of $5,000, better dressing rooms, and more expense money. He asked Ernie Stewart, a college-educated umpire, to send out a letter canvassing major-league umpires about these concerns. When Harridge learned of the letter, he sent Stewart a telegram that accused him of being disloyal to his fellow umpires and that requested his resignation. When Stewart contacted Harridge to explain what had taken place, the latter replied, "Well, when he [Chandler] learns to keep his nose out of my business, he is going to be better off." At a hearing that followed, Chandler remonstrated with Harridge, but to no avail. Stewart was fired. Years later, Chandler admitted to Stewart that his failure to put his "foot down" on Harridge was the first mistake he made in office.[21] The incident also taught Chandler that there were certain "league matters" over which he did not have jurisdiction—the supervision of umpires was one of them.

Chandler's public pronouncements also began to worry baseball owners, some of whom began to look on him as a loose cannon. Making it clear that he thought high school players should be protected from professional baseball until after graduation, Chandler declared in one interview that, when the war was over, he was going to stop "the epidemic of cradle-snatching" that had taken place because of the manpower shortage.[22] Many owners did not feel that high school players should be off limits. When asked in another interview about his attitude toward unionization and the game, a sensitive topic for any business operation, the commissioner replied, "Any fellow has the right to join anything he desires. . . . This country is a voluntary country as far as I'm concerned."[23] Finally, at a flag-raising speech in Baltimore on May 24, Chandler made a ringing speech in which he declared that "My first duty is to America and baseball, not to my employers or the club owners who elected me. . . . With God's help and the fans' support, I will keep the game clean and keep the game going."[24] These were certainly not the words of "a house man," and certainly not in the tradition of Judge Landis, who never gave interviews and never traveled around the country giving talks.

As Chandler's first joint meeting with the owners and the ceremony that would officially make him commissioner approached, a clash with owners over his statements and activities looked imminent. Indeed, rumors abounded that some of the owners were going to attempt to usurp Chandler's authority over baseball's treasury and pass it on to Leslie O'Connor, Landis's former assistant. When the July 12 meeting came, however, Chandler was well prepared. In less than two hours, he whipped through his agenda, leaving the owners speechless. In a fait accompli, he announced to the owners that, in consultation with the two league presidents, he had already offered the secretary-treasurer position to his old college friend Walter Mulbry and that, if anyone objected, he was prepared to pay Mulbry's salary himself. No one did. Chandler also announced that Leslie O'Connor was to be given the title of "special assistant"—a move that undermined any opportunity to shift the responsibility of the treasury from his control.[25]

Sounding almost like Landis himself, the new commissioner told the owners that he had accepted Landis's job and "all of the authority that went with it" and that he would be "the absolute boss" or they could find themselves another commissioner. Then he announced, "I don't want to handicap you. But neither do I want anybody to get the impression I am going to let down the bars. The rights of the players must be protected. The stake of the fans in our game must be recognized. I am going to be helpful, but also tough. I am going to be understanding, but also firm. I was elected unanimously. When I accepted I assumed I would have full powers and I insist upon having full powers and nothing short of it."[26]

Chandler then produced a financial report detailing the expenditures of the commissioner's office for the previous twenty years. Criticizing the owners for thinking that he was not capable of handling baseball's treasury, the former Senator stated, "Gentlemen, when I was Governor of Kentucky, I was directly in charge of more than $70,000,000 of the state's money, and there never was a complaint." At this point, rather than remove funds from Chandler's control, the owners approved a fund of $10,000 for special purposes. Again, in a move strikingly reminiscent of his predecessor, Chandler read aloud from a copy of the 1921 owners' agreement with Judge Landis that stipulated that the owners would respect Landis's decisions and would cooperate with him, even if they believed that he was wrong. Chandler insisted that the owners revive that pact with him or he would not sign his contract. He also added that he would be the sole judge of conduct detrimental to baseball and that, if any owner sought to challenge him, they would need a new commissioner immediately.[27]

Chandler's actions left a definite impression on the owners. He not only pulled a "Landis" on them, he also demonstrated the skills that made him a hard and decisive politician. As the meeting broke up, Cubs' owner Phil Wrigley was heard to say to Larry MacPhail, "Whew! They told me this guy was a backslapper!"[28] By acceding to Chandler's demands, particularly the Landis stipulation, the *Sporting News* wrote, "Chandler virtually restored the clause barring recourse to the courts."[29] Although the agreement might not have withstood a court test, it was a formidable barrier reinforced by peer pressure and the embarrassment that would be brought to baseball if its commissioner resigned.

In spite of this show of strength, Chandler was tested several more times in 1945. First, some owners were bothered by rumors that Chandler, who remained in his Senate office, might be drawing two salaries.[30] Chandler explained that he wanted to vote on the Bretton Woods monetary agreement and the United Nations charter before leaving the Senate and that he would not begin drawing baseball pay until after he had resigned from the legislature.[31] Second, several owners were also upset with Chandler because of a new skirmish with Will Harridge concerning umpires' pay during the World Series. When Chandler suggested to Harridge and a group of umpires that the "men in blue" should receive additional compensation for the World Series beyond what was stipulated by regulation, the American League president was once again incensed. Chandler's interference with the umpires stimulated rumors that the owners had met to discuss buying out Chandler's contract to oust him. William O. DeWitt, general manager of the St. Louis Browns, in an interview some thirty-five years later, confirmed the rumor as he recalled that Tom Yawkey had offered to buy up Chandler's contract himself because the league treasury could not afford it. DeWitt, noted, however, that most of the owners simply wanted to discuss the incident with Chandler.[32]

Finally, at baseball's winter meetings, the minor leagues voted to strip the commissioner of his veto power and to remove baseball's promotional activities from his office. Despite rumors to the contrary, major-league owners refused to support the minor-league actions and instead approved one of Chandler's pet projects—a rule that prohibited baseball from signing high school players unless they had been out of school for more than a year. This action, plus the approval of the commissioner's $50,000 promotional plan the previous August, cemented the commissioner's agenda.

By the end of 1945 it was clear that Chandler's position as commissioner was strengthened. He defeated several moves to reduce the power of the commissionership, he stood up to the owners, and he won approval of his own programs. Owners and baseball executives were not sure of Chandler, but many were still willing to give him a chance. "Chandler is trying," stated Phillies general manager Herb Pennock. "And, because he is trying, he is making mistakes. Politics isn't like baseball. You don't go about things in the same way . . . give the man a chance."[33]

In November 1945, Chandler resigned his seat in the U.S. Senate. After making an emotional speech on the Senate floor, Chandler received the accolades and congratulations of his peers, many of whom jokingly asked to shake his fifty-thousand-dollar hand. In January 1946, the new commissioner shifted his offices from Chicago to Cincinnati's Carew Towers, where he could look across the Ohio River to the shores of Kentucky or to what he called "the promised land." Baseball was about to enter an exciting and tumultuous period.

1946

The St. Louis Cardinals celebrated in the clubhouse
after taking the 1946 World Series from the Red Sox.
From left to right are manager Eddie Dyer, Enos Slaughter,
George Munger, Whitey Kurowski, and Joe Garagiola.

(The Sporting News)

4

The Mexican Baseball Revolution

Danny Gardella was the unlikely catalyst who sparked a baseball revolution in 1946. Teammates thought of the wartime Giants' outfielder as a physical fitness buff and a free spirit. An impulsive character, he entertained fans and players alike by eating dandelions in the outfield grass while walking on his hands or traversing the roofs of Pullman cars while pretending he was a tightrope walker.[1] Gardella was also a renowned prankster who, during the 1945 season, wrote a suicide note and climbed out on a four-inch hotel window ledge just to see roommate Nap Reyes's reaction.[2]

A chance meeting between Gardella and Mexican industrialist and customs broker Jorge Pasquel at Roon's Gymnasium in New York set in motion one of the strangest chapters in baseball history. A 4-F player because of a punctured eardrum, Gardella (.272-18-72) was one of the National League's most productive home-run hitters in 1945. Nevertheless, he still needed to work at the gymnasium to make ends meet. When Pasquel, who was also president of the major professional baseball league in Mexico, learned that Gardella had to work in the off-season, he was incredulous. "That is when he [Pasquel] got the germ of an idea in his mind," recalled Gardella. When baseball veterans returned from the war, Pasquel realized that a surplus pool of major-league talent might be available to play in Mexico at bargain prices. Gardella politely refused Pasquel's initial inquiry regarding his own employment, but they parted with the understanding that Gardella was welcome to a job in Mexico anytime he wanted.[3]

At the onset of spring training in 1946, Gardella's relationship with the Giants began to sour. After arriving late at spring training, he refused to sign a contract that duplicated his $5,000 1945 salary, and he got into an argument with Eddie Brannick, the team's traveling secretary. When manager Mel Ott learned of the exchange, he informed Gardella that he would not be allowed to practice with the team.[4] Gardella knew that the Giants had the upper hand. With a camp full of wartime players and returning veterans, he would have to compete hard to win a spot on the roster. Feeling trapped and unfairly pressured, the angry and frustrated Giant called Pasquel, who dispatched an agent to bring Gardella to Mexico. Before his departure, Gardella told the media, "You may say for me, that I do not intend to let the Giants enrich themselves at my expense by sending me to a minor-league club. They have treated me shabbily, I have decided to take my gifted talents to Mexico."[5]

On Gardella's first night in Mexico, he was chauffeured around in a big limousine. Accompanied by an attractive female escort, he dined at a restaurant where he saw Manolete, the great Spanish matador. The outfielder quickly forgot "the American scene" and signed a contract for $8,000 and was promised a $5,000 bonus.[6] As an unsigned ballplayer, Gardella violated only the reserve clause of his contract with the Giants by jumping to Mexico. This clause, standard in all baseball contracts, bound players indefinitely to the teams that owned their services. It provided the game with stability by preventing players from transferring to other teams and averted bidding wars that favored the wealthiest clubs.

The Mexican League also enjoyed a degree of stability. Although not recognized by professional baseball, the league had been founded in 1924 by Ernesto Carmona, the Mexico City manager, and Alejandro Aguilar Reyes. The latter was better known as Fray Naño, the publisher of *La Afición*, Mexico's daily sports paper. Team owners included some of the country's wealthiest men—bankers, automobile dealers, dentists, and businessmen involved with paper manufacturing, brewing, soft drinks bottling, and the theater. In 1946, the Mexican League consisted of teams representing eight cities or towns (see table 4).

The Pasquel brothers—Bernardo, Jorge, Mario, and twins Alfonso and Gerardo—were the dominant force behind the league. As one contemporary writer noted, "People who grew up with the Pasquels in Vera Cruz find them strong-talking, quick-tempered, hard-hitting, and rolling in dough."[7] They owned banks, newspapers, and at one time ran the national lottery. Several sources estimated their wealth to be equivalent to $60 million.[8] Whereas Bernardo was the financier of the family, Jorge was its spiritual leader. A man of strong passions who bore a passing resemblance to actor Tyrone Power, Jorge enjoyed a reputation for his involvement with beautiful women, luxurious living, and fancy automobiles. Before Mexico's entry into World War II in 1942, Pasquel was on the U.S. State Department's blacklist for trading with the enemy.[9] Moreover, he

Table 4. Teams in the Mexican League, 1946

City	Population[a]	Owner
Mexico City	1,448,422	Jorge Pasquel
Puebla	138,491	Castor Montodo
Monterrey	185,833	Group led by Aurelia Ferrara
San Luis Potosi	57,353	Dr. Eduardo Pitman
Torreon	75,796	Jose Ortiz
Tampico	81,312	H. Fleischman/Dr. Alfred Cantu
Nuevo Laredo	28,872	Frederico Longoria
Veracruz[b]	54,225	Jorge Pasquel

[a] 1940 census figures. *The Sporting News,* March 21, 1946, 2.
[b] The Veracruz Blues played most of their games in Mexico City.

had been acquitted, based on self-defense, of shooting and killing a government border official.[10] Pasquel's fascination with baseball eventually led him to become president of the league.

Before Danny Gardella's appearance in Mexico, the league consisted of players from Mexico, Cuba, Puerto Rico, and the American Negro Leagues. Attractive salaries drew many Negro League stars, such as Josh Gibson, Leon Day, Willard Brown, and Ray Dandridge. Negro League salaries were not competitive, and African Americans encountered little racial bias in Mexico. Other amenities were also available. For instance, Ray Dandridge's family lived in a large rent-free six-room apartment in Mexico City's Chapultepec Park. The Pasquels provided the family with a maid and a tutor for the children. Dandridge's salary was $9,000 for five months of play—a figure far in excess of many major-league incomes in the 1940s. To further cement the relationship, Jorge Pasquel purchased a $10,000 home for the Dandridges in Newark, New Jersey.[11]

With the adoption of strict wartime measures at the beginning of 1945 in the United States, a number of Latin players chose to play in the Mexican League rather than serve in the armed forces or work in defense plants. During the fall of 1945, Commissioner Chandler prohibited major-league players from playing winter ball in Cuba, because of the presence of ineligible players who had played in Mexico. A number of major-league players, such as Mike Guerra, Gil Torres, Lou Klein, Sal Maglie, Dick Sisler, and Fred Martin, ignored Chandler's ruling and played in Cuba anyway. Chandler took no action against these players because he feared that the move would severely diminish the level of play in Cuba.[12]

Far more serious, however, was the threat posed by the Pasquels. With

Jorge and Bernardo Pasquel—the Mexican Raiders. *(The Sporting News)*

Danny Gardella in the fold, offers, containing substantial signing bonuses, were made to Sal Maglie and Adrian Zabala of the Giants, the Dodgers' Luis Olmo, Roland Gladu, and Jean Pierre Roy, the Cardinals' Fred Martin, and Roberto Estallela of the Athletics. The first player to sign was Olmo—a player who was destined to be a fourth outfielder with the Dodgers in 1946. He signed for $40,000, a bonus, performance incentives, and subsidies covering his family's living expenses. At the time of the signing, Olmo announced, "I gave Mr. Rickey every chance in the world to offer me a satisfactory contract, but all my cables, letters, and telephone calls were fruitless." In a lame effort, the Dodgers finally countered with a $12,000 contract offer, but Olmo in reply cabled, "Boost comes a little late, doesn't it?"[13] The size of Olmo's $40,000 contract shocked baseball and led Jorge Pasquel to brag that it was understandable that American ballplayers wanted to come to Mexico, where their salaries were tax free and their living expenses subsidized. Charging that American baseball paid its players "peon salaries," he announced, "I am ready to compete with Organized Ball, dollar for dollar and peso for peso, for the best talent available."[14]

Another major-league player who signed to play in the Mexican League in early 1946 was thirty-year-old native Cuban Adrian Zabala. The slightly built left-hander was 2-4 with a 4.78 earned run average in two months of service with the Giants in 1945. Zabala was extremely disappointed when the Giants' 1946 salary offer came in at the same $4,000 he had received the year before. Not only was he paid $800 a month to play winter ball in Cuba, the Pasquels offered him an $8,000 contract and a $7,000 bonus to sign to play in Mexico in 1946. Realizing his pitching career would soon end, Zabala signed with the Pasquels. Nevertheless, having an American wife and child, Zabala asked the Giants to put him on the voluntarily retired list so he could retain his right to play in the major leagues. Rather than granting this request, the team told him that he would be blacklisted.[15]

Major-league baseball's reaction to the Mexican League threat was swift. The counterattack began in earnest when Clark Griffith, Will Harridge, and Happy Chandler used a trip to Cuba as an excuse to warn players to distance themselves from the Pasquels. Chandler announced that all players who jumped their contracts or violated their reserve status would be banished from baseball for five years, unless they returned to their teams before opening day. Thinking that a two-year ban would not deter players, Chandler later justified the severity of his action, noting, "The question was having the penalty severe enough so that it would deter fellas who might want to do the same thing for quick money. . . . [There was] no trouble with that, I just made it five years and stopped a whole lot of them."[16]

The ban received the support of major-league owners, but it was not universally popular. In Cuba, where it was first announced, fans realized that the decision left home-grown players, who normally played in Mexico, with little room to maneuver and that they might not be able or willing to return to the island to play winter ball. The announcement also smacked of American imperialism.[17] Furthermore, the ban did not prevent the Pasquels from approaching some of the biggest names in baseball. For instance, Cleveland's Bob Feller was offered a three-year deal at $120,000 a year "with all of the money up front in an American bank." "I thanked him very much," recalled Feller, "and did not go."[18]

Ted Williams was also approached and met with Jorge Pasquel in Cuba at the same time Chandler issued his ban. By one account, Williams was offered $500,000 to sign; in another, he was said to have received a blank check. In yet another story, Williams purportedly asked Pasquel whether the Mexican league would give him four strikes instead of three. When the answer was affirmative, he supposedly replied, "Well, I won't come anyway."[19] In a 1988 interview, Williams revealed that the Pasquels offered him $100,000 at a time when he was making $40,000. Although he felt that playing and living conditions in Mexico would not be comparable with the big leagues and he had no intention of leaving the Red Sox, nonetheless he listened to Pasquel's terms. Williams remembered his encounter with Jorge Pasquel clearly: "Jeez!" he exclaimed. "Pasquel had diamonds in his tie and diamonds on his watches, and diamonds on his wrist . . . he didn't have one in his ear, but he had diamonds all over . . . and every time he talked, he kind of splattered you a little bit. But I listened to him and got a commitment from him. But I never really gave it a tumble."[20]

The commissioner's ban failed to stop some players, who, like St. Louis Browns star Vern Stephens, had to see Mexico for themselves. Stephens was the Mexican League's biggest coup. The shortstop was the Browns' best player. He was a power hitter who could run and throw and played a position manned by a weak hitter on most teams. Stephens had one major flaw—although not a drinker, he liked night life. The Browns were so concerned about his nocturnal activities that the shortstop was required to room with the manager on road trips.[21] William O. DeWitt, the team's general manager, said that the Browns tried to tame Stephens's "wild hair" by placing an incentive clause in his 1946 contract giving him a $2,500 bonus for good conduct. Stephens was offended by the clause and countered the Browns' offer of $13,000 with a demand for $17,000.[22]

While Stephens was negotiating with the Browns, he was contacted several times by the Pasquels. Determined to see how far he could push the Pasquels, he asked them for a five-year $75,000 contract with all the money up front and a clause that would allow only him to break the contract. To Stephens's amazement, Jorge Pasquel agreed to his terms and asked, "Can you get to Mexico City in time to play on Sunday?" Dazed by Pasquel's quick acceptance, Stephens explained the situation to his wife and then informed the Browns with the hope that they would make a counteroffer. When they refused, he booked a flight to Mexico.[23]

Like Danny Gardella, Stephens was wined, dined, and feted when he arrived in Mexico. His contract was ready for his signature, a $5,000 check was immediately mailed to his wife, and the remainder of his salary was placed in escrow in a Mexican bank.[24] In his first game, Stephens was cheered by a boisterous Mexico City crowd, and his single in the ninth inning led his new Veracruz team to victory. In spite of the grand reception and his instant success, serious doubts remained in Stephens's mind

St. Louis Browns slugger Vern
Stephens had to see Mexico for
himself. (George Brace Photo)

concerning his new situation. His wife opposed the venture, and when
he attempted to locate accommodations for his family, he found no suitable homes. Other factors also gave Stephens pause. The playing conditions were not up to major-league standards, he missed warm showers
and a friendly clubhouse, and he did not like the food or the language
barrier. Even the faucets, with their C *(caliente)* for hot instead of cold,
confused him. Finally, he was leary of Pasquel's pistol-packing confidants.
His uneasiness was compounded by the suspicion that he was under constant surveillance. Almost everywhere he went, Stephens was accompanied by Mario Pasquel and a bodyguard.[25]

In the meantime, in an attempt to persuade Stephens to return, the
Browns sent scout Jack Fournier and Stephens's father to Mexico talk to
him. DeWitt empowered Fournier to tell Stephens that the Browns would
drop the "incentive" clause and that they were ready to give him the
$17,500 salary he initially requested. In addition, Browns president Rich-
ard Muckerman went to Chicago to persuade Will Harridge to back them
and discuss Stephens' return with Commissioner Chandler.[26] Getting
Stephens to come back was not difficult, because he was already disillusioned with Mexico. On April 5, 1946, he was eating breakfast in his
Monterrey hotel dining room when an American friend informed him

that the Browns were not only ready to meet his demands but that Jack Fournier and his father were in a nearby bar and wanted to talk with him. As was his custom, Stephens's bodyguard joined him for breakfast, but, when the bodyguard went to the men's room, Stephens seized the opportunity and escaped.[27]

Leaving all his possessions behind, Stephens was spirited north to Nuevo Laredo, where he donned his father's overcoat and hat and left Jack Fournier's car two blocks from the border. Nuevo Laredo was Pasquel country, and pedestrian border crossers attracted much less attention. Nevertheless, Stephens was sighted by Erasmo Flores, the general manager of the Nuevo Laredo team. Flores called Alfonso Pasquel, who, instead of calling immigration officials at the bridge in time to stop Stephens, assured the baseball official that Stephens was still in Monterrey.[28] Once across the border, Stephens signed with the Browns and, with Commissioner Chandler's blessing, returned to the major leagues. Although Stephens returned Pasquel's money, Jorge Pasquel was not mollified, complaining that he never even bothered "to say good-bye, and I treat him like family." On April 8, 1946, he announced that Stephens's departure was "an insult to Mexico" and that he would engage a New York firm to sue him for $100,000.[29]

In spite of his difficulties with Stephens, Jorge Pasquel was busy enticing other major-league players to Mexico. Almost coinciding with Stephens's jump came the news that Brooklyn catcher Mickey Owen and a trio of New York Giants players were also headed to Mexico. The three Giants players, pitcher Sal Maglie and infielders Roy Zimmerman and George Hausmann, were fired by Giants owner Horace Stoneham for negotiating with the Pasquels. Sal Maglie was first approached in early 1946 when he pitched for Dolf Luque in Cuba. At that time, Bernardo Pasquel offered him a $7,500 contract with a $3,000 signing bonus. Having just signed a contract with the Giants, Maglie was reluctant to give up major-league baseball. He countered by asking for $15,000. This ended the conversation, and Pasquel gave him his business card and telephone number.[30]

Soon after spring training began, Maglie was contacted by Danny Gardella, who explained that the Pasquels were looking for infielders. Maglie talked to teammates Hausmann and Zimmerman, who both displayed interest. They used Maglie's room phone to contact the Pasquels and quickly came to terms. Hausmann, an adept bunter, was making only $5,000 after two fine seasons as the Giants' regular second baseman. He supplemented his income by working in the winter as a drill press operator. When he approached Mel Ott to see whether he could get a raise, the Giants manager told him he was "lucky to be playing on the ball club."[31]

The Giants also refused to listen to Roy Zimmerman's argument that the expenses of living in New York necessitated a higher salary. The embittered infielder also knew that his playing time would diminish with the return of Johnny Mize from the service.

For Sal Maglie, a trip to Mexico was more of a dilemma. In 1945, he had demonstrated great promise with a 5-4 record and sparkling 2.35 earned run average. Even at age twenty-nine, his career potential in the major leagues seemed good. Maglie loved to pitch and thrived on work, but with so many players vying for positions in 1946, he pitched little during spring training. Maglie was also concerned about his family's financial situation. Furthermore, the Giants' $8,000 salary offer for 1946 paled when compared to the $6,500 he had earned in Cuba during the winter coupled with the Pasquels' offer. Finally, a man he trusted, former Giant great Dolf Luque, was managing in Mexico.[32]

Even though Maglie had committed himself to going to Mexico during the excitement of the other two players' calls to the Pasquels, he was still wavering. His decision was soon determined by the Giants. Somehow manager Mel Ott was warned of the trio's telephone call and convened a team meeting. Before the gathering, he summoned Maglie into his office and berated him for helping the Mexican League steal his players. During the tense meeting that followed, the Giants manager asked each player in the room. "Were you ever contacted by the Mexicans? Are you going to jump?" When he confronted Maglie, the exasperated pitcher replied that he was going.[33] Ott was beside himself with anger. As a result of the meeting, Charles Stoneham released the three players. When the players reached Mexico, Maglie was quoted as saying, "I will make as much the first year, including my bonus, as I would in five years at my present salary with the Giants. Some of the fellows are getting as low as $2,500." Then he added, "Why should players have to work for that cheap wage?" An unforgiving Stoneham commented, "I hope those contracts . . . are worth more than the paper they are written on."[34]

With the Giants' camp still in an uproar, Arnold "Mickey" Owen of the Brooklyn Dodgers was giving Branch Rickey and the Pasquels fits. Owen, drafted into the Navy in 1945, was the Dodgers' first string catcher during the war. He was famous for the passed ball that he had allowed, costing the Dodgers the fourth game of the 1941 World Series. By March 1946, Owen was about to be discharged, and though he made $12,500 with the Dodgers before being drafted, he and his family needed more money. Thinking he would play the Mexican League card against the Dodgers in salary negotiations, he contacted both organizations. Rickey failed to reply, but the Pasquels offered the catcher a five-year contract at $15,000 per year with a $12,500 bonus for signing.[35]

Owen reported the Mexican offer to Rickey and stated, "My wife, Gloria, is urging me to head for Mexico. I want to do what is best for myself and my family. But business ethics are to be considered and my long friendship with you." An appointment was set up with the Dodgers, but it never took place. Instead, Owen signed a five-year contract with the Pasquels that included a signing bonus and assurances that the Mexican League would pay all of his taxes and housing and travel expenses. As the Owen family traveled south, they experienced second thoughts upon hearing of Vern Stephens's return to the United States. After a hurriedly arranged meeting with Alfonso Pasquel in San Antonio failed to calm their fears, Owen announced that he would give the Pasquels their money back and return to the Dodgers. When the *Sporting News* heard of Owen's return, the paper gloated that the outcome of the Stephens and Owen situation constituted "two body blows for the Mexican League." Claiming that the Pasquels had finally extended themselves too far, it contended that Owen's situation should warn other players against going to the Mexican League.[36]

Baseball's optimism, however, was short lived. When Rickey first learned that Owen was going to Mexico, he announced that the catcher would never play for Brooklyn again and that, "if he doesn't decide to go to Mexico, he will either be traded or sold."[37] When Owen contacted Rickey, true to form, the Dodgers' president offered to let him make a deal for himself with another club. As they were headed north, somewhere in Mississippi, the Owens learned that the Pasquels intended to file a $100,000 breach-of-contract suit against them. Completely overcome with indecision, they made an unsuccessful attempt to reach Rickey. Then, in desperation, they recontacted the Pasquels, who invited them to a meeting in Laredo, Texas. Faced with the prospect of never playing for the Dodgers again and with the cloud of a $100,000 suit hanging over them, the Owen family turned around and headed south once again. This time Owen met with Alfonso and Bernardo Pasquel, who made convincing arguments that their promises would be kept by writing out checks for Owen's bonus and first-year salary. Taking no more chances, the Pasquels flew Owen to Mexico City.[38]

Much to the dismay of the major-league owners, efforts by the Pasquels to attract American players accelerated. In late April, pitchers Ace Adams and Harry Feldman jumped the Giants. Then, at the beginning of May, the Pasquels went after members of both the Yankees and the Dodgers. In New York, Bernardo Pasquel publicly vowed that he was not going to leave the city without taking a Yankee regular with him. Offers were made to Snuffy Stirnweiss and Phil Rizzuto, the Yankees' double-play combination. Whereas Stirnweiss refused an offer of $100,000 for five years and a substantial bonus, Pasquel came much closer to signing Rizzuto, who was offered a $60,000 contract and a $15,000 signing bonus. "The Mexican offer made a profound impression on Phil," recalled former teammate Bobby Brown.[39] Rizzuto dined with Pasquel at the Waldorf Astoria and was promised a tax-free salary, a new Cadillac, and free housing in a luxury apartment. The following day, Rizzuto told Pasquel he would sign if he was given the bonus. The Yankee shortstop soon wavered, however, when his wife Cora balked at the prospect of going to Mexico.[40]

The offers to Stirnweiss and Rizzuto spurred Larry MacPhail into action. He sought temporary injunctions in New York against the Pasquels to keep them from tampering with his players. In the meantime, the Dodgers found themselves facing a crisis in St. Louis, where the team was scheduled to play a series with the Cardinals. Having already lost Olmo, Owen, and Roland Gladu, Branch Rickey now learned that the Mexican League had approached Pete Reiser and Stan Rojek. Rojek, an outstanding rookie prospect, was offered a contract for $8,000 and bonus of $10,000 to sign. The potential loss of Reiser, a player of immense talent and the National League batting champion in 1941, really distressed Rickey. After refusing two lucrative offers, Reiser was dazzled by an offer of $100,000 for three years with an immediate advance of $50,000. He could not help being interested—after all, he was making only $12,500 a year with the Dodgers and had just returned from the service, where he had made $50 a month.

Rickey found the Mexican League situation abhorrent. Only a few weeks before, he had chased a Mexican League agent out of the Dodgers' spring training camp and threatened to sue the Pasquels if he ever came back. Sportscaster Red Barber could not recall ever seeing Rickey in an angrier mood. "He hated to lose those ballplayers—he hated to lose Mickey Owen," remembered Barber. "These are players he had developed, trained, and counted on for success."[41] Rickey hurriedly flew to St. Louis, where the team was idled by a rainout. On his arrival, he discovered that Leo Durocher was in the process of persuading Rojek to stay with the team. Rickey then went to work on Reiser—a conversation that resulted in a telephone call to Mexico in which Reiser told the Pasquels he was no longer interested. When pressed for details of the meeting, Rickey's only comment was that he had persuaded Reiser that "he didn't want to be a man without a country." Rickey also announced that he was seeking an injunction against the Pasquels, though he did not see the Mexicans as a permanent threat. "They can't go on paying out such huge sums when it doesn't come in at the gate," he explained.[42]

The Pasquel brothers seemed delighted to take on major-league baseball in the courts. Bernardo Pasquel announced that "he would go to the [U.S.] Supreme Court to establish our right to offer better salaries than are now open to players on the American continent." The Mexicans employed the prestigious New York law firm of Harding, Hess, and Elder, which routinely handled major Mexican-American governmental affairs. The firm's involvement more than hinted that the Mexican government stood behind the league. The stakes were high. The real danger, according to the *Washington Post*'s Shirley Povich, was the Mexicans' constant claim that baseball was an unfair monopoly and that they would welcome a court test based on the legality of players' contracts. By challenging the Mexican League in court, MacPhail and Rickey were playing right into their hands.[43] Fortunately, from the standpoint of major-league baseball, the results of their motions for injunction were mixed, and the potential of a direct clash with the Mexicans over the legality of the reserve clause did not materialize.[44]

The Pasquels, however, were not finished. To legitimize their activities and attract attention, they brought Babe Ruth to Mexico. Ruth made an appearance at the May 16, 1946, Tampico–Veracruz game before a crowd of 15,000. The ailing slugger appeared tired and sounded hoarse as he delivered a brief speech in which he lauded Pasquel for trying to give Mexico the kind of baseball it deserved. Ruth returned to Delta Park after a two-week vacation to put on a hitting demonstration in front of 22,000 fans. With Veracruz manager Ramon Bragana on the mound, Ruth swung at about thirty pitches but hit only two with any authority. Finally, Ernesto Carmona, the manager and president of the Mexico City Reds, brought in a batting practice pitcher to throw to Ruth. "The first thing Babe did," recalled Mickey Owen, who was catching that day, "was to hit one way in the top of those bleachers. People went wild. I don't think that Babe could have taken more than two or three more swings in that high altitude."[45]

The Pasquels got their money's worth from Babe Ruth's appearance. Everyone in Mexico City was talking about the visit—an event that inflated Mexican pride at the expense of the Americans. "It is impossible to be in Mexico City these days without sensing it," wrote Milton Bracker in the *New York Times*, "and wondering what the Pasquels will do next. As one Mexican put it aptly today, 'Nobody really likes Jorge—but he's a national hero.'"[46]

Mexican fans did not have to wait long for Jorge Pasquel's next move. As Babe Ruth headed home, three St. Louis Cardinal ballplayers, Max Lanier, Fred Martin, and Lou Klein, arrived in Mexico. The trio's defection injured team morale and diminished the Cardinals' pennant chances. Lou Klein was the Cardinals' regular second baseman, before he left for the service in 1943, Fred Martin was an excellent right-handed pitcher, and Max Lanier was 6-0 with an earned run average of 1.93 at the time of his departure. In addition, Lanier was historically tough on the Dodgers, the Cardinals' biggest rival. Klein and Martin, who were initially approached by the Pasquels in Cuba, decided to jump because they knew that they would have reduced roles on the Cardinals. When they were approached again, they leaped at the opportunity and begged Lanier to go with them. Lanier accepted the offer because he was disgruntled with Cardinals owner Sam Breadon's tightfisted policies and was amazed by the Pasquels' offer.

The Pasquels courted other Cardinals, including Terry Moore, Enos Slaughter, and Stan Musial. Musial, of course, was the big prize. The St. Louis star was initially contacted by former pitcher Roy Henshaw, who acted as an agent for the Pasquels. In a preliminary agreement worked out between the two men, Musial was to receive a $25,000 tax-free annual salary, a signing bonus of $25,000, and an advance of his first year's salary. Henshaw talked to both Mickey Owen and Jorge Pasquel and told them that Musial planned to go to Pittsburgh to buy a new Chrysler. Henshaw told Owen, "I'm sure he is going to pick up his wife and child in Donora, Pennsylvania, with the new Chrysler and he will drive down there [Mexico]."[47]

On June 14, 1946, Alfonso Pasquel and Mickey Owen met with Musial to close the deal at the Fairgrounds Hotel in St. Louis. As the meeting began, Owen asked Musial whether he had talked to the Mexicans, and he replied, "No, no, I haven't talked to the Mexicans." "Well, you do know Henshaw?" Owen asked. "Yeah, I know Henshaw." Owen then mentioned his own conversation with Henshaw and the terms that Musial had agreed to, and Musial replied, "Yeah, yeah, he talked to me about something like that." "I could see that something was gnawing at him," remembered Owen. Owen then introduced Alphonso Pasquel to Musial, and to Musial's amazement the Mexican placed five $10,000 checks in front of him. Owen's account follows:

> There were five of them. I thought Musial was going to swallow [his] cigar when he [saw] all that money on the table. It would have been peanuts to him now, but then it looked like more money than they had in Donora, Pennsylvania. He wouldn't say much. He just kinda held back and looked at it, bit on his cigar some more, and blew smoke all over the place. I said, "Did you make a deal?" and he said, "Oh I talked to a fella about it." "Do you want to answer a question?" Owen asked. "Have you signed another contract with the ball club [the Cardinals] here, where you won't go to the Mexican League." He said, "I can't talk about that." And I knew he had at the time. I am sure that he signed not only for that year, but for the following year. It was the greatest thing that happened to him that he didn't go.[48]

Max Lanier was disgruntled with Sam Breadon's salary offer. (George Brace Photo)

In 1946, Musial's salary was a paltry $13,500. The amount offered by the Pasquels would have turned any ballplayer's head. In a contemporary account, Musial admitted that he was tempted by the offer. "They made me an offer that was hard to turn down," he noted. "All that money makes a fellow do a lot of thinking before he says no."[49] Although he did not get an immediate raise from Sam Breadon to stay with the Cardinals, he did seek advice from manager Eddie Dyer, who cautioned him about integrity.[50] Referring to his contractual obligations to the Cardinals, Dyer asked Musial what his sons would think if he broke his word.[51] Later Musial told a friend, "I was afraid that every kid who had my autograph or every boy and girl who had my picture pasted in their scrapbook would rip it out."[52] The day following his meeting with Owen and Alfonso Pasquel, he told them no.

Sam Breadon was shaken by the potential loss of Musial. Moreover, he was tipped off by sportswriter Ray Gillespie that the Mexicans were courting Musial again, this time with an offer of $150,000 in cash. In a desperate move, Breadon flew to Mexico to discuss the situation with Jorge Pasquel, who was delighted to meet with Breadon—a man willing to break ranks to protect his own ballplayers. Breadon also provided him with the legitimacy he craved. As a result, the Cardinals lost no more ballplayers to Mexico. Chandler was infuriated by Breadon's Mexican trip. When Breadon refused to appear before the him, the Cardinal owner was fined $5,000 and prohibited from representing his club at the July baseball meetings in Boston. The fine was rescinded only after Ford Frick interceded on his behalf and the Cardinal owner agreed to appear before Chandler. The commissioner scolded Breadon for breaking ranks and told him, "If you are really scared, let's surrender and ask for terms. If not, let's not let Pasquel think he has us on the run."[53]

Although baseball seemed to be on the run, time was short for the Mexican League. Jorge Pasquel and Mexican President Miguel Aleman were cousins and boyhood friends who had grown up together in Veracruz. Pasquel's association with Aleman was well known, and anything he did to tweak the United States' nose was popular in Mexico and helpful to Aleman. The source of Pasquel's money, a mystery to many baseball people, was political. Commanded to raise four million pesos ($850,000) in his area for Aleman's presidential campaign, he raised more. "I did good work," he told Mickey Owen. "I raised nine million and the five million that was left could be spent on baseball."[54] Thus, Mexican baseball was a tool used to help elect Aleman.

Once Aleman was elected on July 7, 1946, the major motive for goading the United States was lost. Aleman was Mexico's first elected civilian president since 1913, and his platform, which was based on industrialization and social reform, depended on good relations with the United States. Indeed, in an unprecedented move between the two nations, the Aleman and Truman administrations exchanged visits in 1947 to mark the "Good Neighbor Policy." When Pasquel's political fund ran dry because of the salaries he paid Americans, teams in the Mexican League had to depend on gate receipts for operation. The league operated on a centralized treasury supervised by Jorge Pasquel. Cities with larger stadiums such as Mexico City and Torreon retained only 25 percent of their gate receipts because they were expected to subsidize teams with lower drawing power.

Borderline teams, such as Puebla, struggled. With a population of not quite 140,000, the city was barely able to support a major-league team. At the beginning of the season, Puebla's eighteen-man squad consisted of eleven Mexicans, five Cubans, two African Americans from the United States, and former major leaguer Nap Reyes. Puebla's payroll was $70,000 for the season, of which Reyes made $10,000. With gate receipts of only $80,000, the team's owner, Castor Montodo, was devastated when he was "forced" to take on pitcher Sal Maglie's high salary.[55] In addition, the higher salaries paid to the American jumpers caused dissension among the other players. Ray Dandridge loaded his family on a train for home when his salary demands were not taken seriously. Jorge Pasquel rushed to the station and prevented the Dandridges from leaving only by doubling the disgruntled player's salary.[56]

Adding to the league's woes was the abysmal condition of its ballparks. The only stadium that approached major-league standards was Delta Park in Mexico City—a structure that seated 23,000. The single-deck grandstand, a green affair, curved from first base almost to the 360-foot sign at the left-field line. On good days, 14,000 fans packed the same hard, narrow boards that supported bleacher fans. Other ballparks in the league were flimsy structures with unpainted stands and patched tin roofs that seated fewer than 10,000 people. Although ticket prices were usually less than $1, this was steep in a country where white-collar workers earned between $2 and $5 per day and laborers earned only 60 cents.[57]

Playing conditions were atrocious. Delta Park was equipped with the only dressing room and showers in the league. Only Delta Park and Monterrey had grass infields—the rest were dirt and, with the exception of the field at New Laredo, hard as rock. Bad hops were the norm. Pitchers, when imperiled by hard grounders up the middle, were best advised to get out of the way. Although all parks had grass in the outfields, underneath lay Mexican clay baked by the sun into a hard crust. Line drives that would be routine singles in the United States often ended up as triples or home runs in Mexico. An added attraction at Puebla was its outfield, replete with scores of gopher holes.

In Tampico, the most infamous park, an oil refinery railroad spur ran through left field about twenty to thirty feet behind second base. Although recessed, the rails still put outfielders in jeopardy, and games often had to be stopped to allow trains to pass. Tampico's location on the Gulf of Mexico also produced hot, heavy, and humid air. Hitters hated Tampico because the wind often blew off the gulf at gale force, sending hard-hit balls to left field back into the infield. If Tampico was a pitcher's paradise, the parks in the interior (Mexico City, Torreon, Puebla, and San Luis Potosi) favored the hitter because at such high altitudes the ball carried well. Moreover, curveball pitchers such as Max Lanier experienced difficulty getting rotation on their pitches. Lanier developed a sore arm trying to work on his breaking pitch and was forced to switch to a change-up.[58] Other pitchers, like Sal Maglie, thrived in Mexico. Maglie, who worked closely with Dolf Luque, developed an outstanding slider by throwing his curve like a fastball and went on to win twenty games in each of his two seasons there.[59]

American ballplayers also had mixed reactions to Mexican food, travel, and accommodations. The Pasquels subsidized the players' housing, which usually consisted of roomy apartments, boarding houses, or hotels. Food caused more of a problem. Although Mexico City boasted scores of excellent restaurants suitable for bland American palates, food available in the countryside was suspect. Fresh vegetables had to be cooked or soaked in chlorinated water, and fruit had to be peeled. Milk was not pasteurized, and familiar American staples like bacon, sugar, and butter were inordinately expensive. Some American players found themselves subsisting on tins of sardines or cans of pork and beans when on the road.[60] Overall, the players were treated well, and those, like Maglie and Fred Martin, who picked up Spanish adapted quickly.

Travel could also be an adventure. Whereas the longest trips were usually made by train, the teams frequently traveled on buses over central Mexico's mountainous, narrow highways, which were characterized by sharp curves and steep grades. Teams taking regularly scheduled buses often found themselves sharing seats with goats, chickens, and other livestock being transported by rural Mexicans to their friends in the city. Moreover, the constant changes in altitude, the rocking and jostling from bad roads, and reckless driving caused some players to become lightheaded, nauseous, and, at times, fearful. Although regular Mexican riders seemed oblivious to the hardships, Maglie and Zabala often flew over the mountains at their own expense to avoid taking the bus.[61]

The level of play and the attitudes of their Mexican teammates bothered the Americans. Discipline on many teams was lax—players regularly smoked and drank beer on the bench. Of course, if you played for one of Jorge Pasquel's teams, the rules were much stricter. Pasquel, who neither drank nor smoked, had his players shadowed to ensure that they did not pick up bad habits. "Every night they checked us in," recalled Mickey Owen. "That is, at midnight, one of his agents would pound on your door and make you sign a note signifying that you were at home and in bed." This practice alienated many players.[62]

Mexican baseball crowds were usually well behaved, but they often celebrated exciting moments in the game by throwing firecrackers on the field or into dugouts. "You didn't know whether you were being shot at [or not]," complained Max Lanier. "They would scare you to death when they would throw one to the mound."[63] Another major aggravation was the manner in which Jorge Pasquel manipulated team rosters and even intervened in games themselves. In one instance, Mickey Owen was arguing a call with umpire Amando Maestri only to find Pasquel at his shoulder trying to help his case. When Maestri threatened to bring his mask down on Pasquel's head, a bodyguard produced a knife. Maestri, the best umpire in the league, resigned after the incident. In another episode, Adrian Zabala was denied a no-hitter when Pasquel overruled an official scorer's decision. Pasquel had offered $1,000 to any pitcher throwing a no-hitter but was not about to make good on his promise.[64]

The event that signaled the downfall of the Mexican League was the departure of Mickey Owen. As manager of Veracruz, Owen was constantly subject to the interference of Jorge Pasquel, who often appeared on the field, sometimes in uniform, and countermanded Owen's instructions to the players. With Veracruz sporting a losing record in July, Pasquel replaced Owen. By midsummer, Owen became increasingly homesick—especially when he learned that the Dodgers were in the thick of the National League pennant race in spite of having two inexperienced catchers. Moreover, the ex-Dodger wanted to reply to the many inquires he received from major-league players requesting information about the money situation and conditions in Mexico. He could not, however, admit to them that he had "made the mistake of his life."[65]

Thoroughly disillusioned with his life in Mexico, Owen sent his young son home in early July and then, with the help of a Mexican taxi driver, crossed the border at Brownsville, undetected, with his wife.[66] Owen left an angry Mexico in his wake. Disparaging remarks about Mexican food, hospitality, and baseball conditions found their way into their newspapers and created great resentment. One editorial in *La Afición* ended with a message to Owen: "It would be wiser for Mr. Owen not to get too close to the international border after his remarks."[67] Jorge Pasquel expressed surprise at Owen's defection, and in September 1946 he filed a $127,500 suit against the catcher. In the meantime, Owen's pleas to the commissioner's office for reinstatement were dashed when Chandler announced that he could find "no good reason" why the catcher's request should be granted.[68]

Suddenly, Owen found himself out in the cold. Banned from major-league baseball, his own difficulties increased in coming years. Nevertheless, his negative comments about his experiences in Mexico, coupled with the commissioner's firm enforcement of his ban, forced major-league players to look at the reality of playing baseball in Mexico. The Mexican League remained in existence until 1948, when it collapsed because of Jorge Pasquel's disinterest and the league's economic woes. The Mexican League affair, however, had an immediate impact on major-league baseball. Hitting the low-payroll Giants, Dodgers, and Cardinals particularly hard, the raids publicized the low major-league salaries. This provided players with increased expectations and new bargaining chips during salary negotiations, following the 1946 season.

The Mexican League threat also brought baseball back to the courts—a venue that, because of the reserve clause, was always fraught with danger. With suits generated by both team owners and the Mexican League, the reserve clause was bound to be exposed to the courts sooner or later. The threat that the Mexican League would challenge baseball's monopoly through its player contracts was real. Finally, with the commissioner's ban on the jumpers firmly in place and with the ultimate collapse of the Mexican League assured, it was only a matter of time before the game would be faced with new player suits demanding reinstatement. Such suits were sure to have the potential of destroying the legal fiction that protected baseball's antitrust status through the 1922 Holmes decision.

5

Murphy Money and More

Following the end of World War II, unions wielded more influence than at any time in American history. Conversion to a peacetime economy, deregulation, and fewer overtime hours caused hourly wages to fall—a situation that caused American labor concern. Labor not only wanted to protect its gains but also to share in America's newfound prosperity. Union-sponsored strikes swept the country between November 1945 and June 1946, including those staged by oil, auto, electrical, steel, and mine workers over wage increases and health and welfare benefits. When a walkout staged by the Railroad Trainmen and Locomotive Engineer Brotherhoods resulted in a national transportation stoppage, President Truman moved quickly to seize the railroads and prevent national paralysis. In all, Truman was forced to take over nine industries to keep the economy moving.

Baseball mirrored this business climate with its low salaries, lack of job security, and rosters overpopulated by returning veterans, and as a result, it attracted union organizers. One such person was Robert Murphy, a Harvard graduate skilled in labor relations and labor law from his experience with the National Labor Relations Board.[1] A former track and field man and ardent baseball fan, Murphy became sympathetic to the plight of major-league players when several of his friends on the Boston Braves complained about their salaries and working conditions.[2] By January 1946, Murphy and his associate, attorney Joseph Doherty, began to implement their idea to unionize baseball players by registering the American Baseball Guild at the Boston city clerk's office. Murphy and Doherty planned to organize players in the major leagues first and then move on to those in the minors.

With the help of several Boston Braves players, who queried their counterparts on other teams, Murphy circulated a letter among the clubs that presented a program incorporating many of the players' own ideas. Murphy recruited players to the Guild's cause by remaining in Boston, a two-team town, and letting the teams come to him. He usually contacted one or two members of each club and asked them to call a team meeting, then appeared and made his case for the Guild. On April 16, 1946, Murphy issued a press statement that announced the formation of the American Baseball Guild. The startling news was accompanied by information that players from more than half of the major-league teams had signed up, including more than half the members on some squads. When told by a reporter that this was the fourth attempt in baseball history to organize a union, Murphy replied that it would be different this time. "Back in the old days, there was no Labor Relations Act," he noted. "Today we have the law behind us, and if ballplayers continue to become interested in the Guild . . . there is no question in my mind that it will be adopted."[3]

In a four-page press release, Murphy explained some of the Guild's goals, including (1) freedom of contract, (2) the right of a player to receive part of his purchase price if sold or traded, (3) the right of arbitration in salary disputes, and (4) the right to join a union. The document also proclaimed that "the days of baseball serfdom would soon be over." Observing that strikes would be rare because of his arbitration plan, Murphy asserted that players would not have jumped to the Mexican League if the Guild had been organized sooner.[4]

The only rejoinder of any note came from the irascible owner of the Washington Senators, Clark Griffith, who predicted that a players' union "would wreck baseball" and would create a situation that would allow the wealthiest teams to corner the best players.[5] Murphy rewarded Griffith's statements by filing charges with the National Labor Relations Board Office in Baltimore against the venerable owner for allegedly engaging in unfair labor practices, accusing him of making derogatory remarks against the Guild, counseling and urging his players to avoid the Guild, and making statements calculated "to intimidate and coerce his players from exercising their rights of self-organization."[6] Griffith called the charges "preposterous" and stated, "Baseball can't exist without the reserve clause and when a union wants to tear that from our game, I'll continue to speak."[7]

As his case against Griffith was pending, Murphy was determined to organize his first team. Ignoring teams with high payrolls, he decided to concentrate on the Pittsburgh Pirates because they played in a union stronghold.[8] The Pirates were owned by Mrs. Florence Dreyfuss and operated by her son-in-law William Benswanger, a mild-mannered man who gave up his insurance business in 1932 to run the team. The 1946 Pirates were a

Robert Murphy, the Harvard-trained labor negotiator who attempted to organize Pittsburgh Pirates' players into his American Baseball Guild. *(The Sporting News)*

diverse group. The team's spring training roster numbered sixty-five men, thirty-six of whom were returning servicemen, seven who played in the minor leagues in 1945, and twenty-two returning wartime players. By the time Murphy approached the team in May 1946, the Pirates were carrying thirty-five players on their roster—ten more than usual because of the presence of service veterans. The Pirates were an old team. The twenty-nine players who made the most significant contributions in 1946 averaged thirty-one years of age. As a group, these twenty-nine players would average only a little more than two major-league seasons after 1946, and most (thirty-nine collective seasons) would be logged by five of their number—Ralph Kiner, Bob Elliott, Ken Heintzelman, Bill Cox, and Elwin "Preacher" Roe.

With a team made up largely of journeymen ballplayers or veterans at the end of their careers, the Pirates were an easy mark. By May, they were in seventh place and obviously struggling. Even the leadership of former Gas House Gang manager Frankie Frisch seemed uninspired. With such large rosters, Frisch and other managers had a difficult time playing and keeping players happy. Moreover, players were increasingly uneasy, because the team had to pare the roster down to thirty in June.

On May 15, Murphy contacted the Pirates' management and informed them that the Guild wanted to discuss a collective bargaining arrangement. The team's first reaction was a statement by vice president Sam Watters that described the Guild as "a new racket."[9] Nevertheless, president Benswanger agreed to meet with Murphy on June 5. An optimistic Murphy told reporters that his relations with the Pirates had been very cordial and that he would try to persuade Benswanger that the Guild was the overwhelming choice of the players.[10] The Pirates' president conferred with Commissioner Chandler and National League president Ford Frick and then announced, "I'm convinced that we do not have a dissatisfied squad and I am sure the whole Guild affair will be settled to everyone's satisfaction."[11] The sports editor of the *Pittsburgh Press,* Chester Smith, reported that the players seemed a little bewildered by all of the turmoil the Guild caused. Explaining that he did not think that the Guild was "trying to run or wreck baseball," one veteran Pirate player noted that "golfers, actors, and others have found some good in organization and if baseball players can do the same, it's worth a trial."[12]

The confident remarks issued by both sides were soon forgotten, as Murphy's meeting with the Pirates' management, held in Benswanger's office, fell into petty bickering and collapsed. Reporters packed the small room, and flashes and clicking cameras served as a constant reminder of their presence. Smith described Murphy as being "red faced, inclined to belligerency, and equipped with a sneer that must be the envy of all sneerers."[13] The Pirates, fearful that their season might be disrupted, refused to agree to Murphy's demands without the active involvement of the National Labor Relations Board.[14]

Charging the Pirates with "dilatory tactics," Murphy indicated that delays might continue through 1948, at which time some of the Pittsburgh players might be "in Peoria."[15] As the afternoon wore on, baseball's first labor negotiations in years deteriorated into exchanges like this:

> MURPHY: "We have nothing to fear."
>
> PIRATES: "Neither have we."
>
> MURPHY: "Oh, you haven't, huh?"[16]

Angry and disappointed, Murphy left the meeting and told reporters that he was going to meet with players before their game with the Dodgers that night to "tell them just what kind of bosses they've got."[17] The Pirates retired to their clubhouse without participating in their normal infield drills. An hour before game time, Benswanger received a call from Murphy, who declared, "Be here in fifteen minutes or you won't have a game tonight." Accompanied by attorney Seward French, the Pirates' president made his first appearance in the clubhouse since he announced the resignation of manager George Gibson in 1934.[18]

Murphy and French engaged in a heated discussion in front of the players. When Pirates management requested more time to consider the Guild's demands, Murphy shouted, "Dilatory tactics!"[19] Before he left, Benswanger told the players, "I haven't had any trouble with a ballplayer since I became president fifteen years ago, and they cannot refute that statement. I have never hurt a ballplayer. I am leaving it up to them to decide whether to play." After management's departure, the players voted to play the Dodgers that night but agreed that, if the Guild was not recognized, they would not take the field against the Giants the following evening, June 7, 1946.[20] Only twenty minutes before game time, the team trotted on the field.

Although the June 6 headline of the *Pittsburgh Press* read "36 Hours Given Club to Accept Baseball Guild," some newspapermen failed to take Murphy or the Guild seriously.[21] There were quips about Second Basemen's Local 307 and overtime pay for extra-inning games.[22] Even President Truman got into the act, when he laughingly denied any intention of taking over the Pirates if they struck. Truman, a native Missourian, admitted, however, that if he did have to take over the game, he would make sure that there would be two good teams in St. Louis.[23]

Murphy's potential strike in Pittsburgh was the main topic of discussion in the nation's sports pages on June 6 and 7. In an attempt to downplay the situation, the Pirates maintained that they did not believe that a strike was in the offing and called for "an orderly, legal" resolution of the impasse.[24]

Murphy defiantly told one reporter, "I guarantee that there will be a strike tomorrow night unless the club comes across. We're going to get tougher. If it goes another day, we're not only going to ask for recognition, we're going to start making actual demands." Murphy demanded that management contact him on the morning of June 7 to negotiate. Then, to place more pressure on the Pirates, Murphy played the labor angle to the hilt as he made an appearance before the Congress of Industrial Organizations (CIO) Steel City Industrial Union Council and told them that there would be no game unless Pirate management consented to an National Labor Relations Board or Pennsylvania State Labor Relations Board election. The audience cheered and unanimously passed a resolution urging the Pirates to comply.[25]

In reality, the Pirates' management took the strike quite seriously. Of the team's thirty-five-player roster, only two, veterans Truett "Rip" Sewell and Jimmy Brown, could be identified as non-Guild members. If the players were to strike, other than forfeiting the game against the Giants, the team had two viable options: (1) call the game because of "threatening weather" or (2) field a makeshift team consisting of non-Guild players, coaches, and sandlot players.[26] While perfectly legal, the weather option was transparent, especially if game-day weather was clear. Therefore, the Pirates, with the support of Commissioner Chandler, planned to put a surrogate club on the field. Such players needed only to sign National League contracts to be legal. Among those recruited were Sewell, Brown, seventy-two-year-old Honus Wagner, and manager Frisch. The commissioner's own special assistant, John "Frenchy" DeMoisey, who was in Pittsburgh working with Pirate officials, was also scheduled to play. Moreover, Commissioner Chandler was prepared to suspend all of the participants for contract violations if the Pirates struck.[27]

The player providing management and the commissioner's office with inside information was Rip Sewell, who openly defied Murphy and told reporters that he, himself, would recruit a team to beat the strike.[28] "I think there are quite a few fellows on the team who will follow me," he said, criticizing Murphy for his ignorance of the game and contending that other channels were available to the players. "We have a commissioner, Albert Chandler, to whom a player can take a grievance," he urged.[29]

Sewell proved to be an obstacle that Murphy could not surmount. A proud Alabamian who believed that unions had a place in society but not in baseball, Sewell rejected Murphy's overtures. When Murphy had meetings with the club, Sewell was excluded. Not long before the strike vote, Murphy accosted Sewell in a Pittsburgh hotel lobby and threatened him for speaking out against the union. "He told me he was going to get somebody to do something or beat me up," recalled Sewell. The Pirates pitcher replied, "You'd better see that you do a damn good job of it, because if you don't, buddy—you know what you're going to get."[30]

Friday, June 7, 1946, was a day of suspense as Pittsburgh's citizens waited to see whether the Pirates would strike. Murphy's morning deadline for the Pirates to contact him passed without word from the team. Scheduled to meet with the players at 5:30 P.M., a full two hours prior to their 7:30 contest with the Giants, the union leader was there at least twenty minutes early. Sewell recalled sitting outside the clubhouse and hearing Murphy pound on the table and shout, "Now fellas, we strike tonight! . . . We've got them tonight. They are not going to let this gate get away."[31] Not long after, manager Frisch came out of his office and "announced in a loud voice: 'Will anyone not connected with the team please leave.' Murphy and a group of newspapermen left and the door was bolted."[32]

A photograph that appeared in many Saturday morning newspapers captured a dazed and nervous Murphy in front of the Pirates' clubhouse door, which bore a sign reading "For players only. Keep out. That means you." The players began their meeting on the strike issue at 6:00 P.M. and, missing batting practice, carried on a heated debate for over an hour and fifteen minutes. By Sewell's account, he was called into the meeting by several players after Murphy's departure. Telling Sewell that Murphy had asked the team to strike, in spite of Sewell's previous declaration that such action was not needed, his teammates urged him to address them. "Well, I told you not to listen to that guy," he reminded them. "You said there was going to be no strike and so he brought it on you tonight. . . . He told you what you are going to do—he is going to unionize the ball club, he is going to have a strike. We all have signed contracts and it is my night to pitch, and I am going out to pitch."[33]

At 7:15, the minor-league farm director, Bob Rice, was called into the meeting and told that the team would play. He came out of the clubhouse and informed Murphy and the newspapermen of the news and then added "that the players had agreed not to talk to anyone and not to reveal the actual count of the balloting."[34] A few minutes later, the Pirates, led by Sewell, filed onto the field to the cheers of 16,000 fans. Many of the details of what transpired at the meeting will likely never be known. The strike vote itself was not for one game but would have committed the team to strike until Guild demands for recognition were met. Newspa-

Truett "Rip" Sewell was an
obstacle that union organizer
Robert Murphy could not
surmount. (George Brace Photo)

permen learned that the final tally was twenty in favor of a strike and
sixteen against—and that the players had agreed to strike only if there
was a two-thirds majority.[35]

All of the players, even Sewell, sympathized with Murphy's rationale
for a strike. Veteran third baseman Bob Elliott, the team's highest-paid
player, simply did not want to go on strike. "There should be a way for
the Guild to get an agreement and avoid such an unpleasant thing. I say
this as one who believes in the principles of the Guild."[36] Nevertheless,
some Pirate players found reasons to vote against the plan. First, Murphy
was an outsider and did not know the game well—a factor that did not
win the confidence of some players. Next, his confrontational style and
abrasive behavior, when contrasted with the kindly demeanor of William Benswanger, alienated some players. Finally, there were players, like
pitcher Ken Heintzelman, who had just returned from the war and feared
that their careers might be jeopardized if they struck.

The one player most trapped by the strike conflict was veteran catcher
Al Lopez. Approaching the end of a long and productive playing career
and aspiring to become a major-league manager, he feared the involve-

ment his position as team captain mandated. Lopez was the most respected man on the team. Consequently, he found himself walking a tightrope—counseling younger players with great potential, such as Ralph Kiner, not to get involved, urging others to take a cautious approach on strike actions, but at the same time coming down on the Guild's side of the issues. Although Lopez respected Murphy, he made sure the Guild organizer knew how unhappy he was that the Pirates were singled out to bear the brunt of the union effort.[37]

The majority who voted to strike were players like pitcher Jack Hallett, who would play only a few seasons more and were making between $3,000 and $8,000 a year. They had the most to gain in establishing a minimum salary of at least $7,500 for rookies and journeymen. These players used the example of Pirates catcher Bill Salkeld, who made less than $6,000. Although frugal, the Salkeld family was financially embarrassed by the end of the 1945 season. Forced to keep his wife and children in a hotel during the season because of tight housing conditions, Salkeld had to borrow $500 to send his family home to California on the train. Even though Salkeld hit .315 in 1945, his 1946 raise was only $500.

The strike-vote defeat left Robert Murphy dazed, but only temporarily. He quickly brought charges against the Pirates before the National Labor Relations Board. In his petition, he accused the team of trying to form a company union.[38] In mid-July, Murphy attempted to organize the Boston Braves—only 60 percent of whom, he claimed, were making $5,000 or more. As a result of Murphy's meetings with the Braves, the players sent a delegation comprised of Billy Herman, Johnny Hopp, and Dick Culler to meet with owner Lou Perini to discuss the Guild's platform. One of the key proposals presented by the players was the need for player representation.

Coupled with the Mexican League raids, baseball's close brush with unionism caused great concern among the owners, who began to realize something must be done to satisfy the players' needs. J.G. Taylor Spink, the publisher/editor of the *Sporting News*, wrote that the entire world was going through a revolution and that America's national game was "passing through that social upheaval, along with bread baking, wheat growing, coal mining, steel puddling, railroading, and meat production."[39]

New York Times sports columnist Arthur Daley reasoned that no one would dare condemn Pirate players for attempting to obtain more money and better conditions, and he argued that just because attempts to unionize ballplayers in the past had failed did not mean that they would always fail. Although he did not profess to be an admirer of Robert Murphy, Daley suggested that player demands regarding an increase in minimum salary,

As captain of the Pirates, veteran Al Lopez found himself in the middle on Guild issues. (George Brace Photo)

a modest percentage of any purchase price, and "a change in the woefully weak and one-sided reserve clause" would be equitable.[40]

Baseball owners were also discontented. Several were concerned because the Giants, Dodgers, and Yankees had taken the Mexican League to court, where baseball's contract, with its reserve clause and ten-day notice of release, would be subjected to judicial scrutiny. The owners were very nervous about baseball's lack of a uniform contract. A disgusted Leslie O'Connor, White Sox general manager and former assistant to Judge Landis, complained, "Judge Landis and I fought twenty-four years to keep baseball out of the courts."[41]

Just as he had during the selection of a new commissioner, Larry MacPhail stepped forward with a proposal that galvanized baseball into action. MacPhail called for the formation of a "company union," player representation on baseball's advisory council, and the formation of an arbitration board to solve salary disputes. Whereas federal labor law prohibited the formation of a real company union, it was time for the owners to listen to MacPhail.[42] They held a series of meetings during the July 8-9 All-Star break, out of which came what was to be known as the Joint Major League Committee. The members included league presidents Will Harridge and Ford Frick and club owners Sam Breadon, Phil Wrigley, Tom Yawkey, and MacPhail. On July 18, the Joint Committee issued an almost revolutionary call for a meeting with the players to discuss baseball reforms and establish a new uniform contract.

Each club was asked to elect a representative to join with the owners in their respective leagues at meetings to be held in Chicago and New York. In addition, the players were asked to select three men from each league to meet with the Joint Major League Committee. Finally, a joint gathering to adopt reforms and to prepare a revised contract form for the 1947 season was scheduled for August 29 in New York. Thus, the machinery was set in motion for the first meetings between players and owners since the National League owners met with representatives of the Player's Fraternity in 1887.[43]

Murphy saw the move as a validation of the reforms suggested by the Guild. "It is obvious that efforts of the Guild to correct injustices to the player are in a large measure responsible for this action by the baseball barons," he said.[44] Unwilling to acknowledge Murphy's role in the move, the owners claimed that Frick was the first baseball official to develop such a plan, in 1936. Refuting Murphy's claim that 40 percent of the Braves players were making less than $5,000, Frick admitted that there were nineteen players in the National League making less than that sum. "I want to admit it is all wrong," he confessed. When asked why he had not done something about it long ago, he weakly stated, "Well, I did. But inertia got hold of me. I drew up this entire reform plan as far back as 1936 [and] I should have had the National League adopt it then."[45]

The players were delighted by the call for representatives. Boston Braves pitcher Johnny Sain mirrored the view of many players when he stated, "Neighbors often disagree on minor matters, but when something big comes along, they forget their petty disputes and stand firmly together. Baseball owners and players are both basically fair, so it should not be difficult to adjust present differences."[46] Each National League team selected two representatives, while the American League was instructed to choose only one, although they could choose an additional representative if they desired. Only two teams, New York and St. Louis, did so.[47]

The teams chose veteran players to represent them. The twenty-five men selected had an average of 11.6 years of major-league experience, and included eight future major-league managers, two Hall-of-Famers, a general manager, a movie actor, and a sportscaster.

The proposals drawn up by the teams were strikingly similar. They included spring training money, the establishment of a minimum salary, a better hitting background at Wrigley Field, the ability of players to realize a portion of their sale price if they were sold, and revisions of rules regarding exhibition games and barnstorming.[48] Foremost among some player concerns was the absence of a pension plan. The drafting of a plan became the pet project of Marty Marion of the St. Louis Cardinals. Known as "Mr. Shortstop," this perennial All-Star was recognized for his slick fielding and range. Marion had enrolled at Georgia Tech with aspirations to become an architect, but he was dissuaded from that path by the persistence of Branch Rickey's brother Frank. The shy but affable Marion, a South Carolinian who could trace his lineage to Revolutionary War hero Francis Marion, was also a respected leader in the Cardinals' clubhouse. Stan Musial noted that while the players "looked up" to outfielder Terry Moore as their "team leader," they looked to Marion as "our spokesman" because he was involved with other aspects of baseball. "He was always talking about trying to improve the conditions for ballplayers."[49] Marion attributed his election as the Cardinals' representative to his teammates' perception that he had "a good business mind." Moreover, they knew he was not afraid to stand up to Cardinals' owner Sam Breadon during salary negotiations. Breadon even admitted to Marion that the ballplayer was the most difficult "businessman" he had encountered—which Marion accepted as a compliment.[50]

Marion envisioned a pension plan supported by radio receipts from All-Star game and World Series broadcasts.[51] While the shortstop did not seek the assistance of an actuary or any committee, he consulted teammates and other players. Rip Sewell remembered discussing the plan with Marion on the train en route to the 1946 All-Star game, and St. Louis sportswriter Bob Broeg recalled sitting in on a discussion of the pension plan between Marion, Terry Moore, and Harrison "Doc" Weaver, the club's trainer. Weaver roomed with Marion because of the shortstop's bad back and had a major influence on the plan's development.[52]

Marion's pension plan called for several different income sources that were designed to build up an annual fund totaling $390,000. Under his scheme, major-league teams would contribute only $2,500 each per year, while five-year players would put in $100 a year and, on reaching their tenth year, would be required to put in a lump sum of $500 or more. These two contributions were intended to collect $80,000 per year. The remainder would be raised through All-Star game receipts ($50,000 per year), the World Series radio fee ($100,000 per year), and a series of interleague games between natural or geographical rivals ($160,000 per year). The plan was designed to provide five-year players with a retirement income of $50 per month and ten-year men with $100 per month.[53]

Player representatives from the two leagues met on July 29, 1946, at separate locations, where they brought their lists of issues together and selected three players each to meet with the Joint Major League Committee in New York on August 5, 1946. The issues raised by the players in rank order are as follows:

National League

(1) A pension plan

(2) A $5,500 minimum salary

(3) A rule forbidding the withdrawal of waivers

(4) Elimination of the ten-day contract clause following release (later replaced by the right to dismiss players for cause coupled with sixty-day severance pay)

(5) A $5 per day spring training allowance to cover incidental expenses.[54]

American League

(1) A minimum salary

(2) A spring training allowance

(3) A rule requiring teams to send out player contracts thirty days in advance

(4) Extension of the postseason barnstorming rule from ten to thirty days

Marty Marion not only instigated the players' pension plan, he also worked hard to cement the players' support in subsequent seasons. (George Brace Photo)

(5) Formation of a permanent players' grievance committee.

(6) Abolition of the practice of cutting a player's salary when he is sent to the minor leagues

(7) Improvement of dugout and clubhouse conditions

(8) A pension plan.[55]

Six players (Joe Kuhel, Johnny Murphy, Mel Harder, Marty Marion, Dixie Walker, and Billy Herman) were chosen to meet with the owners on August 5. Harder characterized the meeting as very positive. "They were very cordial," he noted, "and they wanted to help the situation. They knew what the players wanted."[56] Although minimum salaries received much attention, the pension plan was the most-discussed topic, leading Marty Marion and Larry MacPhail to dominate the discussions. Among the other owners, only Phil Wrigley made significant statements, and it was evident to the players that he supported a pension plan and sided with them on most other issues. Boston's Tom Yawkey also appeared to favor the plan but said little. According to Marion, presidents Harridge and Frick, and his own team's owner, Sam Breadon, remained almost silent throughout.[57]

The players left the August 5 meeting confident that their voices had been heard. Their optimism was rewarded soon after, when MacPhail publicly stated that the players' demands were just and predicted that they would be adopted at a major-league meeting scheduled for August 27, 1946. Conspicuous by its absence was any reference to baseball's reserve clause. In spite of the challenge to the reserve clause that had been posed by the Mexican League raids and some of the owners' court actions to stop the Pasquel brothers, the players continued to accept the reserve clause. This was not lost on MacPhail, who stated, "There is one thing which has been most gratifying. The six player delegates reported to us that not even one percent of their constituencies had made a crack about the reserve clause. . . . It is interesting to us that the players recognize the absolute essentiality of the reserve clause as the foundation rock of our system of Organized Baseball."[58]

When queried about this more than thirty years later, Marty Marion responded, "We didn't think baseball could operate without the reserve clause. . . . They had no television rights—they had none of the money they have to throw around now. And if the players had done what they've done now, there would have been no baseball without the reserve clause." Marion explained further that the owners exercised far more control over the players in the 1940s and there were many good ballplayers in the minors who could be brought up to replace problem players. Players sent to the minors were afraid of being buried and forgotten. In many respects, the players felt almost powerless.[59]

The August 27, 1946, major-league meeting held in Chicago represented a landmark in the history of organized baseball. The Joint Major League Committee presented a report that not only analyzed, assessed, and made recommendations on organized baseball's current situation relative to the issues raised by the players but also provided the game with its first comprehensive planning document. The report that was presented to league owners and their representatives was a chopped-up, makeshift version of a gray-covered report drafted by MacPhail and presented to the Joint Committee only the day before.[60]

The problem with MacPhail's draft report was that it also dealt with controversial and sensitive issues facing baseball, such as the challenge to the reserve clause posed by the Mexican League, baseball's vulnerability in the courts, and the race question. Moreover, attorney MacPhail made several admissions that would have greatly embarrassed the owners had they been made public. For instance, in the report's foreword, MacPhail openly admitted that baseball constituted a monopoly—a combination whose "policies and rules and regulations . . . control every one of us in the operation of our individual businesses." MacPhail also argued that as a viable alternative to arbitration, the option clause in player contracts needed to be strengthened to eliminate any legal grounds for attack. Furthermore, the Yankee president warned that counsel for both leagues were of the opinion that the reserve clause would neither stand up "in an equity court in a suit for specific performance" nor provide the basis for a restraining order to prevent players from playing elsewhere such as in the Mexican League.[61]

An additional revelation was MacPhail's opinion (in the name of the committee) that Murphy would have been successful had he begun by organizing minor-league players first. The report indicated that owners would have faced a "fait accompli" if Murphy had adopted that strategy. Moreover, MacPhail stated that the owners considered Murphy's attempt to organize the players as baseball's "most pressing problem." To protect against unionization and outside player raids, the Yankee president stressed the need for a revised uniform player contract and for an improved relationship between the clubs and their players.[62]

MacPhail also argued that baseball's segregated status quo should remain—a position that would have subjected the game to intense ridicule and criticism if it had been made public in the final version of the report.[63] Baseball's official stance on the race question was that there was no color line. Moreover, MacPhail castigated the owners for failing to take control of the game, their poor organizational skills, their outdated structure, and their inability to develop a central public relations policy.

He pointed out the duplication of effort, lack of coordination, and constant bickering over policies and procedures that characterized league and team offices separated by thousands of miles. In summary, MacPhail charged that baseball faced "an acute situation representing almost total confusion."[64]

With all of its admissions and criticisms, MacPhail's report was not suitable for publication, let alone for submission to the owners. Members of the Joint Major League Committee considered MacPhail's draft unacceptable, and none of them signed it in that form. An edited version was presented to the owners on August 27, and it was this report that was approved.[65]

The fact that MacPhail's report was edited before it reached a vote should not detract from the concessions won by the players or the importance of the document itself to the structure of the game. The deletions did not lessen MacPhail's influence, because most of the recommendations that were approved closely represented the Yankee president's views and vision for baseball. The game was strengthened by the formation of an executive council, consisting of the commissioner as chair, the two league presidents, and two owners. The council's charge was to assist the commissioner in promotional efforts and in maintaining "public confidence in its [the game's] integrity, operations, and methods." Moreover, it was to be used to reconcile regulation and rule differences between the two leagues, particularly as they affected exhibitions, All-Star games, and the World Series. While speculation existed that the creation of the council diminished the commissioner's authority, Chandler was an early supporter of the concept. Indeed, he suggested the council's creation soon after he took office. Claiming that he wanted to guide baseball and not run it by fiat in the style of Judge Landis, Chandler announced, "We have placed baseball on a modern basis and killed the antique and obsolete."[66]

With the player representatives' admission that the reserve clause was necessary to maintain the structure of the game and that the drafting of a new uniform contract protecting baseball against suits was essential, the owners were willing to improve the status of their players with significant concessions. They approved the following: a guaranteed $5,000 minimum salary; the extension of barnstorming after the season from ten to thirty days; permanent player representation; revisions in the uniform players contract;[67] and $25 per player per week for spring training costs over and above transportation, meals, and housing expenses.

Most important was a recommendation that a pension plan be developed, possibly along the lines suggested by the players. Included in the report as possible provisions were the same ideas put forth under Marion's plan. While paying "lip service" to the need for a scheme that would

The first players' pension plan representatives met with baseball's executive council on November 6, 1947. From left to right are Dixie Walker, Brooklyn Dodgers; Warren Giles, Cincinnati Reds; Ford Frick, National League president; Albert B. Chandler, commissioner; Will Harridge, American League president; Benjamin Fiery, American League attorney; Walter Mulbry, secretary-treasurer of baseball; and Johnny Murphy, Boston Red Sox. *(The Sporting News)*

provide the players with "some sort of pension fund, security benefits, and/or group insurance, and/or hospitalization insurance," the following language from the report suggests a lack of unanimity among the owners regarding the pension plan: "Without further conference and discussions with the players' committee, and until their proposals can be studied by actuaries, it is impossible to determine whether or not any such plan is feasible."[68]

Former general manager and owner of the St. Louis Browns William O. DeWitt verified that many of the club owners were disturbed about the possibility of a pension plan—this was particularly true of clubs with poor attendance records, who felt they could ill afford to pay into the plan. In addition, owners such as Sam Breadon of the Cardinals, who had opposed the All-Star game simply because it could continue in perpetuity, resisted the suggestion of a pension plan for the same reasons.[69]

Heralded as baseball's "Magna Carta," the approved plan represented a victory for Larry MacPhail. The Yankees' president led the discussion on behalf of the plan and purportedly warned owners of the dangers they faced if they defeated the proposal.[70] Approval by the players soon followed, and the report was officially adopted. This placed the coup de grace on Robert Murphy's attempt to unionize the Pittsburgh Pirates or any other major-league team. With the players placated for the time being, there was little incentive to back a guild. Furthermore, the Pirates were sold to a new group of owners led by Indianapolis businessman Frank McKinney—a man with a benevolent reputation. With at least partial knowledge of what was to come, the Pittsburgh Pirates voted the Guild down 15-3 in an election held by the Pennsylvania State Labor Relations Board on August 20, 1946. Only eighteen of the thirty-one players eligible to vote participated in the election.

The fiery Murphy acknowledged the setback and prophetically predicted that the owner-dominated committees would never be able to represent the needs of the players adequately.[71] He also muttered wistfully, "The players have been offered an apple, but they could have had an orchard."[72] It would be many years before the players would reach Murphy's orchard.

Although Murphy would be heard from again, as far as the players were concerned, the Guild was a dead issue. Nevertheless, the use of Murphy's name was perpetuated long after he left the scene because the players' incidental expenses during spring training came to be known as "Murphy money." Player representative Mel Harder recalled that the extra $25 per week was supposed to take care of laundry and tips and to provide a little spending money. Even though he was pleased to have it, he laughed, "We never did break even—I can't remember breaking even!"[73]

Although Murphy money was the only visible symbol of baseball's clashes in 1946 with Murphy's Guild and the Pasquel brothers in Mexico, the players gained much more through the encounter. They attained a voice in the game, they established a minimum worth for each player, their salaries began to rise, and they acquired security through a pension plan. The owners were relieved to quash Murphy's attempt to organize major-league players. Thereafter, they were able to strengthen their hold on the game through a revised uniform contract, by continuing to convince the players of the necessity of the reserve clause, and through concessions to the players. Finally, for a brief period, the owners had an opportunity to assess the game and to develop a vision for the future.

6

1946: Season of Tumult

As the nation's industries retooled and the service sector returned to peace-time pursuits, baseball was encouraged to do the same. J.G. Taylor Spink, editor of the *Sporting News*, predicted that the game would far exceed its prewar stature and would lead the nation through a postwar sports boom of unprecedented magnitude. He called for night baseball, renovated and freshly painted ballparks, and the creation of an atmosphere that would prove attractive to the female fans who were drawn to the game during the war. "Without them," he wrote, "the game no longer can exist."[1]

One owner who did not require Spink's urgings was Larry MacPhail. He presided over a series of renovations that made Yankee Stadium the most modern in baseball and increased its capacity to 80,000. Moreover, inspired by Commissioner Chandler's policy of allowing unlimited night games, the Yankee president installed a lighting system capable of generating twice the illumination of any other stadium. Bathed in new paint—"Robin's egg blue, cerulean blue, blue, light greens and dark greens, orange and henna, overlays of silver paint everywhere, [and] chromium plating to great profusion," Yankee Stadium, more than any other park, became a symbol of baseball's renewal.[2]

New lights were also added to Braves Field in Boston, and, only a short time before opening day, the grandstand was painted. Unfortunately, the new paint failed to dry and part way through the Braves' opener, fans, who discovered they had green paint on their hair, eyebrows, and clothes, were taking their complaints to the Braves' office. Issuing an official apology in newspaper advertisements the following day, the embarrassing mistake cost the Braves more than $6,000 in dry-cleaning bills. Nevertheless, the team received good publicity from their offer, and, as Braves president Lou Perini noted, "Nobody can say that it wasn't a colorful opening."[3]

The physical condition and rusty baseball skills of returning veterans was a far greater concern than refurbishing ballparks. In a similar situation during World War I, several players, including Ernie Shore, Dutch Leonard, Hank Gowdy, and Grover Cleveland Alexander, failed to duplicate their prewar successes. Players who returned in 1945, such as Phil Marchildon of the Athletics, Hugh Mulcahy of the Phillies, and the Senators' Cecil Travis, had already demonstrated the difficult transition from soldier to civilian. Only Virgil Trucks, Bob Feller, Buddy Lewis, and Hank Greenberg showed signs of their prewar abilities. On the basis of what he had seen of wartime ball in 1945, Greenberg felt that the veterans should not be too worried. "They aren't going to find the opposition too great," he commented.[4]

When Bob Feller returned to the States, he was sent to the Great Lakes Naval base, in Waukegan, Illinois. "I was lucky," he told a writer, "to be stationed . . . where I could work back gradually into the job of testing my arm. Confidence built up as the arm responded, and when I got terminal leave to rejoin the Indians, I was ready for the big leagues mentally, as well as physically."[5] Realizing that other major and minor leaguers were in poor physical condition because of their war activities, Feller proposed that major-league baseball sponsor a baseball school in January 1946 in Tampa, Florida, for returning veterans. "Mr. Chandler and I had an agreement that if I did this, and they thought it was a great thing for baseball, they would give us an extra month to barnstorm in the fall."[6] As the plan evolved, it was soon enlarged to include younger players between the ages of seventeen and twenty-one. While the players brought their own gloves, shoes, and uniforms, Feller persuaded several sporting goods companies to provide baseballs and bats. A number of outstanding players, such as Lou Boudreau, Spud Chandler, Joe DiMaggio, and Dizzy Dean, also worked as guest instructors. The school, which was well attended by scouts, was a rousing success. Of the 186 men in attendance, sixty-six signed professional contracts.[7]

While Bob Feller rounded into shape at his Tampa baseball school, Ted Williams prepared to make the long cross-country car trip between San Diego and Sarasota, Florida. After spending three years in the service, the Boston star was excited at the prospect of wearing a major-league uniform again. In an interview with Vincent X. Flaherty of the *Los Angeles Examiner*, Williams discussed his chances of reaching statistical goals attained only by Ruth and Cobb. In the same interview, the goal-oriented Williams also admitted that he had made a series of bets on the outcome of the 1946 season with Detroit's Dick Wakefield. Williams was quoted as saying, "That's one bet I'm going to be out there swinging to collect."[8]

Although legal papers documenting the wagers were signed, Williams recalled that "It was all in fun." When Commissioner Chandler heard about the wager, he contacted Williams and told him, "I've been hearing that there have been some bets made. I just want you to know that, if there are, you had better call them off." The players complied. Years later, Williams noted that, of their five bets, the only one he would have lost was a bet that Wakefield would come within $30,000 of Williams's salary—a feat that Wakefield accomplished.[9]

Spring training in Florida and California in 1946 was nothing like many players had envisioned or remembered before the war. First, there was an unprecedented rush on hotel space as war-weary tourists took their first vacations in years. They willingly paid prices that escalated daily. Ball clubs, which made advance arrangements, suddenly found themselves caught in the rush. Four players were often squeezed into one room. Moreover, wartime food scarcities continued. Butter was almost impossible to locate, and brown sugar was commonly substituted for white. Restaurant and hotel service was often poor, and dirty dishes were a common complaint. Prewar wages no longer appealed to waiters, waitresses, and chambermaids.[10] The housing and hotel shortage also led teams to warn players against bringing their families to spring training. Many ex-servicemen ignored the advice. "I didn't see my wife and kids for two years while I was serving in the Pacific theatre," announced St. Louis Browns pitcher Fred Sanford, "and I intend [on] seeing something of them now. They'll be at Anaheim."[11]

Training camps were swollen as returning veterans vied with their wartime replacements for roster places. In many cases, teams were forced to train in two locations instead of one. More than a thousand players competed for just 400 jobs. Baseball agreed to expand the rosters. To allow veterans more time to round into shape, five additional players could be carried by each team until June 15 of the 1946 season. This enabled teams to evaluate personnel and ensured that veterans had every opportunity to earn back their jobs.

Clearly, those in greatest danger of being cut were the wartime players. Nowhere was this more evident than on the world champion Detroit Tigers. By the end of spring training, only thirteen players who participated in the 1945 World Series had made the club, and by season's end only ten remained.[12] On some clubs even solid players who were nearing the end of productive careers were either traded or released. For example, slick-fielding first baseman Johnny Hopp was sold to the Braves to make way for the return of Stan Musial, and with the arrival of service star Bob Dillinger, thirty-four-year-old infielder Don Gutteridge found himself managing the Toledo Mud Hens after several fine seasons with the Cardinals and Browns.

Even more telling was the retirement of Chicago's Tony Cuccinello, who at age thirty-eight had narrowly missed taking the American League batting title in 1945.

Some well-known players, such as Charlie Gehringer, Joe Cronin, Red Rolfe, Paul Waner, and Johnny Cooney, who had been with their clubs in 1941 at the beginning of the war, also retired or were released, while others, such as Paul Derringer, Harland Clift, and Joe Orengo, were sent to the minors and never returned. The Philadelphia Phillies team was almost completely restructured. The only carryover player from 1941 was Vince DiMaggio, and the only player to return from 1945's starting lineup was catcher Andy Seminick.

One of the players not retained by the Phillies was first baseman Tony Lupien. Unlike other wartime players, Lupien also spent six months in the service during 1945. He returned to the Phillies at the end of the 1945 season and, over a twenty-two-day period, played in fifteen games and hit .315. In February 1946, the Phillies sold Lupien to the Hollywood Stars of the Pacific Coast League. As part of the arrangement, the Phillies offered to maintain Lupien's $8,000 salary, even though it exceeded what the minor-league team would have offered him. One of the few Harvard graduates to play professional baseball, Lupien possessed sufficient courage to challenge the Phillies and argued that they had violated the spirit of the G.I. Bill of Rights (the Serviceman's Readjustment Act) by not giving him an opportunity to make the team in 1946. The act stipulated that returning veterans who applied for employment within ninety days of their return must be employed for at least one year.

Baseball maintained its own criteria for returning World War II veterans. Under guidelines issued by Commissioner Chandler in November 1945, a major-league war veteran's contract could not be assigned or optioned to a lower classification unless the player had been retained by the reinstating club for a thirty-day trial or fifteen days of a playing season and not unless the player had cleared waivers in both leagues. The Phillies claimed that Lupien's playing time late in 1945 satisfied baseball's criteria, and general manager Herb Pennock maintained that the team had "leaned over backwards" to give him every chance.[13]

Faced with costs and uncertainties of prosecuting his case in Philadelphia, where the local Selective Service Board would have jurisdiction, Lupien reported to Hollywood in late March. Instead of dropping the matter, however, he counseled other ballplayers on his experiences. One of these was Navy veteran Al Niemiec, who was released by the Seattle Rainers after a thirty-day trial.[14] With the assistance of the Selective Service System, Niemiec filed suit against the team in federal court. The court ruled that baseball players were entitled to the same benefits as other

Table 5. Final Major-League Regular-Season Standings, 1946

American League					National League			
	W	L	%	G.B.		W	L	%	G.B.
Boston	104	50	.675	–	St. Louis	98	58	.628	–
Detroit	92	62	.597	12	Brooklyn	96	60	.615	2
New York	87	67	.565	17	Chicago	82	71	.536	13 1/2
Washington	76	78	.494	28	Boston	81	72	.529	14 1/2
Chicago	74	80	.481	30	Philadelphia	69	85	.448	27
Cleveland	68	86	.442	36	Cincinnati	67	87	.435	29
St. Louis	66	88	.429	38	Pittsburgh	63	91	.409	33
Philadelphia	49	105	.318	55	New York	61	93	.396	35

veterans. Furthermore, it made no difference whether the teams kept the players; the clubs still had to compensate them for what they would have made. The ruling affected 143 former major-league players and an even greater number of minor-league players. Although many of those players failed to return to the major leagues, a few became quite prominent, including Hank Sauer, Frank Baumholtz, Danny Murtaugh, and Jim Konstanty.[15]

Federal judge Lloyd L. Black used the Niemiec case to criticize baseball's treatment of its players and even suggested that the game's antitrust exemption under the 1922 Holmes decision might be subject to reexamination in light of recent U.S. Supreme Court decisions involving interstate commerce. Not only did baseball find itself back in the dreaded courtroom, the Niemiec decision itself was another foreboding sign that the game's legal status was tenuous.

On the field itself, it was evident that the months and years with little opportunity for exercise or play at major-league levels had eroded the skills of many veterans. Older players had particular difficulty. "It was awful tough to come back from the service and start baseball again," recalled Giants pitcher Hal Schumacher. "I remember the running and the terrific exertion that took place trying to get back into shape. . . . Unfortunately, I developed a sore arm which added a lot of difficulty to my problems. As a result, it was not a happy spring, but it was something I wanted to do."[16] Even younger players, such as Ted Williams, had problems, as he complained to one writer, "My legs are in bad shape and my arm is still sore. It stands to reason a fellow is not going to improve by remaining out of the game for three years. And now I come back, and I'm hitting against pitchers I've never seen before, [and] don't know what they throw."[17]

While the 1946 season might have been memorable solely for its overcrowded camps and the challenges presented by labor unrest and the Mexican League raids, it was also an exciting year on the field. In the National League, the heavily favored and talent-laden Cardinals edged out the Dodgers in a surprisingly close race by defeating them in the first-ever league playoff game. In the American League, the Red Sox battered their way to a pennant over the defending champion Detroit Tigers.

The National League Pennant Race

In the National League, the Giants were a major disappointment. Their thin pitching staff was further weakened by the Mexican League raids, and injuries to key batters Johnny Mize and Walker Cooper short-circuited much of the team's power. The seventh-place Pirates, who had been in fourth place in May, never recovered from Murphy's attempt to unionize the team. Promising rookie Ralph Kiner (.247-23-81) and returning veteran pitcher Fritz Ostermueller (2.84, 13-10) led the team. Combative manager Frankie Frisch was fired late in the season, and on August 8, 1946, the team was sold to a group headed by Indianapolis banker Frank McKinney for $2.25 million. Other partners included real estate magnate John Galbreath of Columbus, Ohio, entertainer Bing Crosby, and Pittsburgh attorney Thomas P. Johnson.

The Cincinnati Reds finished in sixth place solely because of their anemic hitting. The strength of the team was a pitching staff that produced fifty-four complete games. Moreover, no Reds starter had an earned run average over 3.24. On September 11, Johnny Vander Meer, famous for pitching two consecutive no-hitters in 1940, worked fifteen scoreless innings against the Dodgers and struck out fourteen. The nineteen-inning contest, which lasted four hours and forty minutes, was at that time the longest scoreless game in major-league history. At the end of a difficult year, respected manager Bill McKechnie was replaced by Johnny Neun.

Although the Phillies finished twenty-seven games behind first-place Brooklyn, their fifth-place finish was the team's best since 1932. Fiery manager Ben Chapman milked as much production as he could from a collection of players that included outfielder Del Ennis (.313-17-73), who earned National League Rookie of the Year honors. With new manager Billy Southworth at the helm, the fourth-place Boston Braves served notice that they were a team of the future. Two young players who had pitched briefly for the team in 1942, Johnny Sain (2.21, 20-14) and Warren Spahn (2.94, 8-5), anchored the pitching staff, former Louisiana State football star and $40,000 bonus baby Alvin Dark made his debut, and Danny

Litwhiler's (.291-8-38) late-season hitting assured the Braves of a first-division finish for the first time since 1934.[18]

The Chicago Cubs discovered how difficult it was to repeat as National League champions, as injuries to key players hurt the team's momentum. Nevertheless, they were still in contention as late as August 16, and they exhibited plenty of courage as a series of brawls on May 22 and 23, headlined by Len Merullo of the Cubs and the Dodger's Eddie Stanky, demonstrated.

The National League pennant race was a battle between the Brooklyn Dodgers, who held first place from the end of May until the beginning of September, and the St. Louis Cardinals. The Dodgers' season began with a bang, as World War II veteran Ed Head pitched a no-hitter against the Braves on April 23. The Brooklyn club reflected the aggressive spirit of their manager, Leo Durocher. The team was led by the superb double-play combination of team captain and shortstop Harold "Pee Wee" Reese (.284-5-60) and second baseman Eddie Stanky (.273-0-36), nicknamed "The Brat." Whereas Reese served as the team's stabilizing influence, Stanky often provided the spark that ignited the Dodgers. A selective hitter with great bat control, Stanky led the National League with an on-base percentage of .436 in 1946. Branch Rickey lauded Stanky when he noted, "If there is a way to beat a team, you may depend on Stanky finding it."[19] Outfielder Fred "Dixie" Walker (.319-9-116) also had an outstanding year for the Dodgers. Nicknamed "The People's Cherce," Walker was easily the most popular player in Brooklyn.

The Dodgers made the 1946 pennant race much closer than the talented Cardinals had anticipated. Rice University athletic great Eddie Dyer, whose personal style of managing was popular with his players, replaced St. Louis manager Billy Southworth. The team was paced by young superstar Stan Musial (.365-16-103), who led the league in batting average, runs scored (124), hits (228), doubles (50), and triples (20) and in the process won his second National League Most Valuable Player award. Musial reluctantly switched from the outfield to first base—a position he was to hold for the next ten years.[20] Third base was manned by George "Whitey" Kurowski (.301-14-89). A courageous, hard-working player, Kurowski overcame a deformed right arm that was described by one teammate as containing more "gristle" than bone below the elbow.[21] Teammates marveled at his throwing ability and the fact that his disability actually allowed him to become a better pull hitter.[22]

The Cardinals also had a superb double-play combination in Marty Marion and Red Schoendienst. Shortstop Marion, who possessed great range, sure hands, and a fine arm, rarely made an error in clutch situations and always made the big play.[23] Second baseman Red Schoendienst was adept at fielding sharply hit balls and ended up leading the league in fielding percentage (.948) at his position. In the outfield the Cardinals had the incomparable Terry Moore (.263-3-28), who was considered to be one of the best defensive center fielders in the game. Unfortunately, Moore returned from the service with two bad knees, which diminished his production. Right field was occupied by the hustling North Carolinian Enos Slaughter (.300-18-130), a throwback to a bygone era. Nicknamed "Country" by his former manager Burt Shotton because of his mannerisms and attire, Slaughter ran hard on every play.

Cardinal pitching was deep, but with the loss of Max Lanier and Fred Martin to Mexico, the ineffectiveness of former twenty-game winner Red Barrett, and Johnny Beazley's injured arm, it needed to be. The team was paced by Murry Dickson (2.88, 15-6), Howie Pollet (2.10, 21-10), Harry Brecheen (2.49, 15-15), Al Brazle (3.29, 11-10), and Ted Wilks (3.41, 8-0). Dickson, nicknamed the "Great Houdini of the Mound," was a trick pitcher who liked to experiment when he was ahead in the count. The right-hander was adept at nibbling at the corners and refused to give in to hitters.[24]

Howie Pollet was a stylish left-hander who relied on control, a moving fastball, and an outstanding change-up. A wiry Oklahoman, Harry "The Cat" Brecheen earned his nickname because of his fielding quickness. Although not overpowering, the left-hander had a sneaky fastball, threw an outstanding screwball, and liberally employed the brush-back pitch as a weapon. He would often yell "Look out!" at the hitter as he was releasing the ball.[25]

The Redbirds' bullpen was led by Ted Wilks and Al Brazle. Wilks, whose real surname was Wilczek, was nicknamed "The Cork" because he was the team's stopper. One of the National League's best relievers in the 1940s, Wilks pitched quickly, threw hard, and tried to get batters to hit the ball directly to fielders.[26] Al Brazle was a lanky sinkerball pitcher whose delivery reminded hitters of a spider coming at them with legs and arms flopping in every direction.[27] Following the trade of Walker Cooper, the Cardinals' catching duties were shared by Clyde Kluttz, Del Rice, and Joe Garagiola. Garagiola, a native of an Italian neighborhood in St. Louis known as "The Hill," was a local favorite. Cardinals owner Sam Breadon told reporters that Garagiola will "have Cooper's catching and hitting skill, with a better disposition to go with it."[28]

Breadon's player transactions, especially the Cooper trade, created resentment among the Cardinals, who were heavily favored to win the National League pennant. Instead, they spent much of the season chasing the Dodgers. Stan Musial, in particular, felt that the Cooper sale set

St. Louis Cardinals players believed that the sale of slugging catcher Walker Cooper seriously handicapped their pennant chances. (George Brace Photo)

the team back for several years.[29] On the last night of the 1946 season, at a testimonial dinner in Breadon's honor, inebriated sportswriter J. Roy Stockton told Breadon, "Sam, it looks like you sliced the bologna a little too thin."[30]

The Dodgers finally relinquished the lead to the Cardinals in mid-August. From that point forward, the two teams vied with one another for the top spot as the suspense and tension mounted. On the last day of the season, the teams were deadlocked at ninety-six wins and fifty-eight defeats, forcing the first best-two-out-of-three playoff series in National League history. St. Louis beat the Dodgers 4-2 in the first game, behind Howie Pollet, who pitched a complete game victory even though his left arm was heavily taped because of a torn muscle. Rookie catcher Joe Garagiola, who had three hits on the day, knocked in two runs as the Cardinals chased Dodger starter Ralph Branca in the third inning. Surprisingly, only 26,012 fans attended the game. Rumors and newspaper stories, which predicted long lines before the contest, apparently scared fans away.[31] In the second game, the Cardinals scored an 8-4 triumph behind Murry Dickson to capture the National League pennant. The Dodgers rallied for three runs in the ninth inning but fell short when relief pitcher Harry Brecheen struck out Eddie Stanky and pinch-hitter Howie Schultz with the bases loaded.

The American League Pennant Race

In the American League, the Boston Red Sox led the circuit from wire to wire. On the verso, the Philadelphia Athletics dropped into last place in mid-April and remained there for the rest of the season. Three of their pitchers, Phil Marchildon, Dick Fowler, and Lou Knerr, tied for the league lead in losses with sixteen apiece. Team dissension marred the St. Louis Browns' season. Jack Kramer (3.19, 13-11), the team's only effective pitcher, was fined for throwing a ball over the stadium roof and jostling umpire Hal Weafer after being pulled from a game. Pitcher Tex Shirley and teammate Walt Judnich got into a fight over a misplayed ball. Only the penitent Mexican jumper Vern Stephens (.307-14-64) had a good year at the plate.

The Cleveland Indians, who battled the Browns for sixth place, finished last in the league in hitting and were saved only by pitcher Bob Feller's tremendous season. Feller (2.18, 26-15), who struck out 348 batters in 371 innings, fell one shy of Rube Waddell's record of 349.[32] Moreover, on April 30, 1946, Feller threw his second career no-hitter, against the Yankees, the first ever against the team in Yankee Stadium. The year also marked a change in Cleveland's ownership, as Alva Bradley sold the Indians to a syndicate led by thirty-two-year-old Bill Veeck, the former owner of the minor-league Milwaukee Brewers.

Fifth place belonged to the Chicago White Sox, who were inspired by tireless shortstop Luke Appling (.309-1-55). Appling led American League shortstops in assists, fewest errors, and double plays. Pitching standouts included Eddie Lopat (2.73, 13-13) and reliever Earl Caldwell (2.08, 13-4).

The Washington Senators were equipped with a mixture of live arms, young talent, and pitching experience and should have fared better than fourth place in 1946. Unfortunately, the hitting of outfielders Buddy Lewis and Stan Spence and first baseman Mickey Vernon (.353-8-85), the American League batting champion, was not sufficient to carry the club.

The preseason favorite New York Yankees were not the sound team they appeared to be on paper. Many of the team's key players experienced difficulty adjusting to their return from the service. Phil Rizzuto suffered from recurring bouts of malaria, Joe Gordon failed to get untracked, and Tommy Henrich was slow to round into playing form after three years in the Merchant Marines. Joe DiMaggio (.290-25-95) underwent a particularly painful year. The Yankee Clipper suffered a torn cartilage in his left knee while sliding and as a result failed to appear in the All-Star game for the first time in eight seasons. Only outfielder Charley Keller (.275-30-101) had an outstanding season. On the mound, the Yankees were led by Spud Chandler (2.10, 20-8), wartime holdover Bill Bevens (2.23, 16-13), and Randy Gumpert (2.31, 11-3). Though the team drew a major-league–record 2,265,512 fans, the team's season was marked by turmoil. In May 1946, manager Joe McCarthy left the team, ostensibly because of poor health. His replacement, catcher Bill Dickey, quit when he became disgusted with team president Larry MacPhail, leaving Johnny Neun to manage the team's last fourteen games.

The defending champion Detroit Tigers could get no closer than twelve games out, in spite of the timely hitting of Hank Greenberg (.277-44-127). Although handicapped by poor defense and inconsistent hitting, the Tigers' strong pitching kept them in the race. The ace of the Tiger staff, Hal Newhouser (1.94, 26-9), crafted eight shutouts while striking out 275 batters—his third consecutive outstanding season.

The Boston Red Sox had winning streaks of twelve and fifteen games at the beginning of the season and so dominated the league that no contender came within ten games of their lead. The team was successful because of the leadership of congenial manager Joe Cronin, the fact that most of Boston's players returned from the war in good physical shape, great hitting, and excellent pitching. In Dave "Boo" Ferris (3.25, 25-6), Tex Hughson (2.75, 20-11), Joe Dobson (3.24, 13-7), and Mickey Harris (3.64, 17-9), the Red Sox had a big four unlike any staff seen in Boston since. The staff ace was Tex Hughson, a 6'3" right-hander out of the University of Texas who averaged eighteen wins in his previous four seasons. Hughson's most effective rotation-mate was Dave Ferris, a strapping right-handed pitcher who was a star basketball player at Mississippi State University. Extremely competitive, he put together winning streaks of six and ten wins on his way to six shutouts and twenty-five victories.

In the infield, the Red Sox had former Detroit Tiger Rudy York (.276-17-119) at first base. Finishing third in the league in runs batted in behind Greenberg and Ted Williams, York's finest offensive game of the season was against the St. Louis Browns, when he hit two grand slams and knocked in ten runs. The Red Sox also obtained third baseman Pinky Higgins, in his fourteenth and last major-league season, from the Tigers. The team's keystone combination of shortstop Johnny Pesky (né Pavescovich, .335-2-55) and Bobby Doerr (.271-18-116) was the envy of every club in the league. After setting a torrid pace during the first months of the season, Pesky slumped and fell below .300, only to rebound in

August. His partner, Bobby Doerr, was undoubtedly the most popular player on the team, and, as team captain, he was also their undisputed leader. Doerr, who returned from the service with his weight more evenly distributed, proved to be much quicker than before the war. Finally, behind the plate was journeyman catcher Hal Wagner.

In right field was Wally Moses, obtained midyear from the Athletics to provide veteran leadership. In center field, the Red Sox boasted one of the American League's best defensive players in Dom DiMaggio (.316-7-73), the youngest of the three DiMaggio brothers to play in the major leagues. Nicknamed the "Little Professor" because his glasses gave him a scholarly bearing, DiMaggio was truly one of the game's underrated players, and his only major handicap was playing in the shadows of his brother Joe and teammate Ted Williams.

Ted Williams's shadow was indeed long. Nicknamed "The Kid," Williams (.342-38-123) finished second in home runs, runs batted in, and batting average, a record good enough to earn him his first Most Valuable Player award. He also excelled in the All-Star game, as he went four for four, including a home run off Rip Sewell's blooper pitch, to lead the American League to a 12-0 victory. Through early May, Williams was on pace to surpass his record-breaking 1941 season, and, according to Cronin, he was hitting the ball "as hard as anyone ever hit it. Yes, as hard as Babe Ruth."[33] Nevertheless, 1946 was a year of frustration for Williams. He was walked constantly. Not only was Williams a selective hitter, but pitchers preferred walking him to letting him hit. His 156 bases on balls was only twenty-six fewer than the combined number of walks issued to three other top American League hitters, Joe DiMaggio, Mickey Vernon, and Hank Greenberg. Even more frustrating was the Boudreau shift, an innovative defense in which Cleveland positioned all of their infielders on the right side of the infield and dared Williams to hit the ball to left field or bunt. Although the Red Sox slugger attempted to drive balls through the defense to right field, he eventually adapted by hitting the ball through the shortstop position. Nevertheless, the defense was at least a contributing factor to Williams's inability to keep his average above .350.

As the 1946 season wound down, so did the Red Sox. Bobby Doerr went into a September slump, Hal Wagner was underweight and badly bruised from countless foul tips, and Dom DiMaggio was pressing to make up for a bruised hip suffered early in the season. Moreover, Boston's pitching began to sour. With the Boudreau shift and countless walks, the season wore Ted Williams down. On Labor Day, Elmer Valo of the Athletics robbed Williams of a home run. Valo crashed so hard into the fence that he had to be carried from the field. Later, in righteous indignation, Williams failed to run out a ground ball and then walked to and from his outfield position. His actions elicited boos from the Boston fans and drew the ire of the local press. The writers also manufactured stories about dissension between Pesky and Williams because of the close batting race. Exhausted, Williams lashed out. "I don't care what they write any more," he said. "I'm tired physically. I'm on the go all the time [and] I wish it were all over."[34]

When the baseball season was extended because of the National League playoff games, the Red Sox kept sharp by playing a three-game exhibition series against a group of American League All-Stars. The games were played in temperatures that hovered around thirty degrees, and in one of them, pitcher Mickey Haeffner hit Williams on the elbow with a sidearm curveball. The bruised elbow prevented Williams from taking batting practice for two days.[35]

The 1946 World Series

With the playoff series against the Dodgers behind them, the St. Louis Cardinals forced the favored Red Sox into a seven-game series. In the opener at St. Louis, the Cardinals went into the ninth inning with a 2-1 lead but let the game slip away when Howie Pollet gave up a single to Tom McBride with two on and two out to tie the score at two apiece. Then, in the tenth inning, Rudy York powered a ball into the left-field bleachers for the winning run. In the second game, Harry Brecheen crafted a three-hitter to beat Boston 3-0. The third game, played in Fenway Park, was determined in the first inning, when Rudy York hit a three-run homer to lead the Red Sox to a 4-0 win. In hurling a shutout, Boo Ferris retired the first thirteen batters he faced.

The fourth game turned into a rout, as the Cardinals pounded Tex Hughson and five other Red Sox pitchers for twenty hits—tying a World Series record set by the New York Giants in 1920. George "Red" Munger scattered nine hits in the 12-3 victory, and every Cardinal in the lineup got at least one hit. Fans viewing the finale in Boston saw the Red Sox prevail 6-3 to take a 3-2 lead in the series. Joe Dobson threw a complete game for Boston, yielding only four hits. He would have had a shutout, had it not been for two errors by Johnny Pesky. Pesky redeemed himself with three hits. Returning to Sportsman's Park, the Cardinals evened the series at three games apiece by beating the Red Sox 4-1 behind steady Harry Brecheen.

The seventh game of the 1946 World Series was one of the most memorable in baseball history. With the score tied 3-3, outfielder Enos Slaughter led off the Cardinals' half of the eighth inning with a single to center

Left, Enos Slaughter's daring dash from first base to score on Harry Walker's hit allowed the Cardinals to win the seventh game of the World Series over Boston. *Right*, Bobby Doerr was the most popular player on the Red Sox team and its undisputed leader. (George Brace Photo)

field. The next two hitters, Whitey Kurowski and Del Rice, were retired, bringing up Harry Walker. The Cardinal outfielder redeemed a miserable personal season by lining a double off Boston reliever Bob Klinger over shortstop Johnny Pesky's head. With the count at two balls and a strike and the steal sign on, Slaughter was running before Walker connected. Not blessed with great speed, Slaughter made what should have been an ill-advised decision to attempt to score. As center fielder Leon Culberson's relay throw came to shortstop Pesky, Slaughter astounded everyone by rounding third base and heading for home plate.

Receiving no warning from his teammates to throw home, Pesky dropped his arm as he turned toward the diamond. The pause caused him to make an off-balance throw that arrived ten feet up the third base line at the same time as the impetuous Slaughter was sliding across home plate.[36] When asked about his decision to make home plate, Slaughter replied, "I just had a hunch I could make it, and I was willing to take the rap if I didn't."[37]

Although the Red Sox rallied in the ninth inning, they failed to score, and the series belonged to the Cardinals. As bedlam prevailed in St. Louis, a photographer caught a disconsolate Ted Williams sitting and staring at the clubhouse floor. Tears, it was said, came later, in the shower and in the cab on the way to the train.[38] None of the Red Sox was more frustrated than Williams. With only five singles, not unlike the experiences of Rogers Hornsby, Babe Ruth, and Ty Cobb before him, Williams's first World Series was a major disappointment. His poor September, sore elbow, the expectation by everyone that he would carry the team at the plate, and the Cardinals' own version of the Boudreau shift all mitigated against Williams's success. Second baseman Red Schoendienst recalled catching several of Williams's line drives that were hit "pretty damn good" while in the shift.[39] Harry Walker explained, "We put the shift on him. . . [and] kept the ball away and Brecheen threw that screwball that he had never seen."[40] Giving clubhouse boy Johnny Orlando his own loser's share of the World Series money ($2,140.89), Williams left Boston for a winter in South Dakota, California, and Florida.[41]

For other Boston and St. Louis players, World Series shares provided a much-needed salary bonus. The limited capacity of the teams' ballparks, however, caused individual shares to be smaller than in any other season since 1918. The winners received $3,742.33 each. Many players felt that the winners should be guaranteed at least $5,000 per player. Thus, when Commissioner Chandler asked the players before the series to sign a waiver agreeing to apply the $175,000 revenue from the Gillette Safety Razor Company's broadcasting rights to the players' pension fund, several Boston players balked.[42]

Whereas the Cardinal players readily signed the waiver, National League player representative Marty Marion was forced to plead with the Red Sox players to change their minds. Marion told the Red Sox that many of them would be out of baseball soon and that they had better take advantage of the plan while they had the chance. Without their cooperation, he noted further, "there would have been no plan at the time."[43] Five Red Sox players still opposed the idea, but after a lecture from teammate Pinky Higgins, several gave in. Finally, before the sixth game, the last two yielded, and Marion was able to give Chandler an affirmative reply.[44]

With the players' pension plan taking form and safe for the moment, the year of tumult came to a close. Fueled by a temporary lack of competition from other distractions and a populace that thirsted for "old-fashioned" entertainment value, the popularity of baseball was at an all-time high in 1946. America's heroes returned from war to a game that, on the surface, seemed unchanged and ageless. Attendance records were shattered, with 18,534,444 fans coming to ballparks as compared with a previous high of 10,951,502.[45] In 1946, baseball remained America's most popular spectator sport.

1947

Joe DiMaggio and Phil Rizzuto were the heart of the
Yankees—the two players the team counted on the most.
(Photographic Archives, University of Louisville)

7

Durocher Finishes Last

Brooklyn Dodgers manager Leo Durocher was rarely characterized as a nice guy. Nevertheless, his suspension by Commissioner Chandler during the 1947 season for conduct detrimental to baseball made him a hero and a martyr in Brooklyn. There is little doubt that Chandler sought to make an example of Durocher. The commissioner used Durocher's vulnerability to prove once and for all that he was as tough on gambling and undesirable behavior as Judge Landis had been. Durocher was also a pawn in a feud between two baseball executives, Larry MacPhail and Branch Rickey, as well as a victim of his own notoriety and indiscretions. How the suspension came to pass and the rationale behind it forms one of the most bizarre chapters in baseball history.

To understand Durocher's situation one must examine his background and temperament. Leo Durocher came from a poor French Catholic neighborhood in West Springfield, Massachusetts. Spoiled by a doting father, he quit high school after an altercation with a teacher. He was a natural athlete who excelled on the football and baseball fields, as well as in the local pool room. Cocky, brash, and self-assured, Durocher joined the New York Yankees as a player in 1925. Although he was a gifted fielder, his hitting was so weak that teammate Babe Ruth nicknamed him "the All-American out."[1]

Durocher's aggressive style and knowledge of the game allowed him to lead the Brooklyn Dodgers to a pennant in 1941 in only his second season as manager. He was a gambling, hunch manager who, as sportswriter Dan Daniel explained, "hit and ran when most managers might have stolen, and he stole when others might have hit and run."[2] He built teams that reflected his character—teams that hustled, scrapped, and outplayed the opposition. He wanted players who "would put you in a cement mixer if they felt like it."[3] Durocher's legendary remark "nice guys finished last" stemmed from a paraphrase of a conversation with Dodger broadcaster Red Barber concerning the kind of men he wanted on his team. Pointing to Eddie Stanky he said, "Look at that little ———. Think he's a nice guy? The hell he is! He'll knock you down to make a play, if he has to . . . that's the kind of guys I want on my club." In contrast, motioning toward the Giants dugout, Durocher stated, "Nice guys! Look over there. Do you know a nicer guy than Mel Ott or any of the other Giants? And where are they . . . in last place!"[4]

The Dodger manager used the threat of the beanball, the knock down, and bench jockeying as psychological weapons. When opposing hitters got an extra base hit, Durocher would remind them to stay loose, saying, "My pitchers got orders about what to do with you the next time you come to bat. They'll knock you down!"[5] "Durocher would say anything," remembered Stan Musial, "like, 'hit him in the head, knock him down.' He was always trying to intimidate you."[6]

Durocher was also the master of sarcasm. One of his favorite targets was Hank Sauer, the Cubs slugger, whose prominent nose reminded everyone of the hood ornament of a popular General Motors car. When Durocher yelled "Pontiac!" Sauer invariably stepped out of the batter's box to regain his composure.[7] Carl Erskine, a young Dodger pitcher, remembered how encouraging Durocher had been to him when he was in the minors. The Dodgers manager lavished praise on Erskine and told him he had a great future. Nevertheless, when Erskine debuted as a rookie for the Dodgers against the Giants in 1949, Durocher reacted differently. Then, as manager of the Giants, he was coaching third base, and he called Erskine some things he had not expected to hear. Erskine was so rattled that he balked in a run for the Giants. Erskine looked over at third and "his heart was broken." Thinking to himself, "Leo! I'm this kid you brought out of the minors," he was devastated. When Erskine mentioned the incident years later, Durocher only recalled, "Aw, I remember that . . . , you were a great young kid, but after all . . . I had a different name on [my uniform]."[8]

Durocher also used psychology to manipulate his team. An outstanding card player, he kept pitcher Kirby Higbe $600 to $800 in debt—a feat that he claimed took little skill because, he noted, Higbe "couldn't beat your aunt in Duluth." As an incentive, he knocked $200 off the debt every time the right-handed pitcher won a game.[9] Durocher's penchant for gambling was entwined with his approach to the game in other ways. As Dan Daniel wrote, "Leo will run a club just as he runs a game of poker. He will deadpan, he will exuberate, he will twit you, he will fool you."[10]

Off the field, Durocher could be charming and captivating. He enjoyed fine clothes, kept company with beautiful women, and cultivated friendships with the rich and famous. It was not unusual to run into actors William Bendix, Danny Kaye, or George Raft in the Dodgers clubhouse. Also frequently seen there was Max "Memphis" Engelberg, the popular New York racing handicapper who provided Durocher and other Dodgers with tips on the morning line.[11]

The Dodger manager also had a violent temper. His domestic life was far from serene. When Durocher's first wife, Ruby, filed for divorce, she charged that he had punched her in the jaw and tied her up with a bed sheet.[12] As a player and manager, Durocher also had several conflicts with umpires and fans. The most serious involved an incident on June 9, 1945, in which he was charged with assaulting John Christian, a veteran who had been heckling him from the stands. Christian testified that he was summoned by a special policeman to meet Durocher under the stands, where both the policeman and Durocher hit him with "a dark object" (a blackjack). Durocher claimed that he simply admonished Christian. Nevertheless, Christian somehow ended up with a broken jaw and multiple bruises. Although Durocher paid Christian $6,750 to settle a civil suit, he and the policeman were brought to trial in Brooklyn on criminal charges.[13] In spite of incriminating testimony by an eyewitness, the friendly Brooklyn jury took only five minutes to acquit Durocher of the charges.

Durocher and Rickey were an odd couple in Brooklyn. Durocher stood for just about everything Rickey found abhorrent, with one exception—he knew how to win. Rickey first acquired Durocher when he was with the St. Louis Cardinals in 1934 and certainly knew everything about him—who his friends were, what character traits he possessed, and what activities he pursued. Sportswriter Red Smith, who thought Durocher was "basically a bad guy," related that Rickey once told him that Durocher "could charm your teeth out, if he chose to, but back him into a corner and he is that same little kid from West [Springfield] . . . with the butt of a pool cue in his hand."[14] Dodgers publicist Harold Parrott described him as Rickey's pet reclamation project.[15] It was, however, a daunting project. When Rickey took over the Dodgers in 1942, he warned the Dodger pilot that he wanted no more gambling in the clubhouse or on the train. To impress Durocher, he fired coach Charlie Dressen, who was known for his habitual gambling. Dressen was later rehired, after promising to reform.[16]

Rickey's warning on gambling had little effect on Durocher's continued friendship with movie star and gambler George Raft. The friendship was so strong that the two men shared living quarters—Raft staying with Durocher when he came to New York and Durocher moving in with Raft at the latter's Hollywood home during the winter. For many years, the two shared cars, clothes, and women.[17] Commissioner Chandler's problem with

Leo Durocher (left) stood for just about everything Branch Rickey found abhorrent, with one exception—he knew how to win. *(The Sporting News)*

the friendship was Raft's connection with the underworld—boyhood friendships in New York with the notorious Benjamin "Bugsy" Siegel and others. It mattered little that other Hollywood celebrities in the 1930s and 1940s, such as Clark Gable, Jean Harlow, Bruce Cabot, and Jack Warner, were also familiar with underworld figures. As Hedda Hopper once said, "Crooks as well as shady ladies liked to mingle with celebrities."[18]

During Durocher's absence because of spring training in March 1944, Raft used the manager's apartment for a floating crap game. When one of the big losers later complained about the game to the Brooklyn district attorney, the news made headlines. Later in 1946, popular syndicated columnist Westbrook Pegler called Rickey and threatened to write a series of columns about Durocher's relationship with Raft unless the Dodger president fired him. Rickey, of course, was aware of Durocher's association with Raft. He knew that Judge Landis had forced Durocher to retrieve four tickets he had given Raft during the 1941 World Series and that, more recently, while waiting to enter the Dodger clubhouse following the team's 1946 playoff loss to the Cardinals, he had been brushed aside by Raft and his bodyguard, who told him, "Just a minute, Pop. Stand back!"[19]

Rickey was worried. Having already signed Durocher for the 1947 season, he could ill afford the bad publicity that Pegler's articles might generate. In an attempt to salvage the situation, he sent his assistant Arthur Mann to visit Chandler in his Cincinnati office on November 16, 1946, to apprise him of Durocher's predicament and to ask him to warn his manager officially to discontinue his association with Raft and other gamblers.[20] Chandler agreed to confer with Durocher and arranged a meeting at the Claremont Country Club in Berkeley, California. There, Chandler demanded that Durocher disassociate himself from Raft, and he produced a list of other individuals whom Durocher was to avoid, including gangsters Bugsy Siegel and Joe Adonis and gamblers Conrad "Connie" Immerman and Memphis Engelberg. The commissioner assured him that, if he agreed to his stipulations and stayed out of the headlines, he would be out of trouble.[21]

Durocher agreed to these strictures and replied, "They'll call me a louse, but I'll do it." Then, much to the commissioner's surprise, he proceeded to unburden himself about his new love affair with actress Laraine Day. When Chandler asked when they were going to get married, the Dodger manager said, "Just as soon as she's divorced."[22] Durocher also related how he had argued with Day's husband about sleeping arrangements in front of Laraine in the couple's bedroom. Chandler, who was shocked by this revelation, told Durocher to stay clear of gamblers and out of bedrooms. "You are going to conduct yourself properly," he warned, "or I'm going to have to discipline you."[23]

Durocher quickly moved out of Raft's house and studiously avoided bad company.[24] Raft, who was very upset by the situation, attempted to see Chandler to protest the decision. According to Chandler, the conversation was brief:

RAFT: "I want to talk to you Commissioner."

CHANDLER: "What about?"

RAFT: "Well, I got a bum rap."

CHANDLER: "You didn't get it from me. George, do you have a baseball contract?"

RAFT: "No."

CHANDLER: "Take your business some place else, because I don't give a damn what you do. I don't have to be responsible for you."

Years later, Chandler explained: "I wasn't going to get involved with George Raft. Why in the hell should I take on George Raft? But Durocher, he's a different proposition—he's got a baseball contract."[25]

If Rickey and Chandler hoped that their actions would enable Durocher to maintain a low profile, they were mistaken. First, the Berkeley meeting was discovered by the press, and there was much speculation on what had taken place there. Second, not long after Rickey's announcement that he was hiring Durocher for another year, Pegler's first column appeared. In it, he described Durocher as "a moral delinquent," linked Raft with Bugsy Siegel and 1920s rum runner Ownie Madden, and compared the Dodger manager's situation with the climate under which the Black Sox scandal broke in 1919.[26]

The timing of Pegler's columns was not propitious for Durocher. The dark shadow of gambling fell over all sports following World War II. In 1945, college basketball was tainted when two players were found guilty of accepting bribes from gamblers.[27] Then, during the fall of 1946, two professional football players, Merle Hapes and Frank Filchock of the New York Giants, were approached to throw the National Football League playoff game to the Chicago Bears.[28] Finally, middleweight boxing champion Rocky Graziano testified to a grand jury that he was offered $100,000 to throw a match against boxer Ruben Shank.[29]

Gambling also threatened minor-league baseball. During the 1946 season, gamblers approached players on the Charlotte Hornets of the class B Tri-State League, and National Association president Judge William Bramham announced the lifetime suspension of outfielder Hooper Triplett for betting $20 on his own Columbia, South Carolina, team.[30] The public became even more aware of gambling when the Evangeline League scandal surfaced—baseball's biggest bribery case since the 1919 Black Sox episode. On January 25, 1947, Judge Bramham suspended five players who were implicated in an attempt to fix the results of the 1946 Evangeline League playoff games between two Louisiana towns, Houma and Abbeville.[31]

The public outcry was not against the players being punished but against the gamblers, who appeared to be escaping attention. Many questioned why Commissioner Chandler had not asked the federal government to pursue the gamblers. Evangeline League president J. Walter Morris was more explicit when he told reporters that, if Judge Landis were still alive, "He'd have been in this matter two months ago."[32] The *Sporting News* also urged Chandler to join with the National Association to meet the gambling threat and stressed that it was the commissioner's duty to check into "all charges, all rumors, all whispers, concerning players, managers, umpires, club owners and other baseball officials."[33]

With baseball so sensitized to the gambling problem, both the major and minor leagues took steps to bar gamblers from ballparks and to publicize the penalties if players failed to report bribe offers to their clubs. On his part, Commissioner Chandler announced the hiring of two ex-FBI agents to keep the game free from gambling. Moreover, he began to use the subject as one of his major speech themes. When he spoke to a Cleveland audience on February 13, 1947, he assured them that baseball's integrity was intact and that he intended to keep it that way. "That means we will deal uncompromisingly with the gambling threat. We'll throw those tinhorns out of our parks and keep them out. We'll do all in our power to protect the player against associations which are undesirable and we expect full cooperation from the players."[34]

If Pegler's columns were not enough to connect Durocher's name with gambling, undesirable associations, and conduct outside society's boundaries, a speech by James A. Farley at the twenty-fourth annual New York Baseball Writers' dinner cemented the relationship. Warning against the erosion of "moral fiber" and "moral standards," the former chairman of the Democratic Party made a clear inference to Durocher's affair with Laraine Day, when he stated, while "I do not want to get mixed up with private affairs . . . what a man does off the field, his personal conduct and reputation away from baseball, certainly are of tremendous importance to the game." To ensure that the connection was made, J.G. Taylor Spink wrote in his *Sporting News* column, "It might be well for baseball to take over jurisdiction in cases like that of Durocher. In the meantime, the matter rests with Leo himself, and with the patience and endurance of Branch Rickey."[35]

Durocher's infatuation with Laraine Day almost guaranteed publicity. The bedroom encounter with Day's husband, Ray Hendricks, described to Chandler at the Berkeley meeting resulted in a suit in which Durocher was accused of breaking up Day's marriage.[36] Day was awarded a divorce on January 20, 1947, but instead of waiting for the mandatory year required under California law, she and Durocher flew to Juarez, Mexico, where she also obtained a Mexican divorce. Then the couple reentered the United States at El Paso, where they were married. Unfortunately for the newlyweds, their escapade became front-page news.

California Superior Court Judge George Dockweiler, who granted Day's first divorce, was enraged by the couple's marriage. Forcing them to return to his court, he threatened to set aside his original decree, reprimanded them for making a mockery of his court, and then made the transcript of the conference public. Durocher, who could not resist verbal retaliation, claimed that the judge was "unethical and publicity-conscious."[37] Not long after, Day's attorneys successfully argued that Judge Dockweiler had shown bias in her case, and he was disqualified from further involvement in her divorce proceedings. Another judge upheld her decree, and one year later Durocher and Day were quietly married in California.

In spite of the happy ending, Durocher's public image was tarnished by the affair. Father Vincent J. Powell, of the Catholic Youth Organization, wrote a letter to the Brooklyn Dodgers' Knothole Club in which he announced that his organization was withdrawing its support for the club because Durocher was "undermining the moral training of Brooklyn's Catholic youths." He assured the team, however, that support would be reestablished if Durocher were replaced.[38]

After telling reporters that he would "go to hell and back" for Durocher, Rickey assured them that once spring training began in Havana, everything would turn around for his manager.[39] In Havana, Durocher banned card games and anything that would give the appearance of gambling on his club. In addition, he studiously avoided contact with anyone outside the media and the team. Claiming that he had been forced to become "a hermit," he told reporters that "Down here I go to the ballpark, come back, have my meals in my room and then read."[40] Regardless of his good intentions, however, subsequent events would lead to his undoing.

Training with the Dodgers in the Caribbean were the New York Yankees. On March 8, 1947, the Dodgers beat the Yankees 17-6 at Stadia Grande before 10,000. The victory notwithstanding, the presence of two known gamblers, Memphis Engelberg and Connie Immerman, in or near boxes assigned the Yankees angered Branch Rickey. Afterward, hinting that there was a double standard, Rickey asked a couple of newspapermen what would have happened had the two men been in Brooklyn boxes as his guests or as the guests of Leo Durocher. Alerted to a potential story, the sportswriters who covered the teams witnessed the presence of the two gamblers in the same boxes at the game on March 9. Dick Young of the *New York Daily News*, looking for a good quote, called Durocher's attention to the presence of the men, and he responded, predictably, "Are there two sets of rules, one applying to managers and the other to club owners? Where does MacPhail come off, flaunting his company with known gamblers right in the player's faces? If I even said 'Hello' to one of those guys, I'd be called up before Commissioner Chandler and probably barred."[41]

An equally incensed MacPhail denied that the two gamblers were guests of the Yankees, and thus began the culmination of the long-standing feud between Rickey and MacPhail—a rift that drove Durocher irretrievably into its web. To understand Durocher's dilemma, one must chart the Rickey-MacPhail relationship, which dated back to 1931, when Rickey, then president of the St. Louis Cardinals, worked out a deal with MacPhail to make the Columbus, Ohio, club part of the Cardinals minor-league system. Two years later, however, even though he had turned the Columbus franchise into an overnight success, MacPhail was fired by Rickey without apparent cause.[42] Although Rickey quickly recommended MacPhail to lead the ailing Cincinnati Reds, the firing was the beginning of a bitter rivalry between the two men. As MacPhail's son Lee noted, "It went back to his time in Columbus. In the beginning he looked up to Rickey. . . . He had different problems. . . . I'm sure a good percentage of it . . . my father was the cause of it. . . . [There have been] things in his personal life that Mr. Rickey didn't approve of . . . maybe his drinking more than Mr. Rickey would have liked."[43]

MacPhail turned a $100,000 profit in 1935 by installing the first lights in the major leagues, hiring Red Barber to announce games over an expanded radio network, and making baseball fun in Cincinnati. He resigned in 1936, not long after having an altercation with a Cincinnati police officer. As a partial legacy to his baseball acumen, the Reds won pennants in 1939 and 1940 with a team largely built by MacPhail.

MacPhail returned to the major leagues in 1937 when he was hired on Branch Rickey's recommendation to run the Brooklyn Dodgers. Over a three-year period he built another pennant contender, which included players Dixie Walker, Pee Wee Reese, Pete Reiser, and Whitlow Wyatt. The Dodgers captured the pennant in 1941, attendance soared, and the team achieved financial stability for the first time in years. Nevertheless, MacPhail's relationship with the team's board of directors and the Brooklyn Trust Company was an uneasy one. His erratic behavior and reputation as an extravagant spender undermined his credibility.[44] Thus, the onset of World War II provided him with a rationale to resign from the team and to rejoin the Army before he was fired.

MacPhail was succeeded in Brooklyn by Branch Rickey, whose relationship with St. Louis Cardinals owner Sam Breadon soured over Rickey's lucrative financial arrangements with the team. Rickey was not an instant success in Brooklyn. He made several unpopular moves, including trading local favorite Dolph Camilli, an act that led him to be hung in effigy by unhappy fans. Rickey became so concerned about the flap that he visited MacPhail at the Pentagon to seek advice. MacPhail likely met Rickey's troubles with mixed emotions. He respected Rickey, but still harbored resentment over his Columbus firing. Moreover, Rickey was now in charge of a team that MacPhail had crafted and that still bore his identity.

MacPhail returned to baseball in 1945 when he joined with Del Webb and Dan Topping to purchase the New York Yankees. Citing MacPhail's unsuccessful attempts to bait former Yankee general manager Ed Barrow while at Brooklyn, *New York Daily Mirror* columnist Dan Parker predicted that the move would now enable him to "pick fights with Deacon Branch Rickey."[45] As Parker anticipated, the two executives clashed over rising ticket prices, and in 1946 MacPhail hired Charlie Dressen away from the Dodgers. Claiming that Dressen was a free agent, MacPhail made the situation worse by publicly criticizing Rickey's treatment of Dressen—a none-too-subtle reminder of his own handling by Rickey.[46] Finally, MacPhail unleashed another salvo against Rickey when, after signing Bucky Harris to manage the Yankees, he announced that Leo Durocher had approached him about the job. Although MacPhail bragged that he could have had him for $35,000, he claimed that Durocher was not given serious consideration.

The Dodgers surmised that MacPhail needed a feud to drum up interest in the Yankees because their pennant prospects in 1947 were not good. They also determined that the best way to retaliate against MacPhail was not through Rickey but through Durocher. In a memorandum drafted by Dodgers traveling secretary Harold Parrott and initialed by administrative assistant Arthur Mann, Parrott recommended that "It was up to Leo to deny emphatically that he sought the Yankee job from MacPhail; and he can enlarge pretty well, I imagine, on the way MacPhail hounded him, trying to get him to take the job." He noted that, when he spoke to Durocher on the phone about MacPhail's remarks, the manager "hit the ceiling" and replied, "I'll let loose a few good blasts" and indicated that his telephone bills would reveal who called who when." Parrott added that he had sent Durocher enough newspaper clippings "to keep the righteous fire of indignation burning under him for some time." Although he suggested that Rickey be given a complete account of the conflict, he asked Mann why the feud needed to be with Rickey and suggested, "Why not with Durocher, whose desirable personality and managing ability is the cause of it all."[47]

Thus, Leo Durocher was set up by his own organization to take on Larry MacPhail. In normal times, Durocher would have been a good choice, but in 1946-47 the Dodger manager was far more vulnerable than most members of the Dodgers staff realized. In a series of well-publicized exchanges, MacPhail and Durocher wrangled over who had approached whom for the Yankees managerial job. The war of words continued through early March 1947, when the two teams met for a three-game series in Caracas, Venezuela. MacPhail was particularly upset over a March 3 *Brooklyn Eagle* column ghostwritten for Durocher by Parrott called "Durocher Says." In the column, Durocher maintained that the three-game series was being played for blood and that MacPhail was out to discredit him because of his refusal to manage the Yankees. The article began, "This is a declaration of war. . . . I want to beat the Yankees because of MacPhail and Dressen." Although Durocher never saw the columns before they appeared, he was confident that he could back up Parrott's words.[48]

Hence, when the two teams returned to Havana, the scene was set for the appearance of the two gamblers in or near the Yankees' box-seat section. Immerman and Engelberg were familiar figures throughout baseball and racing circles. Engelberg was known to some sportswriters as the "betting commissioner."[49] He was such a talented handicapper that Durocher and other players had him mark their cards at the track.[50] Immerman, who during Prohibition earned his living in speakeasies, was briefly the proprietor of Harlem's famed Cotton Club. From 1923 to 1933, he operated Connie's Inn, located at Seventh Avenue and 131st Street, in the middle of Harlem's all-night entertainment district. In Havana, Immerman was the manager and part owner of another Connie's Inn—a well-known casino whose other alleged co-owner was gangster Lucky Luciano.[51]

When MacPhail learned of Durocher's remarks, he was enraged and demanded public satisfaction. He filed official charges against him with the commissioner's office and claimed that he had been libeled and slandered and that what had taken place was conduct detrimental to baseball. While denying that he provided Immerman and Engelberg with their seats, he stated, "This man, Max Engelberg, is a friend of mine, works around racetracks, never has bet on baseball, and will be welcomed in Yankee Stadium any time he wants to come there. However, neither he nor his companion was in my box in Havana, nor were they being entertained by me."[52]

Commissioner Chandler found himself caught in the middle of the dispute between the two clubs. Not wanting to air baseball's dirty laundry further, he tried to persuade MacPhail to withdraw his charges, but to no avail.[53] Unsuccessful, he scheduled a hearing for March 24 to be held in Sarasota, Florida. When interviewed about what might take place at the hearing, Chandler made several statements that gave the impression he might have prejudged the case. In a story picked up by the Associated Press, he reputedly told *Cincinnati Enquirer* reporter Lou Smith, "Somebody may wind up getting kicked out of baseball. I'm taking off my kid gloves, and I intend making things tough for baseball people who won't toe the line and whose conduct I consider detrimental to the game." Even after denying that he made the first statements, he bragged that as governor of Kentucky he had signed death warrants sending men to the electric chair, "so I'm not going to be timid when I get ready to take action."[54]

At the hearing, the Dodgers were represented by Walter O'Malley as acting head of the ball club, Branch Rickey Jr., assistant general manager, Arthur Mann, assistant to the president, and Senator George Williams, an old friend of Branch Rickey who served as the club's attorney. The Yankees were represented by Larry MacPhail and Dan Topping. The judge and jury consisted of Chandler and his assistant, Walter Mulbry. Conspicuously absent was Branch Rickey, who had been called to Ohio to attend a funeral. A last-minute plea by the Dodgers to postpone the hearing until Rickey could be present was denied by Chandler. Rickey's absence was not lost on Durocher, who had been invited to testify on his own behalf. As a Rickey man, he had little faith in O'Malley, who he suspected would do little to protect him because of his own designs on the Dodgers. He also received little solace when he discovered that George Williams had not prepared a brief for the case. Aware of Chandler's remarks and recalling their Berkeley meeting, Durocher told Williams, "I've got a hunch that the Commissioner is laying for me."[55]

In his brief, MacPhail argued that he held Branch Rickey responsible for the pronouncements and press articles, which he claimed impugned by "implication or innuendo" his character and integrity in baseball," and he maintained that there was no feud between the two teams. At no point did he blame Durocher for the affair. When Durocher was called as a witness, he admitted responsibility for the things said in the "Durocher Says" columns and explained that it was "just another rhubarb" and that he and MacPhail had been engaging in such conversation "for years."[56] At Chandler's request, MacPhail read the entire column that appeared in the March 3 issue of the *Brooklyn Eagle*. After he finished, Durocher openly apologized to MacPhail and exclaimed that he still wanted to be friends. According to Durocher, MacPhail tore up the clipping, gave the Dodger manager a bear hug, and said, "You've always been a great guy with me. . . . Forget it, buddy, it's over."[57]

Durocher's relief, however, was short lived. Chandler seemed annoyed with MacPhail's actions and persisted in a different line of questioning directed at the gambling situation on the Dodger club. Durocher explained that he played for high stakes only with Kirby Higbe and that he returned the money he won from Higbe after good pitching performances. When Chandler questioned the Dodger manager about his allegations regarding the two gamblers near MacPhail's box, Durocher attempted to link this point with the Berkeley meeting at which Chandler had warned him against associating with the same men. Chandler did not address the question of who hosted the gamblers.[58] When this phase of the hearing ended, Chandler asked MacPhail if anything else needed to be covered. MacPhail maintained that his specific charges against Rickey had not been satisfied and that he would prefer to have the Dodger president address them in person. Chandler then called for a second hearing to be held on March 29 in St. Petersburg.

Delegations from both teams, including Branch Rickey Sr., attended the second hearing. The Dodger president told the commissioner that he took full responsibility for his statements regarding the presence of the gamblers in or near MacPhail's box, although he denied making any statements detrimental to MacPhail's character as an individual or owner. The second part of the hearing focused on the testimony of Arthur Patterson, the Yankees' traveling secretary and director of publicity, who clearly admitted that he could have "conceivably" provided Immerman and Engelberg with their Havana seats.[59]

Following Patterson's testimony, Chandler excused everyone except the representatives of the Dodgers (Rickey, O'Malley, and Mann). He approached the three men and asked Rickey, "How much would it hurt you folks to have your fellow out of baseball?" Rickey, filled with emotion and with tears rolling down his cheeks, said, "Happy, what on earth is the matter with you?" Chandler pulled a letter from his pocket from a prominent Washington official who had advised him to expel Durocher. Claiming that he had to do something, Chandler calmed the vocal protestations of the three men by telling them that he was only sounding them out.[60]

After talking with the Dodgers about Durocher, the commissioner was closeted with MacPhail for thirty minutes. Based on denials made by Rickey regarding his character that appeared in the press, the Yankee president asked Chandler to issue a statement to the media saying that he felt vindicated by the hearing. The commissioner, however, told MacPhail that the investigation was not completed. Their conversation was heated, and when Chandler left the meeting, he was in a foul mood and said little to reporters.[61]

Chandler officially communicated his decision to Branch Rickey on April 9—the day before the 1947 season began. The Dodgers were shocked to learn that Harold Parrott was being fined $500 for writing a derogatory column about others in baseball and for violating the commissioner's order of silence following the St. Petersburg meeting. Both the Dodgers and Yankees were fined $2,000 each for conducting their controversy in public, and Leo Durocher was suspended from the game for one year for conduct detrimental to baseball. Durocher, the decision read, had not lived up to "the standards expected" of big-league managers and, as a result "of an accumulation of unpleasant incidents" and his involvement in a series of "publicity-producing affairs," was to draw the suspension. In addition, the commissioner ascertained that Charlie Dressen had violated his verbal agreement to serve as a coach with the Dodgers in 1947 and was suspended for thirty days. The last sentence of the decision read, "All parties to this controversy are silenced from the time this order is issued."[62]

Chandler's rationale was not complicated. In an 1980 interview, he explained that he really did not want to hurt Brooklyn, but he felt that Rickey could no longer handle Durocher. He stated, "This thing didn't just happen, it was brought about by a series of incidents. You are just tired of dealing with it, and the only way to deal with it is to just set this guy aside." Incidents that played a role in the decision included Durocher's encounter with John Christian (Chandler called the trial "a fix"), the manager's escapades with Laraine Day, and the publicity resulting from Durocher's association with George Raft. The commissioner explained that he "didn't want to rehash all those damn things, readvertise them, I just said it was an accumulation of unfortunate incidents. . . . I said as little as I could, but I thought that would cover it."[63] His disdain for Durocher was quite clear. "He was tough," Chandler recalled. "He disregarded everybody—everybody was dirt but Durocher, really. He was riding high along with his associates [and] he wasn't particular about who he associated with."[64]

The mystery letter that the commissioner waved in front of the Dodger delegation at the second hearing was from U.S. Supreme Court Justice Frank Murphy, a devout Catholic and avid supporter of the Catholic Youth Organization. Murphy was a close acquaintance of the commissioner and warned him that he would tell the Catholic Youth Organization to boycott the Dodgers if Durocher was their manager in 1947. "What are you going to do about a manager that acts so bad that the kids can't go to the game?" asked Chandler. He recalled that Rickey had told him that Durocher's loss for a year would be "fatal" to the Dodgers. He was unconvinced by Rickey's tears, calling them "fake," and characterized the Dodger president as one of the "most plausible suckers I ever saw in [my] life."[65]

Although Chandler could not establish "hard evidence" that the two gamblers were MacPhail's guests, he suspected that Yankees publicity director Arthur Patterson had given them the tickets and therefore did not hold MacPhail responsible. Chandler also claimed that the Durocher decision had another agenda, which was to warn all of baseball to stay away from gambling and gamblers. He asserted that the decision was meant as a veiled warning to Del Webb, part owner of the Yankees, because of his Las Vegas association with Bugsy Siegel. In 1947, he perceived gambling as a threat and "couldn't afford not to take notice of it." In retrospect, he felt that the decision "scared them pretty good."[66]

The Durocher decision rocked the baseball world and received a mixed reaction. The *Pilot,* the official publication of the Archdiocese of Boston, applauded the suspension, claiming that Durocher had "forfeited his high place as a hero to a multitude of boys." Predictably, J.G. Taylor Spink, long a Durocher detractor, gleefully wrote that the Dodgers and Rickey could no longer protect the "pampered" manager and that Chandler was now "as severe a czar as the late Judge Landis ever hoped to be." Stan Baumgartner of the *Philadelphia Enquirer* warned that "major league own- ers may well take notice," while Joe Williams of the *New York World-Tele- gram* saluted the commissioner with "Nice going commissioner. You looked like Feller out there. Plenty fast." At the same time, Sid Keener of the *St. Louis Star-Times* lauded Chandler for demonstrating "rare courage," but Jimmy Powers of the *New York Daily News* felt that the decision was too lenient. "Landis would have barred Durocher for life long ago," he wrote. Finally, Dan Daniel of the *New York World-Telegram* wrote, "Ye who ask for trouble, verily ye get it."[67]

Many sportswriters who had little sympathy for Durocher still felt that the decision was severe. One of them, Shirley Povich of the *Washington Post,* wrote, "Maybe the punishment was in excess of the crime, but who can shed a tear for Durocher?" Others were critical of the decision be- cause it made Chandler look like MacPhail's agent. Dave Egan of the *Boston Daily Record* described him as MacPhail's "alter ego and office boy," while Jack Clarke of the *Chicago Sun* charged that the commissioner was paying off a political debt to the "campaign manager" who got him into office.[68]

Other writers recognized that Durocher was sacrificed at baseball's altar as a result of the Rickey-McPhail controversy. Red Smith of the *New York Herald-Tribune* wrote, "Happy Chandler proved his courage by throw- ing the book at a couple of hired hands and tipping his hat to the insuffer- able mud-slingers who pay his salary," and Harold Burr of the *Brooklyn Eagle* wrote, "What started as a tempest in a teapot reached too serious proportions. It began with a couple of grown men acting like kids, daring each other to knock the block off their shoulder."[69] Finally, Bill Corum of the *New York Journal American,* who termed the decision "grossly unfair," summed up the position of Chandler's critics when he stated, "no facts have been offered to show that [Durocher] was guilty" of conduct detrimental to baseball. Nor, he added, was Durocher given the opportu- nity to defend himself.[70]

Reaction to the decision was most intense in Brooklyn, where it was viewed as an assault on the borough's entire populace. The suspension amplified Durocher's status as a hero, and Chandler became a villain who was burned in effigy in Brooklyn streets. The commissioner directly felt the wrath of New Yorkers eighteen days later when he appeared at ceremonies honoring Babe Ruth at Yankee Stadium on April 27, 1947. Larry MacPhail was concerned about Chandler's reception and instructed his announcer to introduce the program by saying, "This is Babe Ruth Day, with other personalities on the program entitled to respect as well." Boos were heard the moment the commissioner's name was announced. When he stepped to the microphone, the sound was almost deafening. Holding his head and chin high, the commissioner struck a pose as though standing at attention—in so doing, he delivered a clear message that he would wait out his tormentors. With Yankees announcer Mel Allen in the background trying to quiet the crowd, the commissioner began his presentation with the words "This is Albert B. Chandler." Then, as he paid tribute to Ruth, a small ripple of applause began, which soon erupted into a hearty roar that drowned out the dissenters. "On the applause meter," wrote Shirley Povich, "Chandler had won a clear-cut decision."[71]

Although warned that Durocher might be punished, his one-year's suspension took the Dodgers by surprise. Rickey was astounded that Chandler would take that course of action. The telephone call bearing the news came during a meeting in the Dodgers' front office. When Rickey announced the decision, Durocher blurted, "For what?" Rickey replied, "I don't know."[72] Although Rickey accepted the decision on the surface, he was deeply hurt— Chandler had broken his word to Durocher. According to Red Barber, Durocher did everything Chandler asked. "Nobody was more faithful to his word than Durocher. I don't care what Chandler or anybody else says, I saw Durocher and so did everybody else. The writers were simply aghast— they couldn't believe it."[73]

In an emotional appearance on April 10, Durocher bade his team farewell. He told his players, "You've been a great bunch of boys to work with and, no matter where I am this summer, I'll be rooting for you." Though Durocher was silenced by the decision, Laraine Day was not, and she told reporters that the suspension was "terribly unfair" and that her husband "was condemned without a hearing and denied the right of appeal." After *New York Daily Mirror* columnist Walter Winchell wrote, "If Chandler doesn't stop making himself a national clown—he will make Durocher a national hero," Day wired him the following message: "Thanks from the bottom of my heart. Laraine Day Durocher."[74]

The decision also took MacPhail by surprise. The outcome of the hearings was not what he intended. Before the first hearing, he told a reporter that it was Rickey he was "gunning for." In a 1977 interview, Lee MacPhail noted that his father did not want to hurt Durocher and that he was upset by the decision. "He blamed Rickey," noted MacPhail and then added,

Soon after the Durocher suspension, Chandler withstood a hostile New York crowd on Babe Ruth Day, April 27, 1947. (Special Collections and Archives, University of Kentucky, and Corbis Archive)

"That edict of silence still doesn't sit well in our business—it's hard to enforce."[75]

In the wake of the Durocher decision, everyone survived—at least for the time being. Harold Parrott had his $500 fine returned, Charlie Dressen served his thirty-day suspension and later returned to manage the Dodgers, and the Dodgers found a new manager for 1947 in Burt Shotton. Branch Rickey visited Chandler at his Versailles home on June 5, 1947, in an attempt to shorten Durocher's suspension, but he was unsuccessful.[76] Durocher sat out the entire 1947 season but was reinstated as Dodger manager in 1948. In this sense, he finished last. Nevertheless, he continued to collect his $50,000 salary and spent most of his time playing golf and helping Laraine Day build a new home—not exactly purgatory by anyone's standards![77]

What was accomplished by the Durocher decision? From Chandler's vantage point, he was officially warning everyone about the dangers of gambling. With the Black Sox scandal in the background and the Evangeline affair and other fixes fresh in the public's mind, the suspension of Durocher reestablished a moral tone for the game. The commissioner sincerely felt that he was strengthening the fabric of baseball. In simple terms, Chandler wanted to make baseball safe for the Knothole Club, the Catholic Youth Organization, and the Boy Scouts. Leo Durocher was not one of Frank Meriwell's heroes and was unworthy of emulation. Chandler also silenced critics who felt he had been unable to act decisively, and, to his delight, he received praise comparing him favorably with Judge Landis. Finally, he put an end to a public dispute between two of baseball's most inventive and energetic executives.

Regardless of the immediate results, however, Chandler's decision was ill conceived. He used Durocher as a vehicle to solve several problems, the least of which was Durocher himself. The real problem was the dispute between Rickey and MacPhail. Through the orchestration of Harold Parrott and Arthur Mann, who wanted to protect Rickey, the Dodgers threw Durocher to the lion, and the lion ate him. Moreover, Durocher's off-the-field activities, his association with undesirable elements, his gambling, his own contacts with MacPhail, and the prior warning he had received from the commissioner made him fair game.

There has been much subsequent agreement that Durocher's punishment was too severe. Former Dodgers broadcaster Ernie Harwell commented that Durocher "ran a traffic light, so Happy threw the book at him," and *Washington Post* sportswriter Shirley Povich, who tended to support Chandler, described the decision as "overkill."[78] Although the publicity created by Durocher did not serve the game well, particularly his association with undesirable figures, he certainly had committed no offenses punishable by suspension. Bill Veeck argued that it was inevitable that baseball personnel would meet undesirable characters at the ballpark and elsewhere.

You can't be around and not know some guys. I grew up knowing Mr. Capone. I consorted with him just as a customer. As a customer, he buys a lot of seats, sits in them, and enjoys the game. What he has supposed to have done, has done, or reportedly has done, is none of my business. That is true of McGinty, Morris Kleiman, [and] Melodi in Cleveland— same thing here in St. Louis or Chicago. It's none of our business. I think it [the Durocher decision] was a phony decision. Sometimes commissioners do things to enhance their reputations as being a friend of the pure and a foe of all that is evil. . . . They side with the fan because they are more fans than operators.[79]

Attorney Frederic Johnson echoed Laraine Day's complaint that Durocher was tried and convicted without benefit of a jury. He maintained that baseball was a government within a government and that the conduct detrimental to baseball provision gave the commissioner a roving power that is absolutely illegal under American law.[80] In fact, Durocher did consider a suit against baseball for reinstatement, but, after meeting with the Dodgers ownership, he was counseled not to proceed. Although he was told he might win, Durocher feared he would be blackballed from the game.

Johnson agreed with Durocher's decision not to proceed. He noted that in cases where baseball owners had challenged a commissioner's action, courts had been loath to decide against the game's chief executive. The ruling case, the Lindley decision, would have served as a major barrier to any litigation brought forth by Durocher. In that decision, the court virtually told the owners "that you have made your contract [with Landis], you gave him absolute power, and you have to live with it." Courts are hesitant, maintained Johnson, to challenge "an association contract which is not in its social manifestations of any real consequence except to those right in the enterprise or game."[81]

While Durocher failed to sue, Chandler was the person who eventually lost. His actions did little to enhance his position with most of the owners—especially Walter O'Malley, who witnessed the whole affair and would soon become a major power in the game. In particular, Red Barber noted, Chandler lost the friendship of Larry MacPhail, who "then turned his resentment and anger toward the man he largely made commissioner." MacPhail certainly influenced how Dan Topping and Del Webb viewed Chandler. According to Barber, "time began running out on Chandler on April 9, 1947," the day of the Durocher decision.[82]

8

Jackie Robinson's America

The suspension of Leo Durocher drew baseball's attention away from one of the most momentous events of American social history—the integration of baseball by Jackie Robinson. In 1946, American society was deeply segregated. An African American's place was well defined by law and accepted practice. In the South, home of 77 percent of the country's black population, segregation was public, formal, and direct. Jim Crow laws, poll taxes, and intimidation kept African Americans "in their place." This meant segregated schools, hospitals, waiting rooms and washrooms in railroad stations, dual drinking fountains, and separate milk bars at the five and dime store. In parts of the South, signs in the rear of buses read, "This part of the bus for the colored race."

Racism also abounded in the North, where restrictive property covenants, job discrimination, and poverty left many African Americans imprisoned in the black ghettoes of major cities. Although less obvious, discriminatory practices were visible in the North in 1946. For instance, in a private housing project in Detroit, Michigan, a sign buttressed by two American flags advertised vacancies with the caveat, "We want white tenants in our white community." In Lancaster, Ohio, the birthplace of William Tecumseh Sherman, a restaurant sign read, "We cater to white trade only."[1] In many communities, blacks were barred from municipal swimming pools and first-class hotels and restaurants. Although few exclusionary laws formally existed, the color line was so well recognized by blacks and whites in the North that few African Americans challenged the system.

Nowhere was segregation more in evidence than in the nation's capital. African Americans attended segregated schools, were born, recovered from illnesses, and died in segregated hospitals, and viewed films and plays in segregated theaters, almost in the shadow of the Lincoln Memorial. With the exception of government cafeterias, the YWCA, and Union Station, blacks were not welcome in city restaurants. Nevertheless, World War II heightened African American hopes for equality. They reasoned that, if black men and women served their country in uniform, they should be entitled to full citizenship and its accompanying rights and privileges. Returning black servicemen and women found, however, that as the war ended much of their bargaining power disappeared. In the North only traditional service and menial labor jobs were available, while in the South it was back to sharecropping.[2]

The one ray of hope for African American recognition lay in the realm of sports. In the 1936 Olympics, Jesse Owens electrified the world by winning gold medals in the 100- and 200-meter dashes and in the long jump, thereby defying Adolf Hitler's philosophy of Aryan superiority. The onset of World War II, however, prevented Owens from competing in another Olympics, and his popularity waned. Another well-known hero was Joe Louis, who reigned as the heavyweight boxing champion of the world for twelve years (1937-49). Louis earned millions of dollars and was a household name, but his victories were intermittent, and the connection between racial equality and boxing victories was lost on most Americans. In many quarters, boxing itself was viewed with disdain, and Louis's exploits outside the ring did little to endear him to socially conservative whites.

African American leaders recognized that they needed a sports venue that was followed and respected by the majority of Americans, white and black alike. Only baseball fit their needs. Segregated since 1884, major-league baseball had not fielded a black player since Moses Fleetwood Walker caught for the American Association's Toledo Mudhens. Although sixty blacks played in professional leagues before 1900, a gentleman's agreement between baseball owners had thoroughly segregated the game by the time the U.S. Supreme Court rendered its "separate but equal" doctrine in the notorious *Plessy v. Ferguson* decision of 1896.[3]

Racial segregation was so much a part of the American pastime that African Americans could not even allow themselves to dream about playing in the major leagues. When stars Jimmy Foxx, Lefty Grove, and Lou Gehrig visited Monte Irvin's Orange, New Jersey, school, Irvin was inspired to play baseball. "They were great looking athletes and they looked clean cut. I watched their every move and saw how they conducted themselves. So I said right away that if this is what baseball can do to a person, then I want to become a baseball player." But, unlike most white kids, that is where his dreams died. As Irvin explained, "At that time a black kid could never aspire to play [major-league baseball]—no thoughts of it even, you see? Baseball was the All-American game and everybody played it in one form or another, and I wanted to become a player."[4]

Only the Negro Leagues offered a viable living for young black men who wanted to play professional baseball in the 1930s and 1940s. At the conclusion of World War II, Negro League baseball comprised two major leagues consisting of a loose confederation of twelve teams that in 1945 played as many as sixty-nine league games. An additional 200 exhibition or barnstorming games, played on a daily basis with local or all-star teams, filled in the rest of the schedule. Most of the teams led a nomadic existence because only a few franchises owned ballparks. The greatest showcase for black players, and the premier event of the Negro League season, was the annual East-West All-Star game at Chicago's Comiskey Park. During the war years, the games drew huge crowds. Between the barnstorming tours and the annual All-Star game, black players were bound to attract the attention of major-league owners. Yet, in spite of public statements by baseball officials, including Judge Landis in 1944 and Happy Chandler in 1945, that organized baseball had no official policy barring African American players, few owners, players, or fans failed to recognize the barrier's existence.

Attempts to circumvent the color line failed. Clark Griffith, who witnessed several of black catcher Josh Gibson's prodigious home runs hit in Griffith Stadium, openly admitted in 1938 that the time would come when blacks would play in the major leagues.[5] When faced with a shortage of players during World War II, Griffith even had a meeting with Homestead Grays players Gibson and Buck Leonard in 1943 to discuss the possibility, but nothing ever came of it.[6]

The same year singer/actor Paul Robeson appeared before Judge Landis and the baseball owners to argue on behalf of the entrance of African Americans into baseball. Landis instructed the owners to listen to Robeson but not to ask questions, or make comments.[7] St. Louis Browns official William O. DeWitt recalled that Robeson "made a great presentation. No one asked him any questions, and after he left there wasn't a single word about what he had said. It wasn't even discussed in positive or negative terms."[8] When asked about the meeting the next day by the *Pittsburgh Courier*, Landis said, "Each Club is entirely free to employ Negro players to any extent it pleases, and the matter is solely for each club's decision without any restriction whatsoever."[9]

When Judge Landis died in 1944, baseball's first line of defense against integration disintegrated. Landis's departure proved timely for Branch Rickey, president of the Brooklyn Dodgers, who was quietly scouting black players during World War II. Soon after he joined the Dodgers, Rickey received permission from the team's board of directors to sign black players. While most owners were retrenching and trying to make do during the conflict, by 1943 Rickey was dispatching scouts to Puerto Rico, Cuba, Mexico, and throughout the United States in search of talent.[10]

The rationale behind Rickey's efforts was complex. From Larry MacPhail, Rickey had inherited a Dodger team of aging players and a farm system that was unable to supply enough young talent. On the basis of his experience with the Cardinals, Rickey was determined to build a farm system with new minor-league franchises and hundreds of young players. He also recognized the potential of black players. In 1945, he told Harold Parrott, "Son, the greatest untapped reservoir of raw material in the history of our game is the black race. The Negro will make us winners for years to come. And for that I will happily bear being a bleeding heart, and a do-gooder, and all that humanitarian rot."[11] Rickey knew that the addition of African American players would give the Dodgers a competitive edge.

Nevertheless, Rickey was also aware of the social implications of integration. He was fond of telling people about a black player named Charlie Thomas he had coached at Ohio Wesleyan. During the 1904 season, Rickey took his team to South Bend, Indiana, where a clerk at the Oliver Hotel refused accommodations for Thomas. Rickey argued successfully that Thomas could share his room. Thomas was shaken by the incident. Sitting on the edge of his bed, with tears running down his cheeks, he rubbed his hands continuously and muttered that he would like to make them white. The scene made a lasting impression on Rickey, who later commented, "For forty years I've had recurrent visions of him wiping off his skin."[12]

His Methodist upbringing, the Social Gospel, and other ideas of the Progressive era also influenced Rickey. During his undergraduate days at Ohio Wesleyan and as director of the local YMCA, Rickey helped bring in a number of exciting speakers to Delaware, Ohio, including urban reformers Jacob Riis and Jane Addams; Washington Gladden and Walter Rauschenbusch—the main proponents of the Social Gospel; and Booker T. Washington, the nineteenth-century African American leader. Rickey's background allowed him to pursue black baseball players without self-recrimination over the advantage he would gain against his fellow owners. As Jules Tygiel aptly noted, however, "Rickey was innovative, but he was not impulsive."[13] He was cautious—he knew that breaking the color barrier would take careful thought, planning, and consultation. Time, however, was not his ally. The same war that created opportunities for blacks also placed pressure on Rickey to move more quickly than he wished.

Recognizing that one of the underlying rationales for World War II was to combat racism, the black press used the war as a platform to attract attention to the inequalities minorities faced. Black newspaper writers lobbied for major-league teams to grant Negro League players tryouts. In April 1945, Wendell Smith of the *Pittsburgh Courier* and Isadore Muchnick, a white Boston councilman, put enough pressure on the Boston Red Sox to force them to hold a tryout.[14] Smith recruited Jackie Robinson of the Kansas City Monarchs, Sam Jethroe of the Cleveland Buckeyes, and Marvin Williams of the Philadelphia Stars. All three performed well. At the end of the session, a Red Sox coach commended them, gave them cards to fill out, and told them that the team would be contacting them.[15]

In his autobiography, *I Never Had It Made*, Robinson wrote, "Not for one minute did we believe that the trial was sincere."[16] Jethroe recalled, "Joe Cronin was the manager then, and he just let some coaches run us through some fundamentals. Then they said we all had ability, but that it just seemed that they wouldn't be letting blacks . . . into major league baseball that year. We never heard from them."[17] When queried by reporters who had attended the tryout, Cronin was only able to reply in embarrassment, "The decision is not up to us."[18] He implied that any decision regarding the players would be made by Red Sox owner Tom Yawkey. Ironically, the Red Sox were the first team to hold a tryout for black baseball players and the last, in 1959, in the American League to integrate. Much to Smith's dismay, any national press coverage that the tryout might have stimulated was overshadowed by news of President Roosevelt's death on April 12, 1945.

Only a week earlier, the Brooklyn Dodgers were approached at their 1945 Bear Mountain, New York, spring training camp to hold a tryout for Negro League players David "Showboat" Thomas and Terris McDuffie. Two African American sportswriters, Joe Bostic of the *People's Voice* and Nat Low of the *Daily Worker,* a communist newspaper, sought the tryout as a test of the recently passed New York State Quinn-Ives fair employment practices law, which was to take effect in July 1945. Rickey, who greatly resented the political nature of the ploy, as well as the presence of a representative of a communist newspaper, nevertheless met with the players and conducted a tryout session.

Following the tryout, Rickey blasted the capabilities of the two players, both of whom were over thirty. The Dodger president viewed the tryout session as little more than a publicity stunt, and warned the two men, "I'm more for your cause than anybody else you know, but you are making a mistake using force, dictating in this manner. Like prohibition it [segregation] will fall, because this is a matter of evolution, not revolution. It is a matter of education. You are defeating your aims."[19]

Although the tryout appeared to be a failure, it actually forced Rickey's hand and galvanized him into action. To cover his tracks and give himself more time, the Dodger president created an elaborate subterfuge. He learned that "some substantial people" were supporting a new Negro league called the United States League. He met with the league's promoter, John G. Shackleford, and agreed to assist in drafting the league's constitution to ensure that the circuit would be acceptable to organized baseball. In addition, Rickey also agreed to support a franchise called the Brown Dodgers in the new league, which would play at Ebbets Field. Though neither Rickey nor the Brooklyn Dodgers would have stock in the team, a lease was signed that would give the national league club percentage participation in the Brown Dodgers' gate receipts.[20]

Only a short time after the Bear Mountain tryouts, Rickey called a press conference at which he attacked the character and organization of the Negro Leagues and claimed that they had no written constitutions, rules, official schedules, and, in some cases, written contracts. He then used the forum to announce his involvement with the United States League and the formation of the Brown Dodgers. Many of the black newspaper reporters left the meeting in anger or dismay. The only invited representative of the Negro Leagues, Mrs. Effa Manley, co-owner of the Newark Eagles, asked Rickey why he had not contacted the "official" Negro Leagues if he was so interested in their baseball. He told her that both league presidents had been contacted and that one was not interested and the other had not replied.[21]

Reaction to Rickey's announcement was swift. The African American community feared that another white man was going to take over their turf. Frank A. Young of the *Chicago Defender* accused Rickey of attempting to become the "Abraham Lincoln of Negro League baseball."[22] Bill Mardo of the *New York Daily Worker* viewed Rickey's announcement as a conspiracy by baseball's owners to defuse the anti–Jim Crow forces so that they could be spared further embarrassment. Finally, Washington Senators owner Clark Griffith, who was always good for a Rickey quote, charged the Dodger president with trying to set himself up as the dictator of blacks in the game. He announced that he had written a letter to the other owners, accusing Rickey of "issuing an ultimatum to the Negro American and National Leagues to join 'or else'" and that he was trying to destroy institutions "in which colored people have faith and confidence." Rickey refused to reply to the charges.[23]

Rickey's smoke screen worked beautifully. He kept the Brown Dodgers afloat for one season as even his own scouts failed to suspect that he was searching for African American players for the Brooklyn Dodgers. At the same time, Rickey tried to clear other impediments. The first involved the preparation of the community for integration. An end-Jim-Crow group had been established in New York, and its members had plans to demonstrate outside the Polo Grounds and Ebbets Field. Rickey, with the assistance of Dan Dodson, the executive director of the Mayor's Committee on Unity, persuaded New York Mayor Fiorello LaGuardia to create a city antidiscrimination committee. The mayor appointed a number of distinguished New York citizens to the committee and included Rickey and the Yankees' MacPhail as baseball's representatives. The committee provided Rickey with another Trojan Horse from which he could operate without attracting attention. In addition, the committee appointment gave him access to the ideas and ears of influential community leaders—notably Dr. John H. Johnson of St. Martin's Episcopal Church of Harlem and Judge Edward S. Lazansky. Finally, through Dodson's intervention, the committee persuaded the end-Jim-Crow group to call off their activities.[24]

Although Rickey did not know who was going to integrate baseball, he knew what he had to do to accomplish the task. He had to locate the right player—a great player, one according to Rickey who would "justify himself upon the positive principle of merit." More important, he had to be the right man off the field. He had to be a person who would accept the responsibility of his race and who could bear that burden. Rickey also realized that he had to appeal to black society for restraint. He feared that overindulgence or adulation on the part of African Americans might jeopardize the entire venture. The final hurdle would be the player's acceptance by his teammates—a situation that Rickey could not control.[25]

By summer of 1945, Rickey had received a number of scouting reports. On the basis of the glowing report of scout George Sisler, Rickey decided to take a close look at Kansas City Monarchs shortstop Jackie Robinson.[26] In August, he sent scout Clyde Sukeforth to watch Robinson play in Chicago and to bring him back to Brooklyn for an interview with Rickey if Sukeforth liked what he saw. Robinson was the younger brother of Mack Robinson, the runner-up to Jesse Owens in the 200-meter dash in the 1936 Olympics. He was a Georgia native, a track, basketball, baseball, and football star at UCLA, and during World War II he had entered the Army as an enlisted man and had left as an officer. The only apparent blemish on his record was a court-martial he received for failing to sit in the back of a bus while at Fort Hood, Texas. He was, however, acquitted of all charges. Rickey carefully researched Jackie Robinson. He discovered that Robinson did not drink, smoke, or womanize but that he could be argumentative—particularly in situations with white players and officials. What appealed to Rickey most about Robinson was his maturity. He was twenty-six years old and college educated, and he was accustomed to competing with whites.

The much-chronicled meeting between Rickey and Robinson is one of the most famous events in baseball history. When Robinson was led through the door of Rickey's Brooklyn office on August 28, 1945, by Clyde Sukeforth, both men still believed that the player was being interviewed about a spot with the Brown Dodgers. After establishing that Robinson was not under contract to another team, Rickey asked him, "Do you know why you are here?" Robinson replied, "To play for the Brown Dodgers." "I've brought you here," continued Rickey, "to play white baseball . . . if you will."[27] "I've sent for you because I'm interested in you as a candidate for the Brooklyn National League Club."[28]

Robinson was speechless. He was simultaneously thrilled, scared, excited, and incredulous. Rickey quickly brought him back to reality, "Do you think you could play at Montreal?" Robinson replied affirmatively.[29] For the next three hours, Rickey lectured Robinson on the challenges he would face. Rickey questioned the ballplayer's courage and wanted to know if Robinson had "the guts" to play in the major leagues. The Dodger president became theatrical and assumed a number of roles: the head-waiter who would not seat him; the sportswriter who asked loaded questions; the opposing pitcher who threw at his head; and the racist ballplayer who baited him. He issued almost every epithet at Robinson that the latter was likely to hear.[30] Next, Rickey became the ballplayer who slides into second base with his spikes high and gashes Robinson's leg and then jumps up with a grin and says, "How do you like that, Nigger boy?" "What do you do then?" Rickey asked.[31]

In his autobiography, Robinson recalled the anger that welled up inside him as Rickey challenged him. Robinson recalled replying, "Mr. Rickey, are you looking for a Negro who is afraid to fight back?" and hearing Rickey's thundering reply, "Robinson, I'm looking for a ballplayer with guts enough not to fight back."[32]

As Rickey continued to impress on Robinson the tremendous burden he would face, it became clear to the him that he was being asked to turn the other cheek for the good of his race. To emphasize this point, Rickey produced a copy of Giovanni Papini's Life of Christ from his desk and made Robinson read several passages that emphasized the importance of nonresistance. One of the passages read, "Only he who has conquered himself can conquer his enemies." Later, Rickey explained that this was the most important point in the hiring of an African American by a major-league club. He was asking Robinson to suppress his instinct to retaliate—a request, he noted, that "was almost too much to ask for from any man and particularly Jackie." Robinson, Rickey surmised, had the necessary intelligence and strength of personality for the task, "but he had more and deeper racial resentment than was hoped for or expected."[33]

At the end of the session, Robinson agreed to sign with the Dodgers for a $3,500 bonus and a contract that would pay him $600 a month with Montreal. It was agreed that the contract would be signed the following November and that Robinson would tell no one about his meeting with Rickey except his mother and his fiancée, Rachel Isum. The meeting was the beginning of a long-term partnership between the two men—a partnership built on trust, mutual admiration, and respect.

His scouts having unearthed additional black talent, Jackie Robinson was the cornerstone of his plan to capture America's best black players. Monte Irvin was approached. Irvin was also a college-educated World War II veteran who grew up in an integrated community and had competed against whites in several sports. Before entering the service, he was an established star with the Newark Eagles and, according to Effa Manley, was a favorite among Negro league owners to break the color barrier.[34] Irvin, however, demurred—his time in the service had set him back, and he told Rickey he was not ready.[35]

In early October, Rickey approached other Negro League players, including Don Newcombe, Roy Partlow, and John Wright. Rickey hoped to publicize the signing of several black players at one time. He collaborated with journalist Arthur Mann on a story about Robinson, which was to have been published in a national magazine at the time of the signings. The article identified several players, including Roy Campanella, Newcombe, and the fleet outfielder of the Cleveland Buckeyes, Sam Jethroe. Events, however, derailed Rickey's plans. In a letter to Mann in early October, he told the journalist that he could not go ahead with the article because "other players are in it and it may be that I can't clear the December meetings, possibly not until after the first of the year." He noted that "My purpose is to be fair to all people and my selfish objective is to win baseball games." He indicated that he wanted to extend the November deadline on signing Robinson and wrote, "Quite obviously, it might not be so good to sign Robinson with other and possibly better players unsigned."[36]

Not only was Rickey having difficulty getting players lined up, politics also conspired against him. New York City councilman Ben Davis, a black communist, was making baseball integration an issue in the November elections. Moreover, Mayor LaGuardia was anxious for his Committee on Unity to issue a statement that baseball integration would soon be a reality in New York. The committee drafted a report citing New York City's enlightened racial climate as the rationale for making the New York teams the ideal proving ground for integration.[37] The report, which was critical of the Negro Leagues' lack of structure, also recognized the existence of discrimination in the major leagues and stressed the need for the inclusion of the Negro Leagues within organized baseball.[38]

Larry MacPhail, also a committee member, was displeased with the group's draft and issued a separate report.[39] He announced that the Yankees would not sign players under contract to Negro League teams and that providing tryouts for such players, when there was no intention of employing them, was "pure hypocrisy." He argued that such signings would violate contractual relationships and predicted that the Negro Leagues would fail if organized baseball took their star players. Moreover, the Yankee president cited remarks by Sam Lacey, the influential black sportswriter for the *Afro-American* (Baltimore), to the effect that black players were not ready for major-league baseball.[40] Finally, MacPhail proposed the entrance of Negro League teams into organized baseball "if and when the Negro Leagues put their house in order."[41]

MacPhail's remarks were designed to forestall integration attempts and to put down the "political and social minded drum-beaters" he accused of using baseball as "a publicity medium for propaganda." By suggesting that baseball would take the Negro Leagues in "if and when they would put their house in order," he sought to demonstrate baseball's good intentions toward the Negro Leagues while at the same time placing a vague condition on them that they were unlikely to meet. Baseball's stance might also serve to satisfy the intent of the Quinn-Ives Act. Finally, MacPhail was mistrustful of fellow committee member and rival Branch Rickey. If Rickey was for desegregation, that was reason enough to oppose it.[42]

Rickey could ill afford to appear to be knuckling under to political pressure. His primary rationale for integration, to win ball games, would disappear if everyone felt he was hiring black players to forestall criticism. In addition, the secrecy surrounding his meeting with Robinson was also in danger of breaking down. In his October 5, 1945, article on MacPhail's remarks in the *Kansas City Call*, Don De Leighbur broke the news that Rickey was interested in Robinson and noted, "MacPhail had better cast an eye toward a colored player himself because the 'Great day Is A Comin' mighty soon."[43]

Rickey had to act—he had to sign Robinson before everything fell apart. He contacted Dan Dodson and asked him to get the mayor to hold off his announcement. Then he resigned from the committee to prevent his actions from appearing to be a conflict of interest. Rickey instructed Robinson to fly to Montreal, where on October 23, 1945, he signed an International League contract in the presence of Brooklyn farm director Branch Rickey Jr., and Royals president Hector Racine. Rickey Jr. issued a statement following Racine's announcement of the signing in which he added that this might discourage Southern ballplayers from signing on with Brooklyn and might cause others already on the team to resign, but "they'll be back in baseball after they work a year or two in a cotton mill." He also indicated that the Dodgers "weren't asking for trouble," but if it comes they would not avoid it.[44]

The announcement slowed the pace of Rickey's efforts to quietly gain a monopoly over Negro League players and placed all the burden of integration on Jackie Robinson. Campanella, Newcombe, and Wright were signed the following spring, and Sam Jethroe, who had been mentioned so prominently in Arthur Mann's unpublished article, was not signed by Rickey until 1948. As baseball historians John Thorn and Jules Tygiel wrote, "The early announcement intensified the pressures and enhanced the legend."[45]

Reaction to the signing was immediate. Judge William G. Bramham, a Southerner who was president of the National Association, the governing body of the minor leagues, joked that "Father Divine will have to look to his laurels, for we can expect a Rickey Temple to be in the course of construction in Harlem soon." Intimating that Rickey was a self-styled Moses, he continued, "It is those of the carpet-bagger stripe of the white race under the guise of helping, but in truth using the Negro for their own selfish interests, who retard the race."[46]

Robinson's signing drew mixed reviews from the press. Wendell Smith of the *Pittsburgh Courier* wrote that the event "is the most American and democratic step baseball has made in 25 years." "There's no time like the present" to settle the issue of whether black players are good enough to make the major leagues, wrote John Carmichael of the *Chicago Daily News.* If Robinson "has the guts and ability to stick it out until he can win acceptance in all quarters outside baseball," predicted Red Smith of the *New York Herald-Tribune,* "he'll have no difficulty in the clubhouse. There is more democracy in the locker room than on the street."[47]

Ed McAuley of the *Cleveland News* differed with Smith, when he wrote that integration was a great social question and that he doubted "dugouts, seldom operated on the highest level of mental maturity, are the places to seek the answer." John Wray of the *St. Louis Post-Dispatch* reported that many felt Robinson could not make it. But if he did, there was little doubt that a lot of unpleasantness would develop for Robinson, his teammates, and the spectators.[48] The *Sporting News* all but predicted that Robinson would fail at Montreal. They maintained that not only was he too old but that he would face stiff competition from returning war veterans and players with more skills and experience than he possessed. They noted that "he is reported to possess baseball abilities which, were he white, would make him eligible for a trial with the Brooklyn Dodgers' Class B farm at Newport News."[49]

The Negro League owners were in a quandary over Robinson's signing. Many realized that his very success would sound the death knell of their game. Tom Baird, co-owner of the Kansas City Monarchs, initially wanted to appeal Robinson's loss to Commissioner Chandler but quickly changed his position when both he and J.L. Wilkinson announced that they would not stand in Robinson's way. Wilkinson, a white owner, issued a statement that read, "For many years we have urged Organized Ball to accept Negro players. Whether we get any recompense for Robinson may be considered beside the point. We want Jack to have a chance." J.B. Martin, the president of the Negro National League, remarked, "I admire Branch Rickey for his courage, but the method of signing Robinson raises some problems."[50]

When interviewed years later, Effa Manley was unequivocal when she said, "Branch Rickey raped us." But, "We were in no position to protest, and he knew it. Rickey had us over a barrel." To lose a player to the majors without compensation was unjust; however, "the people would never have understood" if the leagues had taken legal action against Rickey. Blacks would have said, "You prevented that boy from going to the majors."[51] It is unlikely that Rickey ever considered compensating the Monarchs for Robinson. To have done so, even in the absence of a formal contract, would have lent credence to the argument that a legal relationship existed between player and club in the Negro Leagues.

Rickey attempted to downplay the signing. For instance, he told Dan Daniel that Robinson was "not now major league stuff and there is not a single Negro player in this country who could qualify for the American or National League." When asked about the rumor that he had a list of twenty-five other black players to be given tryouts during the coming spring, he replied, "Erroneous, all erroneous. There isn't a single Negro player of major league class." Rickey claimed to have placed Robinson at the highest minor-league classification in Montreal because he was twenty-six and should not have to start with kids at class B.[52] Rickey hoped these answers would relieve some of the pressure on Robinson as well as give himself more time to corner the market on black talent.

Jackie Robinson and Rachel Isum were married in February 1946. When asked whether she expected trouble, Mrs. Robinson replied negatively, "But, if it does come," she said, "then we'll face it together."[53] Spring training in 1946 was difficult for the Robinsons, but trouble did not come from the players. Rickey did everything he could to ensure that Robinson was well received. To keep the player from being isolated, Rickey signed pitcher John Wright, formerly of the Homestead Grays, to a Montreal contract. Then, before the players arrived, he lectured the Brooklyn team on how he wanted them to treat Robinson and Wright. He told them, "We didn't sign either of these boys because of political pressure. We signed 'em because of our desire to have a winning team in Brooklyn. I would have signed an elephant as quickly if the elephant could have played center-field. You have comported yourselves like gentlemen here. And I want you to go on being gentlemen. All I ask of you is that you be yourselves. I would further remind you that Clay Hopper, the Montreal manager, is a Mississippian."[54]

In spite of his baseball knowledge, the choice of Clay Hopper to manage a Montreal Royals team with Jackie Robinson on its roster seemed curious. Hopper owned a plantation in Greenwood, Mississippi, and had deep Southern roots. He was an excellent baseball man who had worked in the Rickey system since 1929. Rickey respected Hopper for his baseball knowledge, his soft-spoken manner, and his ability to work with players.[55] When Hopper was signed to manage Montreal, he knew he would be working with Robinson. Rickey certainly hoped that Hopper's presence and acquiescence in the experiment would set an example for others. The Dodger president hoped that proximity would bring the races together. Nevertheless, the Hopper-Robinson pairing was risky. An example was a story told by Rickey himself. After watching Robinson make several spectacular plays during a spring training game, Rickey placed his hand on Hopper's shoulder and asked, "Did you ever see a play to beat it?" At that juncture, Hopper turned on Rickey, shook him, and "with his face that far from me" recalled Rickey, said "Do you really think that a Nigger is a human being, Mr. Rickey?"[56]

Yet Hopper treated Robinson with fairness and courtesy, and so did his teammates. While they said little to him, the trouble lay with the South itself. Brooklyn and Montreal trained at Daytona Beach, where the mayor welcomed the teams with open arms. Nevertheless, segregation kept the Robinsons apart from the rest of the baseball community. While Jackie's teammates stayed in a hotel, the Robinsons lived in the private home of a local black politician. The Dodgers trained in the white section of Daytona Beach, while the Royals played across the tracks, in the black section of town. Even Robinson's first base hit, on April 2, 1946, underscored the situation as a group of fans ensconced in a cooplike structure in right field, erected specifically for blacks, "literally shook with a spasm of hysteria."[57]

At first, Robinson pressed at the plate—only his spectacular bunting, base running, fielding at second base, and Rickey's determination that he would make good kept him in the lineup. Black fans, who flocked to the exhibition games, made him anxious and caused him to chase pitches out of the strike zone, because, as he told reporter Wendell Smith, "I wanted to get a hit for them because they were pulling so hard for me."[58]

Towns and cities in the South were not receptive to integration. Rickey intended to have Montreal train at a satellite camp at Sanford, Florida, but after a few days, the Robinsons were ordered to pack and return to

Daytona Beach immediately. Red Barber, a Sanford native, recalled, "They ordered the Brooklyn Dodgers to get the Robinsons out of Sanford in twenty-four hours. . . . When you made Branch Rickey make a move like that, . . . it was serious. It had to be!"[59]

Once the Royals took to the road, more problems arose. Games were canceled in Jacksonville and Deland, and the Royals and Dodgers began to receive threatening mail and calls. As the team wended its way north, police with riot guns were employed in Macon, Savannah, and Richmond.[60] In spite of the pressure, Robinson began to hit with authority and continued to do so throughout the entire International League schedule. He had a sensational year. His aggressiveness, audacity, and speed on the base paths and his league-leading .349 batting average helped his team win the International League pennant. He survived knock-down pitches, a riotous crowd in Baltimore that trapped him in the clubhouse well past midnight, a black cat thrown in his path, and outrageous taunting in Syracuse.

Robinson quickly won the hearts and acceptance of the entire Montreal community with his timely hitting and spirited play. This backing was most evident during the Junior World Series, when supporters rallied behind Robinson after the Royals star was resoundingly roasted by fans in Louisville, the American Association champion. Robinson's appearance in Louisville was the first time a black man played professional baseball with whites in that segregated city. Fearing racial strife, the Colonels refused to add more seating to Parkway Field's small five-hundred seat section for black fans. As a consequence, thousands of black fans were turned away. Many retreated to the roofs of adjacent buildings to watch Robinson play.[61]

Robinson came into Louisville in a hitting slump, and the apprehension he felt about playing there further affected his play. Although he played well in the field, Robinson had only one hit in eleven at bats, as the Royals lost two of three to the Colonels. Each time he came to bat he was met with a chorus of boos, off-color remarks, and foul language. "The tension was terrible," he remembered, "I was greeted with some of the worst vituperation I had yet experienced."[62] But when the team returned to Montreal, Robinson discovered that the Royals fans were extremely upset with the way he had been treated in Louisville. To compensate for it, during the first game, they booed heartily every time a Colonel player stepped out of the dugout. In *I Never Had It Made,* Robinson wrote, "I didn't approve of this kind of retaliation, but I felt a jubilant sense of gratitude for the way the Canadians expressed their feelings. When fans go to bat for you like that, you feel it would be easy to play for them forever."[63] The Royals swept the next three games to win the series 4-2.

Robinson came alive, with seven hits. After the final game, the Montreal crowd refused to leave Royals Stadium, chanting, "We want Robinson, we want Robinson." They then paraded winning pitcher Curt Davis, manager Clay Hopper, and Robinson on their shoulders. The Royals second baseman was so deeply moved by the tribute that tears streamed down his cheeks.[64]

Jackie Robinson was one of five black players signed by Branch Rickey to play in the Dodgers organization in 1946. John Wright, who accompanied Robinson to Montreal, played into May and then was optioned to Three Rivers in the Canadian-American League. Roy Partlow, a pitcher for the Philadelphia Stars, was acquired to replace him and remained with the club until July but proved ineffective as a hurler. Two other players, Don Newcombe and Roy Campanella, were assigned to play at Nashua for rookie manager Walter Alston. Newcombe, at the time only nineteen, was a big raw-boned pitcher who had thrown well against the Dodgers in 1945 with the Negro League All-Stars. Campanella, on the other hand, was a twenty-five-year-old professional with nine years of Negro League experience—a record that should have earned him a berth at Montreal with Jackie Robinson. Robinson's troubles in Florida, however, forced Rickey to find suitable places in the North at lower classifications in his farm system. In a telephone conversation overheard by Campanella, at least one team, Danville, Illinois, of the class B Three-I League, refused to take the two players.[65] In retrospect, Newcombe often wondered "just what kind of animals" they were that caused people to reject them.[66] One general manager, Buzzie Bavasi of Nashua in the class B New England League, was willing to take the two players, and Campanella and Newcombe rewarded him by having outstanding seasons. Newcombe went 14-4 with a 2.21 earned run average, and Campanella hit .290 with 13 home runs and 96 runs batted in. The players were treated well in Nashua. Indeed, a local poultry dealer's offer, to award any Nashua player 100 baby chicks for hitting a home run, enabled the catcher to send his father enough chicks to begin a chicken farm outside Philadelphia.[67]

In spite of his stellar season at Montreal, Jackie Robinson's road to the major leagues was still pitted with craters of all sizes. In August 1946, the major-league owners voted almost unanimously to approve a cut-and-paste version of Larry MacPhail's "Report for Submission to National and American Leagues on 27 August, 1946."[68] One of the issues raised by MacPhail in his original version of the report, the race issue, was studiously avoided in the final report by the Yankee president's colleagues, and for good reason. If MacPhail's remarks on race were made public, they would have subjected the game to intense ridicule and criticism. In what baseball historian Jules Tygiel described as a "damning document,"

MacPhail argued that baseball should maintain its segregated status.[69] He asserted that few if any Negro League players were ready for the major leagues and that integration by only a few players would "jeopardize" the viability of the Negro Leagues themselves. Moreover, he reasoned that the revenue earned by major-league clubs from allowing Negro League teams to play in their ballparks would also disappear. MacPhail's crowning argument suggested that black participation in major-league games might attract such large crowds of African Americans at Yankee Stadium, the Polo Grounds, or Comiskey Park that they would discourage white fans from attending games. In a thinly veiled reference to the potential promotion of Robinson to the major leagues, he noted that "the individual action of any one Club may exert tremendous pressures upon the whole structure of Professional Baseball, and could conceivably result in lessening the value of several Major League franchises."[70]

Despite the fact that the race issue was not included in the final report approved by major-league owners, there is little doubt that many were aware of the content of MacPhail's original draft and that the sentiment of many of the owners was against bringing Jackie Robinson up from the minor leagues. Nevertheless, there is no hard evidence to support claims later made by Rickey and Chandler that the owners voted 15-1 to prevent Robinson from playing in the major leagues.[71] Both MacPhail and National League counsel Louis Carroll testified at the Celler Hearings that the owners voted on a much modified version of MacPhail's original draft, which Carroll maintained was objectionable because "it contained characterizations of legal opinions [on the reserve clause] that we did not think were accurate, and should not be contained in a report of that character." Carroll noted further that most copies of MacPhail's original draft were destroyed the day after the owners met on August 27, 1946, because he recognized that there was material in the report that "represented much discussion and controversy."[72]

The prevailing mood of the owners, coupled with the tenor of MacPhail's draft, worried Rickey. According to Chandler's account, it was this concern that spurred the Dodger executive to visit the commissioner's home in Kentucky sometime in late 1946, for the purpose of asking for support. The Kentuckian maintained that he told Rickey, "I'm going to have to meet my maker someday. If he asks me why I didn't let this boy play and I say it's because he is black, that might not be a sufficient answer." Chandler not only promised to assist Rickey, he agreed to assign his assistant John DeMoisey to watch over Robinson during the 1947 season.[73]

The commissioner's support of Rickey was something of a surprise. Chandler, the former governor of a state that maintained segregated facilities, proudly extolled the exploits of a grandfather who had served in

John Hunt Morgan's Confederate cavalry. Personally, he was subject to all of the ingrained prejudices of his region and period. Nevertheless, the signs were there for those owners or writers who paid attention. Soon after his election as commissioner, Chandler was quoted in the *Pittsburgh Courier*, the influential black newspaper, as saying, "If it's discrimination you are afraid of, you have nothing to fear from me." He suggested that the paper quote him as taking the same view that Rickey expressed in a recent interview: "To wit: 'My attitude toward Negro ballplayers is the same as toward any ballplayers. I am in there to win ball games and I like winning ballplayers, whatever their origin or race.'" The same article noted that, while he was governor, Chandler had been an avid supporter of the football program at Kentucky State College, the commonwealth's primary black institution of higher learning.[74]

The commissioner was cited again in the *Pittsburgh Courier,* this time while at the major-league meetings in Los Angeles in December 1946. The article depicted Chandler as being a solid Robinson supporter and quoted him as saying that "from what I have heard since I have been here, Robinson is perhaps the best all-around athlete this country has ever produced."[75] At the least, Chandler's acquiescence in Rickey's plan to bring up Robinson provided the Dodger president with the green light he needed.

Rickey's next hurdle was Brooklyn's African American community. The Dodger president feared that blacks would make such a fuss over Robinson that he would be unable to focus on his play in the field. To counter this possibility, on February 5, 1947, Rickey addressed a group of thirty prominent black citizens at the Charlton Branch Y.M.C.A. and warned them against feting Robinson with banquets, parades, and days, against misbehavior or overzealous displays of pride, and against turning his entry into baseball into a "national comedy." Rickey emphasized that the weight of responsibility was on blacks everywhere, even though "This step in baseball is being taken for you by a single person whose wounds you cannot see or share. You haven't fought a single lick for this victory, if it is one." Rickey's pleas were taken to heart, and committees were formed throughout Brooklyn and Harlem and the message "Don't Spoil Robinson's Chances," was emphasized in churches, lodges, and clubs, and barrooms alike.[76]

The Brooklyn players posed the most formidable barrier to Robinson's entry into the major leagues. Working on his theory of proximity, Rickey wanted the players to embrace Robinson themselves. Early in 1947, he announced that he would not force Robinson on the players, the public, or the press and that he wanted the players to make their own decision after watching him play.[77] To accomplish this, he moved the Dodgers' spring training activities from the segregated South to Cuba and Panama, where he scheduled a series of games between Montreal and Brooklyn. Although Robinson played well for Montreal against the Dodgers in the Panama series, the move almost backfired. The players saw through Rickey's ruse. They reasoned that Rickey would not consult them if he were about to make a trade—they knew that the decision to bring Robinson up was Rickey's alone. Second, though they admired Robinson's bunting ability, they belittled his achievements and noted that he would not be able to bunt his way to the National League batting title as he had in Montreal the previous year. Furthermore, the players realized that it was Robinson's fault that they had to play in the sweltering heat in Panama and Cuba and that they had to endure 1,200-mile plane rides.[78] The last straw for some of the players was the switch of Jackie Robinson from second base to first—the only really weak position in the Dodgers' lineup. This move was a clear sign that Rickey intended to move Robinson from the Montreal club to the Dodgers.

Only days after their arrival in Panama, Rickey learned that Dodgers players were preparing a petition to prevent Robinson from joining the team. Kirby Higbe, a pitcher from South Carolina, tipped off traveling secretary Harold Parrott to the scheme after pangs of remorse and several drinks had gotten to him. Leo Durocher acted quickly on the news by calling a late-night meeting at which he harangued the players for their opposition to Robinson. He told them that "they could wipe their ass with the petition" and informed them that signers would be sent to other teams. In addition, Durocher predicted that Robinson would win the pennant for the Dodgers, so they had better get used to him, because he was only the first of many black players to come.[79] Rickey soon discovered who was involved in the affair. The ringleader was identified as Dixie Walker, a thirty-six year-old Alabaman who was one of the most popular men to ever put on a Brooklyn uniform. Others involved included pitcher Hugh Casey of Georgia, Cookie Lavagetto, Texan Bobby Bragan, and Carl Furillo. Rickey confronted some of the dissidents in personal interview sessions. Only Bobby Bragan, a little-used catcher, stood up to the Dodger president and adamantly refused to play with Robinson and asked to be traded.[80]

By chance, Walker was in Alabama because of an illness in the family at the time news of the petition broke. A few days later, he wrote a letter to Rickey asking to be traded, for the good of the ball club and himself. Although he was pleased that other Dodgers players refused to participate in the petition debacle, Rickey realized that his carefully laid plans had gone awry. Only the quick action of Dodger management had stopped the uprising and saved the team public embarrassment and adverse publicity.

Instead of improving team cohesiveness, Rickey's careful plans decreased team morale. As Harold Burr of the *Brooklyn Eagle* wrote, the team returned from Panama "looking like a crew of ditch diggers which have been working with a pick and shovel building a canal. There was no dryer in the isthmus so that the uniforms were soggy with sweat and filthy. It was hard to hustle in a suffocating suit of armor."[81] Robinson himself was disgruntled. Once back in Havana, he was segregated from the rest of the team, along with Roy Campanella and Don Newcombe in what was described as "a musty third rate hotel" that "looks like a movie version of a water-front hostelry in Singapore."[82] To add further insult to injury, he was unsure of himself at first base and was concerned that the change of position might delay his trip to the majors.[83]

As the 1947 season opened, Rickey's plans for Robinson were almost torpedoed by Durocher's suspension. The Dodger manager had been scheduled to make an orchestrated plea to bring up Robinson but was suspended on the same day (April 9). In the turmoil surrounding the suspension, Rickey announced that he was bringing Robinson up the following day. Many expected Robinson to fail. Sportswriter Cy Kritzer of the *Buffalo Evening News,* who had watched Robinson in the International League, argued that Robinson had played over his head and that, at age twenty-seven, it would only be a matter of time before he would lose his greatest asset, his speed on the base paths.[84] Bob Feller, who often barnstormed against Negro League All-Stars in the off-season and had faced Robinson, was not impressed. He told *Pittsburgh Courier* sportswriter Wendell Smith that Robinson had "football shoulders" and could not handle the high-inside pitch to "save his neck."[85] In later years, the Cleveland Hall-of-Famer explained that he had faced Robinson several times and found that, not unlike many baseball greats (Ruth, Aaron, Greenberg, Foxx, and Mays), Robinson had trouble with baseball's most difficult-to-hit pitch, the high-inside overpowering fastball. In retrospect, he noted, "Maybe I was a little cruel to him, because I was throwing pretty hard and pretty fast when I faced him and he didn't hit it."[86] Stan Musial indicated that the Cardinal players were surprised that Brooklyn would bring Robinson up. "He didn't impress me too much when I saw him in '46. He wasn't graceful . . . and he had a short choppy swing [and] it didn't look like he had a good arm. I figured the guy wouldn't do well in the big leagues [laughing]."[87]

Robinson's first game in a Dodgers uniform was an exhibition contest against the Yankees at Ebbets Field attended by more than 14,000 black fans. Although he failed to get a hit, Robinson was mobbed after the game by youthful autograph hunters. The *Brooklyn Eagle* reported that "hundreds of kids surrounded him and he literally had to fight his way through the press of admirers." It noted further that, "Joe Louis never received such a reception."[88] After going hitless before an overflow crowd in Brooklyn's season opener against the Brave's Johnny Sain, Robinson fell into a deep batting slump—he managed only a bunt single in his first twenty at bats. In an insightful interview after the opening game, Robinson told a reporter, "Give me five years of this and I can make enough money to build my own little place and give my boy a good education, everything will be all right." When asked whether he could hit major-league pitching, he replied, "I realize that to stay in the National League, I'll have to hit . . . I hope I'll hit. I believe I'll hit. I'm sure I'll hit."[89] The pressure on Robinson was tremendous, and it only continued to mount. Burt Shotton, the manager called in by Rickey to replace the suspended Durocher, was very patient with the Dodger rookie. Moreover, second baseman Eddie Stanky and other Dodgers helped Robinson with his positioning at first base.

The Robinsons' domestic situation was also less than happy. The ball club initially provided very little personal support. Jackie, his wife Rachel, and their young son Jackie Jr. were ensconced in a hotel room because of an apartment shortage in Brooklyn. Their only cooking facility was a trunk-mounted portable electric stove that they used to warm Jackie Jr.'s formula. The Robinsons' situation forced them to eat at restaurants in shifts so that one of them could always be with the baby.[90] Rickey also began to feel the pressure. Although he attempted to warn the fans away from Robinson, he had little control over all of the publicity surrounding him. Rickey revealed that Robinson had received more than five thousand invitations to attend social events and make appearances, and he vehemently complained that his new first baseman had become "a sideshow" rather than a ballplayer. "Why, he scarcely has time to change his uniform," Rickey protested. "The boy is on the road to complete prostration."[91] Robinson was also unsettled when black fans cheered his every move. "When I get up to the plate and see how enthusiastic the crowds are and how eager they are for me to make good," he noted, "I grow tense. I want to satisfy them."[92]

On April 18, Robinson finally broke his hitting drought with a home run against the Giants in front of 37,000 fans at the Polo Grounds. The following day, he collected three hits against the Giants before the largest Saturday crowd (52,000) to ever witness a game there. Despite his success, Robinson faced his most difficult test when the Philadelphia Phillies came to Brooklyn for a three-game series. The Quaker City team was managed by the temperamental and fiery Ben Chapman from Alabama. Chapman, who once played in the New York Yankee outfield alongside both Babe Ruth and Joe DiMaggio, was high-strung, pugnacious, and obsessed with winning and possessed an acid tongue that he used freely on umpires. As the Phillies manager, he ruled the club with an iron hand and insisted on verbal participation—jockeying, ribbing, and antagonizing—from the bench at all times.[93]

The first time Robinson stepped to the plate in the series, he was met with a barrage of hate-filled banter from the Phillies bench. They shouted things like, "We don't want you here Nigger," and "Hey, snowflake, which one of those white boys' wives are you dating tonight?"[94] As Robinson himself noted, this was his most severe test. "I have to admit that this day of all unpleasant days in my life, brought me nearer to cracking up than I ever had been."[95] It took all of Robinson's courage to restrain his urge to charge the Phillies dugout. Later in the series, after the Phillies started making references to the Dodgers' "little reconstruction project," Dodger second baseman Eddie Stanky, a native Alabaman, blew up and hollered back at them, "Listen, you yellow-bellied cowards, why don't you yell at somebody who can answer back?" It was a rejoinder that Robinson never forgot. When Rickey learned about Stanky's remarks, he knew that Robinson's teammates had begun to accept him and that his theory of proximity was beginning to work.

Later in the spring, not long before the Dodgers were due for their first series with the homestanding Phillies, Rickey received a call from Philadelphia general manager Herb Pennock, who told him, you "just can't bring the Nigger here with the rest of your team. We're just not ready for that sort of thing yet." When he threatened not to take the field, Rickey responded that he would be happy to accept the forfeit. The Phillies played.[96] According to Harold Parrott, when the Dodgers arrived in Philadelphia, the team's usual accommodations at the Franklin Hotel became suddenly unavailable, and they were told not to return "while you have any Nigras with you!"[97]

Although Commissioner Chandler warned Phillies owner Bob Carpenter against racially oriented bench jockeying, the Phillies were ready to give Jackie Robinson another dose. In an interview with Wendell Smith only a few days earlier, Ben Chapman explained that his team was going to ride Robinson just like any other rookie. He noted, "Robinson can run, he can bunt, he is a good fielder. He is dangerous. We want to see if he can take it. . . . We will try to drive him away from the plate so he will not be able to lay down those great bunts of his."[98]

The Phillies received added ammunition when they learned that Robinson had recently received several death threats as well as letters threatening his wife and child. When the Phillies began their verbal barrage in the Philadelphia series, they took their bats in the dugout and pointed them at him as if they were submachine guns and they were shooting him down.[99] Parrott reported that the racial venom and filth that poured out of the Phillies' dugout was disgusting. Chapman, he noted, resorted to every derisive remark he could think of, including a recounting of "the repulsive sores and diseases he said Robbie's teammates would become infected with if they touched the towels or the combs he used." He ranted about how his own teammates disliked him and how he would not be in majors if he were a "white boy."[100]

In May, Robinson began to hit with authority, and his batting average climbed. Nevertheless, controversy still plagued his presence. On May 9, *New York Herald Tribune* sportswriter Stanley Woodward broke a story telling readers that a threatened player strike instigated by the St. Louis Cardinals players against Jackie Robinson was temporarily averted. Woodward maintained that only the quick actions of owner Sam Breadon and National League president Ford Frick prevented the uprising.[101] Although Breadon refuted the story, Frick admitted that he had passed word on to the team through Breadon that if any players engage in this type of activity, "There will be only one recourse—indefinite suspension from baseball."[102] Many later baseball accounts considered this action to be "Frick's finest hour."

In, *Games, Asterisks, and People*, Frick downplayed the incident and insisted that the actual confrontation between Breadon and the disaffected players took place several weeks before the story broke.[103] In subsequent interviews, Cardinal players insist that, although Robinson's presence was resented, there was no organized plot against him. When the story broke, Bob Broeg, sports editor of the *St. Louis Post-Dispatch*, remembered awakening Cardinal team captain Terry Moore with an early morning call and saying, "I'm sorry to bother you, 'Oldie,' but this is a big one and you had better have the right answer. He [Moore] said, 'Oh, that's absurd,' he swore to me."[104] Stan Musial, who was in a New York hotel sickbed with appendicitis when the story broke, admitted that "there was some feeling there" but denied that there was any scheme against Robinson.[105] Cardinal outfielder Harry Walker noted that there was talk that "when [Robinson] first went on the field, that they [the Cardinals] might not do it [play]," but eventually everyone followed the Dodgers' lead.[106] Another team leader, Marty Marion, noted, "Maybe it [a discussion against Robinson] happened in the hotel somewhere, where I wasn't there, but not in the clubhouse; it never happened in the clubhouse. The Brooklyn Dodgers and the Cardinals were kind of enemies, to tell the truth. We didn't like anybody. . . . Me and Pee Wee Reese were always fighting. . . . I don't think we had any personal love for anybody on the whole club, and I'm sure they didn't for us."[107]

Robinson's baptism by fire continued throughout the season. Slowly but surely, many of his teammates began to rally around him. Of particular note was Pee Wee Reese, who told one writer, "You know, my first feelings about Robinson were that, after all, maybe he's just as good as I am. Now, after meeting him and seeing what a wonderful guy he is, I've reached the conclusion that maybe he's a better man than I am."[108] Reese rallied to Robinson's assistance in tense situations. In Macon, during spring training, Reese stood next to the black player during infield practice not long after a death threat against Robinson. In Cincinnati, Reese quieted a restive, predominantly white crowd, which included his own Kentucky friends and relatives, by openly conferring with Robinson with his arm placed around his teammate's shoulder.[109] His message of acceptance was clear.

Others, such as Rex Barney, Pete Reiser, and Gil Hodges, befriended Robinson, and by early summer even Bobby Bragan asked that his request to be traded be rescinded. Some teammates, such as Eddie Stanky, began to feel much more comfortable with the Dodger first baseman, even to the point of sharing racial references. When both men were on the on-deck circle immediately before the start of a Cubs-Dodger game at Wrigley Field, Stanky pointed to the bleachers, which were filled with enthusiastic black fans instead of the usual sea of white shirts and faces, and exclaimed, "I'm sure glad you're in this league. Some people may not like you, but Stanky does. Thanks for the background pal. Watch me hit today." Robinson and Stanky shared a good laugh over the remarks.[110]

Robinson's steady play (.297-12-74) not only helped the Dodgers win the National League pennant in 1947 and Rookie of the Year honors but also gained him the grudging respect of Dixie Walker. Walker, a close friend of Ben Chapman, could not accept the bench jockeying Robinson received and told the Phillies manager to quit. As the season progressed, Walker and Robinson developed a civil relationship, and Walker even requested that Branch Rickey return the letter in which he had asked to be traded.[111] At season's end, Walker told the *Sporting News,* "No other player on this club with the possible exception of Bruce Edwards has done more to put the Dodgers up in the race than Robinson has. He is everything Branch Rickey said he was when he came up from Montreal."[112]

Robinson also won the respect of his opponents. Willard Marshall, a native Virginian who played against Robinson while with the Giants and Braves, marveled at Robinson's ability to absorb "the shabby treatment" he received. "It was funny to see the ones who were so emphatic about everything," he commented. "Little by little, they came into the fold. There was little Robinson could not do," continued Marshall. "He could run, bunt, throw, steal—he would drive you crazy . . . for four or five years I think he was the best ballplayer around."[113] Pittsburgh slugger Ralph Kiner

Jackie Robinson won the grudging respect of many of his peers on the field and the out-and-out admiration of millions of fans who saw him play or read of his exploits. (George Brace Photo)

agreed, "Robinson went through hell. He got thrown at [and] knocked down [by] everybody—it was just really tough. Being the only black ballplayer in the whole game, everything centered on him."[114]

On July 5, 1947, Robinson was joined in the majors by Larry Doby, a black second baseman from the Newark Eagles. Cleveland president Bill Veeck initiated plans to hire a black player soon after acquiring the Indians in 1946. To illustrate his color blindness, Veeck told the story of how his father, an executive with the Cubs, once directed young Veeck's attention to the color of the money he was counting and said, "Look at it, it's all green. It's all the same, and you can't tell me who put it in the box office can you?' I said, 'No.' That's all he had to say . . . if their money is equal, they are equal."[115] When Veeck called Effa Manley, the owner of the Eagles, and offered her $10,000 for Doby, she demanded more. He agreed to pay her an extra $5,000 if the Indians kept Doby beyond thirty days.[116]

At the time of his signing, Larry Doby was leading the Negro National League with 14 home runs and was hitting .430. At 6'1" and 180 pounds, Doby was a natural athlete who was equipped with a powerful throwing arm, was fast, and possessed tremendous power at the plate. He starred in four sports (baseball, track, basketball, and football) at Eastside High School in Patterson, New Jersey. As captain of several of the teams, Doby earned all-state honors in basketball and baseball and led his school's football team to the state title in 1941. Although offered a basketball scholarship at Long Island University by coach Clair Bee, World War II forced him to enter the Navy, where he spent the next three years.[117] He played basketball and baseball at Great Lakes Naval Base, in Illinois, and then was shipped to the Pacific, where he served as an athletic instructor on Ulithi Island with Washington Senators first baseman Mickey Vernon.[118]

Doby arrived in time for the Indians-White Sox game on July 5, 1947. After a brief talk with owner Bill Veeck, who advised him "that a baseball player is judged on one basis only—what he does with a bat and a glove," he was ushered to the visitor's clubhouse to meet with manager Lou Boudreau and the team.[119] As Boudreau introduced him to each player, some shook his hand, while others refrained. The young man was so concerned about playing in the majors that the racial situation was a secondary matter. "It sort of dawned on me after the game was over and after I got back to the hotel by myself," noted Doby in an interview years later. "I wasn't mature enough to put it in a different perspective until I had been there about three or four years, that those who did not shake were probably doing it from ignorance or maybe from a security point. Maybe I'm taking a job from one of those guys, or he had never dealt with blacks before."[120]

Larry Doby not only had to break the color barrier in the American League, he had to learn to play a new position—first base. (George Brace Photo)

Boudreau was surprised when Bill Veeck informed him of Larry Doby's impending arrival, and he knew his players would be shocked. He and coach Bill McKechnie, the old Cincinnati manager, conducted long talks with the players, some of whom they knew would not accept Doby.[121] On his first day in uniform, Doby was sent to the plate to pinch hit for pitcher Bryan Stephens. White Sox pitcher Earl Harrist struck him out on five pitches. On the following day, July 6, the Indians and White Sox played a double-header. Doby did not play the first game, but he was inserted at first base in the second game. Eddie Robinson, another rookie, was benched, and, when asked if he would loan his first baseman's mitt to Doby, did so with great reluctance. Robinson later explained that he "was incensed," because, "I was fighting for my position, just like anyone else."[122] Doby went one for four, with a scratch hit in his second game. Joe Paparella, who umpired that day, recalled reassuring Doby that he belonged in the big leagues. "He looked white he was so scared," explained Paparella. "Not because he was afraid of the ability he had, it was the fact that he was [playing] first base for the first time in a big league ball game."[123]

According to Indians catcher Jim Hegan, the players did not know how to treat Doby. "At first there was a little coolness. . . . [But] it didn't take long. This was their way of making a living and they weren't going to give it up just because of him. He mixed in well and as long as he did the job that was expected of him, I think he got along fine."[124] Hegan, Bob Lemon, and Joe Gordon were among those who helped the young player acclimate to the major leagues. As Doby himself admitted, the move from the Newark Eagles to the Indians was "a terrific jump. I learned more in the few months I was with Cleveland than I picked up in a couple of seasons with Newark," he remembered.[125]

Unlike the extroverted Jackie Robinson, Doby was quiet and introspective. He found the interviews and other attention he received difficult. Ed McAuley, the sportswriter of the *Cleveland News*, wrote that Doby looked even more youthful when he smiled. "He should smile oftener," he wrote. "When he looks serious, especially in a baseball cap, he looks displeased."[126] By season's end, Doby had thirty-two plate appearances, most of which were in pinch-hitting roles, and had only five hits to his credit, for a .156 average. With a record like that, the Cleveland rookie seemed destined for a trip to the minors in 1948.

Doby's entrance into the American League led the St. Louis Browns to also experiment with African American players. The Browns, who always seemed to be living a hand-to-mouth existence, were desperate to increase their attendance. In 1947, they were mired in last place, and home attendance had slipped below 5,000 fans a game. As a result of pressure from local black groups the team opened their grandstand to black fans in 1946, and in July 1947 team president William O. DeWitt made conditional purchases of two Kansas City Monarch players, Willard Brown and Hank Thompson. He paid the Monarchs $2,500 apiece for the players and agreed to pay an additional $5,000 for each player if the Browns kept them for more than a month.[127]

Brown, a native of Shreveport, Louisiana, was listed as being twenty-six years old but in reality was at least thirty-three.[128] His eleven-year career began with the Monarchs in 1935 and included a stint in Mexico, where he played for the Pasquel brothers.[129] Brown also played against Ewell Blackwell and other major leaguers while serving in Europe dur-

ing World War II. He was a slugging outfielder with speed. One sportswriter wrote that "Brown walks like he has sore feet and runs like he has
wings."[130] Thompson, aged twenty-one and in his second full season with
the Monarchs, was a line drive–hitting second baseman with power. He
attracted the attention of Bob Feller, who described him as being the best
black player his team faced during his fall 1946 barnstorming tour. DeWitt
was mostly interested in Brown's power but obtained two players so they
could keep each other company.[131] Brown, who took a pay cut to play
with the Browns, was not excited about the move. Only the strong encouragement of Monarchs manager Buck O'Neil convinced him that he
needed to give the major leagues a try.[132]

On their arrival, the two players were immediately thrust into the Browns
lineup. Brown started a number of games in the outfield, while Thompson
substituted at second for Johnny Berardino, who was recovering from a
broken arm. Brown and Thompson, however, found conditions in St. Louis
less than desirable. The team was obviously not pleased to have them. Indeed, manager Muddy Ruel was not apprised of their coming and, according to DeWitt, was strongly opposed to their acquisition.[133] The two men
faced other forms of adversity. Brown was forced to use a light pitcher's
bat, because the Browns refused to acquire new bats for him. Moreover,
while they traveled on the train with the ball club, they stayed in black
hotels in Chicago and Philadelphia. Finally, opposition players were no
kinder to the Browns' pair than they were to Robinson or Doby. Bench
jockeying was the order of the day. DeWitt recalled hearing Athletics' coach
Al Simmons holler at Brown, "Hey boy! Put that bat down, pick up my
grip and carry it for me."[134]

Far more disappointing to Willard Brown was the attitude of the team
itself. He was used to winning and could not understand the apathy found
on the club. The team's attitude seemed to say, "We ain't going nowhere—
we'll go out and get this over right quick and then go out and drink a few
cold ones." Brown recalled that some pitchers were so anxious to leave a
game after giving up several runs that they would meet the manager to
hand him the ball long before he reached the mound.[135] Rumors that the
team was loosely run and that there was heavy drinking and card playing for high stakes also square with Brown's comments.[136]

Both Thompson (.255-0-5) and Brown (.179-1-6) failed to hit well enough
to justify their retention. They also failed to significantly increase the number of blacks coming to Sportsman's Park. When DeWitt queried Brown
about this, the outfielder replied, "You've got them out there in the bleachers out in the sun. They are already sun tanned, they don't need no more.
They don't sit up there in the stands. . . . When they do, then you get
somebody in the ballpark."[137] DeWitt tried this approach by instructing

his ticket sellers to sell box seats to the black buyers, who came to the park asking for them as a protest against segregation. This ploy failed to net the Browns more than a hundred ticket sales per game, and it did not come close to rivaling the thousands of tickets sold to black patrons when the Cardinals were playing Jackie Robinson and the Dodgers in the same park. On August 23 the two players were quietly released, and their contracts were returned to the Monarchs.

Thus, with the exception of Jackie Robinson, by the end of 1947, the integration of baseball was not a great success. Larry Doby's future in the big leagues was clouded by his inauspicious start, and the Browns were again an all-white team. Only the Dodgers seemed intent on continuing the experiment. Nevertheless, the die was cast. Jackie Robinson's entrance into baseball irretrievably changed the landscape of the game as it also changed American society.

With regard to the game itself, Robinson's entrance opened up the last great labor supply of untapped baseball players. African American children and even Latin children with dark skin color could now aspire to be major-league baseball players. In addition, Rickey's scouting efforts during World War II enabled the Dodgers to corner the market on black players and thus provided them with a competitive edge over their opponents. Black players were part of the equation that allowed the Dodgers to become a National League powerhouse for the next three decades. Only one team, the 1950 Philadelphia Phillies, would win a National League pennant without significant black stars on their roster during the period 1947-60. Robinson's speed and daring on the base paths changed the way the game was played. The Dodgers star added a new psychological dimension to the game. Encouraged by Rickey, Robinson ran with a reckless abandon not seen since the days of Ty Cobb, as he brought the stolen base back to prominence. Robinson also became a disruptive force whose silent weapons were his ability to break the concentration of opposing pitchers, to throw fielders out of position, and to keep catchers on edge.

Far more important is what Robinson did for African Americans themselves. His entry into organized baseball provided hope for a beleaguered people whose expectations were awakened and raised by World War II. He became a new hero for some—supplanting older ones like Joe Louis and Jesse Owens. Others perceived Robinson as a messiah who was poised to take his people out of Egypt to the land of Canaan. Blacks, particularly from the South, flocked on special buses and trains to cities such as St. Louis, Cincinnati, Philadelphia, and Pittsburgh to behold the phenomenon of a black man in a major-league uniform playing with and against whites. Attendance increased strikingly. On the Dodgers' western trip in June, 1947, the team averaged more than 22,000 fans per game—an exceptional total when one considers that many of the games were week-day afternoon contests. In Chicago, Robinson's presence allowed the Cubs to set an all-time record of 46,572 fans.[138] The friendly crowd practically gave the Dodgers the home-field advantage.[139]

The Dodger hero gave other African Americans a sense of identity and pride. Many blacks lived vicariously through him, living and dying with every throw and swing. Everywhere he went in the black community, he was lionized and feted. The Dodgers became Mr. Robinson's club, not Brooklyn's, kids seeking autographs tore buttons off his coat, and almost every store window in Harlem bore his picture.[140] As MacPhail predicted, black fans deserted the Negro League teams to watch major-league base-ball instead. The Negro National League losses alone were estimated at $100,000.[141] For many owners of Negro League teams, the handwriting was on the wall. They were simply trapped between social change and their desire to make a living.

For whites, Jackie Robinson was a figure they could not ignore. The former football All-American at UCLA was educated, clean-living, and played life by the rules. Robinson earned the grudging respect of many of his peers on the field and the out-and-out admiration of millions of white fans who saw him play or read of his exploits. Robinson was as good as or better than those he played against, and he performed in an institution that was one of the most visibly segregated institutions in America—a game which at the major-league level was played mainly in the North. Jackie Robinson's triumph proved that blacks and whites could work and play together and that proximity could work. Of all the posi-tive steps in race relations, the integration of baseball helped prepare so-ciety for the great changes brought about by the landmark *Brown* decision that was to come seven years later in 1954.

Credit for breaking baseball's invisible color barrier largely belongs to Jackie Robinson and Branch Rickey. In facing the taunts from opposing benches, the unkind remarks from the stands, the death threats from un-known sources, the spikings and brushbacks, and the indignities of be-ing treated as a second-class citizen wherever he traveled, Jackie Robinson gave up his own dignity to gain self-respect for his race—integration will hang forever on his head. Few players with Jackie Robinson's intensity could have withstood the pressure that left him on the verge of a nervous breakdown.[142] Only Rachel Robinson knew the anguish he suffered. To Rickey go the accolades for masterminding the plot behind the Robinson experiment. Few owners were equipped intellectually, organizationally, or otherwise to implement such a plan. The rationale behind Rickey's actions is as paradoxical and complicated as those that converted the Pu-ritans into Yankee traders. Rickey's religious convictions and social and educational background prepared him for the move. Nevertheless, without the profit motive, it is doubtful that he would have attempted the experiment. Others, such as Commissioner Chandler, have also laid claim to Robinson's success. Unlike Judge Landis, Chandler acquiesced in the decision to bring a black player up to the major leagues and provided other assistance behind the scene. Without the commissioner's support, the integration of baseball might not have occurred until well into the 1950s. In a 1956 letter to Chandler, Robinson himself recognized the commissioner's contribution when he wrote, "I will never forget your role in the so called Rickey experiment."[143]

9

1947: Season of Fury

Dodger scout Burt Shotton was in Miami when he received a telegram from Branch Rickey that read, "Be in Brooklyn tomorrow morning, see nobody, say nothing." A few days later he was offered the job of interim manager to replace Leo Durocher. Rickey explained that Joe McCarthy had turned down the Dodgers and that Shotton was the unanimous choice of the Brooklyn coaches and scouts. "You know the way to the Polo Grounds." Rickey told him, "Take my car and drive over there." Shotton never had a chance to refuse the job. "You just don't resist Branch Rickey," he noted, "Somehow he manages to do all the talking."[1]

When Shotton left Cleveland in 1945, he vowed that he would never again put on a uniform.[2] True to his word, as Brooklyn manager he was always seen in the clubhouse or dugout attired in street clothes—a practice that prevented him from appearing on the field during a game. His detractors quipped that, "He's just getting ready for a quick exit. He may leave any moment, and he knows it."[3] Shotton's hiring provided the Dodgers with the stability the team badly needed in a season characterized by Red Barber as the year "that all hell broke loose in baseball." It was also a season with an exciting pennant race in the National League and a World Series to match. Just as Burt Shotton was traveling into the unknown with Jackie Robinson and the rest of the Dodgers, the game itself was reaching a peak of popularity previously unequaled. Throughout baseball, attendance records were surpassed as more than sixty million people poured through turnstiles—an increase of nine million fans over the previous high of fifty-one million in 1946.[4]

Table 6. Final Major-League Regular-Season Standings, 1947

American League					National League			
	W	L	%	G.B.		W	L	%	G.B.
New York	97	57	.630	–	Brooklyn	94	60	.610	–
Detroit	85	69	.552	12	St. Louis	89	65	.578	5
Boston	83	71	.539	14	Boston	86	68	.558	8
Cleveland	80	74	.519	17	New York	81	73	.526	13
Philadelphia	78	76	.506	19	Cincinnati	73	81	.474	21
Chicago	70	84	.455	27	Chicago	69	85	.448	25
Washington	64	90	.416	33	Philadelphia	62	92	.403	32
St. Louis	59	95	.383	38	Pittsburgh	62	92	.403	32

The American League Pennant Race

In the American League race, the hapless St. Louis Browns remained hapless. Failing to clear the league's cellar, none of the team's starting pitchers had a winning record. The pitching was so futile that Browns announcer Dizzy Dean came out of retirement to hurl a game on September 28 against the White Sox. He held Chicago to three hits in four innings and hit a single with a barber pole-colored bat, before he had to leave the game with a pulled hamstring muscle. The Browns lost the game in the ninth inning 5-2.[5] When the Browns drew only 320,474 fans and were faced with paying off major park improvements, general manager William O. DeWitt and president Richard Muckerman decided to dismantle the team.[6] The fire sale resulted in three major trades, which sent infielders Vern Stephens and Billy Hitchcock, and pitchers Jack Kramer and Ellis Kinder to the Red Sox and pitcher Bob Muncrief, infielder Johnny Berardino, and outfielder Walt Judnich to the Indians for nine players and $450,000. The Boston deal involved a cash payment of $310,000—the largest sum ever involved in a player transaction at the time.[7]

The Senators finished a disappointing seventh in 1947, producing an anemic .241 team batting average and forty-two home runs. Only the strong pitching of Early Wynn (3.64, 17-15), Mickey Haefner (3.64, 10-14), and Walt Masterson (3.13, 12-16) allowed the Senators to approach respectability. The season was so woeful that the players almost revolted against manager Ossie Bluege, who was later replaced by Joe Kuhel.

The weak-hitting Chicago White Sox, who finished sixth, were led by Taft Wright and Luke Appling. Wright, a .311 lifetime hitter, had his last great year hitting .324 in 401 at bats. The durable Luke Appling, in his seventeenth season, not only hit .306 but established a new major-league record for games played at shortstop, surpassing Roger Peckinpaugh with 1,986 games played at that position.[8]

The Philadelphia Athletics were the surprise team in the American League. By mid-June, they were only seven games behind the league-leading Yankees. Outfielder Barney McCosky, at .328, and Elmer Valo, at .307, led the team in hitting, while Canadians Phil Marchildon (3.22, 19-9) and Dick Fowler (2.81, 12-11), along with reliever Russ Christopher (2.90, 10-7) and Bill McCahan (3.32, 10-5), led the team in pitching. Rookie McCahan threw a 3-0 no-hitter against the Washington Senators on September 3. Highly regarded rookie first baseman Ferris Fain (.291-7-71) established his credentials for pugnacity when he challenged Boston's Eddie Pellagrini following a collision near third base. The altercation resulted in an indefinite suspension of Fain by Will Harridge.[9]

The fourth-place Cleveland Indians served notice that they would be a team to watch in 1948. Bill Veeck's promotions and the team's improved performance attracted crowds in record numbers to Cleveland's Municipal Stadium. The signing of Larry Doby and several stellar pitching performances added to the team's gate appeal. Right-handed pitcher Don Black hurled a 3-0 no-hitter against his former teammates, the Philadelphia Athletics, on July 10. The Cleveland Stadium crowd of 47,871 was the largest ever to see a major-league no-hitter. Staff ace Bob Feller (2.68, 20-11) struggled through the first half of 1947, but he finished strong to become the American League's only twenty-game winner. He began the season pitching one-hitters against Boston and Detroit and led the league in strikeouts (196), shutouts (5), and innings pitched (299).

Ted Williams's (.343-32-114) triple crown year highlighted the Boston Red Sox's third-place finish. Williams was the first American Leaguer to win the triple crown twice, having already done so in 1941. After midseason, when his average hovered uncharacteristically below the .290 mark, he caught fire. On August 22, he went six for seven against Cleveland in a double-header that catapulted him into the top spot in batting average, a position he never relinquished for the remainder of the season. Although the Red Sox also got good hitting from Johnny Pesky (.324) and Bobby Doerr (.258-17-95), it was not enough to challenge the Yankees after July.

The real race was between the Red Sox and Tigers for second place. The two teams were no more than two and a half games apart most of the season. As usual, the Tigers were carried by their strong arms. Hal Newhouser (2.87, 17-17), however, suffered through a disappointing season. The Tigers lost much of their home-run power when Hank Greenberg was traded to Pittsburgh and only George Kell (.320-5-93) and Hoot Evers (.296-10-67) had good years at the plate.

In July, New York gained an insurmountable lead by winning nineteen games in a row. Through good fortune and by some astute moves, Larry MacPhail pieced together another championship team. He hired Bucky Harris—the boy manager of the Washington Senators during the 1920s. Harris skillfully guided the team through a maze of potentially damaging injuries to key players and provided the Yankees with the stability they had lacked during the previous season. Also fortuitous was MacPhail's inability to consummate several trades that would have sent Johnny Lindell, Floyd Bevans, Aaron Robinson, Billy Johnson, and Joe Page to other teams.

Reliever Joe Page (2.48, 14-8), in particular, had a sensational season. He even earned a save in the American League's 2-1 victory in the 1947 All-Star game—a contest dominated by the Yankees, who had eight players named to the American League squad. Nevertheless, during the beginning of the campaign Page was close to being sent down to the minors. Page was ineffective as a starting pitcher and was in disfavor with Harris because of his off-the-field antics and love of night life. On May 26, 1947, the Yankees played the Red Sox at Yankee Stadium before 74,747 fans. At that time, it was the largest crowd to witness a single game. Harris gave Page one final chance in a relief role, with the Yankees trailing 3-1 in the fourth inning. Page came into the game to face Ted Williams, Rudy York, and Bobby Doerr, with two runners on base and no outs. Williams reached first on an error by the first baseman to load the bases. Page went to three and zero on York and then struck him out with three pitches. He did exactly the same with Doerr and Eddie Pellagrini. The huge crowd roared, and Page embarked on a relief career that saw him register 116 strikeouts in 141 innings and earn a league-leading seventeen saves. Later, Harris admitted that had Page walked York, he intended to send the pitcher to Newark.[11]

Strong pitching was also provided by Allie Reynolds (3.20, 19-8), acquired in an off-season trade with Cleveland, Frank "Spec" Shea, Spud Chandler, Bobo Newsom, and Vic Raschi. The Yankee infield was led by the steady play of shortstop Phil Rizzuto and second baseman Snuffy Stirnweiss—a combination that missed only six games during the season. Tommy Henrich (.287-16-98), who regained his prewar hitting touch, returned to right field, where his strong arm and outstanding defensive skills were best employed. The heart of the team, though, was still Joe DiMaggio (.315-20-97). However, his play in 1947 was interrupted by a series of injuries. Heel problems caused by his flat-footed gait eventually sidelined him. In January 1947, a three-inch bone spur was removed from his left heel. The operation was botched, the incision would not heal properly, and DiMaggio developed a condition called *osteitis*. DiMaggio had a second operation to repair the damage and to graft skin from his leg to close the incision in the heel.

Almost miraculously, he entered the Yankees lineup only a few weeks after the operation. By June, DiMaggio had put together a sixteen-game hitting streak, during which he hit .493, with four home runs and twenty-one runs batted in. At the end of the streak, he was leading the league with a .360 average. Then, by his own admission he "began to press a little" and fell into one of the longest batting slumps of his career. Only when he relaxed did he begin to hit the ball solidly again.[12] Injuries also continued to plague his performance. The Yankee Clipper's arm had bothered him throughout the 1946 season, but in 1947 his arm was usually good for only one throw per game. Although he threw out only two runners all season, opposing teams failed to catch on to his disability.[13] In late July, DiMaggio missed two series with a pulled neck muscle and then missed more time in early August when his heel problem flared up again. After a close batting race, Ted Williams pulled away to hit .343 to DiMaggio's .315. Nevertheless, DiMaggio's dramatic performance earned him the American League's Most Valuable Player award.

The Yankees clinched the American League pennant on September 15. At the victory celebration, as the champagne flowed and the excitement continued, ancient Bobo Newsom, with a twinkle in his eye, circulated among his teammates and placed a dead mouse in Phil Rizzuto's pocket. When Rizzuto discovered the mouse, his entertaining reaction caused Newsom to part with his large chew of tobacco. The old Yankee spirit was back.[14]

The National League Pennant Race

By midsummer, the 1947 National League pennant race was not a foregone conclusion, unlike its American League counterpart. In fact, two tail-end teams, the Philadelphia Phillies and the Pittsburgh Pirates, both ended the season thirty-two games behind the leader. Though tied, the teams were going in different directions. The up-and-coming Phillies were building by spending money on young talent, such as pitcher Curt Simmons, infielders Willie Jones and Granville Hamner, and outfielders Del Ennis and Richie Ashburn. A major surprise was Harry "The Hat" Walker, who led the league in hitting with a .363 average—forty-six points over his nearest rival, Bob Elliott of the Braves.

Conversely, the Pittsburgh Pirates attempted to achieve respectability by buying their way into contention. Although they failed miserably, the

Traded to the Phillies in May 1947 by the St. Louis Cardinals, outfielder Harry
Walker responded by taking the National League batting crown with a .363 average.
(George Brace Photo)

Pirates were far from uninteresting. The new ownership of Frank
McKinney, Thomas P. Johnson, John Galbreath, and Bing Crosby promised the city of Pittsburgh that they would make substantial changes in
the franchise. First, they put $500,000 into renovations of Forbes Field,
and then they acquired Hank Greenberg on waivers from the Detroit Tigers. With the announcement of Greenberg's acquisition, season ticket
sales in Pittsburgh skyrocketed, but when the Pirates attempted to sign
him, he balked. In a series of negotiations that took on soap opera characteristics, the Pirates promised to double his $55,000 Detroit salary, to cre-
ate a bullpen in front of the left-field fence in Forbes Field, making it
easier for Greenberg to hit home runs, and to fly the former Tiger to games
so he could avoid train travel. Galbreath even offered Greenberg's wife,
an avid horsewoman, the pick of any of his yearlings from his Darby Dan
Farm in Kentucky.[15] Though he seriously considered retirement, Greenberg
finally capitulated when the Pirates agreed to give him his unconditional
release at the end of the 1947 season.[16]

In spite of the new owners' changes, the Pirates were a bad team. They were a hard-drinking, fun-loving crew with an average age of twenty-nine.[17] Future Hall-of-Famer Billy Herman was acquired as a player-manager in a trade that sent third baseman Bob Elliott to the Braves. Whereas Elliott went on to become the National League's Most Valuable Player in 1947, Herman was a flop as a manager.

The acquisition of Greenberg (.249-25-74), however, paid dividends for the Pirates. The area in front of the left-field fence was nicknamed "Greenberg Gardens," and by late August nine of Greenberg's seventeen home runs at Pittsburgh had landed there. Far more important was Greenberg's influence over young slugger Ralph Kiner (.313-51-127). Under Greenberg's tutelage, Kiner blossomed as one of the league's premier home-run hitters. Kiner's quick wrist action enabled him to power high fly balls well over stadium fences. With Kiner and Greenberg leading the way, the Pirates established a new attendance mark at 1,283,531, eclipsing by more than 400,000 fans the previous record set during the pennant-winning 1927 season.[18]

Although many players remained, the sixth-place Chicago Cubs were far removed from the 1945 team that won the National League pennant. After leading the league in mid-May, the team gradually fell in the standings. The Cincinnati Reds were separated from the Cubs and the rest of the National League's second division by one player—pitcher Ewell Blackwell (2.47, 22-8). Between May 10 and July 25, Blackwell reeled off a string of sixteen straight victories, equaling Carl Hubbell's 1936 feat. During the run, the lanky right-hander not only pitched sixteen complete games but came within two outs of hurling consecutive no-hitters. His no-hitter was a 6-0 win over the Boston Braves on June 18. In Blackwell's next outing, on June 22 against the Brooklyn Dodgers, the Reds pitcher had a no-hitter going with one out in the ninth inning, when pesky Eddie Stanky grounded a ball sharply over the pitcher's mound, just beyond Blackwell's reach. Jackie Robinson followed with a harmless hit before Blackwell was able to stop the Dodgers for the 4-0 victory. The sidearmer's victory streak was broken by the New York Giants on July 25, when Willard Marshall hit a home run in the ninth inning to tie the score, en route to a 5-4 Giants win.

Blackwell's achievement was the outstanding pitching performance of the era. His appearance, motion, delivery, and speed made him extremely difficult for right-handers to hit. He intimidated hitters. Fellow pitcher Schoolboy Rowe described him best: "He's got a fastball that hops so quickly you can't follow it; a curve that breaks off like a buggy whip—and he throws at you with that sidearm motion that makes you think of a buzzsaw at your stomach. If he ever misses and hits you, the ball will bore a hole right through you."[19]

The New York Giants, proclaimed the "best fourth-place club in years,"

Braves third baseman Bob Elliott, acquired from the Pirates, won the National League's Most Valuable Player award in 1947. (George Brace Photo)

literally wore out National League pitchers as they established a major-league record for home runs in a season, with 221.[20] The 1947 baseballs were much livelier than those used during World War II. Real rubber replaced the synthetic variety used during the war, and superior horse-hide covers were once again available from France and Quebec.[21] The Giants were led by big Johnny Mize (.302-51-138). Nicknamed the "Big Cat," Mize kept pace with Babe Ruth's home-run record into early September before tailing off. His fifty-one home runs set a National League record for left-handed hitters. Mize also established a new National League record by scoring in sixteen consecutive games. Mize was joined in the home-run parade by outfielders Willard Marshall (.291-36-107) and Bobby Thomson (.283-29-85), and catcher Walker Cooper (.305-35-122). Fortu-nately for the rest of the league, the Giants had little pitching beyond Dave Koslo (4.39, 15-10) and twenty-seven year old rookie Larry Jansen (3.16, 21-5).

The third-place Boston Braves, who had two great starting pitchers in Warren Spahn (2.33, 21-10) and Johnny Sain (3.52, 21-12), were the league's best-hitting team, with a club average of .275. They also had the National League's Most Valuable Player in third baseman Bob Elliott (.317-22-113). Though the acquisition of Elliott from the Pittsburgh Pirates for Billy Herman was the theft of the decade, the Braves were poor traders. Over a two-year period (1946-47) the Braves acquired ten players from the Cardinals for more than $200,000 and still had little to show for their investment.[22]

The second-place St. Louis Cardinals ruined their pennant chances by playing miserably during April and May and remained mired in last place until June. Their woes stemmed from weak pitching and from Stan Musial's (.312-19-95) bout with appendicitis and infected tonsils. Musial's recovery was slow, and the Cardinal star did not begin to hit until mid-June. The Cardinals' pitching staff started slowly and fell off in September. Surprising seasons by sinker-baller Alpha Brazle (2.84, 14-8) and former Georgia Tech star Jim Hearn (3.22, 12-7) kept the Cardinals in contention until early fall.

The Brooklyn Dodgers took over first place at the end of June and remained there for the duration of the season. With Jackie Robinson (.297-12-48), Pee Wee Reese (.284-12-73), Eddie Stanky (.252-3-52), and Pete Reiser (.309-5-46) on board, they were the most exciting and unpredictable team in the National League. The club led the league in stolen bases, with 88, behind the daring of Jackie Robinson, and they were defensively sound. Only the Cardinals made fewer errors and more double plays. The team included old timers such as outfielder Dixie Walker (.306-9-94) and Arky Vaughan (.325-2-25) and an array of youngsters from their burgeoning farm system. Gil Hodges and Duke Snider saw very limited action, while others such as catcher Bruce Edwards (.295-9-80), third baseman Johnny "Spider" Jorgenson (.274-5-67), and outfielders Carl Furillo (.295-8-88) and Gene Hermanski (.275-7-39) saw regular playing time.

The Dodgers' thin pitching staff was its Achilles heel. Ralph Branca (2.67, 21-12), a big 6'3" kid who attended New York University during the war, was the anchor of the starting rotation. With twelve older siblings, he proudly wore number 13 on his jersey.[23] Branca, who was second to Ewell Blackwell in strikeouts in 1947, with 148, relied on a live fastball and a sharp-breaking curve. His outstanding game in 1947 was a 7-0 one-hitter against the St. Louis Cardinals on July 18. The bullpen was anchored by Hugh Casey (3.99, 10-4), who led the league in saves with eighteen, and by the steady Clyde King (2.77, 6-5). In August, the Dodgers purchased Dan Bankhead from the Memphis Red Sox in the Negro American League. Although he did not help the team, significantly, Bankhead homered in his first time at bat and earned the distinction of becoming the first black pitcher in the major leagues.

The Dodgers suffered several injuries and scares during the 1947 sea-

Left, With thirty-six home runs, Willard Marshall helped lead the Giants to a new major-league single-season home run record with 221. *Right,* Ewell Blackwell's string of sixteen straight victories was the outstanding pitching performance of the era. (George Brace Photos)

son. On June 4, Pete Reiser slammed into the concrete outfield wall at Ebbets Field while chasing a fly ball. Although Reiser did not sustain a concussion, the talented player was never the same again.[24] In August, the Reds and Dodgers played in a particularly rough series in which Stanky and Reese were both removed from games with spike wounds. Jackie Robinson was also involved in spiking incidents at first base with Enos Slaughter and Joe Garagiola. Finally, as pennant fever mounted in Brooklyn in September, another unusual incident occurred. The Dodgers had two separate games scheduled for Labor Day—one in the morning and the other in the afternoon. Advanced ticket sales for the morning game were so light that broadcaster Red Barber announced several times over the radio that there were "plenty of seats" available.[25] A crowd exceeding Ebbets Field's capacity of 32,000 "came up out of the ground" only a couple of hours before game time catching the Dodgers with only a few ticket windows open. They sold 27,000 tickets in the hour before game time, but vendors had to turn thousands of others away, including entire families. When the crowd became unruly, riot squads were called to contain it.[26]

The Dodgers clinched a tie for the National League pennant on September 19. With the pennant nearly in hand, Rickey finally permitted New York's black population to honor Jackie Robinson with a day. On September 22, citizens from Harlem and other parts of the country honored the Dodgers rookie with a car and other gifts, with a total value of $10,000. Master of ceremonies Bill "Bojangles" Robinson announced, "I'm sixty years old, and I never expected to live to see a Ty Cobb in Technicolor."[27] Only five days earlier, the *Sporting News,* whose editor-publisher originally scoffed at Robinson's signing in 1945, declared the Dodger player the outstanding rookie of 1947.[28]

The 1947 World Series

The 1947 World Series went a full seven games and was one of the most dramatic in baseball history. The Yankees took the first two games 5-3 and 10-3 before huge crowds (the 73,365 first-day crowd was a record) at Yankee Stadium. In the first game, Ralph Branca lost his control in the fifth frame, allowing the Yankees five runs after pitching four hitless innings. In the second game, the Dodgers made several mental errors and played sloppily, as Allie Reynolds struck out twelve and Tommy Henrich collected two hits, including a solo home run. With the series now in Brooklyn, the Dodgers triumphed 9-8 in game three, after taking a 6-0 lead against Bobo Newsom and Vic Raschi. The Yankees came roaring back with two runs in each of the third, fourth, and fifth innings. Joe DiMaggio's two-run homer drove starter Joe Hatten from the mound. The Dodgers held a 9-6 lead in the sixth, but Ralph Branca gave up a run on doubles by Bobby Brown and Tommy Henrich, and then in the seventh he served up the first pinch-hit home run in World Series history to Yogi Berra. Hugh Casey finished the game for the Dodgers.

The fourth game is one of the most famous in World Series history. Little-used Floyd Bevans (3.82, 7-13) was within one out of pitching the

After the Dodgers clinched a tie for the National League pennant, Brooklyn fans hoisted Dodger favorite Pee Wee Reese onto their shoulders and carried him through Pennsylvania Station. (Photographic Archives, University of Louisville)

first no-hitter in a World Series. Great catches by Joe DiMaggio in the fourth inning and by Tommy Henrich in the eighth off drives by Gene Hermanski kept the no-hitter alive. The tension mounted in the bottom of the ninth, as the Dodgers came to bat with the Yankees leading 1-0. Bruce Edwards flied deep to Johnny Lindell for the first out. Carl Furillo walked. Johnny Jorgenson fouled out to George McQuinn. Little Al Gionfriddo was sent in to run for Furillo, and Pete Reiser, who was playing with a broken ankle, was sent to the plate to pinch hit. Gionfriddo, who was safe only because of Berra's high throw, stole second. Reiser then was intentionally passed to put men on first and second. Miksis entered the game to run for Reiser at first. Then, manager Burt Shotton sent in Harry "Cookie" Lavagetto to bat for Eddie Stanky. With the fans on the edge of their seats and cheering every pitch, the crowd noise at Ebbets Field drowned out all other utterances. Lavagetto missed the first pitch—a high outside fastball. Bevans threw him another, and Lavagetto connected with a shot to right field that carried over the outstretched glove of Tommy Henrich and bounced off the wall. Gionfriddo and Miksis scored, and bedlam broke loose in Brooklyn.[29] Mrs. Mary Katherine Lavagetto, lying in an Oakland, California, hospital bed after giving birth to a son, awoke just in time to hear her husband's name called on the radio as a pinch hitter. "It must have been fate," she recalled, "When Harry hit that double that won the game, I just sat down and had a good cry." When the exuberant Lavagetto called, he said, "Did ya hear what happened, Honey? Mr. Shotton told me to talk all I want to; he said the phone bill would be on the club."[30]

The Yankees came back to take the fifth game 2-1, behind the four-hit pitching of Frank Shea and DiMaggio's solo home run in the fifth inning off loser Rex Barney. Upon returning to Yankee Stadium for the sixth game, the Dodgers and Yankees engaged in another slugfest. Neither starting pitcher, Lombardi for the Dodgers nor Reynolds for the Yankees, lasted beyond the third inning. With the Dodgers ahead 8-5 in the bottom of the sixth inning, the Yankees had two men on base with two outs and Joe DiMaggio at the plate. DiMaggio sent a towering fly ball to deep center field off pitcher Joe Hatten. Al Gionfriddo, who had been inserted for defensive purposes, made one of the most discussed catches in World Series history. After the game, he described it for sportswriter Roger Birtwell: "When Joe hit the ball, I started running for the fence. As I got close to the fence, I took a look over my right shoulder. And, I saw the ball coming down way over on the other side of me. So I twisted around and stuck my glove hand—I'm left-handed, you know—and got the ball in it. Then I banged into the fence. It was just boom—boom." Players and spectators near the scene of the catch and World Series films verified that Gionfriddo's catch saved the ball from clearing the fence for a home run.[31]

World Series films also captured DiMaggio kicking up infield dust in dismay as he rounded second base after watching Gionfriddo catch the ball. It was one of the few times the great DiMaggio ever exhibited displeasure during a game. With the Yankees momentarily dispirited, the Dodgers went on to win the sixth game 8-6, with Hugh Casey registering a save in the ninth.

Compared with the excitement of the previous games, the seventh game of the series was almost anticlimatic. The Yankees broke a two-all tie when Bobby Brown set a new World Series record with his third pinch hit of the series to score Billy Johnson in the fourth inning. The Yankees went on to win the game 5-2, behind the outstanding relief work of Joe Page, who allowed only one hit and retired thirteen Dodgers in a row.

With series hero Joe Page and the rest of the Yankees celebrating in the clubhouse, Yankees president Larry MacPhail made a startling statement to the press. With tears running down his cheeks, he announced that he was selling his share of the Yankees. The timing of the announcement was poorly chosen. As sportswriter Tom Meany wrote, "Only MacPhail could take the headlines away from a relief pitcher, who faced 15 hitters and recorded 15 outs."[32] MacPhail, who had vowed to give up ownership if the Yankees won the series, negotiated with his partners, Del Webb and Dan Topping, throughout September. Their tentative arrangement called for MacPhail to continue as general manager of the club at a salary of $50,000 per year. The agreement disintegrated, however, at the Yankees' lavish victory party that evening when an inebriated MacPhail embarrassed the entire organization by punching a sportswriter, firing the head of the farm system, George Weiss, and berating everyone in sight. Within twenty-four hours co-owners Webb and Topping announced that George Weiss was the team's general manager, that they had purchased MacPhail's share of the team for $2,000,000, and that MacPhail was now out of baseball.[33]

Thus ended Larry MacPhail's long and tumultuous affiliation with baseball. With the World Series victory, the Yankees were respectable again. He helped establish new major-league attendance records by fielding an exciting team, refurbishing Yankee Stadium, establishing a stadium club for season ticket holders, bringing lights and night baseball to the park, offering promotions such as free nylons, and sponsoring fashion shows and pregame contests involving the players.[34] Many in the Yankee organization, however, were pleased to see McPhail leave. In a meeting of Yankees' employees not long after MacPhail's departure, Del Webb made a short but pointed speech in which he said, "Everybody relax and get down to calm business. The lion tamer is gone."[35]

While Larry MacPhail's exit from the game created one less problem

Unlike the heralded closers of later decades, 1947 World Series hero Joe Page entered games as early as the third or fourth inning and often pitched them to completion, pouring his fastball by batter after batter. (George Brace Photo)

for Commissioner Happy Chandler, others quickly filled the void. Following weeks of private negotiations, a disagreement between the commissioner's office and Leslie O'Connor, general manager of the Chicago White Sox, over an interpretation of the high school signing rule became public in late October 1947. The high school signing rule, which was drafted by O'Connor himself and passed by baseball in 1946, prevented major-league teams from negotiating with amateur players still attending high schools that were members of the National Federation of Athletic Associations. Following passage of the rule, Commissioner Chandler issued a bulletin stating that he interpreted the intent of the rule to include players attending all high schools. The commissioner's office enforced the rule when one team reported a violation by another. Automatic punishment included loss of rights to the player and a $500 fine.[36]

The White Sox signed George Zoeterman, a student at Chicago's Christian High School, to a contract before his graduation. When O'Connor refused to pay the resulting fine, Chandler suspended him and the White Sox from participating in league activities, whereupon the White Sox executive threatened to take baseball to court. O'Connor's position deteriorated when American League owners met in an emergency meeting and voted not only to support the commissioner's position but also to strip

O'Connor of his membership on the league's executive committee. After recommendations by American League president Will Harridge and Chicago owner Grace Comiskey that he pay, O'Connor reluctantly capitulated.[37] Concerned about bad publicity and the effect of potential court action on the legal structure of baseball, the owners were frightened into supporting the commissioner. Nevertheless, the high school signing rule was not popular among the owners, and the O'Connor skirmish was merely the beginning of an ongoing battle with the owners over the commissioner's zealous enforcement of the rule.

Although major-league baseball established a new record for attendance (19,950,633) in 1947 and continued its rise in popularity, its most recognizable symbol, Babe Ruth, began a long decline that would lead to his death.[38] In November 1946, he entered the French Hospital in New York with what he thought was a bad sinus headache. Neither the Babe nor the public was told that he had a cancerous growth on the left side of his neck. An operation on his neck affected an artery, nerves, and his larynx. Radiation therapy on an inoperable portion of the cancer left him weak and unable to take nourishment except intravenously.[39] Ruth was visited by Commissioner Chandler. The commissioner told him, "Babe, you are a hero to my generation. Every fan in America is pulling for you. I'm going to say a little prayer for you, Babe. God bless you." Tears welled in both men's eyes, and no other words were spoken.[40]

During the three months Ruth was hospitalized, he received 26,835 letters and telegrams (many from young people) and went from 235 to 180 pounds. Wasted by his illness, Ruth was a shell of the man who hit sixty home runs. Once home, he joked with visitor Hank Greenberg that it was the "first time I have been able to look straight down and see my feet for thirty years." Though he never fully recovered and was forced to subsist on a prescribed diet of eggs and beer, Ruth spent most of 1947 giving what little energy he had left to baseball.[41] In April 1947, he signed a contract with the Ford Motor Company to act as a consultant for their American Legion baseball program for boys and announced that "I'm going to back it to the very limit of my health."[42] He appeared at two Babe Ruth days at Yankee Stadium (April 27 and September 28, 1947) and at several ballparks and functions throughout the country. Everywhere his message was the same. In a deep raspy voice, he said, "We— us old-timers have had our chance. You [pointing to the audience] seem to have done well with yours. Now give the kids their chance. They are the America of the future."[43] Ruth, who was mobbed by children and adults everywhere, rarely failed to grant their requests for autographs. It was as though baseball finally realized his value as a symbol of the game just as his fans had for years.

1948

Lou Boudreau, the American League's Most Valuable Player
for 1948, celebrates his birthday. *(The Sporting News)*

10

Miracle on Lake Erie

The sudden departure of Larry MacPhail in 1947 deprived the game of one of its greatest innovators. Nevertheless, the void left by the instigator of night baseball and ballpark modernization was ably filled by William Veeck Jr., who burst onto the baseball scene in 1946 as the new owner of the Cleveland Indians. Indeed, Bill Veeck's promotional activities and marketing techniques during the Pivotal Era shattered existing major-league attendance records and unalterably changed baseball's relationship with its fans. A baseball insider who became an outsider, Veeck's father, William Veeck Sr., was a newspaperman who served as president of the Chicago Cubs from 1917 to 1933. Veeck Jr. grew up with the Cubs, and when his father died early in the Depression, he left Kenyon College and took a job at $18 a week as an office boy with the team. During the next eight years he learned every facet of the Cubs' operation and rose to the position of executive assistant/treasurer of the team.[1]

In 1941, with the very little capital of his own, the twenty-seven-year-old Veeck acquired the bankrupt Milwaukee Brewers of the American Association and over the next three years turned the team into one of the most exciting minor-league franchises in baseball. He cleaned and painted Milwaukee's Borchert Field, greeted fans at the turnstiles, and thanked them when they left. Veeck's first Milwaukee team was so inept that he formed a band that featured manager Charlie Grimm as "baseball's only left-handed banjo player" to keep the fans occupied. The ensemble included the team's radio announcer on washboard drums, the business manager on a homemade bull fiddle, and Veeck himself on a jazzbo (a sliding tin whistle).[2]

Milwaukee was Veeck's promotional proving ground. The unpredictable nature of his unadvertised stunts made them even more attractive to spectators. He gave away anything if there was a good laugh in it—this included ducks, geese and squab, live lobsters, six step ladders at a time, 200-pound blocks of ice, snakes, and cows and sway-backed horses. Peals of laughter would flow through the park as fans waited to see what a recipient would do with the often unwanted gift. Later Veeck was always willing to swap the joke gift for something far more valuable. He even encouraged pregame wedding ceremonies at home plate. During the war, he dramatically increased attendance by scheduling morning games for night-shift employees, complete with a breakfast of cereal and cream, doughnuts, and coffee. Even during rainouts the Brewers president staged activities, including quiz shows and dancing in the aisles to music played by a swing band.[3] Veeck was able to acquire better ballplayers as fan support increased. He was then able to sell players such as Johnny Schmitz, Eddie Stanky, and Dave Koslo to major-league teams for large profits. By 1942, the Brewers were so respectable that they lost the American Association pennant by only half a game to Kansas City. From 1943 to 1945, they won the pennant outright.

In 1943, Veeck's right foot was smashed by the recoil of an artillery piece while serving with the Marines in Bougainville in the Pacific theater. He also developed a bad case of jungle rot in his left leg. After a fourteen-month stay at a U.S. Naval hospital, ten operations, and the loss of part of his foot, Veeck sold the Brewers and moved to Arizona with his wife Eleanor and three children in an attempt to save a failing marriage.[4] Unable to escape baseball's allure, Veeck returned to Chicago and persuaded his old friend Harry Grabiner, a retired Chicago White Sox executive, to join him in an effort to acquire ownership of a major-league team. The Cleveland franchise was the most appealing possibility. The city's business and industry was diversified, and the Indians had a strong fan base, even though the team was badly underpromoted and had not won a pennant in more than twenty years. For a dollar, a fan could buy a box seat behind home plate and be near no one. Finally, if Veeck attracted enough fans, he could take advantage of the city's Municipal Stadium— a structure considered a white elephant by many—which seated 78,000 people.[5]

Veeck was tipped off that the Cleveland franchise could be had for a fair price. Though everyone believed that Indians president Alva Bradley owned the team and that he had no interest in selling it, the controlling stockholders were John and Francis Sherwin of the Sherwin-Williams Paint Company. By developing a then-unusual debenture–common stock scheme, Veeck and Grabiner formed a syndicate to purchase the Indians. Veeck operated clandestinely to reach an agreement with the Sherwins to purchase the team for $2.2 million and secured a $1 million loan from a local Cleveland bank to seal the deal. By the time Bradley learned of the arrangement, Veeck was the new owner of the Indians.[6]

The day the sale was announced, June 21, 1946, Veeck appeared at Cleveland's League Park to mingle with the fans. A constant stream of applause followed him as he wandered through the crowd on his crutches. As Veeck passed through one group of fans, a man patted him on the back and proclaimed, "This is the best darned thing that ever happened to this town."[7] Veeck's quick wit, casual attire, curly blond hair, and boyish good looks quickly won over Cleveland fans.[8] The young executive moved to improve the fans' access to the team. He removed his office doors, installed a ten-line switchboard so the Indians could be contacted by telephone, for the first time in their history, invited 300 small-town editors to Indians games as guests of the team, and offered Cleveland radio stations free broadcasting rights for the remainder of the 1946 season.[9] In addition, ladies' day was reestablished. Bradley had dropped it because it produced little revenue and "women buy no Cokes."[10] Finally, Veeck demanded that his vendors sell larger hot dogs and more peanuts per bag when he discovered that fans were being cheated.[11]

Other changes were implemented that raised staff and team morale. After the new president examined the team's payroll, he gave all office and grounds staff pay raises. Ushers received new uniforms, employees were given raises, and players had their daily meal allowance increased to $5 a day and for the first time were allowed to eat wherever they pleased.[12] Veeck also announced that the Indians were going to play all of their games at Cleveland Municipal Stadium instead of alternating between that facility for Sunday and night games and the 22,500-seat League Park for day contests. "I don't like the idea of our being a road club 154 games a year," he told the press.[13]

Veeck had come to Cleveland with a vision, as he told one reporter, "I'm going to give the fans of Cleveland a lot of fun. But I also plan to give them a pennant. That will come in time."[14] The 1946 version of the Cleveland Indians was unremarkable except for stars Bob Feller and Lou Boudreau. To improve the team, the new owner needed to raise enough capital to acquire better players. He knew that the methods he had employed in Milwaukee would also work in Cleveland. Yet, at the same time, he realized that baseball's establishment would view such promotional activities with scorn. When Will Harridge attended a Brewers game during the war, he was impressed by the great enthusiasm in Milwaukee and told Veeck, "Some day I would like to have you in the American League, but you'd have to eliminate your sideshow tactics."[15] When Veeck acquired the Indians, he told reporters the promotional activities he employed in Milwaukee would not do. "We are in the majors now," he

Bill Veeck was quoted as saying, "I'm going to give the fans of Cleveland a lot of fun. But I also plan to give them a pennant." (Transcendental Graphics)

stated.[16] He also told the press, "You can't substitute Vaudeville for victory."[17] Veeck soon forgot those words, and so did Indians fans.

In July, six-column advertisements proclaiming "We're giving the Indians back to the fans" hit the three Cleveland daily newspapers. The ads enticed readers to come to the ballpark with such slogans as "Bring the Papooses—Reduced Rates," "Telephone Information Service," "New Teepee for a Whooping Tribe," "Radio Broadcasts whenever Possible," "Ladies Day—without Reservations," and "A New Band Will Beat the Drums."[18] On the night of July 23, a crowd of 25,399 came to watch the Indians play the Athletics—a game that would normally draw 7,000. The fans were not disappointed. A fifteen-piece band, attired in Indian costumes and housed in a teepee surrounded by a temporary fence in center field, played "Three Blind Mice" when the umpires appeared on the field. The fence created a bulge in center field and necessitated a change in the ground rules because it made a home run thirty-five feet closer to home plate. Veeck capped the evening off with a spectacular fireworks display.

At an August 1 ladies' day game, Veeck personally handed out 503 pairs of precious nylons to the first 503 women to pass through the gates. Larry MacPhail and the Yankees had recently offered 500 pairs of nylons in a recent promotion. The following day, with the Yankees in town, Veeck put on another terrific fireworks display, which concluded with his version of the dropping of an atomic bomb from a plane, fastened to the top of the scoreboard, onto a battleship rolling in the bleachers below.[19] The planned sequence went awry, and the battleship ended up knocking down the plane.[20] Then, while the pitchers warmed up, Veeck entertained the fans with a five-ring circus that included a juggler at first base, an eccentric dancer at second, a whip act at third, a tumbling act at home plate, and a baton-twirling drum major on the mound.[21] Two days later, on August 4, 1946, the Indians drew 75,595 fans to see a double-header against the Yankees—the second-largest crowd in major-league history. Veeck's "sideshow" was beginning to work.

Veeck came by his love of entertainment naturally. He always loved fireworks and circuses.[22] "My tastes," he wrote in *Veeck—as in Wreck*, "are so average that anything that appeals strongly to me is probably going to appeal to most of the customers."[23] His penchant for entertainment led him to purchase the contract of shortstop Jackie Price from Oakland. Price, who actually appeared in seven games for the Indians in 1946 and hit .231 in thirteen at bats, was a first-class trickster who performed acrobatic feats with baseball equipment. Price's act was phenomenal—he could throw and catch a ball backwards or catch or throw standing on his head, and he could throw almost any number of balls at once. His most impressive trick was to simultaneously throw three baseballs to three players, two of whom were lined up fifty feet apart while the other was located thirty-five feet beyond.[24] Price could also pitch to two catchers abreast of each other, and simultaneously throwing one a fastball and the other a curve.[25] He was also famed for taking batting practice while hanging by his heels from a horizontal bar erected above home plate.[26] Another favorite activity was zooming around the outfield in a regulation Army jeep while shooting a baseball out of a pneumatic tube and then making a split-second backhanded catch while the speeding jeep was somehow on automatic pilot.[27]

While Price's act provided a pregame show for fans arriving at the ballpark, Veeck hired another entertainer, Max Patkin, to enliven the game itself. Patkin was a good minor-league prospect before World War II, but an injury to his arm forced him to stop playing professional baseball. After an operation, he pitched against a number of major leaguers while stationed with the Navy in Honolulu. In one game, Patkin mimicked Joe DiMaggio by following him around the bases after the Yankee Clipper had homered off him. The players and servicemen watching the game loved his antics, and soon Patkin became a minor cult hero in Hawaii. Following the war, Patkin developed a humorous coaching routine while playing for

Wilkes-Barre in the Eastern League. When the score became too one-sided, his manager would send him out to the coaching box to amuse the fans. Lou Boudreau saw Patkin perform and told Veeck about him.[28]

Veeck signed Patkin to a personal services contract at $650 per month and to a $1 coach's contract. The ex-pitcher usually appeared early in a game, dressed in a baggy uniform, and performed ridiculous stunts at first base. He clowned between pitches, stood on his head, ran through series of absurd signs, occasionally lost his pants, and contorted his wonderfully elastic body and facial features to mimic players and umpires.[29] The best physical description of Patkin appeared in *Veeck—as in Wreck*: "He is a hawk-faced, long-nosed, crane-necked, rubber-boned scarecrow," who looks as though he has been put together without a diagram.[30] Patkin "could tie his long body into knots that would have baffled an Eagle Scout," said Veeck in an interview, "and when he went out on the first-base coaching lines people promptly forgot about the Indians—which was about the best thing that could have happened."[31] The fans in Cleveland loved Patkin, and most of the players, many who knew him from the minor leagues, also enjoyed his act.

Veeck also specialized in holding players' nights or days. On August 13, 1946, Veeck held Lefty Weisman Night in honor of the Cleveland trainer's twenty-fifth year with the club. Not only did Jackie Price perform, but Weisman was showered with gifts, including a wheelbarrow filled with $5,000 worth of silver dollars to mark his silver anniversary with the team. The biggest laugh of the evening came when Weisman was told to take his prize off the field but discovered that he could not budge the wheelbarrow. After Veeck milked the joke for all it was worth, he summoned a tow truck, which was waiting underneath the stands, to pull the wheelbarrow off the field.[32] Veeck also honored Lou Boudreau with a day on September 15, 1946, when he presented his manager with a huge gold-plated trophy inscribed, "To the Best Shortstop ever Left Off the All-Star Team."[33] The following year, he honored Mel Harder with a night. Among the gifts the pitcher received was a $2,000 check from Veeck, an automobile, and a prize cocker spaniel. The event drew 56,349 fans.[34]

Veeck's promotions were soon copied by other teams. The Phillies staged a three-ring circus between games of a rainy Sunday doubleheader with the Chicago Cubs and drew 28,409 fans, including more than 10,000 children.[35] As other teams discovered that players' days and nights drew large crowds, the events became the rage in 1947. On August 2, the Boston Red Sox honored Bobby Doerr with $25,000 worth of gifts. The stunned Doerr told fans that he hoped "to remain in Boston for 50 years."[36] A similar night was held for Cincinnati Reds pitcher Bucky Walters. After receiving a new Lincoln car, and numerous checks and gifts, Walters pitched the Reds to a 2-0 victory over the Braves.[37] One of the most extravagant affairs was Cecil Travis Night, held by the Washington Senators on August 15. The beloved Senator received the obligatory automobile, a Hereford bull, Irish Setter hunting dogs, a congratulatory message from General Dwight D. Eisenhower, a $100 check from Connie Mack, and a gift from the umpiring crew, who proclaimed Travis "the most uncomplaining player in the majors."[38]

For the teams, such player events, when planned in conjunction with games against weak opponents, brought in unexpected revenue from gate receipts and concession profits and rewarded them with untold goodwill. The obvious benefit for the players, aside from the recognition itself, was the acquisition of hard-to-obtain automobiles, appliances, and other consumer goods not yet produced in great volume after the war.

Not everyone was enamored with Bill Veeck or with his promotions. Respected managers Steve O'Neill and Joe Cronin were particularly critical of Patkin's presence in the coaching box.[39] They feared that the entertainer would disrupt player concentration. Clark Griffith agreed and complained that Patkin caused his players to laugh and take their minds off the game. Imagine, "the man who hired Nick Altrock and Al Schacht to clown the coaching lines," noted Veeck, "complained that Patkin wasn't dignified."[40] Though Veeck cared little about dignity, Patkin caused problems. He often did things that were on the verge of impropriety. For instance, when Cleveland players failed to produce runs, he would take a newspaper out and read it. As Patkin himself described it, "You know, that's like telling the players that they're horseshit." Invariably Patkin and the entire ballpark would hear Veeck's resonant voice calling, "Max— Max!" and Patkin would get off the ground and put the paper away.[41] The chief blow to Patkin's major-league career occurred in September 1946, when Ray Mack was picked off first base while Patkin was coaching. Boudreau was so irritated that he immediately substituted coach Buster Mills for Patkin, and he rarely allowed the latter to coach again.[42]

Jackie Price proved to be even more self-destructive than Patkin. His major-league career with the Indians was jeopardized when he released some pet snakes on a train filled with a group of female bowlers headed for a tournament.[43] Fortunately, by the 1947 season Cleveland was able to field a much more competitive team, and Patkin and Price were sent to entertain minor-league crowds for the remainder of their contracts. Veeck was rapidly enlarging the team's farm system and was operating a revolving-door policy with the team's roster. In speeches, his repeated description of this situation was "We've got three teams: one here, one coming, and one going."[44] Veeck worked tirelessly to build the team, always energized and always smiling. Even his leg, which continued to be infected, failed to stop him. In early November, his right leg was removed seven inches below the knee. Four hours after being wheeled out of the operating room, a groggy Veeck was on the phone to the *Cleveland Press* sports department to find out what had transpired in the major-league draft.

Veeck also proved to be an astute judge of talent. In October 1946, he obtained second baseman Joe Gordon from the New York Yankees in exchange for pitcher Allie Reynolds. Gordon, who won the American League Most Valuable Player award in 1942, slumped badly in 1943 and continued to slide after returning from the service in 1946, hitting a lowly .210. Veeck offered MacPhail a choice between pitchers Red Embree and Reynolds for Gordon. MacPhail was ready to select Embree until he consulted with Joe DiMaggio, who told him, "I'm off my rocker if I don't take Reynolds."[45] DiMaggio's advice helped the Yankees win six pennants, but Gordon's arrival as an Indian also had an immediate impact. In his first season with Cleveland he hit twenty-nine home runs, drove in ninety-three runs, and provided the team with instant leadership afield. In 1947, Veeck made good on his promise to erect a symmetrical chain-link fence in huge Cleveland Stadium to take advantage of Gordon's power. Moreover, he made the fence low enough (five feet) so outfielders could reach balls that, if uncaught, would be home runs. It was all designed to create excitement. "Time was when fans admired pitching duels," said Veeck. "Now they want action, runs."[46]

In June, Veeck moved the fence again from 320 feet down the foul lines to 362, because Indians' opponents were out-homering them (there was no major-league rule about adjusting fences in 1947). As *Washington Post* sportswriter Shirley Povich cheerfully wrote, "The upshot of it is that the Indians have been taking a beating in the battle of synthetic homers."[47]

By the end of the 1947 season, Cleveland attendance rose to more than 1.5 million, behind only the Yankees and Dodgers at 2.1 and 1.8 million, respectively. Veeck now possessed a corps of avid fans, working capital to acquire players, and a desire to go after major-league attendance records. All he lacked, he thought, was a manager who could lead the Indians to a pennant. When Veeck took over the Indians in 1946, the team's manager was Lou Boudreau, who in 1941, at the age of twenty-four, had become one of the youngest managers in major-league history. Boudreau's critics claimed that he played "dull unimaginative baseball, relieved by wild hunches which generally backfire." He often settled for one run at a time in situations where other managers would play for the big inning—just the kind of conservative strategy that the flamboyant Veeck disliked.[48]

Veeck's dilemma was that Boudreau was not only his manager but also his ball club—the team's most valuable player was also the Indians' undisputed leader on the field. "He showed it in his first big league game," noted sportswriter Gordon Cobbledick. "You had to be there to believe it. Halfway through the first inning, this kid from the bush was running the team—and everybody on the field and in the stands knew it. Damnedest thing I ever saw."[49] Though he won the American League batting championship in 1944, he was far from the ideal ballplayer. He was painfully slow. His legs and ankles, which were taped before each game, showed the wear and tear he put them through as an All-American basketball player at the University of Illinois. Red Smith described him best—"He can't run and his arm's no good. But he plays that spot [shortstop] the way nobody else can play it, and he gets rid of the ball so swiftly the runner never beats his weak throw. Besides which, pitchers say he is the smartest hitter in the league, the hardest to fool, the guy who hits the ball where it's pitched, pushing the outside curve to right, pulling the inside service into the left field seats."[50]

Boudreau was also Cleveland's most popular player. When Veeck first came to Cleveland, rumors abounded that he intended to replace Boudreau with Charlie Grimm or Jimmy Dykes, but in reality his choice was Casey Stengel. The Cleveland president soon discovered, however, that he could not ask Boudreau to step down as manager unless he wanted to take the chance that Boudreau would refuse to play for the Indians.[51] Rather than fire him as manager, Veeck was forced to bide his time. Instead, he made his opinion well known that he did not consider Boudreau a great strategist. In his standard speech, he damned Boudreau with faint praise, saying, "Boudreau is the greatest ball player, bar none, I've ever seen and"—a pregnant pause—"one of the best managers in the league."[52]

By fall of 1947, Veeck was convinced that the time was ripe for parting with Boudreau. He entered into negotiations during the World Series with Bill DeWitt to trade Boudreau, outfielder George Metkovich, and pitchers Red Embree and Bryan Stephens to the St. Louis Browns for shortstop Vern Stephens, outfielder Paul Lehner, and pitchers Jack Kramer and Bob Muncrief. The deal fell through, however, when Veeck refused DeWitt's request to talk to Boudreau about whether he was willing to give up his role as a player-manager. Veeck himself had already leaked news of a deal to several members of the press. When details reached Cleveland on October 3, 1947, via headlines in afternoon papers, the news caused an uproar. The Indians switchboard and local newspapers were swamped with negative calls. That afternoon, Veeck began to field phone calls in his New York hotel room from total strangers protesting the trade, and soon he was deluged by telegrams, one of which came from a Cleveland clergyman and read, "Don't come back to Cleveland if you trade Boudreau."[53]

"If the town's Terminal Tower had fallen into Public Square, the shock would not have been as widely felt," wrote Ed McAuley of the *Cleveland News*.[54] Indians fans, who admired Boudreau, were not only angry that he was going to be traded but were indignant that it was to the lowly Browns.[55] As newspaper headlines in Cleveland ignored the World Series to focus on the Boudreau affair, Veeck returned to town the following day to deal with the public relations nightmare he had created. Petitions against the trade were circulated all along Cleveland's main thoroughfare, Euclid Avenue, antitrade form letters were distributed in parking lots, and in a newspaper opinion poll approximately 80 percent of the respondents favored keeping Boudreau as manager.[56]

As usual, Veeck turned a potential disaster into a minor defeat. He met with several thousand people on Cleveland street corners, in businesses, and in bars and explained that he only wanted to improve the Indians and that he would bow to the will of the people by not trading Boudreau. Without having to acknowledge that the trade was already dead, he assured the fans that it was their opinion that saved Boudreau. Veeck was not unhappy to have all the publicity, even though most of it was negative. He personally replied to each of the five thousand fans who wrote him on the Boudreau situation. He also sent letters to the approximately five thousand fans who had participated in the *Cleveland News* poll. Much to Veeck's satisfaction, speculation on Boudreau's status remained in the news for the next seven weeks until the Browns finally traded Stephens and Kramer to the Red Sox on November 17, 1947. Boudreau was silent throughout the commotion. He had Veeck right where he wanted him and forced the Cleveland president to offer him a two-year contract. In return, Veeck got to name Boudreau's coaches—guaranteeing that Boudreau would have a lot of advisers.[57] The circumstances that led to Boudreau's retention proved quite fortuitous for Cleveland's 1948 pennant chances.

Another Veeck tenet was "keep your players content." As catcher Tom Jordan found out, Veeck was most agreeable to deal with. When Jordan was unsure of his future as a ballplayer, he sent Veeck a letter expressing a desire to retire. Veeck wrote back: "O.K., Retire." When Jordan wrote another letter saying that he had decided to remain in baseball, Veeck replied, "O.K., remain in baseball." Veeck also believed in keeping his players well paid. Salary holdouts were rare because he was usually able to give players what they felt they deserved. Bob Feller, Cleveland's premier gate attraction, always signed quickly when Veeck was president. "Even though his schedule requires him to appear only once in four days," Veeck noted, "I believe he attracts as many fans during the season as Ted Williams or Joe DiMaggio—and Bob should be paid at least as well as they are."[58] Feller's

1947 contract called for a base salary of approximately $50,000, and a series of bonus clauses based on attendance eventually netted Feller an additional $32,000.[59] Veeck used the bonus and incentive clauses with several players as a revenue-sharing device based on the premise that if the team did well, so should the players.

Veeck sincerely cared about his players. When he was with Milwaukee, outfielder Hal Peck had an operation on his arm. The doctor told him that it might respond better if he exercised it and got lots of sun. So Veeck arranged to have Peck stay at his Arizona ranch for the winter. Peck became a Veeck devotee for the remainder of his career.[60] At the beginning of the 1947 season, Veeck promised struggling third baseman Ken Keltner that, in return for a good year, he would receive a bonus. Keltner hit .257 with eleven home runs and seventy-six runs batted in. At the end of the season, Veeck called the third baseman in and asked him why he did not seem interested in the bonus. Keltner replied that he was sorry about his bad year. Veeck said, "Look, I've never had much time to bother about figures. That's why I hire statisticians and bookkeepers. In my opinion you've had a great year . . . here's your $5,000."[61]

He was not above rehabilitating players if he knew they could help the club, but his concern for their welfare went even deeper. When he acquired the Indians, they had a pitcher on the roster named Don Black who was an alcoholic. Veeck paid off Black's personal debts and persuaded him to attend Alcoholics Anonymous. After Black suffered a life-threatening brain hemorrhage almost two years later, Veeck raised $40,000 for him in a benefit night. When Black was well enough to realize what had happened, he told a reporter, "That was certainly swell of Bill, now we can buy a house."[62]

When players joined the Indians or any of Veeck's later teams (the Browns and White Sox), they knew they were going to be treated fairly. His magnanimous nature was legendary. When pitcher Bob Muncrief was traded to the Indians from the Browns in late 1947, Veeck asked Muncrief what he made with the Browns. He then increased it by $2,500 and promised him another $2,500 if the Indians did well at the gate.[63] Ned Garver, who pitched against the Indians in 1948 and later played for Veeck while he was with the Browns, recalled losing two back-to-back 1-0 shutouts against Cleveland and Boston. Veeck sent him a dozen open-collar shirts for each loss. Garver still has not opened Veeck's gifts. Veeck also gave him a leather-bound copy of a *Saturday Evening Post* article on Garver, along with a traveling case and a stainless steel toiletry kit. The baseball executive was also known to wire suits to players after big games and to pick up meal tabs for the entire team. "That was a big deal," Garver noted.[64]

Veeck also employed a little psychology as he shuffled roommates on road trips for 1948. He put Eddie Robinson with Joe Gordon, because he hoped Gordon's positive influence would keep the first baseman from getting down on himself. He put Hal Peck with Jim Hegan after the latter's long holdout because he hoped that Peck "would make Hegan believe that the greatest privilege that could be granted a ballplayer is the privilege of playing for Cleveland." Finally, he placed Johnny Berardino with Pat Seerey because Berardino "is one of those intense fellows who believes the greatest shame in the world is not doing your best every time. He hustles until the last out of every game, and he doesn't sit around crying about his hard luck. I want to expose Seerey to that spirit."[65]

By 1948, the team was a big business that left Veeck with little margin for error if it failed on the field. Indians business manager Rudy Schaffer projected that the team needed seasonal attendance exceeding a million fans for it to break even. Veeck's overhead, which was largely driven by the salaries of 782 employees, was the largest in team history by a wide margin. Indians personnel were broken down as follows: seasonal employees: 179 ticket-takers, 187 ushers, 122 special policemen, and 117 scorecard boys; regular employees: 20 office workers and executives, 5 dining room staff, 28 scouts, 58 players, and a grounds crew of 56. These figures did not include concessions or farm-system personnel.[66]

Veeck was determined not only to make the Indians a financial success but also to assault Larry MacPhail's recent attendance record of 2,265,512 established in 1946. In addition, he wanted to avenge his father, who held the previous record set in 1920. "As for myself," Veeck observed, "I would feel sore as hell if I had piled up an amazing record like 1,485,166 admissions for one season and some guy had come along and picked it all to pieces, the way MacPhail has."[67] During the 1947 season, he publicized the Indians by giving more than five hundred speeches throughout Ohio. His schedule was so overwhelming that on some days he made three presentations. Hal Lebovitz recalled offering to drive Veeck on a trip to Seville, Ohio, in hopes of getting a good story. The affable Veeck foiled Lebovitz's plan by sleeping all the way to Seville and back. Veeck's speeches were filled with corny jokes and old baseball stories—the kind that Midwestern crowds seemed to enjoy.[68] But, more than anything else, Veeck was the attraction. His relaxed style, open shirt, infectious smile, wittiness, and candor captivated almost everyone he met. "I do it because I think it gets results," he told a sportswriter. "People will remember they saw me and will come to see the team play."[69]

A consummate planner, Veeck left little to chance. Before the 1948 season, he conducted a media blitz that covered most of Ohio, western Pennsylvania, and western New York. Between January 1 and opening day, the Indians mailed out 35,000 pieces of literature about the team per month; they distributed 7,000 window posters, and just before opening day mounted 350 "Welcome Indians" street cards on telephone poles around town. More than a hundred banks, stores, and restaurants were supplied with picture displays of Cleveland players, and almost 350,000 schedules were mailed. In addition, the team offered Indians sketchbooks through 2,500 newsstands and distributed ten motion picture films to local movie houses. Stories about the team were mailed to 1,800 newspapers (dailies, weeklies, and school and trade papers), and Veeck appeared on radio at least twice a week.[70]

The Indians also targeted female customers—as Veeck himself wrote, "We wooed women shamelessly." Instead of treating women as "men customers in dresses," Veeck paid special attention to them by renovating and enlarging women's restrooms, giving away nylons and orchids as gate attractions, and providing baseball clinics for the uninitiated.[71] His most famous ploy was the installation of a nursery in Municipal Stadium's tower D.

From opening day through the remainder of the 1948 season, everything clicked for the Indians. On April 20, 73,163 fans streamed through the gates to see the Indians play the Browns, establishing a major-league record for an opening-day crowd. In four home dates, against the Browns, Tigers, and White Sox, the Indians drew 208,391 paid admissions—another record.[72] Veeck and the Indians targeted a scheduled double-header against the Yankees on May 23 as the date they wanted to break the major-league attendance record. Veeck was bedridden following his fourteenth leg operation but promoted the game furiously, achieving an advance sale of 57,000 tickets.[73] Only a continuous drizzle prevented the crowd of 78,431 from breaking MacPhail's 1938 record. Business manager Schaffer estimated that 40 percent of the crowd came from outside Cleveland and that every community in northeastern Ohio was represented. Veeck also got the railroads and bus companies to organize excursions to the game. His strategy worked. More than a hundred buses and twelve special trains carried fans to the game from places as far as Rochester, Niagara Falls, and Buffalo, New York; Erie and Pittsburgh, Pennsylvania; Toledo, Mansfield, Springfield, Zanesville, and Youngstown, Ohio; and even Detroit, Michigan, where the Tigers drew 35,000 themselves on May 23.[74]

Much of the overflow crowd lined Veeck's chain-link outfield fence—it was the first time in the history of Municipal Stadium that spectators were allowed on the field. Veeck, who watched the game on television from his hospital bed, could not contain his own enthusiasm. He escaped from his room early in the game, hailed a cab, and, though in great pain, reached the stadium press box in the third inning. Even though the Indians split the doubleheader with the Yankees and failed to break the attendance record, the game was a tremendous public relations and financial success. In the first game, Joe DiMaggio hit three home runs off Bob Feller and Bob Muncrief, and Joe Page shut the Indians down in the bottom of the ninth with the bases loaded to win 6-5 in what announcer Mel Allen described as "one of the tensest moments in sports" he had ever witnessed. By one account, "concessionaires sold five tons of hot dogs, 50,000 boxes of popcorn, and enough beer and cokes to float a battleship."[75] Nevertheless, Veeck was so disappointed that the Yankees still held the attendance record that he went back to his hospital bed to sulk and plan for the next time the Yankees returned to Cleveland.[76]

Then, on Sunday, June 20, the Indians unexpectedly broke the record during a Father's Day double-header against the Philadelphia Athletics. The Indians and Athletics were one and two in the league standings at the beginning of the week, and the team and its radio announcers promoted the game heavily with a "Bring Your Dad to the Game" message. Nevertheless, advance ticket sales were moderate. As the day turned warm and sunny, special trains and buses came pouring into town all morning. In a day when interstate highways systems were but a dream, sportswriter Ed McAuley wrote,

> Traffic arteries for 100 miles in all directions were clogged with private cars headed for Cleveland. As early as noon the bridges leading to the Stadium were thick with fans. And at 1:00 the last seat in the park was occupied and the public address horns round the Stadium started blaring "Standing Room Only." That didn't discourage the customers. They crowded three deep behind the lower deck seats. They overflowed the stands and stood, perhaps 5,000 of them, on the grass behind Veeck's fence-within-a-fence. Some of them found vantage points on the concrete runways beside the bleachers and stood there for the five hours—about 450 feet from home plate.[77]

In the sixth inning of the second game, Veeck received word that a new record had been established. As he swung through the aisles on his crutches, "wave after wave of applause followed him through the stands." When he reached the public-address system microphone, he began to speak: "Ladies and gentlemen, I want to take this opportunity to thank you on my own behalf and on behalf of the Cleveland club, for your attendance here today. The attendance today is eighty two thou——" Veeck's voice was lost in the thunder from the stands. A moment later he continued, "82,371, a new record. Thank you very much."[78] To top off a great day, the Indians won both games.

On September 28, Veeck sponsored a Joe Earley Night against the Chicago White Sox, in honor of Cleveland's fans. Earley was a twenty-six-year-old night watchman at a local automobile plant and a war veteran who wrote a local newspaper complaining that the ordinary fan should be honored with a night instead of a star baseball player. Veeck agreed. The promotion drew 64,000 fans, several of whom received typical Veeck gag gifts. Onto the field came an old Model T car, overflowing with beautiful girls, followed by livestock of almost every description. One customer got a sway-backed horse, and another was awarded three stepladders. One woman received four squirming rabbits. Another got a crate of leghorn pullets that, by design and to the great glee of the crowd, proceeded to escape all over the field. The Earleys received a yellow 1949 Ford convertible and countless gifts, including household appliances, clothes, luggage, and books. In addition, the first 20,000 women through the turnstiles received orchids flown in from Hawaii at a cost of $30,000. The team donated $1,000 to the American Cancer Society, and Indians fans also donated an undetermined amount.[79]

Veeck and the Indians set other attendance records, including a single game record of 86,288 fans during the final 1948 World Series game played in Cleveland. The Indians had never drawn more than a million fans in any season during their forty-five-year history before the coming of Bill Veeck. During Veeck's four-year tenure, the Indians averaged more than 1.7 million fans a year. The miracle on Lake Erie occurred during 1948 chiefly because the conditions were perfect for Bill Veeck. He built an exciting ball club, several of his players had outstanding years, Cleveland was starved for a pennant-winning team, and Veeck was one of the few owners who knew how to cultivate and entertain his guests—not bad for a team that operated in one of baseball's smallest markets and that in 1946 was still so penurious that it demanded the return of all foul balls hit into the stands.

Veeck proved that the time-honored method of depending on the local newspapers to market a team was archaic and out-moded thinking.[80] He gave the game and the team back to its followers. He gave Clevelanders, an ethnically diverse lot, a common experience and a topic everyone could discuss. Most important, the baseball renaissance in Cleveland meant that the community prospered as never before. Retail businesses, restaurants, hotels, and cab companies benefited directly from the additional one million people who came from out of town that year because of the Indians.[81]

At age 34, Bill Veeck reached the apex of his career as an owner. Although he would own the St. Louis Browns and the Chicago White Sox twice, Veeck was never able to duplicate the excitement of the miracle on Lake Erie. In November 1949, he sold the Indians to a group headed by businessman Ellis Ryan because he needed a large sum of money as part of his divorce settlement with his first wife, Eleanor.[82] Veeck's restless nature and the need for new challenges were also motives for parting with the team. As Veeck himself noted, the new owners paid a huge sum "largely for the goodwill we had built up in Northern Ohio in three and a half years. They bought one of the largest and most enthusiastic fan populations in the major leagues."[83] In 1950, the Indians possessed an advance sale of over a million tickets. The team's popularity continued through 1956, after which it began to erode because of poor performance on the field.

11

Ownership Has Its Privileges

The Pivotal Era was a transitional period for ownership. For a brief time following World War II, baseball maintained a firm grip on the attention of a sports-starved public. Radio was still broadening baseball's appeal and attracting the interest of millions of fans, many of whom had never seen a live game. Television, which was just entering the barroom, did not overtake the living room until the end of the era. The huge surge in attendance between 1946 and 1949 was fueled by the success of night baseball—an evening attraction that encouraged family attendance. By 1948, only Chicago's Wrigley Field was without lights.[1] Thirteen franchises established new team attendance records during the era. The New York Yankees surpassed the previous major-league attendance record of 1,485,166 set by the Chicago Cubs in 1929 six years in a row between 1946 and 1951. Nevertheless, their high mark of 2,373,901, established in 1948, was easily surpassed by Cleveland's record attendance of 2,620,627 set during the same season. Several teams recorded unprecedented profits. Of baseball's sixteen major-league teams, only the Boston Red Sox, with their high payroll and burgeoning farm system, failed to show a profit for more than two seasons during the era.[2]

Prospective owners, with wartime profits in their pockets, were attracted to the game as a diversion and potential tax shelter, and current owners found themselves with a huge influx of returning players, a public hungry for the return of prewar baseball, and the potential, at long last, of making a profit. The need for change was inevitable. When Del Webb, Larry MacPhail, and Dan Topping acquired the New York Yankees from the estate of Jacob Ruppert in 1945, then–Yankee president Ed Barrow ran the entire operation by himself. "If a player needed a dozen bats," recalled Webb, "he had to get the okay of Barrow. . . . Baseball," he added, "needed bigger operational methods."[3]

Although wedded to tradition, even the game's old guard—the Mack, Griffith, Comiskey, and Stoneham families—were not immune to change. Now in his eighties and always standing straight and looking stately in his dark suit and old-fashioned starched high-collared shirts, Connie Mack, the president of the Philadelphia Athletics, more than any other figure represented baseball's greatest symbolic strength—its continuity.[4] A piece of living history, Mack played with or managed almost three generations of players and went on to win nine pennants and five World Series. When the Depression cut into attendance and profits, however, Mack dismantled his 1933 and 1934 pennant-winning clubs. From that point, the hapless A's were a perennial second-division team, finishing last nine times and seriously contending again only during the 1948 pennant race.

The A's maintained a modest farm system and a scouting corps of ten. Nevertheless, in the 1940s a constant flow of players, such as Lou Brissie and Joe Coleman, were sent Mack's way by an adoring network of friends and admirers.

The Athletics also suffered from competing in a two-team city. Fortunately, before 1950, the Philadelphia Phillies were even less competitive than the Athletics. Moreover, the Phillies also used Shibe Park and paid the A's 10¢ out of every admission for its use, and the football Philadelphia Eagles paid them 15 percent of their gate for each home game. Between the two clubs, the A's earned $175,000 in 1950. The concessions department, which was the A's most profitable unit, also operated during all events at Shibe and at nearby Temple Stadium.[5]

Mack's players revered him. "To the players he was 'Mr. Mack' in conversation, but 'The old man' when they spoke of him to others."[6] In 1945, at age eighty-three, Mack was still relatively sharp. He never wore a uniform in the dugout, and hung his coat on a hook above a chair in which no one else dared sit. From this vantage point, he commanded the field with a wave of his score card, and everyone paid close attention. Former A's player Charlie Metro recalled that Mack "knew everything that was going to happen. He knew the potential of what a guy could do . . . [and] he made fantastic moves."[7] So identified was Mack with his scorecard that, on the celebration of his fiftieth year as a manager in 1944, President Roosevelt sent him a telegram that read, "Long may your scorecard wave."[8]

Although Mack was revered, he was not a tin God. In 1950 Red Smith noted his paradoxical characteristics when he said that Mack could be "reasonable and obstinate," "courtly and fierce," "kind-hearted and hard fisted," "autocratic and shy," and "completely lovable."[9] Grantland Rice wrote that Mack "could swear colorfully at the proper time."[10] Players rarely forgot a Mack tirade. Metro was present at a 1945 meeting called by Mack after the A's loss to the Browns on a single by Pete Gray. Having lost fifteen of the last sixteen games, Mack was frustrated. "Gentlemen," he began, "that was atrocious, disgusting, and embarrassing. To be beaten by a one-armed ballplayer when I've got ballplayers who have two arms and two legs. Now God dammit, I'm not mad; God dammit, I'm not mad." Then, hitting the table hard enough to make the ashtray jump high into the air, he exclaimed, "[But] if that one-armed so-and-so beats us again, there won't be another ballplayer here with two arms!"[11]

As the 1940s passed, Mack gradually lost his hold on the team. In 1950, family members fought over control of the club, with Mack's two oldest sons, Earle and Roy, temporarily emerging victorious. To purchase the team's outstanding stock, the three Macks (Connie Sr., Earle, and Roy) pooled their resources and borrowed money from a friend. They then mortgaged Shibe Park to pay off their short-term loan.[12] This deal put the franchise in a financial hole from which the family never emerged. The mortgage and the rising popularity of the Phillies doomed the franchise in Philadelphia. As Red Smith noted, "The last owners to go broke were Roy and Earle Mack, and they did that on merit."[13] Tired from a busy schedule, ticker-tape parades, and other events spawned by the celebration of his golden jubilee year with the A's, Connie Mack Sr., officially retired in October 1950.

Mack's retirement left Washington's Clark Griffith as the last of the old guard in control of a franchise. During his own playing career, Griffith, nicknamed the "Old Fox," used scuffed balls, spitters, guile, and intimidation to compile a record of 236 wins and 139 losses. In 1901, he helped Ban Johnson and Charles Comiskey found the American League, and eleven years later he purchased a 10 percent interest in the Washington Senators. He also managed the Senators—a team that finished no higher than sixth place during its first eleven years. Indeed, by 1911 the parody about Washington—"First in war; first in peace, and last in the American League"—was a favorite with baseball fans everywhere.[14] Griffith turned the team around, however, with second-place finishes in 1912 and 1913. By 1919, Griffith entered into an agreement with William Richardson, a wealthy Philadelphia grain dealer and exporter, allowing him to gain full control of the club.

With players and managers such as Walter Johnson, Heinie Manush, Ossie Bluege, Joe Judge, Goose Goslin, Sam Rice, Bucky Harris, and Joe Cronin, his teams won pennants in 1924, 1925, and 1933. Although the Senators remained competitive through the war years, they finished in the league's first division only twice (1943 and 1945). The team was a family affair. The Griffiths, who had no offspring of their own, took in seven children when a brother of Mrs. Griffith died. They adopted two of them—Calvin, who became vice president of the club, and Mrs. Thelma Griffith Haynes, the wife of pitcher Joe Haynes. The others included a niece, Mildred Robertson Cronin (the wife of Red Sox general manager Joe Cronin), Sherry Robertson, a utility player with the Senators, and nephews James and William Robertson, who managed the concessions at Griffith Stadium.[15]

As a family-run business, the Senators existed on the financial edge and the team cleared a million in attendance only once (in 1946, with 1,027,216) through 1951. Griffith was cautious by nature, sometimes argumentative and contentious, and he did not adapt easily to change. For instance, he was an outspoken opponent of night baseball until President Roosevelt asked him to provide World War II workers with an opportunity to attend night games. As attendance increased dramatically, Griffith reversed course and the Senators ended up scheduling more night games than any team during the war.[16] Griffith was also slow to embrace a strong farm system and employed just three scouts, relying heavily on superscout Joe Cambria, who operated over the entire Western Hemisphere and kept the Senators well supplied with players from both sides of the Rio Grande.[17]

When Griffith's benefactor, William Richardson, died in 1950, the latter's share of the team was acquired by John Jachym, a thirty-one-year-old ex-Marine who once scouted for Branch Rickey. Griffith disliked anything affiliated with New York, wanted nothing to do with a Rickey disciple, and froze Jachym out of the club's operation. Jachym told reporters that, had Griffith accepted him as a partner, he would have created a downtown ticket office, initiated season ticket sales, hired new scouts and a public relations director, installed a new scoreboard that would have included National League results, and purchased the triple-A Buffalo franchise for Washington. In the spring of 1950, Jachym sold his shares at a substantial profit to H. Gabriel Murphy, a Washington insurance broker and old Griffith friend. Murphy, the new silent partner, was named vice president of the Senators.[18]

Once Griffith regained control, he refused to abandon his outmoded management style. Instead, he decreased the Senators' farm system from ten clubs in 1950 to six in 1951.[19] The Senators' backwardness and Griffith Stadium's lack of modern amenities and insufficient parking led historian David Voight to observe that in 1950 the A's and Senators both "resembled a general store in a supermarket era."[20]

Another team that began the Pivotal Era looking like a general store operation was the Chicago White Sox—the only franchise continuously owned by one family since its inception. Charles Comiskey, better known as the "Old Roman," formed the team soon after he and Ban Johnson founded the American League in 1901. During World War I, Comiskey built a powerhouse that took American League pennants in 1917 and 1919. The White Sox, however, never fully recovered from the Black Sox scandal of 1919. The team finished in the first division of the American League only six times between the scandal and 1950. As the Pivotal Era dawned in 1946, the White Sox were led by Grace Reidy Comiskey, Charles's daughter-in-law. Mrs. Comiskey, the daughter of a Chicago street car conductor, had three children—Dorothy Rigney, the club's treasurer and wife of former pitcher John Rigney, Grace Comiskey, an assistant secretary with the team, and twenty-year-old Charles A. Comiskey II.[21]

Grace Comiskey operated in the shadow of her famous father-in-law. She absorbed all of the criticism and heard the occasional taunt from a disgruntled fan, "Why don't they put in old lady Comiskey?" She operated on the philosophy that women were not allowed in the "inner baseball circles to correct things" and depended heavily on, first, Harry Grabiner and, then, Leslie O'Connor, Judge Landis's old administrative assistant, to run the team.[22]

The designated savior of the Sox was young Chuck Comiskey. Mrs. Comiskey prevented the team from being sold in 1939, on the premise that the club would some day come under young Comiskey's direction.[23] Although his mother retained the title of president, Chuck Comiskey took over the club in late 1948, following two years of training in the White Sox farm system.

Comiskey soon hired Frank Lane, a former Cincinnati sportswriter, football and basketball referee, and president of the American Association, as the team's general manager. Lane was a breath of fresh air in Chicago. The attendance boom allowed him to spend money freely on new talent. The Comiskey family, which lived for years on what could be squeezed from the ball club, was often criticized for its penurious ways. Chicagoans were used to hearing the claim, "They wouldn't spend $1.98 for Joe DiMaggio."[24] Lane would later earn the sobriquets "Trader Lane" and "Frantic Frank" for making 192 moves involving 298 players during his six seasons as general manager of the White Sox.[25] Many of the players acquired by Lane, including Nellie Fox and Billy Pierce, provided the nucleus for respectability in the 1950s and led the club to the American League pennant in 1959. But it was a pennant that the Comiskey family would not enjoy.[26]

Another owner who lived almost entirely off the earnings of his team was Horace Stoneham. He inherited the New York Giants in 1936 on the death of his father, Charles C. Stoneham. The elder Stoneham, along with fellow stockholders John McGraw and Judge Francis X. McQuade, acquired controlling interest in the team in 1919. The senior Stoneham amassed a fortune on the curb market in the financial district on Broad Street.[27] As a so-called "bucket-shop operator," both he and his customers wagered on the rise and fall of securities. Stoneham also speculated with his customers' money.[28] Moreover, he was a gambler who owned a race track and associated with a number of gangster types. Although Stoneham's questionable financial deals kept him tied up in litigation, he refused to give up the Giants. He was also adamant that his son Horace would someday inherit the team.[29]

Although he matriculated at Fordham, Horace Stoneham's real education began after he went west to work in a California copper mine. The venture was approved by his father, who hoped that the experience would curb his son's wayward behavior and drinking habits. When young Stoneham returned to New York, his father made him learn how to run a baseball club—everything from the sale of tickets to grounds keeping and secretarial work. As an owner, Horace Stoneham was reclusive.[30] He kept to his office on Forty-Second Street and his father's window in the clubhouse.[31] According to Bill Veeck, Stoneham had two occupations in life— he owned the Giants and he drank.[32] Since Stoneham rarely appeared in public, Eddie Brannick, the team's traveling secretary, also served as the club's spokesman. Nevertheless, Stoneham was very much in charge, participated in league meetings, influenced club policies, and was an astute trader. From the late 1930s through the mid-1940s the Giants put together one of the most impressive groups of sluggers ever assembled in the National League, but they could not contend. Thus, after Leo Durocher was hired in 1948, Stoneham allowed his new manager to reshape the team by adding speed and defense through shrewd trades and the acquisition of African American players. The strategy resulted in two pennants and allowed Stoneham to live off his baseball revenue well into the 1970s.

Another class of owners, the gentleman sportsmen, assumed control of their clubs in the mid-1920s and during the Great Depression. Several of these owners, notably Tom Yawkey of the Red Sox, Philip K. Wrigley of the Cubs, Walter O. Briggs of the Tigers, and Powel Crosley of the Reds, were wealthy men. Yawkey and Wrigley inherited their wealth. The Red Sox owner, who was a millionaire at age sixteen, was adopted, after both his parents died, by William Yawkey, then owner of the Detroit Tigers. The Yawkeys made their money in mining, timber, tin, and oil. At the time of Tom Yawkey's death in 1976, it was estimated that he was worth as much as $200,000,000.[33]

Philip K. Wrigley was the son of William Wrigley, the founder of the Wrigley chewing gum empire. The senior Wrigley parlayed the popularity of the Juicy Fruit, Spearmint, and Doublemint gum labels into a $40 million enterprise. When Wrigley died in 1932, his son inherited not only the gum company but also Catalina Island off the coast of Southern California, hotels, other buildings, and the Chicago Cubs. Following World War II, Wrigley's personal wealth increased to more than $100 million as gum sales experienced a phenomenal rise.[34]

Detroit's Walter O. Briggs and Powel Crosley of Cincinnati were self-made-millionaire industrialists. Crosley was an engineering genius who turned his ideas into pioneering manufacturing efforts such as automobiles and radios, refrigerators, and other appliances. His radio station, WLW in Cincinnati, with its 50,000-watt transmitter, was the most powerful station in the world in 1935.[35] With no other prospect in sight during the height of the Depression, Crosley was approached by Larry MacPhail to purchase the Reds from the Central Trust Company of Cincinnati. Crosley was a lapsed baseball fan who personally broadcast the first Cincinnati baseball game ever heard on radio.[36] His rationale for purchasing the team was to keep it in Cincinnati and maintain the city's baseball heritage. Although MacPhail appealed to Crosley's civic pride, both men were undoubtedly aware of the promotional value that the Reds would provide WLW.[37] Conversely, Crosley's support allowed MacPhail to purchase the players he needed to make the Reds a contender.

When Walter O. Briggs died in 1952, he was said to have amassed a fortune of more than $50 million. In the business world, Briggs "was known as a man with uncanny judgment, lightning like decision [capability] and cold common sense."[38] He began his career working in a Michigan Central car shop at age fifteen and at the turn of the century got a start in the automotive business. In 1909, he organized the Briggs Manufacturing Company, which soon became the major supplier of automobile bodies for the Ford Motor Company and the largest independent manufacturer of auto bodies in the United States. Briggs was credited with perfecting "the mass production methods that brought millions he comfort and convenience of the closed car."[39] A lifelong baseball fan, Briggs bought into the Detroit Tigers in 1920 and purchased the controlling interest in the club following the death of owner Frank Navin in 1935.

For all four men, ownership of a team was akin to having an expensive hobby. Tom Yawkey was the most avid fan of the group. He wintered at his South Carolina estate and resided in New York and Boston during the summer. Unlike the other three owners, he left the day-to-day operations of his business, Yawkey Enterprises of New York, to others and instead focused his attention on his team. He was close to several players, notably Ted Williams, and often appeared in the clubhouse. He also occasionally suited up to take batting practice long before a game.[40] Yawkey rarely

Depicted in these two photographs (top, from left to right) are Clark Griffith, Tom Yawkey, and Boston Red Sox general manager Joe Cronin; and (right) Commissioner Chandler and Connie Mack. Clark Griffith and Connie Mack represented the game's old guard and were venerated by many, including Chandler. Red Sox owner Tom Yawkey, a millionaire by age sixteen, was a gentleman sportsman. (Special Collections and Archives, University of Kentucky)

interfered with the team's front office operations, which were run by Eddie Collins and Joe Cronin.[41]

Briggs employed a series of general managers/executive vice presidents to run the Tigers, including Jack Zeller, George Trautman, and Billy Evans. In 1940, Briggs fell ill and was left partially paralyzed. At that time, he insisted that the Tigers acquire the best talent possible, and he defied usual baseball wisdom by purchasing a number of veteran ballplayers. When asked why, he explained, "My life is not certain. I want to be the head of a winning ball club before I'm called out at the plate." In 1940, the Tigers won the pennant.[42]

For Wrigley, ownership of the Chicago Cubs was a bittersweet experience. The Cubs were his father's hobby, not his—the mechanically oriented son was much more at home tinkering with his collection of antique automobiles. He was modest and shy, and, as Chicago sportswriter Ed Burns noted, "William Wrigley reveled in the spotlight just as his son P.K. shunned it."[43] Wrigley refused to take full control of the club until 1934, when he said, "When you own the club, you get the blame for what happened, so you might as well be president."[44] After the Cubs won pennants in 1935 and 1938, the unpredictable Wrigley appointed newspaperman Jim Gallagher to be general manager of the team in 1940. Wrigley challenged Gallagher, one of the owner's most severe critics, to make the Cubs better. Since winning the pennant in 1945 with Gallagher at the helm, the Cubs have not won another. When the Cubs finished last in 1948 for only the second time in their history, Wrigley blamed himself for not taking control of the team. "Unfortunately," he apologized, "I own many different businesses. I don't have time."[45]

Of the four owners, Cincinnati's Powel Crosley was the least involved with his team. He refused "to dictate team policy" and explained that his philosophy was "to put the best available baseball men in charge and give them free rein."[46] Fortunately, the Reds received excellent leadership from Larry MacPhail and then from Warren Giles and Gabe Paul. Crosley allowed the inventive MacPhail to promote the team and approved of his ideas to install lights and introduce night baseball. Giles capitalized on MacPhail's work. Following the latter's departure in 1936, Giles built a modest farm system and added key players, such as pitcher Bucky Walters, to bring the Reds back-to-back pennants in 1939 and 1940. Giles accepted the presidency of the National League in 1951 and was succeeded as general manager by his faithful lieutenant of fifteen years, Gabe Paul. Though Cincinnati was baseball's smallest market, the Reds treated their players well—their salaries attained acceptable levels, and they stayed at first-class hotels on the road. Nevertheless, the team's modest farm system failed to produce enough players, particularly pitchers, for the Reds to become contenders during the 1950s.

The gentleman sportsmen were followed during the 1940s by a new generation of owners, the capitalists. These were men with money, either earned or inherited, who were looking at the game as a financial opportunity and operated their clubs as businesses. In Boston, construction company owners Lou Perini, Guido Rugo, and Joe Maney, better known as the "Three Steam Shovels," purchased the Braves from Bob Quinn in 1943. In the same year, DuPont heir Bob Carpenter purchased the Philadelphia Phillies from William Cox. Two years later, the Yankees were acquired by Del Webb, Larry MacPhail, and Dan Topping from the estate of Jacob Ruppert. Although MacPhail was a baseball man, Topping and Webb were from totally different backgrounds. Webb was a contractor, while Topping had inherited his wealth. Finally, in 1947 the Pittsburgh Pirates were sold by the heirs of Barney Dreyfuss to a group that included Indianapolis banker Frank McKinney, lawyer/businessman Thomas P. Johnson of Pittsburgh, real-estate tycoon John Galbreath from Columbus, Ohio, and Hollywood entertainer Bing Crosby.

Of the four teams, only the Pittsburgh Pirates failed to achieve success during the 1940s. The team was previously owned by Florence Dreyfuss, Barney's widow. Under Dreyfuss, the Pirates had won National League pennants in 1901-3, 1909, 1925, and 1927. Following Dreyfuss's death in 1932, the team was operated by his son-in-law, William Benswanger, a classical pianist who never spent more than the Pirates took in. By 1946, beautiful Forbes Field was in poor physical condition, and the Pirates' morale, shaken by Robert Murphy's attempt to unionize them, had fallen to an all-time low. The Pirates were sold to a group organized by McKinney in August 1946 for $2.25 million. The purchase included four minor-league properties and Forbes Field.[47]

McKinney, the son of an Indianapolis fireman, had quit high school to take a job as a bank messenger. He eventually became a bank president and treasurer of the Democratic National Committee. As a boy, he dreamed of owning a baseball team, and the Pirates was his third, following part-ownership of the Louisville and Indianapolis minor-league franchises.[48] One of his partners was John Galbreath, a Columbus developer and real estate man. Galbreath, an Ohio University graduate, was the president of the Ohio Board of Realtors and a long-time friend of U.S. Senator John Bricker of Ohio. The millionaire maintained extensive real estate holdings in Ohio, West Virginia, Alabama, and Pennsylvania. During the late 1940s and early 1950s, he planned and built a huge development west of Columbus. He also purchased the Terminal Tower complex in Cleveland for $30 million and was president of a company that built a thirty-five-story skyscraper in downtown Pittsburgh to house the Mellon Bank and U.S. Steel.[49] As a thoroughbred horse owner and breeder, Galbreath also sought and received Commissioner Chandler's blessing to own a piece of the Pirates.

The other two partners in the Pirates' quartet of owners were Tom Johnson, a Pittsburgh attorney, and entertainer Bing Crosby. Johnson, the scion of a wealthy and established Pittsburgh family, provided the new ownership with a hometown flavor.[50] Crosby, on the other hand, gave the team instant excitement. As a screen and radio star, he was at the height of his popularity, and his beautiful baritone voice was heard constantly over the airways. Crosby loved golf, horse racing, and baseball, raised and raced thoroughbreds, and retained a large financial stake in the Del Mar racetrack near San Diego. In the early 1940s, he attempted to buy into the Boston Braves, which were then owned by Charles Francis Adams, but failed when a jockey scandal at Del Mar led Judge Landis to squelch the deal.[51]

The Pirates' new management poured money into the team. "If it will help give Pittsburgh a winner," said McKinney, "we'll buy the Brooklyn Bridge."[52] They purchased reluctant star Hank Greenberg from Detroit, built a bullpen area in left field nicknamed "Greenberg Gardens" to enable Greenberg and Ralph Kiner to hit more home runs, and restored Forbes Field to its old grandeur. While the park sparkled, Greenberg Gardens was a disappointment. Some Pittsburgh fans joked, "They call it Greenberg Gardens, because everybody hits home runs there but Greenberg."[53] By the mid-1950, the new owners had spent $5,021,450 and had gone through 123 players, two managers, and six coaches and finished seventh, fourth, and sixth in consecutive years.[54]

At the end of 1950, the Pirates were in last place, with only Ralph Kiner's prodigious home run hitting to attract fans.[55] McKinney became discouraged and in 1950 sold his interest in the team to his former partners. Galbreath, the new majority stockholder, became president. Realizing that he needed help, Galbreath brought in a skilled hand to run the team—none other than Branch Rickey himself.

Pennsylvania's other National League team, the Philadelphia Phillies, was also beset with a multitude of problems. During the 1934-43 period, the Phillies were the doormat of the National League, with a .344 overall winning percentage. Under the ownership of Gerald Nugent, the team existed off the sale of players to other teams. By 1943, the Phillies were deeply in debt to the National League. The league took over the club and allowed lumberman William Cox to purchase it. Cox, however, was caught betting on the team and was thrown out of the game by Judge Landis. In late 1943, the team was purchased for $450,000 by Robert R.M. Carpenter Sr. to provide his son with a challenge. Carpenter was a multimillionaire partner in E.I. Du Pont de Nemours, of Wilmington, Delaware. As a former director, he was instrumental in transforming Du Pont from a company that almost exclusively manufactured explosives to one featuring diversified chemical production.[56]

Robert Jr., who was an end on Duke's 1939 Rose Bowl team, attempted to work for Du Pont, but his heart was in sports. Determined to give sports his full attention, Carpenter became a promoter, a fight manager, and operated both women's and men's basketball teams. In 1940 he became half-owner of the Wilmington franchise in the Interstate League—an affiliate of the Philadelphia Athletics. In view of his limited experience, the elevation of Robert Carpenter Jr. to president of the Phillies at age twenty-eight seemed a potential disaster, the classic example of the rich kid being handed a new toy. Red Smith once described Carpenter as "a princeling of the blood scion of the vast Du Pont empire, who eats bologna on pumpernickel only when he feels like it."[57] Such was not the case. Carpenter distinguished himself from other sportsmen owners by treating the team as his main business.[58] "Baseball is a sport," he noted, "but it is a sport that should pay for itself, just like any other business. What I want is dollar and cents results."[59]

Unlike the Pittsburgh Pirates, the Phillies did not wave their money around. Instead, they hired former Red Sox and Yankee star pitcher Herb Pennock to run the team. Pennock, nicknamed the "Squire of Kennett Square," was a Scotch-Irish Quaker renowned for his photographic memory and calm, gentlemanly demeanor. Umpires loved him because, as a player, he never disputed a call.[60] Not long after Pennock was hired, Carpenter was inducted into the army, and the job of resurrecting the Phillies fell to the new general manager. Pennock enlarged the Phillies farm system and used Carpenter money to sign a number of good young players to bonus contracts, including Granville Hamner, Stan Lopata, Richie Ashburn, Bubba Church, Robin Roberts, and pitching phenom Curt Simmons.

When Simmons was signed, Philadelphia sportswriter Frank Yeutter wrote that "the only scout who wasn't parked on the Simmons front porch that day was Daniel Boone."[61] After Pennock died unexpectedly in 1948, Carpenter assumed the position of general manager himself. After spending approximately $3,500,000 on the team over a six-year period on salaries, bonuses, player acquisitions, scouting, and a farm system, Carpenter's patience was rewarded with a pennant in 1950—the first by the Phillies since 1915.[62]

Unlike Carpenter, the management of the Boston Braves did not have the patience to stay the course. The "Three Steam Shovels," construction magnates Lou Perini, Joe Maney, and Guido Rugo, acquired the Braves in

1944. As capitalists, they adopted what they described as "a business man's approach" to solving baseball problems.[63] If something did not work right away, they would alter course and try something different. They purchased a majority interest in the team for $250,000 because they were tired of being asked to put up money to cover the club's routine operational bills. The Braves were a perennial second-division team, completely run down, debt ridden, and out of financial resources. In addition, they faced stiff competition from the more popular Red Sox, who played in the more attractive Fenway Park. The Braves' low attendance figures inspired one newspaper man to write that "the club frequently played to more pigeons than paying guests."[64]

Perini, Maney, and Rugo first met as competitive bidders on numerous construction projects and later combined forces on larger projects such as deep-pressure tunnels, ordnance depots, and highway and airport construction. Among their projects was the Tuscarora Mountain tunnel, in Pennsylvania, and the Park River Conduit, in Hartford, Connecticut.[65] All three men had similar backgrounds. Maney began his career as a timekeeper on Boston's Washington Street subway tunnel.[66] By 1931, he had formed the C.J. Maney Company—a concern that by late 1945 was doing $30 million worth of postwar construction contracts.[67] Rugo, the treasurer of the Rugo Construction Company, was the son of the Padua stone mason who founded the company business.[68]

The leader of the group and team president was Perini, whose Italian immigrant father, a bricklayer by trade, formed the family construction company. In 1935, Perini became president of B. Perini and Sons—a multifaceted company that eventually did business all over the world, building dams, tunnels, highways, watersheds, army camps, docks, office buildings, pipelines, industrial plants, and airports. In the decade before he took over the Braves, Perini's company did more than $100,000,000 worth of business.[69] Not all of his business was untainted. In 1937, for instance, Perini and Maney pleaded guilty to income tax–evasion charges stemming from kickbacks given to a Massachusetts politician during the construction of the Quabbin Dam. The partners were fined heavily but escaped a prison sentence.[70]

To his credit, Perini operated the Braves with panache and imagination. For night games, he outfitted the team with satin uniforms, installed neon foul poles, employed marching bands, and set off fireworks. The Braves gave away automobiles and free trips to spring training, placed suggestion boxes around the ballpark, and became the first major-league team to offer fried clams at their concession stands.[71] The Three Steam Shovels were fortunate to inherit executive John Quinn, a Boston College graduate whose father Bob had run the team since 1936. With the infusion of new financing, Quinn and the new owners were determined to make the Braves a competitive force in the National League. Between 1946 and 1948, they spent more than $500,000 to renovate single-decked Braves Field, installed lights, and expanded their farm system from one team during the war to fourteen by 1948. Finally, they lured manager Billy Southworth away from the Cardinals with a large contract offer.

The most difficult task was the acquisition of players. The Braves purchased so many players from the Cardinals that they became known in the Midwest as the "Cape Cod Cardinals." Boston even offered the Cardinals a blank check for Marty Marion and Whitey Kurowski. While none of the ex-Cardinal players helped the Braves, other acquisitions, such as Bob Elliott, Earl Torgeson, Jeff Heath, Nelson Potter, Eddie Stanky, Mike McCormick, and Alvin Dark, proved propitious. After an investment of $3.5 million, a National League pennant, and four profitable seasons in succession, the team was out of debt and showed a surplus of $4,537.00 in 1949.[72]

Perini, Maney, and Rugo purchased Braves Field in 1949 and made plans to increase its capacity from 39,000 to 55,000, but then disaster struck. First, the Braves faltered on the field. Second, when attendance declined throughout the major leagues in 1950, the Braves found that they were unable to compete with the Red Sox and Tom Yawkey's millions. They experienced a rapid loss of attendance, from a high of 1,455,439 in 1948 to 487,475 in 1951.[73] With the magic gone, Perini and his partners seemed powerless to prevent the slide. Instead, the Braves president began to look wistfully at the possibility of expansion on the Pacific Coast or in Milwaukee—the location of the Braves' triple-A farm club, where a new stadium was under construction.[74] As Bill Veeck cruelly noted, Perini proved in Boston and in his later ventures that he "had no capacity whatsoever for harnessing the enthusiasm of the winning years to carry them [the Braves] through the poor ones."[75]

As in Boston, clubs in two-team cities were especially vulnerable, and St. Louis, with the Browns and Cardinals, was another good example. The Mound City was the smallest baseball market to support two teams. Between 1901 and 1944, the combined attendance of the teams exceeded one million only twice (1922 and 1928). The lack of larger metropolises to the south, the already tight scheduling of games dictated by train travel, and the great distances to the West, mitigated against league expansion. Rickey's influence, and his creation of the farm system, was in part responsible for the continued existence of two teams in St. Louis between 1936 and 1953. The farm system changed the operational philosophy of baseball forever, as it reinvigorated the minor leagues, allowed small-market teams to compete with the rest of the league, and, in the case of the Browns, allowed such teams to stave off bankruptcy.[76]

Owning a baseball franchise in St. Louis was a constant struggle. When Sam Breadon became the majority owner and president of the Cardinals in 1920, Rickey continued running the team. While Breadon approved all transactions, it was Rickey's farm system, ability to judge talent, and expertise and genius as general manager that propelled the Cardinals to seven National League pennants between 1926 and 1942. Although highly successful, the Cardinals failed to draw more than 762,000 admissions in any season during the period. The lack of fan support caused Breadon to explore moving the team to Detroit in 1931. Rickey also irritated Breadon because he received most of the credit for the Cardinals' success and because his percentage of the team's profits, which he received in addition to his base salary, continued to increase. By 1941, he made approximately $88,000.[77] After selling his Pierce-Arrow dealership in 1936, Breadon was left with little to do.[78] Wanting to run the Cardinals himself, he deposed Rickey in 1942. Although the Cardinals won pennants in 1943, 1944, and 1946, the move eventually led to a period of decline. The Cardinals' continued success was not a tribute to Breadon's leadership, but instead to the great depth of the organization assembled by Rickey.

Sam Breadon in many ways typified the image of the hard-boiled, uncommunicative, tight-fisted owner. He was a native New Yorker who turned the $35 he made selling molasses-coated popcorn during the 1904 St. Louis World's Fair into a career in the automotive business. He vowed that he would never be poor again. By 1917, his successful Pierce-Arrow dealership and investments in property and bonds allowed him to buy stock in the nearly bankrupt Cardinals. After loaning the team more than $20,000, the team's board of directors asked him to assume the presidency, in 1920. In 1921, Breadon made a lease arrangement with Phil Ball, the owner of the Browns, who agreed to share Sportsman's Park with the Cardinals as cotenants. This enabled Breadon to sell rundown Robison Field to the St. Louis Board of Education for $200,000 and to put the Cardinals on a sound financial footing. During the next twenty years, Breadon's low-budget operation was dictated by the realities of St. Louis baseball.[79]

Rickey and Breadon maintained a modest payroll by developing young players and shipping them elsewhere when they reached higher salary brackets. Though Breadon could be quite generous in private (he assisted pitchers Grover Cleveland Alexander and Mort Cooper in times of need), he was unable to recognize the economic realities brought about by World War II. Unwilling to pay stars like Stan Musial what they were worth, he lost many players to the Mexican League.

In 1947, Breadon, who was fighting prostate cancer, sold the Cardinals to Postmaster General Robert Hannegan and St. Louis attorney Fred Saigh for $4,060,800. The terms of the sale, which was engineered by Saigh, were astonishing. Hannegan and Saigh anted up only $60,800 in cash to close the deal. The purchase was consummated through short-term loans with the First National Bank and the St. Louis Union Trust Company ($3,000,000), loans of $350,000 and $550,000 from Sam Breadon, and a $100,000 loan from Mrs. Mark Steinberg (wife of a St. Louis broker and former minority Cardinal stockholder). The cash portion of the purchase was $10,000 in capital and $50,800 cash described as surplus. The purchasers essentially used the team's existing assets to acquire the club. They purchased the team's $2.6 million in accumulated profits and then mortgaged their three top minor-league parks at Houston, Columbus, and Rochester for $1.5 million. These loans were secured by property Sam Breadon intended to use for a new stadium, which was also acquired in the deal, and by two buildings owned by Saigh.[80]

Hannegan, who resigned his position as Postmaster General to take over the presidency of the team, was an unabashed baseball fan who as a boy sold peanuts at Robison Field. A popular football player at St. Louis University, he was a powerful St. Louis political figure who became Chairman of the Democratic National Committee during the Truman Administration. Suffering from hypertension, he was able to serve as president of the team for only a year. Saigh and Hannegan each had the right of first refusal on the sale of the other's stock. When Hannegan came to Saigh in 1949 with a $1.2 million offer from Joseph Kennedy, Saigh was forced to match the bid. Saigh later noted, "It wasn't worth that much. He was only in it a season without an outlay of a penny. As you know, I haven't thought too much of the Kennedys since that time."[81]

Saigh was a casual baseball fan who thought the Cardinals might be a good investment. He became increasingly interested when Hannegan's outside activities forced him to become more involved in the team's operation.[82] The son of a Syrian immigrant, Saigh practiced law in St. Louis for more than twenty years before becoming affiliated with the Cardinals. Although seemingly unpretentious and even shy, Saigh was outspoken and combative at times. Not long after taking over the team, he became locked in a struggle with the Browns over what became the initial battle between the two teams for St. Louis. Following the sale of the Cardinals to Hannegan and Saigh, the Browns demanded that the more-popular Cardinals cease broadcasting their away games because it was hurting their attendance. In addition, when negotiations to obtain more reasonable rental terms from the Cardinals broke down, the Browns unsuccessfully sued their tenant.[83]

The St. Louis Browns franchise was the "sick man" of the American League. Ice magnate Phil Ball, who died in 1933, was the last owner able

"Dear Miss Lonelyhearts—I'm jealous of the Cardinals

Everytime they're in town my husband and sons want to spend all their time with them, while I sit home alone. What shall I do?

Dear Dejected:

Go see Stan Musial hit a home run. It'll change your whole life.

Once you've tasted the action, thrills, suspense and relaxing fun of baseball, you, too, will be in love with the Cardinals. You will share a common interest with your menfolk, you will have a new interest in life, and your troubles will be over.

Why not start tomorrow night? Join them at Sportsman's Park to see the Cardinals play the Brooklyn Bums. You owe it to yourself and to the men in your life.

P.S. • Cards vs. Bums Wed. night and Thurs. afternoon, too.

In two-team towns like St. Louis, female fans became the object of much marketing attention. "Your troubles will be over," assured this 1951 Cardinals advertisement, if you only join your "menfolk" at Sportsman's Park. (Courtesy of the St. Louis Cardinals Baseball Club)

to subsidize the team out of his own pocket. The Browns were so un-loved in St. Louis that between 1932 and 1936 the team averaged a little more than 98,000 fans a year. One game in 1933 was attended by only thirty-four fans.[84] In 1937 the heirs of the Ball estate sold the team for $350,000 to Donald L. Barnes, the owner of a small investment firm, and William O. DeWitt. In late 1941, Barnes almost moved the team to Los Angeles. Arrangements were made with the Cubs to buy their Los Ange-les Pacific Coast League franchise, American League owners gave their consent, and a new American League schedule, which provided for air and long-distance train travel, was drafted. The move was canceled, how-ever, when the bombing of Pearl Harbor by the Japanese on December 7, 1941, convinced the American League that the West Coast was not a safe place for major-league baseball.[85] After the team won its only pennant in 1944, Barnes sold his stock to Richard Muckerman, another Browns stock-holder, leaving the club with $750,000 in assets.[86] Muckerman, heir to the St. Louis City Ice and Fuel Company, retained William O. and Charles DeWitt to run the team. Not unlike Phil Ball, Muckerman indebted the Browns further by acquiring and renovating Sportsman's Park and build-ing a new minor-league park in San Antonio and a new training facility in Florida. Nevertheless, attendance continued to ebb—when the Browns finished seventh in 1947, 200,000 fewer fans came through the gates than during 1946. By the end of the 1947 season, the club was almost $2 mil-lion in debt. William O. DeWitt saved the team from disaster by selling or trading players to the highest bidder. DeWitt specialized in playing con-tending teams such as the Yankees, Indians, and Red Sox against each other. He sold Jack Kramer and Vern Stephens to Boston for six players and $310,000, in late 1947, and journeyman pitcher Sam Zoldak to the Cleveland Indians for $100,000 during the 1948 pennant race. During the two-year period, he received about a million dollars in cash in various transactions.[87]

In 1949 Muckerman sold his interest in the team to the DeWitts. Hav-ing sold soda pop at Sportsman's Park in 1913 and worked as office boy under Branch Rickey soon after, the acquisition of a major-league team was a dream come true for William O. DeWitt. Unfortunately, the terms of their deal left the team seriously undercapitalized. The American League, which guaranteed a note to Muckerman, also loaned the DeWitts $300,000 so they could make their first payment. With an uncompetitive team and low attendance assured, it was not long before the DeWitts re-alized they could not survive. In 1950 rumors abounded—first that the team would be sold to a Baltimore group and then another that William Zeckendorf would move the Browns to Houston. Finally, in June 1951, it was announced that Bill Veeck was about to acquire the Browns and that he intended to keep the team in St. Louis.[88] The battle of St. Louis was on again—this time in earnest and to the death.

A battle for regional supremacy was also fought in New York—one of the few urban areas capable of supporting several teams. The battle for New York dated back to 1903, when Ban Johnson, president of the American League, outmaneuvered the powerful Giants, who wanted sole possession of New York, by shifting the Baltimore Orioles to the city. The new entry, first called the Highlanders and then the Yankees, did little to challenge the supremacy of the Giants for the next twenty years. This changed, however, when owners Jacob Ruppert and Ed Barrow acquired several key players, including Babe Ruth, Carl Mays, Waite Hoyt, and Herb Pennock from Harry Frazee, the New York theater entrepreneur who owned the Boston Red Sox. The deals provided the Yankees with the players they needed to begin an American League dynasty.

Throughout the early 1920s, the Giants and Yankees went head to head, but after 1925 Babe Ruth's popularity and twelve American League pennants allowed the Yankees to capture New York. After Ruppert's death in 1939, the Yankee franchise began a slow decline. Swept of their best talent by the war, they finished third and fourth in 1944 and 1945. The Yankees under Ed Barrow, George Weiss, and Joe McCarthy were still capably run, but Ruppert's estate was controlled by bank executors who considered the team a bad investment. In 1945, the franchise was sold for $2,850,000 to a group that included Dan Topping, the owner of the Brooklyn Dodgers football club, Phoenix contractor Del Webb, and Larry MacPhail. Following two turbulent but profitable years, Topping and Webb bought out MacPhail for $2 million after the Yankees' World Series win in 1947.

With MacPhail's departure, George Weiss was appointed general manager. As the original architect of the Yankee farm system, he poured new resources into an organization that supplied the Yankees with three or four new major leaguers per year. Cold and calculating, Weiss was both tight with a dollar and an outstanding administrator. Much of the Yankees' success in the next fifteen years must be laid at his feet. Not unlike Weiss, Topping and Webb were businessmen first and sportsmen second. As capitalists, they looked at the team as a profitable diversion. Not long after buying the Yankees, Webb noted, "I invested in the Yankees strictly from a business viewpoint."[89] He compared the team with his construction company and said that the old methods of running the team "just could not survive." The Yankees under Colonel Ruppert were a rich man's toy that had never paid a dividend. Topping and Webb installed a budget system because, according to Webb, "We had to know just how much each unit cost to operate. We had to know which farm was losing, and how much, which was profiting, and how much."[90]

By the time he acquired his interest in the Yankees in 1945, Webb was head of one of the largest contracting firms in the United States and was worth an estimated $10 million. A high school dropout, Webb turned to carpentry when his dream of becoming a major-league baseball player evaporated because of illness and injury. When a contractor with whom Webb was working abandoned a grocery store project, Webb completed the store with the grocer's money and the Del E. Webb Construction Company was born. According to former player and friend Art Nehf, Webb "came to Phoenix without a dime and parlayed a saw and hammer into a million dollars."[91] In the fast-growing city of Phoenix, he built filling stations, theaters, and chain stores. After expanding his enterprise to Los Angeles and Chicago, Webb was positioned to take on over $100 million worth of government-contract work during World War II. At the height of the war, he employed more than 25,000 workers and built several huge military installations—"including air fields, army and navy training bases, hospitals, and prisoner of war camps." In the years immediately following the war, Webb's company was involved in hundreds of projects in twenty-six states.[92]

Webb was also acquainted with the rich, the famous, and the notorious. He was a partner with Bing Crosby in Bing Crosby Productions and the Decca Record Company. In addition, he built the Flamingo Hotel— the first luxury gambling casino in Las Vegas—in 1947. Webb's client for the Flamingo was notorious criminal Benjamin "Bugsy" Siegel. Siegel was under great pressure to make a success of the hotel, which was financed by Albert Anastasia and other East Coast underworld figures. When workmen could not obtain scarce wartime construction materials, Siegel threatened them. As head contractor, Webb complained to Siegel that his methods intimidated the workers because they were aware of his reputation. Siegel admitted to Webb that he had personally killed twelve men, but, on seeing Webb's reaction, he laughed and said, "There's no chance that you'll get killed. We only kill each other."[93] On June 21, 1947, Siegel's investors foreclosed on him by gunning him down in his living room. Webb was left with the Flamingo—a circumstance that eventually led him to invest in other gambling properties in Las Vegas. By 1964, it was speculated that Webb had $90 million invested in Las Vegas, making him the largest single investor in town and a potential baseball liability.[94]

Webb's partner, Dan Topping, inherited his wealth. He was the grandson of John A. Topping, one of the cofounders of the Republic Iron and Steel Corporation. In addition, his mother was the daughter of Wall Street financier Daniel G. Reid, who amassed a $140 million fortune in tin plate, tobacco, steel, banks, and railroads. Topping was so wealthy that Larry MacPhail once told him, "Hell, you weren't born with silver spoon in your mouth. You were born with a gold one."[95] Although a graduate of the Wharton School of Finance, sports, not business, captivated him. In 1934, Topping invested in the Brooklyn Dodgers football team and eventually bought out his co-owners Shipwreck Kelly and Red Cagle. Not long after, he withdrew from Lloyd and Topping, an advertising firm that held the Lifesavers account, to take over the helm of the Dodgers.[96] The tanned and well-heeled Topping was married six times and earned a reputation as a playboy. His third wife, figure skater Sonja Henie, who became an American citizen when she married Topping on July 4, 1940, was never shy when money was involved. When MacPhail took her to a baseball game at Yankee Stadium and tried to explain it to her, she said, "Never mind zat. What is ze gross when zis place is sold out?"[97]

In spite of his reputation, Topping was a hands-on operator, who, after MacPhail's departure, ran the Yankees for sixteen years. He often arrived at Yankee Stadium at 7:00 A.M. and remained long after others left. Webb, on the other hand, was always traveling on company business and rarely saw more than ten or twenty games a year. Webb served as the team's representative at league meetings and soon became one of the most influential owners in baseball.

Of course, there was another team in New York—the Brooklyn Dodgers. In 1946, Brooklyn, with its three million residents, was the third most populous city in the United States, following New York and Chicago. During World War II, Brooklyn sent more men and women into the armed services than did thirty-six states.[98] Following the war, Brooklyn was a community in transition. With the construction of new highways and the retooling of the auto industry, a large segment of Brooklyn's middle class fled to the suburbs. The largely white population was replaced by African Americans and Puerto Ricans. The team and Jackie Robinson's arrival in particular provided the community with a much-needed identity—the one ingredient that the entire borough was willing to support. No team was more identified with a community than Brooklyn.

It was in this environment that Rickey laid the foundation for one of the game's most celebrated dynasties. Rickey, along with attorney Walter O'Malley and John L. Smith, the president of Charles A. Pfizer & Company, the makers of penicillin, purchased three-quarters of the team's stock for approximately $1 million in 1943. Rickey busied himself rebuilding the Dodger's depleted farm system. While other owners slept, he spent more than $100,000 on free agents and quietly cornered the market on young talent. By 1946 the Dodgers, with twenty-two affiliates and more than 400 players, maintained the most extensive minor-league system in baseball.

In 1947, Rickey opened Dodgertown at a surplus naval base at Vero Beach, Florida. There he housed, trained, and instructed his entire orga-

nization. The camp contained barracks, hangars suitable for indoor workouts, cottages for married players, a swimming pool, office space, a dining hall, a theater, and an airstrip for his private plane. By 1949, Dodgertown
housed more than 600 players and was equipped with four diamonds, a
sixty-yard cinder track, two pitching machines, four batting tees, two sets
of string targets for pitchers, and two sliding pits. Dodgertown cost the
team approximately $250,000 a year to operate—a figure that included
expenses for payroll for more than a hundred employees, maintenance,
laundry, medical support, heating, entertainment, travel, and food. Aside
from the team's normal entourage, the Dodgers employed fifteen umpires, seventeen grounds keepers, two doctors, seven trainers, and three
property men. The largest expense was travel, which alone cost $75,000.[99]
With a motto borrowed from the Navy, "take all you want and eat all you
take," Dodger players consumed more than 1,200 meals per day, including tons of beef and thousands of gallons of milk and Florida orange
juice.[100]

Beyond being astute in the business of baseball, Rickey was a natural
teacher. Baseball historian Robert Smith described him as "the Paul Brown
of baseball, treating the game as if it were a scholarly discipline, outlin-
ing its techniques on blackboards, insisting on earnest attention."[101] In
the morning, Rickey conducted half-hour lectures on everything from
baseball fundamentals to personal matters such as diet, hygiene, ethics,
and religion. During the afternoon, he often instructed young players on
the art of pitching or hitting.

To know Rickey was to be fascinated by him. Red Smith once wrote,
"Branch Rickey is a God-fearing, checker-playing, horse-trading, cigar-
smoking, double-talking, non-alcoholic, sharp-shooting blend of elo-
quence and sincerity and enterprise and imagination and energy and
independence and profundity, and guile."[102] His energy was boundless.
He was restless—always on the move and rarely idle. According to Smith,
if Rickey was traveling somewhere in an automobile, he would grab the
wheel and dictate a letter to his son or an assistant. Indeed, time was so
precious to him that while with the Cardinals, he was known to call DeWitt
into the men's room so he could dictate a letter to him while he was sitting in a stall.[103]

Rickey stood far above other baseball executives. None possessed his
intelligence, and only Larry MacPhail and Bill Veeck were more auda-
cious. He was respected, but distrusted, by his counterparts. According
to Red Smith, "His reputation as a dealer was, 'don't drink and keep your
hands in your pockets, otherwise he will hornswoggle you.'"[104] "The greatest proof of Rickey's genius," noted Veeck, "was that you always knew

what he was doing—except when he was doing it to you."[105] A master of circumlocution, Rickey employed his superior language skills, powers of persuasion, and preparation to confuse and entrance his trading partners. With so much surplus talent available in the Dodger system, trading with Rickey was inevitable. By 1950 almost 15 percent of all major-league players traced their development to Rickey farm systems at St. Louis or Brooklyn.[106]

While Branch Rickey had no peer when it came to shrewd trading, he himself was no match for Dodger counsel Walter O'Malley. O'Malley, a native New Yorker, got his start handling bankruptcies during the Depression. Over the next decade, he acquired interests in the Long Island Railroad, the Brooklyn Borough Gas Company, a beer company, hotels, and other assorted businesses.[107] His work on behalf of the Brooklyn Trust Company led the bank's president, George McLaughlin, to appoint O'Malley counsel for the Brooklyn Dodgers in 1941, replacing Wendell Willkie. O'Malley acquired a quarter interest in the team in 1944. O'Malley's stake in the team was financial, and he was always looking over the Dodger president's shoulder, criticizing any move he thought was unsound. They argued over losses Rickey incurred through his investment in the football Brooklyn Dodgers, over beer advertising, over Rickey's poor relations with certain sportswriters, over Rickey's air travel, over his "extravagant" spending, and over the acquisition of Vero Beach as a training site.[108]

In addition, O'Malley and co-owner John Smith were well aware that Ebbets Field, the darling of Brooklyn fans, was outdated, filled with poor seats located behind pillars, and just too small. Smith grumbled ominously, "All we know is that we cannot enlarge Ebbets Field. Either it has to come down and a new plant built on the present property, we move or just go on patching up the old stands."[109] Moreover, as successful as the team was on the field, overall attendance was disappointing. After 1947's record attendance of 1,807,526, the team averaged only a little over 1.4 million fans per year during the next three seasons, a period that included their 1949 pennant win. Although Ebbets Field, which had a capacity of 31,902, was small by major-league standards, the team averaged a little more than 18,000 fans per contest.[110]

Not unlike his St. Louis operations, the Dodgers' profit margin was greatly enhanced by Rickey's player sales. From 1945 to 1948, the Dodgers' net income after taxes was $1,725,114.40. During the same period, income from the sale of players was $1,413,325.00.[111] While Walter O'Malley recognized the need to increase attendance and sell off surplus players, he was very unhappy with Rickey's contract, which provided that he would receive 10 percent of the sale price from each player transaction. This arrangement not only made Rickey the highest-paid executive in baseball but, in O'Malley's opinion, created a conflict of interest.[112]

By 1950, the Dodgers organization was split into pro-Rickey and pro-O'Malley camps. With Rickey's contract coming up for renewal at the end of 1950, O'Malley gained the support of Mrs. May Smith (John Smith died on July 10, 1950) and successfully blocked Rickey from being re-hired by preventing discussion of Rickey's contract at board meetings. Rickey's original five-year contract expired in 1947, and he was given one-year extensions in 1948 and 1949.[113] Although not officially fired, he had no choice but to seek an outside buyer for his stock or sell it to O'Malley and Smith. In addition, according to a prior agreement the co-owners could match any outside offer. O'Malley confidently concluded that he could purchase Rickey's share for $600,000 or approximately double what he had paid in 1944.[114] To his dismay, he was outmaneuvered when New York real estate tycoon William Zeckendorf appeared with an offer of $1 million for Rickey's stock. Unknown to Rickey, Zeckendorf was recruited by John Galbreath of the Pirates, who was interested in attracting the Dodger president to Pittsburgh. Zeckendorf also stipulated that he was to be awarded a fee of $50,000 should one of the partners match his offer. O'Malley quickly met Zeckendorf's offer rather than have an aggressive partner who might also wish to retain Rickey's services.[115] As Red Smith wrote, "Zeckendorf received $50,000 for his trouble, Rickey got his million, and O'Malley's enduring hostility."[116]

Pledging to give the "Bums" back to the fans, O'Malley set his sights on winning a pennant. With more than a tinge of jealousy, he complained that "Rickey will receive credit for all Dodger successes for years to come, and the incumbent administration only the blame."[117] Though his prophecy came true, during the next thirty years O'Malley became the most powerful and influential owner in baseball.

With the Korean conflict threatening to take some of the game's best players, major-league ownership retrenched at the end of the Pivotal Era. The players now received pension benefits, minimum salaries, Murphy Money, and were represented in baseball's counsels. Although several teams, such as the Yankees, Red Sox, Tigers, and Cardinals, failed to hire African American players, the integration of baseball was firmly in place. The reserve clause, which was temporarily imperiled because of Congressional scrutiny by the Celler Committee, would survive several legal challenges. As Americans purchased cars, left for the suburbs, and became enamored with their television sets, the postwar attendance boom bottomed out. With the exception of the Cubs, night baseball became a staple of most teams.

The owners who would run the game for the next fifteen years—the O'Malleys, Webbs, Toppings, Yawkeys, Galbreaths, Carpenters, Perinis, and Wrigleys—were in their ascendancy. The game became more business oriented in its operation and in its impersonal approach to fans and players alike. Clubs would bow to the reality of economics in two-team cities and would soon escape Boston, Philadelphia, New York, and St. Louis for new territory. Owners who lived entirely off the game's profits were also on the endangered species list. The general store operation all but disappeared with the demise of Connie Mack, Clark Griffith, and the Comiskeys, during the 1950s. Horace Stoneham and Calvin Griffith adapted by expanding their farm systems, as did gentlemen sportsmen Powel Crosley, Tom Yawkey, Phil Wrigley, and Walter Briggs.

Outside of the potential for expansion, the owners who dominated baseball at the end of the Pivotal Era lacked a vision for the game. Not unlike owners before them, they were unable to act in concert or to conduct in-depth planning. When they did act, their efforts were usually knee-jerk reactions to crises. Television's potential was an enigma for most, and competition from other professional sports such as football was not recognized until several sports had surpassed baseball in popularity. Unfortunately, the game's two most dynamic executives, Bill Veeck and Branch Rickey, found themselves in weak positions at the end of the Pivotal Era. By the time Rickey joined the Pirates, almost every team had a viable farm system and was signing young talent with astonishing bonuses. Rickey could no longer surprise his competitors with talent off farm teams or from the Negro Leagues. With limited financial and player resources, it took him a long time to build the foundation for the pennant-winning 1960 Pirates.

Bill Veeck had even less capital to work with in St. Louis. Moreover, his situation was rendered hopeless when Fred Saigh was imprisoned for income-tax evasion and the Cardinals were sold to beer baron August Busch in 1953. Veeck could not compete with Busch. Nevertheless, it is doubtful that leadership from Veeck or Rickey, had it been available, would have been accepted by the other owners. Rickey was admired, feared, and heartily disliked by many of his peers. Bill Veeck was even more unacceptable. Described by some as an iconoclast, no one burned more bridges than Veeck.[118] With leadership in the hands of Walter O'Malley and Del Webb, as always, the game marched blithely along.

12

1948: Indian Summer

A fat, wrinkled man reached his hand through the flowers and affectionately placed his palm on the Babe's clasped hands. Within seconds, he was rushed away by the two policeman who guarded the casket. "I loved the man," he apologized, "I loved that man." The mourners passed the Babe at the rate of a hundred persons a minute—kids clinging to baseball bats and mitts and adults alike, all hoping to get one last glimpse of an American icon.[1] More than 100,000 persons viewed the body as it lay in state in the rotunda of Yankee Stadium from 5:00 P.M. on August 17 to 7:00 P.M. the next day.[2] More than 5,600 mourners crammed St. Patrick's Cathedral to witness Cardinal Spellman officiate the Babe's funeral mass, and in spite of a downpour, 70,000 people lined the procession route to the Gate of Heaven Cemetery in Mount Pleasant, New York.[3]

Ruth's death on August 16, 1948, momentarily diverted America's attention from the Berlin airlift and the worsening situation in Europe. In spite of his follies and excesses, Americans identified with Ruth as with no other sports figure. His feats, both fact and fiction, were written into American folklore long before his death. Ruth's love of life, baseball, and his unselfish devotion to children made him worthy of emulation. As Robert Creamer noted in his beautifully crafted biography of Ruth, "Glutton, drunkard, hell-raiser, but beloved by all—except the Japanese during World War II. The Japs shouted, 'To hell with Babe Ruth!' the ultimate insult to GIs on Guadalcanal."[4] Ruth's heroics, the pennants and home runs, made everyone forget the Black Sox scandal. Ruth, along with Jack Dempsey and Bobby Jones, were the central American sports figures of the 1920s. According to Dan Daniel, "Together they made over the sports pages." They spurred sports writing to new heights. Ruth was the most

Table 7. Final Major-League Regular-Season Standings, 1948

American League					National League			
	W	L	%	G.B.		W	L	%	G.B.
Cleveland	97	58	.626	–	Boston	91	62	.595	–
Boston	96	59	.619	1	St. Louis	85	69	.552	6 1/2
New York	94	60	.610	2 1/2	Brooklyn	84	70	.545	7 1/2
Philadelphia	84	70	.545	12 1/2	Pittsburgh	83	71	.539	8 1/2
Detroit	78	76	.506	18 1/2	New York	78	76	.506	13 1/2
St. Louis	59	94	.386	37	Philadelphia	66	88	.429	25 1/2
Washington	56	97	.366	40	Cincinnati	64	89	.418	27
Chicago	51	101	.336	44 1/2	Chicago	64	90	.416	27 1/2

recognizable figure in America, always a patient and willing target for autograph seekers.[5]

The 1948 season was Ruth's "Indian Summer"—the last time he traveled south for spring training and the last time he heard the cheers and applause of adulation in a major-league park. A 1947 operation, which only partially eradicated a malignant tumor between his inner ear, brain, and neck, left him with a raspy voice and an inability to eat solid food. On June 13, 1948, Ruth made his final appearance at Yankee Stadium to celebrate the structure's twenty-fifth anniversary. For two weeks before the event, the Babe behaved like an excited child and even insisted on having his prized uniform sent out for cleaning, though it was already spotless.[6] On the big day, the weather was damp and rainy. Ruth was the last of the old timers to be announced. When his turn came, he slowly emerged from the Cleveland dugout and was met with a thunderous ovation. Leaning on a bat borrowed from Bob Feller, in his hoarse, croaking voice, he said, "I'm proud that I hit the first home run in this stadium. I am thrilled. It is a marvelous privilege to come back here and to see thirteen men of 1923 playing together again. It makes me proud." According to Dan Daniel, "as the Babe walked away from the mike, tears streamed down his face. There was a lump in many a throat, and there were some 50,000 in the park, despite the early rain."[7] Following his hospitalization, Ruth ventured out in public one last time, on July 26, to attend the premier of the *Babe Ruth Story*, a mostly apocryphal account of his career, starring William Bendix. Because of the physical strain, he left twenty minutes into the screening.[8] Three weeks later, he was dead.

Throughout the 1948 season, baseball's popularity remained at an all-time high. Driven by exciting pennant races in each league, attendance records were broken in Boston and Pittsburgh in the National League and Boston, Cleveland, Detroit, New York, and Philadelphia in the American League. While baseball writers picked the Yankees and the Red Sox to battle it out for the American League pennant and the Braves and Cardinals to do so in the National League, in a portent of things to come, the Braves and Indians topped spring training's Grapefruit League standings.

The National League Pennant Race

For the city of Chicago, with both its baseball teams finishing last, 1948 was a lost season. Although the cellar-dwelling Cubs received career years from outfielder Andy Pafko (.312-26-101) and left-hander Johnny Schmitz (2.64, 18-13), at season's end, club owner Phil Wrigley publicly apologized for his team's performance.

The Cincinnati Reds' 1948 season began in January when shortstop Eddie Miller gave a speech in which he made disparaging remarks about several teammates and predicted a last-place finish for the team.[9] Although Miller was quickly traded to the Phillies, his predictions were close to the mark, since the team finished only a half game ahead of the last-place Cubs. Bright spots for the Reds included outfielder Hank Sauer (.260-35-97), who became the first Cincinnati Red to hit more than thirty home runs in a season, Ken Raffensberger (3.84, 11-12), who one-hit the Cardinals twice (May 31 and July 11), and Johnny Vander Meer (3.41, 17-14), who enjoyed the last great season of his career.

The Philadelphia Phillies continued their metamorphosis in 1948, as several new stars emerged, including rookie Richie Ashburn (.333-2-40) and pitcher Robin Roberts (3.19, 7-9). Ashburn was so fast that Joe DiMaggio described him as being "jet propelled," and Joe Cronin insisted that he had "a motor in his pants."[10] The outfielder set a National League rookie record by hitting in twenty-three games in a row and easily led the league in steals, with thirty-two. Outstanding seasons also were enjoyed by knuckleballer Dutch Leonard (2.51, 12-17) and outfielder Del Ennis (.290-30-95).

Although the New York Giants quickly surged to the front and held first place through early June, their pitching suddenly disintegrated and their hitting became erratic. By July 12, the Giants were in fourth place, eight games back. On July 16, owner Horace Stoneham announced the retirement of manager Mel Ott and the signing of Dodger manager Leo Durocher, the first outsider to manage the Giants since 1902. Most of the players were dumbfounded by the news. Infielder Bill Rigney recalled, "We hated the Dodgers. He [Durocher] was our worst enemy." Nevertheless, Durocher took charge quickly. "Let's see who the hell can play here and who can't play and why the team's not playing better," he told the players.[11] One of the players who knew he would not be there long was Willard Marshall. "Everybody in those days hated Durocher. He was peppy and arrogant and got everybody a little teed off. I knew that he didn't care for me as a ballplayer and he [would] get rid of me as soon as he could, but that was his prerogative."[12] Even though outstanding years were turned in by Sid Gordon (.299-30-107), Larry Jansen (3.61, 18-12), Sheldon "Available" Jones (3.35, 16-8), and slugger Johnny Mize (.289-40-125), Durocher was no miracle worker, and the Giants finished in fifth place.

The Pittsburgh Pirates finished an astonishing fourth, under freshman manager Billy Meyer, who moved to reestablish discipline on the team. The Pirates, who were fun to watch, were still a mixture of savvy veterans, rookies, and Dodger castoffs. "Old-timers" Elmer Riddle, Truett "Rip" Sewell (3.48, 13-3), and forty-year-old Fritz Ostermueller teamed up with Bob Chesnes (3.57, 14-6) to lead the pitching staff. The prodigious home run hitting of Ralph Kiner (.265-40-123), the team's only superstar, allowed the Pirates to establish a new attendance mark of 1,517,021. Unfortunately, the Pirates were an aging team that peaked in 1948.

Although the third-place Dodgers were very talented, they were not a solid team. They possessed three great catchers, no natural first basemen, an abundance of unproven infielders, and the 1947 rookie of the year. Branch Rickey compounded the muddle before the 1947 season by replacing manager Burt Shotton with Leo Durocher. Though he felt almost duty bound to return the suspended Leo Durocher to that post, Rickey knew that the uncontrollable Durocher was a liability.[13] The trade of Eddie Stanky to the Boston Braves for Bama Rowell, Ray Sanders, and $60,000 to make room for Jackie Robinson at second base left the Dodgers without the spark plug that ignited the 1947 team.

Several misfortunes befell the Dodgers: Pete Reiser suffered from a recurring ankle injury, relief pitcher Hugh Casey injured his back in a fall at his Brooklyn tavern and never regained his form, and sore-armed Ralph Branca (3.51, 14-9) was lost for part of the season. Furthermore, as a result of consuming too much food on the banquet circuit, Jackie Robinson reported to training camp thirty pounds over his normal playing weight. As he struggled to round into shape, Robinson was even put on waivers.[14] On a more positive note, Robinson was no longer considered an oddity. The Negro fans have stopped "whooping it up every time I make a simple play," he noted, "They're used to me—all except the bus loads that come up for Sunday or night games on the road, usually in St. Louis and Cincinnati." In addition, he was now free to express his opinion. "I say what I want to say," proclaimed Robinson. "I do what I want to do. Nobody seems to care, and that's the way I like it."[15] On August 24, he was ejected from his first game for heckling an umpire. By now, some of the pressure was off.

With the Dodgers mired in sixth place through the month of June, Rickey could not ignore the mounting criticism of his team. He decided to cut Durocher loose, but, when he had traveling secretary Harold Parrott inform Durocher of Rickey's intentions, the manager refused to resign. Rickey's dilemma was quickly solved after Horace Stoneham removed Mel Ott as the Giants manager and asked for permission to approach Durocher. When Durocher learned that he was authorized to deal with the Giants, he asked Rickey, "And what if I don't take it?" Rickey replied, "You'll still be manager of the Dodgers, but there won't be any future in Brooklyn for you."[16] Durocher wisely departed. Under Burt Shotton, his replacement, the Dodgers recovered and briefly took the lead at the end of August, but during the next month they faded to finish third. The major positive note as the season closed was Rex Barney's September 9 2-0 no-hitter against the New York Giants.

After leading the field in May, the St. Louis Cardinals spent the remainder of the season battling Brooklyn and Pittsburgh for second place. With their starting lineup and five top pitchers averaging thirty years of age, the Cardinals were on the verge of being an "old" ball club. Outfielder Terry Moore retired after a superb career, Marty Marion's trick knee reduced his mobility and effectiveness at shortstop, and injuries cut into Whitey Kurowski's and Red Schoendienst's seasons. Nevertheless, Schoendienst set two major-league records, by hitting eight doubles and a home run in three straight contests.[17] With the exception of Harry Brecheen (2.24, 20-7), who led the league in earned run average and strikeouts with 149, and reliever Ted Wilks (2.62, 6-6), the pitching staff also struggled.

In hitting, the team was carried by Enos Slaughter (.321-11-90) and Stan Musial (.376-39-131). After going hitless in his first thirty-four trips of the season, Slaughter went on a rampage in August, as he put together the second of two seventeen-game hitting streaks. Musial's awesome season allowed him to become the first National League player to win three Most Valuable Player awards, and his .376 average was the highest average since Arky Vaughan hit .385 in 1938. Morever, due to a rainout, Musial lost a home run that would have tied him with Ralph Kiner and Johnny Mize for the home run title and would have earned him the Triple Crown.[18] Musial's four five-hit games in one season tied the major-league record set by Ty Cobb in 1922 and established a new National League record.[19]

With the exception of the Dodgers' charge in late August, the Boston

Rookie Alvin Dark (left) combined with veteran Eddie Stanky (right) to give the Braves an outstanding double-play combination through midseason, 1948. Paired as roommates, Dark credited Stanky with his development. (George Brace Photos)

Braves were comfortably ensconced in first place throughout the season. Serious Billy Southworth did an outstanding job with a team that possessed little speed and no great power hitter. The quiet leader of the team was Bob Elliott (.283-23-100), who followed his MVP year with another outstanding season. Another team leader was Earl Torgeson (.253-10-67), who occasionally held court in the clubhouse. Torgeson, a fiery, rough-and-tumble competitor, shared first base with the smooth-fielding veteran Frank McCormick (.250-4-34).

The Braves also made several key acquisitions. Two of these acquisitions were rookie Alvin Dark (.322-3-48) and former Dodger Eddie Stanky (.320-2-29), who formed the team's keystone combination. Dark, a $45,000 bonus baby out of Louisiana State University, was the prospect that scout Ted McGrew had assured president Lou Perini would make the Braves forget about their quest of Marty Marion. Although he broke his ankle near the season's midpoint, Eddie Stanky provided the Braves with the leadership they badly needed. After he was traded, Stanky vowed, "The Dodgers will not win the pennant this season without me."[20]

Other newly acquired players also contributed. Enigmatic Jeff Heath (.319-20-76), purchased from the St. Louis Browns, enjoyed a great year, before he broke his ankle at the end of the season. Outfielder Jimmy Russell and catcher Bill Salkeld, who were acquired from the Pirates for Johnny Hopp and Danny Murtaugh, also made major contributions. Rounding out the Braves' attack was steady outfielder Mike McCormick and hard-hitting Tommy Holmes (.325-6-61), whose twelve- and thirteen-game hitting streaks propelled him to a third-place finish in the league batting race.

The Braves' great strength was their pitching. In the bullpen, the team had Bobby Hogue (3.23, 8-2) and veteran Clyde Shoun, along with spot starters Red Barrett and Nelson Potter. The latter duo won several key late-season games for Boston. Two other hurlers, Kentuckian Vern Bickford (3.27, 11-5) and South Carolinian Bill Voiselle (3.63, 13-13), also pitched well for the team. Bickford, a solid pitcher in his rookie year, received a four-figure raise following the All-Star game after going 5-2 as starting pitcher.[21] Voiselle, acquired from Giants in 1947, beat his former teammates four times in 1948.

The bellwethers of the Braves pitching staff were Warren Spahn (3.71, 15-12) and Johnny Sain (2.60, 24-15). Spahn struggled through most of the season. He experimented with off-speed pitches and, as a result, lost something off his fastball. He was also distracted by his wife's pregnancy. Johnny Sain, in his finest season, carried the club through mid-August.[22] As the Dodgers and Braves fought for first place, the all-Boston attendance record for a five-game series was shattered when 151,519 attended the series between the two teams that ended August 16. With both the Braves and Red Sox leading their respective leagues in September, pennant fever raged in Boston. The crucial games of the year were played in a doubleheader against the Dodgers on Labor Day, September 6. More than 40,000 fans saw Spahn pitch thirteen innings to beat Brooklyn 2-1. Spahn, who had an outstanding move to first base, picked off Jackie Robinson twice. In the second game, Sain threw a 4-0 shutout. With three weeks left in the pennant race, the two pitchers, in an unprecedented move even for the late 1940s, started twelve of the team's last seventeen games.[23]

Behind Spahn and Sain, the Braves won fourteen of fifteen games through September 21, to break the pennant race wide open. Sain won six games in nineteen days without relief, and, over a twenty-nine-game period, he pitched nine games without relief—winning seven of them. In five of the nine games, he pitched with only two days rest. Spahn pitched four complete games in a row and won them all. According to the *Sporting News*, "At one point during the Braves' winning streak, Sain and Spahn pitched eight of eleven games played by the team—and won all eight without relief."[24] The feat immortalized the two pitchers in baseball lore.

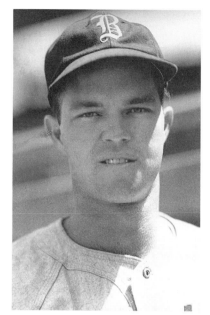

In September 1948, Warren Spahn (left) and Johnny Sain (right) pitched eight of eleven consecutive games for the Boston Braves and won all eight without relief. The feat immortalized the two hurlers in baseball lore. (George Brace Photos)

The initial phrase "Spahn and Sain, two days of rain," which later was more commonly known as "Spahn and Sain, and pray for rain," was certainly a fitting tribute to the efforts of two great pitchers.[25]

The American League Pennant Race

The 1948 American League pennant race was one of the most exciting in league history. Never before had four teams (Cleveland, New York, Boston, and Philadelphia) been so tightly clustered in the standings. Only six percentage points separated the first- and fourth-place clubs as late as August 3. The same could not be said of the bottom four teams, however, none of which contended at any time during the season. The basement-dwelling Chicago White Sox were led by Luke Appling (.314-0-47), who at age forty-one was still their only legitimate star. He made his two thousand five hundredth hit at midseason. The team was so punchless that outfielder Bob Kennedy, a lifetime .246 hitter at the time, started off the season in the cleanup spot. After a 9-26 start, the White Sox were so desperate for power that they traded Kennedy to Cleveland for pitcher Al Gettel and inconsistent slugger Pat Seerey (.229-18-64). Seerey supplied bursts of power, including a four-homer game on July 18 to beat the A's 12-11. The feat, which had been accomplished only by Lou Gehrig and Chuck Klein, did not cure the team's woeful hitting.

Excitement was generated in Washington only when President Truman appeared to throw out the first pitch in the season opener. Not unlike the White Sox, the Senators' hitting attack was anemic. Having connected for only five team home runs by the beginning of June, the Senators took out some of their frustrations on the umpires. In July, the team's bench jockeys got to veteran umpire Bill McGowan, who lost his temper, used profane language, and threw his ball and strike indicator during a game. McGowan's actions led to a formal complaint by the Senators and a ten-day suspension by American League president Will Harridge. Thereafter, the Senators were a marked team. The umpires were so fed up with them that in one game umpire Red Jones ordered pitcher Ray Scarborough out of the game for bench jockeying when in fact he was 450 feet away in the Senators' bullpen.[26] With the exception of Scarborough (2.82, 15-8), most of the Senators had off years. The team was simply bad. As manager Joe Kuhel stated, with an air of resignation, "I can't make chicken salad out of chicken shit."[27]

The fact that the St. Louis Browns finished above the Senators and White Sox is a testament to the weakness of those teams. Nevertheless, several Browns players, including Jerry Priddy (.296-8-79), Bob Dillinger (.321-2-44), Al Zarilla (.329-12-74), and catcher Les Moss, had excellent years. The 1948 season also marked the debut of right-handed pitcher Ned Garver (3.41, 7-11). The largest crowd of the year in St. Louis, 17,992, witnessed a pitching duel between Satchel Paige and Garver in which the latter beat the Indians 4-3 and knocked in the winning run in the bottom of the tenth inning.

The fifth-place Detroit Tigers were very disappointing. They were hampered by injuries to star third baseman George Kell (.304-2-44), who missed sixty games that year because of a fractured wrist early in the season and in late August when a wicked one-hopper by Joe DiMaggio fractured his jaw in two places. With only Pat Mullin (.288-23-80) and Hoot Evers (.314-10-103) having good years, the Tigers chronically left men on base.

Although several exciting prospects, including Art Houtteman, Ted Gray, and Billy Pierce, debuted in 1948, Tigers pitching was also less than satisfactory. Pitching ace Hal Newhouser (3.01, 21-12) began the season poorly, as he nursed a sore arm into the All-Star game. During the second half, however, he carried the team.

The fourth-place Philadelphia Athletics were one of the most amazing stories of 1948. Connie Mack spent $75,000 acquiring his whole 1948 team, whereas Tom Yawkey of the Red Sox spent $375,000 on the acquisition of four players from the Browns.[28] The A's pitching staff was filled with World War II combat veterans, including Bob Savage, who was wounded twice in Italy, left-hander Alex Kellner, who was aboard the USS *Callahan*, the last U.S. ship sunk during the war, Phil Marchildon, who was shot down and captured in Germany while serving in the Royal Canadian Air Force, and Lou Brissie, who was hit by a German shell that killed eleven men around him and shattered his leg.

Although the A's received an excellent year's play from Joe Coleman (4.09, 14-13), Dick Fowler (3.78, 15-8), and Carl Scheib (3.94, 14-8), they were counting heavily on Phil Marchildon to be the staff ace. Unfortunately, the trauma of the war and the chronic influenza that he picked up in prison camp returned and caused him to be ineffective. Marchildon never won another major-league game after 1948.

The A's were in the thick of the American League race until September, largely because of their great defense and timely hitting. The infield of Ferris Fain, Hank Majeski (.310-12-120), Pete Suder, and Eddie Joost ended the year fielding .981, only a point lower than the American League season record. Joost set an American League record by shortstops by playing forty-one consecutive errorless games and handling 225 chances without an error. In addition to Majeski's career year, the A's also got excellent hitting from outfielders Elmer Valo (.305-3-46) and Barney McCosky (.326-0-46). Nevertheless, key injuries to Valo, McCosky, and Joost, along with a lack of depth, doomed their fine season.

As Labor Day passed by, Philadelphia slipped badly at 9½ games off the pace, and Cleveland appeared to be faltering at 4½ back, while the Yankees trailed the league-leading Red Sox by a half-game. But, in a major surprise, Cleveland battled back to catch both front runners and to throw the lead into a three-way tie on September 24. Of the three teams, the Yankees were the odds-on favorite to repeat in 1948. To counter moves made by the Red Sox, they strengthened their pitching with addition of Red Embree from the Indians and Eddie Lopat (3.65, 17-11) from the White Sox. Pitchers Allie Reynolds (3.77, 16-7) and Vic Raschi (3.84, 19-8) completed what became the Yankees' "great triumvirate" for the next five seasons. Raschi was also the star of the 1948 All-Star game played in St. Louis, as he drove in two runs and received the win in the American League's 5-2 victory. Although support was forthcoming from Tommy Byrne and Spec Shea, Joe Page (4.26, 7-8) was not nearly as effective as he had been in 1947. In August, complete games were scarce and relief pitching was questionable.

Yankee highlights included Snuffy Stirnweiss's record of seventy-one errorless games at second base, which erased the old major-league mark of fifty-nine set by Bobby Doerr in 1943. Yogi Berra (.305-14-98) and Tommy Henrich (.308-25-100) also had outstanding years. Henrich switched from the outfield to first base and responded with the best year of his career. The Yankees remained in contention because of Joe DiMaggio's incredible season. Although the Yankee Clipper (.320-39-155) faced constant pain because of a sore heel, pulled muscles, a trick knee, and bone chips in his right elbow, he missed only one regular season game. DiMaggio began the season in spectacular fashion with a 450-foot home run off Washington's Mickey Haefner at Griffith Stadium, and on May 23 he slammed three home runs to beat Cleveland and Bob Feller 6-5 in front of a crowd of 78,431.

DiMaggio's torrid hitting continued throughout the season, but by late September the bone spur in his heel was so painful that he could barely play. With the Yankees eliminated from contention, DiMaggio got four singles against the Red Sox, who remained in the race with the Indians. When the Yankee's last single bounced off the left-field wall, DiMaggio was barely able to reach first base.[29] He was removed for a pinch runner and later recalled, "As I limped off the field the Boston fans, who knew I was hurting and probably should not have been playing at all, gave me an ovation, despite what I had been doing to their team that day. That was something I'll always remember."[30]

The Boston Red Sox almost bought themselves a pennant in 1948, with the acquisition of pitchers Jack Kramer (4.35, 18-5) and Ellis Kinder (3.74, 10-7) and infielder Vern Stephens from the Browns and outfielder Stan Spence from the Senators. Before their arrival, the Red Sox staff was in a shambles. Tex Hughson, Dave Ferris, and Mickey Harris had arm problems, and Joe Dobson (3.56, 16-10) underwent an appendectomy. Fortunately, major contributions came from left-hander Mel Parnell (3.14, 15-8), a finesse pitcher with great stuff, and veterans Earl Johnson and Denny Galehouse.

The Red Sox, who led the league in runs with 907, scored often and in quantity. Ted Williams (.369-25-127) carried the Red Sox through June with a .374 average, eleven home runs, and forty-two runs batted in. Then, in early July, Williams suffered a pulled cartilage roughhousing in a Pullman car with teammate Sam Mele. Not only did Williams miss two weeks of playing time, the injury reduced his ability to hit with power for the remainder of the season.

The presence of Stan Spence (.235-12-65) and Vern Stephens (.269-29-137) in the Red Sox lineup prevented hurlers from pitching around Williams. Along with Bobby Doerr (.285-27-111), Stephens, who in August led the league in runs batted in, provided Boston with one of the most potent keystone combinations of all time. An excellent fielder, Doerr also set an American League record with 411 chances without an error in seventy-two straight games, breaking Snuffy Stirnweiss's record set earlier that season. Another pleasant surprise in the infield was rookie first baseman Billy Goodman (.310-1-66).

With both Boston teams leading their leagues in September, World Series fever captured the city. The Red Sox, however, began to lose momentum when, in addition to Ted Williams's loss of power, they temporarily lost Doerr to a leg injury. The September 24 three-way tie between the Yankees, Red Sox, and Indians was broken when the Red Sox and Yankees lost two games each to the Senators and the A's respectively, and the Cleveland Indians, behind excellent pitching performances by Gene Bearden and Bob Feller, won two games against the White Sox. Cleveland appeared to be in the driver's seat with three games left and a two-game lead. Detroit dampened Cleveland's prospects, however, when the Tigers took two games from the Indians in the season's last three-game series. Hal Newhouser, whom Lou Boudreau described as throwing "aspirin tablets," defeated the Indians 7-1 on the final day of the season.[31] Meanwhile, Boston fans were delighted when the Red Sox won their last two games against the Yankees, 5-1 and 10-5, to force the first playoff game in American League history.

Indians manager Lou Boudreau surprised the Red Sox by selecting knuckleballer Gene Bearden (2.43, 20-7) to start the one-game playoff in Boston's Fenway Park. During the 1948 season, the left-hander's earned run average led the American League, and he was almost unhittable. His knuckleball, which was thrown with three fingers rather than the usual two, dipped sharply just as it reached the plate. The pitch acted like a sharp-breaking spitball rather than floating to the plate as most knuckleballs did. In many respects, it was remarkable that Bearden was pitching at all. He had been a machinist's mate aboard the cruiser USS *Helena* when it was sunk during World War II. He spent two days on a life raft in a semiconscious state with head and leg injuries. An aluminum plate was fitted in the back of his head and another, which was held together by a screw, was placed over his knee.

Boudreau knew that Bearden's knuckleball would be difficult to drive over Fenway Park's dreaded "green monster" left-field wall. As Boudreau recalled, "If he was on, I knew he would give me five or six good innings and I had everyone else in the bullpen including Feller, Lemon, and Gromek. I would have used them all for a one-hitter if I had to."[32]

Red Sox manager Joe McCarthy had a surprise of his own. In a move that Boston writers second guessed all winter, he started veteran Denny

Galehouse against the Indians. Galehouse pitched eight shutout innings against the Indians in relief earlier in the season, and McCarthy's other starters were tired from the grueling pennant race.[33] Boudreau himself played the greatest game of his career, going four for four at the plate. He smashed two home runs to accompany a three-run homer by Ken Keltner, as the Indians beat the Red Sox 8-3. Bearden yielded only five hits, including Bobby Doerr's three-run home run for his twentieth win of the season.

The Cleveland Indians' miraculous season was the story of propitious moves by Bill Veeck, outstanding performances by veteran players and rookies, who in some instances played beyond their normal capabilities, and just plain luck. One key to the Indians' success was an excellent pitching rotation that included not only Gene Bearden but also Bob Lemon (2.82, 20-14), Steve Gromek (2.84, 9-3), and Bob Feller (3.56, 19-15). The stopper on the staff was converted infielder Bob Lemon, who had an excellent natural sinker, a curve, and a splendid slider, which made him tough to hit.[34] Lemon pitched ten shutouts in 1948 and a 2-0 no-hitter against Detroit on June 30 that was witnessed by 49,628 fans—the largest crowd ever to see a no-hitter at the time. The Indians' bullpen was anchored by Russ Christopher (2.90, 3-2) and Eddie Klieman (2.60, 3-2), with the former earning a league-leading seventeen saves. Other pitchers included Sam Zoldak (2.81, 9-6), acquired by Veeck from the Browns for $100,000, and Don Black. On September 13, Black suffered a cerebral hemorrhage and collapsed at the plate while batting against the St. Louis Browns. The following week, Veeck staged a Don Black night and turned the proceeds, $40,000, over to Black and his wife. Black never returned to the game.

The Indians' most controversial pitcher was Negro League star Satchel Paige (2.47, 6-1). Veeck was heartily criticized by many for signing a pitcher whom many thought might be close to fifty, and there were accusations that the signing was nothing more than a publicity stunt. The *Sporting News* also made racial inferences, when it charged that "public opinion would not have been so aroused if Veeck had hired a 50 year old Caucasian."[35] Paige, however, soon proved he could still pitch and impressed his new teammates. Batterymate Jim Hegan recalled Paige's first start on August 13, when 51,013 fans, many of them black, crammed into Chicago's Comiskey Park: "He didn't have many pitches—mainly a fastball," noted Hegan. "His greatest asset was control—all you had to do was put your glove up. I don't care where you put it, he could hit it . . . he could throw strikes over [a] gum wrapper."[36] So many people streamed in to see Paige pitch that 15,000 fans were turned away. Just before starting time, the pressure of the crowd at one of the entrances became so heavy that the gates collapsed," wrote Ed McAuley. "Hundreds of fans—whether they had tickets or not—poured through the breach."[37] Paige threw a nine-

A converted infielder with a live arm that made baseballs do unpredictable things, Bob Lemon possessed a sinker that never seemed to have a bottom. (George Brace Photo)

inning shutout. On August 20, before 78,382 fans, the largest crowd ever to witness a night game, Paige shut out the White Sox again. This time he pitched a three-hitter, to run his scoreless string to twenty-six innings for his fifth victory in six weeks. Veeck sent the *Sporting News* a telegram, which read "Paige pitching—no runs, three hits. He definitely is in line for the *Sporting News* Rookie of the Year Award. Regards. Bill Veeck."[38]

Paige became an instant gate attraction and the darling of Cleveland's media. In spite of all the attention, Satchel Paige remained Satchel Paige. Although friendly with his teammates, he was rarely with them when he could be with his black friends located in every city. Paige gave Lou Boudreau fits—he dumped a day's catch of fish in the team's shower, disregarded curfews, and maintained his own schedule. When Boudreau fined him for "indiscretions" such as missing a July game in New York, he simply made light of them—"Mr. Boudreau fined me $100. Fifty for

Satchel Paige still had pinpoint control when he was signed by Cleveland in 1948. "He could throw strikes over a gum wrapper," recalled catcher Jim Hegan. (George Brace Photo)

missin' the game and fifty for missin' the train to Boston that night. And he gave me a baseball schedule, too. That $100 guaranteed I would keep lookin' at it."[39]

The easygoing Paige's roommate was Larry Doby (.301-14-66), whose speed, excellent fielding, and power potential became readily apparent in 1948. Although not as intense as in the previous year, he was still struggling to prove himself and his race. As Bob Lemon recalled, "It was strapped on him—he took some of the harassment personally. I can't put myself into that situation, but when you had to stay at other hotels and weren't allowed into restaurants that other players went into . . . it would create a little problem. It didn't take him long to adjust."[40] The turning point came in May when Doby crashed a home run that hit the top of the center field wall in Washington—the longest since Ruth cleared the wall in 1922. Doby's home run hit a loudspeaker set atop a thirty-five-foot wall, the base of which was 408 feet from home plate, and then it bounced onto the field. Only the loudspeaker, which was not present in Ruth's time, prevented the ball from clearing the wall.[41] A converted infielder, Doby made several spectacular catches and delivered key hits that contributed to the team's success.

Beyond Doby, the Indians' roster sported an unusual number of outfielders. Hank Edwards and Thurman Tucker were lost to injuries early in the season, and two others, Walter Judnich and Bob Kennedy, failed to deliver at the plate. However, Hal Peck, another little-used outfielder, made several key pinch hits during the campaign. Finally, the unsung hero of the outfield was University of Oklahoma graduate Dale Mitchell (.336-4-56), who finished third in the American League batting race. Mitchell was a contact hitter who hit to the opposite field and could fly around the base paths.

The Indians catching corps was headed by Jim Hegan (.248-14-61), a receiver respected by everyone for his defensive prowess. Al Rosen recalled Hegan's great agility behind the plate and his fine throwing arm. "He could do everything well," noted Rosen, "he just couldn't hit. If Jim Hegan had been able to hit .280 or .285, he would be in the Hall of Fame."[42] Backing up Hegan was Joe Tipton (.289-1-13), a fun-loving, hard-scrapping receiver who later left baseball amid gambling charges. While substituting for Hegan in June, he had nine consecutive hits.

The Indians' greatest strength in 1948 was its infield. At first base was fan favorite Eddie Robinson (.254-16-83). A World War II veteran, Robinson suffered damage to his leg when a Navy doctor destroyed a key nerve. After many operations, he was forced to wear a brace attached to his baseball shoe.[43] At third base was veteran Ken Keltner (.297-31-119), the slick-fielding infielder whose diving stops ended Joe DiMaggio's great hitting streak in 1941. At age thirty-one, Keltner was nearing the end of a fine career.

Backing up the Indians' keystone combination of Joe Gordon (.280-32-124) and Lou Boudreau (.355-18-106) was Johnny Berardino, a part-time actor who entertained roommates with long excerpts from Shakespeare. Veeck obtained him for $50,000 to keep him out of Yankee hands and then had the handsome player's faced insured for $100,000.[44] The 1947 acquisition of second baseman Joe Gordon from the Yankees for Allie Reynolds proved even more important. At age thirty-two, Gordon had already played on five pennant-winning teams with the Yankees. The friendly veteran proved to be an outspoken and decisive team leader who pushed his teammates to excel.[45] He was a smooth fielding, even acrobatic infielder, with power. Coupled with Lou Boudreau, the duo was described by Eddie Stanky as "the greatest second base combination I have ever seen."[46]

Player-manager Lou Boudreau won the Most Valuable Player award in the American League and a place in the Hall of Fame because of his 1948 performance. Until Alex Rodriguez hit .359 in 1996, no shortstop had topped Boudreau's .355 average for four decades. The trade talks between the Indians and Browns involving Boudreau and Vern Stephens during the previous winter spurred Boudreau into action. "It was an incentive to me just to prove to him [Bill Veeck] what I could do, and perhaps do better, while I was still managing," he remembered.[47] Nevertheless, Boudreau was an unlikely hero. After breaking his ankle three times, this former University of Illinois All-American basketball player was the slowest player in the game since Ernie Lombardi. He had flat feet and lacked the range usually required of the demanding shortstop position.[48] He made up for his inadequacies through intelligence—he studied every hitter in the league and knew exactly where to position himself. Although Boudreau had an awkward-looking stance, Indians vice president Hank Greenberg noted that he had "everything" as a hitter—"fine coordination and perfect vision . . . his form is flawless."[49]

As a manager, Boudreau was constantly second guessed by Veeck. Several times during the season, Greenberg had to persuade Veeck not to replace Boudreau.[50] Others, like Gordon Cobbledick of the *Cleveland Plain Dealer*, agreed that Boudreau was "inspirational" and had the confidence of his players but felt that he "over-managed" and "theorized" too much."[51]

No one disputed Boudreau's courage. He did everything in his power to get the Indians to win. On August 1, he stole home to beat the Red Sox and end an eight-game losing streak against them. Earlier, Boudreau had caught in a game in which the team used twenty-three players. Finally, after being sidelined in mid-August with a variety of ailments, including a badly injured ankle, the Indians manager came off the bench to deliver a key pinch hit that tied the score and allowed the Indians to beat the Yankees before 73,434 fans. When Boudreau limped to the plate, Veeck, who was in the press box, reportedly remarked, "Even if Boudreau doesn't get a hit, this is the most courageous thing I've ever seen in baseball."[52]

The 1948 World Series

After the exciting pennant races and the American League playoff game, the 1948 World Series between the Braves and Indians was dull by comparison. The most excitement came in game one in Boston, as the Braves beat the Indians 1-0 behind Johnny Sain, who waged a pitching duel against Bob Feller. All of the action occurred in the eighth inning with one out and two men on for the Braves. On a timed pick-off play, Feller suddenly whirled around and threw a perfect strike to Boudreau, who slipped behind pinch runner Phil Masi at second base. The trapped Braves catcher dove for the bag and was apparently tagged out, but umpire Bill Stewart, who was also caught off guard by the play, called him safe. Boudreau protested vigorously, but the call stood. The next batter, Tommy Holmes, drove a single down the third base line, past the diving Ken Keltner, to drive Masi home for the only score of the game. Although he threw a two-hitter and pitched brilliantly, Feller lost his best opportunity to win a World Series game. Photographs taken of the disputed play clearly showed Boudreau applying the tag while Masi's outstretched hand was at least a foot away from the bag. Ten years later, Stewart admitted to Feller that he had blown the call, and, after the umpire's death, Masi told Boudreau that he also knew he was out.[53]

In game two, the Indians beat the Braves 4-1 on runs driven in by Larry Doby, Lou Boudreau, and Joe Gordon, after the Braves scored in the first on a run driven in by Bob Elliott off winning pitcher Bob Lemon. Warren Spahn was the loser. Gene Bearden continued his pitching mastery by shutting out the Braves in Cleveland 2-0 on a five-hitter in game three. The Indians scored in the third on a throwing error by Alvin Dark and again in the fourth on a single by Jim Hegan. The losing pitcher was Vern Bickford. The fourth game of the series was a pitchers' duel between surprise starter Steve Gromek and Johnny Sain. The Indians triumphed 2-1 when Larry Doby clouted a 410-foot homer off a high fastball thrown by Sain. The Indians also scored in the first on a single by Mitchell and a double by Boudreau. The Braves scored their lone run in the seventh, on a home run by Marv Rickert.

The Indians established a new World Series attendance record in game five, as 86,288 fans, including 8,500 who stood behind the team's chain-link outfield fence, jammed into the park. They saw the Braves route Bob Feller 11-5 on two homers by Bob Elliott and a solo home run by Bill Salkeld. Warren Spahn won the game in relief of Nelson Potter, as he held the Indians to one hit in five innings of work and struck out seven. After returning to Boston for game six, the Indians finished the series when Bob Lemon beat Boston 4-3 with relief help from Gene Bearden. Bearden entered the game with a 4-1 lead and the bases loaded and one out in the eighth inning. A sacrifice fly by Clint Conaster and a double by Phil Masi scored two more runs before Bearden got out of the inning. In the ninth, Bearden was in trouble again after walking Eddie Stanky, but the Braves self-destructed when Sibby Sisti bunted into a pop-up double play.

Indians players celebrated mightily on the train trip home. Veeck threw a party, and players shot champagne everywhere, ruining the upholstery of three cars. The next day the players were given a victory parade on Euclid Avenue. The street was strewn with roses and confetti and lined with more than 200,000 fans.[54] Jack Ledden described the action:

> Flags flew over the happy scene, banners were waved frantically while whistles and horns tooted. School children carried signs saying: "We knocked the Beans out of Boston." Thousands of balloons floated down from buildings. A few spectators thrust packages containing gifts into the car bearing Louis and Mrs. Boudreau and President Bill Veeck. Ticker tape fluttered out of windows in Public Square and all along the avenue. Bankers, stenographers, bellhops, policemen, bus drivers and executives jockeyed for positions near the line of march so they could wave to the victorious players. Public Square was a mass of humanity with some 100,000 jammed into the six-block area. Street cars and buses were stalled and boys and girls climbed atop them to get a better view of the Indians. As the parade struggled into movement toward University Circle, two miles away, the biggest cheer in Cleveland history shattered the air. It ignited like a fuse and continued its din until the line of cars disbanded near Western Reserve University.[55]

The series win evoked a sense of pride and joy in Cleveland unlike any other in the twentieth century. For once, this diverse city was joined by an event that all could celebrate. Most thankful of all was Bill Veeck, who realized just how thin his margin was. Veeck rewarded everyone in the Indians organization—and if you were like Ada Ireland, who worked twenty-four hour shifts at the switchboard during the series, you received a new car.[56]

1949

Vern Stephens, Ted Williams, and Bobby Doerr—in 1949 the
Boston Red Sox were the best hitting-machine in baseball.
(Photographic Archives, University of Louisville)

13

Gardella's Folly

Commissioner Chandler's five-year ban on the Mexican League jumpers was the beginning of a saga that almost brought baseball's perpetual reserve clause to its knees long before the 1975 McNally-Messersmith case. Unlike the Federal League jumpers of 1914, who were quickly reinstated following their league's collapse, Chandler's ban was implemented. When catcher Mickey Owen presented himself at Chandler's Cincinnati offices following his flight from Mexico in August 1946, he was rebuffed. This reaction sent a message that baseball would not take back its prodigal sons. While in the short-term this policy successfully discouraged others from jumping to Mexico, the long-term effect was that baseball's structure was placed in grave danger.

In addition, Chandler's ban left the remaining Mexican League jumpers right where Jorge Pasquel wanted them—with few options except to play in his league. Pasquel sued Owen for $127,500 for breach of contract and damages and then offered the catcher's fellow jumpers, most of whom had no written contracts, reduced salaries to play in Mexico for the 1947 season. "I didn't talk to Max Lanier or Lou Klein," Pasquel noted, "because they know that they must reach a new understanding with me regarding their salaries for 1947. Lanier was paid $25,000 in 1946. He won only five games for my Veracruz team. That's $5,000 per victory, and that's too much. Klein also wasn't the player in Mexico that he was in Cuba this winter."[1] After learning of Lanier's plight, Branch Rickey lamented with a twinkle in his eye, "Poor Lanier, Pasquel is an assassin of careers."[2]

Financial losses from the previous season caused the Mexican League to begin with only six teams in 1947: Veracruz, Mexico City, Monterrey, Tampico, Torreon, and Puebla. With only Danny Gardella, Ace Adams, and Mickey Owen permanently absent, most of the jumpers eventually, if not reluctantly, returned to play in Mexico.[3] Lou Klein, who won the Cuban League batting championship during the winter, signed on May 16, but Lanier held out until early June. The former Cardinals pitcher failed in an attempt to market his services elsewhere. In April, he sent a telegram to the Cleveland Rosenblooms, the 1946 National Baseball Federation champions, that read, "Heard that you had a baseball club. I would like to pitch for you this summer. If you would be interested wire me collect," signed, "Max Lanier, Former St. Louis Cardinal pitcher." The Rosenblooms wrote back that they were flattered but could not take him, even without pay, because they were amateurs. Other teams could not come close to his $15,000 salary demand.[4] Finally, Lanier capitulated and made his season debut on June 26, losing 1-0 to Tampico.

Although the league still boasted many good players, including Cuban pitcher Sandy Consuegra, Mexican batting champion Bobby Avila, a plethora of former Negro League stars such as Theolic Smith, and jumpers Klein, Hausmann, Gladu, Maglie, Zabala, Martin, Carrasquel, Reyes, and Olmo, it was far from a financial success, even with the reduced salaries. Moreover, hot weather, poor conditions, and miscommunication continued to take a toll on foreign players. Former Detroit shortstop Murray Franklin left in August following a fight with the Tampico manager, and Lanier quit at midseason after a salary dispute. He later explained, "They cut my pay in half, and they are doing the same thing to the other Americans down there. I had a letter from Jim Steiner and he said most everybody on his team got paid only half what they were due the last week. That's the way they do business down there, so I came home."[5]

It was painfully clear that the jumpers missed major-league baseball. "Financially, I have no regrets," complained Lanier, "but I miss the major league life now, and I'd give anything to be back. There's nothing like it."[6] Another player who missed the game was former Giants pitcher Ace Adams. Sportswriter Furman Bisher reported that Adams was "living like a king" on his 650-acre farm in Georgia's peanut and cotton country. Although he made three times more money in Mexico than with the Giants, Adams stated, "I'm tickled pink not to have to return. I never gave my going back a second consideration, anyway, because it's not our kind of baseball—it's strictly second-rate." Relegated to pitching in a semipro league at age thirty-five, he added, "being on the black list is sorta like being a criminal. If I could only get that lifted. It'll hang over my head and folks won't remember me for my National League records, only as the guy who was banned for five years because he went to Mexico. . . . I think I did the right thing."[7]

For Mickey Owen, Chandler's ban was the beginning of a long nightmare. After being sued by Jorge Pasquel, Owen countersued for $93,908.56, claiming that Pasquel had fired him as manager of the Veracruz club without justification.[8] The suits, which continued into 1952, when Pasquel won a final verdict, left the Owen family bankrupt. To pay their 1947 legal fees and taxes, the Owens sold some of the very properties that they had acquired with Pasquel's bonus money. Owen, who attended auctioneering school in Iowa, sold his two Greene County, Missouri, farms and then auctioned off his own livestock. The former Brooklyn catcher quickly tired of the life required of traveling auctioneers and quit.[9] In desperation, Gloria Owen even wrote a letter to President Truman admitting that their Mexican venture was a mistake and pleading with Truman for relief. "We are in debt to our lawyer, income tax, and have no way to earn a living as my husband knows nothing but baseball," she wrote. The letter was referred to the Veterans' Administration, which sent it to Commissioner Chandler, who in turn politely replied that he would give "full consideration to all the things that you have said to the President."[10]

During the summer of 1947, Owen barnstormed around the Midwest with a group of semipro players. On occasion minor leaguers played with the team under assumed names. In addition, Owen's team was invited to play in the *Denver Post*'s semipro tournament at Merchant's Park, the home of the Denver Western League club. Realizing there might be a problem, former U.S. Senator Edwin C. Johnson, the Western League president, wrote to Chandler for permission to include Owen's team and stated that "the *Denver Post* claims they will lose the best drawing team if Mickey Owen is not permitted to play so I hope you will offer no objection." The commissioner reminded Johnson that ineligible players were not permitted to play in a professional ballpark, and he declared further that any men playing with or against an ineligible player would become ineligible themselves.[11]

Chandler's ruling had a chilling effect on the ineligible players and ultimately led to Danny Gardella's suit against baseball. During the summer of 1947, Gardella played for the Gulf Oilers, a semipro team on Staten Island. His presence on the team caused the Cleveland Buckeyes to cancel a game against the Oilers at the last minute. "The announcer asked the spectators not to hold the action against the players of the Negro National League, because they could not afford to risk the penalty imposed upon players who play against an outlaw."[12] A disgruntled fan who was in attendance that night reported the incident to dentist Conrad Meibauer. Meibauer told another patient, attorney Frederic Johnson, about it and then arranged a meeting between Gardella and Johnson.[13]

Frederic Johnson, a graduate of Yale University and Harvard Law School, was interested in baseball from childhood. When he was secretary to New York Supreme Court Justice Julius Miller, Johnson wrote a legal treatise on baseball published in the *United States Law Review* in 1939 predicting the downfall of the reserve clause.[14] Johnson recognized that Gardella's situation might provide a case that could make his prediction come true. Gardella's violation was against the reserve clause and not his contract—baseball had never argued in court that the reserve clause was legally binding on its players. George Wharton Pepper, who argued the Federal League case, claimed that players had only "an honorary obligation" to comply with the reserve clause.[15] After meeting Gardella on September 17, 1947, Johnson signed the ballplayer to a 50 percent retainer and sued baseball.[16]

"I wanted to make sure that baseball wouldn't interfere with my contract with Gardella," recalled Johnson, "so I served my notice of it with the Willkie firm."[17] Ten days later, they contacted Johnson and told him that his arrangement with Gardella was "champertous" and that he would have to withdraw it or risk being removed as Gardella's attorney by court order.[18] Johnson fought this point in court and won, when the judge determined that he must charge Gardella a preliminary fee of $60. When Gardella's case was argued on its merits before the U.S. Federal Court in the Southern District of New York in early October, 1947, Judge John Bright reserved judgment on it. Bright, however, died before he could issue a verdict, and the case was not handled by Bright's successor, Judge Henry R. Goddard, until July 1948. Goddard refused to overrule the 1922 Supreme Court decision and dismissed the case on the basis that it was out of the court's jurisdiction. Nevertheless, in his remarks, he noted that a reversal and distinction of the Federal Club case was now possible if the case were appealed on the basis of an expanded interpretation of the commerce clause of the United States Constitution and with the introduction of baseball's relationship with radio and television. It was Goddard who tipped Johnson off to these distinctions and strengthened Gardella's case. Mark Hughes and Louis Carroll, the attorneys representing baseball, attempted to get Johnson to settle, but he refused because he believed he could get a reversal. Hughes and Carroll were incredulous when Johnson demanded a $200,000 settlement.[19]

As the Gardella suit progressed, Mexican League players headed for the Havana Winter League during 1946 and 1947. The league's four teams (Cienfuegos, Havana, Almendares, and Mariano) played their games in the newly constructed Grand Stadium in Havana. Team rosters were liberally sprinkled with players from the Mexican League, in defiance of major-league rule 15 (b), which had been amended in 1946 with the intent of banning or fining players or owners who played against or hired ineligible players. The ban meant that Cuban players could no longer play winter ball in their own country or in Mexico if their team included ineligibles. One of the best-known baseball men affected by the rule was

Mike Gonzalez, a longtime player (since 1915) and coach with the St. Louis Cardinals who also managed and owned the Havana entry in the Winter League. Gonzalez's pleas that Cuban baseball be exempted from the rule failed. He resigned from the Cardinals after the 1946 World Series.[20]

Another league, the National Federation (Havana, Oriente, Matanzas, and Camaguey), which played its games at the old Tropical Park, was established to give eligible Cuban players a place to play. Organized baseball promised to stock each team with three professional players. The Cuban owners hoped for star players but instead received rookies who played poorly. Opening-day crowds of 7,000 at Tropical Park for National Federation games and 31,000 at the Grand Stadium for the Cuban Winter League, the largest crowd ever to see a game in Cuba, quickly established the pecking order of the two leagues.[21] After two months of operation, Grand Stadium crowds were averaging 20,000, whereas Tropical Park games were attracting fewer than a thousand admissions per game.[22] By season's end, the National Federation had lost $81,147.[23]

The Cuban Winter League, on the other hand, was a great financial success. During one game, more than 45,000 fans flocked to see a pitching matchup between Mexican jumpers Max Lanier with Almendares and Fred Martin of Havana.[24] In an exciting finish, Almendares defeated Havana in a playoff series to take the championship. Lanier won the first game of the series, and then for an extra $500, he pitched the team to a 9-2 victory with one day's rest. The former Cardinal was carried off the field by a crowd of excited fans. He recalled stuffing $100 bills that had been thrust into his hand in the clubhouse into his pockets—when he got home, he discovered that he had been given almost $1,700. "We almost never got out of the ballpark," he recalled. "They had to run a taxi underneath the stands. I tried to get out once and they nearly tore my coat off . . . they weren't bad—they just wanted a souvenir."[25] Lanier made $1,500 a month plus living expenses to play in Cuba.[26] Mike Gonzalez did even better. As team owner of the Havana Club, he cleared more than $50,000 in 1946-47.[27]

Of course, Gonzalez's ban and the fact that Chandler's action completely disrupted baseball in Cuba did not play well in the press. Cuba's sportswriters were almost unanimous in their support of Gonzalez. Jose Losada of the *Prensa Libra* called for "national homage" of "vindication for Gonzalez for the wrong done by 'Feliciano Chandler.'"[28] The national director of sports for Cuba, Luis Rodriguez, went to see Commissioner Chandler at the 1946 winter meetings in Los Angeles, but he was told that there was nothing the commissioner could do about the Cuban Winter League, because it was blacklisted. Calling Chandler "uncooperative," Rodriguez described organized baseball as a "commercial, imperialistic monopoly." The Cuban sports official threatened to lodge an official complaint with the U.S. State Department and explained, "We in Cuba feel that baseball was perfectly willing to use . . . Cuban players during the war, when there was a manpower shortage, but now that the war is over, they are through with us. Cubans, who play in the United States during the regular season, cannot return to their homeland and play during the winter."[29]

Stung by this criticism and the success of the Havana Winter League, organized baseball moved to become more competitive in Cuba during the 1947-48 season. They agreed to bring the Cuban Professional League into organized baseball in return for the league's promise not to employ ineligible players. Mike Gonzalez was accepted as an eligible owner, although he was still banned from returning to the Cardinals, and the league switched to the new Grand Stadium. Although the teams were restricted to ten players from organized baseball, the players received were of a much higher caliber than of those who played in 1946-47. Rickey sent the league a list of eighty players from the Dodgers' farm system. Players on the list who later reached the major leagues included Dee Fondy, Monty Basgall, Frank Laga, Toby Atwell, Carl Erskine, and Solly Hemus, Cuban stars Minnie Minoso, Witto Aloma, and Conrado Marrero, and Negro League players Henry Kimbro, Hank Thompson, and Sam Jethroe. Rickey announced, "I have done all I can personally. . . . All the Cuban League needs is a strong start. Then it will beat down the ineligibles with its own momentum."[30]

By January 1948, the Cuban Professional League was outdrawing the Liga Nacionale two to one, with receipts of $25,000 and Sunday crowds averaging 18,000. At season's end, in late February, the organized baseball–backed league recorded gate receipts totaling more than $500,000. Conversely, one of the Liga Nacionale's teams (Santiago) disbanded, and two of the league's remaining owners bailed out, forcing Tomás de la Cruz, the president of the players' association, to take over the teams.[31] When the 1948-49 season commenced, only the Cuban Professional League remained.

The Mexican League opened its season in 1948 with six teams (Monterrey, Mexico City, San Luis, Puebla, Tampico, and Veracruz) and minus its American and Cuban stars.[32] Jorge Pasquel's refusal to pay his players more than $1,000 per month scuttled any chance of their return. Moreover, Pasquel faced a palace revolt when, on October 25, 1947, the owners met while he was on a hunting trip and deposed him as commissioner of the league. Alejandro Aguillar Reyes, the country's foremost baseball expert, was named to replace him. Although Pasquel retained his title as president of the league and still owned the Veracruz club, it was the intent of the league's owners to end Pasquel's stewardship. Reyes calmly proclaimed that the league would continue to honor its commitments but it would now emphasize the development of young Mexican players over the use of highly paid Americans.[33]

Reyes's appointment was viewed by Chandler and major-league owners as a positive step. With the Gardella suit pending, the timing of Reyes's ascendancy was propitious. It was reported that the State Department, which was unhappy about the war between organized baseball and the Mexican League, had requested that Cardinals owner Bob Hannegan intercede with Chandler to set up "peace negotiations." In January 1948, Walter Mulbry, the treasurer of baseball and Chandler's chief administrative assistant, conveniently took a vacation in Mexico. While there, he visited Mexico City and met with Reyes, in an attempt to set up discussions on bringing the Mexican League into organized baseball.[34]

Only days after Reyes's meeting with Mulbry, Jorge Pasquel returned to the limelight—this time in New York, where he denounced any attempt at peace between the Mexican League and organized baseball. Describing the meeting between Reyes and Mulbry as "inconsequential," he exclaimed, "If Chandler wants to do anything, he must come to me personally. Nothing can be done by a tourist. Jorge Pasquel is the head man in Mexican baseball." Undermined by Pasquel, Reyes resigned, and the negotiations failed.[35] At a January 30 meeting at the Waldorf-Astoria, the National League discussed the peace proposal and rejected any attempt to reduce the five-year suspension of the jumpers. National League president Ford Frick was angered by Pasquel's remarks and by the fact that he had not been informed in advance of Mulbry's trip.[36] Chandler defensively replied that it was the Mexicans who had contacted him first and then noted that the return of the Federal League players in 1915 established a precedent for the jumpers' return "when the men who conduct that league decide to operate according to our rules and regulations."[37] A month later, Mexico's president Miguel Aleman prohibited Pasquel from making any further public remarks on baseball, but the damage was done.[38]

The Mexican League limped through the summer of 1948. Wet weather, the untimely deflation of the peso, and the absence of the American and Cuban players contributed to poor attendance. By the end of July, San Luis Potosi and Tampico were dropped from the league, all of the ballparks were boarded up, and the remaining teams were moved to Parque Delta in Mexico City to cut down on travel expenses. Reports estimated that the league lost 2,500,000 pesos ($500,000) during its last three seasons.[39] Despite these setbacks, Pasquel remained a potent force. In August, he was criticized by writer Pino Sandoval in *Present* magazine. On August 23, the printing plant that published *Present* and other magazines was "mysteriously" raided by twenty-five gunmen, who destroyed the operation's equipment and beat two employees. In a full-length advertisement appearing in his newspaper *Excelsior*, Pasquel denied that he was "the #1 millionaire" in Mexico and for the first time admitted that he had suffered great financial losses. "During more than eight consecutive years, it has only caused me losses and annoyance," he wrote. "As a business, it does not exist and never has existed. The scarce entrance money obtained from the games hardly covers the salaries of players and employees."[40]

The Mexican League ended its season five weeks early, with Monterrey being declared the winner on September 19, 1948. The teams' four remaining managers were summoned and told that their season was over and that Pasquel was not going to pay the players "a single cent more." In disbelief, the players congregated outside Pasquel's plush offices the next morning, but were told that there was no money and were advised to leave.[41] At a league meeting on October 28, 1948, the Pasquels finally yielded control of the Mexican League. Dr. Eduardo Quijano Pitman, a San Luis Potosi dentist, was named the new commissioner. He announced that the league would be completely reorganized for 1949 and that there would be no further player raids on organized baseball.[42]

Instead of returning to Mexico in 1948, eighteen of the jumpers formed a barnstorming troupe called "Max Lanier's All-Stars." An agent booked the team for approximately eighty games, and it won all of them. Starting in Monroe, Louisiana, they traveled on a tourist bus to Michigan, Iowa, Nebraska, and Missouri. Entertainment was provided by Danny Gardella, who was easily persuaded to sing "Danny Boy" or opera pieces in his beautiful tenor voice.[43] At one stop, Gardella "enthralled" an entire town by playing Sibelius's Second Symphony over the bus's loudspeaker while the rest of the team went into a restaurant to eat.[44]

The trip was expensive. "You just had to have a game every day," recalled Lanier. "Staying at the motel every night and traveling by bus wasn't exactly cheap. Our expenses ate up any profits."[45] In many places, thousands of fans turned out to watch them play, but as 1948 wore on, the fact that they were ineligible to play against professional teams caught up with them. Negro League teams would not play them, and they could not play in parks affiliated with organized baseball—the very venues that allowed them to attract crowds large enough to turn a profit. Chandler's edict also caused players to shy away from them.

Lanier and several of the players ended up losing money on the venture. Sal Maglie lost about $2,000 in travel expenses because he brought his wife Kay along, and Lanier dropped about $8,000 because he had to purchase the bus, equipment, and uniforms. Fortunately, he was able to sell the bus and recouped a major portion of his loss.[46] By the end of 1948, it was clear that barnstorming was no longer a viable option for the jumpers. "I'm not especially against Happy Chandler—I suppose he had a job to do—but he tried to stop us from playing," remembered Lanier. "We knew we couldn't play in professional ballparks against professional ballplayers, but he shouldn't have tried to stop us from playing against colleges and semipro clubs. But he did."[47]

As 1948 came to a close, Frederic Johnson argued Gardella's case on appeal before the Second Circuit Appellate Federal Court for the Southern District of New York. Three eminent jurists, Harry W. Chase, Jerome N. Frank, and Learned Hand, heard the case. On February 10, 1949, the tribunal released their decision—a 2-1 declaration that Gardella's case be remanded to a lower court for a jury trial. In his dissent, Judge Chase argued that the 1922 Holmes decision should be upheld. He saw no distinction between the original argument that the telegraph did not make baseball interstate commerce and Johnson's claim that television and radio made it so now. Organized baseball was shaken by the rationale employed by the majority. Both Hand and Frank maintained that baseball's connection with radio and television gave the game an interstate character that might bring it within the purview of the antitrust laws. Noting that the concept of interstate commerce had changed since the Holmes decision, Hand also remarked that the Supreme Court had overruled many of the cases based on that decision during the previous twenty years.

Even more devastating was Justice Frank's observation. Citing the thirteenth amendment, he described baseball and the use of the reserve clause as "an enterprise holding men in peonage." "Only the totalitarian-minded," he pontificated, "will believe that higher pay excuses virtual slavery." Referring to baseball's claim that millions of Americans depended on the game for diversion and that it could not continue without the reserve clause, Frank replied, "the public pleasure does not authorize the courts to condone illegality and . . . no court should strive to ingeniously legalize private (even if benevolent) dictatorship."[48]

Johnson was ecstatic over the appellate court's decision. He now had baseball right where he wanted it—on the run. In addition, in Gardella he had a client who, after spending the off-season making $36 a week as an orderly in a Mt. Vernon, New York, hospital, was quite sympathetic.[49] Quoted in the *New York Times*, Gardella stated, "It's just too bad if my case is hurting baseball because I've been hurt pretty badly myself. They say I'm undermining the structure of the baseball contract. . . . Let's say [instead] that I'm helping to end a baseball evil."[50] In a speech at the City College of New York, Jackie Robinson came out in support of the former Giant. Gardella, he noted, did not want to destroy the reserve clause; he

Mickey Owen traveled thousands of miles to persuade other Mexican League jumpers to drop their suits against baseball. *(The Sporting News)*

simply wanted compensation for "his inability to make a living" as a result of the ban.[51] The spectacle of a wartime ballplayer taking baseball to court, let alone threatening its very foundation by challenging the reserve clause, was incongruous to many baseball insiders.

Baseball reacted with determination. Ford Frick announced that baseball would take the Gardella case "all the way to the Supreme Court."[52] Clark Griffith assured everyone that Gardella's case would not be well received in the Supreme Court. "For the life of the trade, you've got to keep the ball player in his own association," he argued. "If they are allowed to move around every fall, it would destroy their profession."[53]

In a speech in Wilmington, Delaware, Chandler noted, "No major league player receives less than $5,000 a year and some of them get close to $100,000. If that's slavery or servitude, then there's a lot of us who would like to be in the same class." The decision also troubled several owners and club officials, who blamed Chandler for the court challenge. Many, like Edgar Feeley, the Giants' attorney, felt that once the threat of the Mexican League had dissipated, Chandler should have reinstated the jumpers.[54]

Chandler worked diligently to derail Gardella's suit. On January 13, 1949, Mickey Owen traveled to Versailles, Kentucky, to meet with the commissioner. Owen, considering an offer of a public relations position with the Coors Brewing Company, wanted to learn if there was any hope that baseball would reinstate the jumpers in the near future. Chandler was encouraging and told him that he felt reinstatement was just "around the corner," perhaps even by spring training. They reached an agreement. In return for credit toward his pension for his years of service between 1937 and 1945, Owen pledged not to sue baseball.[55]

Owen then traveled more than 8,000 miles to spread Chandler's "good news" to the jumpers and to ask them to drop any plans they might have for suing baseball. With the help of Fred Martin and Roy Zimmerman, he drafted a reinstatement petition that was signed by eleven players. The trio then visited Danny Gardella, in Yonkers, where they told him that their reinstatement was assured if he would drop his suit.[56] Gardella put the three men off until he could consult with his attorney. Johnson forbade Gardella from discussing his case, and he also refused to talk with Owen. Both Gardella and Johnson felt that Owen's mission had Chandler's blessing, but Owen denied the allegation and stated, "I want to play baseball, not destroy it. Baseball must have the reserve clause. It does not seem that in justice to Organized Ball, Mr. Chandler will be able to act on our appeal with the Gardella case pending."[57] Years later, still angered by what he considered tampering with his client, Johnson complained, "Baseball was as crooked as hell on me, because they tried to talk Danny Gardella out of the case."[58]

With Gardella's refusal to drop the case, Chandler was unwilling to reinstate the jumpers. A dispirited Mickey Owen appeared on the radio show *We the People* and asked the show's listeners for help. "I feel I have been punished enough," he complained. "I did not commit a crime. I believe that a five year sentence was too severe; why, five years represents the average life of a ballplayer in the game." When host Dan Seymour asked why he had jumped to the Mexican League, Owen simply replied, "Bad judgment."[59] Nevertheless, he honored his commitment to Chandler. After the appeals court's decision in the Gardella case, Owen was deluged with calls from attorneys who wanted to take his case because he had violated only his reserve clause and not a contractual agreement. Many of the lawyers were astounded when he refused. Owen recalled that one Philadelphia lawyer called him "the dumbest SOB he ever talked with."[60]

Max Lanier and Fred Martin, however, had no such commitments, and through attorney John L. Flynn filed a $2.5 million suit against baseball in federal court in New York. In the suit, they claimed triple damages, charging that baseball was a monopoly in violation of the Sherman and Clayton antitrust laws. They also sought reinstatement until their case was settled.[61] The Lanier-Martin case was argued on March 15, 1949, before Judge Edward A. Conger in the District Court of the United States for the Southern District of New York. Counsel for baseball argued that only Commissioner Chandler had the power to reinstate the players. Thus, the court had no jurisdiction in the case. For the plaintiffs, Flynn stressed the unilateral character of players' contracts, which he claimed "completely violate the liberty of the players." This suit, he argued, was a case of "men against monopoly, [and] human rights against property rights."[62]

As the threat to baseball loomed larger, Chandler took steps to bring in legal reinforcements. U.S. Senator George Wharton Pepper, who had argued the Federal Case on behalf of baseball in 1914, was ruled out because he had admitted on the record that the reserve clause was not enforceable after a player's contract expired and that it "was only an honorary obligation."[63] Instead, Chandler selected former Justice Department attorney John Lord O'Brian of the famed Washington legal firm of Covington and Burling.

The pressure brought to bear on baseball by the litigation was reflected by Commissioner Chandler's remarks delivered at a dinner at the University of Florida on April 5, 1949, to the effect that he would quit fighting the suits if he "was doing anything wrong or illegal." Assured of the correctness of his position, Chandler maintained that he would fight "until the Supreme Court of the United States tells me I'm wrong." To counter arguments that Judge Landis might have acted differently, he noted, "I followed in the footsteps of a myth, and I'll tell you that following a myth is not easy. I have Judge Landis's files for reference, but have had no personal word from him on what to do in the many difficult situations which abound in my office."[64]

Eight days later, in a speech delivered in Baltimore, Branch Rickey charged that the reserve clause was opposed by persons of "avowed Communist tendencies who deeply resent the continuance of our national pastime." Maintaining that the reserve clause had worked out "splendidly," Rickey continued, "As far as I know, players favor the clause unanimously." Johnson assailed Rickey's remarks and stated, "Rickey has had dictatorial powers so long he doesn't recognize the true principles of American life. Name calling is the last resort for a beaten man. The treatment Rickey has accorded baseball players would have made Simon Legree blush for shame."[65] In early April, District Court Judge Edward A. Conger refused to grant Lanier and Martin's motions for immediate reinstatement, stating that "the issues of law are too doubtful for any sort of pre-judgment in the matter." He also denied a similar motion filed on behalf of Gardella.[66] Both cases were appealed to the Second Circuit Appellate Federal Court in the Southern District of New York.

In the meantime, with the exception of Mickey Owen, who was playing semipro baseball in Winner, South Dakota, most of the Mexican jumpers were off playing baseball in Mexico, Venezuela, or Canada.[67] The Quebec Provincial League, where the majority of the jumpers were playing, was operated by Albert Molini of Montreal. The six-team league consisted of towns (Drummondville, Granby, St. Johns, Sherbrooke, Farnham, and St. Hyacinthe) ranging in population from 5,000 to 47,000. They were all located within fifty miles of each other, which allowed the teams to play twice in the same day—an afternoon game in one town and a night game in another. A ninety-game schedule culminated in an early September playoff between the two leaders. To attract the jumpers to Canada, the league's owners paid salaries far in excess of their receipts. In Drummondville, a town of 30,000, the club paid Max Lanier a salary of $10,000. The team pledged $6,000, and the other $4,000 was subscribed by the town's merchants in just two hours to prevent Lanier from signing with another team. Drummondville, which was managed by Stan Breard, also employed Gardella, at $7,000, Sal Maglie, at $5,000, Roy Zimmerman, at $700 per month, and a Puerto Rican first baseman named Victor Pellot (later known as Vic Power). Sherbrooke's roster included Fred Martin, Adrian Zabala, Harry Feldman, and Roland Gladu, while Alex Carrasquel and Lou Klein joined St. Johns, which was managed by Red Hayworth. Granby, having no Mexican League jumpers, had ex-Washington Senator pitcher Tex Shirley on its squad. With most of them making at least $2,500 for the season, the jumpers were not starving in Quebec.[68]

On June 2, 1949, the U.S. Court of Appeals refused to order baseball to reinstate Gardella, Lanier, and Martin and upheld Judge Conger's decision that the disputed questions of law and fact in the cases needed to be settled by a jury trial. In a unanimous opinion, Judge Learned Hand noted, "We are all agreed that the bare allegations in a complaint that the defendants make contracts with broadcasting and television companies will not support the jurisdiction of the court." Nevertheless, the court urged that the antitrust suits be tried as soon as possible.[69] The decision, while not a victory for baseball, provided Commissioner Chandler with a long-awaited opening. On June 5, he announced that the jumpers' bans were being reduced from five years to three and that, in spite of the pending suits against baseball, all of the jumpers were now free to return to the game. After citing Owen as a major influence in his decision, Chandler telephoned him in front of several newsmen and said, "Get your bag packed, boy, and get to your club right away."[70]

Chandler noted that he had waited to rescind the ban until it was "clear that I could act under no compulsion and without being justifiably accused of retreating from any situation." Only Frick and American League president Harridge knew of his decision in advance.[71] The move was designed to take away the players' public support and to defuse and discourage litigation against baseball. It also divided the ballplayers so they could be conquered one by one. In lifting the ban, Chandler instructed the players and ball clubs that players were entitled to a thirty-day trial, at which time they would be kept, traded, or released.

Not surprisingly, the players did not all come back at once and not all of them got the welcome they expected. For instance, Bill DeWitt refused to take Red Hayworth's collect call from Quebec and told the operator he would talk to the catcher only if he paid for his own call. Lanier, of course, felt he was worth more than $15,000 and scoffed at Fred Saigh's initial offer of $11,000. This demand did not endear Lanier to his old teammates, either. Enos Slaughter summed up the Cardinals' feelings when he said, "We'd still like to see those boys with us, but if they think the Cardinals owe them something for the time they've been gone, we think they're wrong. We've got harmony on this club, and we don't want any dissension or dissatisfaction. We could have won the pennant in '47 and again last year if we had a pitcher like Lanier and a utility infielder like Klein, so we lost money, too."[72] Other players, such as Luis Olmo, who was second in the Venezuelan League in hitting, were under valid contracts. Indeed, the co-owner of Olmo's team wanted a $10,000 indemnity for the player's services.[73]

Moreover, there was no guarantee that the players would be competitive in the major leagues. Four of them were twenty-nine (Gardella, Olmo, Feldman, and Reyes), and the remainder were thirty or older. As it turned out, only a few returned to make an impact. Six of the jumpers never appeared in another major-league game, and three others made only cameo appearances in 1949 or 1950.[74] Mickey Owen, whose career lasted until 1954, was sent to the Cubs. Between 1949 and 1950, the careers of Roberto Ortiz and Luis Olmo were less than spectacular. Adrian Zabala, who in his first two games back in 1949 beat St. Louis and shut out Cincinnati, got into a dispute with Leo Durocher over his salary and how he was being used. Zabala developed a reputation for being difficult and was sent to the minor leagues, never to surface again.[75]

Sal Maglie refused to leave Quebec during the 1949 season because his Drummondville team was in the pennant race (he won eighteen games in the regular season and five in the playoffs in 1949) and the Giants had offered him only $5,000 to return. In addition, Maglie realized that he would get only one more shot with the Giants and felt he was not in shape.[76] The most active owner in luring players back to his team was Fred Saigh of the Cardinals. He signed Lou Klein for $6,500—exactly what he made when he jumped the Cardinals in 1946—but promised to pay him for the remainder of the season regardless of whether he stuck with the Cardinals, was traded to another team, or was sent down to the minors. Klein, the first of the jumpers to reappear in a major-league uniform, did so well in his first two weeks that Saigh raised his salary an additional $2,500. When asked what he would pay Martin and Lanier when they returned, Saigh replied that, if they pitched like Harry Brecheen, he would put them in Brecheen's salary bracket.[77] Saigh's generosity, so unlike that of his predecessor Sam Breadon, quickly got the attention of Fred Martin, who signed on June 24. Lanier signed five days later for $23,000 and the promise that he would receive pension benefits retroactive to 1938.[78]

By the end of August 1949, Lanier and Martin were so pleased with their return to St. Louis that they allowed Fred Saigh to talk them out of their suit against baseball. Lanier announced, "We were treated swell when we came back. We found a new order in the Cardinal organization, more considerate. Mr. Saigh was understanding and said he would do his best to see that we could stay in baseball . . . so, when Mr. Saigh talked to us about our suit, we were willing to give up something too."[79] In spite of the Lanier-Martin settlement, the Gardella suit loomed large on the horizon. Although he failed in an attempt to see the commissioner's records, Johnson obtained permission to take a deposition from the commissioner at a pretrial hearing on September 19, 1949. Rather than take his case to the U.S. Supreme Court, Johnson wanted baseball to settle. He realized that Gardella could not collect damages, because he made more money in Mexico and Quebec than he made playing for the Giants in 1945. Johnson wanted to do everything he could to scare baseball officials into settling the case.[80]

As the tension surrounding the hearing heightened, Chandler began to worry. Saigh's success with Lanier and Martin did not escape his attention, and the night before the hearing Chandler cabled Saigh and asked him to call. When Saigh telephoned, the commissioner asked Saigh to take the next available plane to New York. Arriving at 11:30 that evening, Saigh was ushered into Chandler's bedroom by his aide Walter Mulbry. According to Saigh, the commissioner was sweating and shaken. He looked pale and scared. Chandler asked him to sit on the bed and then shook his shoulder and said, almost crying, "I want you to go see Johnson. The case comes up tomorrow, and I don't want it to." When Saigh asked why Chandler had called him, the commissioner replied, "Well, you are a lawyer. I know you are a damned good negotiator. I want you to call the man up now." By Saigh's own account, he arrived at Johnson's apartment on the west side of Central Park at about 1:00 or 1:30 in the morning, and they talked until 3:00. "I settled it with him," Saigh recalled. "I think it cost baseball—I can't give you the exact figures—around $150,000. Some players got $25,000. Lanier got the most."[81]

Johnson's recollection of the late-night visit differs markedly from Saigh's version. "I knew they would pull something," he recalled. Saigh wanted Johnson to go to breakfast with him to discuss a settlement, but Johnson refused because he suspected that it was a ploy to keep him from getting to the hearing—so Saigh came up to see him. Johnson wanted to throw Saigh out, but his wife insisted that he listen to the Cardinals owner. According to Johnson, Saigh offered him a $60,000 settlement, but when he refused, Saigh kept him up until 4:00 A.M., and, contrary to Saigh's version of the meeting, no settlement was negotiated.[82]

The following morning, Johnson arrived at the courthouse long before Chandler. He had alerted the press, to ensure publicity, and was well prepared for the hearing. Johnson and Chandler had been classmates at Harvard Law School and had not seen each other for twenty-eight years. When the commissioner appeared, Johnson greeted him with "Hello, Happy, how are you?" and Chandler turned his back on him. "It wasn't to be rude," recalled Johnson. "He just seemed afraid of me. He didn't know anything." Though extremely tired, Johnson was still able to conduct the hearing without notes.[83] According to the *Sporting News,* he put on a real show, "astounding witnesses by reciting all 463 clubs in the 61 professional leagues from memory." He did this to demonstrate the interstate nature of baseball and to impress those in attendance with his baseball knowledge. In addition, he quizzed Chandler on the game's relationship with television and radio and got him to admit that baseball earned $150,000 from its radio rights and $65,000 from television rights.[84] At several points, Chandler denied that he had attempted to punish the players. "I tried to get them to live up to their obligations and responsibilities. This was a fight against baseball in the United States. These players joined a group who said they were going to kill baseball in the United States." Johnson also successfully proved that he knew far more about the game's history than did the commissioner. When queried about the game's early history, the commissioner admitted that his knowledge went back only to 1909, when, as a boy, he had joined a gathering around Corydon's telegraph office to hear the Pittsburgh-Detroit series "tap-by-tap."[85]

During the second day, Johnson attacked the reserve clause, in an attempt to demonstrate how the players were being exploited.[86] By the afternoon of the second day, Johnson had made his point. John Lord O'Brian came to him and said, "I think I'll leave you boys to settle." Johnson sent another attorney, Fred G. Morritt, over to one of the judges, and the case was settled for $60,000. The parties agreed not to announce the settlement until after the World Series, when the impact of the deal would receive less media attention.[87] Saigh, who played an important role in the final settlement, agreed to take Danny Gardella, who did not want to return to the Giants. His only regret was not taking Sal Maglie, whom the Giants also wanted to unload. "I didn't take him," he stated remorsefully, "because I didn't have room for him on my roster. That was one of the worst mistakes I made in baseball."[88]

Gardella did not want to settle and repeatedly complained to Johnson about his doubts. Gardella later reflected, "It was baseball which was so wrong—so undemocratic for an institution that was supposed to represent American freedom and democracy. I thought it was quite wrong . . . if you sue someone for something, why should money appease you? It is like Judas taking money and saying, 'I'm being bought off.' Apparently my lawyer thought it was all right—I agreed to give him half the settlement."[89] Johnson was sure that Gardella was bluffing and told him sharply, "You do it!"[90]

Chandler was pleased to have the case settled and announced to reporters, "I'm so relieved. If I were a drinking man I'd get drunk."[91] Thirty-five years later, he maintained that baseball's attorneys were afraid of the reserve clause and felt they could not win the Gardella case. "I didn't know the terms of the settlement," he remembered. "They paid for it, but how much I do not know because I was not privileged to sit in the negotiations for the settlement."[92]

Commissioner Chandler received most of the credit for the Gardella settlement and for blunting the threat to the reserve clause. Ed McAuley applauded him for the timing of the announcement, and Dan Daniel predicted that Chandler would be offered a new contract as a result of his

Danny Gardella nearly brought baseball's reserve clause to its knees. "It was baseball which was so wrong—so undemocratic," he complained. (George Brace Photo)

handling of the case.[93] In spite of this praise, Chandler's role in the Mexican League affair was suspect, and the Gardella settlement showed him at his weakest. If Chandler had taken action following the 1947 season, when it was clear that the Mexican league was not a viable enterprise, it is unlikely that suits would have been brought against baseball.

Unlike Landis, Chandler failed to keep baseball out of the courts and played into Johnson's hands during the pretrial hearing. Undoubtedly, many owners felt that the hearing demonstrated the vulnerability of the reserve clause and needlessly placed baseball's antitrust exemption at risk. If the Gardella case had reached the Supreme Court, it is difficult to speculate what decision the court would have reached. In subsequent cases that challenged the reserve clause, specifically Toolson, the Vinson and Warren courts refused to challenge baseball's 1922 exemption.[94] It was not until football player William Radovich, in a case very similar to Gardella's, won a decision in 1957 that the Supreme Court acknowledged that baseball's exemption was an aberration.[95]

For Chandler, the pretrial hearings and subsequent settlement of the Gardella case were far from his finest hour. Instead of handling the Gardella case with vigor, preparing assiduously for the pretrial hearing, and involving himself in the settlement, he appeared apprehensive, indecisive, and purposely distanced himself from negotiations. In addition, by requesting Saigh's eleventh-hour assistance, he lost Saigh's respect. As Saigh later recalled, he "weakened on him from then on."[96]

The victory also allowed the owners to continue to hide behind the reserve clause in an atmosphere of false security. It would be "business as usual" for the next several decades. As for Danny Gardella, he had one at bat for the Cardinals in 1950 and then was sent down to Houston, where he batted .211. Disgruntled because of his situation, he muttered something to a reporter about being paid off by baseball to settle his case. Saigh gave Gardella his unconditional release. As a farewell stunt, Gardella borrowed a coat and traveling bag and leaped onto the Houston outfield fence as he waved good-bye. "I've been climbing outfield fences all my life," he joked, "so I might as well leave Houston climbing one."[97] For all his efforts, Gardella earned $30,000—the rest was folly.

14

A Stepchild in Peril, The Minors

The minor leagues reached the height of their prosperity and success during the first five years (1945-49) of the Pivotal Era. On the verge of extinction during the Depression, minor-league baseball was saved by night baseball and the Shaughnessey playoff system. The strong leadership provided by North Carolina judge William Bramham, who took over the presidency of the National Association in 1932 at a time when only ten leagues remained, also helped. Bramham forcefully placed the leagues on a sound financial footing and demanded integrity from the association's members.[1] Baseball quickly recovered from the manpower shortage during World War II and put forty-three leagues into operation in 1946. Thus, the minor leagues were poised to entertain a public temporarily flush with savings and few places to spend it.

Municipal bonds were issued for the construction of ballparks in Cedar Rapids, Omaha, and San Antonio. League attendance records in Nashville, Atlanta, New Orleans, and Memphis were smashed as the Southern League drew 85,276 on opening day 1946. Montreal drew 200,000 fans to watch Jackie Robinson on his first home stand, as 1946 minor-league attendance reached 32 million. Attendance hit a record 40,635,366 in 1947, only to be topped by almost a million in 1948. Twenty-one of the operating fifty-eight minor leagues established new attendance records, including the Texas League, which reached two million for the first time. By 1949, organized baseball operated in every state except Wyoming and Vermont.[2]

This period of prosperity, however, was short lived. As baseball historian Neil Sullivan wrote, "No period in the history of the game has been more disastrous for minor-league baseball than the 1950s. In 1949, nearly 42 million people paid to watch teams compete in fifty-nine minor leagues.

Ten years later, attendance barely surpassed 12 million, and only twenty-one leagues operated."[3] The decline was precipitous. Attendance in the major leagues dropped 14 percent in 1950 and 17 percent in the minor leagues—a decline of 7,338,274 admissions. Contemporary apologists cited the Korean conflict, bad weather, weak clubs in large-market cities, and record installment buying by the public as the cause.[4] Baseball scholar David Voigt placed the blame squarely on radio and television broadcasting, which, he maintained, destroyed "much of the local interest in minor-league teams."[5] Neil Sullivan, however, argued that broadcasting was only the vehicle of the minor leagues' downfall and that they were destroyed by a "prosperity" that all of baseball should have been able to share. According to Sullivan, their collapse "was but one result of major league greed."[6]

The main culprits were the farm system and the major leagues' inability to adopt a systematic approach to television. The farm system discouraged local owners from developing their own players and made them totally dependent on major-league teams for their supply of players. As Sullivan noted, the debate over the minor leagues is a debate over their purpose.[7] Do they exist to provide entertainment for the local populations they serve, or is their purpose to provide major-league teams with talent? Branch Rickey, the founder of the modern farm system, and Commissioner Landis clashed over this argument. Landis envisioned an America where free enterprise reigned and teams developed their own talent—eventually selling it to the major leagues for a handsome profit. In 1939, in the "Cedar Rapids" decision, the commissioner "freed" seventy-four Cardinal players by ruling that Rickey secretly controlled two teams in the same league. Two years later, he declared ninety-one Tiger minor leaguers free agents and charged Detroit general manager Jack Zeller with making a series of secret agreements with lower minor-league teams that allowed the Tigers to control scores of players not officially listed as their property.

After Landis punished the Tigers in 1940, the team dismantled its farm system. Zeller adopted Judge Landis's position with the zeal of a new convert. "We're cutting each other's throats by paying exorbitant bonuses to young players and absorbing heavy minor-league losses," he said. "Let's dump the whole farm plan. We could sign and train talent collectively and then distribute the players through an expanded draft system."[8] By the beginning of 1946, of the 230 minor-league teams affiliated with major-league chains, 125 were attached through working agreements. Zeller was particularly critical of this situation and noted, "Working agreements make parasites of most minor-league clubs and have no lasting value."[9]

Former minor leaguer Ross Horning described major-league baseball's relationship with the minor leagues as a form of mercantilism in which the balance was tipped in favor of the major leagues. Citing the three-veteran limit employed in the lower minors, he observed that the rule limited the ability of minor-league teams to acquire non-rookie players. "If a local ballclub owner could hire ballplayers who had experience," he testified before the Celler Committee in 1951, "then the quality of his base-ball team would rise." Major-league teams wanted players who were pros-pects, and no others.[10]

Most major-league owners cared little about being responsible to their minor-league counterparts. They viewed the minor leagues as a proving ground for the development of talent. It was survival of the fittest. By be-coming a farm club or developing a working arrangement with a major-league team, minor-league clubs yielded control and mortgaged their futures. Local franchise owners and fans often resented lost talent and pen-nant races when they were stripped of players. Only a few teams, notably the Cardinals, regularly refused to interrupt minor-league pennant races. Rarely was there even an admission that such responsibility existed. Per-haps the most famous is the advertisement taken out in the *Minneapolis Tribune* by Giants owner Horace Stoneham when he brought Willie Mays up to the major leagues, in 1951. In late May, Mays was leading the Ameri-can Association with a .477 average, and his promotion caused an uproar in Minneapolis. The advertisement read: "We feel that the Minneapolis fans, who have so enthusiastically supported the Minneapolis club, are entitled to an explanation for the player deal that on Friday transferred outfielder Willie Mays to the New York Giants. We appreciate his worth to the Millers, but in all fairness, Mays himself must be a factor in these considerations. On the record of his performance since the American As-sociation season started, Mays is entitled to his promotion and the chance to prove that he can play major-league baseball. The New York Giants will continue in our efforts to provide Minneapolis with a winning team."[11]

Although farm teams lacked stability, other sources of talent, such as "industrial leagues, colleges, semipro leagues, and the military were less reliable sources than Class D," the lowest minor-league classification.[12] With ninety players on major-league rosters in 1946, the Cardinals farm system was a shining example of productivity.[13] Even the Detroit Tigers returned to the farm system following World War II. Indeed, in 1948 Com-missioner Chandler stripped the Tigers of ten players, including future major leaguers Bill MacDonald and Bill Serena, for operating under an illegal oral agreement with the Dallas club of the Texas League.[14] In spite of the penalty, by 1948 the Tigers were back to prewar levels with 225 players in a twelve-club system, with a goal of reaching 300 players.[15]

The Brooklyn Dodgers developed the largest and most successful farm system during the postwar years. Branch Rickey's organizational genius was again at work. By emphasizing "quality out of quantity," the Dodgers by 1947 were stocking farm clubs with players developed through tryout camps at Pensacola, Florida; Thomasville, North Carolina; and San Bernardino, California. The camps, which were like college campuses, had bowling alleys, swimming pools, and other recreational facilities. The players ate at well-stocked training tables. At Pensacola, the players were divided into nine teams. Each team had a manager who was responsible for familiarizing himself with his players' capabilities and personalities. Scouts watched every workout and game and then gathered with Dodger staff at the end of each day to analyze talent well into the night. At the beginning of the minor-league season, more than a thousand men had been evaluated.[16]

By 1949, the Dodgers were running more than 700 men through a player college each summer at Dodgertown, in Vero Beach, Florida. As with the tryout camps, little time was wasted—players, known by their numbers, were rigidly scheduled for activities. Rickey attempted to reduce training to a science. By the time a player was ready for assignment, the Dodgers knew almost everything about his strengths and weaknesses. They measured his speed, arm strength, throwing accuracy, agility, and sliding capabilities. At the plate, they studied his batting stance, stride, swing, and bat speed. With pitchers, they clocked velocity and measured control.[17]

The talent Rickey developed paid handsome dividends for the Dodgers system. During the six-year period beginning in 1946, Dodgers-affiliated clubs won thirty-four titles—a feat not matched by any other team, including the New York Yankees, who won only thirteen. Averaging twenty-four affiliates a year, the Dodgers won pennants at a .239 rate compared with the Yankees' .124 rate, based on an average of seventeen affiliates per year. The Dodgers were particularly dominant in the triple-A and double-A classifications, with Montreal winning pennants in 1946, 1948, and 1951, St. Paul and Hollywood capturing titles in 1949, and Fort Worth taking Texas League championships in 1946 and 1949. So strong were the Dodgers in triple-A that two teams, Montreal and St. Paul, met in the Junior World Series in 1948. In the same year, twenty-two of the twenty-seven Dodger affiliates finished in the first division, and nine won postseason titles. In contrast, the Yankees won most of their titles (eight) during this period in the low minors. Only three players (Pee Wee Reese, Mike McCormick, and Billy Cox) on the 1949 Brooklyn Dodger World Series roster were not products of the Dodgers farm system, while many of the Yankees' star players, including Joe DiMaggio, Tommy Henrich,

Gene Woodling, Ed Lopat, and Allie Reynolds, were acquired through other means. It was not until 1950-51, with the arrival of Gil McDougald, Mickey Mantle, Jackie Jensen, and Whitey Ford, that the Yankees farm system consistently produced major-league talent.

The St. Louis Cardinals also, courtesy of Rickey, maintained an extensive farm system with approximately nineteen affiliates per year during the period. Although Houston and Columbus usually enjoyed good success, the Rickey touch was missing. Of the team's top prospects in the late 1940s, only Harvey Haddix made a major impact. It was not until 1954-55 that the system turned out Wally Moon, Ken Boyer, Joe Cunningham, Brooks Lawrence, Larry Jackson, and Bill Virdon.[18]

On the other end of the spectrum were the teams that maintained small farm systems—the Senators, Athletics, Tigers, White Sox, Red Sox, and Reds, all of which averaged fewer than ten affiliated clubs per year during the period. Clubs like the Red Sox and Reds preached that their smaller systems gave players more personalized attention. Gabe Paul of the Reds noted, "Any educator will tell you that the smaller the group, the easier it is to instruct."[19] Red Sox farm director George Toporcer described Rickey's operation at Brooklyn as a "Cecil DeMille mob scene." "Rickey," he crowed, crams his players "with baseball technique the way a 'black market' tutoring school crams errant pupils for their college mid-year exams."[20] Nevertheless, teams with smaller farm systems had a difficult time competing with the likes of the Dodgers. In 1949, for instance, the Red Sox, White Sox, and Reds failed to have a single winner in the minor leagues. Washington had the worst record, with only two of its teams ranking in the first division.

Staffing an organization with top-flight scouts was also an essential ingredient for success. Following World War II, teams quickly built small scouting armies. In 1947, the number of major-league scouts increased from 227 to 317.[21] Instead of hunting talent over wide territories, as they had before the war, scouts were now assigned to specific areas. The Cincinnati Reds argued that their 1947 scouting staff of twenty-five was searching for quality and not quantity. "Our program centers around the scouts instead of the clubs," maintained Fred Fleig, supervisor of the Cincinnati farm system, "and it is our firm opinion that it is easy to find a place for players to play, if they are good men."[22]

The increase in the scouting population almost coincided with the decrease in baseball talent. World War II broke the Depression, and after the conflict there was a rising demand for professional services. The G.I. Bill of Rights also provided previously unavailable educational opportunities to millions of men. With a portion of their potential labor pool drying up, several teams attempted to compete by offering prospects large bonuses when they graduated from high school.[23] To discourage this practice, the major and minor leagues adopted a rule that placed handicaps on the former free-handed bidding for the contracts of prospective stars. The so-called bonus rule provided that any player signed by a major-league team for $6,000 or more was thereafter identified as a bonus player and could be assigned to a minor-league team for only a year. Thereafter, the bonus player was kept on a major-league roster unless placed on irrevocable waivers. The rule proved to be unmanageable and led to "a lot of bitter recriminations and charges of subterfuge and 'under the table' dealing."[24] Furthermore, it did not prevent an onslaught of signings that caused clubs with small markets, as represented by the Cincinnati Reds' president Warren Giles, to complain loudly that the exorbitant bonuses being paid to "untried" teenagers were violating "all principles of sound business practice."[25]

The bonus rule was scrapped in 1951, and the signings continued. Many teams were burned by players who never developed. Examples of such signings include Pittsburgh pitcher Paul Pettit for $100,000, Cleveland pitcher Billy Joe Davidson for $150,000, and Red Sox pitcher Dick Pedrotti for $75,000. Other clubs, however, used their scouts to capture some outstanding talent. No team was better at judging bonus players than the Philadelphia Phillies. They paid $6,500 for Granville Hamner, $15,000 for Bob Miller, $25,000 for Robin Roberts, and $65,000 for Curt Simmons—who formed the core of their great Whiz Kids team of 1950.

The downsizing of the minors in 1948-49 was inevitable. As the supply of ballplayers dwindled, and the cost of running a farm system rose, major-league teams began to cut back on their affiliations with farm clubs. The New York Yankees estimated that it cost them in excess of $4 million between 1946 and 1950 to scout, develop, and acquire major-league ballplayers. The cost doubled from approximately $500,000 per year in 1946 to a million in 1949.[26] As the Pirates cut their farm teams from nineteen to thirteen and reduced their scouting staff, general manager Roy Hamey explained, "The margin of profit in one successful minor-league club is so small, with the tremendous overhead of bonuses, salaries, traveling expenses, etc. that it takes six or seven to overcome a loss that can be incurred in one losing team."[27] Cincinnati's Gabe Paul maintained that the Reds' scouts were able to sign only seventy-five players a year. "That's 7½ per team with 10 teams," he stated. "A working agreement used to mean that you would allow the minor-league team to dig up its own players and the major-league club would pick one or two for a certain lump sum agreed upon before the beginning of the season. Now a working agreement means that the major-league team will supply all the players and pay all the bills."[28]

By 1950, the majors were affiliated with fifty-three fewer clubs than they had been during 1948, and by 1952 that figure was reduced by an additional forty-six teams. Even the Dodgers downsized. Rickey explained that baseball, like the rest of society, had simply overexpanded and had taken farming beyond its limit in its enthusiasm following the war. "The need to protect your players is the horse, expansion is the cart," he noted. "Don't buy a farm and then stock it with players."[29] By 1949 the Chicago Cubs were down to ten clubs, from twenty in 1947. Not only was their system not producing players—their best prospect was Ransom Jackson—but it had run a deficit of $100,000 in 1949. Jack Sheehan, Cubs director of minor-league clubs, explained that "big farm chains simply can't be maintained by the average big league club anymore. We found, for instance, that the cheapest we can operate a Class D club is $35,000. If you are lucky, you'll escape at a loss of $20,000. A Class C club requires about $50,000 for operation and one in Class B $60,000. You seldom make any money on these three low classes. From Class A on up, if you happen to have a good team, you have a chance to show a profit. But you have to be lucky to wipe out the losses incurred down below."[30] In spite of these arguments, however, figures provided by a Senate investigation in 1953 indicated that, until 1950, the net cost to all major-league teams of owning minor-league subsidiaries never exceeded $400,000 and that, during the four years immediately following the war, minor-league systems actually subsidized major-league profits.[31]

While the player supply was dwindling, radio and television, far more insidious creatures, were also sapping the strength of the minor leagues. As early as 1948, Frank Lawrence, the owner of the Portsmouth, Virginia, club in the Piedmont League, predicted that "Television will be baseball's cancer."[32] Evidence of television's effect first appeared in 1948, when major-league teams in New York, Chicago, Boston, and Washington began to televise their games. Most television sets were located in barrooms. Many tavern keepers resented television because it drew far more beer sales than whiskey. Nevertheless, they needed television to keep up with their competition. In Jersey City, a community of 360,000, there were 600 taverns, and 90 percent of them had television sets. Early in the 1948 season, the Jersey City Giants experienced turnouts of 121 and 345 on successive afternoons when Dodger and Giant games were telecast. Attendance fell in Milwaukee and Baltimore because of Chicago and Washington television, while attendance dropped by almost 60 percent in Albany, which received televised New York games via Schenectady. In addition, the New England League, which had several cities within viewing range of Boston, also suffered a decline in attendance.[33]

In 1948, a television set was a big box with a small screen. The number of cameras in use was limited, and the announcer remained almost as important in describing the game as he was on radio. In spite of the fact that fans were not able to take in the entire field, they could still see the players and the action. Most important, television viewing was free and the small weekly payments that it took to purchase a new television set were less than the price of admission to a game. Once television caught on, fans stayed home in droves. Not only did major-league games vie with minor-league games, television itself competed with the game. The medium also popularized other sports, including football, basketball, wrestling, boxing, bowling, and golf. It further diluted America's leisure dollar.

Television grew so quickly that the owners were unable or unwilling to develop a common approach to the medium. Even the astute Branch Rickey could not predict how baseball, and other American sports, would some day be dominated and shaped by television. He did, however, see its immediate future quite clearly. Suppose television "arrives at a point at which its presentation of a ball game is perfect, a point at which a color picture will show every detail?" he asked. What if "the ownership of video sets becomes so widespread, and the quality of television programs, particularly after dinner becomes so alluring that folks stay home to watch the screen and forget all about the game at your ballpark? Huh?" He continued, "This thing requires intense study."[34]

When it became obvious that Baltimore, Newark, and Jersey City would experience the lowest attendance in the International League, league president Frank Shaughnessey called for the cessation of night games and for a home territory rule that would ban televised regular-season major-league games beyond a fifty-mile radius. He also warned that baseball would be unable to escape the threat of television as it had radio. "Remember this," he noted, "radio aroused curiosity in the fan. Television satisfies it."[35] In late 1948, both the National Association and the major leagues adopted Shaughnessey's rule.

The allure of television also was felt by minor-league owners. With television cameras located behind home plate and first base, the Louisville Colonels announced in March 1949 that all of their home games would be televised on WAVE television and sponsored by the Oertel Brewing Company. At the beginning of the season, at least twelve other triple-A or double-A teams also planned telecasts. Among those teams was the Newark Bears. The Bears were at one time the top New York Yankee farm team and the pride of the International League. The franchise won league pennants seven times between 1932 and 1942 and boasted such players as Charlie Keller, Yogi Berra, and Vic Raschi. Although runners-up in the 1948 pennant chase, they were last in the league in attendance with 170,506. In spite of improved bus service and park beautification, the team drew a 1949 opening day crowd of only 11,000 instead of the expected 20,000.[36]

Following opening day, attendance declined precipitously. Three consecutive afternoon games in April drew 403, 174, and 210. Rumors began to circulate that the club would be moved. As the team sank lower in the standings, league president Frank Shaughnessey charged that Newark lacked civic pride. In Newark City Hall, officials took umbrage at his remarks and attacked the Yankees for taking away their good players. One city commissioner complained that the Bears "are merely kidnapping bait for the Yankees." Then, on June 25, 1949, the *Newark Star-Ledger* announced that it was dropping the Bears from the International League standings and listing them instead under exhibition baseball, "because they obviously don't belong in triple A competition." The Bears took the unprecedented action of asking for the recall of sportswriter Jim Ogle, who reported on the team for the paper, and left themselves on the road without coverage. At the end of the season, the franchise was moved to Springfield, Massachusetts. Although few blamed television for the team's demise, the Bears were its first real casualty.[37]

In the meantime, an even more monumental decision was made—Commissioner Chandler was forced to remove baseball's territorial restraints on broadcasting. The catalyst was radio network owner Gordon McLendon, who re-created New York Yankees games in the Dallas area without baseball's permission. When baseball moved to stop McLendon, he threatened to sue and maintained that their restrictions were a prima facie violation of the antitrust laws. The Dallas club in the Texas League eventually submitted to pressure from Western Union to grant McLendon permission to re-create the games for a fee. After his Liberty Network became successful, other stations approached baseball for similar arrangements. When baseball balked, broadcasters threatened to sue and brought their case to the formal attention of the Justice Department. Upon studying the matter, Attorney General Tom Clark, an old political friend of Chandler, informed the commissioner and his attorney, John Lord O'Brian, that baseball would have to change its rule on territorial rights, although the Justice Department would allow a game-time exemption.[38] Chandler was caught in an untenable situation. If he refused to cooperate, baseball would again be threatened with court action that would undoubtedly jeopardize the reserve clause. As he finally realized, one of his major roles as commissioner was to keep baseball out of the courts. In late October, Chandler ruled that the fifty-mile broadcasting limit was no longer in place and that "clubs may no longer ban broadcasting of others' games except during hours of their own contests."[39] In explaining his decision,

Chandler stated, "I had to think of the over-all picture; it was the best we could do."[40]

Chandler's decision hastened the collapse of the minor leagues. By 1950, American communities accustomed to hearing only the All-Star game and World Series on radio were now being reached by Mutual's Game of the Day, the Liberty Network, or the expanded major-league networks.[41] Major-league baseball had arrived. In the same year, the Colonial League, whose franchises were located in New York and Connecticut, collapsed and the Jersey City club, which shared Newark's fate, moved to Ottawa. The destruction continued.

Although Chandler's vested interest lay with the major leagues, his advocacy for the minor leagues made the broadcast decision a difficult one. He reveled in rags-to-riches stories—to have played and umpired in the low minors and then to become commissioner. "That illustrates what a grand nation we live in," he exclaimed. "In what other country in the world could something like that happen?" The commissioner was in great demand as a speaker and as a representative of baseball. His papers attest to the hundreds of speaking engagements he fulfilled in the minors. The minors, for the most part, represented small-town America, where Chandler was most comfortable and effective. The engagements also fit his style—a little handshaking here and there, an entertaining presentation, questions and answers, ribbon cutting, praise and kidding, and, of course, singing. For example, he made an address before 545 fans the annual baseball banquet in Elmira, New York, on February 5, 1947, and pledged to protect the integrity of baseball against the evil forces that threatened all sports. Following his after-dinner speech, Chandler used his clear tenor voice to perform three solos, including "My Old Kentucky Home," accompanied on the accordion by Atlanta musician Graham Jackson. Then, as a finale, Chandler and Jackson formed a quartet with Eastern League president Thomas H. Richardson and Elmira mayor Leo Williamson. The group brought the house down with renditions of "Down in the Old Cherry Orchard," "When You Wore a Tulip," "Mother Machree," and others.[42] Some major-league owners were embarrassed by Chandler's antics and compared his actions unfavorably with Judge Landis's conservative demeanor.

As long as their own broadcasting interests were protected, major-league owners were willing to sacrifice any rights the minors possessed. This same vested interest determined their attitude toward the Pacific Coast League's desire to become a third major league. Led by league president Charles "Pants" Rowland, the Pacific Coast League lobbied for major-league status from 1946 through 1951. By 1947, the league's eight teams

(Los Angeles, Hollywood, Sacramento, Seattle, Portland, San Diego, Oakland, and San Francisco) served a combined population of almost eight million people. Los Angeles, with a metropolitan area of 3.7 million people, and San Francisco, with 2.3 million, certainly were major-league cities, and Seattle and Portland, with populations of 631,000 and 650,000, respectively, were not far behind. Charles Rowland argued that thirteen million people lived between San Diego and Seattle and that in ten years the figure would be twenty-five million. "We're a major league right now," he claimed.[43]

There was little doubt that the Pacific Coast League was a cut above the other triple-A leagues. Pacific Coast League players were paid above major-league minimum salary levels, teams traveled exclusively by air and stayed at the best hotels, and their players were treated like major leaguers. The San Francisco Seals ball club, owned by Paul Fagan, had lights as effective as those at Yankee Stadium, an infield manicured by a Scottish golf course groundskeeper, and an immaculate stadium constantly maintained by scores of employees. Fagan also insisted that his ballplayers be presentable at all times and provided them with electric razors, sterilized combs and brushes, clean handkerchiefs, freshly shined shoes, and a free barber shop.[44]

Rowland's critics argued that the league, with its small ballparks and poor lighting—with the exception of Seals Stadium—was insufficient to support major-league franchises. Although teams were capable of paying salaries in the $10,000 to $15,000 range, they would not be able to support the $125,000 salary that stars such as Ted Williams commanded. On their part, Pacific Coast League owners and fans decried the major-league draft, which allowed major-league teams to draft one player off a minor-league team for $10,000—a paltry figure in view of the $50,000 bonuses that untried players were receiving at the time. The draft forced teams in the Pacific Coast League and in other leagues, which owned their players outright, to sell them before the draft if they wished to receive their full value. Players such as Gene Woodling, Gus Zernial, Irv Noren, Jackie Jensen, and Bob Chesnes were sold for sums that in some cases exceeded $50,000. Only on rare occasions, however, was a truly good player left unprotected. The real issue was the inability of the Pacific Coast League to keep home-grown talent while teams remained subject to the draft. Under these conditions, it was impossible for the clubs to develop the talent they needed to bring the level of play in the league up to major-league levels. Thus, the situation perpetuated the Pacific Coast League's minor-league status.

The real battle was over Los Angeles and San Francisco. Pacific Coast League owners knew that if either or both cities were added to the National or American Leagues, their league, which also had teams in Oakland and Hollywood, would be severely hurt. In 1946, the owners moved to discourage outsiders from bringing a major-league team into league territory by agreeing that unanimous consent from all the owners would be required before a major-league team could move in. Moreover, they got the major leagues to agree that the league would be indemnified based on compensation determined by an arbitrator. In 1948, Edwin Pauley, a wealthy oilman and Democratic Party politician, decided not to buy the St. Louis Browns from Richard Muckerman and move them to Los Angeles. There were too many impediments: Muckerman wanted too much per share for the team, and Pauly would have to indemnify owners in the Pacific Coast League, including Phil Wrigley, the owner of the Los Angeles club. Pauley estimated that the entire transaction would cost him around $8,750,000.[45]

Nevertheless, major-league owners continued to eye the Pacific coast and were in no hurry to approve the league's annual requests for relief from the draft or to allow them to achieve eventual major-league status. Although at times he appeared to favor granting the Pacific Coast League relief from the draft, Commissioner Chandler fought a rear-guard action against both campaigns during his tenure. In 1947, after touring the West Coast cities in the league, he stated, "I am in favor of every section of the country having major-league baseball, if they can support it. . . . As the old umpire said, 'They're either out or safe and they ain't nuthin' until I call it.'"[46] Chandler did come up with a plan that would have expanded each league to ten teams by placing new teams in San Francisco and Los Angeles. The plan failed only because two American League teams refused to support it.[47] When Ford Frick took office in late 1951, Pacific Coast League owners were in open revolt and threatened to bolt the National Association and operate as an independent league. Frick mollified the owners by arranging for the league to have a new 4-A classification. Then, after having to confess during the Celler Hearings that there were no standards or provisions established to admit teams, Frick devised a formula that provided for the entrance of entire leagues at the major-league level if they could meet three requirements: a total market of 15 million people; stadiums with a capacity of at least 25,000 seats; and an aggregate attendance of 3.5 million or more in the last three seasons. Unfortunately for Pacific Coast League supporters, after 1949 the circuit was no longer in a position to muster enough attendance to meet the final requirement.[48]

Hindsight tells us that West Coast population growth did explode as envisioned by Clarence Rowland and that there were several cities in addition to San Francisco and Los Angeles with major-league potential

(San Diego, Seattle, and Portland). If other major western cities, such as Denver and Phoenix, had been included in a major league formed in 1947 or 1948, and the National and American Leagues had reduced their weak two-team towns by sending the Browns, Braves, and Athletics packing to Midwestern or Southern locations, it is difficult to believe that the game would not have prospered. Instead, major-league owners chose to prop up weak teams and in 1956 allowed two of baseball's strongest franchises to flee baseball's most lucrative market for greener pastures in San Francisco and Los Angeles. The owners' inability to plan and work cooperatively, their own personal vested interests, and their greed prevented them from taking advantage of a great opportunity.

While the Pacific Coast League was a great place for a ballplayer, the road to the major leagues was still a long and arduous one. With more than 8,000 men competing for 400 major-league roster spots in 1948, most never made it to the "show." In addition, in the minors salaries were low, conditions poor, and travel unforgiving. Players were shunted from team to team pretty much at the whim of the organization that owned them. In spring training, players received free room and board but no salary. A player's first pay day was May 1. In triple-A, the maximum salary was $6,000, although players were paid more under the table, and there was no minimum. In double-A, the mean monthly salary in 1951 was $526, whereas in single-A it was $313, in B it was $235, in C it was $192, and in D it was a meager $160.[49] The average minor-league salary was $2,100. If a player saved $1,000 on that salary, the sum was easy to exhaust in March and April. In addition, it was difficult to find winter employment—few employers would hire a temporary worker for five months. The tenuous state of being a minor-league baseball player was made worse by the lack of job security. Players could be released at any time and then would have to pay their own way home, just as they did at the end of the season. Traded players lost deposits and advanced rent, and players sold to a lower classification could have their salaries cut. There was no pension plan or medical benefits for players. If a player was injured, he was in danger of getting two weeks pay and a release.[50]

Travel on the longer trips in triple-A was by rail, although usually by coach. In the lower classifications, it was generally by antiquated bus or automobile. Many trips were long, and some were dangerous. Bus disasters during the Pivotal Era almost completely wiped out two teams. On June 24, 1946, eight members of the Spokane team of the Western League were killed when their team bus left the road and plunged 300 feet down an embankment in the Cascade Mountains. Many of the survivors were badly burned when the bus caught fire following the accident. One player, Jack "Lucky" Lohrke, who only a few years later made the majors with the New York Giants, had left the bus only fifteen minutes before the crash. He had received a call from the team's president to report to San Diego.[51]

The second bus crash involved the Duluth Dukes of the Northern League, taking the lives of four players and their manager/driver George Treadwell. The crash occurred after a truck carrying dry ice hit a rough spot in the road and careened out of control, rammed the Duluth bus, and pitched it into a ditch on its side. All but three of the occupants of the bus were pulled from the wreckage before the vehicle was engulfed in flames. The survivors included Red Schoendienst's brother Elmer and future Cleveland Indians manager Mel McGaha. In both cases, funds (more than $55,000 in Spokane and $81,000 in Duluth) were raised to aid the families of the victims and the injured. The most touching gift was from three Eau Claire, Wisconsin, children (ages 3½, 5, and 7) who operated a sidewalk soft-drinks booth for five days and raised $52.30.

Accommodations on the road were usually the best hotels available in smaller communities and mediocre lodgings in larger cities. Most class C and D ballparks lacked clubhouses, so players were forced to change in their hotel rooms. At night they often returned dressed in their sweaty soiled uniforms. "Therefore," recalled Ross Horning, "you don't wind up in the best hotels in the city for obvious reasons."[52] In 1947, most players in class C and below received a food allowance of $2.50 a day—insufficient in some areas, but comparable to Federal government per diems. Of course, conditions were even worse if you played for an independent team like the class C Topeka Owls, of the Western Association. The Owls paid their players $2 per day meal money and saved money by placing three or four players to a room on the road. At home, the team provided a bunk house that looked like a chicken coop for players who did not have accommodations in town. Teams in class C played anywhere from 120 to 150 games a season, a game each day and twice on Sundays, and traveled as much as twelve hours between destinations.[53]

The level of play in the low minors was simply "throw the ball and catch it." Play was punctuated by wild pitches, errors, and walks. In the higher minors, players were expected to pick up fielding and hitting tips. At the triple-A level, pitchers and hitters began to study each other's characteristics. Pitching became more refined, as hurlers possessed better control, and managers were able to play percentage baseball.[54] Umpiring was also uneven, and rabid fans often treated umpires poorly. Profanity and bottle showers marked some contests, and it was not unusual for fans to "pass the hat" to pay players' fines. In 1946, the games got so out of hand in the Florida State League that Judge Bramham threatened to suspend play in the league.[55] In 1947, fans in San Francisco and Sacramento almost rioted on two occasions. On July 4, after umpires chased the Angels' manager and a player out of the game, fans held up the contest several times by throwing cushions, lighted sparklers, and firecrackers onto the field.[56] The most ingenious breakup of a free-for-all occurred during a July 26 contest between Cedar Rapids and Kewanee. Following three separate altercations in the seventh inning, a wild melee broke out involving players, spectators, umpires, and the police. While the wild group threw punches, wrestled, and grappled with each other in front of home plate, public address announcer Bob Hahn placed a recording of "The Star-Spangled Banner" on the loudspeaker system. This brought everyone to attention, and by the time the music had ended, tempers had cooled.[57]

Making the "big leagues" was difficult. There were so many men in several of the major-league chains that if a player did not take the field when injured or when a major-league scout was watching, he might not have another chance. Pitcher Harvey Haddix, who went on to win 136 major-league games, provides the classic example. At age twenty-two, he earned rave reviews while pitching for Winston-Salem in the class C Carolina League in 1947. When a Cardinal scout was dispatched to watch him pitch, he discovered that Haddix was sick in bed with a temperature of 104. In spite of his weakened condition, Haddix left his sickbed and threw a one-hitter against the Durham Bulls.[58] The young pitcher finished the season and led the league with a 19-5 record, with 268 strikeouts in 204 innings and an earned run average of 1.90. Nevertheless, Haddix toiled for three years at the Cardinal's triple-A club in Columbus, Ohio (winning 42 games), and spent an entire season in the service (1951) before he was brought up to St. Louis in 1952 at the age of twenty-seven.

Al Rosen, who hit 192 home runs in seven full seasons with the Cleveland Indians, is another player whose early career suffered because he was playing in a system full of talent. In Rosen's case, he was a third baseman playing behind All-Star Ken Keltner. After great seasons at Pittsfield in 1946 and Oklahoma City in 1947, where he was named the Texas League's Most Valuable Player, Rosen was "loaned" to Kansas City. There he broke an American Association record by hitting five home runs in succession over July 27 and 28, 1948, at St. Paul's Lexington Park. The 1949 season was Rosen's most frustrating. It was obvious that Ken Keltner was having difficulty with his legs and could not match his 1948 performance, but Lou Boudreau, the Cleveland manager, was not keen on playing rookies and was reluctant to take Keltner out of the lineup. Only Keltner's virtual inability to field without great difficulty convinced the Indians to release him and start Rosen instead in 1950. Rosen finished 1950 with 37 home runs, 118 runs batted in, and an average of .287.[59]

Other players such as Ray Jablonski, Hank Sauer, Frank Baumholtz,

Left, Gene Woodling had trials with Cleveland and Pittsburgh before making the Yankees in 1949. (George Brace Photo) *Right,* Cleveland's Al Rosen, who was blocked by All-Star Ken Keltner, was typical of potential stars who languished in the minor leagues. (Transcendental Graphics)

Gene Woodling, and Jim Konstanty spent considerable time in the minors before they finally made the major leagues. Players who were "on the bubble," not knowing where they were going, had to maintain a degree of flexibility. Little Bobby Shantz of the Philadelphia Athletics, who at 5'6" defied the theory that someone that small could not be an outstanding pitcher, was optioned out to Buffalo on May 3, 1949. No sooner had Shantz begun the drive for Buffalo from Philadelphia when owner Connie Mack discovered that two of his starters had sore arms and changed his mind about Shantz. He contacted the Pennsylvania State Police, in an attempt to stop the pitcher, but to no avail. Shantz, who was not speeding, recalled seeing one state trooper trailing him, but when he rounded a curve and pulled off on a side road, the trooper went whizzing by. When Shantz reached Buffalo he was ordered to park his car under the stands and to take a train to Detroit. Three days later, Shantz pitched nine no-hit innings in long relief against the Tigers.[60]

Of course, being purchased by a major-league team was not always a welcome occasion. Al Widmar, who won twenty-two games for Baltimore in the International League, was purchased by the St. Louis Browns, who had the rights to two Oriole pitchers through a working agreeement. In 1949, Widmar's salary was $5,000, and at season's end he was given a bonus of $3,000. After he received a contract from the Browns for $6,000 for the 1950 season, he balked. When the Browns told Widmar that he would have to go on the voluntarily retired list if he did not accept their terms, the pitcher threatened to sue baseball. The impasse was eventually mediated by Commissioner Chandler, who persuaded the Browns to give Widmar a raise.[61]

Conditions were very different in the class D leagues. At the beginning of 1948 there were twenty leagues with 154 teams from Ada, Oklahoma, and Nyack, New York, to Oshkosh, Wisconsin, and Thibodaux, Louisiana. This is where professional baseball met grassroots America. Life in class D was rudimentary and personal. The Kitty League provides an excellent example of class D existence. Initially called the Kentucky-Illinois-Tennessee League when it was founded in 1900, the league became part of professional baseball in 1922. It was one of the initial stops for such players as Red Schoendienst, Dusty Rhodes, Vern Stephens, Bob Buhl, Chuck Tanner, and Tony Kubek. In 1948, the league consisted of eight teams: the Owensboro (Ky.) Oilers (Braves), the Mayfield (Ky.) Browns (St. Louis), the Hopkinsville (Ky.) Hoppers (Independent), the Madisonville (Ky.) Miners (White Sox), the Fulton (Ky.) Chicks (Senators), the Union City (Tenn.) Greyhounds (Indians), the Cairo (Ill.) Egyptians (Dodgers), and the Clarksville (Tenn.) Colts (Independent). The towns ranged in size from Owensboro, with a population of around 30,000, to Fulton, which at 3,000 prided itself in being one of the smallest towns in America to have a professional baseball team.

Support and ownership for the teams came from local industries. Fulton was a railroad town on the Illinois Central. As a junction point, it served several lines. The town was a center for dispatching bananas shipped from New Orleans to all parts of the country. Union City and Clarksville were meat-packing and tobacco centers, Owensboro had oil interests and an electric light bulb plant, and Hopkinsville, where the Kitty League was founded, was in close proximity to Camp Campbell, an Army training center. Madisonville was a mining center, while Cairo, a bustling river town, was the headquarters of several barge companies, and Mayfield was the home of two large clothing factories.[62]

Teams operated on a 125-game schedule, playing seven days a week with double-headers on Sundays, Memorial Day, Labor Day, and the Fourth of July. Travel was by school bus over paved two-lane highways through rolling dark-leaf tobacco country. Playing fields ranged from Owensboro's 1,500-seat stadium with its immaculately kept grass infield to Fulton's 800-seat wooden bandbox. Skin infields scraped by cars, rutted outfields created by grazing cows or wet tire tracks, and lights so low that players would lose high flies and pop-ups were more the norm. Madisonville's field was so uneven that outfielders running to catch fly balls disappeared from the vision of spectators sitting at field level. The mound was built on a hill, and if a player hit the concrete block fences he "could run until the cows came home." At Union City, the outfield was spacious and shaped somewhat like the Polo Grounds, while at Cairo players and fans alike spent much of their time fending off some of the largest and most voracious mosquitoes in America. Players' uniforms, hand-me-down woolen affairs, were hot and heavy. For a pitcher "a sauna bath wasn't necessary—you would walk to the mound and break a sweat."[63]

For a small rural town like Mayfield, Kentucky, with a population of 7,000, the ballplayers provided a window to the world. Baseball brought in players from several different ethnic backgrounds and from all over the country. Before World War II, outside of a handful of World War I veterans, few from Mayfield had ever traveled across America, let alone Europe. With only two movie theaters in town, the ball team was the summer's main form of entertainment and, next to politics down at the courthouse, its most discussed topic. This was even true of African American fans, who were forced to sit in segregated seating. Opening day was always marked by a parade featuring fire trucks carrying the players and bands, including those of the Merritt and Curley Clothing Companies and from local high schools. The president and general manager of the Mayfield team was the county court clerk and a high school teacher and coach by trade. He also doubled as bus driver, traveling secretary, and "father confessor" for the players. He arranged promotions like sweepstakes with ticket stubs where fans could win merchandise from local stores. There were weddings in which newly married couples paraded under an arch formed by the crossed bats of Mayfield players, with home plate serving as the altar. For the price of a ticket, you could be an invited guest. There were Boy Scout and Girl Scout nights, races, and throwing and hitting contests. Other attractions included baseball clown Al Schacht and the bearded House of David team.[64]

The young men who came to Mayfield before and after the war soon ingratiated themselves with the local population and became adopted Mayfieldians. They roomed alone or in pairs in private homes with "foster" parents, ate in downtown restaurants, attended local churches, and occasionally dated and married local girls. Although they were not saints, there was a good feeling between the players and the townspeople. For young boys, they were heroes, and for local churches a boon for attendance.[65] To belong to the local Knot Hole Club, every boy under fourteen who attended Sunday School received a ticket to one of the following week's games (Sunday doubleheaders excluded). The plan was so popular that Sunday School attendance boomed and the club had to construct additional bleachers to seat the youngsters.[66] Women were highly visible at games—they sold tickets, kept score, ran the concession stands, and sat in the bleachers. Following the war, the games also attracted scores of bobby-soxers.

For most ballplayers, many of whom were veterans, Mayfield was a comfortable five-month interlude in their lives. Immediately after the war, the dollar was still "as big as a bed sheet." With salaries of at least $250 a month, many paid their hosts a modest $2 a week in rent. While they often got invited out for meals, food was inexpensive. A loaf of bread was 12¢, a five-pound bag of flour was 32¢, a hamburger was 35¢, and bacon sold for 37¢ a pound. If you wanted to buy your favorite girl a new dress at Newberry's, it would cost $2.60, and if you wanted to really splurge and take her via bus to Nashville to see the Grand Ole Opry, a round trip ticket cost $3.00.[67]

The forces that brought much of minor-league baseball to its knees in the late 1940s and early 1950s also directly affected the Kitty League. Although an admission ticket was only $1.00, St. Louis television, first received in Mayfield via Paducah in 1953, proved stiff competition. Families who used to walk to the ballpark bought automobiles and took vacations away from home in places like Kentucky's new Land between the Lakes recreation area. The formation of Kentucky Lake brought an upsurge of swimming, boating, and other aquatic activities. Stock-car racing and outdoor theaters also appeared. Attendance during the Pivotal Era went from a high of 361,985 in 1947 to a low of 267,141 in 1951. In 1955, the Kitty League disbanded.[68]

The minor leagues, which reached their apex in activity and attendance during the Pivotal Era, were well on their way to extinction by the end of the period. Major-league baseball failed to realize the value of grass-roots baseball. Only the artificial support of major-league teams would keep a skeletal minor-league organization alive during the ensuing three decades. By its own greed, and inability to plan and work in concert, baseball failed to meet the threat of television and instead was eventually swallowed by the industry itself. When faced with the broadcasting issue, Commissioner

Chandler and the owners sacrificed the minor leagues to protect the reserve clause and to protect their own television profits. Furthermore,
major-league baseball failed to take advantage of the opportunity to expand to the west coast and into minor-league territory in a logical manner. Through its own lack of foresight, baseball was at least partially
responsible for its own decline in popularity in the coming decades.

15

1949: Pinstripes Prevail

World powers were deeply immersed in the Cold War by 1949. As the new baseball season commenced, the North Atlantic Treaty Organization was established, the Alger Hiss spy trial began, and the Soviet blockade of Berlin was lifted. In June, the last U.S. occupation forces from World War II were quietly withdrawn from Korea. Hollywood producers, intent on capitalizing on baseball's popularity, rushed in to make a quick dollar. Several baseball movies appeared, including *It Happens Every Spring*, *The Stratton Story*, and *The Kid from Cleveland*. When Commissioner Chandler read the script of *It Happens Every Spring*, which starred Ray Milland as a clumsy chemistry professor who discovers a chemical compound that will make a baseball do strange things, he forbade major-league players from playing roles in such an "undignified" film. Instead, he approved their participation in *The Stratton Story*—the tale of the Chicago White Sox pitcher who lost a leg in a hunting accident and returned to pitch in the majors. The movie, which starred Jimmy Stewart and June Allyson, also provided roles for eleven major-league players. *The Stratton Story* was proclaimed to be the first really believable baseball film because it portrayed real players instead of actors "who looked like they were waving good-bye to the *Queen Mary*."[1]

Conversely, *The Kid from Cleveland* was a movie that Chandler should have "canned." Although it included Cleveland owner Bill Veeck, manager Lou Boudreau, Johnny Berardino, and fifteen other players in its cast, the amateurish film proved to be a box-office bust. The story, which revolved around the Indians' 1948 championship season and a batboy who was saved from juvenile delinquency, was viewed with great disdain by Veeck and Boudreau. "I have one unwritten law at home that I adhere to," said Veeck. "I never allow my kids to mention or see that

Table 8. Final Major-League Regular-Season Standings, 1949

American League					National League			
	W	L	%	G.B.		W	L	%	G.B.
New York	97	57	.630	–	Brooklyn	97	57	.630	–
Boston	96	58	.623	1	St. Louis	96	58	.623	1
Cleveland	89	65	.578	8	Philadelphia	81	73	.526	16
Detroit	87	67	.565	10	Boston	75	79	.487	22
Philadelphia	81	73	.526	16	New York	73	81	.474	24
Chicago	63	91	.409	34	Pittsburgh	71	83	.461	26
St. Louis	53	101	.344	44	Cincinnati	62	92	.403	35
Washington	50	104	.325	47	Chicago	61	93	.396	36

abortion." Boudreau, who also thought the movie was "a dog," complained that the making of the film during the beginning of the 1949 season was a major distraction to the whole team. It was filmed at Cleveland's League Park in the mornings during home stands from April through early June, and Boudreau remarked that, for the team, "it was like being on the road every day."[2]

Other baseball news included the release of thirty-two-year-old Pete Gray by Dallas of the Texas League. The one-armed outfielder, who was only hitting .214 at the time, announced that he was going back to his billiard hall in Nanticoke, Pennsylvania, and speculated that he might even try motion pictures. Sore-armed Hal Bevans, the former Yankee pitcher who almost completed a no-hitter in the 1947 World Series, was reportedly playing softball in Salem, Oregon. Finally, soft-spoken Charley Gehringer, who was part of 1949's newly elected contingent to Baseball's Hall of Fame, missed his induction to get married at age forty-six.[3]

On the field, the "Summer of '49" was one of the most exciting in baseball history. Both pennant races went to the wire, with the Yankees nudging out the Red Sox and the Dodgers outlasting the Cardinals.

The American League Pennant Race

The last-place Washington Senators suffered through their worst season since 1909. Owner Clark Griffith got so frustrated with his team that he fired Mickey Haefner, one of his most reliable pitchers, for not fielding a bunt that cost the team a game. Earlier in the season, Haefner had thrown a one-hitter against Cleveland. The Senators' only bright spots were first baseman Eddie Robinson (.294-18-78) and rookie outfielder Clyde Vollmer.

In St. Louis, the DeWitt brothers acquired the Browns for more money than it cost Del Webb, Dan Topping, and Larry MacPhail to buy the Yankees in 1945. Nevertheless, the seventh-place Browns were a much more viable franchise than were the Senators—at least they had a good farm system and a number of promising players, including Ned Garver (3.98, 12-17), second baseman Jerry Priddy (.290-11-63), third baseman Bob Dillinger (.324-1-51), outfielder Dick Kokos (.261-23-77), and catchers Sherm Lollar and Les Moss. The biggest surprise was first baseman Roy Sievers (.306-16-91), who captured the Rookie of the Year award in the American League.

The sixth-place White Sox also had a forgettable year. Their only power threat, outfielder Gus Zernial, suffered a broken collar bone and was lost for sixty days. Playing in spacious Comiskey Park, no Sox player hit more than seven home runs all season. Only strong pitching from Randy Gumpert (3.81, 13-16), Bill Wight (3.31, 15-13), Billy Pierce (3.88, 7-15), and Bob Kuzava (4.02, 10-6) saved the Sox from ignominy. Moreover, ill-tempered manager Jack Onslow made life miserable for the team. He clashed openly with several players, including catcher Joe Tipton, who subsequently was dealt to the A's for second basemen Nellie Fox. Fox, a future All-Star, became a fixture in the White Sox infield for the next fourteen seasons.

Athletic's owner Connie Mack uncharacteristically announced that his team had a chance to win the pennant in 1949.[4] The A's infield was outstanding, with Ferris Fain at first, Pete Suder at second, Eddie Joost at shortstop, and Hank Majeski at third. The strength of the A's was their starting pitching behind rookie sensation Alex Kellner (3.75, 20-12) and veterans Joe Coleman (3.86, 13-14), Lou Brissie (4.28, 16-11), and Dick Fowler (3.75, 15-11). Outfielder Sam Chapman (.278-24-108) also had a career year. The A's possessed little bench strength, and the untimely losses of Hank Majeski, who was beaned by Early Wynn, and Barney McCosky, because of a bad back, hurt their pennant chances. By August 19, when more than half a million people turned out for a ticker-tape parade in New York City in honor of Connie Mack, the A's were in fifth place for good.

The fourth-place Detroit Tigers bounced between fifth and second most of the season, before catching fire in late August. They won eighteen of twenty games, including ten in a row, to challenge Cleveland for third place. On September 8, they took a double-header from the Indians 10-0 and 4-1, behind Hal Newhouser and Ted Gray, to derail Cleveland's pennant chances. Newhouser's bid for a no-hitter was spoiled by Lou Boudreau in the seventh inning as he connected for the Indians' only hit of the game. Injuries hampered 1949 batting champion George Kell (.343-3-59), who broke his toe, and pitcher Ted Gray (3.51, 10-10), who was sidelined with a concussion after being struck by a batted ball while in the dugout. Meanwhile, Art Houtteman (3.71, 15-10) made a miraculous comeback early in the season after suffering a near-fatal skull fracture in a spring training automobile accident. Outstanding seasons were enjoyed by Vic Wertz (.304-20-133), rookie Johnny Groth (.293-11-73), Hoot Evers (.303-7-72), and pitchers Hal Newhouser (3.36, 18-11), Fred Hutchinson (2.96, 15-7), and hard-throwing right-hander Virgil Trucks (2.81, 19-11).

Cleveland's season began miserably. The players who had outstanding years in 1948 failed to produce. Ken Keltner struggled, and Joe Gordon was not nearly as explosive at the plate. Pitchers also began to pitch Lou Boudreau high and tight. The Indians' manager, whose stance put him perilously close to the plate, was hit five times by mid-May. In addition, 1948 pitching sensation Gene Bearden was totally ineffective. It was rumored that New York manager Casey Stengel had ordered his players to lay off Bearden's first couple of pitches, because he knew that the Cleveland pitcher had difficulty consistently getting his knuckleball over the plate.

Larry Doby (.280-24-85) distinguished himself by hitting several long home runs. One of them, which traveled an estimated 500 feet, cleared the scoreboard at Griffith Stadium—a deed previously accomplished only by Babe Ruth. After Doby's ball hit the building across the street, the Senators received an irate call from a mother who complained that someone had thrown a ball on her roof and she could not get her kids to sleep. When the attendant tried to explain that it was a batted ball, the mother hung up in disbelief.[5]

In Cleveland, Charlie Lupica, a druggist, erected a four-foot platform on a flagpole and proclaimed that he would not come down until the Indians moved into first place. Meanwhile, his drugstore, located below, was doing a thriving business. In July, the Indians caught fire behind the excellent pitching of rookie Mike Garcia (2.36, 14-5) and veterans Al Benton (2.12, 9-6), Early Wynn (4.15, 11-7), and Bob Lemon (2.99, 22-10). Staff ace Bob Feller (3.75, 15-14), hampered by injuries, continued to struggle—often having difficulty with his control beyond the fifth or sixth inning. After climbing to within 4½ games of the lead, in mid-August, the Tribe sputtered. On the night of September 23, Veeck held a mock funeral procession and ceremoniously buried the Indians' 1949 pennant hopes. In typical fashion, it was a night of celebration. He moved Charlie Lupica, pole and all, by lift truck to the stadium, where the druggist was joined by his family. They received a four-poster bed, a bathtub full of soda, bicycles and puppies for the children, a cooking range for Mrs. Lupica, and a Pontiac sedan.[6]

The New York Yankees, who topped the standings most of the season, suffered through seventy-one separate injuries. Yankee depth, grit, and manager Casey Stengel helped them overcome adversity. As a young man, Stengel eschewed a career as a dentist to concentrate on baseball. Brash and scrappy on the field, he also earned a reputation as a comedian. His most famous antic occurred in 1918 when he returned to Brooklyn after being recently traded to Pittsburgh. As he approached the batter's box for his first at bat, he was met by a chorus of boos and derisive remarks. Stengel turned toward the noisy Ebbets Field crowd, doffed his cap, and out flew a bird. The symbolism of the gesture was not lost on the crowd, which broke into peals of laughter. As a manager, Stengel guided some terrible second-division teams at Brooklyn and Boston and amassed an unimpressive .435 win-loss percentage. Nevertheless, his three years as manager of Oakland in the Pacific Coast League, where he was named minor-league manager of the year in 1948, drew the attention of Del Webb.

On the day he was hired by the Yankees, reporters persuaded Stengel to don a Yankee uniform and to pose behind a baseball as though he were gazing at a crystal ball. The resulting photographic caricature did little to dispel Stengel's reputation. When Stengel made his first appearance at training camp in 1949, he was still an enigma to his players. As Eddie Lopat recalled, "We knew that he was a funny guy and a clown," but, we decided, "to bide our time and see how he operated."[7] The new Yankees manager found himself in a precarious and pressure-packed position— where he was expected to win the pennant with a team of established veterans who failed to realize their potential in 1948. Weiss, who hired detectives to follow Yankees players around during the 1948 season, fired Bucky Harris because he felt Harris was too lenient with his men. With this in mind, Stengel announced that a midnight curfew would be strictly enforced and that henceforth Yankee players would be restricted to attendance at the nearby dog races only on Thursday nights. "I don't want to be a Simon Legree and the players will find me a very pleasant guy to work with," he said, "but I want to say that I did not come to the New York club with the idea of letting anybody make a sucker out of me."[8]

The players resented the dog racing restrictions, and several, including Joe DiMaggio, ignored them. When confronted by Stengel, DiMaggio gracefully retreated. Nevertheless, DiMaggio never really accepted Stengel as a manager. Stengel also received a rocky reception from the press— particularly from Bucky Harris supporters. Nevertheless, he went out of his way to make himself available to New York sportswriters and succeeded in making himself a popular buffer between his team and the media.[9]

George Weiss recognized that the team needed an overhaul for the 1949 season. Several of his key players were on the downside of their careers.

Tommy Henrich, "Old Reliable," at age thirty-six, could not be relied on forever; Charley Keller's disk problem rendered him ineffective; and DiMaggio's increasingly frequent injuries threatened to make him a mere mortal. Weiss acquired Pacific Coast League batting champion Gene Woodling for $125,000 from the San Francisco Seals and brought up Dick Kryhoski and Hank Bauer from Kansas City and infielder Jerry Coleman from Newark. In an attempt to bolster Yankees pitching, Weiss acquired Fred Sanford (4.64, 12-21, in 1948) from the Browns for pitchers Red Embree and Dick Starr, catcher Sherman Lollar, and $100,000. Nevertheless, after his big three (Reynolds, Raschi, and Lopat), the team's pitching remained suspect. Joe Page was coming off a mediocre season, and young Bob Porterfield and promising but erratic Tommy Byrne were still unknown quantities.

As the season unfolded, so did Stengel's problems. During the winter, DiMaggio had an operation on his right heel to remove a bone spur similar to the one removed from his left heel in 1947. Although the operation was declared a success, DiMaggio was in constant pain and struggled through spring training. The somber DiMaggio explained to reporters that he had no idea when his heel problem would clear up and told them, "Please deny that I have any intention of retiring."[10] Stengel wanted DiMaggio to remain with the team as a pinch hitter and to boost team morale, but the Yankees hero could not bear to remain on the bench and not contribute.

DiMaggio's injury forced Stengel to platoon Bauer (.272-10-45), Woodling (.270-5-44), Cliff Mapes (.247-7-38), and Johnny Lindell (.242-6-27) in the outfield. Although platooning was not a new managerial strategy, Stengel was of necessity forced to take it to another level. In the infield, both his second-base and third-base situations were unsettled. At third, he had Bobby Brown (.283-6-61), a hard-hitting youngster who was studying to be a physician, and Billy Johnson (.249-8-46), a good fielding, hard-nosed competitor who could hit with power. In spite of their strengths, they both had glaring weaknesses. Brown, in spite of a tremendous work ethic, was an erratic fielder, and Johnson was a slow runner who was prone to hit into double plays.[11] Stengel loved speed and often made the statement that "he didn't want those guys who took one swing and made two outs."[12] Competing at second were Snuffy Stirnweiss (.261-0-11), an infielder with speed and excellent range, and rookie Jerry Coleman (.275-2-42), a nervous World War II veteran who was a superb infielder. In truth, the Yankees had no genuine first baseman. Dick Kryhoski and Tommy Henrich (.287-24-85) were platooned early in the season, but the former became Stengel's scapegoat and was farmed out to Oakland during the last half of the season.[13]

In spite of injuries to Keller and Porterfield, Yankee pitching, led by Allie Reynolds (4.00, 17-6), Vic Raschi (3.34, 21-10), Ed Lopat (3.26, 15-10), Tommy Byrne (3.72, 15-7), and Joe Page (2.59, 13-8); the hitting of Yogi Berra (.277-20-91); and inspired infield play of Phil Rizzuto (.275-5-64) kept the Yankees ahead of their competition by at least five games through July. At the end of June, DiMaggio (.346-14-67) made a dramatic return. One morning he awakened to find that he had no pain in his heel. After missing sixty-five games, he debuted against the Boston Red Sox at Fenway Park on June 28. His two-run homer against Mickey McDermott led the Yankees to a 5-4 victory. The next day, the Red Sox led the Yankees 7-1 in the fifth—a seemingly insurmountable lead even at Fenway. In the fifth, DiMaggio launched a three-run blast to make the score 7-4. Then in the eighth, with the score tied at 7-7, DiMaggio hit a solo shot to break the tie, and the Yankees went on to a 9-7 win. In the final game of the series, the Yankee Clipper came to the plate in the seventh inning against Mel Parnell with the Yankees clinging to a 3-2 lead. After working Parnell to a full count, DiMaggio smashed a ball against the steel towers in left field to lead New York to a 6-2 win and a series sweep. DiMaggio's return, which netted him four home runs and nine runs batted in, was one of the most spectacular comebacks in baseball history and raised the team's morale considerably. On July 4, the Red Sox came to Yankee Stadium, where they dropped a double-header, thanks in part to DiMaggio's fifth home run, and fell twelve games back.

The Red Sox were seemingly buried for good, but then injuries and the long season began to take its toll on the Yankees. Vic Raschi, who had been sensational during the first half of the season, tired and dropped four in a row. Then, on August 7, they lost Yogi Berra, when his thumb was broken by a pitch from the Browns' Dick Starr. The resourceful Weiss acquired first baseman Johnny Mize from the Giants for $40,000 on August 22, after several National League clubs waived on his $32,500 salary. Six days later, during a double-header against Chicago, veteran Tommy Henrich crashed into a wall at Comiskey Park and broke two vertebrae in his back, and Johnny Mize pulled his right arm out of its socket. The Yankees entered the home stretch in September with Henrich ensconced in a body cast and Mize unable to raise his right arm.

In the meantime, the Boston Red Sox, led by manager Joe McCarthy, were on fire. After a slow start, their pitching jelled behind Ellis Kinder (3.36, 23-6), Mel Parnell (2.77, 25-7), and Joe Dobson (3.85, 14-12). Kinder, who gave up baseball in 1942 to work as a pipe fitter with the Illinois Central Railroad, possessed a great curveball and a change-up second in the American League only to Hal Newhouser's. A notorious hard-drinker, he was often at his best after a long night. Mel Parnell, whose nickname

If pitchers could be sent to the Hall of Fame in tandem, New York Yankee hurlers Allie Reynolds, Vic Raschi, and Eddie Lopat would be "shoo-ins." Between 1948 and 1951 the trio recorded 239 wins and threw 178 complete games while leading the Yankees to three American League pennants and World Series championships. (George Brace Photo)

Mel Parnell, a stylish left-hander, flourished in Fenway Park as he won seventy-six games for the Red Sox between 1948 and 1951. (George Brace Photo)

was "Midnight" because he was so effective under the lights, became an even better pitcher after he broke the ring finger on his throwing hand in 1947. A knot developed around the break between the middle and top joints of the finger and it allowed him to improve his curveball dramatically. The Red Sox were also the best-hitting machine in baseball in 1949, with Billy Goodman (.298-0-56) at first base, Bobby Doerr (.309-18-109) at second, Johnny Pesky (.306-2-69) at third, Vern Stephens (.290-39-159) at shortstop, and Birdie Tebbetts (.270-5-48) behind the plate. In right field, newly acquired Al Zarilla (.281-9-71) joined Dom DiMaggio (.307-8-60) in center field and Ted Williams (.343-43-159) in left field.

By mid-July, Tebbetts, Pesky, and Goodman were hitting around .300, Stephens was leading the league in home runs and runs-batted-in, and DiMaggio was leading the league in hitting with Williams close behind. On August 10, DiMaggio's thirty-four-game hitting streak was stopped by Vic Raschi. DiMaggio, who labored under the shadows of his brother Joe and his outfield partner Ted Williams, finally drew the attention he richly deserved. After the streak was over, he remarked, "It was a matter of going after bad balls to keep the streak alive. Now I can just devote all my attention to just hitting."[14] DiMaggio was also an excellent defensive player with a reputation for having a great arm. Williams also had one of his best seasons and missed winning the triple crown by .0002 points to

George Kell of the Tigers. On the final day of the season, he went hitless in two official trips to the plate, while Kell banged out two hits in three at bats to edge the "Splendid Splinter" .3429 to .3427. Williams tied teammate Vern Stephens in runs batted in, with 159, and led the league in home runs with forty-three and in all other offensive categories except triples. The Boston outfielder was also the hero of the 1949 All-Star game, played at Ebbets Field. Williams made a running catch of Don Newcombe's bid for a hit with the bases loaded, preserving the American League's 11-7 victory. Williams's dominant performance won him the American League's Most Valuable Player award.

In August, Boston caught pennant fever as the Red Sox won nineteen games during a twenty-three game homestand. Bobby Doerr went on a tear in late August and, during a fifteen game stretch, hit .422. The Red Sox were almost unbeatable at home, taking sixty-one of seventy-seven games played at Fenway Park, including all eleven against the A's. By mid-September, they trailed the Yankees by only two games. On September 18, the Yankees lost Joe DiMaggio, who was stricken with viral pneumonia. On September 26 the Red Sox took the lead after defeating the Yankees 7-6 in a game that was decided in the eighth inning on a hotly contested call by umpire Bill Grieve over a squeeze play.

With two games remaining, the Red Sox met the Yankees head-on at Yankee Stadium. Boston had a one-game lead and needed only one victory to clinch the pennant. In the first game, the Red Sox jumped to a 4-0 lead in the third, as both starter Allie Reynolds and reliever Joe Page were wild. In the third, with the Yankees up, Tebbetts began to needle Phil Rizzuto. He told the Yankee shortstop that, with this game in the bag, the Sox were going to pitch former Yale star Frank Quinn the following day. When Rizzuto returned to the Yankee bench, he angrily passed on Tebbetts's remarks. The challenge seemed to galvanize the Yankees.[15] Page recovered his control and shut down the Red Sox through the next six innings. The Yankees scored two each in the fourth and fifth to tie the score, and in the eighth Johnny Lindell homered to break the tie and win the game. In the finale on October 2, Vic Raschi hooked up with Ellis Kinder. Trailing 1-0, McCarthy removed Kinder in the eighth for a pinch hitter. In the bottom half of the inning, reliever Mel Parnell gave up a home run to Henrich and a single to Berra. When Tex Hughson came in to take over, he was touched for three more runs to give the Yankees a 5-0 lead. In the ninth, Doerr tripled over Joe DiMaggio's head, scoring two runs. DiMaggio, who was still recovering from pneumonia, collapsed as he started to run for the ball. The proud Yankee walked off the field to a thundering ovation and was replaced by Mapes. The Red Sox scored another run on a hit by Billy Goodman, and, then with two outs, Tebbetts came to bat. With many on the Yankee bench making reference to his remarks on Quinn, Tebbetts popped out to Henrich, and the Yankees clinched the pennant 5-3.

As usual, Red Sox writers gave no quarter in castigating Tom Yawkey and his team for the loss when a pennant seemed such a sure thing. "They weren't hungry enough," read the headlines. "The 'millionaires' were too highly paid," "they are a group of individuals who are only worried about their batting averages." Williams, with his $100,000 salary and unproductive performance in the final two contests, bore the brunt of the criticism.[16] Scant attention was paid to the courageous team that beat them. Williams was shaken by the loss. Little did he know that he would never come close to playing in another World Series.

The National League Pennant Race

The Cubs and Reds fought a spirited battle for the basement in 1949, with the Chicago Cubs prevailing. The Cubs had spent more than $2 million to purchase players since 1945 with little to show for their efforts. Only sluggers Hank Sauer (.291-27-83) and Andy Pafko (.281-18-69) enjoyed stellar seasons for the Cubs. The Reds pinned their hopes for 1949 on a comeback by ace Ewell Blackwell (4.23, 5-5), but the lanky pitcher failed to recover from an operation to remove a diseased kidney. The bellwether of the Reds' staff proved to be Ken Raffensberger (3.39, 18-17), who finished third in the league in wins and second in complete games. Cincinnati started the season quickly, winning twenty of their first thirty-six games, but they then dropped thirty-four of their next forty-seven. The Reds' leading hitters were Ted Kluzewski (.309-8-68) and Walker Cooper (.280-16-62). On July 6, Cooper had the game of his career, going six for seven with three three-run home runs and ten runs batted in to lead the Reds to a 23-4 victory over the Cubs.

Ralph Kiner (.310-54-127) was the main attraction in Pittsburgh as he led the National League in home runs and runs-batted-in. On September 11 and September 13, Kiner hit four consecutive home runs against the Cubs and the Phillies to become the first player in major-league history to accomplish the feat twice. He also tied a major-league record by hitting four grand slams in a season.

The New York Giants again maintained their reputation for slugging, but this time in a different vein. In an odd incident, Leo Durocher was accused of assaulting a Giants fan, Fred Boysen, as the teams walked across the field to their clubhouses following an April 28 game at the Polo Grounds. Commissioner Chandler suspended Durocher for five days pending an investigation but reinstated him after finding contradictory evidence. Boysen's attorney later dropped all the charges. As a result of the incident, a ruling was issued banning fans from entering the playing field following games.

After a fast start that kept them in first place until the beginning of June, the Giants suddenly slipped. Durocher, who was already unhappy with his team, persuaded Horace Stoneham to begin unloading his sluggers. Walker Cooper was sent to Cincinnati for veteran Ray Mueller, and in August the Giants let Johnny Mize go to the Yankees for $40,000. In 1949, former Negro League stars Monte Irvin and Hank Thompson made their debuts with the Giants, and Dave Barnhill and Ray Dandridge were assigned to Minneapolis in the American Association. Thompson (.280-9-34) became the team's regular second baseman, while Irvin saw limited action. Excellent seasons were turned in by Bobby Thomson (.309-27-109), Willard Marshall (.307-12-70), and Whitey Lockman (.301-11-65) as well as pitchers Larry Jansen (3.85, 15-16), Monte Kennedy (3.43, 12-14), and Sheldon Jones (3.34, 15-12). Hard-luck pitcher Dave Koslo (2.50, 11-14) led the league in earned run average.

The 1948 National League champion Boston Braves fell apart. Determined not to have a team letdown in 1949, manager Billy Southworth established a set of rigid rules and drove his players hard with two three-hour workouts daily during spring training. Moreover, the manager began to drink heavily to calm his nerves.[17] With first baseman Earl Torgeson sidelined by a shoulder separation and Johnny Sain hindered by a sore arm, the team fell to fourth place in June. By midsummer, Southworth's drinking had taken a toll on the Braves, and infielders Eddie Stanky and Alvin Dark were suspected of leading a faction of players seeking the manager's ouster.[18] In late July Stanky openly clashed with Southworth, and two players, Jimmy Russell and Earl Torgeson, got into an altercation with three soldiers after curfew. With his team disintegrating, Lou Perini sent Southworth home on leave and placed the team under coach Johnny Cooney.

The Braves failed to recover and only Warren Spahn (3.07, 21-14), who led the National League in wins, strikeouts, and complete games, had an outstanding year. The dissension led the Braves to trade Dark and Stanky to the Giants in December 1949 for Sam Webb, Willard Marshall, Sid Gordon, and Buddy Kerr. It was a deal that would come back to haunt Boston.

The third-place Philadelphia Phillies were beginning to come of age. The pitching staff led by Robin Roberts (3.69, 15-15) and reliever Jim Konstanty (3.25, 9-5) was a pleasant surprise. Unpredictable Russ Meyer (3.08, 17-8) pitched a one-hitter against Boston on September 8, and veteran Ken Heintzelman (3.02, 17-10) also enjoyed his best campaign. Hank

Borowy (4.19, 12-12) a throw-in as part of the trade that brought Eddie Waitkus to the Phillies, discovered a baby cereal that calmed his nervous stomach and allowed him to pitch effectively. The major blow to the Phillies' pennant hopes was the loss of Waitkus in June when the first baseman was shot and seriously wounded by a deranged girl in a Chicago hotel room.

Although he did not duplicate his 1948 performance, Richie Ashburn (.284-1-37) remained one of the National League's most exciting young players. His stolen base totals were cut because manager Eddie Sawyer disliked his head-first slides and refused to let him run. While the Phillies' team batting average was not high in 1949, the team often exhibited surprising bursts of power. One of these occurred on June 2, when they beat the Reds 12-3 and broke several records in the process. In the eighth inning, they hit five home runs (two by Andy Seminick and one each by Del Ennis, Willie Jones, and Schoolboy Rowe), a triple, and a double as they scored ten times. Seminick homered three times in the game, tying a National League record, and his two home runs in the eighth tied a record held by several players. Willie "Puddin' Head" Jones also tied a major-league record against the Braves on April 20 when he doubled in four consecutive trips to the plate. Leading hitters for the Phillies included Jones (.244-19-77), Del Ennis (.302-25-110), and Andy Seminick (.243-24-68).

The Phillies also played in the most disorderly game of the season. In the ninth inning of the second game of a double-header, fans rioted after a call by umpire George Barr went against their team. Many of the 19,000 spectators "tossed soft drink and beer bottles, beer cans, vegetables, cards, and papers on the field for fifteen minutes until Umpire-in-Chief Al Barlick forfeited the game to the Giants." Immediately after the call, umpire Lee Ballanfant was hit in the back of the neck by a bouncing bottle and in the cheek by a flying lemon. Barlick was spattered in the back by an overripe tomato, while Barr, who made the call, came through the disturbance unscathed.[19]

The battle for first place in the National League was almost as exciting as the race in the junior circuit. With Burt Shotton again at the helm, Branch Rickey bragged that it was the best team with which he had ever been associated. "The team has defensive class, a punch that might develop suddenly into a devastating attack and a strong bench," he stated. "The pitching alone may disappoint and first base is still a question mark."[20] Rickey's prediction was close to the mark for this was the team that would become known as the "Boys of Summer"—a group whose core players would continue to play for the Dodgers for most of the next decade. At third base was Billy Cox, a tremendous glove man whose World War II experiences still stalked him. At shortstop was Kentuckian Pee Wee Reese

(.279-16-73), the team's captain and quiet leader. A slimmed-down Jackie Robinson (.342-16-124), no longer restrained by Rickey's edict of silence, was prepared to go to war at second base. First base, which quickly ceased being a question mark, was placed in the huge hands of Gil Hodges (.285-23-115), the converted catcher who became one of the best first basemen of all time. After the first month of the season Bruce Edwards went down with a sore arm and relinquished his position to Roy Campanella (.287-22-82). Campanella went on to catch five consecutive All-Star games (1949-53) in their entirety. In center field, the Dodgers boasted Duke Snider (.292-23-92), who, much to the dismay of opposing pitchers, finally located the strike zone. In right field was Carl Furillo (.322-18-106), who not only could hit with power and for average but also possessed one of the best arms in the league—a skill that earned him the nickname "The Reading Rifle." Only left field, ably manned by Gene Hermanski (.299-8-42) in 1949, remained in doubt.

On paper, the Cardinals, led by manager Eddie Dyer, were no match for the Dodgers in the field. At the corners, they had Nippy Jones (.300-8-62) at first base and Eddie Kazak (.304-6-42) at third. Although both enjoyed their best major-league seasons, neither packed the hitting power expected at their positions and both suffered debilitating injuries during the second half of the campaign. The Cardinals' double-play combination was one of the best in baseball, when slick-fielding shortstop Marty Marion (.272-5-70) was not suffering from back problems. His partner, Red Schoendienst (.297-3-54) was just coming into his own at second base. Behind the plate, the Cardinals had Del Rice, a fine defensive catcher, and the confident Joe Garagiola. Chuck Diering, who possessed excellent defensive skills but lacked power, played center field. Flanking him in left field was Enos "Country" Slaughter (.336-13-96)—a warhorse from the end of the Gas House Gang era whom Dyer nicknamed "Old Aches and Pains." The incomparable Stan Musial (.338-36-123), who led the league in total bases and finished second in the league in just about every offensive category, held forth in right field.

The pitching staff provided the Cardinals with a decided edge. They were so deep that they traded veteran Murry Dickson to Pittsburgh for $125,000—a controversial deal that upset manager Eddie Dyer and might have cost them the pennant.[21] To add insult to injury, five of Dickson's twelve wins in 1949 were against the Cardinals. Nevertheless, the Cardinal staff, led by Howie Pollett (2.77, 20-9), Harry Brecheen (3.35, 14-11), Al Brazle (3.18, 14-8), and Red Munger (3.87, 15-8), enjoyed an outstanding year. In addition, right-handed relievers Gerry Staley (2.73, 10-10) and Ted Wilks (3.73, 10-3) registered nineteen saves between them. The Dodgers began the season with a starting rotation that consisted of Ralph

Don Newcombe overpowered hitters with his sinking fast ball to fashion a 17-8 mark and capture the National League Rookie of the Year award. (Transcendental Graphics)

Branca (4.39, 13-5), Joe Hatten (4.18, 12-8), Preacher Roe (2.79, 15-6), and Rex Barney (4.41, 9-8). Neither Barney, who possessed lightning speed, nor Hatten could regain his 1948 form, and Branca was a perfectionist who, at age twenty-three, was still battling to control his emotions. Only the wily Roe, who was known to include an occasional spitball in his repertoire, was dependable.

Fortunately, relief came in the form of former Newark Eagles pitcher Don Newcombe (3.17, 17-8). At 6'4" the tall, hard-throwing hurler was an imposing figure on the mound. In his rookie season, Newcombe was just wild enough to keep hitters loose, and his fastball resembled an aspirin tablet as it approached the plate. Although he pitched well during spring training, the Dodgers returned Newcombe to the minors at the beginning of the year because they claimed that he had not matured enough. Newcombe, upset with his demotion, went home instead and had to be persuaded by his wife to return to Montreal. Nevertheless, Rickey knew Newcombe's value and placed a $300,000 price tag on him shortly after rumors circulated that Warren Giles of the Reds had offered $250,000 for the young player.[22]

At the beginning of the season the Cardinals struggled and were in seventh place with a 10-15 record. Stan Musial, who was having difficulty getting untracked, was hitting .217. Inevitably, Lawton Carver of the *International News* suggested that the Cardinals trade Musial. Cardinals owner Fred Saigh, who rarely backed down from anyone, issued an angry denial that he had any intention of trading Musial and placed a $2,000,000 value on him. "That's how much Musial means to me at the gate and to the Cardinals!" he exclaimed. "I would have to have my head examined if I sold or traded Musial. It would be impossible to give up a player like that and continue to live in St. Louis."[23] After winning only twelve of their first twenty-nine games, the Cardinals went on a rampage to overtake the Dodgers and grabbed first place for the first time on June 24. The following day, they relinquished the lead again to the Dodgers, who held first place until July 24, when Stan Musial hit for the cycle to tear the Dodgers apart 14-1.

The force behind the Dodgers' success in 1949 was Jackie Robinson. Free to speak out at last, he made up for lost time. During spring training he got into a shouting match with rookie pitcher Chris Van Cuyk and was quoted in a newspaper account to the effect that opponents "had better be prepared to be rough this year, because I'm going to be rough on them."[24] Robinson's actions earned him a visit from Commissioner Chandler. In his autobiography, *I Never Had It Made*, Robinson recalled, "I told the Commissioner exactly how I felt and that, while I had no intention of creating problems, I was no longer going to turn my cheek to insults. Chandler completely understood my position, and that was the end of our interview."[25] The commissioner accepted Robinson's explanations but warned him against future outbursts. The incidents, however, continued. In July, the Dodger second baseman almost came to blows with Schoolboy Rowe when the Phillies pitcher openly encouraged Ken Heintzelman to knock Robinson down. Later, in September, Robinson was thrown out of a game against the Cardinals when he protested umpire Bill Stewart's calls by clasping his own throat in a manner to indicate that the umpire had choked on the call. Later in the game, Red Schoendienst drove a ball off the leg of Robinson's substitute at second base, Eddie Miksis, to win the game 1-0.

The same fury that drove Robinson to protest bad calls also pushed him to new heights elsewhere. His fielding, hitting, and daring on the base paths made the difference in many games. After leading the league in stolen bases, winning the batting title, and driving the Dodgers to a pennant, Robinson was named the National League's Most Valuable Player. His on-base percentage, at .432, was second only to Stan Musial's .440—a figure that represented twenty-one additional walks. Tony Cuccinello, then coaching for the Cincinnati Reds, insisted that the only way to beat the Dodgers was to keep Robinson off the base paths. Manager Bucky Walters replied sarcastically, "Yeah, but how are you going to do it?" Cuccinello replied, "Kidnap him before the game."[26]

In late July, St. Louis again ascended to first by sweeping a three-game series from Brooklyn. With the exception of a three-day period in August, they remained on top until September 29. Although at the end of September the Cardinals led the Dodgers by a game and a half with five road games remaining, they were a tired and beaten-up club. Even worse, they had to play a three-game series against Pittsburgh—a team that harbored bad feelings toward the Cardinals. During the spring, Rip Sewell accused Joe Garagiola of calling a pitch that beaned Stan Rojek. Later in August, the benches of both teams emptied when Enos Slaughter ripped his spikes into Danny Murtaugh's chest with a high slide. The encounter ended with manager Billy Meyer chastising Eddie Dyer for the Cardinals' rough play. "Do that to the Dodgers, you bums," shouted Meyer, "Why pick on us? We're not going anywhere. If that's the way you want to play, we'll play your way. You've been asking for it all year and we can give it to you now." Meyer wanted to beat the Cardinals so badly that, in the next game between the two teams, he put Cliff Chambers, who was scheduled to pitch against Cincinnati, in the bullpen instead. In the eighth inning, Chambers entered the game. When Slaughter led off the eighth, Chambers worked the count to two strikes and then sent the Cardinal outfielder to the ground with a close pitch. The fourth pitch came in on Slaughter's legs, and he had to "skip rope." The Cardinals outfielder got his revenge, however, on the next pitch, which he lined off the right field foul pole for a triple. The inspired Pirates went on to win the game in the tenth inning on back-to-back doubles by Murtaugh and Rojek.[27]

The Pirates exacted even more revenge by beating the Cardinals 6-4 and 7-2. The last game of the series represented Murry Dickson's fifth win against the Cardinals. The Cardinals limped into Chicago and lost the first two games to the Cubs. Meanwhile, the Dodgers lost to the Phillies and, with one game left, only a single game separated the two teams. On the final day of the season and after four consecutive losses, the Cardinals finally beat the Cubs 13-5 to give Howie Pollett his twentieth win. In their closing game, Brooklyn took a 5-0 lead into the fourth inning behind Newcombe, but the Phillies rallied for four runs in the bottom of the frame and then tied the game at 7-7 in the sixth inning. The game was not decided until the tenth inning, when Brooklyn scored twice to win 9-7. It was the first time in major-league history that both pennant races had gone down to the last day.

The 1949 World Series

The 1949 World Series lacked the excitement of the two pennant races. In the first game Tommy Henrich, who only a month earlier had been wrapped in a body cast, homered in the top of the ninth inning to break a scoreless tie and a pitching duel between Allie Reynolds and Don Newcombe. In losing 1-0, Newcombe gave up only four hits and struck out eleven, while winning pitcher Reynolds threw a two-hitter and struck out nine. In the second contest, Preacher Roe scattering six hits to best Vic Raschi 1-0. Roe's performance was particularly gutsy because he pitched much of the game in great pain as a result of having been hit by a line drive on the fourth finger of his right hand. Later in the game, Roe's fingernail had to be drilled out by a doctor to drain a pocket of blood. The Dodgers' lone run came in the second inning when Gil Hodges singled Jackie Robinson home after the latter's double

The third game at Brooklyn was a well-pitched contest between Ralph Branca and Tommy Byrne. With the score knotted 1-1 going into the top of the ninth with two out and the bases loaded, Branca gave up a two-run single off the right-field fence to pinch hitter Johnny Mize. Jerry Coleman then singled in another run off reliever Jack Banta. In the bottom of the inning, the Dodgers rallied for two runs on solo home runs by Luis Olmo and Roy Campanella, but it was too little, too late. With Brooklyn down two games to one, Newcombe took the mound for the Dodgers in the fourth game. He was knocked out of the game in the fourth inning, as the Yankees scored three runs behind doubles by Bobby Brown, Cliff Mapes, and pitcher Eddie Lopat. New York added three more runs in the fifth, when Bobby Brown tripled off reliever Joe Hatten with the bases loaded. The roof caved in on Yankee starter Eddie Lopat in the sixth inning. After getting two outs, he gave up four runs on singles to Reese, Cox, Robinson, Hodges, Olmo, Campanella, and Hermanski. Allie Reynolds, who was summoned to relieve Lopat, struck out pinch hitter Johnny Jorgenson to end the inning. Reynolds held the Dodgers hitless in the bottom three frames to preserve the win.

The final encounter between the two teams was barely a contest, as the Yankees held a 10-2 lead after six innings, largely because of Dodger starter Rex Barney's wildness. Barney gave up five runs on three hits and six walks in his three innings of work. The Yankees then pounded relievers Jack Banta and Carl Erskine for five more runs on a home run by Joe

DiMaggio and run-scoring extra-base hits by Gene Woodling and Bobby Brown. The Dodgers rallied in the seventh inning to score a run on hits by Duke Snider and Gene Hermanski and then chased Vic Raschi in the seventh inning, with three more runs on a sacrifice fly by Jackie Robinson and a bases-loaded double by Gil Hodges. Yankee reliever Joe Page came in and shut the Dodgers down. He was particularly spectacular in the ninth, when, after yielding a double to Eddie Miksis, he struck out Duke Snider, Jackie Robinson, and Gil Hodges to allow Yankee pinstripes to prevail 10-6.

After the series, many of the Yankee players were feted in hometown celebrations. Stengel received his in a two-block parade attended by thousands at his home in Glendale, California. In an interview with writer Al Wolf, Stengel admitted for the first time, "If we hadn't won [the pennant] I was ready to step aside and no hard feelings. Now they seem to want me to stay on a while. So that's that." Faced with a flurry of requests for speaking engagements and a mountain of mail, Edna Stengel sighed, "And here I thought the baseball season was over." Stengel replied, "A baseball season is never ended. You play 'em all over during the winter, awake or asleep. The only difference this winter is that they'll be pleasant dreams instead of the nightmares I used to have at Boston and Brooklyn."[28] Thus began the ascendancy of Casey Stengel and the New York Yankees.

1950

Phil Rizzuto received the 1950 American League's Most
Valuable Player award from league president Will Harridge.

(The Sporting News)

16

"Who Were Those Guys?"

Ruth Ann Steinhagen, a tall, thin Chicago clerk-typist, was infatuated with Cubs bachelor Eddie Waitkus. In a nightly ritual, she covered her bed with photographs and press clippings of the first baseman. She included baked beans in her diet because Waitkus was from Boston, and she studied Lithuanian because he was of Lithuanian descent. As a regular ticket holder at Wrigley Field, she often stood with other bobby-soxers to watch the players pass outside the park, and once she almost got close enough to touch Waitkus. The prospect of such contact nearly caused her to faint. Steinhagen believed that she carried Waitkus's intellectual being with her and that she could commune with him. In 1948, he was traded to Philadelphia, so Steinhagen switched her allegiance from the Cubs to the Phillies. Knowing that she could not have him in "a normal way," she plotted his murder and her suicide to keep others from possessing Waitkus.[1]

Steinhagen purchased a .22 rifle at a pawn shop and then made reservations under the name Ruth Anne Burns at the Edgewater Beach Hotel—a popular accommodation for road teams. On June 14, 1948, the day the Phillies arrived to play the Cubs, she attended the game with a friend but left in the seventh inning to return to the hotel. There, she gave a bellhop a note to deliver to Waitkus. It read: "It is extremely important that I see you as soon as possible. We're not acquainted, but I have something of importance to speak to you about. I think it would be to your advantage to let me explain it to you. As I am leaving the hotel the day after tomorrow, I'd appreciate it greatly if I could see you as soon as possible. My name is Ruth Anne Burns, Room 1279-A. I realize that this is a little out the ordinary, but, as I said, it's rather important."[2]

Hours passed. Steinhagen debated on whether to kill Waitkus or to simply ask him to sleep with her. She eventually decided to explain the whole plan to him, leaving herself at his mercy. Sure that Waitkus would call the police, she wrote a letter to her parents, apologizing for her actions. By 10:30, she retired, thinking that Waitkus would not call. She was awakened by the phone—it was Waitkus. "What's so darned important?" he asked. Steinhagen was irritated by his informality and abruptness. "I hadn't figured a guy like him," she later told psychiatrists. "I thought he would ask me what is it all about but he was so informal." Steinhagen told him that she could not discuss the matter on the phone and asked if he would stop by in the morning. When he said no, she asked if he could come up that night for a few minutes. He replied affirmatively.[3]

Steinhagen was scared but determined that she "would settle this once and for all and really kill him." She decided she would stab him with a knife when he arrived at her door. But, Waitkus foiled her plan. As she opened the door, he barged right past her and sat down in a chair, as he asked, "What do you want to see me about?" Steinhagen, now even more irritated, said, "Wait, a minute I have a surprise for you." Producing the rifle from a closet, she pointed it at Waitkus and ordered him to stand by the window. "Baby, what is this all about?" questioned Waitkus. He stammered out the same question again, which further infuriated Steinhagen, who exclaimed, "For two years you have been bothering me and now you are going to die." With that, she shot him. Waitkus stood motionless, and then suddenly crashed against the wall and fell to the floor. He kept asking Steinhagen, "Baby, why did you do it, oh, why did you do it?" Instead of committing suicide, Steinhagen lost her nerve and called for a doctor.[4]

Steinhagen's bullet passed through Waitkus's lung and buried itself in the heavily muscular part of his back near the spine. Having escaped serious injury during four landings in the Pacific during World War II, Waitkus now lay in a hospital bed fighting for survival. He could have easily been a scholar instead of a ballplayer—he was an excellent student, who graduated twelfth in a class of 700 from Latin High School, in Cambridge, Massachusetts. Waitkus majored in mathematics and languages and was fluent in Lithuanian, Polish, German, and French. Although he attended Boston College for a few months, he quickly realized that academics and professional baseball were incompatible.[5] Following a successful minor-league career and his Army tour, Waitkus played three full seasons with the Chicago Cubs, where he earned a reputation as a slick fielder and an excellent hitter.

After five operations, Waitkus began to recover. As he lay in the hospital, he was deluged with sympathy letters. A few of the writers demanded that he forgive the girl "or vengeance would be theirs." "You'd have thought I did the shooting, not the other way around," Waitkus noted. In

Eddie Waitkus escaped injury
during four Pacific landings
in World War II only to be shot
by a woman who suffered
from a split personality.
(George Brace Photo)

explaining his side of the story, he claimed that he had checked with the room clerk after receiving Steinhagen's note and found that its signer, Ruth Anne Burns, had given her address as Portland Street, Cambridge, Massachusetts—his home town. When she told him it was important that she see him, he thought they might have mutual friends. Confronted with Steinhagen and the gun, Waitkus remembered that "She had the coldest face I ever saw. Absolutely no expression."[6]

On June 30, 1949, Ruth Steinhagen was declared insane and was sent to the state mental hospital at Kankakee. "A psychiatrist for the court reported she suffered from a split personality."[7] Waitkus missed the remainder of the season. Phillies owner Bob Carpenter sent the first baseman to Florida for the winter and ordered the team trainer, Frank Wiechec, to work with him until he was fully recovered. In spite of two ugly scars on his back and the mental anguish caused by the event, the patient responded well enough to become a major contributor in the 1950 pennant race. Nevertheless, the incident, which bore a striking resemblance to the plot in Bernard Malamud's first fictional work, *The Natural* (1952), was a stark warning to ballplayers that off the field they were neither anonymous nor immortal.

The problems with bobby-soxers, teenage girls who idolized ballplayers as heroes and sometimes as sex objects, reached new heights in the 1940s and 1950s. Most were well-behaved young women who formed fan clubs for their favorite players and attended games to root for them. Others waited outside ballparks after games to get an autograph or some form of recognition. When in large groups, their behavior sometimes became unruly and overwhelming for players who were trying to reach subway stations, taxi cabs, or private automobiles. Eddie Waitkus identified Chicago as the "badlands of bobby-sox fans. It seems as if ninety percent of the autograph seekers are teenage girls," he noted. "If you ignore them, they flick ink on the back of your suit. They really take advantage of you."[8] "Tell 'em off," he added, "and they become violent." Unlike the boys, "the girls know they have two strikes on you because of their sex," he complained.[9]

Players seeking to avoid confrontations with the bobby-soxers often waited for hours after games to make their escapes. In Cleveland, however, where Jim Hegan and Dale Mitchell were favorites, the players never seemed to outlast the bobby-soxers, day or night. "We can keep them from clustering around the players' exit, and we try to prevent them from molesting the players to excess. But these gals outstay us," explained one officer detailed to protect the players. "It's murder for some of those players when they try to get away. I've seen some of the boys leave part of a coat behind, just to make it into a cab."[10]

Mash notes received by players were more serious. While most were the result of innocuous teenage crushes, others appeared to be more dangerous. In 1950, one Phillies player received a note from a girl, which warned, "Either make a date with me, or I'll shoot you." The club asked authorities to investigate the girl.[11] Players were also fair game for female fans who not only knew where they lived but followed every move they made and discovered their routes to and from the ballpark, their favorite eating establishments, and where they sent their laundry. During the late 1940s, Richie Ashburn's parents moved to Philadelphia. Soon they took in several other young Whiz Kids. When a local newspaper ran a story on the players, the Ashburns made the mistake of giving their address. From then on, the home was assailed by women callers requesting dates or making marriage proposals.[12] When traveling on the road, ball clubs were subject to siege. Callers located room numbers and awakened players with continuous phone calls. Pillows slept on by players disappeared to become souvenirs, and napkins were swiped from players' laps as they ate in hotel dining rooms or restaurants.[13]

The Waitkus shooting and the onslaught of the bobby-soxers failed, however, to affect most players. For them, anonymity was not difficult to achieve. It was not until television appeared in Texas in the early 1950s, for instance, that Yankee third baseman Bobby Brown remembered being recognized outside of New York City.[14] Most players were identified with middle-class America, while others emerged from even more humble circumstances. A profile of the 382 players whose records appeared in the 1951 edition of *The Baseball Register* yields interesting information about those who played during the Pivotal Era.[15] The median age of the group was twenty-nine. The five youngest players were twenty-one years old, whereas only five players in the game were thirty-eight or older. The lack of younger players reflected the great backlog of talent in the minor leagues. Only nine players were without minor-league experience, while 224 spent at least four years in the minors. In addition, 238 of the players listed had four years of major-league experience or less. World War II, which severely cut into playing careers, created this situation; moreover, 136 of the 230 players who were veterans had at least three years of wartime service.

Using birthplaces as an indicator of geographic distribution, only ninety-seven players were born in the South or in former slave states. Of them, five were African Americans (Larry Doby, Luke Easter, Monte Irvin, Jackie Robinson, and Dan Bankhead). This seems to damage the impression that opposition to integration among ballplayers was so strong because so many white players came from the South. The most populated states were also those most heavily represented by ballplayers in the major leagues, with California leading the way with forty-eight players, followed by Pennsylvania with thirty-eight, New York with twenty-nine, Illinois with twenty-three, and Michigan with nineteen players. Nine states were unrepresented.[16] Seventeen players were foreign born, with Canada and Cuba each providing five. California's climate, which allowed year-round play, and the proximity of major-league franchises in the other four states seem to explain baseball's popularity in those locations. Of the 383 players listed, only 113 were born in urban areas of 50,000 people or more. Detroit led the way, with thirteen players, followed by Los Angeles and St. Louis, with ten each, and New York and Chicago, with seven each. Most players were born in little places like Moosup, Connecticut; Shickshinny, Pennsylvania; Midvale, Ohio; Comanche, Oklahoma; Grants Pass, Oregon; or Paris, Texas. The game during the Pivotal Era, not unlike the game before it, was still played by men who grew up in small towns and rural areas.[17]

Thirty-two nationalities were listed opposite ancestry as part of the players' biographical data. With the exception of those listed as African American (9), Jewish (4), and American Indian (2), information gathered closely paralleled European immigration patterns. Nationalities listed were as follows: German (69), Irish (56), English (47), Scotch-Irish (36),

Polish (28), Italian (27), Dutch (21), and French (12).[18] Education also reflected the general population, with ninety-one players listing at least a semester of college or university study. Only twenty-eight players possessed college degrees, and just five had graduate training. Birdie Tebbetts, a graduate of Providence College with a degree in philosophy, did postgraduate work at the University of New Hampshire. Tommy Upton, who studied at Bucknell and the University of Pennsylvania, used his graduate work at the University of Southern California to become a math teacher. Paul Calvert, the trilingual French-Canadian pitcher, graduated from the University of Toronto with a master's degree in commerce, and Vic Raschi, the superb Yankee pitcher, pursued graduate work at the College of William and Mary.

Baseball's most famous collegian was Dr. Bobby Brown, who earned four World Series rings with the Yankees while studying medicine at Tulane University. At age fifteen, Brown was a celebrated baseball prodigy whose father took him on a big-league tour of all sixteen clubs to showcase his son's hitting ability and beautiful swing.

In 1942 Brown became a premed student at Stanford University, but he left in 1943 when the Navy asked all premed students to enter the V-12 program. Brown enlisted and was first sent to UCLA and then to Tulane. At Tulane, Brown found time to play baseball, and after hitting .440 during the 1945 season attracted a flock of scouts. Instead of facing the dilemma of pursuing medical school or playing baseball, he was determined to do both. Tulane's three-semester system made it possible. As the most sought-after free agent in the country, Brown was signed to a contract by Larry MacPhail of the Yankees under a bonus arrangement that paid him $35,000 over a three-year period. By missing much of spring training and taking his books with him on the road, Brown was able to fit in two-thirds of a year's worth of schooling. To play ball and study, too, he gave up all holidays and remained in school during all recesses, including Christmas. In the spring of 1950, Brown earned his medical degree. After playing with the Yankees in parts of eight seasons and a stint in the military, Brown left baseball in 1954 to become a heart surgeon. In retrospect, Brown was one of the few major-league players to satisfy two such burning ambitions—but the division came at a price.[19] "I think because of my medical career I felt quite certain that I was never able to really reach my potential as a ballplayer," he recalled.[20]

Other athletes attempted two-sport careers—usually baseball in combination with either football or basketball. Most, however, ended up choosing between one or the other, and those with the talent for it usually selected baseball because of its stability and economic potential. Bobby Brown noted that "All the athletes with talent . . . usually gravitated to-

The Cincinnati Reds offered Frank Baumholtz a $10,000 bonus to give up a promising professional basketball career to concentrate on baseball. (George Brace Photo)

ward baseball."[21] Professional football, golf, basketball, and tennis salaries were not comparable to baseball's higher levels. In the tradition of such greats as Frankie Frisch, Mickey Cochran, and Christy Matthewson, those who gave up promising football careers to play baseball during the Pivotal Era included Alvin Dark, a star halfback at Louisiana State University; Charlie Keller, who played at Maryland; Sam Chapman and Jackie Jensen, both All-American backs who played at California; Snuffy Stirnweiss, a back at North Carolina; and Spud Chandler, a kicker at the University of Georgia. Only Pennsylvania's Chuck Bednarik, who later starred with the Philadelphia Eagles, and Chicago Cardinals halfback Charlie Trippi gave up baseball to play professional football. Trippi, another University of Georgia athlete, quit the Atlanta Crackers after leading the Cardinals to the National Football League championship in 1947. An unprecedented $100,000 four-year contract provided the incentive to leave baseball.

In basketball, the major two-sport athlete was Frank Baumholtz. The Ohio native was an All-American on the Ohio University team that played in the National Invitational Tournament in 1941. After serving in the Pacific during World War II, Baumholtz returned to play professional basketball with the Youngstown Bears in 1946 and went on to become the star forward and leading scorer for the Cleveland Rebels of the Basketball Association of America in 1947. He also finished second in hitting to Ted Kluzewski in the Sally League with Columbia, South Carolina. At age twenty-eight, he was undecided on whether to pursue a basketball or baseball career. "I want to give baseball one more year," he stated. "It is no use batting around the minors. With the years lost by the war I don't want a career of minor-league ball now. Baseball ruins the basketball season and if I don't make the grade, I don't want to mess up two sports."[22]

Baumholtz became the Reds' leadoff hitter in 1947 and was hitting over .300 when a series of family hardships and medical expenses almost brought him to his knees financially and psychologically. Knowing that he needed the extra $4,000 salary from the Rebels, he was determined to resume his basketball career. At the end of the season team president/general manager Warren Giles called him into his office and raised his salary to $10,000 and then presented him with a bonus check for $10,000. As Giles began to recite reasons why Baumholtz should give up professional basketball, the outfielder interrupted and said, "You have just talked me into it" and thus ended his basketball career.[23]

Front-office personnel were rarely as magnanimous at salary time as Giles was with Baumholtz. With the exception of Bill Veeck, who rarely allowed his players to leave negotiations dissatisfied, most general managers and presidents were unappreciated by the players. Many general managers operated on the philosophy that the first contracts they sent players did not really reflect what they thought a player was worth and, furthermore, that it was their job to make the players believe that they were overpaid. Conversely, some of the players believed that they should never sign immediately and that they should never let the club know that they were satisfied. *Cleveland Plain Dealer* sportswriter Harry Jones cited the case of Indians outfielder Hank Edwards, who never returned his contract until the day before spring training began. When Veeck asked the recalcitrant outfielder whether he was satisfied, he replied, "Sure I'm satisfied. I just hang on to it so you'll get the impression I'm not satisfied and send me a new one with more money." In another instance, infielder Johnny Berardino's contract was slashed by 25 percent—a cut that both Veeck and the player knew was coming after Berardino's poor 1948 season (he hit only .198). When Berardino became a holdout and was asked by Veeck for an explanation, he exclaimed, "Look, don't cut me 25%. Just cut me 24%. Leave me a little self-respect."[24]

Most players negotiated their own contracts, and in doing so they often found themselves at a distinct disadvantage. One of the few exceptions was Cardinals second baseman Red Schoendienst, whose wife always represented him.[25] Most negotiators for the ball clubs were tough, and even irascible. The most negative was William O. DeWitt, whose Browns were always strapped for funds. DeWitt's chief tactic was to get a ballplayer to sign for less by disparaging his season, no matter how much improvement he had made, and by presenting a laundry list of the club's financial woes.[26] DeWitt's counterpart with the Cardinals, Sam Breadon also had a reputation as a miser. "Sam Breadon was tough. He was a hard-nosed guy," recalled Stan Musial. "You couldn't negotiate . . . with him. He had his points. He would offer you a contract and that was it. You didn't have much leeway."[27] Fellow Cardinal Harry Walker also complained that Breadon had a habit of counting the previous year's World Series money against the coming year's salary—a negative incentive at best. The players were also aware that Branch Rickey received incentive money if he signed players below a salary cap set by Breadon.[28]

As a negotiator Rickey was, as usual, in a class by himself. In one instance, he learned that an excellent minor-league prospect, who was hitting .320 at the time, wanted to see him because he felt he was not getting enough money. Rickey invited the player to meet with him. During their conversation, Rickey convinced the player that he might not be major-league material, and, instead of asking for more money, the minor leaguer ended up pleading with Rickey to save his job.[29] Another general manager suspected of getting a slice of salary savings was the Yankees' George Weiss. He was also prepared to criticize the players.[30] As Vic Raschi recalled, Weiss was tough to deal with and never looked at a player during negotiations. "You always got the impression," noted Raschi, "that he was thinking, 'What's this guy want and how can I get rid of him in a hurry.'" In 1952, after Raschi slipped to sixteen victories, he wheedled a good contract out of Weiss, but the general manager warned, "Don't you ever have a bad year." When Raschi finished with thirteen wins the following year, he was traded to the Cardinals.[31]

Another difficult negotiator was Hank Greenberg, who became Cleveland's general manager in 1950. "Hank never forgot he was a player," remembered Al Rosen. "When you would go in to see him, he would tell you about his records. If you were in your third year, he would tell you what he did in his third year, etc. It made you very uncomfortable." Not only did Greenberg make unfair comparisons, "He was absolutely stone cold deaf to anybody's pleas for more money," recollected Rosen. "One year there were four of us holding out. The total package for the four of us was $6,000. How does that sound today?"[32]

It was also difficult for a player to renegotiate a salary in midseason. Mickey Vernon, the Senators' first baseman, was leading the American League in hitting in 1946 with a .360 average and decided that, at $9,000, he was entitled to an adjustment. When he approached owner Clark

Griffith, he was told to return to the field. Griffith, who eventually awarded Vernon a modest bonus, told reporters, "Don't forget, we gambled on him last year too. We agreed to pay him $9,000 with no certainty he wouldn't be a complete bust." Shirley Povich of the *Washington Post* agreed with Griffith when he wrote, "No player is ever given a salary cut in midseason because he is having a poor year, and by the same token he has no right to expect a midseason raise."[33]

By 1950, the average major-league baseball player's salary was $11,000. Outstanding veteran players were making much more. Examples included Tommy Henrich at $40,000, Joe Gordon at $35,000, Birdie Tebbetts at $25,000, and Virgil Trucks at $22,000. In an era when a three-bedroom ranch bungalow sold for $13,800 in Chicago, a new Frigidaire refrigerator was advertised at $200, a pound of bacon was 63¢, a pound of coffee was 77¢, a loaf of bread was 13¢, and a fifteen-pound bag of potatoes sold for 84¢, a ballplayer's salary compared quite favorably with salaries earned by U.S. Senators, at $12,500. Of the major professions, only physicians, with an average income of $12,324, made slightly more. In comparison, baseball players fared much better than attorneys, $8,349, dentists, $7,436, and school teachers, $2,794.[34] With per capita consumption at $1,266.45, the ballplayer's income looked very inviting.

Several major drawbacks, however, dulled the glitter of major-league careers. With 26.7 minor-league players waiting in the wings for each major-league position, compared to 5.9 in 1990, players played while injured or risked losing not only starting positions but sometimes roster spots.[35] Others hid injuries suffered in the minor leagues for fear that they would ruin promising major-league careers. Frank Baumholtz almost tore the little finger from his throwing hand in 1947 when he collided with an outfield fence. The injury impaired his throwing, but he told no one.[36] Pitchers were especially vulnerable. Boston Red Sox 1946 staff aces Boo Ferris (25-6), Tex Hughson (20-11), and Mickey Harris (17-9) all suffered debilitating arm injuries that either ended or severely hampered promising careers. Moreover, the cost of rehabilitation often fell to the players themselves. Even Eddie Waitkus was forced to appear before the Pennsylvania State Workmen's Compensation Board in an attempt to collect $4,800 from an insurance company for medical expenses incurred as a result of his shooting.[37]

Career longevity at the major-league level was another problem for players. With playing careers averaging only five years, Frank and Betty Bell Baumholtz realized that they could not squander their resources. As children of the Great Depression, they were cognizant of the value of money. With no income from basketball, three children to send through college, and two residences to maintain, the Baumholtzes developed five-

year plans designed to achieve long-term goals. They set aside large portions of each paycheck to be left untouched. Their plan included frugal
household management and limited restaurant visits. At the end of each
season, Baumholtz took a winter job selling clothes with a large Cleveland
department store. Without dipping into their baseball resources, the
Baumholtz family lived on their off-season income.[38]

Only a few players, notably Ewell Blackwell, had their paychecks
stretched out over a twelve-month period. Most players were paid during the baseball season, which usually necessitated careful financial planning and, in most cases, some form of supplemental income. Finding
off-season employment was not easy, and players were glad to take what
was available. Virgil Trucks worked for the mayor of Birmingham for $25
a week writing up citations for people who illegally dumped ashes from
their coal stoves onto the street. He later went to work on the Alabama
Great Southern railroad as a switchman—a job Trucks held for many
years.[39] Working in clothing stores was one of the most popular off-season jobs. Bob Porterfield, who was also a carpenter, worked in a men's
clothing store in Bluefield, West Virginia, as did Farris Fain in Oakland,
California. Johnny Vander Meer clerked in a Cincinnati store in the late
1940s, while in 1950 Don Newcombe assisted with merchandising in a
men's clothing store in New York. Other such employees included Rex
Barney, who worked for Abraham & Straus, in Brooklyn; Phil Rizzuto
and Gene Hermanski, who were employed by a Newark men's shop;
and Sid Gordon, who sold suits on Pitken Avenue in Brooklyn. Another
popular form of off-season employment was working for beer companies—many of which already maintained close ties with ball clubs as spon-
sors. In 1951, Tommy Henrich and Snuffy Stirnweiss were salesmen for a
Miller High Life distributor in New Jersey. In Cleveland, Bob Kennedy
worked for Erin Brew (Standard Brewing Company of Cleveland), Larry
Doby was employed by the Pabst Brewing Company, and Al Rosen
worked for Budweiser.

Other forms of off-season employment were more varied. Ted Wilks of
the Cardinals worked in an Oswego Falls, New York, power plant, catcher
Sal Yvars was a post-office worker in White Plains, New York, and Phil
Masi was employed by a Chicago printing company. Stan Rojek, who
was an early riser, worked as a milkman at his father's dairy—A.J. Rojek
Dairy, in Tonawanda, New York. Kirby Higbee sold insurance in Columbia, South Carolina, while Howie Pollett worked with the Eddie Dyer
Insurance Company in Houston—a company owned by the former Cardinal manager. Another popular off-season occupation that allowed players to trade on their names was car sales. Following his tremendous 1947
season, Ewell Blackwell was ready to sell cars in Cincinnati over the win-

ter. But, after two weeks on the job, the hard-luck hurler was called to California to care for his ill mother. Nevertheless, before he left, he sold eight Lincoln/Mercury vehicles, plus a new station wagon to the Reds.[40]

Other players developed second careers during the off-season. Utility infielder and aspiring actor Johnny Berardino signed a joint contract with Bill Veeck and movie producer Richard K. Polimer in 1948 that allowed him to act in the off-season and play baseball in the summer. In addition, under the contract Berardino's dark and handsome face was insured for $100,000.[41] Another Cleveland Indian, pitcher Gene Bearden, used his fine 1948 season as a springboard to work in the movies. He appeared in *The Stratton Story* and also had a part in *And Baby Makes Three*. Pitcher Ralph Branca, a crooner of some note, embarked on a singing tour in 1950. He also organized and played in basketball exhibitions between baseball players and local teams. Other baseball players found off-season jobs connected to sports. Dave Koslo, who was also on the sales staff of the Walters Brothers Brewery, served as the football expert for radio station WNAM in Menasha, Wisconsin. Jim Tabor, who starred in basketball at Alabama, coached a prep team in South Boston, while Pirate third baseman Frank Gustine coached baseball at Waynesburg College in Pennsylvania.

Some players were employed by the ball clubs in the off-season. Mel Harder and Bob Cain worked in the Cleveland Indians' ticket office, whereas others, such as Phil Cavarretta of the Cubs and Dizzy Trout of the Tigers, gave after-dinner speeches on behalf of their teams. The witty Trout told audiences that the secret to his pitching success was that "Nobody likes to hit a man with glasses." The Tiger pitcher also operated an off-season business cleaning and polishing bowling balls. In 1947 Trout, whose salary was in the $20,000 range, moved his family of six into a fourteen-room house. The entire third floor was reserved as a gallery where he could exhibit his extensive gun collection and pictures of his Tiger teammates.[42]

Other players were even more entrepreneurial and their businesses extended year round. Senators' teammates Walt Masterson and Al Evans owned a dry cleaning and laundry firm in 1946, which they sold at a profit. In 1947, Masterson sold automobiles. Then, in 1948, he opened a new theater, the Globe, in Arlington County, Virginia. Red Sox outfielder Al Zarilla manufactured lamps out of baseballs and bats. Tiger infielder Don Kolloway operated Kolloway Kollision Service in Detroit and as a premium gave away free autographed baseballs to any customer having his auto repaired there. Del Ennis, the talented Phillies outfielder, who also trained to become a stockbroker, went into the Christmas tree business with Phillies coach Benny Bengough. Snuffy Stirnweiss ran a baseball school in Bartow, Florida during the off-season. Employing Yankee teammates as instructors, in 1948 he also bought control of the Greenville, North Carolina, ball club in the Coastal League.[43]

The restaurant business also provided opportunities for players. As an early Christmas present, pitcher Frank Shea purchased a coffee shop in downtown Naugatuck, Connecticut, for his father to operate. Perhaps the most famous restaurant was Dodgers relief pitcher Hugh Casey's steak and chop house at 600 Flatbush Avenue in Brooklyn. The establishment had a thirty-foot mirrored bar, a jukebox by the door, and booths for cozy dining. Decorated with photographs of famous Dodgers, it became the hangout of choice for Dodgers players and their families.[44] Although none of the players were as fortunate as Ty Cobb, whose investment in the Coca Cola Company earned him tens of thousands, several were stockholders or company officers. Billy Herman invested in a Louisville paint manufacturer, Johnny Mize had stock holdings in a Florida orange juice company, and Jack Kramer was on the board of directors of the Tony Bonelli Spaghetti Company of Belleville, Illinois.

Many ballplayers combined off-season employment with hobbies and outdoor activities such as hunting, fishing, and golf. Other activities or hobbies commonly listed in the *Sporting News Baseball Register* included bowling, basketball, woodworking, boating, sketching, training and raising dogs, watching football, photography, skiing, music, skating, mechanics, movies, billiards, and electric trains. While some activities, like hunting, occasionally imperiled players, few accidents like those that wounded Monty Stratton or Hal Peck occurred.

Another potential form of income for ballplayers was the endorsement of products. Unfortunately, companies were most interested in stars. Other players usually drew attention only because of a no-hitter or a key hit in a big game. Of course, for players with the Yankees, Giants, or Dodgers it was easier to get endorsements because of New York's huge market. Johnny Mize allowed his name to be used by first-class New York tailoring establishment, and Willard Marshall, the Giants outfielder, endorsed Chesterfield cigarettes, though, like many players, he did not smoke.[45] Giants teammate Bobby Thomson, another nonsmoker, also signed on with Chesterfield after his successful 1949 season. In 1950, Thomson had an off-year and was dropped by the company. In 1951, after he hit his historic home run, the cigarette company suddenly rediscovered Thomson. On October 4, 1951, newspapers were filled with "full-page Chesterfield ads," recalled Thomson, "and there was Bobby Thomson all over them. I guess the folks didn't realize after the big night that I was no longer with them." When Thomson threatened to take legal action against the company, a settlement was reached.[46]

Most players were unsophisticated regarding endorsements. When

Cleveland Indians' Ken Keltner shows son Randy (9) how to stab "hot" grounder. Veteran infielder spends spare time coaching his two boys in diamond sport. "Any good training program includes eating the right kind of food," says Ken. "My number one training dish is milk, fruit and Wheaties."

At right . . . youngest Keltner, Jeff (5), proudly points to dad's name on autographed bat.

Champions start young!

Sandlots of hometown Milwaukee is where Ken Keltner began playing baseball. Early training paid off . . . last season Keltner slammed 31 homers for peak performance of eleven-year Big League career. A Wheaties eater over 12 years!

Want *your* youngsters to develop the energy and endurance of true champions? Then start 'em young! See that they eat like champions. Include lots of Wheaties, nourishing whole wheat flakes. Yes, champions do . . . why don't you? Eat Wheaties!

"Wheaties" and "Breakfast of Champions" are registered trade marks of **General Mills**

Keltners team up at breakfast table . . . with lots of Wheaties, milk and fruit on hand. Mom serves Jeff . . . and now watch the boys dig in! "Wheaties go over big with everybody at our house," says Big Leaguer Keltner. Second helping good . . . these 100% whole wheat flakes! Wheaties are plenty nourishing, too. Give you three B vitamins, also minerals. Best energy proteins. At your house tomorrow . . . have America's favorite whole wheat flakes—Wheaties.

"Breakfast of Champions"

Although companies were usually interested only in stars, endorsements were offered to players who drew attention because of a great season, a no-hitter, or a big hit in a key game. *(Left)* Ken Keltner and his family appeared in advertisements for Wheaties, and *(right)* Bobby Thomson endorsed Bromo Seltzer. (Courtesy of General Mills, Inc., and Randy and Jeffrey Keltner; Courtesy of Warner-Lambert Company and Robert Thomson)

Browns pitcher Ned Garver won twenty games in 1951, he received endorsement offers from Wheaties, Gillette, and several other smaller companies. Rather than handle them, Garver turned the business over to the team's traveling secretary, Leo Ward.[47] Those players with real agents had a much better chance of attracting endorsements. Dom DiMaggio hired Jessie Stearns, a Virginia radio station employee, to handle his endorsements, which included an optical firm (he wore glasses), a cigarette testimonial, and playing cards.[48] Following a fifty-homer season at Syracuse, slugger Hank Sauer employed Louis N. Gordon as his agent. Gordon secured a contract with Wheaties—"The Breakfast of Champions"—for Sauer during the player's rookie year with the Cincinnati Reds. Players signed Wheaties contracts with the stipulation that they eat and enjoy the cereal and that General Mills, the cereal's manufacturer, might publish the player's testimonial. Moreover, the player had to fill out a questionnaire on the reverse side of the contract that asked the following questions:

> How often do you eat Wheaties?
>
> At what meal?
>
> At what other meal?
>
> What other foods do you eat at breakfast?
>
> With cream or milk?
>
> Sugar?

Under the contract, players received a case of Wheaties every six weeks, plus cases for home runs. In 1948, Sauer hit 32 home runs and received numerous cases at his Cincinnati home. In the winter, however, he worked as a set designer in Hollywood and asked his agent to take the cereal. "My wife and I haven't any children," Gordon explained, "and there must be 60 boxes of Wheaties to a case. Did you ever see 60 boxes of Wheaties in a small apartment?"[49]

Pittsburgh Pirates star Ralph Kiner also signed a contract with Wheaties for $500 a year—a sum he characterized as "a ridiculous amount." In addition, his 1949 contract called for a case of Wheaties for every home run he hit, and that year he hit fifty-four. "I had Wheaties all over the garage," he remembered, and "I couldn't [even] get the car in."[50] Most players, like pitcher Bob Cain, were forced to settle for a $250 fee and new clock provided by the Bowman Chewing Gum Company, the major producer of baseball cards during the Pivotal Era.[51]

For the thousands of children who opened the packages of cards with hopes of capturing a Rizzuto, Mize, Williams, or Spahn, the life of a ballplayer seemed ideal—a profession worthy of emulation. It mattered little that the odds of playing major-league baseball were incredibly small. During the long days of summer, baseball was the game of choice for children of all ages, whether they played on rural fields, city sandlots, playgrounds, alleys, suburban backyards, or small-town diamonds. Amateur baseball, which was not yet dominated by Little League, was led in the 1930s and 1940s by Junior Baseball, sponsored by the American Legion.[52] By 1947, there were 204 players under contract to major-league teams who had participated in American Legion baseball leagues.[53]

During the Pivotal Era, children could identify with players whose backgrounds were similar to their own and who were removed by only a decade or less in age. Players like Andy Seminick, Red Schoendienst, and Bobby Shantz came from modest circumstances. If you were from a Pennsylvania mining town, you could look to see the example set by scrappy Phillies catcher Andy Seminick—one of ten children born into a family of Russian immigrants in Muse, Pennsylvania. When Seminick graduated from high school in 1937, he took up his father's occupation as a coal miner. Baseball was his escape from the mines.[54] Red Schoendienst, whose father was a prison guard at the Illinois state penitentiary, grew up in Germantown, Illinois, also a mining community. His favorite pastimes, fishing and baseball, did not include school. At age sixteen, he left school and joined the Civilian Conservation Corps, earning a wage of $30 a month. After an eye injury kept him out of the service, on a lark he attended a Cardinals tryout camp at Sportsman's Park. After the first day of tryouts, Cardinal scouts compared notes and discovered that Schoendienst was the only boy to receive exceptional ratings out of the 398 candidates. Schoendienst, who achieved a dream shared by almost all sandlot players, was on his way to the big leagues.[55]

At 5'6" tall, "Little" Bobby Shantz not only defied the odds of becoming a major-league baseball player, but in 1952 he was voted the American League's Most Valuable Player. Yet, throughout his career, Shantz was forced to convince skeptics that his height was not a handicap. As was the case for many players, Shantz's greatest supporter was his father. Wilmer Shantz worked for Bethlehem Steel near Pottstown, Pennsylvania. Discouraged from playing professional baseball by his own father, Wilmer Shantz vowed that his own sons would not suffer the same fate. In 1929, he purchased a new home with a huge backyard where he could throw with both his sons. When the Depression hit, the Shantz family had little money to spend on equipment. They saved breakfast cereal box tops and sent them away for balls. A family friend at a local school gave them the boxtops from the school's cereal supply. Like fathers before and after, Wilmer Shantz used baseball as a vehicle to share valuable time with his sons. Later, Bobby claimed that the games of "ball and strike" they played in the backyard "had a lot to do with the control I mastered as a big leaguer."[56]

Other ballplayers' fathers were not as easygoing as Wilmer Shantz. Eddie Stanky's dad was a leather glazer and a frustrated semipro ballplayer who was determined that his son would succeed in baseball. According to Stanky, his father started teaching him the game when he had barely begun to walk. "No kid stuff, either," explained Stanky. "We didn't just play catch. I wasn't permitted to throw underhanded like most kids do. With me it was sidearm and overhand right from the beginning. With my father, it was serious business. It was his mission in life."[57] Don Mueller, whose timely hitting earned him the nickname "Mandrake the Magician," was under even more pressure. He was the son of Walter Mueller—who played outfield for the Pittsburgh Pirates in the 1920s—and the nephew of Heinie Mueller, another outfielder, who compiled a .282 batting average with four teams over an eleven-year career. Walter Mueller had high expectations for his sons—he was determined that both would be better ballplayers than he had been. "Dad cracked the whip," recalled Mueller. "I always liked to go fishing on Sundays, but to him Sunday meant just two things—church and baseball." Mueller Sr. made his teenage sons promise that if either was signed to a professional contract, the boys would split the money between them. When Don Mueller signed with the Giants in 1944, his brother Leroy received half of his $6,000 bonus. It was Leroy's only professional paycheck—a tropical disease acquired in the Pacific theater during World War II made it impossible for him to play professional baseball.[58]

The glamour of a major-league career during the Pivotal Era was not everything adoring fans imagined it to be. Until the advent of Murphy money, players were completely responsible for their own spring training expenses. Moreover, the barnstorming trips made by teams as they headed north before the season began were often miserable. When the Indians and Giants broke camp in Arizona, they stopped each day to play each other in a different town along their rail route. "It was terrible," Willard Marshall recalled. "You always had a satchel full of wet clothes. They didn't have four or five sets of uniforms in those days, they had one or two. They were made out of flannel and boy they were hot. You [would] get them full of water and it was like carrying around [extra weight]."[59]

Players also purchased their own gloves and shoes, and not unlike other commuters, whether at home or on the road, they were responsible for the taxi, bus, subway, or streetcar fares that got them to and from ballparks. While on the road, they were given a daily food allowance of $6.00. When Bill Veeck unilaterally paid his players a $7.50 per diem, he angered his fellow owners in both leagues. Intercity travel, which was generally by train, received mixed reviews from players. Cleveland's Bob Lemon enjoyed the long train rides and fondly remembered the friendships formed in the men's room, where players would talk baseball over a case of beer. "I learned more baseball," noted Lemon, "in the men's room or washroom on a train than I did in the clubhouse."[60] Other players despised train travel. Ralph Kiner complained, "To me train travel was terrible. I never fit in a bunk right and I never slept well. And of course it wasn't like taking the Super Chief—you always got the milk runs. You got on at midnight and [when] you stopped at every city on the way . . . the engineer would joggle you all over the place."[61]

Airline travel in the late 1940s was far from predictable and was often a bumpy, unpleasant experience. Malfunctions also caused concern. On a Chicago–St. Louis flight in early 1946, for instance, the Red Sox had a scare when they went through bad weather and their aircraft's tail wheel would not come down. Sportswriter Dan Daniel chronicled another trip between Detroit and New York in which the pilot of his aircraft had to skirt several disturbances. The passengers were being served dinner when the plane hit another storm system and momentarily seemed to be out of control. "Up went the steak [and] up went the coffee," wrote Daniel. "Down it came—and you should have seen Joe Trimble of the *New York News*. They had to rush him and his clothes to the cleaners. It was not a pleasant experience."[62] It is little wonder that Yankees such as Bill Wight, Frank Crosetti, Red Ruffing, and Floyd Bevans opted to travel by rail. In 1947, when Larry McPhail issued an ultimatum that all Yankee players would fly, eight team members defied him, and, with the exception of Crosetti, all received bills for their travel. MacPhail rescinded his order to avoid a team mutiny and because he knew player contracts stipulated that players were entitled to first-class rail tickets.[63]

Travel during the season was also hard on families. Road trips averaged between twenty-one and thirty days. Wives with children operated as single parents—almost totally responsible for their children's upbringing. When teams returned to play homestands, family schedules were again disrupted. On teams such as the Cubs, which played at unlighted Wrigley Field, fathers shared dinners after games with their families on a regular basis. The increase in night games elsewhere, however, played havoc with family routines, with players returning home early in the morning only to have to return to the park late the same morning for the next day's contest. As Casey Stengel commented, "As a general thing, night baseball is a player problem. If we had nothing but night ball, the players would not kick. But 1:30 on Monday, 8:30 on Tuesday and Wednesday, then 2:30 on Thursday, with 8:30 on Friday—well your stomach begins to holler, 'Hey, what's going on? I can't take much of this.'"[64]

Many children shared in their fathers' profession by attending games with their mothers. Cynthia Wilber, the daughter of catcher Del Wilber and author of *For the Love of the Game*, wrote, "For myself, my brothers, and other baseball kids, the parks were our playgrounds, our home turf, and the adults in our lives were America's ballplayers. The sights and sound of the ballpark and the nagging smells of popcorn, hot dogs, beer, and sweat mingle together in our memories of the way it was."[65] Of course the park was not without its dangers—including to players' children. Then seven years old, Donnie Doerr still remembers a day in 1950 when he was sitting in the Red Sox dugout before a game with the Cleveland Indians and was struck by a wild throw made by Billy Goodman. Doerr suffered a cut lip and lost a tooth. Nor were children sitting on the bench immune to foul language and other events. During a 1947 game in Brooklyn, Cardinals third baseman Whitey Kurowski was put out of a game after an argument with an umpire. Kurowski's five-year-old son Slug, who wore a Cardinal uniform on the bench, witnessed the whole affair. As Kurowski left the field, his son followed him silently into the clubhouse. "You got put out of the game, didn't you, Daddy?" asked Slug. When Kurowski nodded his head, Slug said, "Then we had better take off our suit, hadn't we?"[66]

Baseball wives were expected to assume a secondary role to their husband's careers. Violet Dickey, wife of Yankee great Bill Dickey, once wrote in the *Saturday Evening Post* that "The game takes precedence over all other aspects of a player's life during three recognizable periods: for three months when he's training to play the season. (This includes floor pacing before contract matters are settled.) For six months when he is playing the season. For three months when he is relaxing from playing the season." Ever the realist, Dickey continued, "The girl who thinks she can supplant baseball in a player's mind and heart is not only a foolish optimist but her own worst enemy. She must be satisfied to beat out hunting or fishing for second place."[67] Although written in a caring vein, Dickey's portrayal of her husband cast ballplayers as self-centered individuals with little time for wives or concerns outside their own environments.

Della De Ruiter Boudreau, wife of the Indians' player-manager, provided a typical example of what was expected of many baseball wives. During the Cleveland Indians' championship season in 1948, the Boudreaus owned a house in Harvey, Illinois, and rented a second home in Cleveland Heights during the summer, which, by agreement, they were to vacate on Labor Day. Della Boudreau, who raised the couple's three children, attended most Indians games, while Barbara, 9, Sharon, 5, and Louie Jr., 2, were in the care of a babysitter. Though she cheered for her husband and team during the game, she remained totally in the background, often waiting patiently for him in the car until after his interviews were finished and he had showered and dressed. When the team was on the road, the Boudreaus kept in contact by mail. The Indians' manager expected a letter waiting for him in every city. Baseball, which the Boudreaus treated as a business, was rarely discussed at home.[68]

Only a few players were married to career women or those with independent incomes. Even fewer were married to celebrities. Hank Greenberg married Caral Gimbel, a member of the department-store family who maintained her own stable of horses, while All-American swimmer Zoe Ann Olsen was attached to Jackie Jensen, and Ralph Kiner married tennis professional Nancy Chaffee. Dodgers pitcher Dan Bankhead's wife studied music at Northwestern University and sang with several big-name bands. Strong women were often viewed with a sense of wariness by baseball officials. Even such an avowed family man as Branch Rickey was skeptical of a woman's involvement in family financial affairs, when he noted, "I encourage a man to consult his wife about any offer I make him. I think she should be part of any important decision that is made. But on the other hand, there are wives who 'manage' a player, dominate him until he loses initiative and aggressiveness."[69]

Younger wives were also suspected of being adverse influences. In 1949, Phillies manager Eddie Sawyer banned players' wives from all trips and from spring training in 1950 because he thought it would enhance the teams' pennant chances. The ban caused a wave of indignation among the players' wives. "I'd like to [wring] his neck," complained one disappointed wife. "Who does he think he is? I get a tan every year in Clearwater that carries me through the whole year. Who wants to stay home and keep house for two months? And what is my husband going to be doing while I am at home washing dishes?" Explaining that his ball club was young, Sawyer reasoned that the absence of the players' wives from trips and spring training would allow his team to keep their minds on baseball instead of shopping trips, stage show tickets, marital disagreements, and late-night dinners. In a secret ballot, 75 percent of the Phillies players supported their manager's position.[70]

Divorce among professional baseball players was uncommon, but nevertheless present. Only in rare situations was the divorce predicated on conflicting professions. In 1947, Helen Blankenship Brazle sued Al Brazle for divorce in Little Rock, Arkansas. The St. Louis pitcher claimed to be taken completely by surprise, having previously been given assurances that his wife would give up her lucrative job to join him in St. Louis.[71] More common were divorces caused by players who acted irresponsibly with family finances or were simply poor husbands or fathers. Pitcher Bobo Newsom, one of baseball's most traveled players, was slapped with a $3,869 claim by the Internal Revenue Service, charging that he owed them that amount from his 1947 income tax return. Only a year later, in 1949, Newsom was indicted by a Laurinburg, North Carolina, grand jury in 1949 for nonsupport of his two teenage children. Divorced from Lucille Newsom six years before, he was in arrears for three months of payments at $150 per month. Sheriff Jessie C. Gibson resignedly noted, "I guess everything will be all right, even though we'll have to try him, now that the grand jury has indicted him. If he doesn't come home, we'll have to extradite him."[72]

Another player with serious marital and financial difficulties was former Cardinals pitcher Mort Cooper. Cooper was a gritty hurler, who when he pitched chewed aspirin tablets to dull the pain caused by bone chips in his elbow.[73] During his seven-year stint with the Cardinals, he earned more than $125,000. Cooper's distinguished career collapsed, however, after the 1946 season. In 1945, following nine years of marriage, Bernadine Cooper filed for divorce, contending that, among other complaints, her husband had a violent temper. The divorce decree ordered Cooper to pay $100 a month in alimony and $200 a month in child support. A subsequent court battle divulged just how convoluted Cooper's situation had become. During his own court appearance, Cooper sued to gain custody of his son Lonnie and to stop making alimony payments. Noting that he had made $15,000 during the past two seasons, Cooper explained that, after deductions for taxes and living expenses, he was lucky to have $5,500 left at the end of the season. Cooper testified further that he had fallen behind in his alimony payments because of $10,000 in bad debts incurred in the purchase of a nightclub and package liquor store. According to Bernadine Cooper's testimony, the former pitcher was a heavy spender who quickly squandered the World Series checks he earned in 1943 and 1944. She also testified that Cooper had installed a $2,500 basement bar and a recreation room equipped with slot machines and poker tables in their former home.[74]

Unfortunately, Cooper's travails did not end with his divorce. In October 1948, Cooper was jailed for passing three bad checks—two at the Mark Twain hotel in St. Louis and another at the Squire Clothing Company in Cincinnati. Former Cardinals owner, Sam Breadon, who only a few years before sold both Cooper brothers because he was angered by their holdout, put up $2,000 bail for Mort. Seemingly embarrassed by Cooper's predicament, Breadon told reporters, "Mort's such a good-hearted fellow . . . he was probably the smartest pitcher in the business. But when it came to outside interests involving money, he was just like a little child. He never did have any sense of business or of handling money."[75] Cooper died in 1958 at age forty-five.

Players' wives confronted other vices, too—particularly chewing tobacco and alcohol. The use of both substances, which was as old as the game itself, was often indulged in by young players as a sign of manhood and acceptance. Others, such as Phillies outfielder Johnny Blatnik, used the chewing habit as a crutch. In 1946, when Blatnik found himself in a deep slump in the minors, catcher Joe Tipton gave him some tobacco. That same day Blatnik broke out of his slump with three hits. From that day on, he was a confirmed tobacco chewer. The first time his wife saw him with a chew, she refused to cook dinner for him and told him not to come home. Blatnik ate out![76]

Far more serious were drinking problems. Alcohol was the drug of choice during the Pivotal Era. While most players' substance-abuse problems were covered up by reporters, some of whom were alcoholics themselves, a few players made headlines. The classic case was Don Black, a pitcher acquired by the Indians in 1947 at the waiver price because Connie Mack gave up on him. Roger Peckinpaugh advanced him $1,500, but Black squandered it on alcohol. After being sent down to Milwaukee, he was hit hard and ended up with an 0-5 record. Bill Veeck, who knew Black was an alcoholic and deeply in debt, bought him from Milwaukee. To keep him from drinking, Veeck sent half of Black's salary to his wife and used the remainder to pay off Black's debts. The Indians president then put Black on a dollar-a-day allowance and forced him to come by the office every day to pick it up. Veeck stationed a representative of Alcoholics Anonymous outside the office, who engaged Black in conversation each day. Not long after this arrangement began, Black joined the organization. Black stopped drinking, paid off his debts, and on July 10, 1947, threw a no-hitter against his old teammates, the Philadelphia A's.[77]

Alcohol also may have affected, if not altered, other promising careers. That is what Branch Rickey surmised was the case with Pete Reiser, the talented outfielder of the Brooklyn Dodgers. When Reiser won the National League batting championship in 1941, with a .343 average, 14 home runs, and 76 runs-batted-in, he appeared to have the whole package—speed, power, a great throwing arm, and an excellent batting eye. Reiser, however, was a reckless player who refused to yield to any man or object. In 1942, his stubbornness led him to suffer a concussion from running into the center-field fence in St. Louis's Sportsman's Park. The impact resulted in migraine headaches and caused the fusion of two vertebrae at the base of his neck.[78] Later that season, Reiser broke his ankle sliding into first base in a game against the Phillies. Afterward, he was not the same ballplayer—indeed, his injuries were so bad that in 1943 he was initially turned down for induction by the Navy until they discovered he was a major-league baseball player.[79]

In January 1945, Reiser wrote to Rickey and requested a $2,000 advance to cover a number of expenses, including the cost of a divorce and medical bills. Rickey refused because Reiser already owed the team $1,250. Also, Rickey had heard some "really ugly stories" from more than one source concerning Reiser's drinking. Noting that he believed Reiser's request confirmed the reports of his drinking, Rickey lectured, "If a man is going to drink and drink to excess, and from time to time and not infrequently goes hog wild about it, there usually isn't any cure for it. He doesn't get any better and he doesn't quit. He goes from bad to worse and in time it gets him."[80] In 1947, Reiser collided with the outfield fence at Ebbets Field and almost died—he was paralyzed for ten days. After this injury, his career plummeted. In 1948, the Dodgers traded Reiser to the Boston Braves for Mike McCormick. Buzzie Bavasi, who witnessed the transaction, recalled that Rickey "was exceptionally honest. He told those people that Reiser might not measure up because of certain shortcomings. But they wanted him anyway, and finally Mr. Rickey let him go."[81]

Trades were often hard on ballplayers and their families. In 1946, George Kell was traded by Connie Mack to the Detroit Tigers for Barney McCosky during his third full season with the Philadelphia A's. Kell had deep respect for Mack and could not understand why he had been traded. Indeed, at the time he felt rejected. When Kell confronted Mack about the trade, the venerable owner replied, "Son, you are going to be a good ballplayer. You are going to make a lot of money, but not in Philadelphia, because I can't pay you. In Detroit you can do it. You will play well, and they will pay you well." As magnanimous as Mack's motive for making the trade seemed after that reply, the deal still placed the Kell family in an awkward situation. The Kells, who had a young baby, were living in a small apartment in Philadelphia. "We didn't have any money," Kell recalled, "and there were no provisions then for being traded. They didn't pay your way. They didn't give me a dime. They didn't say sorry." Kell was on the road with the Tigers, and there was neither time nor resources for them to search for housing in Detroit. In addition, in 1946 housing was virtually unobtainable in some locations. When he complained about his situation, he was told, "Well, that is your problem." Their dilemma was solved when Kell's younger brother took a train from Arkansas to Philadelphia to retrieve the family and take them home. Nevertheless, the bitterness of this experience remained with Kell.[82]

By 1950, good housing was still difficult to find for ballplayers with young families. During his third full major-league season, Gil Hodges hit four home runs in a game. While his teammates were elated over the feat, the event was even more meaningful to Jean and Gil Hodges for another reason. "I hope it brings us a place to live," said Hodges to writer Dick Young as he glanced at his wife and six-month-old son. "We've tried ev-

After Connie Mack traded future All-Star George Kell to the Tigers, he told him, "Son, you are going to be a good ballplayer. You are going to make a lot of money, but not in Philadelphia." (George Brace Photo)

erything to get a decent home to rent," added Jean Hodges. "We're living with my folks and there just isn't enough room. We've advertised, but didn't have any luck. Maybe, now something will happen."[83]

Few families, however, had as unsettling a season as that of first baseman Johnny Hopp in 1949. The Hopps maintained a permanent home in Hastings, Nebraska, and leased a home in Pittsburgh for the summer. On May 16, Marion Hopp and her two children Tarilla, 10, and Johnny, 5, arrived in Pittsburgh following a three-day car trip. When Johnny Hopp returned that night, he awakened Marion to announce that he had been traded to Brooklyn for Marv Rackley. While the news meant an instant change of venue, it also provided an opportunity to play for a team with a chance to win the pennant. The Hopps drove the family car to St. Louis, where the Dodgers were playing. Marion Hopp and the children traveled on to Hastings to await further instructions. Hopp rented a home in Brooklyn—no small feat—and then told his family to come by train. They arrived on Sunday, June 5, and Hopp met them for breakfast and then left for the game while Marion Hopp returned to her new home to unpack. The following day, not long after she purchased $30-worth of groceries, the Hopps learned that the trade was off because Rackley had a sore arm.

Although the family traveled more than 5,000 miles in three weeks, Marion Hopp met the turn of events stoically. "I was ready to swoon," she said, "But . . . I realized it's all part of baseball. But Johnny and I have had less than a day together since spring training. We had subleased our home in Pittsburgh to the Les Flemings and now I'll have to go there and start looking again." The family's bad luck continued the remainder of the summer, when Johnny Sr. was struck in the face during infield practice and suffered two black eyes and a broken nose and Johnny Jr. had an emergency appendectomy ten days later. Nevertheless, little Johnny was delighted to return to Pittsburgh, because, as he commented, "Now I can have my Pittsburgh uniform again."[84]

Another couple suffering from mixed emotions because of trade was the Pafkos. When Andy Pafko learned that he had been traded from the Cubs to Brooklyn after eight years in Chicago, he was elated. "It's just like having a man you just met on the street hand you $5,000," he exclaimed. The trade meant a higher salary and, because the Dodgers were loaded with talent, less pressure to carry his team. Furthermore, he would no longer have to face his nemesis, Dodgers pitcher Don Newcombe. But when he told wife Ellen the news, she was devastated. "You can't blame her," explained Pafko. "All her roots are in Chicago. All her relatives and friends live there. She's lived there all her life." The thought of leaving their home and moving was traumatic, but, Pafko added, "She's getting used to it now, though, especially when she starts thinking about that World Series check."[85]

For pitcher Eddie Lopat, who was traded from the White Sox to the Yankees in 1948, there was little question about the result. "I have no complaint about Chicago. But Chicago will not win the pennant, and New York will. It feels marvelous to be with a team which is hailed everywhere as the potential winner, with a club which creates a lot of stir no matter where it goes, no matter where its players are spotted. It's great to be a Yankee."[86]

Often a player was the last to know about a trade. St. Louis pitcher Murry Dickson learned about being traded to the Pirates when a Leavenworth, Kansas, neighbor called to tell him that he just heard the news on the radio. The surprised Dickson waited another four hours before the story was confirmed on the radio. The next day, the transaction was in the newspaper headlines. Four or five days later, a letter arrived from Fred Saigh, telling him about the trade. At about the same time, he received a letter from the Pirates' general manager, Roy Hamey, with a contract calling for a salary that at that point was Dickson's best ever.[87]

Others were not so fortunate. Ed Klieman was traded to the Senators only a year after he bought a house in Cleveland. "It never fails," sighed Klieman. "You buy a home and then you're traded. I hope I get the pay in Washington that I did here, or I may stay on my job at the Allerton Hotel."[88] Other players, such as pitcher Jack Kramer, who was sent from the Red Sox to the Giants on waivers in 1950, reacted bitterly to the news. "That McCarthy is the most ornery man I know. He's just plain vindictive," Kramer continued. "When you are winning he's all for you, when you're not going so well, he avoids you like you've got a disease."[89] In 1950, when Gene Bearden was traded from the Indians to the Senators, he was extremely unhappy and demanded compensation for being traded to a fifth-place team from a team that he felt was certain to share in World Series money. Cleveland general manager Hank Greenberg had a ready answer—major-league rules prohibited a traded player from being voted World Series money and also forbade any extra payment to a player at the time of his sale.[90]

Most major-league players during the Pivotal Era had a comfortable life but few rights or benefits. They had uniform contracts, a $5,000 minimum salary, a modest pension plan, and spring training money. Issues raised by American and National League player representatives during the era are an indication of player concerns and of their vulnerability. They included providing released players with travel expenses and separation pay and traded players with moving expenses, and a guarantee of medical coverage in case of game-related injuries. Other issues stemmed from game conditions such as the players' request that owners not schedule double-headers the day after a night game and that all fields should have uniform lighting and outfield warning tracks. Finally, there were matters that directly affected the family. These included proposals prohibiting restrictions on wives attending spring training, a policy to allow double expenses for players who maintained two residences (their own homes and houses in their playing city), and a provision to provide moving expenses for players at the end of the season.[91]

Although they were often idolized, players were little different than the fans who came to watch them. The vast majority were World War II veterans who were not educated beyond the twelfth grade. Most players were Caucasian and of European descent. In addition, more than half were from rural areas or towns with populations under 50,000. Their salaries, while comparable to those earned by physicians, in most cases did not make up for the short duration of their careers. In many instances, major-league ballplayers worked in the off-season at professions with which most working- and middle-class people could identify. There were few significant opportunities to earn major endorsements or other outside income. Players also had little control over their own destinies—a fact virtually ignored by baseball fans but well understood by baseball families. Finally, though players rarely fraternized with opponents, they shared basic values and goals. After catcher Birdie Tebbetts was traded to Cleveland by the Red Sox, he was asked what he thought of the Indians. He replied, "Really a great bunch of guys. So were the Red Sox. To me, most ball players are good guys . . . they follow a set pattern that I think I understand—being one myself."[92]

17

The Great Triumvirate and Other Stars

Hank Greenberg was shocked when he heard radio reports of his sale to Pittsburgh. The news was confirmed by a telegram from general manager Billy Evans, which read, "This is to inform you that your contract has been assigned to the Pittsburgh club of the National League trust you will find your new connection a most profitable one."[1] After leading the league in home runs and runs batted in 1946, Greenberg had been unceremoniously dealt to the Pirates without a phone call, personal contact, or any explanation whatsoever from the Tigers. To add insult to injury, the other American League teams allowed him to be waived out of the league without putting in a claim. Not unlike Babe Ruth, who was released by the Yankees in 1934 so he could join the Boston Braves, a great star was discarded and shunted off to the National League.

The acquisition of Greenberg allowed Pittsburgh to sell close to $400,000 in advance tickets. Greenberg, however, was so embittered by the transaction that he was ready to quit. Only prolonged negotiations by John Galbreath, in which the Pirates promised the slugger a series of incentives, persuaded him to come to Pittsburgh.[2] The Hank Greenberg of 1947 was not the Hank Greenberg of old—hitting only .244 with twenty-five home runs. Greenberg's most important contribution, however, was his friendship with young Pittsburgh slugger Ralph Kiner. Greenberg stressed the need for a disciplined and structured approach to the game and worked tirelessly on Kiner's hitting. Finally, as Kiner noted, "He gave me confidence and showed me how to relax."[3] Kiner the student learned his lessons well, and as one giant left another star was born. At the end of the 1947 season, Greenberg retired to become vice president with the Cleveland Indians.

As Greenberg's case illustrates, the stars of the game in the Pivotal Era

Table 9. Great Players of the Pivotal Era, by Position and League

Position	American League	National League
Catcher	Yogi Berra	Roy Campanella
First base	Hank Greenberg	Stan Musial
Second base	Bobby Doerr	Jackie Robinson
Shortstop	Lou Boudreau	Pee Wee Reese
	Vern Stephens	
	Phil Rizzuto	
Third base	George Kell	Bob Elliott
Outfield	Joe DiMaggio	Richie Ashburn
	Ted Williams	Ralph Kiner
		Duke Snider
		Enos Slaughter
Pitcher	Bob Feller	Ewell Blackwell
	Bob Lemon	Larry Jansen
	Ed Lopat	Don Newcombe
	Hal Newhouser	Robin Roberts
	Mel Parnell	Johnny Sain
	Vic Raschi	Warren Spahn
	Allie Reynolds	Jim Konstanty
	Joe Page	

were almost as expendable as their less-skilled and lower-paid counter-parts. Nevertheless, they often stood well above other players. They were impact players—for a season, several years, or over a long career. They were acclaimed by their own peers, by their managers, coaches, team owners, and fans. They played in All-Star games and won Most Valuable Player awards. They were the great pitchers, fielders, and hitters of the Pivotal Era. In other cases, they were the catalysts or leaders who inspired their teammates to win pennants and the World Series. Finally, in most cases, they were the most highly remunerated players in the game. They were the great players of the era.

The stars of the Pivotal Era were children of the Depression. In all cases, they came from middle-class or blue-collar families. Several were the sons of immigrants. Joe DiMaggio's father was a San Francisco fisherman from Palermo, Sicily, and Yogi Berra's father, a brickmaker, had toiled in the same Milan brickyard as Joe Garagiola's dad. Robin Roberts's parents were from England and Wales. His father was a coal miner. Tigers pitcher Hal Newhouser's parents, who were of German and Czech descent, immigrated to Michigan from Austria. Newhouser's dad, a gymnast, was a wood-pattern maker in a Detroit auto plant. Stan Musial's father, who was from Poland, settled near Pittsburgh in the industrial community of Donora. Lukasz Musial worked in the American Steel and Wire plant, and the Musials' modest home sat on a hill overlooking the town's smoky steel and zinc mills. Musial's mother, Mary Lancos Musial, was hospitalized during a smog inversion that hit Donora on October 30, 1948, and led to the deaths of twenty-one people.[4]

Hard labor was no stranger to the parents of most of the stars. Joe Page's dad was a Pennsylvania coal miner. Duke Snider's father worked in the pits of the Goodyear Tire and Rubber Company in Los Angeles, handling hot molding equipment, Lou Boudreau's dad was a machinist in Harvey, Illinois, and Richie Ashburn's father ran a machine shop in Tilden, Nebraska. Bobby Doerr's father worked for a telephone company in Los Angeles. Bob Feller, Enos Slaughter, and Larry Jansen were all raised on farms, while Johnny Sain's dad was a mechanic in Havana, Arkansas, and "Pop" Lemon, Bob's father, owned a filling station in Long Beach, California.

Other fathers were in the retail or wholesale business. Warren Spahn's parents raised six children on one floor of a two-family house in Buffalo, New York, living on Ed Spahn's salary as a wallpaper salesman. Roy Campanella's father had a Model-T truck and sold fruit, vegetables, and fish in the Logan section of Philadelphia. Campanella, one of four children, recalled, "None of us Campanella kids honestly knew there was a depression on! Daddy saw to that. You can be poor, but if your daddy's business happens to be food, you sure aren't going to be hungry."[5] Vern Stephens's father worked for a creamery during the day and was a minor-league umpire at night, while Flugin Ewell Blackwell, the father of the lanky Reds pitcher, was employed by a fruit-packing firm in Fresno, California.

Don Newcombe's father was a chauffeur for a northern New Jersey family, and Phil Rizzuto's dad was a trolley car motorman in Brooklyn. "I used to bring him lunch," remembered Rizzuto. "I'd meet him on a prearranged corner, hop on the car with his lunch box, and ride a couple of stops with him. I used to think that was the greatest thing in the world, riding with Pop like that."[6] Two other parents employed in the transportation industry were Mel Parnell's father, a diesel engine expert with the Illinois Central Railroad in New Orleans, and Carl Reese, who moved his family to Louisville when Pee Wee was twelve to take a job as a railroad detective with the Louisville and Nashville Railroad.

In only a few instances did both parents work outside the home. This was the case of San Diego's Ted Williams, whose father was a photographer and whose mother was a missionary with the Salvation Army. May Venzer Williams was a social force in San Diego. Nicknamed "the Angel of Tijuana" and "Salvation May," she worked tirelessly, remembered her son, in "the seamiest sections of San Diego, and across the border into Tijuana, going into jails to minister to people and even into the red light districts if she thought she could get a contribution."[7] Ralph Kiner's mother, who was an Army nurse during World War I, returned to work after her husband died when Ralph was just four. "She's the person who made it possible for me to play baseball," noted Kiner. "If it weren't for her, I'd be lucky to be driving a truck."[8] Mallie Robinson, Jackie Robinson's mother, was also the sole support of her family of five. In 1919, when Jerry Robinson deserted Mallie, she abandoned her Georgia roots and moved her family to Pasadena, California, where she found work as a domestic doing washing and ironing. Mallie's job, which required long hours, and welfare payments barely enabled the Robinsons to stay together. "Sometimes there were only two meals a day," recalled Robinson in his autobiography, "and sometimes we wouldn't have eaten at all if it hadn't been for the leftovers my mother was able to bring home from her job. There were other times we subsisted on bread and sweet water."[9]

Only a few of the stars' parents attended college. One exception was George Kell's father, superintendent of schools in Kell's hometown of Swifton, Arkansas. Both of Allie Reynolds's parents attended college. His father, a half Creek Indian, was a Nazarene evangelist in Bethany, Oklahoma. Reynolds's mother, the former Mary Smith Brooks, was a state field worker for the Women's Christian Temperance Union. According to one account, the former school teacher "probably sold more Oklahoma youngsters on a life of total abstinence than any woman in the state."[10] Another collegian was Irving Elliott, Bob Elliott's father. The elder Elliott starred in baseball and track at Stanford University and was intensely proud of his son. Irving Elliott's critical booming voice was often heard at Bob's games if the Boston Braves' third baseman made an error or had a rough at bat. Once, when a fan took exception to Elliott's remarks and almost caused an altercation, his son rushed over to the screen and told the fan, "Don't get excited—he can say anything he wants because it's all in fun. That's my dad."[11]

While the sons of upper-class parents were playing tennis, golf, and polo, baseball was often the game of choice for children from middle-class or blue-collar backgrounds. Football was also popular, but to play the game professionally almost automatically meant going to college—an option that was beyond the reach of most youths. During the Pivotal Era, baseball was one of the few games, because of its remunerative possibilities, that promised its participants a piece of the American dream—a family, a car, and a house. Ten of the thirty-three stars were from California, where they had the distinct advantage of being able to play baseball year-round. Ralph Kiner and Ted Williams were never far removed from local playgrounds and diamonds. But even in colder climates, such as Springfield, Massachusetts, where Vic Raschi was raised, or New York City, the home of Eddie Lopat, children had ready-made facilities. On Yogi Berra's block in St. Louis's Italian section, the future Yankee catcher had about twenty-five playmates who loved sports. "School let out at 3:20, and if you didn't get back home, into your overalls and out on the street by 3:25, you might not get into the game," recalled Berra. "We'd play till suppertime, and if it was still light, we'd come right back after supper and play some more. We played everything—baseball, corkball, softball, soccer, roller hockey, [and] football. Some nights we kept going so late the cops came along and ran us off."[12]

When children's games turned into potential careers, however, parents were not always supportive. This was particularly true of immigrant parents who knew little about baseball. Berra's parents prevented his three older brothers from signing contracts because they believed that baseball was "an idle pastime." Finally, when Berra received a $500 offer from the Yankees, Yogi's brothers persuaded their father to give his consent. Joe DiMaggio, whose brothers Vince and Dom preceded him into the game, also ran into parental skepticism. Papa DiMaggio could not understand why his son did not take to the family fishing business. Joe disliked going to sea so much that he would hide under the bed until his father had left. When he first started playing sandlot ball, his father was particularly disdainful of his son's scuffed shoes and torn pants. "Too many shoes, too many pants," he would say.[13] Nevertheless, after Joe and Dom reached the majors, Papa DiMaggio became a fan and anxiously awaited the box scores in the morning papers.[14]

In other instances, the interest of stars in the game was actually driven by a father who loved the game. In 1932, Bob Feller's father laid out a field on the banks of the Raccoon River—a stream running through their Van Meter, Iowa, farm. Although Bill Feller's dream of attracting big-league scouts to the field to watch his son pitch never materialized, crowds as large as 1,000 paid 35¢ apiece to see Bob pitch against local teams. Moreover, Bill Feller's dream field provided the competition that ultimately allowed his son to realize his potential as a pitcher.[15] Enos Slaughter's father, a tobacco farmer in Roxboro, North Carolina, instilled his love of the game into each of his five sons. By their teen years, all of the boys were playing on the same weekend baseball team. Enos, the best athlete in the family, honed his throwing skills winging rabbits with rocks. In 1934, he persuaded his father to allow him to play for a cotton-mill team in Durham, North Carolina—a venture that earned Slaughter a tryout with the Cardinals.

Duke Snider, who was given a bat, ball, and glove as soon as he was able to walk, credited his father's frustrated ambition for his own career. "I was an only child," recalled Snider, "and he spent all his spare minutes teaching me. He taught me more about baseball than any other person."[16] The Slaughter and Snider scenarios were replayed several times over by other stars and their fathers. Ewell Blackwell, Joe Page, Warren Spahn, Vern Stephens, Bob Lemon, Richie Ashburn, Lou Boudreau, Pee Wee Reese, and Bobby Doerr all had fathers who worked with them incessantly. In addition, many of them played on American Legion teams that were sometimes coached by a father. For stars such as Ted Williams, Joe DiMaggio, Ralph Kiner, Jackie Robinson who either were fatherless or whose parents cared little for the game, surrogate dads in the form of neighbors, coaches, or older brothers provided guidance and encouragement at different stages of their development.

Ironically, the three most dominant hitting stars during the Pivotal Era—Joe DiMaggio, Stan Musial, and Ted Williams—were not motivated by fathers but played the game for entirely different reasons. Shy and aloof by nature, Joe DiMaggio disliked school so much that he quit to take a series of short-lived jobs to help his close-knit Italian family. Although baseball came easily to him, he did not take the game seriously until he discovered that his ability to hit brought him instant recognition in his neighborhood. When brother Vince was signed by the San Francisco Seals, it opened Joe's eyes. "If Vince can get dough for playing ball," DiMaggio recalled thinking, "then I can too."[17] After Joe also signed with the Seals in 1933, it was his hitting that propelled him to the majors in 1936. Unwilling to overanalyze his skill, in his 1947 autobiography DiMaggio explained, "It always has been a theory of mine that hitting is a God-given gift, like being able to run fast or throw hard."[18]

Ted Williams never conceded that hitting is a God-given talent. Hitting was work and required constant practice.[19] As a precocious five year old in San Diego, he asked the man across the street to pitch to him. Later, he worked hours at a time hitting and pitching with a local playground instructor who was a former minor leaguer. He also spent many hours at the playground hitting balls to local boys who shagged his flies just for the privilege of watching him hit. Although there were other pursuits in his life—fishing, hunting, flying, and driving—hitting was the quest. Williams's goal "was to be the greatest hitter that ever lived."[20] He perfected his swing against phantom pitchers in his backyard—a practice he continued in front of mirrors or even in the outfield during games long after he reached the majors. Williams's hitting and prodigious home runs attracted the attention of major-league scouts, but he signed with the hometown San Diego Padres to please his mother.[21]

The third member of the great triumvirate, Stan Musial, began his ca-

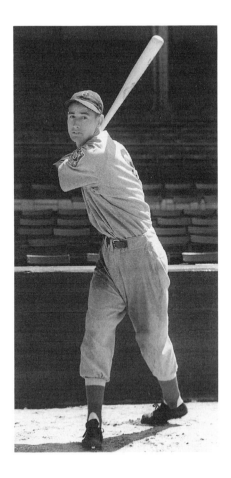

When the Great Triumvirate returned to the game in 1946, their youth had been taken by the War. *(Top left)* Ted Williams, 1939, *(top right)* Stan Musial, 1941, and *(right)* Joe DiMaggio, 1936. (George Brace Photo)

reer in the minor leagues as a pitcher. Musial followed the lead of neighbor Joe Barbao, a former minor-league pitcher who taught him how to throw a curveball. When Musial reached his midteens, Barbao found him a spot on the local zinc mill team, pitching against adults. Although Lukasz Musial was a big fan of Babe Ruth, he wanted his son to attend college. Moreover, Musial was a superb basketball player and was almost sure to get a basketball scholarship. He took his dilemma to the school librarian, Helen Kloz, who recognized that he was much more motivated to play baseball than to attend college. "You can't afford to lose your head," she told him. "But, you can afford to follow your heart."[22] When the St. Louis Cardinals offered Musial a contract, his father adamantly refused to give his parental consent. When the disappointed son began to shed tears, Mary Lancos Musial intervened. "Lukasz, why did you come to America?" she asked. "Because it's a free country," he replied. Then, drumming her point home, she said, "And in America a boy is free not to go to college too."[23]

In 1940, Musial hurt his shoulder—an injury that curtailed his pitching career and led to a switch to the outfield. By late 1941, his torrid hitting led to a trial with the St. Louis Cardinals, where he hit over .300 for the next sixteen seasons.

A common trait among the stars of the Pivotal Era was self-confidence. This was particularly true of the great triumvirate. Musial saw his first major-league game at Forbes Field when he was in high school, and afterward he told the sportswriter who had invited him that he was sure he could hit big-league pitching. In an interview not long after he returned from the service in 1946, he stated simply, "I know I can hit."[24] In his book *Lucky to Be a Yankee*, Joe DiMaggio stressed that the "first requisite of the good hitter is confidence. No player can be a hitter without it. If there is fear in your heart . . . you might as well give up baseball."[25] Lefty Gomez, DiMaggio's mentor when he first arrived with the Yankees, told interviewer Maury Allen that DiMaggio "had more confidence than any hitter I have ever seen. He just knew he was good."[26] "How you think is vastly important," Ted Williams once told Grantland Rice. "I could have led the league the first time I was in it, but I didn't think I was that good. A big mistake. Now, I have kidded myself into thinking I am the greatest hitter in baseball. Maybe I am not . . . [but] you are only going to be as good as you think you are."[27]

How good were the three stars? Only Babe Ruth, Lou Gehrig, Jimmie Foxx, and Al Simmons, in the era before them, posted better or comparable offensive numbers and possessed their rare combination of power and overall hitting ability. While Ty Cobb, Tris Speaker, Rogers Hornsby,

Harry Heilmann, and Joe Jackson all played in the dead-ball era, there is little evidence in their careers to suggest that they would have become power hitters. Unlike in the decades that followed, during the Pivotal Era the sacrifice fly rule was not in effect, strike zones were large, mounds were high, and the pitching, when every team had at least one ace, had not yet been watered down by expansion. The talents of all three players were held in awe by their peers. When Williams stepped into the batting cage, remembered Tommy Henrich, "the rest of us would stop warming up for the game as long as he was swinging, just so we could watch the Master."[28] Ned Garver recalled that "No one told you to stop [when DiMaggio entered the cage]. We would be playing catch along the sidelines in Yankee Stadium, and he would step to the plate, and we would stop and watch him. That is how majestic he was. I remember looking around and the ushers and the people gathering in the ballpark were stopped and watching [too]."[29]

Each of the three had his own distinctive hitting style and philosophy. DiMaggio was a line-drive hitter with power. He had a short, level swing with a classic follow through. As he came to bat, DiMaggio went through a ritual of stubbing his right toe in the dirt behind his left heel before he entered the box. Once in the box, he rubbed dirt on his hands, tapped the plate with the bat, and then set his feet about four feet apart.[30] As Joe McCarthy told Maury Allen, "He had this open stance and he stood straight up when he hit the ball. Once he got set at the plate that was it. He didn't move."[31] In an interview with Frank Graham, DiMaggio explained that he never took his eyes off the pitcher. "That's the reason you never see me move around at the plate," he continued. Although pitchers often hid the ball and sometimes used twisting motions in their deliveries, DiMaggio always attempted to keep the ball in sight so he could discern the pitcher's release point. By hitting into the pitcher with a short slide step, he was able to keep his eyes focused on the pitch.[32]

Compared to DiMaggio's classic style, Musial's stance looked completely unorthodox. He stood far off the plate, in the back of the box, in a crouched position that reminded White Sox pitcher Ted Lyons of "a kid looking around the corner to see if the cops were coming."[33] Then, when the pitcher went into his motion, Musial would bend his right knee like a cocked rifle, and, as the ball was delivered, he uncoiled "with all the power of a steel spring. To most hitters this would be fatal," explained sportswriter Stan Baumgartner, "but Musial can stop his unwinding at any time, halt his swing, and let the ball go by."[34] Even though he employed a twelve-inch stride toward the pitcher and six inches toward the plate, Musial's quick wrists allowed him to reach outside pitches and to turn on inside ones. Concentrating on an imaginary vertical zone in front of the plate, Musial would determine where he would hit the ball as it crossed through the zone.[35]

Ted Williams was the ultimate zone hitter. He created his own hitting zone—a box that enabled him to factor by percentage where he wanted to connect with a pitch. Following the advice of Rogers Hornsby, his hitting mentor at Minneapolis in 1938, Williams always attempted to get a good pitch to hit.[36] Williams's patience and planning at the plate made him an extremely selective hitter.

Although not as selective as Williams, DiMaggio and Musial were also discriminating hitters. When Musial came back from the war, he explained that he was no longer the free swinger that he had been in 1943. "I think now about the pitchers, what they throw, and what their stuff does. I try to figure what they'll throw me in the clutch. I hit the pitch I want, not the one they want me to hit."[37] DiMaggio, on the other hand, was willing to hit any ball close to the plate if the situation so dictated. The selectivity of the power hitters was reflected by the number of times they struck out. Between 1946 and 1951, Musial averaged thirty-four strikeouts a season, or one in every eighteen at bats. DiMaggio averaged twenty-nine strikeouts, which worked out to one in every sixteen at bats. Finally, Williams averaged forty-two strikeouts a season, or one in every twelve at bats. Williams, the all-time leader in on-base percentage at .483, led the American League in that category in each of his seasons, with the exception of 1950, when he was injured. Musial led the National League in on-base percentage in 1948 and 1949 and finished second to Eddie Stanky three other times.

American League umpire Joe Paparella, who began his major-league career in 1946, recalled that Williams "did not know what a borderline call was. He had a strike zone that was the best I ever saw in my life. He could count the stitches on the ball coming in from the pitcher. He could tell if the ball was that far [an inch] outside. He had a great pair of eyes." Williams, noted Paparella, could tell by the spin on the ball "when the pitch was going to break." All three of the great hitters went out of their way not to antagonize umpires. Occasionally Musial might gape at a bad call, DiMaggio would whistle, and Williams would simply march back to the dugout if he was called out on strikes. Each knew that umpires represented an edge—and other players believed that umpires rewarded them for not showing them up when they made bad calls. Regardless of motive, however, each of the great sluggers appreciated good umpires. A case in point is Paparella, who received a mysterious package in the mail in December 1951. He opened it to discover a gold watch inscribed "To a great guy and a great umpire," from the newly retired Joe DiMaggio.[38]

Endless and often futile arguments have been made in an attempt to determine who was the greatest ballplayer during the Pivotal Era. Musial, as an all-around player, certainly dominated the National League during the period, and DiMaggio was a favorite of many of his peers and teammates because of the almost effortless grace and skill he employed in not only hitting but also in his fielding and throwing. Nevertheless, most players agreed with former Yankee teammate Gene Woodling when he stated, "DiMaggio was probably the best all-around ballplayer I ever played with, but in just hitting alone, Williams [was the best during] my career."[39] In the box, Williams stood with his front foot on a line even with the front of the plate and approximately a foot away, with his feet spread a little more than two feet apart. With his bat almost perpendicular to the plate, he would stride into the ball, cocking his hips as the pitch was on the way. Williams contended that it was in the hips that a hitter developed most of his power.[40] Nevertheless, most observers marveled at Williams's power and bat speed and attributed it to his quick wrists. It was the same quickness and ability to wait until the last possible moment that also distinguished Musial and DiMaggio from their peers.

Hall-of-Famer Al Simmons was one of Williams's most ardent supporters: "Only a fellow with wrists like Williams could hit like he does. He doesn't ever seem ready. He's fidgeting at the plate, moving his arms. Most of us have to get set to hit. He can swing at the last moment and get his full power into the swing. You can't fool a batter with a pair of fast powerful wrists like Williams. I have seen him pull pitches into right field that were actually past him before he swung. I didn't see how he could do it."[41]

Bill Dickey, the great catcher of the New York Yankees, described Williams's hitting as remarkable. "I never saw a hitter who could swing as late as he does and hit the ball as good," contended Dickey. "I swear I've thought a million times we had him fooled, but at the last second he'd take that swipe at the ball and hit it safe. Sometimes, it just seemed like he hit it right out of my glove."[42] Another Williams adherent was Harry Walker, a fine hitter in his own right. "He just overpowers the ball and the pitcher. The rest of us are overpowered by the pitcher and the best we can do is meet the pitch and drive it on the line." As Williams lined a ball over first during batting practice, Walker continued, "look at that. That ball was almost past him, yet he swished his wrists in the last fraction of a second, when the ball wasn't more than four inches from his bat, and drove it into right."[43] Bill McKechnie, whose major-league career began in 1907 and who was long respected as one of the most astute baseball men in the game, summed up Williams the hitter when he said, "I've seen a lot of hitters in my day, but none as good as Williams. He's the best, over a long stretch, in my time."[44]

Hitting was more than just a matter of mechanics and wrist-strengthening activity for Williams, it was also a great cerebral exercise. Williams was a baseball intellectual who turned the art of hitting into a science. He always maintained that "hitting a baseball is the single most difficult thing to do in sport," and it was the sheer joy and challenge of this quest that kept him coming back season after season.[45] He studied the effect of aerodynamics on a baseball, after learning about the Bernoulli effect during flight training in World War II; he analyzed and catalogued opposing pitchers according to what they threw, where, when, how, and in what situations. In addition, Williams knew the count, the pitcher, and the situation for each of his first 300 home runs. He constantly sought and absorbed information that, during batting confrontations, would enable him to use a pitcher's own tendencies to defeat him. The information he gathered turned him into a calculating guess hitter who based his thinking on probabilities.

Williams sought information on opposing pitchers from any credible source: teammates returning from an at bat, umpires during rain delays, and opposing pitchers themselves during All-Star games, exhibitions, and spring training. Each time he saw a new pitcher for the first time, the encounter represented a new challenge. Bob Cain, then pitching for the Detroit Tigers, struck Williams out with a curveball on a 3-2 count the first time he faced him. "It was the last time I had an advantage," recalled Cain. "There was one man who remembered all pitchers and what they threw him."[46] Ned Garver, the rookie sensation for the Browns in the late 1940s, also remembered Williams as a great hitter. "If he were the second hitter in the inning," noted Garver, "he would be in the on deck circle trying to time me and measure me. If a new pitcher came into the league, he would come over and talk to our good hitters and ask them what he would throw in different count situations. The first time I ever faced him, he struck out—I think that was the last time [I struck him out] until fourteen years later."[47] Williams had the upper hand with most pitchers, including Tiger right-hander Virgil Trucks: "Williams hit me pretty good. He took me downtown a lot. I was a power pitcher. It was just power against power. Mel Parnell told me that that is what Williams said about me. He loved to hit not only against me, but the Detroit ballclub, because we wouldn't try to piddle around. We would go after him. He liked that. It was a challenge to both of us. If he hit the ball out of the park, he hit my best pitch."[48]

After the 1946 All-Star game, Cubs manager Charlie Grimm was asked how to pitch to Williams. The only way, he replied, is to "run a pipe line under the plate to the catcher and pitch through it."[49] The ultimate compliment to Williams, although he did not fully appreciate it, was the Boudreau shift. On July 14, 1946, during the first game of a double-header

Ted Williams was a baseball intellectual who turned the art of hitting into a science. (Photographic Archives, University of Lousville)

at Fenway Park, Lou Boudreau had the best day of his career, hitting four doubles and a home run. The Indians lost the game, however, 11-10, as Ted Williams destroyed the Tribe with three home runs, including a grand slam. By the time Williams came up the second time in the second game he had already doubled down the line to clear the bases again. In an attempt to defeat Williams, Boudreau shifted his entire team to the right side of second base, with the exception of left fielder George Case, who was positioned about thirty feet from the infield in shallow left-center. When Williams saw what was happening, he stepped out of the box and laughed.[50] "What you are doing," remembered Indians' pitcher Mel Harder, who had done the same to Babe Ruth, "is taking the power away from that hitter—his line drives and everything else. You've got more chance to get those line drives. Of course the long ball is gone."[51]

Here was a challenge of major proportions. The Indians were willing to give up a single to left to prevent Williams from doing more damage to right. "I knew Ted Williams," recalled Boudreau. "I knew that he would take any challenge as long as he was a hitter. He challenged that shift—he could [have gone] to left field [or] bunted the ball the first time at bat—we had nobody on the left side of the diamond. So if he had bunted the ball, my shift would have failed."[52] With Indians pitchers still pitching him carefully, and outside, Williams grounded out and walked twice.

The shift did affect Williams's hitting. Lou Boudreau's charts told him that the Indians were 37 percent more successful with the shift against Williams than without it.[53] Moreover, in the eighty-three games before the shift was employed, Williams hit .352 with twenty-six home runs and eighty-two runs-batted-in, whereas in the sixty-seven games after the shift was introduced, he hit .316 with twelve homers and forty-one runs batted in.[54] Michael Seidel, in his insightful biography *Ted Williams: A Baseball Life*, noted that the shift was "the greatest challenge to Williams as a guess hitter." The maneuver altered his thinking pattern because it eliminated "the need for Williams to guess, and consequently the advantage he gained from guessing."[55] Williams, himself, later confessed that the shift caused him problems. "Everybody was saying—and the Boston writers were writing—that I wasn't trying to hit to left, that I was too stubborn, that all I cared about was ramming the ball into the teeth of that shift, getting base hits in spite of it," wrote Williams in *The Science of Hitting*. "The fact was," he admitted, "I was having a hard time learning to hit to left."[56]

Williams really did not feel comfortable against the shift until 1948, when he finally followed Paul Waner's advice to step back from the plate. On June 6, 1948, he went five for eight against the Tigers and had three hits to left field. Moreover, nine of his last thirteen hits were to left field against shifted defenses. Williams had finally adjusted.

The three great-hitting stars made other difficult adjustments. All three were reluctant heroes. Of the three, Stan Musial was the most easygoing in temperament and the most accessible to the public. He was soft-spoken, modest, and even shy. Many working-class Americans identified with Musial's image as a family man who enjoyed an occasional beer or a good cigar. Also, he enjoyed the companionship and complete confidence of his teammates. In 1949, Musial's telephone number was still listed in the St. Louis directory, even though he received calls at all hours. He received thousands of pieces of mail a year from fans and one year gave away more than 5,000 autographed photographs. Musial loved children, and he sent autographed baseballs (at $18 a dozen) to the disadvantaged or handicapped. In addition, the St. Louis star was deluged with requests for donations. Fame also brought trouble. In 1948, a thief broke into the Musial home in St. Louis and stole a large sum of money, jewelry, and

Stan Musial was the most accessible member of the Great Triumvirate. In 1949
Musial's telephone number was still listed in the St. Louis telephone directory.
(Photographic Archives, University of Louisville)

Musial's 1946 Cardinals pennant ring. The thief was caught, but the jew-
elry was never recovered.[57]

Although Musial received media attention in St. Louis, it was not as
overwhelming as the coverage accorded Williams in Boston or DiMaggio
in New York. Nonetheless, as one of the most recognizable and respected
sports figures in the United States, Musial lacked the privacy enjoyed by
most ballplayers. He was very popular in Brooklyn, where he earned his
nickname, "The Man," because of his heavy hitting at Ebbets Field during the 1946 pennant race. In 1948, he hit .500 with four home runs and
twelve runs batted in at Ebbets Field. Musial's positive relations with
fans faltered only once, when he was buffeted by a crowd before a double-
header at Sportsman Park on August 30, 1948. On that occasion, he twisted

his knee when his spikes got caught on a cement walk as he grappled with a man who had attempted to take his photograph.[58]

Compared to Musial, DiMaggio and Williams lived in a fishbowl. They paid the price of being stars. Both were deluged with requests for autographs wherever they went, and they were hounded by writers and photographers. DiMaggio suffered the most. He was painfully shy and uncommunicative even with teammates. Moreover, as Dan Daniel wrote, Joe "does not like demonstrative appreciation and he abhors adulation. DiMaggio is uncomfortable, off the field, in a group of more than half a dozen."[59] Nevertheless, he was the game's most popular symbol—an icon with whom everyone could identify—immigrant, blue-collar worker, the white-collar commuter, and the well to do. To many he represented what was good in baseball and what was good about America. He was graceful, modest about his own superior skills, and the undisputed leader of a team that won eleven pennants during his thirteen-year career. His fifty-six-game hitting streak in 1941 was viewed as a superhuman feat. To many he was America's greatest hero.

DiMaggio was so well recognized that Yankee announcer Mel Allen once wrote, "Walking down the street with him is an experience. Heads twist and turn like those in a tennis stadium. Dining out is a hobby of his, even though he can never eat a meal without a steady stream of people dropping by his table for an autograph or a brief word."[60] Like Musial, DiMaggio quickly learned to be wary of crowds and of fans. He was often the first player to arrive at the ballpark and the last to leave. After a night game, it was not unusual to find him still there at 2:30 in the morning with only the night watchman present. Still, many fans attempted to outwait him. To leave earlier meant running a gauntlet of well-wishers and autograph seekers and the risk of having a sports coat, shirt, and pants ripped to shreds. On one occasion, he reached his car safely only to have to stop because a thirteen-year-old boy was hanging on to his fender and would not let go.[61]

DiMaggio took many of his meals at Toots Shor's restaurant—a popular hangout for celebrities from the sports and show-business worlds. He was given a permanent table, which overlooked the entire dining area but was not within view of the curious, where he could eat in peace or join with friends of his own choosing. It was here that he met with sportswriters such as Red Smith, Jimmy Cannon, Bill Corum, and several others, who always accorded him a very positive press. DiMaggio was used to preferential treatment by the press, and it was understood that if a writer was befriended by DiMaggio, he was not supposed to betray his private life in the press. DiMaggio's unwitting press agent was sportswriter Jimmy Cannon of the *New York Post*, one of the most widely read writers in the city.

According to David Halberstam in the *Summer of '49*, Cannon not only helped to create the legend of Joe DiMaggio "the great athlete but, even more significant, DiMaggio as the Hemingway hero, as elegant off the field as on it."[62] Roger Kahn, in *The Era*, does Halberstam one better, noting that it was not Cannon who created the image but DiMaggio himself. "Joe DiMaggio," wrote Kahn, "and nobody else invented Joe DiMaggio."[63]

The Pivotal Era was not kind to DiMaggio. He was stricken with an ulcer in 1944, suffered through a divorce in 1946, and developed a sore arm in 1947. He played with two constantly aching knees, developed pneumonia in 1949, and had two extremely painful bouts with bone spurs in his heels that required surgery in 1947 and 1949. Adversity became DiMaggio's constant companion. His calm exterior and carefully controlled emotions did not reflect the intensity that lay within. He felt responsible for carrying the Yankees and brooded over any perceived failure on his part to do so. An example is Al Gionfriddo's famous catch of DiMaggio's long drive during the 1947 World Series. When asked by reporters to comment on the play, he replied, "Nice catch." Later, DiMaggio admitted to Yankees co-owner Del Webb that he had gotten into his automobile after the game and driven around the countryside by himself, unable to sleep that night.[64] DiMaggio's intensity was betrayed by his habits. He consumed cups of coffee and chain smoked a pack of cigarettes before each game.[65] Furthermore, when the Yankees were at bat, the star would often steal a smoke in the runway.[66]

DiMaggio's temperament, his fame, and his bouts with various physical problems often kept him apartment bound. On the road, he was also sequestered—so much so that teammate Eddie Lopat once quipped that "DiMaggio led the league in room service."[67] As DiMaggio's considerable skills eroded during his last three seasons, so did his relationship with the press. "Being deadpan was my way of playing when I first came up," he told one writer. "But in late years, it has been getting harder for me to conceal my emotions. You know, I take those ball games to bed with me." When asked, "Don't you think it would be easier on you if you let off a little steam once in a while instead of letting it cut you up inside?" he replied, "I'm a ball player. Not an actor."[68] Injuries and his rundown condition made 1951 a particularly exasperating season for DiMaggio. Nevertheless, he was still full of pride and vinegar. After having a rare good day in August, when he hit a home run and a triple to beat the Senators, he vented his anger on several writers, some of whom had suggested that Stengel should bench him:

> You are darn right that I wanted to make you writers look bad. I'll always try to make you look bad. Just because I have a bad day, you guys

want to fire me. Some of you guys are the ones who washed me up in 1946. But here I am, five years later. How are you going to explain the hits I made today? Are they going to fire me every time I have a bad day. Did anyone ever see me give up on a fly ball in the outfield? Bet your life, no. The only thing I am interested in is to win the pennant again this season.[69]

Unlike DiMaggio, Ted Williams was often full of vinegar and had few writers in his corner. Moreover, he made it difficult on those who did support him. He often wore his fragile feelings on his shirt sleeve, and was easily nettled by the one boo in a crowd of cheers and by anything negative written in the press. He was such a perfectionist that when he failed to live up to his own expectations, he would react in a childish manner. Indeed, he was a child who never really grew up—and perhaps never wanted to. Not unlike DiMaggio, there were many times when he failed to understand why his genius and incredible skills could not be appreciated and accepted at face value. Both DiMaggio and Williams craved attention, appreciation, and reaffirmation; but they wanted it on their own terms. At times, Williams was temperamental, profane, and unable to control his emotions. The Boston player's difficulties can be traced to his famous 1940 tirade. The Red Sox were playing poorly and Williams was suffering with a sore back, and he lashed out against Boston, the fans, his teammates, and team management. Williams's remarks were written up in full by Boston sportswriter Austin Lake. From that time forward, in a market with too many newspapers, a number of Boston writers went after Williams like a group of famished sharks whenever there was the slightest hint of controversy.

Williams's major nemesis in the press was Dave Egan, a Harvard-educated lawyer-turned-sportswriter. Egan was a barely functioning alcoholic who Ed Linn, in *Hitter*, noted "had two prime distinguishing characteristics. He could turn a phrase and he had the integrity of an alley cat."[70] Another fellow writer commented, "Egan can do more with fewer facts than any newspaperman I ever read. He's the most facile man with a rumor that you ever read."[71] Egan's humor and outrageous prose appeared in the *Boston Record*, a Hearst tabloid with a circulation of more than half a million readers. The paper specialized in sex scandals, sports, and lambasting Ted Williams. Egan's charges against Williams were legion: he was not a team player; he was only for Ted Williams; Williams is feuding with Johnny Pesky or Vern Stephens, or he's not talking to Dom DiMaggio, or he wants to be traded to the Yankees. Although most of these charges had no basis in fact, they sold newspapers and served to place most of the Red Sox's woes squarely on Williams's shoulders at a time when Boston was usually long on hitting and short on pitching.

Williams retaliated by developing an antagonistic attitude toward the press—a disposition that at times motivated him to even greater performances on the field. Nevertheless, his constant feuding with sportswriters was often blamed for poisoning the atmosphere between the team and the press—a charge Williams has never denied.[72] Williams's worst offense during the Pivotal Era occurred on May 11, 1950. He dropped a fly ball during a double-header loss at Fenway and was roundly booed by many of the 27,000 fans in attendance. Williams responded with obscene gestures. He later apologized. "I am sorry I did that stuff," he explained. "Those fans were on me. I had a cold and I was burning at them."[73] Later he added, "Maybe I should not have done it. But when you're straining to win, and have just hit a home run worth four runs, it seems unfair to be booed for an error which hurt you more, inside, than it did those who are riding you."[74] Noting that Williams had been the target of fan abuse in left field for years, writer Steve O'Leary summed up the case for the Boston writers who supported Williams: "He has taken this going over, sometimes in white-lipped rage and sometimes snapping back angry retorts from behind his glove. But he still refuses to recognize that the majority of Boston fans are for him, just as he heaps his scorn on the entire press corps for the sins of one or two of the membership of the craft. He has never acknowledged applause or praise, but he's quick to resent boos or criticism."[75]

In June 1950, at Williams's behest, the Red Sox banned writers from their clubhouse until thirty minutes after the game—a rule that made the reporters' jobs much more difficult. A year later, Williams's opinion of writers had not mellowed. "Not all baseball writers are bad. I know the few good ones," he generously remarked. "But if I had my way, none of them would be allowed in any clubhouse. In a few years, there'll be no newspapers—only television and radio. That'll be great. There are two things I'd like to get rid of—night games and baseball writers."[76]

As a reluctant hero, Williams was happy to leave all of the other baggage that went with fame behind him once he left the ballpark. He was almost always restless—a bundle of energy and enthusiasm seeking whatever knowledge or information he needed to fulfill his current quest or to satiate his intense curiosity. He was a voracious reader of fishing and hunting magazines. Away from baseball, he simply wanted to be left alone to pursue his own agenda. He disliked making speeches and attending formal occasions where he was supposed to wear ties and meet people with whom he was uncomfortable. Nevertheless, something in his childhood, perhaps even his mother's work with the Salvation Army, imprinted Williams with a social conscience and a marked desire to associate with those in need. This urge led him to make countless visits to veterans and

Table 10. Theoretical Career Statistics, Had Ted Williams Not Served in the
          Armed Forces

	G	AB	H	R	2B	HR	RBI	BB	AVG	SLG
Actual Statistics:										
	2,292	7,706	2,654	1,798	525	521	1,839	2,019	.344	.634
Theoretical Statistics:										
with WWII years										
	2,733	9,251	3,209	2,200	642	617	2,205	2,433	.347	.642
with WWII and Korea years										
	2,938	9,996	3,452	2,375	690	663	2,380	2,652	.345	.637

NOTE: G = games played; AB = at bats; H = hits; R = runs; 2B = two-base hits;
      HR = home runs; RBI = runs batted in; BB = bases on balls (walks);
      AVG = batting average; and SLG = slugging percentage.

children in hospitals during the Pivotal Era. His only request was that photographers not be present and that his visits be kept out of the press. It is a topic that Williams is still reluctant to discuss, and he would only reply, "Heck, some kid that is sick or anything, you've got the time to go, certainly you go. You get ten times more credit for that [than you deserve]. Sometimes it's a pretty good deal, though."[77] Those closest to Williams, like Johnny Orlando, the Red Sox clubhouse man, swore by him. After the 1946 World Series, Williams was so disconsolate over his team's loss and his performance that he gave his World's Series share to Orlando. "Ted has a heart as big as his batting average," said Orlando. "If you are nice to him, he'll give you the shirt off his back. . . . He hates to be in the limelight. His big fault probably is that he can't get it into his head that he is a big sports figure and, as such, must be in the public eye."[78]

As veterans themselves, many of the stars could easily identify with hospitalized or disabled veterans. Although most came through the conflict completely unscathed, they all knew they were fortunate to be playing baseball again. During the last year of the war, Williams told Furman Bisher, "This war is tough on everyone. I've still got two arms, two legs and I'm healthy. For that I'm thankful and I know I'm lucky."[79] In spite of their luck, World War II stole some of the stars' greatest years. Hank Greenberg lasted only two seasons after the war and Joe DiMaggio was no longer the player of his youth. In the absence of injury, Bob Feller's victory total might have easily been 353 wins instead of 266 and he might have recorded 3,502 strikeouts instead of 2,581—such figures would have made him eighth in both lifetime wins and strikeouts. Even more impres-

Table 11. Theoretical Career Ranking and Statistics, Had Ted Williams Not Served in the Armed Forces

	Batting Average	Runs Scored	Home Runs	RBIs	Walks Drawn
1.	Ty Cobb (.366)	**Ted Williams (2,375)**	Hank Aaron (755)	**Ted Williams (2,380)**	**Ted Williams (2,652)**
2.	Rogers Hornsby (.358)	Ty Cobb (2,245)	Babe Ruth (714)	Hank Aaron (2,297)	Babe Ruth (2,056)
3.	Joe Jackson (.356)	Hank Aaron (2,174)	**Ted Williams (663)**	Babe Ruth (2,209)	Joe Morgan (1,865)
4.	Ed Delahanty (.346)				
5.	⎰ Tris Speaker (.345)				
	⎱ **Ted Williams (.345)**				

sive is what might have happened to Williams if he had not lost almost five full seasons to World War II and the Korean conflict. According to the projections in table 10, if Ted Williams had not served in the military during World War II or Korea, he would have connected for an additional 798 hits, including 142 more home runs, and he would have knocked in another 541 runs.[80]

Ted Williams's projected offensive statistics in table 11 would have tied him for fifth place for career batting average, first in runs scored, third in home runs, first in runs batted in, and first for walks drawn.

Players returning from the service in 1946 were also motivated to improve their salary situations to make up for lost time. Salaries were a visible measure of stardom. Babe Ruth's 1930-31 $80,000 salary was the standard by which players were judged. The first to break the $80,000 barrier was Hank Greenberg, when he received $115,000 to play for Pittsburgh in 1947. Although his base salary was only $40,000, Bob Feller likely cleared $80,000 in 1947 and 1948 because of attendance incentives in his contract. During the years 1949 through 1951, Joe DiMaggio made $100,000 per season, and during 1950 and 1951 Ted Williams's salary reached $125,000. DiMaggio's salary represented about 15 percent of his team's expenditures on salaries, and Williams's salary was about 23 percent of the entire Red Sox payroll.[81] Nevertheless, two factors prevented even those players who surpassed Ruth's salary from equaling Ruth's effective purchasing power. First, the dollar in 1931 was worth 63 percent more than the 1951 dollar, meaning DiMaggio needed to make $163,000 to equal Ruth's 1931 salary. Moreover, the tax rate was much higher in 1951 than in 1931. DiMaggio, for instance, owed more than $49,000 in taxes in 1951, while Babe Ruth paid only $10,512 in taxes on his 1931 salary.[82] Taxes took huge chunks from the stars' salaries. In 1947, if Bob Feller made $80,000, his take-home pay was only $32,300. At $75,000, Ted Williams's take-home pay was $31,130 as opposed to $18,753 in 1946 on a $40,000 salary.[83]

Table 12. Highest Player Salaries ($) during the Pivotal Era

Player	Year					
	1946	1947	1948	1949	1950	1951
Greenberg	75,000	85,000	retired			
Feller	70,000[a]	72,000[b]	82,500	72,500	50,000	50,000
DiMaggio	43,750	43,750	70,000[c]	100,000	100,000	100,000
Williams	40,000	75,000	80,000	85,000[d]	125,000	125,000
Boudreau	45,000[e]	45,000	49,000	62,000	62,000	45,000
Newhouser	45,000	60,000	50,000	60,000	53,000	42,000
Musial	13,500	31,000	36,000[f]	50,000	75,000	80,000
Robinson	...	7,000	12,500	17,500	35,000	50,000
Kiner	5,000	10,000	35,000	40,000	60,000	65,000
Rizzuto	12,500[g]	15,000	20,000	25,000	35,000	50,000

[a] Feller's 1946 base salary was $50,000. Because of incentive clauses he made more.

[b] Feller's 1947 base salary base was $40,000. He made more because of attendance incentives in his contract ($32,000) (*Sporting News,* September 10, 1947, 14). Other sources indicate he made as much as $85,000 in 1947 (*Sporting News,* January 14, 1948, 3). When asked about other players, Bill Veeck said, "My dealings are with Feller, I don't have to sign Williams or Newhouser" (*Sporting News,* January 15, 1947, 4).

[c] DiMaggio's 1948 contract called for a base of $50,000 and included attendance incentives.

[d] Williams' base salary was $85,000. He also received bonuses based on Boston's final finish in the standings. In 1950, his base salary was $90,000 plus bonus money, which brought his salary to $125,000.

[e] Boudreau's salary was $25,000 to manage and $20,000 to play. He would continue to earn $25,000 to manage through 1950. In 1951, he was signed by the Red Sox strictly as a player.

[f] Musial's 1948 salary includes a $5,000 increase awarded during 1948 All-Star break.

[g] Rizzuto was given a $5,000 bonus for remaining with the Yankees instead of signing with the Pasquel brothers and playing in the Mexican League.

Many players, of course, also had incomes from outside baseball, but only the top stars were able to cash in on their fame. The most entrepreneurial star was Cleveland Indians pitcher Bob Feller. Feller lost almost four full seasons to the war. Although he could have initially avoided the war (he had a III-C draft status because his father was dying of cancer), he went anyway. "I thought it was the thing to do to be in the war and help win it," he recalled. Besides, "I was in the public eye."[84] Feller viewed the war as another sacrifice that went with duty. Being responsible was not new to him. He built his parents a new home in 1940 and put his sister through school, and when his father died in 1943, he found a companion for his mother. While Feller was aboard the battleship USS *Alabama*, he did a lot of thinking about his return to baseball, envisioning how he might maximize his earnings in the years he had left and how, through such avenues as barnstorming against Negro League stars, he might supplement his income. "I had it all laid out," he remembered. "I knew what I was going to do and I knew the people personally that I was going to have get the black clubs together—the Kansas City operator, Mr. Wilkinson and Satchel Paige and many others that I wanted to oppose us."[85]

Feller's sense of timing was excellent. The nation was hungry for baseball—especially those regions rarely exposed to major-league baseball. By playing against Negro League stars, he added a competitive element sure to bring out the curious. After a trial venture at the end of the 1945 season, Feller persuaded Commissioner Chandler to allow players to barnstorm during a thirty-day period following the 1946 season. Always the political horse-trader, Chandler exacted a promise from Feller that his All-Stars would play in the Kentuckian's hometown of Versailles. The Cleveland right-hander put the entire operation together himself during the 1946 season. Using $50,000 of his own money—one of the few players in baseball who could do so—Feller chartered two DC-3 aircraft and hired a staff that included trickster Jackie Price, an "airplane crew, a trainer, a physician, a secretary, a lawyer, a publicity man, and an advance man."[86] His team included Stan Musial, Johnny Sain, Eddie Lopat, and Mickey Vernon, while Satchel Paige fielded his own team, which included Quincy Trouppe, Buck O'Neil, Hank Thompson, and Sam Jethroe. Feller also invited Ted Williams and Hal Newhouser to join him, but fearing air travel or possible injury to their stars, the Tigers and Red Sox both offered $10,000 incentives to keep them from playing. Some owners were also apprehensive that the players would make a large profit and thus raise their expectations for higher salaries during the following season. "We went first class all the way," Feller recalled. "Everybody profited by it, including the fans. They got to see the greatest Negro players against the greatest white players [and] the racial rivalry was terrific. It was just like it was the World Series every day."[87] In thirty-five games, Feller's all-stars played in front of 271,645 fans on a tour that began in Pittsburgh on September 30 and ended on the West Coast in late October. The tour earned each of Feller's players between $1,700 and $6,000. Musial, who joined the group following the World Series, earned $6,200 on the trip—a much larger amount than his $3,757 share for winning the World Series.[88]

Feller, who served as both team manager and road secretary, maintained a torrid pace during the tour by pitching at least two innings per

Bob Feller, one of the twentieth century's greatest pitchers, was also the Pivotal Era's most entrepreneurial star. (Photographic Archives, University of Louisville)

night—usually against Paige. In addition, he met with local officials and fans everywhere and still had time to tend to the needs of his entourage. He stretched himself so thin that one evening he pitched two innings in Sacramento, flew all night to New York to do a radio program, and then flew back two hours later to fulfill another engagement in Bakersfield, California, the following day. Feller was an indefatigable worker who seemed almost indestructible. Some, like Indians manager Lou Boudreau, worried that he was taking on too much. "Bob is, by all odds, the hardest worker in baseball," noted Boudreau. "Even on days when he isn't pitching, he is running and doing calisthenics, almost literally by the hour. I've never known an athlete who trains as conscientiously, and the results speak for themselves." Nevertheless, stated Boudreau, "I don't believe anyone can keep up that pace year after year."[89]

The tour was also a tremendous financial gamble on Feller's part. "He signed everyone to guaranteed contracts," remembered pitcher Bob Lemon. "You can run into weather in October. We were very fortunate."[90] Feller not only covered all of the air travel, he also carried "millions of dollars of liability insurance if either ballclub, black or white, went down. That is why I had to incorporate Rol-Fel," he explained.[91] As a result of his barnstorming endeavors, Feller became the first modern ballplayer to incorporate. Incorporation also allowed him to organize and shelter a plethora of other income-producing activities, including endorsements for Popsicle, Wheaties, Gillette, and the Wilson Sporting Goods Company. Had he not refused offers from tobacco and brewing companies, his portfolio would have been larger. Moreover, Feller wrote a daily newspaper column, hosted a weekly radio show, received payment for magazine articles, and authored a book entitled *Strikeout Story*. Feller even had a clause in his contract that allowed him to participate in barnstorming for thirty days following the completion of a season. Although not assured of receiving permission from the commissioner to barnstorm in 1947 as he had in 1946, the confident pitcher proclaimed, "If I don't get it, it will cost the Cleveland ballclub some money." By 1947, his total income increased to $150,000. In a poll conducted at the end of the year by the American Business Institute of Research, Feller and Cleveland owner Bill Veeck finished one and two behind Henry Ford II as the most admired business executives under forty.[92]

Feller's success, though admired by many of his fellow players, earned him the enmity of the owners. During the winter of 1946, Musial made a speech at the Dapper Dan Dinner in Pittsburgh at which he noted that he would rather go on a barnstorming tour with Feller than play in another World Series because he could make three times as much money. "Some of the owners did not like that," remembered Feller, "[and] they tried to kill barnstorming. It was a matter of who was handling the money, they or us."[93] At their midsummer meeting in 1947, baseball's executive committee did move to limit barnstorming to a period beginning no sooner than ten days following the last World Series game. Clark Griffith, who blamed Feller and his barnstorming trip for Mickey Vernon's season-long hitting slump in 1947, was suspected of being behind the move. In exasperation, Feller exclaimed, "No employer should be able to tell his men how much they can earn, or where and when they can earn it, once they've fulfilled their contract obligation for the season." Noting that year-round participation did not hurt ballplayers, he stated, "When I was in the South Pacific with the Navy, I pitched almost every day winter and summer. Certainly the players are tired at the end of the season. But how long does it take to rest up? Four months? That's silly."[94]

Feller's own star went into modest decline following the 1946 season. Although he won ninety-two more games during the Pivotal Era, including two twenty-win seasons, he hurt his back in 1947 and began to lose something off his fastball. In addition, he was roundly criticized for flaps over whether he would participate in the 1947 and 1948 All-Star games and for his failure to win a game during the 1948 World Series. Feller's considerable skills and greatness as a pitcher worked against him. When he did not win key games or served up a home run in the wrong situation, he was not given the benefit of the doubt accorded mere mortals. Instead, he was roundly booed—a payback by many fans who felt that his well-publicized outside activities and entrepreneurship were now costing him on the field. When Feller failed to win a game in two attempts during the 1948 World Series, his losses were cheered around the country. Indeed, even loyal Cleveland fans booed him. After he was knocked out of the second game, recalled writer Frank Graham, "the hooting and jeering" from the Cleveland crowd of 86,288 was "deafening."[95] Even Bill Veeck got into the act as he made light of Feller's miseries following the 1948 season by joking, "I've been working for Feller, but next year the tables will be turned. Bobby's going to work for me."[96]

Barnstorming, like Feller, reached its zenith in 1946. Barnstorming trips put together in subsequent seasons by Feller and others never matched the success of his 1946 tour. Several factors contributed to its demise. First, the executive committee's action to limit barnstorming to ten days following the World Series increased the chance that games would be subject to inclement weather. Second, with the availability of automobiles, appliances, and other manufactures, in addition to other competing recreational activities, baseball was forced to contend for its share of family income. Third, the arrival of and widespread use of television captivated American audiences and kept them home. Finally, Jackie Robinson's entry into the major leagues effectively eliminated racial rivalry as a box-office attraction.

Robinson's star status also allowed him to reach out for the American Dream. It was not until halfway through his first season that Branch Rickey allowed him to endorse products. Soon Robinson's smiling face adorned advertisements for Bond Bread and, although he did not smoke, Old Gold cigarettes.[97] After receiving a World Series share of $4,000, Robinson signed up to make a tour that included three vaudeville acts in Washington, New York, and Chicago, at $2,500 an appearance. Each appearance was a carefully scripted eight-minute performance featuring questions and answers between Robinson and Monte Hawley. The Apollo Theatre in Harlem was a sellout for every performance, and by the time Robinson's tour ended in California, it was rumored that the trip had netted him more than $50,000. He also appeared in the South during the winter of 1948, touring with a dance band and stopping at Negro colleges, where he gave students baseball talks. The exciting player was wined and dined across the country. He received the Comiskey Cup, as Rookie of the Year, in Chicago and was honored by the Bruin Club in Los Angeles. A vignette of Robinson's life was carried on national radio, and sportswriter Wendell Smith was actively preparing a full-length biography. At twenty-eight, the

Jackie Robinson's star status allowed him to reach for the American Dream.
(Photographic Archives, University of Louisville)

"old" rookie was on a fast track to take advantage of his opportunities while they lasted. When asked how much longer he expected to play, Robinson replied, "From three to five years. I figure I can't last as long as some of the other fellows in the game, because I've been taking part in all sports—baseball, football, track, basketball."[98]

Robinson's off-season activities caused Rickey great concern. Not only had Robinson put on more than twenty pounds, his rejection of the Dodger president's first salary offer was accompanied by some curt remarks. In Rickey's mind, Robinson's sudden fame and opportunities might spell potential disaster for integration. Rickey feared the type of remarks made by one Dodger organization critic who exclaimed that, "Jackie was 'nigger rich' [and] could not stand prosperity." It took a meeting between the Robinsons, Unity Committee members John Johnson and Dan Dodson, and Rickey to straighten out the situation—to assure Robinson of a higher salary and at the same time get him refocused on baseball.[99]

Robinson not only concentrated his efforts on baseball, going on to win the National League's Most Valuable Player award in 1949, he also achieved continued success outside the game. By 1949 he was the most sought-after celebrity in the National League, with offers to sell appliances at $1,000 a week, to become a partner in a butcher shop, and to make lecture tours. When he took on a six-day-a-week radio program at $400 a week, he became the first African American sports commentator to broadcast daily over a New York station. By 1950, with all of his endorsements for miniature bats, baseball gloves, candy bars, and clothes, Robinson surpassed Feller as the player with the most outside activities. In the same year, he also played the lead role in a Hollywood movie based on his career—*The Jackie Robinson Story*. Robinson signed a $35,000 contract for the 1950 season, making him the highest-paid player in Dodgers history. At the beginning of 1950, a close friend speculated that up to that point Robinson would clear more than $135,000 in earnings from the movie, his baseball salary, and endorsements. Although the price was great, Robinson also proved that a black man could be successful in American society both on and off the field.[100]

Other stars also fared well off the field, particularly after big years. For instance, following Cleveland's exciting 1948 season, Lou Boudreau's portrait appeared on several billboards along major Cleveland thoroughfares advertising Sealtest milk and ice cream.[101] In 1947, Ralph Kiner earned $17,500 in outside income through endorsements, barnstorming with Bob Feller, and writing a column for the *Pittsburgh Sun-Telegraph*. The Pittsburgh star combined with Pirates announcer Bob Prince to form Kiner Enterprises in 1951, a year in which his fourteen endorsements were expected to increase his income by $20,000 to $30,000.[102] Yogi Berra, who supported a wife and son in addition to his parents, moved from St. Louis to New Jersey, not only to better his family's quality of life but also to enhance his business opportunities. In 1951 he told the *Sporting News*:

> I have to dress like a Yankee, live like a Yankee, act like a Yankee. That takes dough. I am paying in on annuities. I also am buying Savings Bonds. I figure them bonds are a fine investment. If they ain't—well, then nothing is worth a dime. We are buying a home in Jersey where Larry, Jr. can grow up in the country, and I can drive over the George Washington Bridge to the Stadium in not much more than half an hour. I don't want to go on renting other people's places in New York each season, and I want to have a home of my own. Another thing, if I spend my winters in New York, I can get into some business. I believe I can make better connections than I could in St. Louis.[103]

In St. Louis, Stan Musial's family made the most of his connections as they agreed to do endorsements for shoes, soap, toothpaste, and antacid tablets in national magazines.[104] Musial's biggest investment was his partnership in Stan's and Biggie's, a well-known St. Louis restaurant. Adding his name to an already popular dining spot, Musial not only increased the business's profitability but, according to partner Biggie Garagnani, after being in business for just one year "we have outgrowed [*sic*] our place, and we are planning to build a new one."[105] Musial, like many other stars of the era, also received offers to endorse such national products as Gillette, Wheaties, and Chesterfield cigarettes. Tobacco companies, such as Liggett and Myers, were very aggressive in going after athletes for endorsements, even though many players did not use their products. These advertisements were particularly prominent in national magazines like the *Saturday Evening Post*, where they depicted the stars of the past or previous season either with cigarettes in their hands or in their mouths. According to George Kell, when he was approached by Chesterfield he informed them that he did not smoke. "We want to pay you anyway," they explained, and assured him that the ad would merely say, "Chesterfield is my cigarette." The endorsement was short-lived because Kell's father disapproved and told him, "That is in terrible taste—I don't like that." Stung by his father's criticism, Kell discontinued the endorsement.[106] In addition to such familial disapproval, players were not always free to endorse products of their choice because of restrictions in their contracts. For example, two Dodgers players were forced to turn down a $3,000 offer from a tobacco company because another cigarette company sponsored Brooklyn games.[107]

Endorsements or personal appearances were refused for other reasons, too. Ralph Kiner refused to do beer advertisements because he did not

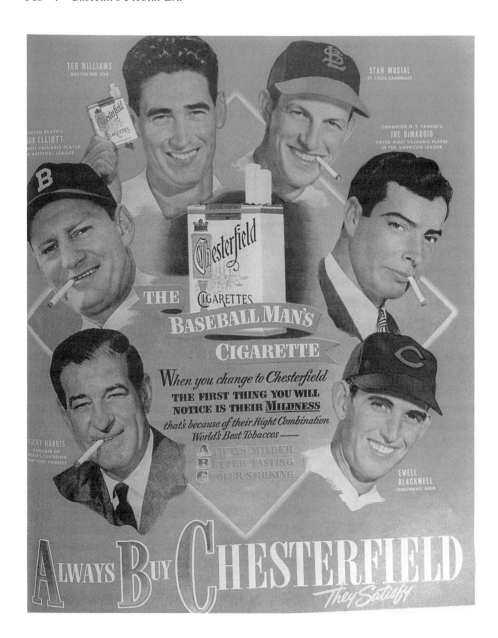

Tobacco companies, such as Liggett & Myers and R.J. Reynolds, were particularly aggressive in going after athletes for endorsements. (Courtesy of Liggett & Myers)

As late as 1950, Pittsburgh's Ralph Kiner was being touted as the only bona fide threat to Babe Ruth's home run record. (Photographic Archives, University of Louisville)

want to tarnish his image, and Joe DiMaggio turned down $5,000 to appear on the Milton Berle television show because he might look "silly on the kidding end of a comedy sketch."[108] Ted Williams turned down two movie roles in 1949—one a remake of Ring Lardner's *Elmer the Great* and the other a baseball movie for children planned by Bing Crosby—largely because the outside income would increase his tax liability.[109] Thus, outside income, for those who could generate it, was both a blessing and curse and often did not amount to as much as the public imagined. DiMaggio, for instance, cleared only a little more than $10,000 in outside income after taxes in 1947, in spite of earnings from the sale of baseball gloves, royalties on his book *Lucky to Be a Yankee*, several radio and exhibition game appearances, and the winners' share of the 1947 World Series. On a salary estimated to be approximately $43,000, his take-home pay was $22,280.50—not a sum that would challenge Howard Hughes.[110]

The money generated by endorsements was as temporary as the fame that made them possible. For instance, as late as 1950, Pittsburgh's Ralph Kiner was being touted as the only bona fide threat to Babe Ruth's home run record. Kiner became the most popular sports figure in Pittsburgh. Adoring fans ruined his convertible, and he received more than a thousand letters a month in the dead of winter. "Ralph is our gate," admitted general manager Roy Hamey. "No player in the game is so important to his team."[111] Nevertheless, Kiner's ascendancy was fleeting, and by 1950, Pittsburgh attendance began a steady decline in spite of his presence. Moreover, at age twenty-nine, Kiner's skills slowly began to erode—a situation that did not escape the attention of Pittsburgh general manager Branch Rickey, who arrived on the scene in the autumn of 1950. Mounting losses, Kiner's high salary and outside business interests, and his special privileges and role as player representative were all reasons Rickey used in a two-year campaign aimed at Pirates owner John Galbreath to rid the team of its hero. In a March 1952 memo, he even quoted manager Billy Meyer, who noted that "Kiner may be in front of quick deterioration. If so the market can pass completely at the end of the coming season."[112]

Although Rickey let it be known throughout the 1952 season that Kiner was available, he almost made Meyer's prophecy come true by waiting to deal Kiner in mid-1953 to the Cubs in a trade involving nine other players and $150,000 cash.[113] Not only was Rickey crucified in Pittsburgh by irate Pirate fans for trading their hero, he also gained Kiner's lasting enmity. "He traded me and I never liked him," remembered Kiner. "I thought he was the biggest hypocrite that was ever in the game," he continued. "He was really the father of all the unrest in baseball. He had all of the players and all of the money and never let the two get together. I certainly do not want to detract from his brilliance, but he was cheap. He was extremely hard to deal with and just ground the screws into all the players."[114] Kiner played through only two more seasons. Without Pittsburgh's Greenberg Gardens and the city's adulation, he was just another fading superstar. Now he realized how his friend Hank Greenberg felt in 1946—expendable, mistreated, and without his old identity. Even the career of a star during the Pivotal Era was fleeting.

18

1950: Year of the Whiz Kids

On June 26, 1950, Americans were jolted by the news that a Soviet-equipped and -trained North Korean army had invaded South Korea and was threatening the capital, Seoul. President Truman rushed troops to Korea to stem the tide and dispatched a fleet to protect Formosa from possible invasion by Red China. The Korean conflict reversed American military retrenchment, and the draft, which had been reinstituted in 1947, again threatened baseball. There was fear that America might be faced with World War III and that baseball and other professional sports might have to cease operation. Fans and owners alike were not reassured when Commissioner Chandler agreed that baseball might have to be shut down if total mobilization became a reality.[1] His friend Ty Cobb disagreed, noting, "Let us mobilize baseball as we have done in the past in the camps, overseas and at home. In concentrating on the big things, let us not forget the small ones. If we do that, if we play the game as we always have, we'll win."[2]

The nation was also paranoid about the specter of communism. Driven by fear and the demagoguery of U.S. Senator Joseph McCarthy, this was the beginning of an era (1950-54) that would bear his name. Baseball, which prided itself as being the most loyal and patriotic of sports, was not immune to McCarthy's call. For instance, the New York Yankees stopped their practice of flying a flag after each day's game to alert those passing by the stadium of the outcome. A blue flag was flown for victory and a red for defeat. When the Yankees received numerous politically motivated complaints about the red flag, they switched to blue and white banners for victory and red and white for defeat. The whole practice was ended, however, when the Danish ambassador called to lodge a complaint that his nation's flag was being used as a symbol of defeat.[3]

The year 1950 also marked Connie Mack's jubilee in baseball. Mack signed his first professional contract with Meriden of the Connecticut State League in 1884—Grover Cleveland's first year as president. The octogenarian was feted in every American League city with days and dinners. In Philadelphia, 600 attended a $50-a-plate dinner in his honor, with the proceeds designated for scholarships at the University of Pennsylvania. The following day, Mack received a scroll signed by all of the diners and by more than a million fans. Mack also cut a record for Joe DiMaggio's radio program, and his life story was aired over the *Cavalcade of America* program and on other national radio shows. In addition, television personality Ed Sullivan moved his variety show, *The Toast of the Town*, and its entire production crew of 107 from New York to Philadelphia just to do a special program on Mack.[4]

Where Connie Mack represented fifty years of continuity, the owners of the perennial also-rans Chicago Cubs and the St. Louis Browns experimented with innovative ideas in an attempt to improve their clubs. Well-intentioned Cubs owner Phil Wrigley was convinced that his team's eighth-place finish in 1949 was due to a lack of spirit. "They just haven't had the will to win," he complained. To get his team's attention, he replaced easygoing manager Charlie Grimm with hard-driving Frankie Frisch, who Wrigley predicted would "tongue-lash" the Cubs into shape. But instead of sending the Cubs off to baseball "boot camp," Wrigley invited the team to spend the ten days before spring training at his Catalina Island estate, where they went hiking, fished, played golf, hunted, or enjoyed other leisure activities. Such "strenuous" activity was intended to make the players "feel like they're on a real team and give them the urge to pull together and win," he explained. Citing what he had learned from his World War I experiences, Wrigley noted that "Spirit is the most important factor in victory. If it helps to restore winning spirit in the team, it's worth the price."[5]

While the Cubs were relaxing on Catalina Island, the St. Louis Browns were having their emotions profiled in an attempt to improve their mental well-being. The team hired psychologist Dr. David Tracy to work with the players. "With my treatment the club should finish fifth and may even climb to fourth," predicted Tracy. "The Browns are merely the victims of negative suggestion," he added.[6] Pleased with the media attention that Tracy's activities drew, William O. DeWitt hired the psychologist for the remainder of the season at $200 a month. "If he can help us sell tickets as well as relax our kids and make them more confident, so much the better," he explained.[7]

In a desperate move, the Browns also threatened to oust the Cardinals from Sportsman's Park. They claimed that the transfer of ownership from

Table 13. Final Major-League Regular-Season Standings, 1950

American League					National League			
	W	L	%	G.B.		W	L	%	G.B.
New York	98	56	.636	–	Philadelphia	91	63	.591	–
Detroit	95	59	.617	3	Brooklyn	89	65	.578	2
Boston	94	60	.610	4	New York	86	68	.558	5
Cleveland	92	62	.597	6	Boston	83	71	.539	8
Washington	67	87	.435	31	St. Louis	78	75	.510	12 1/2
Chicago	60	94	.390	38	Cincinnati	66	87	.431	24 1/2
St. Louis	58	96	.377	40	Chicago	64	89	.418	26 1/2
Philadelphia	52	102	.338	46	Pittsburgh	57	93	.373	33 1/2

Breadon to Saigh and Hannegan had violated the terms of their lease agreement. The real motive behind the action was a desire to get the Cardinals to renegotiate the lease and pay more rent. The Cardinals paid the Browns $35,000 per year in rent, and they shared maintenance costs of approximately $130,000 per year. The Browns insisted that maintenance costs should be on a per capita basis, since the Cardinals easily outdrew them. While Judge Richard Aronson ruled that the transfer was not a violation of their agreement, the testimony in the trial revealed publicly for the first time how Hannegan and Saigh had purchased the Cardinals with only $60,000 and further that Hannegan had received $700,000 in cash and stocks valued at $300,000 when he sold his share of the team to Saigh in January 1949. The testimony later led to Saigh's imprisonment for income-tax evasion.[8]

The Cubs and Browns owners were rewarded for their efforts with seventh-place finishes in 1950. The races in both leagues went to the wire, with the Yankees edging out Detroit and Boston in the American League and the youthful Philadelphia Phillies winning their first pennant since 1915 by holding off the surging Dodgers and Giants.

The American League Pennant Race

The eighth-place Philadelphia A's pitching staff, which initially looked deep, literally dissipated. At one point in the season, the team had only six able-bodied pitchers. Envisioning a pennant during the previous winter, the A's shelled out $100,000 and four players to acquire Bob Dillinger (.301-4-50) and Paul Lehner (.309-9-52) from the Browns, but both proved to be disappointments.[9] Only outfielder Sam Chapman (.251-23-95) and shortstop

Eddie Joost (.233-18-58) enjoyed good seasons at the plate. With Mickey Cochran and Jimmy Dykes running the club, the 1950 season marked the first time in fifty years that an A's team was not guided from the bench by a Mack. With fewer than 310,000 fans attending home games (down 515,000 from 1949) and a $400,000 payroll, the Athletics were in deep financial difficulty. Only their concession rights at Temple Stadium and Shibe Park and their percentage on admissions at Philadelphia Eagles and Phillies games (15¢ and 10¢, respectively, on each ticket) enabled them to stay solvent.[10]

When Browns' attendance continued to falter and Dr. Tracy's meetings became a nuisance, Bill DeWitt quickly severed the team's relationship with the psychologist. The Browns suffered through another dismal year in 1950. Not unlike the Athletics, the Browns continued to live from hand to mouth. Their attendance of 247,131 was almost 24,000 admissions short of the level attained in 1949. Forced to sell off their minor-league franchises in Springfield, Illinois, and Elmira, New York, they still experienced difficulty meeting their payroll.[11]

The sixth-place Chicago White Sox fired unpopular manager Jack Onslow and replaced him with Red Corriden after an 8-22 start. Improvement during the season was shown particularly by White Sox hitters, who broke the previous home run record of seventy-four at Comiskey Park, set in 1934. Gus Zernial (.280-29-83) and Eddie Robinson (.311-20-73) led the homer parade. Luke Appling's long and distinguished career ended in 1950 as he retired with a .310 lifetime batting average and established a new major-league record for most games played at shortstop, with 2,218.[12] Appling was supplanted by smooth-fielding Chico Carrasquel—a Venezuelan native who teamed with second baseman Nellie Fox to establish a double-play combination that was to last for the next six years.

Determined to increase the Senators' home run output, Clark Griffith brought in the outfield fence at Griffith Stadium and installed an additional 1,000 seats. One wag commented that the Washington owner had simply put in "1,000 more empty seats."[13] Though the Senators actually hit five fewer home runs in 1950 than in 1949, the team prospered under the guidance of manager Bucky Harris. Harris persuaded Griffith to make several trades which strengthened the Senators. New players acquired included Irv Noren (.295-14-98) from the Dodgers, second baseman Cass Michaels from the White Sox, first baseman Mickey Vernon (.306-9-65) from the Indians, and Cuban pitchers Connie Marrero and Sandy Consuegra. In spite of their improvement, the team remained in fifth place from May to the end of the season.

From June through the end of the season the Cleveland Indians were in contention in spite of several roster changes. This was the last season

Nellie Fox escaped Connie Mack's Athletics in 1949 to form famous double-play combinations with Chico Carrasquel and Luis Aparicio. (George Brace Photo)

with the tribe for several members of the 1948 world champion team, including Ken Keltner, Lou Boudreau, Joe Gordon, and Gene Bearden. Al Rosen (.287-37-116), who won the 1949 American League home run title, took over third base, while second baseman Bobby Avila and shortstop Ray Boone (.301-7-58) often spelled Gordon and Boudreau as the team's double-play combination. Infielder Luke Easter (.280-28-107), a thirty-five-year-old rookie formerly of the Negro League Homestead Grays, finally overcame injuries to capture the first base job. The only man to hit a home run over the center field fence in the Polo Grounds, Easter also hit some tape measure shots during 1950. The team's leading hitter was Larry Doby (.326-25-102), who survived a beaning in an exhibition game against the Dodgers and proceeded to feast on American League pitching in the last half of the season.

Indians' pitching, which was again strong, was led by Bob Lemon (23-11, 3.84), Bob Feller (3.43, 16-11), Steve Gromek (3.65, 10-7), Mike Garcia (3.86, 11-11), and American League earned-run-average leader Early Wynn (3.20, 18-8). The team's season virtually ended in September when the lowly Browns beat the Indians in four straight games to knock them out of contention. General manager Hank Greenberg was so incensed by the losses that he vowed, "We may lose the pennant again in 1951, but it will not be with the same team."[14]

The third-place Boston Red Sox experienced adversity throughout the season. Manager Joe McCarthy left the team under duress because of alcohol-related problems in early June and only Ted Williams (.317-28-97) and the leadership of replacement manager Steve O'Neill kept the team within striking distance at six games back.[15] Then, at the 1950 All-Star game at Chicago's Comiskey Park, disaster struck when Ted Williams fractured his elbow against an outfield fence while chasing a drive off Ralph Kiner's bat. In spite of the temporary loss of Williams, the Red Sox continued to win behind the heavy hitting of outfielders Al Zarilla (.325-9-74) and Dom DiMaggio (.328-7-70) and infielders Johnny Pesky (.312-1-49), Vern Stephens (.295-30-144), and Bobby Doerr (.294-27-120).

Two youngsters, first baseman Walt Dropo (.322-34-144) and utility man Billy Goodman (.354-4-68) also made major contributions. Dropo won the American League Rookie of the Year award while Goodman's versatility was described by one writer as like having a "jack-knife with 22 different gadgets."[16] Although Williams returned, the team's hitting faltered in mid-September when they were only a half game out of first place. Red Sox pitching, always suspect, also faded. Only Mel Parnell (3.61, 18-10) could claim an earned run average under 4.00. Although Red Sox bats cooled, the team batting average at the end of the season was an incredible .302.

The Detroit Tigers held first place for 119 days only to relinquish the position to the Yankees in mid-September. Managed by ex-Yankee third baseman Red Rolfe, the team was driven to excel. The Tiger infield was ably filled by Don Kolloway at first base, Jerry Priddy at second, Johnny Lipon at shortstop, and All-Star George Kell (.340-8-101) at third base. The Tigers received outstanding production from outfielders Hoot Evers (.323-21-103), Johnny Groth (.306-12-85), and Vic Wertz (.308-27-103). Evers was a spectacular defensive outfielder when healthy; Wertz reached his potential when Rolfe allowed him to hit against both right-handed and left-handed pitching, and Groth, a talented but enigmatic youngster, never again lived up to the potential he demonstrated in 1950.

Virgil Trucks's sore arm hampered an able staff led by Dizzy Trout (3.75, 13-5), Fred Hutchinson (3.96, 17-8), Hal Newhouser (4.34, 15-13), and Art Houtteman (3.54, 19-12). The Tigers' weak bench and bullpen eventually proved no match for the Yankees. Moreover, Red Rolfe's high expectations could only drive a team so far. Indeed, his intensity sometimes created adverse reactions. "He'd say things that just didn't sit well with a ball player in the heat of battle. Some of the players just disliked him intensely," recalled Tiger George Kell.[17]

In a pennant race, the New York Yankees always seemed to have an edge, and 1950 was no exception. They were good, sometimes very good, but rarely during the Pivotal Era did they win a pennant race without a struggle. Was there a mystique or tradition that made players perform better when they donned Yankee pinstripes? In 1950, players such Tommy Henrich and Joe DiMaggio were still connected to the great teams of the 1920s and 1930s led by Lou Gehrig, Lefty Gomez, and Red Ruffing. In addition, two members of the Yankees' coaching staff, Frank Crosetti and Bill Dickey, were also part of those teams. Henrich was one of the most vocal torchbearers. In 1949, he told one reporter, "It's something more than just tradition. It is a mental almost physical lift for a player to put on a Yankee uniform. I like to tell the young players new to the club about this pride in being a Yankee. I like to tell them about the days when the Yankees walked out on the field and threw terror into the ranks of the opposition simply because they were Yankees."[18] Younger players quickly received the message. "Anybody who played with the Yankees in those days," recalled third baseman Bobby Brown, "was quite aware of their success and tradition and realized that they were part of something that was awfully good in sports."[19]

Not only did the Yankees have a great tradition from those two decades, there was a Yankee way of doing things, much of which could be traced back to Joe McCarthy's reign as manager. When announcer Curt Gowdy first joined Mel Allen in 1949 to cover the Yankees over radio station WINS, he noticed that "the players, from DiMaggio on down, came to the ballpark wearing suits and ties and changed into pinstriped uniforms reminiscent of Wall Street."[20] Pitcher Ed Lopat, who joined the team in 1948, remembered that the Yankees "were very conscientious, all business-like, and [there was] no horsing around." Nevertheless, he added, "If you walked into the clubhouse before the game, you would think that we're all crazy—the bedlam that was created—fellows arguing, playing dominoes, cribbage—agitating one another. But we had a bell that went off five minutes before game time. When we ran from the clubhouse to the dugout, the complex changed completely. Everybody was ready for business."[21]

There was also an air of invincibility about the Yankees. "They had confidence in their ability," continued Lopat. "They didn't make many mistakes [and] it's a game of mistakes."[22] "When you are bought by a club like the Yankees," recalled outfielder Gene Woodling, "you are in awe, because they did nothing but win." Nonetheless, Woodling and his teammates knew that it took more than pinstripes to win games, and there was the added incentive not only to win pennants but to perform well as a player—namely money. "The funny thing about baseball—it's called a baseball team," continued Woodling. "But you are paid as an individual. If you win a pennant, but you hit .230, you will get a pay cut."[23] As if this incentive was not enough, Yankees players had a system of policing themselves that was also passed on from one generation to the next. "If a young player wasn't bearing down," Allie Reynolds related to interviewer Dom Forker, "a veteran would tell the youngster that he was fooling around with his Series money. The players policed themselves. Not the manager."[24] In at least two instances, Joe DiMaggio took aside Yogi Berra and with uncharacteristically pointed remarks corrected his attitude.[25] Woodling, who described himself and several of his teammates as "red-asses," remembered how he and Hank Bauer got on Mickey Mantle in 1951. "He was a kid who would get mad when he would strike out. He would pout in the outfield and short-leg us. We straightened that out in a hurry." Finally, even among the veterans themselves, you "didn't use the word 'nice hustle.' That was an insult," continued Woodling. "You were supposed to do that!"[26]

The little extra that helped the Yankees win also came from the front office. George Weiss always seemed able to make the right transaction or bring up a rookie at the right time from the Yankees' well-stocked farm system. By early June, it was apparent that Joe Page was having an off year, and the Yankees bullpen was struggling. With the contenders not wanting to help them, Weiss looked to the Browns for help. To get the ingredients the team needed, he was forced to send several young players (Jim Delsing, Duane Pillette, and Don Johnson) along with veteran Snuffy Stirnweiss and $50,000 to the Browns for pitchers Tom Ferrick (3.29, 9-7) and Joe Ostrowski (3.65, 3-5) and two minor leaguers.

The Yankees also continued to profit from moves that they did not make. Although Weiss thought veteran Johnny Mize was through, he feared that the Tigers would claim him on waiver, so he reluctantly retained him. With Henrich's (.272-6-34) bad left knee acting up and Joe Collins's (.234-8-28) inability to become a consistent hitter, Mize (.277-25-72) began to see more action at first base. On July 8, he got four hits against the Browns, including two home runs. During July and August, Mize's hitting carried the team, and at one point Stengel even moved Mize into the fourth spot and slumping DiMaggio (.301-32-122) to the fifth slot.

The Yankees also received support from several rookies, including Billy Martin and Whitey Ford. Martin was a brash, pugnacious kid with some talent, a wealth of confidence, and great abilities as a bench jockey. The rookie who really contributed was Whitey Ford (2.81, 9-1). A native of New York City, he was as cocky as Martin but was far less abrasive. When asked about his confidence, he told Dan Daniel, "I have been in four leagues since I started playing for money and I've got by in every one of them. So why shouldn't I do the same up here? It's the same game."[27] Ford won eight straight games, all against second-division ball clubs. His performance won him the *Sporting News*'s Rookie of the Year award.

Ford complimented strong performances by Yankee starters Allie Reynolds (3.74, 16-12), Vic Raschi (4.00, 21-8), Eddie Lopat (3.47, 18-8), and Tommy Byrne (4.74, 15-9). In addition, infielders Jerry Coleman, Bobby Brown, Billy Johnson, outfielders Gene Woodling and Cliff Mapes, and catcher Yogi Berra (.322-28-124) all made major contributions to the Yankee pennant drive. Hank Bauer (.320-13-70), in his second full year with the club, was outstanding. The ex-Marine platoon sergeant, who saw combat in the Pacific on Okinawa, Guam, and Guadalcanal, was awarded two Purple Hearts and was twice decorated with Bronze Stars for valor. Stengel, who loved Bauer's aggressive spirit, initially envisioned him as DiMaggio's successor. Strong, confident, and equipped with a great arm, one observer likened him to Enos Slaughter because "he runs like him, hustles like him, throws like him and he's just beginning to hit like him."[28]

The real story throughout the 1950 season for the Yankees was the play of shortstop Phil Rizzuto (.324-7-66), whose 200 hits allowed him to capture the American League's Most Valuable Player award. Rizzuto attributed his sudden hitting prowess to Johnny Mize's hitting advice and to a series of off-season eye exercises prescribed by doctors to correct a depth-perception problem. After Rizzuto went hitless in his first eleven at bats of the season, Rizzuto borrowed Mize's bat—a taped Louisville Slugger with a thick handle and barrel that, according to Rizzuto, "looked and felt like something used on a wagon train on 'Death Valley Days.'"[29] Nevertheless, Rizzuto began to hit. The Scooter also sparkled at shortstop, where he established several fielding records, including fifty-eight consecutive errorless games.

Rizzuto was valued highly by his teammates. When asked about the difference between playing with the Browns and the Yankees, pitcher Tom Ferrick replied that hard-hit balls went to the outfield, but "with the Yankees, I just turn around and watch Rizzuto and the other guy, Coleman, reel off a double play. Rizzuto gets the balls that go by other shortstops and that's the main reason why pitching for the Yankees is such a good deal."[30]

On August 30, the Yankees took a double-header from Cleveland to regain first place. Nevertheless, their hopes were dimmed when DiMaggio left the first game with pain in both knees and his left instep. In spite of collecting his two thousandth career hit, the Yankee Clipper experienced a rocky season that saw him benched for the first time in his career for anemic hitting. As the race tightened at the beginning of September, Stengel noted, "We must trust in the Lord, drink plenty of orange juice, stay out of drafts, and fight like hell."[31] Not taking a chance on the Lord, Weiss acquired veteran first baseman Johnny Hopp on waivers from the Pittsburgh Pirates for $35,000. Hopp, who hit .333 for the Yankees in nineteen games, hit a home run off Al Widmar to win one key game for the club. In addition, Mize continued his hot hitting with three home runs in a game against Detroit on September 13. The Yankees' real savior, however, was DiMaggio. When he returned to the lineup in early September, Dan Daniel reported that he looked "tired and jaded. . . . He did not hit, he dropped a fly ball and gave Boston two runs."[32] Then, on September 10, he regained his form as he hit three 400-plus-foot home runs and a double in a single contest—the first ever to accomplish the feat at spacious Griffith Stadium. DiMaggio fashioned a nineteen-game hitting streak and batted .373 with nine home runs and thirty runs batted in. For one month, he was the Yankee Clipper of old. Teammate Bobby Brown expressed it best when he said, Joe DiMaggio "could rise to the occasion as well as anyone I ever saw."[33] The Yankees clinched the pennant on September 29.

The National League Pennant Race

Although the Philadelphia Phillies held first place from late July until the end of the season, the Dodgers and Giants took the pennant race down to the wire. Conversely, the eighth-place Pittsburgh Pirates gradually sank from second place in April to last in July. Ralph Kiner (.272-47-118), the National League home run champion, continued to be Pittsburgh's major gate attraction. On April 22, Kiner hit a 500-foot homer that cleared the left-field scoreboard by fifty feet, carried over a road, and lodged in a Schenley Park tree. Suitably impressed, as were all of Kiner's teammates, Rip Sewell remarked, "If Kiner had cut that drive up into small pieces, he would have had enough singles to last him for a month."[34] With Kiner as an attraction, the Pirates drew more than 1.1 million fans in 1950 (the third-highest total in the league).

The Chicago Cubs were not only the worst-fielding team in the National League, they also established a new season record for team strikeouts, with 767. The Cubs' infield was anchored by shortstop Roy Smalley (.230-21-85), who possessed unusual "pop" for a player at his position. The outfield was led by All-Stars Andy Pafko (.304-36-92) and Hank Sauer (.274-32-103). Cubs pitching also showed some strength behind Johnny Schmitz, Frank Hiller (3.53, 12-5), Paul Minner, and Bob Rush (3.71, 13-20).

After losing thirty-eight of their first fifty-three games, the Cincinnati Reds finished sixth by playing at a .500 clip thereafter. The Reds mysteriously traded Walker Cooper to the Braves in May for infielder Connie Ryan. Although the move stabilized their infield, Cooper's departure left the Reds with two unproven catchers: Dixie Howell and John Pramesa.

Cincinnati's power was supplied by big first baseman Ted Kluzewski (.307-25-111), who kept another promising rookie named Joe Adcock (.293-8-55) in the outfield. Ewell Blackwell (2.97, 17-15) regained the form that made him one of the most feared pitchers in the league, and Ken Raffensberger and Howie Fox also made Reds starting pitching respectable.

St. Louis' fifth-place finish was a major disappointment. The veteran pitching staff of Howie Pollet (3.29, 14-13), Harry Brecheen, Max Lanier, Al Brazle, Red Munger, and Gerry Staley averaged thirty-three years of age. Of the group, only Staley was destined to pitch well into the 1950s. Veterans Red Schoendienst and Marty Marion still anchored the infield, but Marion's back would hasten the end of his fine career. In spite of being thirty-four years old, Enos Slaughter (.290-10-101) could still hit and field with anyone, and the incomparable Stan Musial (.346-28-109), who at age thirty won the National League batting championship, shuttled back and forth between first base and the outfield. Injuries to Nippy Jones, Ted Wilks, Bill Howerton, Chuck Diering, Tommy Glaviano, and Stan Musial hampered the Cardinals. The most serious injury, however, was Joe Garagiola's season-ending shoulder separation suffered on June 1 against the Dodgers. The young catcher, who was hitting .348 at the time, never attained such lofty levels again. On the brighter side was second baseman Red Schoendienst, who went fifty-seven games at second base and handled 320 chances without an error, setting new records in both areas. Schoendienst also became the hero of the 1950 All-Star game when he homered off Detroit's Ted Gray in the fourteenth inning to give the National League a 4-3 victory. After piloting the team to one first-place finish and three seconds, manager Eddie Dyer resigned after the team went into a disastrous slump in August.

The fourth-place Boston Braves received outstanding starting pitching from Vern Bickford (3.47, 19-14), Warren Spahn (3.16, 21-17), and Johnny Sain (3.94, 20-13). Spahn led the National League in victories and strikeouts, Sain regained his pitching form, and Bickford led the league in complete games. Bickford, who was described by one writer as "an aggressive and mean eyed employee on the mound, but quiet, gentlemanly off the field," also threw a no-hitter against the Dodgers on August 11.[35] The Braves led the league in complete games with eighty-eight, of which seventy-seven were registered by their "Big Three." Boston, however, had virtually no bullpen and finished dead last in the league with only ten saves.

The arrival of Sam Jethroe (.273-18-58), the first African American to play on a Boston team, was the major story of the year. Nicknamed "The Jet," Jethroe "could throw, he could run, and he could hit," recalled teammate Willard Marshall. He was also tough. "I saw him charge a line drive one night in Philadelphia and he got hit right in the mouth with it," noted

Marshall. "It knocked his teeth out and everything else. They wanted to [take him out]. He got up and stayed in the ball game."[36] Jethroe's Boston initiation was difficult. He was hampered by a sore arm in spring training and struggled at the plate. Typical of Boston's thoughtful writers, Harold Kaese wrote, "Jethroe can carry the ball from center field to the infield just as fast as he can throw it. This is symptomatic of Jethroe's talent. He is handcuffed by fly balls, can't throw and the feeling is he won't hit big league pitching. He can run period."[37]

Jethroe silenced his critics by getting off to a fast start with nine hits in his first twenty times at bat, including a home run and two doubles. He also led the league in stolen bases with thirty-eight. Only a badly sprained ankle, suffered at midseason, kept him from stealing more. At the end of the season, Jethroe was named the National League's Rookie of the Year.

The Braves sacrificed defense for power. With such hitters as Earl Torgeson (.293-23-87), Bob Elliott (.305-24-107), Sid Gordon (.304-27-103), Walker Cooper (.329-14-60), and Tommy Holmes (.298-9-51), they finished second in the league in runs scored and third in home runs.

Despite all of their strengths, though, the Braves were an unbalanced and troubled team. Youngsters Del Crandall and Johnny Antonelli were still several seasons from stardom, and the team's veterans failed to produce. The team's gamble failed and now it was stuck with a number of players over thirty. One of the Braves starting pitchers noted, "The very thing we went out and got, power, was the thing that ruined us. It blew up in our faces. Our sluggers were trying to hit the ball out of the park every time they got up. And these guys just don't hit good pitching. How many times would a single, or a double, have won a game for us?"[38] With attendance down and a roster of aging veterans, the Braves were headed in the wrong direction.

Unlike the Braves, the third-place Giants were in disarray at the beginning of the season rather than at the end, as a pair of early seven-game losing streaks ruined almost all hopes of winning the pennant. With only two returning starters, Bobby Thomson (.252-25-85) and Whitey Lockman (.295-6-52), making major contributions, it is little wonder that the Giants had difficulty finding themselves. The pitching staff was a major question mark. One hopeful, veteran Kirby Higbe, attended a South Carolina revival and in the heat of the moment promised a youthful evangelist named Billy Graham that he would win ballplayers to Christ. "I'm no preacher, but I'll do the best I can," said Higbe. "Fine," replied Durocher when told of Higbe's remarks. "If it helps his pitching, I'll send for this Graham fellow immediately."[39] Although Higbe's new mission failed to bring him personal success, Durocher obtained two superb starting pitchers almost out of thin air in Jim Hearn (2.49, 11-4) and Sal Maglie (2.71, 18-4). Hearn regained his confidence to throw eleven complete games—all wins. Maglie, who also won all twelve of his complete games, threw a curveball pitch resembling a slider that exploded past hitters. Coupled with Larry Jansen (3.01, 19-13), Dave Koslo (3.91, 13-15), and Sheldon Jones (4.61, 13-16), the Giants suddenly found themselves with quite a pitching staff.

Durocher also added former Negro League players Hank Thompson (.289-20-91) and Monte Irvin (.299-15-66) to the mix. Thompson, who had been up with the Browns in 1947, was an excellent fielder who could hit with power. At the age of thirty-one the versatile Irvin, the great Negro League star, was finally getting the chance he turned down in 1946. In addition, with Alvin Dark (.300-8-51) and Eddie Stanky (.279-16-67) as their pivot combination, the Giants already bore Durocher's mark. Even though the Giants' manager and his second baseman rarely got along, Durocher once told Willard Marshall with regard to Stanky that "I can hate you like a snake, but if you can play baseball, I want you."[40] By season's end, it was also clear that the Giants would be future pennant contenders.

The second-place Dodgers were the odds-on favorite to repeat for the pennant in 1950. Branch Rickey put together a team that used the intimate confines of Ebbets Field to lead the National League in almost all offensive categories, including batting average (.275), runs scored (855), home runs (184), and slugging average (.434). With a lineup that included power hitters in Gil Hodges (.283-32-113), Roy Campanella (.281-31-89), Carl Furillo (.305-18-106), and Duke Snider (.321-31-107), there was little wonder that expectations were high. Moreover, the Dodgers led the league in team defense. The Brooklyn infield of Hodges, Jackie Robinson (.328-14-81), Pee Wee Reese, and Billy Cox led the league in double plays, and Hodges, Robinson, and Cox possessed the league's highest fielding percentages at their respective positions. Cox was such a great fielder that sports writter Joe King once wrote that the infielder "turns blazers into double plays with such nonchalance that he might be lighting a cigar or showing a card trick at the same time."[41]

The Dodgers continued to experience weak pitching. Talented Rex Barney, who could not regain his control, would soon be out of baseball. Ralph Branca was hampered by a sore leg and sore arm, and Dan Bankhead was ineffective. Young Carl Erskine, the farm system's best prospect, was also a question mark. After an exciting rookie year in 1949, he floundered at the beginning of the season and was sent to Montreal, where he remained until August. Even Preacher Roe (3.30, 19-11) and Don Newcombe (3.70, 19-11) went through periods of injury, leaving only Erv Palica (3.58, 13-8) unscathed.

The Dodgers reached rock bottom in early August, when they lost four straight, including two games to the league-leading Phillies. They found themselves 6½ games off the pace. Exonerating his friend, Burt Shotton, from blame, Branch Rickey made an unusual speech charging his team with being complacent.[42]

Although it is doubtful that Rickey's speech caused the Dodger revival, the team came close to overtaking the Phillies. Late in the season, two extraordinary events occurred. On August 31, Gil Hodges became only the sixth man in baseball history to hit four home runs in one game, as the Dodgers beat the Braves 10-1.[43] Then, on September 8, Don Newcombe started both games of a doubleheader against the Phillies, winning the first with a three-hitter 2-0 and leaving the second game at the end of seven innings down 2-0. The Dodgers went on to win the second game in the ninth 3-2. The feat was the result of some good-natured kidding between Shotton and Newcombe. The big Dodger right-hander was on a streak, having allowed only four earned runs in his previous fifty-two innings—a period in which three of his previous five starts resulted in shutouts. With the Dodgers so short of effective pitching and Newcombe so hot, Shotton told him, "You can do two if you pitch a shutout in the opener."[44]

At season's end, with the Phillies in an apparent free fall and only two games left, the Dodgers met Philadelphia on September 30 in a two-game series at Ebbets Field trailing only by two games. The Dodgers took the first game 7-3, behind Erv Palica, thereby making the last game of the season, on October 1, critical for both clubs. In a matchup between Robin Roberts, who was starting his third game in five days, and Don Newcombe, the game was tied at 1-1 going into the ninth. Only a perfect throw by Richie Ashburn, which nailed Cal Abrams by twelve feet at the plate, and clutch pitching by Roberts saved the Phillies from a potential Dodger rally in the ninth. In the tenth, the Phillies clinched the pennant, 4-1, on a dramatic three-run homer by outfielder Dick Sisler. With the Dodgers' season at an end, Walter O'Malley forced Rickey to sell his stock in the team. The same fate faced Burt Shotton, who was replaced by Charley Dressen. "I wasn't fired because of my record," complained Shotton. "It's just that O'Malley wanted an organization without any Rickey men in it. The deal I got this time made me a little sour."[45]

The 1950 season was anything but sour for the Whiz Kids of Philadelphia. Following Sisler's home run, Roberts retired the Dodgers in the bottom of the tenth, allowing the Phillies to seize their first pennant in thirty-five years. With the victory, pandemonium broke loose in Philadelphia. In a scene reminiscent of V-E Day, fans poured into the streets and began to celebrate. Horns sounded, bells rang, and whistles tooted all over town. Thousands jammed into the area surrounding the city's courthouse, and few telephone books survived joyous fans looking for a source of confetti. As later described by city historian Frank Brookhouser, when the team arrived at the 30th Street Station, it had to make its way "through a happy mob of 30,000 fans—old ladies, old men, teenagers, tots—which broke through police lines. Phillies pennants, caps and buttons were sold by the thousands before buses took the players to the Hotel Warwick while passing motorists blasted their greetings on horns." Thousands of well-wishers gathered outside the hotel, where owner Robert Carpenter threw a party for the team, and the city continued to celebrate well into the night.[46]

The Phillies' success was neither sudden nor unexpected by knowledgeable baseball people. With an organization built from the bottom up by Herb Pennock and with such ex-Yankees as scout Johnnie Nee, coaches Benny Bengough and Dusty Cooke, and manager Eddie Sawyer guiding it, the Phillies were poised to win. Pennock believed in youth and developed an excellent scouting system. Carpenter studied at Pennock's knee for three years before the latter's untimely death in 1948. Manager Ben Chapman strongly suggested to outside sources that Carpenter needed another strong baseball man to guide the Phillies. After hearing of his remarks, Carpenter replaced Chapman instead.[47] Unlike Rickey, Carpenter went after size rather than speed and ignored African American players until 1958, when black scouts William Yancey and Judy Johnson were added to the staff. The Phillies' big advantage was money—they led the vanguard of teams who offered players bonuses. "With the Carpenters, money was no object," recalled scout Jocko Collins. "You always tried to get the last shot in the bidding, because you could say to the mother and the father: 'Talk to the other scouts. Get the best offer. And whatever it is, we'll give you five thousand more.'"[48] In 1950, Stan Baumgartner figured that the Whiz Kids cost Carpenter only $370,000 to sign and $3.5 million to develop. The signing bonuses used to acquire the Phillies ten bonus players on the 1950 championship team ranged from Curt Simmons's $65,000 to Bubba Church's $3,000. Twelve other players were purchased or acquired through trades. Two of them (Seminick and Ennis) were already with the team when Carpenter acquired it, and one (Mike Goliat) came to the Phillies as a free agent.[49]

The heart of the Phillies was manager Eddie Sawyer. Sawyer, who toiled as a manager in the Yankee system for several years, taught biology at Ithaca College in the off-season. Quiet and introspective, he understood young men, and, having managed at Utica and Toronto, he already knew many of the young Phillies. He rarely upbraided the culprit when mistakes were made. Instead, he was a confidence builder. "Ability is half confidence," he once noted. "Build up a man's confidence and you build up ability. Knock his confidence down and you kill his ability." Nevertheless, because he had a photographic memory, his players knew he never forgot a mistake—it was a memory so sharp that when he was at Ithaca

College he knew every student's name and hometown.[50] In return, the players called him "Skipper" and treated him with great respect.

With an average roster age of twenty-seven, the team was young by 1950 standards. Players ranged in age from Curt Simmons, at twenty-one, to veterans Bill "Swish" Nicholson, Ken Heintzelman, and Blix Donnelly, all of whom were thirty-five. With thirty-one-year-old Eddie Waitkus and thirty-year-old Dick Sisler as anchors, the Phillies' starting lineup also averaged twenty-seven years of age. Smooth-fielding Waitkus (.284-2-44) surprised his teammates with his comeback. Andy Seminick recalled that when Waitkus first reappeared in the clubhouse after being shot that "he looked like a ghost. He looked terrible."[51] Waitkus's recovery allowed Sisler (.296-13-83), a power-hitter whose father was the great George Sisler, to return to right field. Sisler carried the team in the early part of the season when in May he made eight straight hits, a home run and seven singles. Center fielder Richie Ashburn (.303-2-41) rebounded from a mediocre 1949 season. "I had a swelled head last year," Ashburn told a reporter. "I laughed at the advice given me by veterans, thought the big leagues were a snap and got the best lesson a fellow can ever get."[52] Rounding out the outfield was strong-armed left fielder Del Ennis (.311-31-126), the National League's runs-batted-in leader. Ennis was a hometown boy who rarely got the credit he deserved in Philadelphia. A true hitter, Ennis soaked twenty-four bats in crankcase oil for six months between seasons. Observers reported that balls seemed to jump off Ennis's bats, which weighed an additional four ounces and seemed more solid and tight-grained as a result of the soaking.[53]

The most untried regular was infielder Mike Goliat. Ordinarily a third baseman, second base was a new position for him at the beginning of 1950. Fortunately for the Phillies, the peppery Goliat proved to be an excellent clutch hitter and experienced the best season of his career. Goliat's keystone partner, Granny Hamner (.270-11-82), was the team captain, leader, and player representative. A feisty, scrappy player, Hamner, according to J.G. Taylor Spink, was "a driver—needling, jibing, cussing, praising, anything to get the best out of the other men." Hamner was a self-made infielder who possessed enough power at the plate to make himself dangerous.[54] Willie Jones (.267-25-88), who rounded out the infield at third base, was a character. Nicknamed "Puddin' Head" after a popular song title during his youth, Jones was not a good-looking prospect when he first came to the Phillies in 1947. Manager Ben Chapman ordered Jones, overweight and equipped with a cheap glove and old, ill-fitting shoes, to wear a rubber suit to sweat off the weight and gave him new equipment. After hitting .307 at Terre Haute in 1947, the Phillies sent him to Toronto, but he initially failed to report. Apparently, Carolyn Jones,

Veteran catcher Andy Seminick
was the only player on the Whiz
Kids who played with the Phillies
in 1945. (George Brace Photo)

who was pregnant at the time, refused to go because she feared that if her child were born there, it would not be eligible to become president of the United States. Always a dangerous hitter, Jones became a proficient third baseman through hours of daily practice.[55]

Backstop Andy Seminick (.288-24-68) also came into his own as a leader and handler of pitchers in 1950. He was so improved behind the plate that such experts as ex-catcher Gabby Street praised him as the best catcher in baseball.[56] The Phillies' pitching staff was anchored by Curt Simmons (3.40, 17-8) and Robin Roberts (3.02, 20-11). Simmons was one of the team's major surprises in 1950. His herky-jerky motion prevented batters from picking up the ball readily. Moreover, the left-handed Simmons's crossfire delivery, which came from the direction of first base, intimidated left-handed hitters. His pitching repertoire consisted of two fastballs—one that took off and another that dipped—an excellent change-up, and a hard-breaking curve.[57] Robin Roberts, the bellwether of the staff, was a paragon of consistency all season long. Now one of the best pitchers in the game, he not only led the league in games started (39) but was among the leaders in complete games (21), innings pitched (304), strikeouts (146), and shutouts (5). Three of his shutouts were in succession.

The Phillies also profited from the sudden development of two other young starters—Bubba Church (2.73, 8-6) and Bob Miller (3.57, 11-6). A poised and confident starter, Church was a control pitcher with a smooth three-quarter delivery who was most effective when he kept the ball low. Miller was even more of a surprise than Church. The Phillies thought so little of Miller that they left him exposed to the draft in 1947. Nevertheless, he turned heads in 1949 with a spectacular season at class B Terre Haute. Miller's greatest asset was an unpredictable sinking fastball that exploded when it got about fifteen feet from the plate. The other major contributor on the pitching staff was reliever Jim Konstanty (2.66, 16-7), who led the league in saves (twenty-two) and established a modern record with seventy-four appearances in a single season. Only Joe Page in 1949 and Firpo Marberry of the 1924 Senators exceeded Konstanty's save total. He achieved fame so quickly as a reliever in 1950 that he received mail simply addressed "Relief pitcher."

Although the Phillies had some excellent hitters, it was their pitching staff that carried them through the season. After taking over first place from the Cardinals in late July, the team burned up the league in August. An August 12 altercation between Andy Seminick and Bill Rigney of the Giants led to a brawl that seemed to spark the team. Nevertheless, after establishing a seven-game lead, the Phillies began to unravel until, by the last day of the season, a win by the Dodgers would have forced a tie. Waitkus, still weak, lost fifteen pounds. Curt Simmons was lost when his National Guard unit was called to active duty. Bubba Church was incapacitated for several days when he was hit by a line drive in mid-September, and Bob Miller came up with a sore arm. Finally, Andy Seminick injured an ankle when Monte Irvin slammed into him during the team's last series with the Giants. Without the heroics of Richie Ashburn, Robin Roberts, and Dick Sisler in the team's last contest with the Dodgers, the Phillies might not have taken the pennant. Eddie Sawyer attributed the team's slide to the its weak bench. Forced to play his regulars each day, the Phillies manager noted, "Our boys were dead tired."[58]

The 1950 World Series

The Phillies were still a tired team when they met the Yankees in the 1950 World Series. Although the Yankees swept the series in four games, the first three were hard fought and quite close. Sawyer surprised everyone in the first game, which was played at Philadelphia's Shibe Park, by asking reliever Jim Konstanty to face the Yankees' Vic Raschi. It was Konstanty's first effort as a starter since 1948, when he was with Toronto. The big right-hander allowed the Yankees only five hits but still lost 1-0 because Raschi threw a two-hitter. The Yankees scored in the fourth inning on a double by Bobby Brown, who advanced home on two fly-ball

Although Robin Roberts had great stuff, it was his poise that impressed others. Umpire Al Barlick once described him as "having the outward disposition of an oyster," because he betrayed so little emotion. (George Brace Photo)

outs. The second contest was a pitchers' duel between Robin Roberts and Allie Reynolds in which the Yankees prevailed 2-1. The Yankees scored first in the second inning on singles by Reynolds and outfielder Gene Woodling. The Phillies tied the game in the fifth when Mike Goliat singled, was moved to third on a bad-hop grounder by Waitkus, and scored on a fly out by Ashburn. Roberts, who had the Yankees hitting under his fastball most of the game, ran out of luck in the tenth, when Joe DiMaggio led off the inning with his seventh career World Series home run—a shot into the upper tier of the left-field stands.

Momentum continued in New York's favor as the series shifted to Yankee Stadium and Eddie Lopat was matched up against veteran Ken Heint-

Richie Ashburn was a speedster on the bases and a superb outfielder. A great contact hitter, Ashburn was an outstanding lead-off man and often led the league in on-base percentage. (George Brace Photo)

zelman. The Yankees scored first in the third inning, when, with two outs, Phil Rizzuto walked, advanced to third on a throwing error by Seminick, and scored on a single by Jerry Coleman. The Phillies went ahead 2-1 by scoring runs in the sixth on a double by Del Ennis and a single by Dick Sisler and in the seventh inning on a single by Granny Hamner, Seminick's sacrifice, and a single by Mike Goliat. Heintzelman was outstanding until, with two outs in the eighth, he lost his control and walked the bases full. Reliever Jim Konstanty came in and got pinch hitter Bobby Brown to hit a routine grounder to shortstop Granny Hamner, who inexplicably

Jim Konstanty's twenty-two saves and 16-7 record helped propel the Phillies to the National League pennant. The National League's Most Valuable Player was the surprising starter in the opening game of the 1950 World Series. (*The Sporting News*)

fumbled the ball, allowing the tying run to score. With Russ Meyer on the mound, the Yankees scored the winning run after two outs in the ninth on several close plays. Woodling was credited with a single on a ball bobbled by Jimmy Bloodworth and then advanced to second on hard-hit grounder by Phil Rizzuto, which was barely blocked by Bloodworth. He then scored when Jerry Coleman's long fly to left-center landed just out of reach of outfielders Jack Mayo and Richie Ashburn. The final game was dominated by Whitey Ford's pitching, as the Yankees won 5-2. The Yankees' rookie left-hander kept the Phillies at bay through the ninth but lost his shutout when Woodling dropped a fly ball with two men on. The Yankees knocked starter Bob Miller out of the game with two runs in the first inning on an error by Goliat, a single by Berra, a passed ball, and a double by DiMaggio. They struck for three more in the sixth inning off Konstanty when Berra homered, DiMaggio was hit by a pitch and scored on Bobby Brown's triple, and the latter tallied on a line drive to center by Hank Bauer.

The 1950 World Series was played in the shadow of the Korean conflict. At Commissioner Chandler's direction, a silent prayer for peace was offered prior to the National Anthem at the beginning of the first and third games. Curt Simmons, who had pitched so brilliantly for the Phillies during the season, was already in khakis. Although ineligible for the series, he returned on furlough to pitch batting practice to his teammates. Whitey Ford was next: he was drafted only two weeks after winning game four. "To say I was shocked was an understatement," recalled Ford. "One day I was sitting on top of the world . . . and the next day I faced the prospect of army life, basic training, peeling potatoes, long marches, and all the rest."[59] With Americans again engaged in combat, Joe DiMaggio and Lefty O'Doul traveled to Japan in late October on a goodwill tour, where they played in exhibitions, lunched with General Douglas MacArthur, and visited wounded soldiers at numerous base hospitals. In mid-November, they flew to Korea, where they visited hospitals near Seoul and Pukchong. On one trip, they flew in a small L-17 observation plane in bad weather and landed at an improvised strip so they could visit a newly established field hospital. In order to take off, a siren was sounded to clear a small-town street so their plane could use it as a runway. On his return, DiMaggio told reporters that the prevailing perception in the United States that the war was merely a police action was incorrect. "It looked like an all-out war to me," he stated. "And the boys want the people in this country to know they're not just a police force. They want credit for what they are doing, and I don't blame them."[60] It was credit that would be long in coming.

1951

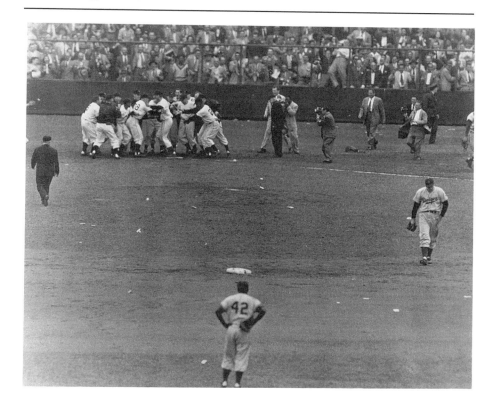

Few sporting events electrified the sports world like Bobby
Thomson's playoff game-winning home run. (National
Baseball Hall of Fame Library, Cooperstown, New York)

19

Chandler's Waterloo

Until the evening of December 11, 1950, baseball's winter meetings were remarkably quiet—no major trades or transactions were announced, and there seemed little of a controversial nature to report. Most of the legion of baseball writers covering the St. Petersburg meeting were having a night on the town some thirty-three miles away in Tampa. Unbeknownst to most of them, the National and American League owners were meeting in executive session at the Soreno Hotel to discuss the next day's agenda, which included the renewal of baseball commissioner Happy Chandler's contract. St. Louis owner Fred Saigh recalled jesting with a couple of reporters, including Dick Young of the *New York Daily News*, and telling them that they should remain in town because the news was going to be "right here." "What do you mean?" they asked. "I think the commissioner is going to get five votes against him," Saigh replied. Knowing that Saigh was the only outspoken enemy of the commissioner among the owners, the reporters all laughed and went on to dinner.[1] The writers realized their mistake later that evening when they received frantic phone calls from their papers or listened to quick radio bulletins in their cars that announced that the owners had voted not to renew Commissioner Chandler's contract.

Some reporters did hear rumors that Chandler's reelection might not go smoothly. Dan Daniel ran into Frank Yeutter at 2:00 P.M. and the Philadelphia sportswriter told him, "There definitely is trouble. I know that Bob Carpenter of the Phillies has been in some secret conferences which plan to oust the Commissioner. There may be a real revolution within the next few hours."[2] Daniel went on an investigation of his own but was reassured by the owners that he talked to that they were unaware of any revolt. Later that afternoon, Daniel found it difficult to contact many of the owners. The ones he did reach assured him that they knew nothing. "Those men were telling the truth," wrote Daniel. "Those behind the revolt had taken care not to approach magnates whom they knew to be irrevocably tied up with Chandler." The whole thing might have exploded, he added. "Had the Commissioner known beforehand about the meeting which was to repudiate him," Daniel noted, "he might have been able to stop the fight." At 7:00 that evening, Daniel attended a dinner in St. Petersburg sponsored by the Yankees and held in honor of the New York writing delegation. George Weiss, the host, was conspicuously absent. After a series of speeches, Daniel arose to introduce the evening's final speaker, Roy Hamey, when he was interrupted by Yankee publicist Red Patterson, who had just returned from taking a phone call. "You men had better get back to the Soreno," Patterson shouted. "All hell's broken loose." When Daniel's group of reporters reached the hotel, they were met by Yankees owner Del Webb, who told them of the meeting and the results. The first ballot was nine to seven, he related. The second was eight to eight, and the third, nine to seven. "The voting was secret," he added. "So there is no way of your finding out which seven were against the Commissioner."[3]

Chandler's downfall was not precipitated by one specific instance but instead was instigated by a minority of baseball's major-league owners who either came to the conclusion that the commissioner had outlived his usefulness or held specific grievances against him. This is not to assume, however, that Chandler was universally beloved by the rest of the baseball world. For instance, for many Eastern sportswriters, Chandler simply failed to measure up to their expectations. Although he was the antithesis of Landis, the Judge cast a long shadow over his conduct and his decisions. New York and Boston sportswriters, in particular, were unable to reconcile Chandler with the image projected by his predecessor. A man who possessed a folksy Southern twang, an instant toothy grin, and a natural tenor voice and who would sing "My Old Kentucky Home" at the slightest urging was not considered dignified enough to be taken seriously. During his tenure, writers tagged him with a number of derisive appellations. Such critics called Chandler "an indifferent Commissioner, but a pretty good ham actor," "the Kentucky windbag," "Unhappy Chandler," "The Kentucky Duce," The Great White Father," and "a handshaking baby-kissing practitioner of the arts."[4]

What really irked baseball writers was the commissioner's inability to handle criticism. Chandler was a man who demanded absolute loyalty—one was either for him or against him. Gray was a color he did not recognize. When a reporter penned a column he did not like, he often wrote him a pointed letter. Red Smith remembered receiving such a letter in

Eastern sportswriters, especially those from New York City, failed to identify with the image Chandler projected. A man who would sing "My Old Kentucky Home" at the slightest urging was not considered dignified enough to be taken seriously. (Special Collections and Archives, University of Kentucky)

1946 taking him to task for a column he had written on Judge Bramham's stand on the gambling scandals. After demanding that Smith turn over any evidence on gambling he had in his possession, Chandler included a short clipping written by Arch Ward as "a sample of what decent sportswriters were writing in this country."[5]

Chandler's failure to approve Bill Corum of the *New York Journal-American* as a World Series radio sportscaster because of his criticism of the Durocher decision earned him "the enmity of virtually all of the important sportswriters in the business—particularly in New York, noted Shirley Povich of the *Washington Post*. "He entirely underestimated the power of the press."[6] According to sportscaster Red Barber, Chandler forfeited any chance he had of reconciliation with the writers by placing baseball's headquarters in Cincinnati instead of in a two- or three-team town such as Chicago or New York. He not only eliminated American League writers but isolated himself from New York's powerful press corps and thus had little chance to make a favorable impression on them. "Chandler could win in Kentucky," exclaimed Barber, "but you can't be this country boy around those hard-nosed New York writers."[7]

Although Stanley Woodward of the *New York Herald-Tribune* gleefully claimed that "the sportswriters are the boys who dethroned Happy," they really had little direct influence on the result.[8] Indeed, in some respects Chandler precipitated his own downfall when he made a surprise request at the 1949 baseball winter meeting that owners consider the renewal of his contract a full two years in advance. Chandler claimed that he had other opportunities and needed to know their intentions. He left some owners with the impression that he was trying to use the commissionership as a political springboard.[9] The proposal engendered heated debate. American League president Will Harridge, who produced old minutes to show that Judge Landis had never received approval for a contract renewal more than a year in advance, argued vehemently against the precedent. His argument persuaded two of Chandler's staunchest allies, Connie Mack and Clark Griffith, to vote against the proposal, which failed 11-5 in spite of the impassioned sponsorship of Chandler's friend Frank McKinney of the Pirates.[10]

Chandler's temporary defeat did not go unnoticed by Fred Saigh, the most outspoken of Chandler's enemies among the owners. Saigh first soured on Chandler when he was called in by the commissioner to settle the Gardella case. "I saw a scared man," he recalled. A man "who was not willing to stand up and fight for the job he was hired for."[11] Saigh was also displeased with Chandler's handling of the Martin-Lanier case. According to Saigh, all sixteen owners were in agreement on reinstating the two pitchers. Chandler, however, agreed to fight their suit and then, shortly before trial, suddenly dropped it, necessitating a settlement that likely cost the Cardinals in excess of $40,000.[12] At the same time that Saigh was assisting with the Mexican League settlements, Chandler had him under investigation. With fellow politician Bob Hannegan no longer involved with the Cardinals, Chandler felt free to investigate Saigh's original purchase of the team and his acquisition of the remainder of the team's stock from Hannegan. Rumors abounded in St. Louis that Saigh had used Hannegan as a front to provide himself with respectability and that the money to purchase the team had come from mysterious outside sources. Robert Boyle, the former FBI agent hired by Chandler to conduct the investigation, compiled a seventeen-page report that provided details concerning Saigh's background, associations, police record, business transactions, and other involvements.[13] Even though the report contained information detrimental to Saigh's reputation, there was little evidence that could substantiate the rumor that Saigh and Hannegan were "fronts" for someone else in the Cardinal sale. Nevertheless, the report contained enough information on Saigh to whet Chandler's appetite.

A little over a year later, Saigh appeared on Chandler's plate again. Saigh and Branch Rickey had agreed to make up a rained-out game on a Sunday evening instead of playing it as the second half of a double-header. Saigh printed tickets for the game and sold them out. When a St. Louis Baptist preacher wrote to Chandler, complaining that the game conflicted with his radio program, Chandler called Saigh and asked him not to play the contest.[14] He argued that Sunday night games "would cause us to forfeit the support and good will of thousands of religious people in this country" and that the rescheduling might be construed as an attempt by Saigh to earn two gates in one day. Saigh countered with several arguments, including the facts that no Missouri law banned Sunday night games; such Sunday night events such as hockey, basketball, auto races, and the Municipal Opera had failed to draw criticism from church; the National League allowed Sunday night games with the consent of the home team; and Sunday night games were commonly played in the minor leagues.[15] Saigh resented Chandler's intervention in what he considered a "league matter." Fortunately, Saigh decided to yield. If he had fought Chandler on the issue, not unlike Phil Ball and his battle with Judge Landis, he would have given the commissioner a reason to punish him. Dan Parker reported that at least one source close to the commissioner had heard Chandler say that he was "prepared to banish Saigh from baseball if he defied his order to cancel the disputed game" and that other remarks indicating the commissioner's intent to "kick that fellow out of Baseball" had also reached Saigh's ears.[16]

Saigh's American League counterpart was Del Webb of the Yankees.

Reporters speculated that his opposition to Chandler was based on disgruntlement over the commissioner's decision in the Wakefield case.[17] The real reasons, however, were much more personal. First, Chandler also had Webb investigated because he wanted to learn more about his alleged connection with Las Vegas gamblers and specifically about his role in the construction of the Flamingo Hotel. In addition, Chandler knew that Webb was having tax problems with the federal government.[18] The commissioner asked Walter Mulbry, baseball's secretary-treasurer, to direct the investigation. Mulbry, Chandler's classmate at Transylvania University and his administrative assistant dating to his governorship, became friends with Webb and confided to him the details of the investigation.[19] Second, Webb was also displeased with the way the commissioner handled his job—he wanted a commissioner who did things in a businesslike manner and who did not jump to conclusions.[20]

Webb once told a sportswriter that his greatest thrill in baseball was deposing Happy Chandler. "It might sound strange for me to call that exciting," he noted, "but the club owners were in a tizzy because they were unhappy with Happy and they didn't dare to do anything about it. I told them I'd arrange to get rid of him and we did."[21] Webb joined forces with Saigh and three other owners to ensure that Chandler would not get the twelve votes he needed for reelection at the St. Petersburg meeting. He recruited Lou Perini of the Boston Braves, Bob Carpenter of the Phillies, and William O. DeWitt of the Browns. Perini often complained that Chandler paid more attention to the Red Sox when he came to Boston. Much more serious, however, was his resentment toward Chandler after he lost Jack "Lucky" Lohrke in the 1946 baseball draft as a result of a decision by the commissioner. The commissioner's office claimed that the Braves had not immediately forwarded a check with the signing papers and that Lohrke was therefore a free agent. At the draft the angry Perini attempted to get his fellow owners to pass on Lohrke, but the Giants immediately selected him.[22]

In addition, both the Braves and Phillies were embittered when they lost a bidding war with Branch Rickey for the services of pitcher Carl Erskine. In a bit of skullduggery, the Dodgers signed Erskine in 1946 for a bonus of $3,500 while he was still in the Navy. After playing several games at Danville in the Three-I League, Chandler declared Erskine a free agent at the end of the season because the Dodgers had violated a directive that teams could not sign servicemen before they were discharged. According to Erskine, it was the Braves who alerted Chandler to the violation, but he noted further "I think they [the Braves] would have [also] signed me with no questions." Because of the pleadings of Rickey and the fact that Erskine really wanted to sign with the Dodgers, Chandler blinked at his own regulation and allowed the Dodgers to re-sign the pitcher for an additional $5,000 bonus. Chandler justified the action, claiming that the wording of the directive might have been subject to misinterpretation.[23] In a statement that seemed transparent to the Phillies and Braves, he noted, "I am convinced the Brooklyn Club would suffer through an honest error if Erskine were awarded to another club."[24] The re-signing was accomplished quickly and prevented the Dodger rivals from reentering the bidding. With Erskine's entrance into the Brooklyn rotation in 1950, both Perini's and Carpenter's memories were refreshed.

Carpenter was seen canvassing other owners regarding their votes before the surprise meeting on December 11. While he later told reporters that he was doing it simply "for his own benefit," he was clearly heavily involved in the plot against Chandler. Never really pleased with the commissioner, Carpenter reportedly complained about Chandler's efficiency and purportedly once stated, "I tried for thirty days to get a decision out of the commissioner's office and he was never in. . . . Instead, he was running around the country making speeches."[25] The fifth member of the quintet was William O. DeWitt, who told the Cardinals owner that he agreed with his position on Chandler and that "he had his vote in his back pocket."[26] Chandler angered DeWitt and Browns owner Richard Muckerman at least twice. First, when Chandler unsuccessfully attempted to block Dizzy Dean's appearance on the mound in 1947 and then again when he attempted to stop the Browns from including All-Star tickets in their season-ticket package in 1948. Now that the DeWitt brothers controlled the team, they had another problem—they were indebted to the American League. In purchasing the team, the brothers put up $50,000. The American League loaned the club $300,000, and Richard Muckerman accepted a note from the DeWitts for $600,000 with the ball club as collateral. DeWitt wanted to support American League president Will Harridge, who helped him get the loan.[27] Will Harridge, who clashed several times with Chandler over the supervision and pay of umpires, was no friend of Chandler either.

When the owners gathered to hold their "rump" meeting in Dan Topping's room at the Hotel Soreno, Webb and Saigh possessed the five votes needed to stop Chandler's contract renewal. "Topping and Yawkey sort of ran the thing [meeting]," remembered William O. DeWitt. "They had booze all over the place and everybody was drinking. Stoneham got drunk and couldn't talk. It was a stormy meeting. They said, 'Look, there is only one way to handle this, and that is to pay this man off for the rest of his contract and get rid of him.'"[28] When the first straw vote taken resulted in an 9-7 tally in favor of renewal, they decided to take an official ballot, which resulted in an 8-8 count. While the identity of the other three votes against Chandler is uncertain, the best possibilities seem to be Tom

Yawkey of the Red Sox, Charles Comiskey of the White Sox, and Phil Wrigley of the Cubs. Both Yawkey and Comiskey indicated that they were not surprised by the vote, when queried immediately following its announcement—a possible indication that they knew ahead of time that the commissioner was in trouble.[29] Although he carefully refrained from giving any indication of how he voted, Yawkey was not particularly close to the commissioner and often complained about his performance. When Grace Comiskey, the owner of the White Sox, heard that her son might have voted against Chandler, she was reportedly incensed and was quoted as saying, "There is no reason the White Sox should oppose Chandler. Some influence must have been brought to bear on my son. I wasn't consulted, so I didn't even know there was such a movement afoot. I will have a nice talk with Chuck when he returns."[30] DeWitt recalled that Charles Comiskey told him that his mother wanted him to vote for Chandler but that he was not going to do it. "I'm sure he did not vote for Chandler," noted DeWitt. "Webb talked to him all the time. Webb was around talking to everyone. Webb and Yawkey were the most influential owners in the American League."[31]

The vote change from 9-7 to 8-8 may have belonged to Phil Wrigley. According to Saigh, Wrigley represented one of the five original votes against Chandler's request for early consideration of contract renewal. Why Wrigley opposed Chandler remains a mystery. His wife, for one, was fond of the commissioner. Chandler "never could conceive [that] Wrigley voted against him," Saigh commented. At the St. Petersburg meeting, Wrigley was the only one in doubt, he added. "Wrigley would talk one way one day and another the next. But after the meeting in St. Petersburg, and the reasons were given, Wrigley went straight down the line against him."[32]

As the owners prepared to meet for their annual winter meeting in St. Petersburg, Chandler made one more gaffe that caused them immediate concern. One of the reasons he was chosen commissioner in 1945 was to keep the game going during the last year of the war. In 1951, when asked about baseball's continuance during the Korean conflict, Chandler took a stance almost diametrically opposed to that position. He stated that baseball must be prepared for the worst—even shutting down. Though Chandler later claimed to have been misquoted, the damage was done.[33] For the owners, having players sent off to war was one thing, but shutting the game down was another.

The owners' vote took almost everyone by complete surprise. Sportswriters, like Cleveland's Ed McAuley, who cited Chandler's integrity and promotional activities as commissioner, took his reelection for granted. "The chance that Chandler will be bounced out of his $65,000 a year swivel chair in Carew Towers," noted McAuley, "is about as remote as the prospect that the St. Louis Browns will win the pennant."[34] As news leaked out regarding the commissioner's multimillion-dollar television negotiations with Gillette to secure the players' pension plan, Dan Daniel was moved to write that his "situation was never as solid as it is today." In addition, Giants owner Horace Stoneham assured the New York writer that Chandler deserved reelection and that he would vote for him. Citing only Saigh's apparent opposition, Daniel quipped, "The contract is as good as in Albert's pocket." Les Biederman received the same assurances from Pirates co-owner John Galbreath, who told him, "Commissioner Chandler has done a fine job and I don't think there's any doubt he'll be re-elected."[35]

No one was more shocked by the initial vote than Chandler himself. When asked in later years about the St. Petersburg results, with more than a hint of bitterness, the former commissioner admitted as much. "Yes, originally I hadn't known that there was that many [votes against me]. Although I knew [about] Webb and Topping, and Perini and Saigh. I knew Frick was undercutting me—I knew he wanted the job and he was trying to undermine my influence. And so was old Harridge. He was the biggest fuddy-duddy I've ever seen, by God! He did just what those owners wanted."[36] According to Shirley Povich, who was close to Chandler, the commissioner was simply "naive" in underestimating the opposition against him. "If Happy had a failing," recalled Povich, "he imputed to everybody a liking for Happy Chandler. It wasn't true. He was never too discerning as far as who his enemies were." When Chandler first heard rumors in 1949 that some owners might try to buy up his contract, he asked his old friend Clark Griffith, "They won't do this to me—will they, Mr. Griffith? These are all my friends." When the Washington owner tried to warn him against some of the owners like Branch Rickey, Chandler simply brushed the opposition off.[37]

Wrigley and Webb were delegated to break the news to Chandler, who was attending a party given by Atlanta Cracker owner Earl Mann in the Vinoy Park Hotel. Following a ten-minute conference, Chandler requested that the owners take another vote. When he discovered that the final vote was 9-7, the following day (December 12, 1951) he announced to the press that he intended to remain in office until the completion of his term in 1952. "I have never run away from a situation," he noted. "And certainly I am not disposed to retreat from the one now confronting me."[38] It was also learned that Chandler refused several overtures by the owners to buy out his contract if he would leave office at once.[39] The same day, he appeared before the owners, who were again meeting in executive joint session. There, standing at the end of a long table separating the owners of the two leagues, he challenged any of them to stand up and tell him why he was being repudiated. Having agreed ahead of time to remain silent, everyone just listened. Finally, according to Saigh, Walter O'Malley addressed the commissioner and stated, "Mr. Commissioner—although I didn't vote against you, I think it is the prerogative of this group to have their own Commissioner." With his face flushed and tears in his eyes, Chandler replied, "This is a horrible shock to me and my family. I left a berth in politics that would have been mine forever and now I find myself a free agent. I am going to fight it." He then pointed to Spike Briggs and said, "Briggs, don't you have anything to say?" The startled son of the Detroit owner replied, "Well, Mr. Commissioner, the vote's in."[40] After Chandler's departure from the meeting, the owners announced that their vote was unanimous to appoint a search committee to find a new commissioner as soon as possible. Moreover, they also voted to abolish both the high school signing and bonus rules—two of Chandler's favorite measures.

Unlike old generals, old political campaigners rarely fade away. Commissioner Chandler was determined, if not confident, that he could regain the three votes necessary to win back the commissionership. The timing of his first act, the signing of a long-term television contract for the rights to the All-Star game and the World Series between baseball and the Gillette Safety Razor Company and the Mutual Broadcasting System, could not have been better. The commissioner concluded several months of negotiations by signing a six-year $6 million contract with the two companies on December 26, 1950. Coupled with the baseball's radio rights to the two events, which had been sold for $1,195,000 in 1949, the deal ensured the long-term stability of the players' pension fund. During a meeting held on November 16, 1950, Chandler had obtained the owners' approval to apply most of the World Series money to the plan. The contract was astonishing when compared with the $100,000 baseball received each year between 1934 and 1946 for radio rights to the two events. Television had begun its ascendancy by the late 1940s, and by 1950 baseball was earning a total of $875,000 for the rights. The deal was one of the outstanding achievements of the Chandler commissionership.

Nevertheless, the commissioner's critics were quick to pounce on the transaction. "If the package was worth $800,000 in 1950 when television's scope is still limited to the eastern half of the U.S., and by no means all of that," asked Dan Parker, then "the question being asked by baseball and television folk is: 'What will the series rights be worth three or four years hence when the networks should cover the country like the canals on Mars?'"[41] "Television is in its infancy," Saigh stated. "Television rights worth $1,000,000 today may be worth several million two or three years from now. Furthermore, signing such a contract so soon after his repudiation by the owners seems in bad taste." Wrigley, coming to the commissioner's defense, refuted Saigh's remark when he said, "It came as no surprise to me and shouldn't have to anybody else who was in the meeting. The commissioner discussed the matter at that time, mentioned the proposed figure and asked for opinions. There were no objections at that time and I don't see why there should be now."[42]

Indeed, if anything, the risk was on Gillette's part. They were gambling $7.3 million that the World Series would go more than the minimum four games in each year of their contract.[43] In reply to others who pointed to baseball's slipping attendance and criticized a close relationship between television and the game, Chandler replied that television was not causing the attendance drop, but instead it was the game's "archaic organization." Pointing to census figures showing wholesale population shifts in the United States, the commissioner noted that the great work now facing baseball was the need for "a competent and exhaustive study of the entire setup, to realign the baseball structure on modern lines. What we must have," he continued, "is the mechanism to develop the highest quality of baseball for the fans everywhere, a goal which is not possible with the disturbing distribution of power, from very strong to very weak, existing in so many leagues."[44]

The Gillette deal buoyed Chandler's supporters. Moreover, it allowed him to develop a strategy to regain the commissionership. First, Chandler was temporarily safe from being immediately ousted from office, because, at Judge Landis's insistence, it would take a 16-0 vote to abrogate his contract. Not long after the St. Petersburg vote, Horace Stoneham made it clear that he would cast a vote to block any attempt to annul Chandler's contract.[45] Second, with several owners still potentially behind him, the commissioner could create a stalemate by blocking any nomination put forth by the search committee appointed to find his successor. Third, Chandler sought to have his name reentered as a candidate for the position. As long as he was a candidate, potential aspirants would be loath to have their names considered for the job. With these factors in mind, Chandler decided to rally his support among owners already predisposed to him, to take his case to the public through a series of speeches, to persuade several owners who voted against him to support him, and, finally, to force a meeting at which his name would again be thrown into nomination.

The commissioner's office called the next meeting for March 12 at the Shoremede Hotel in Miami Beach. Convened ostensibly to submit a screened list of candidates to the owners, Chandlerites hoped that the meeting would turn out to be a successful referendum on his own candidacy. Florida was chosen as the site of the meeting because Chandler knew that Connie Mack, Walter Briggs, and Clark Griffith would all be able to attend this time. During the early winter months of 1951, Chandler hit the banquet circuit like the seasoned campaigner he was. He delivered speeches in Chicago, New York, and Boston—locations where he was the least popular with writers and owners. His speeches were perceived as an attempt to get the fans' backing on his behalf and to get them to persuade the owners of his popularity. In Boston, his presentation turned into a Chandler rally. In New York, in the presence of friend and foe alike, he told the audience that the American public is baseball's real board of directors and that during the previous two months, as long as baseball's strife had been up for a public airing, Americans wanted to obtain all of the facts. "Unfortunately," he noted, I have been able to give them only arguments for the defense; the full brief filed by the plaintiff has never been placed in my hands."[46]

Chandler's greatest champion among the owners was the outspoken Clark Griffith. Speaking of the opposition, the venerable Senators' owner complained, "They haven't yet cited a single reason why they want to impeach him. . . . The game is greater than the personal prejudices of the club owners, and we should never forget that we have the public to answer to." Griffith and Warren Giles in the National League coordinated attempts by Chandler loyalists to swing votes. In a letter to the commissioner in late January, Griffith wrote, "I have five clubs in the American League pledged and two more, which are St. Louis and Chicago, tell me that they will vote with the majority. Giles tells me that he only has four votes in the National League but he is working on Carpenter and O'Malley to see if he can't get them in line."[47] Also helping Chandler plot strategy was Pan American executive Roger Doulens. Doulens, whom Shirley Povich referred to as "Mr. Pan American," was an ardent baseball fan based in Washington. He volunteered to assist Chandler in hopes of gaining a job in the commissioner's office if Chandler was reelected.[48]

The owners most heavily targeted by Chandler forces were Bob Carpenter, the DeWitt brothers, Chuck Comiskey, and Lou Perini. Of these men, the most perplexing to Chandler was Carpenter. Although he denied that he was part of the leadership group that ousted Chandler, rumors that he voted against the commissioner in St. Petersburg took Chandler by surprise, because it was through Carter Glass, a friend of Robert R.M. Carpenter Sr., that Chandler learned in 1945 that he might be considered for the commissionership. Later, Carpenter Sr. warned Chandler, "You've got to watch these baseball people. They're all right—fine men—but some of them would cut your throat if they had a chance."[49] By early March 1951, from statements that he was making in the press, it looked as though Chandler forces had converted Carpenter. The young owner was quoted as saying that he had nothing against Chandler and that he had always been fair to the Phillies. In addition, Carpenter told sportswriter Joe Reichler shortly before the meeting, "I'm going to the meeting with an open mind. Unless some name sticks out as being far, superior to Chandler, I'm going to vote for him."[50]

Griffith was sure that the swing vote for Chandler would come from the DeWitt brothers and maintained that "They have assured me that they will go along with the American League majority. If they hold to their word, that means they will have to vote for Mr. Chandler's reelection."[51] In spite of Griffith's claims, William DeWitt recalled only being approached by Branch Rickey. "You know, he's a good Christian man," pleaded Rickey. "If you can influence the St. Louis vote, I think you ought to vote for him," he continued. DeWitt recalled that he did not make a commitment to Rickey.[52] With Bill Veeck in the picture as owner of the Browns, DeWitt's vote would also be his. According to Veeck, he instructed DeWitt to do whatever he wanted at the Miami Beach meeting. "We knew we had no way of saving Chandler," recalled Veeck. "He had no chance of winning."[53]

Comiskey was equally vexing to Chandler. Though his mother was a Chandler ally and general manager Frank Lane a good friend, he seemed to have little influence over the White Sox owner's son. "Father [Benedict] Dudley is contacting Chuck Comiskey directly," wrote Roger Doulens to Chandler in February. "We had been under the impression that he had been squared away and your information was disquieting. Frankly, my contacts with the White Sox are extremely weak. Also I negate the good Father's ultimate strength, insofar as Comiskey is concerned."[54] Chandler's own attempt to influence Comiskey may, however, have been his undoing. Comiskey made a courtesy call on Chandler while in Cincinnati to attend a draft meeting during early 1951, and Chandler pulled out a dossier on Fred Saigh, and said, "Here, read this!" Comiskey was taken aback. "I didn't go there to learn anything about anybody," said Comiskey angrily, "I just wanted to say hello. I'd never seen the Commissioner's Office." It "was right there," maintained John Carmichael of the *Boston Globe*, that "White Sox support of Chandler began to waver."[55]

Key portions of Chandler's dossier on Saigh were also leaked to sportswriter Vincent X. Flaherty, through whom, in a blatant attempt to discredit Saigh, they appeared in one of his pieces in the *Los Angeles Examiner*. The seventeen-page report contained information that did little to enhance Saigh's reputation. The dossier documented Saigh's business ventures, altercations, and lawsuits and his penchant for accumulating parking tickets. In addition, it noted that he clerked at Bass and Bass—a firm that specialized in serving mobsters in and around St. Louis and that he had first made news because of his association with Nellie Tipton Muenche, a courtesan and notorious blackmailer. The report also explored the mysterious financing that allowed Robert Hannegan and Saigh to purchase the Cardinals in 1947, but it only came to the conclusion that the two men were fronts for someone else. While Robert Boyle, the report's creator, may have been plowing fertile ground, the dossier contained circumstantial evidence at best.[56] Referring to Flaherty as a "Chandler stooge" and calling the entire episode a "smear campaign," Saigh told J. Roy Stockton, "The only construction I can place on the development is that Chandler finally realized that he has no chance of remaining in the commissioner's office."[57]

Boston sportswriter Bill Cunningham charged the Chandler campaign with using tactics against its foes that included bribery, character assassination, and anti-Semitism. He cited not only Flaherty's column but also a letter-writing campaign out of Kentucky that, in unspeakable language, attacked Fred Saigh, who is of Syrian descent, accusing him of being Jewish. Moreover, he claimed that Lou Perini was offered the option of returning to the lucrative St. Petersburg spring training site, if he would double-cross Fred Saigh and vote for Chandler.[58] Perini's failure to support Chandler was especially irksome to Doulens, who was a big Braves fan and an acquaintance of the Boston owner. In early February, Doulens wrote to Chandler, "I'm still the fatal optimist on the subject of Mr. Perini and hope to have some Christian talks with him in Bradenton within the next couple of weeks."[59]

Doulens and Chandler were also concerned about keeping their own loyalists from suggesting other candidates who might overshadow Chandler to the search committee. With men such as Fred Vinson, J. Edgar Hoover, and James A. Farley out of the competition, Chandler would still seem to be the best candidate for the position. When it appeared that Cleveland owner Ellis Ryan might suggest Ohioian Frank Lausche for the post, Doulens encouraged Chandler to call Ryan in Tucson. Noting that Ryan's wife was a Kentuckian, he wrote, "If Ryan's slip is beginning to show, let's put on some stronger elastic." Also noting that John Galbreath seemed interested in Ohio Senator John Bricker, Doulens told Chandler, "You can bet I'll work Mr. Galbreath over plenty when he gets to Miami Beach." The Pan American executive also expressed concern over Clark Griffith's statements. "He comes out with a positive, powerful statement in your behalf and then weakens it by about 50 percent," complained Doulens, "by saying 'if Chandler is not reelected, they will find themselves in a fight to name a new commissioner.' Don't let him concede an inch," he demanded.[60]

By the end of February, Chandler ceased making speeches and the opposition was uniformly quiet. As the day of the St. Petersburg meeting approached, reporters queried owners on their voting preferences. Those openly advocating Chandler for the job included Ellis Ryan of the Indians, Warren Giles of the Reds, Horace Stoneham of the Giants, and Billy Evans, who represented the Tigers. Even the vacillating Phil Wrigley seemed on board, when he was quoted as saying, "This is very serious business and it deserves open-minded consideration from all. We have a fine list of candidates and after looking them over, Chandler seems to be the best man." Moreover, Carpenter and DeWitt provided hope when they gave indications that they would attend the meeting with open minds. Finally, a hopeful Horace Stoneham noted, "I think Chandler's chances of reelection are brighter than ever right now."[61]

The great fear of the Chandler camp was that the vote would be a closed ballot. Without an open ballot, the owners were not accountable. "The game belongs to the fans," noted Griffith. "If the rascals will stand up and be counted so baseball fans the country over know how they voted, we will rectify the terrible mistake made at St. Petersburg." Griffith also employed his trump card—a threat to derail any attempt to elect a replacement for Chandler, exclaiming, "The situation is reversed this time. At St. Petersburg they needed only five votes to deny Chandler a new contract. At Miami, they'll need 12 to install another man and we have the votes to stop them."[62]

Major-league owners gathered at Miami Beach on March 11 to hold separate league meetings on the commissioner's post. The anti-Chandler camp laid their groundwork well as they persuaded a majority of owners to consider only Chandler's name on a ballot at their joint major-league meeting the following day. Moreover, their argument that the owners should vote by secret ballot, based on precedent set at their St. Petersburg vote and during Chandler's election in 1945, also carried. Both measures were passed in the American League, despite strong opposition from Griffith.[63] A joint statement was issued by the two leagues announcing the decisions. The results spelled disaster for the Chandler camp. Griffith reportedly told one friend, "We can't win now. Even Tom Yawkey has deserted us."[64] Nevertheless, Chandler forces were still trying to capture votes as late as the morning of March 12. According to Red Smith, opposition owners received calls from Chandler operatives, who were saying, "Look, Happy has 13 votes lined up, so its in the bag. Why don't you come over and make it 14 for the sake of appearances?"[65]

The joint meeting, held in the ballroom of the Shoremede, was almost anticlimactic. Perini was seen heartily shaking hands with Webb before it commenced. Chandler knew that the odds in favor of his reelection were long—in fact, it was rumored that friends had dissuaded him from re-signing the night before.[66] On his way to the meeting, he told a group of reporters that "the condemned man ate a hearty breakfast and proceeded to the guillotine."[67] After opening the meeting, Chandler turned the gath-ering over to Wrigley and left. Griffith again pleaded for an open ballot. Perini, however, carried the day, when he replied, "I did not campaign against the commissioner, although you all know I shall vote against him. I have never insulted your intelligence by trying to tell you how you should vote. How you vote is your business and for that reason we should have a closed vote." Only Griffith and Connie Mack, both of whom cham-pioned Chandler, spoke. Instead of the fiery speech some owners expected, Griffith gave an academic performance on the history of the commissioner-ship and said he would vote for Chandler.[68]

The vote, which again was 9-7, broke along similar lines when com-pared to the St. Petersburg balloting. In spite of all his lobbying and cam-paigning, Chandler was unable to convert the owners to his side. Webb, Saigh, Perini, DeWitt, and Carpenter are known to have voted against him. Of the three other likely candidates, Yawkey, Comiskey, and Wrigley, the latter seems most likely to have returned to Chandler's camp. Some contemporary accounts mentioned John Galbreath as a possible vote against Chandler, but this seems doubtful.[69] It was Galbreath who was dispatched by the owners to inform Chandler of their decision, to discuss their terms, and to bring him back to the meeting. Chandler considered him a friend—and it was Chandler's decision allowing horsemen to own ball clubs that allowed Galbreath to invest in the Pirates in the first place. Recognizing this, Perini readily admitted that the owners had sent Galbreath as their emissary to Chandler because he was a known sup-porter of the commissioner.[70] Finally, Galbreath, himself admitted that he was chosen to speak to Chandler because of their friendship.[71]

Chandler agreed to cooperate with the owners if they would allow Dick Butler and the rest of Chandler's staff to remain in baseball. The one exception was Walter Mulbry, whom the commissioner wanted fired. Chandler was convinced that Mulbry's perfidy had supplied his enemies with the ammunition that cost him his job, and he was intent on revenge. As the commissioner returned to the meeting, he told reporters, "We held the meeting on the home grounds. I wore my Confederate suit and a Texas hat. We gave them a battle, but that's the end of it."[72] Following his return, the commissioner addressed each owner with a moving fifteen-minute performance. According to DeWitt, Chandler discussed the accomplishments of his commissionership and then personally addressed each man in an attempt to get them to accede to his opinions.[73] At the end of his performance, with tears flowing down his cheeks, he asked the owners to withhold their announcement until he had time to call his family. "I had hoped to be reelected," he told reporters following the meeting, "but I don't want to embarrass the game of baseball by continuing an impossible situation. I had the majority of votes, but was a victim of the voting rules. Some of the men who said they would vote for me didn't tell me the truth."[74] Following the meeting, most of the owners shook hands with the commissioner. Only Carpenter and Perini openly told Chandler that they had not voted for him, and Perini simply said, "I'm sorry I couldn't see eye to eye with you, but the best of luck." As Chandler departed and other meeting participants dispersed, a victorious Fred Saigh was seen turning to speak into a television camera while Will Harridge busily gathered up all the torn ballots that had been carelessly left behind on the meeting table—such was the scene that ended Happy Chandler's baseball career.[75]

Although defeated, Chandler was determined to remain in office until a satisfactory settlement could be reached and a replacement could be chosen. Regardless of his wishes, however, other forces were at work. First, a spate of lawsuits, inspired by the Gardella case, were being filed to challenge the reserve clause. Subpoenas for information were eventually served on the commissioner's office in the Prendergast, Corbett, Kowalski, and Toolson suits. In addition, on May 18, 1951, Congressman Emanuel Celler announced that he was launching a congressional investigation into baseball's status as an entity exempt from antitrust laws. The investigation posed a potential threat to the reserve clause and to baseball's protected status based on the 1922 Holmes decision. Citing the recent cases against baseball, television and radio's increased presence, their vast farm systems, and other business activities that cross state boundaries, Celler noted that the committee would also examine the allegation that baseball was interstate commerce.[76]

Chandler's attorneys, John Lord O'Brian and W. Graham Claytor, urged Chandler to leave baseball as soon as possible. They feared that if Chandler waited much longer to resign, he would be drawn into the congressional investigation and that critics would claim he resigned under fire. Second, they argued that the longer he waited the more difficult it would be for him to obtain an equitable indemnity agreement from baseball—his bargaining power would be lessened. Finally, they maintained that if the Attorney General opposed an exemption for baseball or if a substantial number of congressmen came out against the reserve clause as a result of the investigation, many of the owners already hostile to Chandler might see him as a convenient scapegoat. Above all, they warned the commissioner that "if extreme caution is not used you may find yourself personally involved, not only in expense but endangered by damage suits of various sorts."[77]

Taking his attorneys' advice seriously, Chandler signed a severance contract with baseball on June 21, 1951. Under its terms, Chandler was indemnified by baseball against any legal actions against the game and was awarded $65,000 in severance pay—the sum he would have earned had he fulfilled his contract. In return, he volunteered to assist with baseball's defense in suits then pending against the game and to cooperate in the congressional investigation. Chandler left baseball much the way he entered the game. Following his last official act as commissioner, the dedication of a new stadium at Reading, Pennsylvania, on July 15, he sang "My Old Kentucky Home" to an audience of 5,000.[78]

Chandler's political acumen, applied with great success in Kentucky, failed him in baseball. Instead of cultivating Tom Yawkey and up-and-coming power brokers like Bob Carpenter and Walter O'Malley, he chose as his allies the grand old men of baseball—Connie Mack, Clark Griffith, and Walter Briggs. These were his heroes. It was also a group derisively referred to as "the horse and buggy class" by Cardinals' owner Fred Saigh.[79] Moreover, Chandler's support among many of the other owners was never particularly strong. Bill Veeck believed that most owners were basically ambivalent toward the commissioner and maintained that if Chandler's supporters had taken the initiative at St. Petersburg, "They'd have lined up enough votes to renew his contract before some owners who didn't care much one way or the other had committed themselves to the opposition."[80] Gordon Cobbledick of the *Cleveland Plain Dealer* postulated that the owners really did not want Chandler in the first place. After being railroaded by Larry MacPhail into hiring him, they spent the next six years talking about buying out his contract and putting in a man they really wanted. "If it all sounds slightly screwy," noted Cobbledick, "that's only because you don't know how the great game of baseball conducts its business. It was, to anyone familiar with the zany industry, perfectly normal."[81]

There were several other reasons why Chandler might fail an owners' litmus test. First, he was not the tractable defender of the owners' interests that many had envisioned. Tom Yawkey reportedly complained to his fellow owners that Chandler is "the players' commissioner, the fans' commissioner, the press and radio commissioner—everybody's commissioner but the men who pay him."[82] Second, Chandler jeopardized baseball's structure by not reinstating the Mexican League players when it became clear that the league was no longer a threat. Instead of finding a means of repatriating the jumpers, his hard stance invited lawsuits challenging the reserve clause. Though the Gardella case was settled out of court with minimal monetary damage, its notoriety spawned additional cases and a congressional investigation. Third, some owners felt that Chandler played favorites. A case in point involved his friendship with Frank McKinney of the Pittsburgh Pirates—the executive who championed Chandler's attempt at reelection in 1949. In 1950, Chandler approved the signing of pitching prospect Paul Pettit by the Pirates in what some owners thought was an apparent violation of the commissioner's own pet regulation, the high school signing rule. Pettit signed a contract with a Hollywood movie agent while still in high school. Bob Cooke, the sports editor of the *New York Herald-Tribune*, investigated the deal and alleged that the agent had consulted with McKinney during the summer of 1949— long before he signed Pettit. Thus, he acted as a sports agent—a clear violation of the rule.[83] According to Red Smith, the owners should have known better than to hire a politician as commissioner. "They went out and hired a man trained in the school of pork-barrel patronage and log-rolling politics," he noted. "Happy's entire experience was calculated to teach one lesson: reward your friends, blast your opponents."[84]

Chandler's greatest crime was that he alienated the wrong people. Knowledge that he was being investigated by Chandler was the last straw for Del Webb, who already associated the Kentuckian with MacPhail anyway. Webb was one of the strongest owners in baseball. It was his lobbying in the American League that ultimately sealed Chandler's fate. In a 1978 interview, Commissioner Bowie Kuhn succinctly summed up Chandler's demise when he stated, "Commissioner Chandler in carrying out his job, and he carried it out with courage, I believe, . . . created some animosity between himself and some people in baseball, and it showed up."[85] For an active and independent commissioner, the task of making rulings that adversely affect players, umpires, league presidents, and owners can easily become a dangerous one. This was especially true during the period 1945-84, when a commissioner needed the support of at least three-fourths of the owners to remain in office.

While Chandler's tenure as commissioner was at times tempestuous, his motives were sound and his integrity remained intact. His accomplishments are lasting ones. First, he presided over the game during one of its periods of greatest popularity. Attendance records were shattered in both the major and minor leagues.[86] Although he did not create the conditions necessary for the game's popularity, he unquestionably served as an able promoter of the game. Research in the commissioner's trip files verifies that he promoted baseball through hundreds of speeches across the country, in small towns as well as large cities.[87] In addition, he enhanced the game's image by diverting funds to support amateur base-

The commissioner with two young admirers in Rochester, New York. Tom Yawkey once complained to his fellow owners that Chandler was "the players' commissioner, the fans' commissioner, the press and radio commissioner— everybody's commissioner but the men who pay him." (Special Collections and Archives, University of Kentucky)

ball. Second, through his efforts, a contract was signed for television and radio rights to the World Series and All-Star games, which secured the players' pension plan. After his contract was terminated, there was con-siderable discussion among players of hiring Chandler—always regarded as a players' commissioner—as their own commissioner.[88]

Finally, Chandler's fair-mindedness compelled him to support the breaking of the color barrier. During spring training 1946, he told reporter Wendell Smith, "I think every boy in America who wants to play profes-sional baseball should have the chance, regardless of race, creed, or color. I have always said—and I repeat it now—that Negro players are wel-come in baseball."[89] The social impact of the breakthrough on segregated American society was enormous. Jackie Robinson's forum was second only to the American presidency, and even the president was not on view 154 times a year.

As commissioner, A.B. Chandler was neither a visionary nor a crusading reformer. He was at heart a baseball fan, a man who wanted to take the commissioner's position off its pedestal, to humanize it, and to share himself and the game with its followers. In this he succeeded admirably. Faced with difficult and even critical decisions during one of American history's most pivotal social eras, he let his conscience guide him. Although he took legal risks with his handling of the Durocher suspension and with the Gardella case, the Kentuckian met challenges with determination. A consistent friend of the athlete, Chandler was never the pliable officeholder some expected. To his credit, Chandler left the game in a stronger position than he found it. At the very least, he should be remembered as a good commissioner, a man who used his abilities to the utmost to imbue the game he loved with fairness and stability.

With Chandler eliminated as a candidate, the committee appointed to find his successor could now move forward unimpeded. Rejecting several candidates from a list that included Stuart Symington, George Trautman, Frank Lausche, Emmett "Rosey" O'Donnell, Milton Eisenhower, Douglas MacArthur, and J. Edgar Hoover, the owners finally settled on two of their own—Reds' president Warren Giles and Ford Frick, president of the National League. When the owners seemed hopelessly deadlocked between the two, Giles suddenly withdrew, clearing the way for Frick's election. Frick, whose chief adherent was Walter O'Malley, was seen by his backers as a man whose baseball background would enable him to heal the rift in the owners' ranks caused by the Chandler upheaval, whose knowledge of the game would allow him to avoid pitfalls, as someone who would be good at public relations, and above all as a loyalist who would support their interests. Frick did not disappoint them. After being unanimously elected, he indicated his thanks and stated that "he would back them 100 percent."

With Frick in office, the owners were blessed with a known quantity who possessed such admirable traits as stability, predictability, flexibility, and a penchant for keeping baseball's counsel with his pat reply, "That's a league matter." Frick was a company man who, in uninspiring fashion, presided over the game from 1951 through 1965. Instead of facing the major issues of the day, such as increased competition from other sports and leisure activities, labor relations, reserve clause challenges, realignment and expansion, the demise of the minor leagues, attendance issues, and the rise of television, he allowed the owners to run amok. As historian David Voight noted, "At a time when critical leadership was needed, Frick offered none."[90] Many of the gains of the Pivotal Era were squandered, including the goodwill between owners and players, the game's great popularity across the country, the ability to harness broadcasting, and the opportunity to develop a plan that would provide quality baseball across the country. The proverbial voice in the wilderness, Clark Griffith, warned his fellow owners when he said, "Those who want Frick or a big business man forget that the commissioner is not merely an employee of the major-league club owners. The commissioner represents the fans, he represents the players, he represents the game. I want a strong national figure. I want the big stick. I am against saddling the new commissioner with a board of directors, and making just a phony figurehead out of him."[91] Of course, they did not listen.

20

1951: "The Shot Heard 'Round the World"

A mixed chorus of boos and cheers greeted President Harry S Truman as he threw out the ceremonial first pitch at the Senators' home opener on April 20, 1951. It was the president's first major appearance in public since he removed General Douglas MacArthur from his command in Korea and the Far East. His reception at Griffith Stadium was in stark contrast to the ticker-tape parades and hero's welcome accorded MacArthur during the previous week and marked the first time a U.S. president was heckled at a baseball game since Herbert Hoover was met with the chant of "We want beer" during the 1931 World Series in Philadelphia. MacArthur himself used baseball as a political venue, making appearances at all three of New York's ballparks a few weeks later. As the hero of the hour, he was accorded a box draped with a five-star flag and entered and departed to the tune of the old barracks ballad "Old Soldiers Never Die"—a reference to his famous speech to a Joint Session of Congress only days before. Baseball showered the general and his family with gifts, including a gold lifetime pass to Dodgers games, orchids for Mrs. MacArthur, Charley Dressen's cap, a Giants windbreaker, and two autographed baseballs from Leo Durocher for nine-year-old Arthur MacArthur. Furthermore, when young Arthur arrived at Yankee Stadium, he was seen clutching a glove given to him by Joe DiMaggio. In an address before the game, MacArthur said, "It has been many years since I saw the Yankees play and two names I knew well are now missing—Babe Ruth and Lou Gehrig. Unlike the old soldier. . . these men died. But American sports fans never will let their memories fade away."[1]

While Truman stewed over MacArthur's popularity, the Korean conflict was beginning to have an impact on baseball. Although not at its apex, the military draft stripped the game of several young stars, including Curt Simmons, Art Houtteman, and Whitey Ford, and it was beginning to make itself felt in the minor leagues as well. Baseballs were also in short supply because the government curtailed civilian use of horsehide. Baseball, which contracted for 10,000 dozen balls in 1950, possessed an adequate supply for 1951 but now encouraged fans to return balls hit into the stands so that they could be sent to the armed forces. In many ballparks, fans who refused to return foul balls were strenuously booed. In addition, the government's Wage Stabilization Board ruled that baseball salaries were not exempt from regulation and that teams could not pay their players more than their top salaried player received during the previous year. Thus, Stan Musial was unable to collect a $25,000 raise over his 1950 salary of $50,000. The ruling penalized players on clubs in which the salaries of the highest-paid player was comparatively low. For instance, Giants Eddie Stanky and Larry Jansen could not receive raises exceeding the $30,000 top salary Bobby Thomson received in 1950.

America's political climate also reached a repressive and intolerant state in 1951. With the loss of China to the Communists, the revelations and charges of subversion and treason intensified by the Hiss and Rosenberg scandals, the threat of global war against Communism manifested by the Korean conflict, and the specter of self-recrimination raised in Congress by Joseph McCarthy and his followers, few Americans or American institutions escaped the Red Scare. Any idea even remotely identified with Soviet philosophy or noncapitalistic enterprise could be discredited simply through guilt by association. For instance, when Cardinals owner Fred Saigh suggested that visiting teams should share in the profits from home television agreements, Walter O'Malley, who would stand to lose the most if the idea was adopted, labeled the proposal "socialistic." Why doesn't Fred go all the way with his socialism?" continued the sarcastic O'Malley. "Why doesn't he continue the thought, and call for an equalization of players' salaries, no matter where they play? To be logical, why does he not demand a common treasury, with all clubs share and share alike?"[2] O'Malley's ridicule of Saigh effectively closed the issue.

Most unexpected were O'Malley's own labor difficulties with the Dodger Sym-Phony—a group of unpaid musicians who had entertained Dodgers fans for thirteen seasons with their disharmonious behavior. During the 1951 season, Local 802 of the American Federation of Musicians charged that the nonunion members of the Sym-Phony were unfairly competing with union artists. A union official even offered to recruit union members who would play "even lousier than the Sym-Phony."

Table 14. Final Major-League Regular-Season Standings, 1951

American League					National League			
	W	L	%	G.B.		W	L	%	G.B.
New York	98	56	.636	–	New York	98	59	.624	–
Cleveland	93	61	.604	5	Brooklyn	97	60	.618	1
Boston	87	67	.565	11	St. Louis	81	73	.526	15 1/2
Chicago	81	73	.526	17	Boston	76	78	.494	20 1/2
Detroit	73	81	.474	25	Philadelphia	73	81	.474	23 1/2
Philadelphia	70	84	.455	28	Cincinnati	68	86	.442	28 1/2
Washington	62	92	.403	36	Pittsburgh	64	90	.416	32 1/2
St. Louis	52	102	.338	46	Chicago	62	92	.403	34 1/2

O'Malley reacted by declaring that the Sym-Phony was part of the fans' self-expression and that he would not pay its members a nickel. When Brooklyn fans learned of the union's demands, the Dodgers received hundreds of letters in protest. Later the union backed down, claiming that it really just wanted the Sym-Phony's two union members to stop violating union rules by playing with the group. O'Malley retaliated by proclaiming August 13 "Music Appreciation Night" at Ebbets Field and offered free tickets to fans accompanied by a musical instrument. The evening was a booming success, as more than 2,400 fans brought their instruments and even succeeded in drowning out the newly reconstituted (without its two union members) Dodger Sym-Phony with their self-expression.[3]

The Browns were singing a different tune as St. Louis native Helen Traubel, a renowned Wagnerian soprano who made her debut at the Met in 1939, bought a small interest in the team. "I love those Browns," Traubel told reporters. "It's a team I have followed since my childhood and one which will get the crowds again, once it begins to win regularly. And it's going to do that even though I may have to go out and find a few infielders and pitchers."[4] Less sanguine about the Browns' chances was former Cleveland owner Bill Veeck, who began 1951 by making his acting debut as a member of the cast of "The Man Who Came to Dinner" at Cleveland's Hanna Theatre. When the play folded after one week, because of poor attendance, Veeck was out of another job but as usual not at a loss for words. Comparing the play with the Browns, he said, "It was like a day game in St. Louis—strictly for park employees and friends." With regard to his own performance, he noted, "It was like putting Sarah Bernhardt in at second base. Everybody would be incensed. The theater people would think she was out of place there and the baseball people would know she was." Adding that the theatre had no hold on his interests, he admitted, however, that "baseball still has."[5]

Although at that time few reporters realized that Bill Veeck had his sights on the Browns, even Veeck's wizardry would prove incapable of lifting the team out of last place in 1951. At the other end of the standings were the Yankees, who outlasted Cleveland in the American League, and the New York Giants, who beat the Dodgers in a best-of-three playoff series after overtaking Brooklyn in one of the most remarkable pennant races of the century.

The American League Pennant Race

The last-place St. Louis Browns were so dismal that by late May they were already 17½ games out of first place, and attendance was paltry. A small five-car parking lot in front of a house near Sportsman's Park illustrated the team's plight. When the Cardinals played, the lot was full. But when the Browns played, the woman who collected money for the parking lot used the property to hang out her laundry.[6]

The team's only bona fide star was pitcher Ned Garver, a young farm boy from Ney, Ohio, who at 20-12 in 1951 became the first pitcher in major-league history to win twenty games for a team that lost more than a hundred games in a season. Furthermore, he was the first pitcher to win twenty for a last-place team since Hollis Thurston did it for the White Sox in 1924.[7] Of the team's first twenty-four wins, Garver took credit for twelve. "I think the team had more confidence on days I pitched," recalled Garver. "I think they felt that if they scored some runs, that had a chance to win." Nevertheless, winning twenty games for a team of the Browns' caliber (they finished last in hitting at .247 and fielding at .971) was an amazing feat. With only four starts left, Garver's record was only 16-12. Garver won his next three starts and then pitched against the White Sox in the season finale. With the game tied 4-4 in the sixth inning, Garver homered over the center-field fence. Noting that it was one of the biggest thrills of his life, he remembered, "I saw that ball disappear into the bleachers over the Sealy Mattress sign. I said to myself, 'There you've got it, now make it hold up. You've got it—now make it stand up!'"[8]

The greatest excitement in St. Louis, however, was the arrival of Bill Veeck on July 4. After acquiring more than 75 percent of the team's stock from the more than 1,400 stockholders, Veeck began to work his magic. He set off fireworks, signed holdout Frank Saucier, brought in pitcher

Ned Garver became the first pitcher in major-league history to win twenty games for a team that lost more than a hundred games in a season. Garver won his twentieth on the last day of the season with a sixth-inning home run. (George Brace Photo)

Bill Veeck threatened to shoot midget Eddie Gaedel if he dared swing at a pitch. Gaedel's work with the Browns gained him instant fame and many more appearances. (*The Sporting News*)

Satchel Paige, hired comics Jackie Price and Max Patkin, persuaded the fire department to hose down Sportsman's Park, and, with his wife Mary Frances, went on perpetual tour to drum up business wherever speaking engagements could be arranged. Veeck would introduce his topic by apologizing for his team but promising a much better edition the following year, as he stated, "We've got rid of half our players and we mean to get rid of the rest as soon as possible."[9]

It was on the occasion of the American League's fiftieth birthday that Veeck pulled off the most infamous stunt in baseball history. During the break between a double-header with the Tigers on August 19, 1951, Veeck served ice cream and cake to those in attendance and entertained them with juggling and tumbling acts, Max Patkin's contortions, and old cars and fireworks. Then, the Browns' owner rolled out a huge birthday cake and, to the delight of the crowd, out popped little Eddie Gaedel, a 3'7" 65-pound midget attired in a Browns uniform bearing number ⅛ . But Veeck was not finished. The Browns' owner schemed to replicate James Thurber's story, "You Can Look It Up," in which a midget is sent to the plate with the bases loaded.[10] Veeck signed Gaedel to an official American League contract for $100 a game and mailed it to Will Harridge's

Although pitcher Bob Cain was amused by the stunt, he recalled that he "just lobbed them up there and some of them would have been a strike to an ordinary man." (George Brace Photo)

office the evening before the Detroit double-header. Then, with only a handful of team officials, including manager Zack Taylor, in his confidence, he sent Gaedel to the plate to bat for Saucier in the bottom half of the first inning. Home-plate umpire Ed Hurley was understandably perplexed. "What should I do?" he asked crew chief Joe Paparella. "I don't know," he replied. "If he is under contract in the last forty-eight hours, you have to let him hit because there is nothing in the American League regulations or rules that you have to have size to play ball. But, maybe he's not under contract, let's find out."[11] When Taylor produced a valid contract and a copy of Veeck's telegram to American League headquarters announcing Gaedel's addition to the Browns' roster, Hurley reluctantly waved the midget into the batter's box.

Although he was shocked by Gaedel's appearance, "we thought it was amusing at the time," recalled Tiger pitcher Bob Cain. Catcher Bob Swift, who attempted to play along, got down on his knees, placed one hand on the ground, put his head on his hand and held his glove up as a target. Hurley, who was not noted for his good humor, forced Swift off the ground. "I was kind of leery of throwing too hard," recalled Cain. "So I just lobbed them up there and some of them would have been a strike to an ordinary man. But, with the way Bill Veeck taught him to spread his feet out and bend over like DiMaggio, why, I didn't have much of a strike zone."[12] Veeck, who threatened to shoot Gaedel if he dared swing at a pitch, breathed a sigh of relief when he walked on four pitches. After he was replaced by pinch runner Jim Delsing, Gaedel took a leisurely departure, repeatedly waving his cap in the air to a crowd of 18,000 cheering fans. Shaken by the event, Cain walked another batter and gave up a hit before he regained his composure to prevail in the game by a 6-2 score.

On the following day, Will Harridge banned the use of midgets and announced that Gaedel's "participation in an American League championship game comes under the heading of conduct detrimental to baseball." "I am criticized and overruled after all my efforts and hard work," replied Veeck in half-mockery. "They [league executives] say I am embarrassing the American League by drawing crowds to Browns' games at Sportsman's Park, a baseball graveyard for several years."[13] Gaedel's appearance with the Browns catapulted him into instant fame and netted him several thousand dollars from subsequent appearances. The added income proved a nice supplement to the checks he received as a Chicago office worker with the *Drover's Daily Journal*.

When Veeck returned to the American League, he announced that the Browns would remain in St. Louis. "I have come here to accept a challenge and the Browns are it." He then noted, "Let me assure you that we have no plans to disturb the Cardinals either. This city is big enough to support two major-league teams. We'll go along minding our own business and in no way will we interfere with the operation of the Cards." Nevertheless, as he admitted in *Veeck—as in Wreck*, the new Browns owner realized that St. Louis was unable to support two teams. Moreover, he fully intended to drive the Cardinals out of town—a situation that placed the two teams at loggerheads for the next two years.[14] Only fate, in the form of the forced sale of Fred Saigh's interest in the Cardinals to August Busch, interfered with Veeck's dream.

The seventh-place Washington Senators captured ten of their first thirteen games behind the surprise pitching of Conrad Marrero and Sandy Consuegra. Nevertheless, injuries and tired arms took their toll as the season progressed, and only the acquisition of ex-Yankees Don Johnson (3.95, 7-11) and Bob Porterfield (3.24, 9-8) saved them from disaster. Regulars

Mickey Vernon (.293-9-87), Eddie Yost (.283-12-65), and Gil Coan (.303-9-62) all had respectable years, but with one of the weakest benches in the league, the team could not recover from the loss of outfielder Irv Noren (.279-8-86), who was disabled with a broken jaw.

A key injury also derailed the Philadelphia Athletics, who lost first baseman Ferris Fain (.344-6-57) when, in a fit of anger after popping out, he broke his foot kicking first base. Excellent seasons were enjoyed by pitcher Bobby Shantz (3.94, 18-10), infielder Eddie Joost (.289-19-78), and outfielders Elmer Valo (.302-7-55) and Gus Zernial (.268-33-129). Zernial, who was acquired from the White Sox early in the season, led the American League in home runs and runs batted in. His first six home runs were hit in pairs in three consecutive games to tie a record set by Yankee great Tony Lazzeri.

Injuries, a depleted pitching staff, and a lack of fresh talent were all reasons why the Detroit Tigers slipped into fifth place in 1951. George Kell (.319-2-59) missed several games because of a fractured finger; with the exception of Vic Wertz (.285-27-94), Tiger outfielders went into a prolonged slump; and staff pitching ace Art Houtteman and top pitching prospect Ray Herbert were both drafted by the military. To make matters worse Hal Newhouser (3.92, 6-6), who won his first four starts, went down with a sore arm. With the Tigers slumping badly, former Tiger great Charley Gehringer was named to replace Red Rolfe as manager.

Ensconced in first place as late as mid-July, the Chicago White Sox created the most excitement in the American League race. General manager Frank Lane pulled off a brilliant three-team trade to acquire outfielder Minnie Minoso (.324-10-74) from Cleveland. Minoso, a Cuban native, was a complete player who could field, hit, and run. In one game against the Red Sox he scored on a ball hit to Dom DiMaggio only thirty feet behind second base. Failing to heed the third base coach's protest to stop, Minoso yelled over his shoulder, "Too late, too late, I gone." When startled catcher Matt Batts went to make the tag on the speeding runner, all he got was air as Minoso slid across the plate.[15]

With a team to his liking, cerebral manager Paul Richards noted, "We haven't many stars, but we do have a hustling, fast, running ball team, and we have a chance."[16] In May the White Sox put together a fourteen-game winning streak that captured the imagination of pennant-starved Chicago fans. Minoso and outfielder Jim Busby (.283-5-68) combined to steal fifty-seven bases to help the White Sox lead the American League in that category. Other players having good years included Eddie Robinson (.282-29-117), acquired from the Senators, pitcher and American League earned-run-average leader Saul Rogovin (2.48, 11-7), and smooth south-paw Billy Pierce (3.03, 15-14). The team's double play combination was the best in the American League. Second baseman Nellie Fox adopted a bottleneck bat, which allowed him to spray balls to all fields and give Phil Rizzuto competition as the league's premier bunter. Flashy short-stop Chico Carrasquel so impressed Casey Stengel that he jokingly attributed his skills to the fact that he could understand only a little English and therefore missed all of the bad advice that usually confused most young players.

The White Sox bubble burst in late July as the team collapsed after losing a four-game series to the Washington Senators. Having led the league by a game at the All-Star break, the Sox trailed Cleveland, New York, and Boston by 2½ at the end of the month. Though they were able to get no closer, they established a new Comiskey Park attendance record, at 1,328,324, and broke the million mark for the first time in their long history.

In spite of crippling injuries to Walt Dropo, Vern Stephens, Bobby Doerr, and Lou Boudreau, the Boston Red Sox found themselves only three games out with eight games left in the season. Unfortunately, they lost all of their remaining games, to finish eleven behind the Yankees. The season began with Ted Williams (.318-30-126) as the biggest question mark. The left-elbow injury suffered in the 1950 All-Star game continued to bother him. Although he started the season slowly, he went on a hitting binge in May that included a seven-for-thirteen day (a homer, triple, three doubles, and five runs batted in) as the Red Sox swept a Memorial Day double-header against the Yankees. Through July 16, Williams was hitting .338 and led the league in runs batted in with eighty.

Other players made major contributions during the team's pennant surge. During May, outfielder Dom DiMaggio (.296-12-72) put together a twenty-seven-game hitting streak (the second-longest of his career), and Clyde Vollmer's sixteen-game hitting streak helped carry the Red Sox in July. Vollmer (.251-22-85) drove in sixteen runs during the streak and had key hits that led to seven straight Red Sox wins. Pitchers Mel Parnell (3.26, 18-11) and Ellis Kinder (2.55, 11-2) also had outstanding seasons. Kinder, now used almost exclusively in relief, led the league in saves with fourteen and in appearances with sixty-three.

The second-place Cleveland Indians had great pitching, but finished seventh in the league in hitting with a .256 team average. Cleveland's pitching was sensational in July, as they won twenty-two of twenty-seven. Then, in August the Indians put together a twelve-game winning streak, enabling them to maintain a slim lead over the Yankees. After having their winning streak stopped 4-0 by Tommy Byrne of the Browns, Al Lopez lamented, "If our big fellows start hitting we could crack this thing wide open."[17] Such was not the case however, as Luke Easter (.270-27-103) suffered from recurring leg injuries, and sluggers Al Rosen (.265-24-102) and Larry Doby (.295-20-69) failed to equal their 1950 numbers. Indians hitters provided only seven runs in five contests with the Yankees and Red Sox in late August. Nevertheless, the team was still in the race as late as mid-September, when, leading New York by one game, they dropped a two-game series to the Yankees. Thereafter, New York won nine of their next twelve, and Cleveland finished in second place, five games behind, after dropping five of their next eight games.

Cleveland was led by Bob Feller (3.50, 22-8), who won more than twenty games for the sixth time and pitched the third no-hitter of his career, against Detroit, on July 1, 1951. Feller became only the third pitcher to throw three no-hitters and the first to throw all three in the twentieth century.[18] Furthermore, Cleveland had two other twenty-game winners in Mike Garcia (3.15, 20-13) and Early Wynn (3.02, 20-13), making them the first club since the 1931 Athletics to have three twenty-game winners in a season. Rounding out Cleveland's big four was Bob Lemon (3.52, 17-14), who was considered by many to be one of the toughest pitchers in the league to hit.

Uncertainty also plagued the New York Yankees at the beginning of the 1951 season. Whitey Ford was in the service, Bobby Brown was scheduled to be called to active duty, the team had an ineffective bullpen and no regular first baseman, Joe DiMaggio's career was in doubt, and Stengel was about to put two rookies, named Mantle and McDougald, into his starting lineup. With Brown a question mark, rookie Gil McDougald (.306-14-63) was tapped to battle veteran Billy Johnson for third base. McDougald, the 1950 Texas League's Most Valuable Player, was so impressive that Johnson was traded to the Cardinals, and, when Brown discovered he would not have to serve in the military in 1951, the rookie was platooned between third and second. Elsewhere in the infield, Phil Rizzuto (.274-2-43) had a solid season, and first base was covered by committee (Joe Collins, Johnny Mize, and Johnny Hopp).

In the outfield, the season's story was switch-hitting Mickey Mantle (.267-13-65)—a nineteen year old from Commerce, Oklahoma, who in 1950 at Joplin, Missouri, had terrified class C Western League pitchers by hitting .383 with 26 home runs and 136 runs batted in.[19] Yankees general manager George Weiss, who was not enthused about rushing Mantle to the majors, failed to include money for the teenager's travel expenses with the letter ordering him to spring training camp in mid-February 1951. Mantle, who needed the money, simply continued to work as an electrician's assistant in a Commerce lead-zinc mine. As February began to wane, and he had heard nothing from the Yankees, his friends in the mine teased him that he could not "trust them dead gummed carpetbaggers from Noo York." When the rookie failed to show up at spring training, Yankees farm director Lee MacPhail, who could not reach Mantle because the family had no telephone, asked some newspapermen to locate him. They did, and the next day Mantle's picture, depicting him in overalls with a smile across his smudged face, appeared on the Associated Press wire accompanied by a story that proclaimed, "I haven't gotten my ticket yet."[20]

The embarrassed Yankees quickly dispatched scout Tom Greenwade, the man who signed Mantle, to Commerce with the expense money. A couple of months later, after Mantle's impressive spring training, J.G. Taylor Spink wrote in the *Sporting News*, "Here was a youngster worth a fortune as a ball player, yet the Yankees had neglected to ask him about his financial situation and had permitted him to go 400 feet underground, in the damp and cold, to work as an assistant electrician for something like $40 a week. An advance would have tided Mickey over."[21]

Under the tutelage of coach Tommy Henrich, Mantle readily adapted to a switch from the infield to the outfield. In addition, tremendous shots, including a 430-foot line drive off the center-field wall at Los Angeles's Wrigley Field, awakened the Yankees to Mantle's offensive potential. Mantle's raw skills—particularly his great speed and his powerful hitting—so impressed Stengel that the Yankees manager was determined to keep him with the team. Even Joe DiMaggio was moved by Mantle's performance. "Mickey Mantle is the greatest prospect I can remember," he stated. "Maybe he has to learn something about catching a fly ball, but, that's all. He can do everything else. If he's good enough to take my job, I can always move over to right or left."[22] Later, when asked by sports writer Frank Graham whether Mantle reminded DiMaggio a little of Arky Vaughan, the Yankee Clipper replied tersely, "He doesn't remind me of Vaughan or anybody else. I never saw anybody like him before."[23]

In spite of his excellent early season performance, Mantle was awed by his surroundings. After leading the Yankees in home runs and runs batted in, the rookie went into a horrendous slump in July. American League pitchers discovered that he would go after fastballs up and in and that, out of frustration, he would follow pitches out of the strike zone.[24] Moreover, the youngster's batting problems also caused him to lose his concentration in the field. With Mantle striking out at an alarming rate, the Yankees sent him down to Kansas City on July 12, where he languished until the end of August.

Although DiMaggio periodically gave Mantle instructions on where to play hitters, the two were not close. DiMaggio (.263-12-71) had troubles of his own. His attempt to reunite with his former wife Dorothy Arnold failed, his mother, Rosalie DiMaggio, passed away, he suffered from a series of physical disabilities, and his considerable talents were in decline. His shoulder still occasionally popped out, and he often was limited to one throw a game—a secret that other teams amazingly failed to discover. Pain was now his constant companion. He suffered from bad knees, a sore leg, and an arthritic back. To compensate, he dropped his bat and was hitting a lot of balls to right field. Once, when he hit a home run to right, he complained to teammate Billy Martin that "Anybody could hit a piss home run to right."[25] Moreover, pitchers discovered they could get him out with the slider. "He felt bad about it," Eddie Lopat told writer Maury Allen. "He knew he just couldn't handle the pitch." DiMaggio's struggles were evident to other teammates, including Rizzuto, who told Allen, "I used to watch him and it was agony for him just getting in and out of a taxicab.[26]

DiMaggio had warned everyone that 1951 might be his last year, but that did not make his season more palatable. As he struggled, he withdrew from his teammates and the media. Rumors that he was feuding with Casey Stengel surfaced in early July, after the manager replaced him in front of a large Boston crowd at the beginning of the second inning with the Yankees trailing the Red Sox 6-1. DiMaggio, who prided himself in cultivating reporters, now became almost unapproachable. "Nobody is trying to fire Joe," wrote Dan Daniel. "Nobody except Father Time, a terrible, soulless, vindictive guy."[27]

Fortunately for the Yankees, Yogi Berra (.294-27-88) stepped in to provide the team with clutch hitting and field leadership. The catcher also captured the American League's Most Valuable Player award. Hank Bauer (.296-10-54) and Gene Woodling (.281-15-71) also contributed in limited roles. The real success story of the 1951 Yankees was their pitching. From the Browns, George Weiss acquired Stubby Overmire, a little left-hander who was most effective if he pitched once a week, and from the Senators Bob Kuzava (3.61, 11-7), who performed well in both starting and relief roles. Rookie Tom Morgan (3.68, 9-3) ably replaced Whitey Ford, and the Yankees' big three of Eddie Lopat (2.91, 21-9), Vic Raschi (3.27, 21-10), and Allie Reynolds (3.05, 17-8) were outstanding.

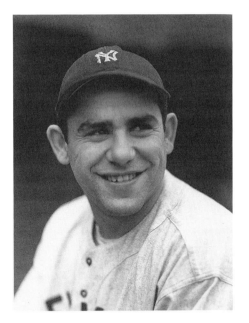

Catchers Yogi Berra and Roy Campanella won their leagues' Most Valuable Player awards. By 1951 Berra was a seasoned veteran whose clutch hitting and field leadership made him the dominant catcher in the American League. Roy Campanella, who combined great defense with a powerful swing, was the premier catcher in the National League. Quick and agile behind the plate, the Dodger threw out two-thirds of the runners who attempted to steal on him. (George Brace Photo; Photographic Archives, University of Louisville)

With Joe Page, who tore a muscle in his pitching arm in spring training, no longer with the club, Reynolds became the team's closer even though he hurled sixteen complete games in twenty-six starts. The dual role took its toll on Reynolds, who told interviewer Peter Golenback that "The muscles in my arm drew so tight that I couldn't put my hand in my pocket."[28] Reynolds also threw two no-hitters. The first was a 1-0 triumph over Cleveland's Bob Feller on July 12, with Gene Woodling's seventh-inning home run making the difference. His second no-hitter was an 8-0 triumph against the Boston Red Sox at Yankee Stadium during the first game of a double-header on September 28. In that game, Reynolds retired the last Red Sox batter, Ted Williams, twice, when catcher Yogi Berra failed to catch the first of two towering foul pop-ups.

Reynolds dominated his old team, the Cleveland Indians, all season by allowing them only two runs in thirty-six innings. The Indians were even more disgruntled when George Weiss provided the team with pennant insurance by sending prospect Lew Burdette and $50,000 to the Boston Braves for veteran Johnny Sain. Sain, who won his first start, a 3-1 victory over the Athletics, proved invaluable. For Indians manager Al Lopez, 1951 would be the first of nine times that one of his teams would finish second to the Yankees.

The National League Pennant Race

The Chicago Cubs successfully battled the Pirates for last place, although through May they were a surprise contender, trailing the Dodgers by only 3½ games. An extended losing streak in June dropped them out of contention and into seventh place. Severe injuries to infielders Roy Smalley and Bill Serena were serious handicaps. Hank Sauer (.263-30-89) led the team in hitting after the All-Star break. On the mound the Cubs were led by steady right-hander Bob Rush (3.83, 11-12) and veteran knuckleballer Dutch Leonard (2.64, 10-4), who won most of his games in relief. Cubs manager Frankie Frisch could not withstand the team's poor performance and was replaced by first baseman Phil Cavarretta on July 21. During the final ten days of his tenure, Frisch was ejected four times by umpires, including three straight days in Brooklyn. Owner Phil Wrigley was not amused.

The Pittsburgh Pirates were dreadful, but with Branch Rickey in charge, certainly not boring. Rickey promised that the Pirates would be adventurous and more respectable than in 1950. But, as adventurous as he tried to be, as biographer Murray Polner noted, "The truth was that his old wiz-ardry had become obsolete."[29] Rickey's success was copied by everyone. There was simply no new way to gain an edge, and there was no quick fix. The Pirates' farm system was almost threadbare, and the team roster was full of deadwood. At first, money flowed freely. John Galbreath bought Rickey and his staff a $150,000 airplane, and bonus contracts totaling $496,000 were offered to youngsters such as Paul Pettit during Rickey's first eleven months.[30] Indeed, Pettit's $100,000 contract covered Pettit's wedding, which included a honeymoon in Hawaii and $750 in expense money. Older players, primarily from the Cardinals and Dodgers, were acquired in a constant stream.[31] Rickey the innovator and mechanic contin-ued to tinker, as he introduced the batting tee and a cradle—a cage that sprayed balls in different directions and was designed to replace the game of pepper. In addition, he was still in the business of molding and shaping players. "He liked the married player," recalled infielder Pete Castiglione. "He figured they would be more family, they would stick to their condi-tioning and would live a normal life [instead of being] out in bars trying to pick up women."[32] In his spring-training lecture on marriage, he called the single men on the team "matrimonial cowards" and even offered infielder Stan Rojek $1,000 if he would get married.[33]

In spite of Rickey's efforts, little that he did seemed to work. He tried to convert Ralph Kiner into a first baseman, he gave first baseman Dale Long three different catcher's gloves, and he attempted to challenge mild-mannered catcher Ed Fitz Gerald to take charge of the team by offering a $100 reward any time he punched an opposing player in the nose—all to no avail. The team's reputation was so low that when crooner Bing Crosby had difficulty gaining admittance to a spring training game because an attendant did not recognize him, one wag wrote, "passes are about the only dividend Bing can collect for his $250,000 investment in the Pirates."[34]

In spite of their seventh-place finish, the Pirates did have some bright spots. Outfielder Gus Bell went five for five against Cincinnati Reds ace Ewell Blackwell on April 22, including a home run, three doubles, and a single—the first time Cincinnati writers could remember anyone going five for five off Blackwell. Fans could catch a glimpse of the team's future as outfielder Frank Thomas made his major-league debut and pitchers Bob Friend (4.27, 6-10) and Vern Law (4.50, 6-9) were paired for the first time. Right-hander Murry Dickson (4.02, 20-16) carried the team much of the year, racking up more than 30 percent of the Pirates' victories. Finally, perennial slugger Ralph Kiner (.309-42-109) again led the league in home runs, slugging average (.627), and runs scored (124) and established a new

National League record for bases on balls with 137. Nevertheless, he failed to finish the season with his accustomed rush of home runs, and for the first time in several seasons, Kiner's bat was not a sufficient reason to come watch the Pirates. Consequently, attendance was off by 16 percent, falling below a million for the first time in since 1946.

Pitchers Ewell Blackwell (3.45, 16-15) and Ken Raffensberger (3.44, 16-17) were the only standouts on the sixth-place Cincinnati Reds. Raffensberger threw a 7-0 one-hitter against the Cubs on September 2 in the first game of a double-header. Bobby Adams charged a grounder that might have rolled foul had he let it go and missed Eddie Miksis on close play at first in third inning. Raffensberger, who threw only sixty-nine pitches in the game, was almost nominated by manager Luke Sewell to start the second contest of the twin bill. Although their pitchers finished second in the league in shutouts, the Reds' .248 team average placed them last in hitting. Through July 17, the Reds made only one roster move, dispatching rookie Wally Post to Buffalo and acquiring Barney McCosky from the A's.

Although pitchers Robin Roberts (3.03, 21-15) and Bubba Church (3.53, 15-11) and outfielder Richie Ashburn (.344-4-63) turned in strong performances, the 1950 National League champion Philadelphia Phillies finished below .500 and tumbled into fifth place. Starting slowly, the team languished in seventh place through the beginning of June, and by mid-July they were all but eliminated from the race. Their downfall could be attributed to Curt Simmons's loss to the service, injuries to Andy Seminick, Dick Sisler, and Del Ennis, and reliever Jim Konstanty's ineffectiveness. With eleven families expecting or having just added newborns, one writer even intimated that the Phillies' domestic situation might have been a contributing cause.[35] Nevertheless, Eddie Sawyer made no alibis for the team. When asked early in the season about their chances of repeating, he said simply, "We aren't good enough."[36]

In spite of a quick start out of the gate, the Boston Braves faltered and again finished in fourth place. Manager Billy Southworth resigned in June and was replaced by veteran outfielder Tommy Holmes. With the exception of Sam Jethroe (.280-18-65), the Braves were still ponderous and slow and largely depended on the home run power provided by Earl Torgeson (.263-24-92), Bob Elliott (.285-15-70), Sid Gordon (.287-29-109), and Walker Cooper (.313-18-59). Shortstop was also a weakness, since neither Buddy Kerr nor rookie Johnny Logan could generate much offense. Finally, Braves pitching also suffered when sore-armed Johnny Sain proved ineffective and Vern Bickford (3.12, 11-9) broke a finger in August. Nevertheless, rookie Chet Nichols (2.88, 11-8) led the league in earned run average, and Warren Spahn (2.98, 22-14) was the league leader in complete games (26) and finished second in strikeouts (164) and innings pitched (311). The Braves' major concern was their precipitous 48 percent drop in attendance. Moreover, the 1951 figure of 487,475 represented only a little more than a third of the Red Sox's attendance of 1.3 million. The team printed up 23,000 questionnaires to be handed out to fans asking for their suggestions on how rebuild fan interest in the Braves, but it was readily apparent to all that the National League's days in Boston were numbered.

The Cardinals again depended on a veteran cast to carry them into third place in 1951. Red Schoendienst (.289-6-54) and Enos Slaughter (.281-4-64) were steady as usual, and superstar Stan Musial (.355-32-108) had a gigantic year to lead the league in batting average, triples (12), and total bases (355). In the infield, Billy Johnson (.262-14-64), acquired from the Yankees, temporarily solved the team's third base problem, and rookie Solly Hemus (.281-2-32) proved a solid substitute for new manager Marty Marion at shortstop. After pitcher Gerry Staley (3.81, 19-13) no other member of the Cardinals' pitching staff recorded more than eleven victories. Marion, who was impatient with ineffective hurlers, substituted according to the situation and often pitched his starters in relief or out of turn. Cliff Chambers (4.38, 14-12), who pitched a 3-0 no-hitter against the Braves on May 6, 1951, while with Pittsburgh, also proved effective in spots.

The Giants-Dodger interborough rivalry reached its peak in 1951. Baseball in Brooklyn was a religion—a part of the community's fabric. Giant fans, however, were scattered all over the remainder of the city and its suburbs. When the two teams met, sparks flew. "We didn't even talk to those fellows," recalled Bobby Thomson. "We would pass them and would hardly nod to them. Gil Hodges was the only Dodger player that everybody felt was—well, he was a very fine person."[37] Dodger unfriendliness toward the Giants was just as intense but tended to be directed toward their ex-manager Leo Durocher. When beanball wars erupted between the two teams, it was Durocher who was blamed. After one beanball incident, Brooklyn outfielder Carl Furillo actually charged the Giants' dugout in an attempt to get at Durocher. "I didn't hate the ballplayers," he told interviewer Peter Golenback, "I hated Durocher. I hated his guts."[38] Durocher's demeanor on the third-base coaching line and the knowledge that he would do almost anything to win added fuel to the fire.

The Dodgers were the class of the National League in 1951. They featured an All-Star lineup with Roy Campanella (.325-33-108) behind the plate,

By 1950 and 1951, Duke Snider was putting up numbers in sufficient quantities to live up to Branch Rickey's prediction that the young outfielder would be the "next Musial." (George Brace Photo)

Gil Hodges (.268-40-103) at first base, sure-handed Billy Cox (.279-9-51) at third, and were anchored up the middle by steady Pee Wee Reese (.286-10-84) at shortstop and the spectacular play of Jackie Robinson (.338-19-88) at second base. In the outfield were power-hitters Duke Snider (.277-29-101) and Carl Furillo (.295-16-91), and on the mound were hard-throwing right-handers Don Newcombe (3.28, 20-9) and Ralph Branca (3.26, 13-12), crafty Preacher Roe (3.04, 22-3), and youngsters Carl Erskine (4.46, 16-12) and Clyde King (4.15, 14-7). Newcombe, in particular, was overpowering, as he shut the American Leaguers down on two hits in the final three innings of the 1951 All-Star game in Detroit to preserve an 8-3 National League victory. Nevertheless, the Dodgers were not the overwhelming favorites to take the National League pennant. Based on their solid finish in 1950, the Baseball Writers of America picked the Giants to win in a preseason poll.

Contrary to preseason predictions, the Giants stumbled badly coming out of the gate, as they lost eight straight in April to the Braves, Dodgers, and Phillies and fell into last place at 2-12. A combination of bad luck and poor fielding were credited with the string of losses. "The more the Giants lost, the madder they became," wrote writer Ken Smith. "They broke bats on home plate in disgust, kicked buckets and growled of their fate. Before long they were pressing and straining so hard that all semblance of normal play disappeared." Though they broke the streak on April 30, by beating the Dodgers 8-5 at Ebbets Field, the Giants realized they had placed themselves in a deep hole. Nevertheless, feisty Leo Durocher refused to give up. "Let the other clubs talk now, poke fun at us, make wisecracks about us. There is a long way to go before the season is over. We'll show them yet," he huffed.[39]

By mid-June, the Giants had passed the .500 mark, but they still trailed the Dodgers by six games. Then, just before the June 15 trading deadline, general manager Buzzie Bavasi pulled off a deal that seemed to assure the Dodgers the pennant when he acquired outfielder Andy Pafko (.249-18-58) along with infielder Wayne Terwilliger, pitcher Johnny Schmitz, and catcher Al Walker from the Cubs for outfielder Gene Hermanski, infielder Eddie Miksis, pitcher Joe Hatten, and catcher Bruce Edwards. The trade caused an uproar among other clubs in the league and appeared so slanted in favor of the Dodgers that one rumor had Duke Snider coming to the Cubs in 1952 for $200,000 as additional compensation. J.G. Taylor Spink wrote, "In some quarters, the deal was called the biggest steal since Harry Frazee dealt off his Boston stars to the Yankees," while other writers referred to it as a "barefaced swindle."[40] Pee Wee Reese recalled talking to players on other teams who after the Pafko trade told him, "Now you'll probably win it by 30 games."[41] Finally, Fred Saigh, who also attempted to acquire Pafko, complained bitterly that "It will be bad for the league and bad for Brooklyn too. We won't draw, and they won't either if they push too far ahead."[42]

Not only were the Dodgers winning during the summer of 1951, by August 7 they had taken nine of twelve from the Giants and during the next two days swept three more from them to increase their lead to twelve and a half games. After the final game of the series, Charlie Dressen and several of his players, including Jackie Robinson and Ralph Branca, taunted the Giants through a wooden door that separated the two teams' dressing rooms at Ebbets Field. "Eat your heart out, Leo!" they shouted. "So that's your kind of team?" "The Giants are dead," they bragged as though the race was over. Finally, to top off the frivolity, Dressen engaged several of his players in a chorus of "Roll out the barrel, we got the Giants on the run."[43] The Dodgers' insensitive remarks undoubtedly angered the Giants and provided them with an added incentive during the remainder of the season. Alvin Dark, who broke the story to the press after the season, remarked, "You just can't treat human beings like they treated us and get away with it."[44]

The inspired Giants won their next sixteen games—the longest winning streak in the National League since 1935. Eight of the games were decided by a single run, and seven were won by the Giants on late-inning rallies behind big hits and big plays. Although Giants' fans were slow to catch on to what was happening (only 9,000 turned out to watch the team go after its seventeenth victory), according to writer Arch Murray, "They had the Dodgers across the bridge in Brooklyn reeling and shaking watching the scoreboard with frozen faces as they saw the Giants moving up and up and up."[45] By August 28, the Giants were only five games out.

There were many heroes during the streak. The foremost was Leo Durocher, who seemed to make all the right moves. Earlier in the year, he moved Whitey Lockman (.282-12-73), a fine fielder, to first base and inserted strong-armed Monte Irvin (.312-24- 121) in left field. Then, in May, the Giants brought up Willie Mays (.274-20-68) to play center field. The twenty-year-old outfielder was signed by the Giants in 1950 by scout Eddie Montague, who described Mays as "the greatest young ballplayer I had ever seen in my life or my scouting career."[46] Beginning the season at triple-A Minneapolis, Mays was sensational, hitting .477 in the team's first thirty-five games. He made incredible plays in the outfield and hit the ball so hard that one of his line drives put a hole in the fence at Borchert Field. When Mays was called up, he pleaded with Leo Durocher to leave him in triple-A because he was sure he could not handle big-league pitching. A shocked Durocher asked him, "What are you hitting now?" "Four seventy-seven," replied Mays. "Well," intoned Durocher sarcastically, "Do you think you can hit two-fucking fifty for me?" When Mays replied in the affirmative, Durocher ordered him to get on the next plane to New York.[47]

The Giants stuck with the youngster, nicknamed "The Say Hey Kid" because of his penchant for using "Say Hey" to get people's attention, through an initial one-for-twenty-five drought. When Mays surfaced from his slump, he provided the team with a real spark. Durocher also made a

(*Top, left*) Although Monte Irvin was thirty years old when he reached the major leagues in 1949, he was still a superb player. In 1951, his timely hitting carried the Giants through much of the season. (*Top, right*) Larry Jansen, the most overlooked pitcher during the Pivotal Era. The father of seven had great control and a fine curve. He once quipped that when he went on picnics he would let "everybody else collect his kids, and [then he would] take what's left." (*Left*) Sal Maglie was the only Mexican League jumper to return with great success. Under the tutelage of pitching great Dolf Luque, Maglie developed a curve he could throw consistently on the outside part of the plate. (George Brace Photo)

propitious move on July 21 when he shifted Bobby Thomson (.293-32-101) from center field to third base. When Thomson's hitting picked up dramatically and he began making sensational plays look routine, Durocher extolled, "There isn't a better third baseman in the league right now." Thomson attributed his improved hitting to a new closed stance and to the fact that playing third base kept him so busy that he did not have time to brood over his hitting.[48] Thomson had another motive. When he shifted to third base, the Scotsman was hitting only .220, and Durocher "made it clear that my chances of staying with the Giants depended on the success of this 'experiment,'" recalled Thomson.[49] Moving Thomson to third base allowed Durocher to put Don Mueller (.277-16-69) in right field. Nicknamed "Mandrake the Magician" because of his uncanny bat control, Mueller hit five home runs in two days, to beat the Dodgers 8-1 and 11-2 on September 1 and 2, and in the process tied a major-league record.[50]

The Giants' pitching staff, anchored by starters Larry Jansen (3.04, 23-11), Jim Hearn (3.62, 17-9), and Sal Maglie (2.93, 23-6), was equally responsible for the team's success. The trio chalked up fifty-one complete games between them. The fourth and fifth starting slots were ably filled by veterans Dave Koslo (3.31, 10-9), Sheldon Jones, rookie Al Corwin, and former Ohio State blocking back George Spencer (3.75, 10-4). Spencer won four games during the streak—three in relief and a 4-2 start over the Dodgers, which, according to Durocher, was the key game in the Giants' streak. "That gave our guys the first idea that the Dodgers weren't supermen and we made the most of it," noted Durocher. "I don't think the Dodgers have been the same since."[51]

The Giants' streak ended when Sheldon Jones lost a pitching duel to the Pirates' Howie Pollet 2-0 on two unearned runs on August 28. After the Giants streak was ended and rookie Clem Labine beat the Reds to extend their lead to six games, the Dodgers sang in the showers for the first time in weeks. Afterward, a relieved Preacher Roe noted, "Of course, you have to realize we have to win ourselves or we don't deserve to win the pennant. But, it sure was rough, I'll admit."[52] By September 19, the Giants' season looked as though it were over. Ken Smith's headline in the *Sporting News* read, "Giants' Pennant Bid Fades, But Lip's Men Can Hold Heads High." Joe King's column heading read, "Brooks Breathing Easier, Rest Pitchers for Series." To bring his point home King wrote, "If the Giants won all remaining 16 games, the Dodgers would have to drop eight of their 19 to blow the pennant."[53]

The Giants kept coming, in spite of the odds—and the Dodgers began to slip precariously. Although the Dodgers never really slumped (they were 13-11 between August 9 and September 1, and 11-10 between September 1 and September 25), they were losing games with uncharacteristic play and obvious anguish. In a double-header loss (6-3 and 14-2) to the Braves, the Dodgers made three errors in the second inning of the nightcap. Then, on September 27, Don Newcombe lost a pitchers' duel to Chet Nichols, 4-3, on a disputed call by home-plate umpire Frank Dascoli, who ruled that the Braves' Bob Addis slid under Roy Campanella's tag to score the winning run. Campanella and coach Cookie Lavagetto were thrown out of the game, and the Dodgers cleared their bench during the subsequent argument. On September 28, a Dodger loss to Philadelphia, while the Giants were idle, deadlocked the two teams in the standings. The next day, both teams won, and on the final day of the season, September 30, the Giants beat the Phillies behind Larry Jansen, 3-2, while the Dodgers struggled with the Braves. Down 6-1 after three innings and 8-5 after five innings, the Dodgers needed a spectacular play from Jackie Robinson, who caught an Eddie Waitkus line drive only inches off the ground with the bases loaded. Robinson's save sent the game into extra innings and enabled the Dodger star to tag the Phillies Robin Roberts for a home run in the fourteenth inning to win the game for Brooklyn and to force a three-game playoff series.

The Dodgers and Giants split the first two games of the best-of-three series, with Jim Hearn triumphing over Ralph Branca 3-1 in the opener at Ebbets Field and Clem Labine beating the Giants 10-0 on a six-hitter in the second game at the Polo Grounds. The rubber match, played on October 3 at the Polo Grounds, saw Don Newcombe locked in a pitchers' duel through seven innings against Sal Maglie. In the eighth, the Dodgers erupted for three runs on singles by Duke Snider and Pee Wee Reese, a wild pitch by Maglie, followed by singles by Andy Pafko and Billy Cox. With a 4-1 lead going into the bottom of the ninth inning, the Dodgers looked like a sure bet to win the pennant. Nevertheless, in the top of the ninth, the Giants' leadoff hitter, Alvin Dark, reached base on an infield hit, and Don Mueller singled him over to third. With two men on, outfielder Monte Irvin came to the plate. Giants announcer Ernie Harwell remembers:

> My own personal feeling was that the Giants didn't have a chance because Newcombe was throwing very hard. He was terrifically effective. It got to the point where the Giants looked like they weren't going to touch him. Newcombe looked awful powerful going into the ninth inning and they had the lead. When they began—it looked like they might rally there in the ninth inning, my feeling again was that if anyone was

going to break up the game, it was going to be Monte Irvin. Because Monte over those last five or six weeks had been fabulous. He'd knocked in a lot of runs. He hit line drives all over the place. He had one of the best performances I have ever seen over that span of time. Well, he came up and popped up. To me—I thought it was all over.[54]

At this point, the goat of the game for the Giants was Bobby Thomson. The third baseman pulled a rally-killing base-running blunder in the second inning, when he hit a ball down the third-base line and, with his head down, almost overran the lead runner at second base. Whitey Lockman, who had singled, was not about to challenge strong-armed left fielder Andy Pafko, and thus Thomson was an easy run-down victim for the Dodgers. Now in the ninth, after Monte Irvin popped up for the first out, Thomson's roommate, Whitey Lockman, doubled to left, scoring a run and sending Mueller to third, where he injured his leg on his slide. Thomson was the next hitter, and this is his account:

And now we come in for our last at bats. I'll never forget the dejection that I felt. We are just dead—don't have a chance. Then pretty soon a couple of fellas get on. Hey, things are starting to come to life. I realize that I might get a chance to hit. I had hit well for the last three months of the season and had confidence in myself at bat. I think we were all numb anyway at that point. And all of a sudden here we are. Don Mueller slid into third and injured his leg severely. I was the next hitter and feeling very badly for Don and my mind was totally off the ball game for that brief period. They carried Don off the field and made a pitching change that I was totally unaware of. The game is about to resume and I am walking down to home plate and Leo [Durocher] came up and put his arm around me and said, "Bobby, if you ever hit one, hit one now." And I remember thinking, "[Leo] you are out of your mind." I remember walking back to home plate swearing at myself, which is unusual. I have never done that before. What I was saying to myself was "Don't get over anxious. Wait and watch. You SOB, give it a good shot." I got in the box and now I realize Branca is pitching. Well, goodness me, he threw the first ball right over the plate. Why I took it, I do not know. Now the next pitch, I can remember his winding up and throwing and I just got a glimpse of it. It was high inside . . . and I jumped on it. The thing took off, and I thought, "I've got a home run." And then all of a sudden the darn thing started to sink—it must have had tremendous overspin. And then I thought it's not a home run, it is just a base hit. According to the films, which I had to wait to see, I was only half-way to first base when I saw the ball disappear. Then I lost control. I just remember jumping up into the air, and jumping around the bases—just a feeling of exhilaration that I have never experienced before—just unbelievable.[55]

Bobby Thomson, the "Flying Scot," was not even sure he would be with the Giants in 1951. After hitting his famous home run, he recalled "jumping up into the air, and jumping around the bases—just a feeling of exhilaration that I have never experienced before—just unbelievable." (George Brace Photo)

The choice of Ralph Branca to pitch in relief of Don Newcombe in this situation remains a matter of controversy. Branca had given up three home runs to Thomson in 1951, including one in game one of the playoffs. Nevertheless, according to coach Clyde Sukeforth, of the two pitchers warming up, Erskine and Branca, the latter was the only one who was ready. After the Dodger right-hander fired his first pitch for a strike to get ahead of Thomson, he recalled, "The next pitch I had wanted to waste, so I threw a fastball up and in, and I might have aimed it." After Thomson hit the pitch all Branca could remember saying was "Sink, sink, sink."[56] As left fielder Andy Pafko looked up to see the ball clearing the wall to give New York an incredible 5-4 win, Giants announcer Russ Hodges's voice was captured on tape over radio station WMCA for all to remember, as he said, "There's a long drive. . . . It's gonna be . . . I believe . . . " and then, letting all caution go, he shouted five times "The Giants Win the Pennant, The Giants Win the Pennant," followed by "They are going crazy! They are going crazy! and the Home Run of the Century, the Shot Heard 'Round the World." After the home run, Dodgers announcer Red Barber simply allowed the Polo Grounds' crowd noise to filter through his WMGM mike. Following a commercial, he attempted to put the game in perspective by telling his listeners that hundreds of service personnel had lost their lives in Korea that week and that the Dodgers and their fans would get over the loss of the pennant.[57]

Thomson's home run is considered one the most dramatic moments in all of sports history. The scenes it evokes—Thomson jumping gleefully around the bases while Jackie Robinson watches him touch every bag; his leap into a joyous throng of teammates at home plate; the bedlam that broke out among the fans at the Polo Grounds; the utter disbelief experienced by Dodger fans; and the great agony suffered by pitcher Ralph Branca as he lay prone on the clubhouse steps—are etched in baseball history forever. Moreover, the playoff series was the first sports event ever televised from coast to coast. "It was the most famous home run ever made," noted New York sports writer Gary Schumacher, "He hit it in 3,000,000 living rooms, to say nothing of the bars and grills."[58] Not unlike Pearl Harbor, millions of people can still tell you exactly where they were and what they were doing when Thomson hit his home run. Writers have struggled in their attempts to give the event real meaning. Divine intervention plays a role in Thomas Kiernan's book—*The Miracle at Coogan's Bluff.*[59] Ray Robinson wrote that Thomson "transcended the cold statistics of the game's record books to enter the realm of folklore."[60] Harvey Rosenfeld cogently argued that it framed and helped define one of the great rivalries in sports history and that "myriads of baseball fans . . . continue to marvel at the feat that seems unbelievable."[61] Even the great Red Smith was at a loss for words when he wrote in his column the following day, "There is no way to tell it. The art of fiction is dead. Reality has strangled invention. Only the utterly impossible, the inexpressibly fantastic, can ever be plausible again."[62]

The 1951 World Series

There was little chance that the 1951 World Series would be able to top the National League playoff series for drama—but the teams tried. In the first contest, at Yankee Stadium, Monte Irvin rapped three singles, belted a 440-foot triple, made a great catch to rob Hank Bauer of a home run, and stole home off Yankees starter Allie Reynolds in the first inning to lead his team to a 5-1 victory. Unlikely starter Dave Koslo, the oldest Giant player at thirty-one, scattered seven hits and threw a complete game to hand Reynolds his first series loss. The Yankees evened the series by beating the Giants 3-1 in the second game, as left-hander Eddie Lopat bested Giants ace Larry Jansen in a pitchers' duel. Although Monte Irvin continued strong performance with three more hits, the Giants were no match for the Yankees, who scored on bunt singles by Phil Rizzuto and Mickey Mantle and a bloop single by Gil McDougald in the first, a solo home run by Joe Collins in the second, and singles by Bobby Brown and Eddie Lopat in the eighth. The game was most memorable for an incident in the fifth inning, in which Mickey Mantle and Joe DiMaggio both went after a fly ball hit by Willie Mays. Mantle caught his foot on a drainage cover and his knee buckled, tearing several ligaments and sending him to the hospital.

At the Polo Grounds the Giants took the third game, 6-2, behind Jim Hearn. The Giants scored five unearned runs off Yankee starter Vic Raschi in the fifth inning after Eddie Stanky dropped kicked a ball out of Phil Rizzuto's glove. The Yankees argued vehemently that Stanky should have been called out for interference and that he had not touched the bag, but to no avail. Subsequent singles by Alvin Dark and Hank Thompson, an error by Yogi Berra, and a home run by Whitey Lockman ended Raschi's nightmare inning. The Yankees knotted the series again in the fourth game, when Joe DiMaggio broke out of a zero-for-eleven series slump by singling in the third frame and homering with Yogi Berra aboard in the fifth inning to give the Yankees a 4-1 lead. The Yankees scored two more runs in the seventh inning to clinch the game 6-2, as Allie Reynolds beat Sal Maglie.

The Yankees hammered five Giants pitchers in the fifth game, en route to a 13-1 victory behind the steady pitching of Eddie Lopat. The game featured a third-inning grand-slam home run by rookie Gil McDougald—only the third time the feat had been accomplished.[63] The Yankees captured the World Series in the sixth game with a hard-fought 4-3 win at Yankee Stadium. Dave Koslo and Vic Raschi were locked in a 1-1 pitching duel until the sixth, when outfielder Hank Bauer tripled with the bases loaded to put the Yankees up 4-1. The Giants made a game of it in the ninth inning, when they loaded the bases against reliever Johnny Sain with no outs. Bob Kuzava replaced Sain and gave up two long run-scoring fly-outs before retiring pinch hitter Sal Yvars on a low line drive that Hank Bauer snagged with a sensational sitting catch.

The 1951 season marked the end of the Pivotal Era. It was a year of transition that saw Bill Veeck return to baseball with a midget among his usual bag of tricks but that also witnessed a continued attendance drop as America's love affair with television, the automobile, and other leisure activities began to take their toll. The year marked a new transition in the commissionership, symbolized by Ford Frick throwing out the first pitch of the 1951 World Series as his first official sanctioned act in office. Nineteen fifty-one was also the year that Mickey Mantle and Willie Mays broke into the game and demonstrated flashes of future greatness. Finally, it was the year that saw the departure of future Hall-of-Famers Joe DiMaggio and Bobby Doerr. Doerr went quietly as was his style, but DiMaggio, who wished to go quietly, could not. After all there was only one DiMaggio, and he represented the end of an era.

21

Baseball Then and Now

Many of baseball's gains during the Pivotal Era were squandered or allowed to languish during the following decades. Ford Frick's election as baseball commissioner in 1951 ensured that baseball would backslide. "When the clubs pushed me out in 1951," noted Frick's predecessor Happy Chandler, "they had a vacancy and decided to keep it. So they named Ford Frick."[1] Although Chandler's comment is harsh, Babe Ruth's ghostwriter was a fan, an insider, and a known quantity who did not threaten the owners. He believed that the game did not need a policeman and that the commissioner's job was to administer baseball's rules, not to make them, and certainly not to tell the owners what to do. "The game, in the final analysis," Frick noted, "is in the hands of the players and fans and they are the only policemen needed."[2]

Frick's hands-off policies allowed the owners to ignore the lessons of the 1940s as well as the expansion and minor-league issues raised by the Celler Committee hearings. No antitrust legislation was generated by the hearings and the U.S. Supreme Court upheld baseball's exemption when it refused to consider the antitrust issues raised by *Toolson v. New York Yankees* (1953).[3] As long as the reserve clause and baseball's antitrust exemption were protected, the owners were satisfied. Walter O'Malley and the New York Yankees team of Dan Topping and Del Webb effectively ran the game during Frick's regime. Organized planning during the period was for all practical purposes nonexistent. Replying to a question about potential expansion into Los Angeles and San Francisco–Oakland, the country's fifth- and seventh-largest markets, Frick explained that he was giving a lot of thought to the matter but that "I rarely tell in advance what plans I have in mind. I like to turn them around several times in my own mind before sharing them with others," he continued. "Then I prefer to have accomplishment speak my piece."[4]

Instead of placing expansion teams in the two areas, baseball allowed Walter O'Malley and Horace Stoneham to take two relatively secure franchises out of New York in 1957, lining their own pockets in the process. Baseball's initial wave of expansion, while eliminating the problem of having two-team competition in small markets, was also serendipitous. The most logical was Lou Perini's move in 1953 from Boston to Milwaukee, where a new stadium, a rebuilt team, and high fan interest created almost instant success for the Braves. On the other hand, the St. Louis Browns' move to Baltimore eventually compelled two moribund Washington Senators franchises to flee the nation's capital.[5] Bill Veeck and the Browns were forced to leave St. Louis because they could not compete with the vast resources of new Cardinals' owner August Busch. Veeck's poor financial condition and his propensity to alienate his fellow American League owners allowed Del Webb to negotiate a deal that awarded the Browns to Baltimore and at the same time sent Veeck packing. Veeck's departure left an intellectual and creative void in the game. Among owners and executives, only Branch Rickey, whose influence was now diminished by poor health and the lowly status of the Pittsburgh Pirates, retained any global vision for baseball.

Webb also engineered the shift of the Athletics to Kansas City in 1956. The move enabled the Yankees to send their Kansas City minor-league franchise to the growing Denver area and allowed Webb's construction company to build a new stadium for the Athletics. As a result of the move, Webb established a puppet franchise in Kansas City, where the A's in essence became another Yankees farm club. When Frank Lane, Cleveland's general manager, traded Roger Maris to Kansas City in 1958, there was little doubt that he would soon be playing in a New York uniform. The Yankees used the Kansas City connection to keep them in first place for the next five years.

Baseball's lack of central planning and its owners' inability or unwillingness to work in concert severely handicapped the game's capacity to deal with changing times. During the 1950s, as they developed a love affair with the automobile and the interstate highway system, Americans became increasingly mobile. At the same time, the rapid migration of America's middle class to the suburbs solved the postwar housing crisis and created new leisure-time activities. Many clubs that owned inner-city ballparks, which were designed to fit within the confines of local neighborhoods, now found themselves with inadequate parking facilities and located in areas considered undesirable by potential fans. Moreover, many of the parks themselves, were poorly maintained, run down, and outmoded.

Night baseball also lulled the owners into a false sense of security. When they discovered that five times as many people were free to attend a night game as an afternoon contest, with the exception of the Chicago Cubs, all of the teams developed evening schedules. Night baseball led sports columnist Red Smith to write, "Baseball at night is strictly a theatrical spectacle. It is vain to argue that night baseball bears scarcely any recognizable resemblance to the pleasant game of hot, lazy afternoons which Americans grew up loving, for owners are in business for profit. But night baseball is all business."[6] With turnstiles humming at unprecedented rates through the late 1940s, owners believed that their bonanza would continue. Competition from television, however, quickly dispelled that notion.

When televised baseball first took root in the late 1940s, the game had an excellent opportunity to seize the initiative. Instead, baseball's lack of unity prevented it from harnessing the medium—indeed, television eventually consumed baseball. Unlike professional football and basketball, in which teams shared network contracts, baseball owners went their separate ways, making whatever deals their local markets would bear. Television was a paradox for baseball—whereas it exposed and educated more fans to the game, nighttime television personalities and programs, such as Milton Berle, Imogene Coca and Sid Caesar, and Armstrong Circle Theatre, created stiff competition. Furthermore, the medium literally transformed other lesser sports such as football, basketball, golf, bowling, and hockey into viable leagues or circuits as they became popular with a new viewing public. As baseball historian David Voight noted, "What ensued was a broad exposure to sports that turned Americans into sports generalists. In time this would make baseball's claim to being the national pastime a shopworn myth, as watching sports on television became the national pastime. Such a prospect in 1950 was beyond the ken of baseball men still reveling in their newfound prosperity."[7]

Most baseball officials were dumbfounded by television. A case in point was National League president Warren Giles, who stated, "Surveys to determine the effect of television on baseball attendance so far have been only fragmentary and, in my judgment, not conclusive. I doubt if anyone is qualified to state with any degree of accuracy at this time whether or not the telecasting of baseball games has an adverse effect on the attendance at home games."[8] Although the club owners realized that giving their product away might bear some correlation to their attendance woes, they attacked the problem with inertia. In a 1951 article, respected reporter Grantland Rice urged baseball to study the problem, "and soon, unless they want to begin staging their games exclusively in TV studios."[9]

Other owners, such as Walter O'Malley and Webb, however, saw potential profits in television. By 1951, the Giants, Dodgers, Yankees and Cubs were televising all of their home games, the Phillies aired all of their day games, and the Tigers were selectively broadcasting a slate of thirty-five contests. The Pittsburgh Pirates were the only team not to televise home games. Teams in the large markets soon became dependent on broadcasting money. For instance, the Dodgers' income from radio and television in 1955 exceeded their player payroll by more than $250,000. Conversely, however, the attendance of New York's three teams dropped by more than 2.4 million between 1947 and 1957. In *The Era*, sportswriter Roger Kahn discounts the importance of this loss of attendance, adding, "Interest, as opposed to attendance, never flagged. The ballplayers were godlike. The managers were giants in the earth. The Era was the greatest age in baseball history."[10] Perhaps, in the short term, Kahn is correct. Television expanded baseball's horizons. Nevertheless, over the long term, baseball's falling attendance represented not only lost income but also the potential for declining interest. Baseball's slow pace and relatively long periods of inaction did not lend itself to the medium as well as intercollegiate and professional basketball and football. Moreover, most of baseball's season is played in good weather at a time when fewer viewers are housebound.

Even more serious was the rapid deterioration of the minor leagues. The die was cast when rule 1 (d), which placed restrictions on broadcasting major-league games during hours when minor-league teams were playing home games, was completely abandoned at the end of the 1951 season.[11] Instead of finding ways to share television revenue, the minor leagues were allowed to wither on the vine. Attendance continued to drop precipitously, from approximately 27.6 million in 1951 to little more than 12 million in 1959. "The majors were forced to accept a market economy," wrote Neil Sullivan in *The Minors*, "a condition they had labored to avoid throughout their history. The ruin of the minors followed not so much from the major's venal decisions as from their inept calculations of self-interest within the new market of baseball broadcasting."[12]

Television revenues also led to polarization among several of baseball's interest groups by pitting small-market owners against large and players against employers. Having helped establish "a company union" through baseball's system of player representation and a pension plan, under Ford

Frick the owners proceeded to ignore the players. The owners did not want to share broadcasting profits with the players, they would not provide accountability on monies in the pension fund, and they refused to meet with the players' lawyer. "In 1953 we had a mess of difficulties," recalled player representative Ralph Kiner. At the Atlanta meeting, he and Allie Reynolds attempted to continue the pension plan, but "they refused to allow our attorney, J. Norman Lewis, into the meetings. We had knock-down drag-out battles. They refused to meet with us—then they did. Finally we reached total disagreement."[13] Baseball's intransigence led directly to the formation of the Major League Baseball Players' Association in 1953 and ultimately to the hiring of Marvin Miller as the association's executive director in 1966—an event that marked the point of no return between labor and management.

Today, television revenue, not receipts from baseball attendance and concession sales at the ballpark, is the driving force behind baseball's economic well-being. Without a substantial television contract, clubs could not pay the astronomical salaries to which players have become accustomed. Expansion, divisional play, and World Series games played on cold October nights, often continuing long after children have gone to bed, are all the result of television.

Aside from the influence of television, the game of today, is very different from its predecessor in the Pivotal Era. "Though the rules are basically the same," wrote baseball commentator Peter Gammons, "today's game is a distant cousin of the one played in 1950, just as that version was far removed from its counterpart in 1910, the heart of the dead-ball era. In 1950, baseball was a slow plodding affair, featuring sluggers like Gus Zernial and Walt Dropo, who could hit the long ball and not much else, and speedsters like Dom DiMaggio, who led the American League that year with fifteen stolen bases."[14] To say that one form of the game is superior to the other is like attempting to weigh the virtues of apples versus oranges. Nevertheless, it is instructive to compare today's game with the past—particularly as it is viewed by Pivotal Era participants, most of whom are quick to point out its differences.

With the entry of Jackie Robinson and more black and Latin players, speed and stolen bases became a major factor in the game. One only has to examine Luis Aparicio and the "Go-Go" Sox of 1959, and later the great years experienced by Maury Wills, Lou Brock, and Rickey Henderson, to see the effect it has had on the game. Players today are twice as likely to steal bases as they were during the Pivotal Era.[15] Of course, the game's strategy was geared more to the sacrifice bunt, the hit-and-run, and the home run in the 1940s. Could teams have run more? The Yankees' Gene Woodling thought so, but he explained that it just was not part of the team's strategy. He remembered Casey Stengel saying, "Who on my ball club doesn't go first to third and second to home? I don't have to move them up. I don't have to take the bat out of the hitter's hands." And, added Woodling with some disdain, "You would get run out of ball games for stealing third—particularly in close games."[16]

Most players from the Pivotal Era readily admit that today's players are bigger, more muscular, and are better athletes. Winter jobs prevented most Pivotal Era players from lifting weights and working out during the off-season. "The players today make more great fielding plays in one week or one series than I would see in one month in the big leagues years back," noted former Cubs manager Charlie Metro, and "they are faster." Regardless, Metro maintains that many of today's players are not in great physical shape, because they fail to condition themselves properly. Citing the great number of ballplayers on the disabled list at any one time, he notes that at the beginning of the 1991 season there were ninety-three players on the list, the equivalent of four teams—or approximately $41 million worth of talent. "Broken bones are excusable," he explains, but not "a hamstring pull, a sore elbow, or a pulled tendon. If you run you didn't have hamstring pulls. We conditioned them. I used to run them until they were sterile," he laughed.[17]

Of course, placing a man on the disabled list today is one way of protecting management's huge investment. Moreover, unlike the 1940s, there is little fear that if a player leaves the lineup because of injury that he will be replaced by an equally talented player from the bench. Umpire Joe Paparella recalled an incident behind the plate in which catcher Yogi Berra's fingernail was pushed all the way back but he refused to leave the game. "There was blood all over the place," remembered Paparella, but "he never missed an inning."[18] Moreover, with the minor leagues at their apex, each position was usually several players deep. Baseball was literally where the money was in professional sports. "All of the athletes with talent, as they were going through high school, if they had any professional aspirations, usually gravitated toward baseball," observed Yankee great Bobby Brown. "So the competition for the good athletes was greater in those days. Players today are just as great—but the competition was a lot tougher because of the number of players trying to reach the big leagues. The competition to make a team and stay on the team was tougher."[19]

Another common complaint expressed by veterans is how watered down major-league talent has become today. "There are too many play-ers who don't belong here," stated Tiger announcer George Kell.[20] In ad-dition, players with any talent are sometimes rushed to the major leagues, and the way they play the game is a source of embarrassment for some veterans like outfielder Willard Marshall, who decried their lack of in-struction, noting, "There are too many errors. These are not just funda-mental errors, they are stupid errors. Six or seven errors [in a game] is unbelievable."[21] "People can't understand . . . what kind of ballplayers we had in those days," explained former Reds and Cubs outfielder Frank Baumholtz. They were super. . . . In those days if you were a regular player and you hit .265, you would end up in the minor leagues the next year. . . . If you had a bad year, you would take a 25 percent cut. You were paid one year at a time and you were paid for the coming year for what you did the previous year—period."[22] "Let's face it, they have thinned the talent out," remarked Gene Woodling. But "if you take the good ballplayers off twenty-eight and put them back on sixteen [teams], I think it would equalize itself."[23]

The players' surroundings and equipment have also changed. In the 1940s and 1950s, each park had its own idiosyncrasies and character. With the exception of Tiger Stadium, Wrigley Field, and Fenway Park, the old steel structures that replaced the wooden grandstands of the nineteenth century are gone. Many were replaced by homogeneous, symmetrical multipurpose structures and domed stadiums in the 1960s and 1970s. Surrounded by huge parking lots, often equipped with artificial turf, sym-metrical field measurements, and electronic scoreboards, the atmosphere of the game has changed, as have the playing conditions. Fortunately, during the past decade, a new trend has emerged in the form of Camden Yards in Baltimore—a modern but intimate stadium designed, like the old parks, to fit the confines of an existing inner-city neighborhood. To some purists, such as Bobby Brown, the entertainment factor in many parks has gotten out of hand. "Games were played for the sake of games. People went out to watch the game. You didn't have a sign board that told you to charge, to cheer, or clap. You didn't have an organ blaring at you."[24] On the other hand, the hype and carnival atmosphere in some parks would eternally please Bill Veeck. Conditions in the dugout and clubhouse are inarguably much better. Spacious, air-conditioned club-houses, clean showers, and large dugouts are the rule rather than the exception. Infielder Pete Castiglione remembered the long double-head-ers on hot summer days without air conditioning: "They had a little am-monia on the bench with a pail. They would slap it on your face—to get your breath and to try to revive you. You put your arm and your wrist in there to cool your hands off."[25]

A far more insidious innovation is artificial turf, a much-maligned substitute for natural grass. First installed when it was ascertained that grass would not grow in the Astrodome, synthetic turf also appealed to clubs with outdoor parks because it was cheaper to maintain than grass and greatly reduced the number of rained-out contests. Artificial turf, however, has several serious drawbacks. First, it is hard on outfielders diving for balls and on players' legs. "I worked a couple of games on Astroturf," remembered Joe Paparella, "and you start to feel it after five or six innings. It's like running on concrete. I know it is going to shorten the careers of ballplayers two or three years."[26] It also altered the game's defensive strategy. "It takes away the aggressiveness of the outfielders when a ball can hit the carpet and bounce over the fielder's head," observed announcer Ernie Harwell. Furthermore, "in the infield it takes away the lateral range of an infielder [because] the ball gets by too quickly."[27] Good hitters from the past, however, eye artificial turf with envy. "If they had the synthetic turf when I was playing—me being a guy who hit up the middle. I would say that my batting average would have been up to 20 to 25 percent higher," noted Frank Baumholtz.[28] "There should be a .400 hitter on artificial surfaces," opined .300 hitter George Kell.[29] The installation of artificial turf also meant the demise of the groundskeeper's stratagems—particularly the tricks employed by the Bossard families in Cleveland and Chicago—no more watered-down base paths, slanted foul lines, and ankle-length or razor-cut grass.

The padded outfield walls and backstops in most parks and batting helmets provide players with more protection than ever before. Indeed, most injuries, unlike those suffered by star Yankee outfielder Earle Combs in 1935 or Pete Reiser in the 1940s, are rarely life threatening. Baseball uniforms, gloves, and bats have also improved. Baseball uniforms and styles have gone from itchy wool or heavy flannel outfits with low-stirruped stockings worn at the knee to blended knits with high-stirruped stockings often worn down to the ankle. Now styles are a crazy mix with mostly low-stirruped stockings and high-topped spikes. Whatever the design, today's players are far more comfortable than were their Pivotal Era counterparts. Former National League batting champion Harry Walker agrees, "The uniforms are different. They are tighter and better to run in. If you had a pair of pants like we wore, and put it as tight as we had it, you couldn't get your leg up properly in those things. But today they stretch when you stretch. All you have to do is look at the Olympics and see what has happened. The swimming trunks are tight and they're greased so they slide through the water—resistance. But when we ran, it was like a tent. They would be big flared-out pants that would sometimes weigh six to eight pounds when you would get through sweating."[30] Gloves are huge in comparison to those used in the 1940s. Giants' great Hal Schumacher remembered how most catches were made in the palm of your hand instead of in the web, where balls would usually glance off the player's small mitts. "The glove today helps fielders and helps knock down batting averages. They make some wonderful plays—they are incredible."[31] "I used a small glove that they would laugh at today," chuckled outfielder Harry Walker. But, you didn't miss the ball—you used your hands. The former All-Star went on to explain how the quick transfer of the ball from mitt to throwing arm was a great advantage for those who caught the ball with two hands.[32]

With the increased size of gloves, players no longer stuck them into their large back pockets, nor, with a rule change in 1954, were they allowed to leave them on the field when it was their turn to hit. Out of all those interviewed for this book, amazingly, only umpire Joe Paparella recalled seeing a glove obstruct a play in the field. "Oh, yes!" replied Paparella, "Lots of times they [players] would stumble, especially the infielders. When they would go out on a short pop fly, as a rule they would be looking up at the ball and all of a sudden they would be stepping on a glove and it would throw them off kilter."[33] Far more common was Frank Baumholtz's reply, "In all the years that I played, with the gloves laying out there, I never saw a ball that was hit off the bat that hit a glove."[34] Instead they remembered, with some glee, how players used to stick gummy chewing tobacco down the fingers of Phil Rizzuto's glove or how Pete Suder would stick a rubber snake underneath it as it lay in the grass.[35] Gene Woodling summed up the rule change: "It was more God-danged trouble after they started bringing them in, because it happened all the time that you would make the last out in an inning . . . now you are out on second base because you ran the ball out. . . . If somebody doesn't bring your glove out, you got to go all the way back—damned nuisance! It did not affect the game at all—and do you realize how long they threw their gloves on the field? . . . About seventy-five years."[36]

Bats are also different. Today's players use lighter (30-ounce-plus), thin-handled bats with hollowed-out barrels modified to increase bat speed. During the Pivotal Era, large-handled bats were used by singles hitters like Nellie Fox, while sluggers like Joe DiMaggio and Hank Greenberg used bats weighing 38 to 40 ounces. "The average bat in those days was 33 [ounces] and now they are going down to 31 and 30 ounces," explained former manager Al Lopez. "It gives you a faster swing, but you miss more. We used to concentrate more on making contact with the bat."[37] Statistics verify Lopez's words—hitters during the Pivotal Era were more selective.[38]

The Pivotal Era was known for its home run hitters, but today's hitters are even more prodigious.[39] One rationale was put forth by Joe Paparella: "They didn't have that ball they are swinging at today. Cripes, you take that ball today and it looks like a jackrabbit. There is no doubt about it in my mind [that they are playing with a lively ball]. This ball is like a rock. It is like a golf ball, it is so tight."[40] There is little proof, however, that the balls have been altered since Australian yarn was first wrapped around the spheres to end the dead-ball era in 1920.[41] A more plausible reason might be the lowering of the mound from fifteen inches in height to ten in 1969 and to a shrinking strike zone. During the late 1940s, the strike zone extended from the batter's shoulders to the top of the knee. "Today you have a little bitty box to pitch in," complained pitcher Virgil Trucks. "Hitters know they are going to get two of three pitches in that strike zone if the pitcher is a fastball pitcher. If it is not there, they will take it—and if it is, they will hit it out of any ballpark."[42]

The American League, of course, has added another element—the designated hitter—to the battle between pitcher and hitter. Baseball purists view the designated hitter with disdain. Many pitchers during the Pivotal Era were excellent hitters—Don Newcombe, Early Wynn, Bob Lemon, Johnny Sain, and Eddie Lopat come readily to mind. Surprisingly, though, many veterans take an opposite view and echoed Barney McCosky's sentiments when he recalled how futile it was to watch Detroit and Cleveland pitcher Al Benton hit. He "just waved at the ball," remembered McCosky. Noting that the designated hitter allowed great players to have longer careers, McCosky also argued that both leagues should be the same.[43]

Although hitters seem to have the upper hand in the 1990s, hitters from the Pivotal Era did not have to face an army of pitchers each game. During the 1940s and 1950s, a starting pitcher's durability was the key, and a complete game was as much a matter of pride as it was a statistical goal. For instance, in 1951 pitchers threw 938 complete games as opposed to 275 in 1995. "There are very few fellas today that know how to lock up a ball game with a one- or two-run lead," stated pitching expert Al Lopez. "That goes back to the manager who says, 'Give me five or six good innings and we can take it from there.' Now pitchers feel if they go five or six good innings, they have done their job."[44]

"In 1948 the relief pitcher was generally a washed-up starter," recalled

Ernie Harwell. "Now the bullpen man can be the top man on the team," he added. "Also we have the bullpen by committee—you have the long man, the short man, and the closer."[45] In the 1990s, during certain situations, hitters will face left-handed or right-handed specialists employed for only one or two outs. Furthermore, almost every team has a closer for the last inning who is capable of firing the ball by hitters at more than ninety miles per hour. Though the Pivotal Era boasted few great relief specialists, every team had an ace or stopper and several had more than one. Today, only the Atlanta Braves can muster a starting pitching staff to rival those of the Cardinals, Giants, Indians, Yankees, and Tigers of the 1940s or 1950s. There is little doubt that expansion seems to be the real reason pitching is thinner today than it was during the Pivotal Era.

Another huge difference between the game today and that of the Pivotal Era is free agency. Every veteran of the 1940s and 1950s has an opinion on the reserve clause. Although most are willing to concede that today's players are entitled to whatever remuneration they can get, they defend the reserve clause. "We took it [the reserve clause] in our years, because that was the way it was," stated pitcher Mel Harder. "We lived with it. I didn't mind being tied up with Cleveland all my life. [Today] players can go from one club to another. I don't think that's good for the game."[46] "When we signed a contract, we were theirs for life," noted pitcher Bob Cain. "The way it is now, it is going to come back and haunt the owners. Sooner or later you are going to end up with all the good ballplayers on just a few teams . . . the ones that have the money."[47] "I never thought I was being abused," reflected Ned Garver, who in 1952 became the highest-paid player in Browns history with a salary of $25,000. "I thought that the club owner had a sizable investment." Nevertheless, Garver was singled out to testify at the Celler Hearings in 1951 as an example of a star who was helplessly toiling with a last-place team. Garver sent them a deposition. "My only proposal was that if a guy didn't get a chance to play in a certain length of time, that he get to move," remembered Garver. "I always thought that Yogi Berra killed off several really fine catchers. He caught about every day, and everybody in the Yankee chain [Charlie Silvera, Ralph Houk, and Elston Howard] who was a good catcher, had no chance."[48]

Most Pivotal Era players found other employment after baseball—jobs with private businesses in public relations or sales; the post office or other governmental agencies; selling insurance, running restaurants, golf courses, gas stations, or automobile agencies; working as truckers, in law enforcement, or as security officers; as farmers or ranchers; or as school-teachers and coaches. Several are still active in baseball as coaches, scouts, or announcers. Only a few, like television personality Joe Garagiola and actors Chuck Connors and Johnny Berardino, achieved fame outside of the game, and only Bob Feller and the members of the great triumvirate were able to continue to capitalize on their fame. Joe DiMaggio was noted for his advertisements for New York's Bowery Bank and for Mr. Coffee. Many players are deceased—some tragically. Jackie Robinson died of complications from diabetes in 1972 at age fifth-six, George Stirnweiss was lost in 1958 when his train toppled into a river, and amiable Luke Easter was murdered in 1979 while serving as a security guard. Many former players are dependent on their baseball pensions. Others, including players' families, Negro League players, and those not served by the pension plan, have been assisted by B.A.T. (the Baseball Assistance Team), an organization that, through a grant program, is underwritten by the commissioner's office. Today B.A.T. is headed by chairman Ralph Branca. Underscoring the plight of many players, Branca noted, "Of the first seventy-eight people we helped, ten were former teammates of mine and probably twice that many were former colleagues who I had played against."[49]

Many "old veterans" have difficulty reconciling their salaries and current pension benefits with today's player salaries and benefits. "If the damn club owners are stupid enough to give it to them, more power to them," commented Willard Marshall.[50] Frank Baumholtz, who would like to see better pension benefits so that he did not have to work at age 73, was equally appalled at modern salaries. "When you are talking about Barry Bonds, a lifetime .275 hitter for seven years getting $43 million, I can't conceive of this. The salary schedules in the big leagues are so out of hand—when you get a .220 hitter sitting on the bench making $800,000 a year, there is something wrong. Unless they can get a grip on things, a lot of bad things could happen in the foreseeable future."[51] "Without the pension plan, I wouldn't be here!" exclaimed Barney McCosky, who like many older players bears resentment against the Major League Baseball Players' Association for refusing to recognize their needs: "You think they would say, 'Well, there's not that many old guys left. Let's give them something. We didn't have television money.' But no—they had their lifestyle, this is ours, so 'to hell with them.' That's not fair. We always talk about that. That's one thing about us. You walk down the street and you see an old ballplayer and you can go up to him and shake his hand and talk to him. You can't do that with these guys today—no way."[52]

Bob Cain, whose pension benefits are based on his five years in the majors, agreed with McCosky: "We started the pension plan and at that time we were putting in half and the ball club was putting in half. Since

'57 the ballplayers don't put a dime in the thing. The owners, the ball clubs, and receipts from the All-Star game and World Series games goes into the fund. Since 1957, a player who has ten years service can retire at $90,000 per year. They will not bring the ones who retired prior to that into it. Wynn and Branca are fighting for us. Wynn says, the least that they could do is to provide us with medical benefits. To hell with the dental, few of us have our original teeth anyway."[53]

During the 1990s, baseball has become even more selfish. The 1994-95 strike and loss of the 1994 World Series was an unmitigated disaster. The strike, which was the eighth major-league work stoppage in twenty-two years, served to almost completely divide and polarize baseball into three groups—the owners, the players, and the fans.[54] Though the strike is over, the same issues that divided management and the players (salary caps, salary arbitration, revenue sharing to assist small-market teams, and free agency) remain unresolved. Fortunately, after a five-year hiatus, baseball finally selected a permanent commissioner in former Milwaukee Brewers owner Alan H. Selig. He will be carefully observed to see if he can provide baseball with the leadership it requires. By selecting an insider, baseball's owners sent a strong message that they do not want regulation, interference, or leadership from someone outside the game. With the exception of Ford Frick and William D. Eckert, often referred to as the "Unknown Soldier," Commissioners Bowie Kuhn, Peter Uebberoth, A. Bartlett Giamatti, and Francis T. Vincent Jr. proved to be far more influential and powerful than many owners liked.

Today's players are intent on protecting fifty years of hard-fought gains that have earned them job security, better conditions in the workplace, and enormous salaries. In addition, they now have marketing agreements that annually bring them more than $100 million from the sale of baseball cards and other memorabilia. Players are treated like royalty. They live in a world of briefcases and investments, travel first class, and even receive $65 a day in meal money. Many justify their status by comparing themselves to other performers in the entertainment world. While a number, like Cecil Fielder and Cal Ripken Jr., give generously of their time and wealth, others are ambivalent or even hostile toward fans or toward the idea that the public might look at them as role models. Barry Bonds, who signed a six-year contract in 1993 that with incentives could earn him $54.75 million, is well known for his disdain for the fans and was once quoted as saying, "If fans pay $10 to go see *Batman*, they don't expect to get Jack Nicholson's autograph."[55] In their defense, players are increasingly suspicious that the "tame" autographs sought by adults or even children will soon be sold at a profit. During the 1980s and early 1990s, when baseball went through a popularity renaissance, prices for baseball cards and other memorabilia skyrocketed.[56]

The 1994 baseball strike greatly widened the gulf between players and a fan base that already has great difficulty identifying with the men on the field. As sportswriter Thomas Boswell wrote, "The truth is, nobody cares about any explanation baseball may have to offer except, perhaps, why $1 billion a year—net after expenses—isn't enough to satisfy 700 players and 28 owners."[57] Many diehard baseball fans took the strike personally and refused to return, and baseball attendance fell by 17 percent in 1995.[58] What baseball failed to realize, or simply chose to ignore, was that once the game's continuum was broken, so was its spell over the fan. What has made baseball the national pastime, and what has separated it from other sports, is the proprietary interest that its followers have developed. Red Smith once wrote, "The relationship between a store and its customers is purely a business one. Between a ball club and the fans, it is vastly more intimate."[59] Baseball's followers, including those sitting on the bench of the U.S. Supreme Court, can no longer deny the business aspects of the game—a situation they have consciously chosen to deny by rewarding the game's participants with the status of legends. Moreover, as commentator Don Beck recently argued, the strike greatly impaired a "vulnerable addiction" based on the game's "myths, rituals, and historic meaning—[which have been] interwoven into our collective psyche."[60]

Not only has baseball turned off some of its traditional followers, its fan base is also shrinking. Currently, the game's largest group of fans are fifty years of age or older. Those in their forties follow football, while those in the group between twenty-four and forty are most attracted to basketball.[61] Today's leading sports heroes are basketball star Michael Jordan and a plethora of athletes from other sports. In addition, many members of the Nintendo Generation find baseball boring—it is slow, it lacks constant action, and it does not feature instant gratification. According to a recent survey by marketing firm Teenage Research Unlimited, baseball finished a poor fourth to basketball, football, and hockey in popularity.[62] Moreover, the survey showed that baseball was, like other professional sports, becoming a pastime for the wealthy. Ticket prices, which by 1994 cost a family of four an average of $95.80 to attend a game, were discouraging families with moderate incomes from coming.[63]

An even more serious slippage for the game is the suspicion that in the 1990s fewer and fewer children are playing some form of baseball. Almost gone are the days when games were played in neighborhood lots, crowded back alleys, or green pastures—when children would spend summers playing for hours and taking turns hitting tens of times a day. Soccer has become popular with many middle- and upper-class children. For most African American children, many of whom view baseball as a white man's game, the sport of choice is basketball. Baseball has already lost a generation of youngsters who will not be taking their children to the park. Should baseball lose its historic stability and its continued presence in the lives of Americans, the game will have little meaning. Post World War II baseball was so popular because it was an inexpensive way of reintegrating our lives into the routine of the familiar—it was a means of reestablishing our identity after a horrendous experience. Baseball was a game we played as children, shared with our parents, and grew up to share with our own offspring. While baseball's future may seem clouded, the game has survived the Black Sox scandal, the depression, world wars, poor leadership, and other shortcomings. The game's built-in resiliency may save it again. The 1998 season's astounding home run race between Mark McGwire and Sammy Sosa, the end of Cal Ripken's remarkable consecutive-game streak, and the New York Yankees' dominating 114-win season have renewed nationwide interest in the game. Hopefully, baseball will not squander the opportunity to once again become the national pastime.

Notes

Chapter 1. Winds of Change

1. "Wobblies" was a nickname for members of the Industrial Workers of the World.

2. See *Standard Oil Co. of Indiana v. U.S.*, 166 *Federal Reporter*, 376-96.

3. John G. Taylor Spink, *Judge Landis and Twenty-Five Years of Baseball* (New York: Thomas Y. Crowell, 1947), 71.

4. David Voight, *From the Commissioners to Continental Expansion*, vol. 2 of *American Baseball* (University Park: Pennsylvania State Univ. Press, 1983), 130.

5. Frank Graham, "Kenesaw Mountain Landis," Baseball Magazine (February 1945), 292.

6. Spink, *Landis*, 226-29.

7. Robert Feller, interview with William Marshall, December 27, 1979, A.B. Chandler Oral History Project, Special Collections and Archives, Univ. of Kentucky Libraries (hereafter cited as Chandler Oral History Project).

8. *Federal Baseball Club of Baltimore, Inc. v. National League of Professional B.B. Clubs and American League of Professional B.B. Clubs*, 259 U.S. 200, 42 Supreme Court, 465.

9. Shirley Povich, interview with William Marshall, March 29, 1976, Chandler Oral History Project.

10. Povich interview.

11. Franklin Delano Roosevelt, Washington, D.C., to Judge Kenesaw Mountain Landis, Chicago, (copy) in the A.B. Chandler Papers, box 162, Special Collections and Archives, Univ. of Kentucky Libraries (hereinafter cited as the Chandler Papers).

12. Ed Fitzgerald, "Hank Greenberg: A Study in Success," *Sport* (March 1951), 86.

13. For a list of players, see *Baseball Magazine* (April 1946), 378-79.

14. *Sporting News* (April 12, 1945), 7. The players included Frank Gustine, Al Lopez, and Bob Elliott (Pirates); Stan Hack, Claude Passeau, and Bill Nicholson (Cubs); Mel Ott, John Rucker, and Billy Jurges (Giants); Rick Ferrell, Dutch Leonard, and George Case (Senators); Marty Marion (Cardinals), George McQuinn (Browns), Rudy York (Tigers), and Frank McCormick (Reds). The Athletics had Dick Siebert and Frankie Hayes and the White Sox had Bill Dietrich and Mike Tresh. Others included Dixie Walker and Mickey Owen (Dodgers), Lou Boudreau and Jeff Heath (Indians), and Pete Fox and Joe Cronin (Red Sox). The Yankees, Phillies, and Braves had no 1941 players in their starting lineups at the beginning of 1945.

15. William Meade, *Even the Browns: The Zany True Story of Baseball in the Early Forties* (Chicago: Contemporary Books, 1978), 189.

16. Ibid., 189-97.

17. Hank Greenberg, *Hank Greenberg: The Story of My Life,* ed. Ira Berkow (New York: Times Books, 1989), 150-51.

18. Bob Feller, *Strikeout Story* (New York: A.S. Barnes, 1947), 227.

19. Stan Musial, interview with William Marshall, May 17, 1978, Chandler Oral History Project.

20. Harry Walker, interview with William Marshall, May 11, 1988, Chandler Oral History Project.

21. Ibid.

22. Yogi Berra with Tom Horton, *Yogi Berra: It Ain't Over. . .* (New York: McGraw-Hill, 1989), 136-49; *Sporting News* (March 29, 1945), 11.

23. *Sporting News* (April 6, 1949), 2.

24. Al Silverman, *Warren Spahn: Immortal Southpaw* (New York: Sport Magazine Library, Bartholomew House, 1961), 48-51. Another battlefield commission was awarded to Jack Knott, who was appointed from first sergeant to first lieutenant at New Haven, Germany, March, 1945. *Sporting News* (March 29, 1945), 11.

25. Frank Baumholtz, interview with William Marshall, December 10, 1992, Chandler Oral History Project.

26. *Sporting News* (November 2, 1944), 11.

27. August Donatelli, interview with William Marshall, March 18, 1988, Chandler Oral History Project.

Chapter 2. "No One Is Qualified"

1. *Sporting News* (March 29, 1945), 11.

2. Mel Harder, interview with William Marshall, June 1, 1988, A.B. Chandler Oral History Project, Special Collections and Archives, Univ. of Kentucky Libraries (hereafter cited as Chandler Oral History Project).

3. Dan Daniel, "Wartime Baseball 'Rationing' Finds Fans Tolerant, Eager for Game," *Baseball Magazine* (April, 1944), 368.

4. Harry Walker, interview with William Marshall, May 11, 1988, Chandler Oral History Project.

5. William O. DeWitt, interview with William Marshall, September 29 and October 1, 1980, Chandler Oral History Project.

6. *Sporting News* (December 28, 1944), 3.

7. *Sporting News* (March 1, 1945), 4.

8. *Sporting News* (February 1, 1945), 1.

9. Ibid.

10. *Sporting News* (January 4, 1945), 10.

11. *Sporting News* (February 22, 1945), 10.

12. *Sporting News* (March 1, 1945), 1-2; (March 22, 1945), 8; and (March 29, 1945), 2.

13. *Sporting News* (April 19, 1945), 1-2.

14. Dan M. Daniel, "Senator Chandler Eminently Fitted for Vital Job as Baseball Commissioner," *Baseball Magazine* (July 1945), 255.

15. Branch Rickey, Memorandum, April 25, 1945, the Branch Rickey Papers, Library of Congress, box 27 (hereafter cited as Branch Rickey Papers).

16. Ibid.

17. Ibid.

18. Ibid. Rickey had read Carpenter's letter before it was introduced and knew that the Phillies owner favored Ford Frick. In his memorandum, he noted that he had attended a meeting on the previous Friday (April 20, 1945) with the Carpenters and Herb Pennock of the Phillies, Bob Quinn, and Lou Perini of the Braves, Horace Stoneham of the

Giants, and Tom Yawkey. All of the clubs in attendance, with the exception of the Braves, favored Ford Frick as commissioner. The Braves wanted James A. Farley, with Frick as their second choice. All agreed that Chandler would be their third choice if the other two men could not be elected. Rickey also knew of MacPhail's strong support of Chandler.

19. Ibid.

20. Ibid.

21. Ibid. J.G. Taylor Spink speculated that Farley might have rejected the position if an offer were made and that this hurt his candidacy. He was making $70,000 a year with Coca-Cola. According to Spink, "He had expressed interest in the baseball job, but had added that if elected, he would have to be given 24 hours to consider, and confer with Mr. Woodruff of Coca-Cola." *Sporting News* (May 3, 1945), 5.

22. Rickey, Memorandum, April 25, 1945, Branch Rickey Papers. The swimming pool was constructed by a Louisville contractor and family friend Ben Collings. It became a campaign issue in the 1944 senatorial election, with Chandler's opponents claiming that the pool was constructed using much-needed war materials. Chandler disputed this claim and asked a Senate committee to investigate the charges. The committee reported that the charges were groundless.

23. Ibid.

24. Ibid.

25. A.B. Chandler, interview with William Marshall, August 15, 1980, Chandler Oral History Project.

26. *Sporting News* (February 22, 1945), 2.

27. Ibid., 10.

28. Vincent X. Flaherty, "The Life Story of Albert B. 'Happy' Chandler," *Baseball Guide and Record Book, 1946* (St. Louis: Charles C. Spink and Sons, 1946), 111-14.

29. Charles P. Roland, "Happy Chandler," *The Register of the Kentucky Historical Society*, no. 85 (Spring 1987), 141.

30. Flaherty, 116-18.

31. Roland, 143-44.

32. Ibid. Centre College's football team was coached by future National League umpire Charlie Moran. Centre's claim to fame was its 1922 win over football power Harvard University—a game in which Chandler helped Centre by scouting the Harvard team.

33. Ibid., 147.

34. Terry Birdwhistell, "A.B. 'Happy' Chandler," in *Kentucky: Its History and Its Heritage*, ed. Fred Hood (St. Louis: Forum Press, 1978), 208-9.

35. Ibid., 211-12, 214.

36. Roland, 158-59.

37. Flaherty, 124.

38. Birdwhistell, 218.

Chapter 3. 1945: Season of Hope

1. *Sporting News* (June 28, 1945), 5, and (March 22, 1945), 6. Gray's legal surname is Wyshner.

2. At the time, this was the third-highest sale price in history. Joe Cronin was sold by the Senators to the Red Sox in 1934 for $250,000 and a player, while the Cardinals sent sore-armed Dizzy Dean to the Cubs in 1938 for $185,000 and three players.

3. See Dan Daniel, "Standout Deal of Baseball Season," *Baseball Magazine* (October, 1945), 369-70.

4. For the inside story on the Borowy deal, see William F. McDermott, "Upside-Down Man," *Colliers Magazine* (October 6, 1945), 53.

5. *Sporting News* (August 2, 1945), 2.

6. Hank Greenberg, *Hank Greenberg: The Story of My Life,* ed. Ira Berkow (New York: Times Books, 1989), 155.

7. *Sporting News* (October 4, 1945), 25.

8. Ibid., 10, 12.

9. Clifford Bloodgood, "The Tigers—In Seven Games," *Baseball Magazine*, December, 1945, 235-36.

10. J.G. Taylor Spink, *Baseball Guide and Record Book, 1946* (St. Louis: The Sporting News, 1946), 159-61.

11. *Sporting News* (May 3, 1945), 3.

12. Leland S. MacPhail to A.B. Chandler, April 27, 1945. Chandler Papers, box 162.

13. Ibid.

14. Ibid.

15. Ibid.

16. *Sporting News* (February 8, 1945), 4.

17. *Sporting News* (June 7, 1945), 6.

18. Ed Danforth, *Atlanta Journal* (April 15, 1946); Jimmy Cannon, *Paris Post* (December 19, 1945).

19. Joe Estes, *Blood-Horse*, May 12, 1945.

20. A.B. Chandler, interview with William Marshall, September 10, 1980, A.B. Chandler Oral History Project, Special Collections and Archives, Univ. of Kentucky Libraries (hereafter cited as Chandler Oral History Project).

21. Ernie Stewart, interview with Larry R. Gerlach, *Men in Blue* (New York: Viking Press, 1980), 123-25. See also testimony of Ernie Stewart, U.S. Congress, House of Representatives, *Study of Monopoly Power: Organized Baseball* (Washington: Government Printing Office, 1951), ser. 1, pt. 1, 933-38. For Harridge's viewpoint on this incident, see testimony on pages 927-41.

22. *Sporting News* (December 20, 1945), 10.

23. *Sporting News* (May 3, 1945), 2.

24. *Sporting News* (May 31, 1945), 6.

25. *Sporting News* (July 19, 1945), 5.

26. Ibid.

27. Ibid.

28. Ibid.

29. Ibid., 12.

30. William O. DeWitt, interview with William Marshall, September 29 and October 1, 1980, Chandler Oral History Project.

31. *New York World Telegram* (June 27, 1945); A.B. Chandler interview, September 3, 1980, Chandler Oral History Project.

32. DeWitt interview.

33. *Sporting News* (October 18, 1945), 16.

Chapter 4. The Mexican Baseball Revolution

1. Charlie Metro, interview with William Marshall, June 13, 1991, A.B. Chandler Oral History Project, Special Collections and Archives, Univ. of Kentucky Libraries (hereafter

cited as Chandler Oral History Project); "Gardella the Unfathomable," *Baseball Magazine* (October 1945), 371-72.

2. Ibid. Giant teammate Adrian Zabala tells a slightly different version of this story. Adrian and Mary Zabala, interview with William Marshall, March 2, 1989, Chandler Oral History Project.

3. Danny Gardella, interview with William Marshall, August 27, 1980, Chandler Oral History Project.

4. Ibid.; *Sporting News* (February 28, 1946), 14.

5. Frank Graham, Jr., "The Great Mexican War," *Sports Illustrated* (September 19, 1966), 119.

6. Gardella interview.

7. Milton Bracker, "Mexico's Baseball Raiders Ride Again," *Saturday Evening Post* (March 8, 1947), 27.

8. Kyle Crichton, "The Hot Tamale Circuit," *Collier's Magazine* (June 22, 1946), 63.

9. *Sporting News* (June 12, 1946), 2.

10. See Teodulo M. Agundis, *El Verdadero Jorge Pasquel: Ensayo Biographico Sobre un Caracter* (Mexico City: Gráfica Atenea, 1957), 95-102.

11. Delores and Ray Dandridge, interview with William Marshall, November 12, 1979, Chandler Oral History Project.

12. *Sporting News* (November 22, 1945), 18, and (March 14, 1946), 2.

13. *Sporting News* (February 28, 1946), 2.

14. Ibid.

15. Zabala interview.

16. A.B. "Happy" Chandler, interview with William Marshall, September 15, 1980, Chandler Oral History Project.

17. *Sporting News* (March 21, 1946), 2.

18. Robert Feller, interview with William Marshall, December 27, 1979, Chandler Oral History Project.

19. *St. Louis Post-Dispatch* (August 2, 1946), 4c; *Sporting News* (March 14, 1946), 2.

20. Ted Williams, interview with William Marshall, March 17, 1988, Chandler Oral History Project.

21. James Toomey, interview with William Marshall, September 29, 1980, Chandler Oral History Project.

22. William O. DeWitt, interview with William Marshall, September 29, 1980, Chandler Oral History Project; Al Hirshberg, "Vern Stephens—Junior Red Sock," *Sport* (August 1949), 18.

23. Hirshberg, 18.

24. Ibid., 19; Accounts of the amount of money involved in the Stephens-Pasquel deal differ radically. An earlier report, which appeared in the *Chicago Tribune*, indicated that Pasquel guaranteed Stephens $15,000 per year for five years, tax free, plus a $5,000 bonus, plus all of his expenses paid. The *Chicago Tribune*, April 9, 1946, 23. In Hirshberg's article on Stephens, the arrangement was for $175,000 for five years. In an interview with Frank Graham in the 1960s, Stephens maintained that the entire transaction was worth $250,000. He indicated that Pasquel sent $25,000 to Stephens's wife and placed the remainder in a Mexican bank. See Graham, op. cit., 124. The most conservative figure is employed here because it squares with other contemporary accounts and with offers made to other players.

25. *Sporting News* (April 11, 1946), 2.

26. DeWitt interview.

27. Graham, 124-25.

28. *Sporting News* (April 11, 1946), 2.

29. *Chicago Tribune* (April 7, 1946), pt. 2, 2; (April 9, 1946), 23

30. Sal Maglie, "I'm the Luckiest Guy in Baseball," *Sport* (September 1951), 74.

31. Sal Maglie, interview with William Marshall, May 25, 1981, Chandler Oral History Project.

32. Ibid. See also Stanley Frank, "How the Giants Found a Pitcher in the Doghouse," *Saturday Evening Post* (May 1951), 152.

33. Maglie interview.

34. *Brooklyn Eagle* (April 1, 1946).

35. Mickey Owen, interview with William Marshall, May 27, 1980, Chandler Oral History Project.

36. *Sporting News* (April 11, 1946), 10.

37. *St. Louis Post-Dispatch* (April 9, 1946), 4c.

38. Owen interview.

39. Robert Brown, interview with William Marshall, September 11, 1985, Chandler Oral History Project.

40. *New York Times* (June 9, 1946), 2L.

41. Walter "Red" Barber, interview with William Marshall, June 27, 1987, Chandler Oral History Project.

42. *Brooklyn Eagle* (May 5, 1946); *Sporting News* (May 9, 1946), 2.

43. *Sporting News* (May 16, 1946), 10.

44. While the Yankees were initially successful in obtaining a temporary injunction, the case for permanent action lingered into oblivion in 1947. The Dodgers' injunction against the Pasquels was dismissed in late May 1946, on the basis of jurisdictional questions.

45. Owen interview.

46. Milton Bracker, "Ruth's Visit Stirs Interest of Fans," *New York Times* (May 16, 1946), 25L.

47. Owen interview.

48. Ibid.

49. *Sporting News* (June 19, 1946), 2.

50. According to Musial, he met with Breadon, but the Cardinal owner did not give him a raise at that time. Musial had another meeting with Breadon, in August, at which time he was given a $5,000 raise because he was having a good season. Stan Musial, interview with William Marshall, May 17, 1978, Chandler Oral History Project.

51. Barber interview.

52. *Sporting News* (December 18, 1946), 4.

53. Chandler interview, September 15, 1980.

54. Owen interview.

55. *Chicago Tribune* (April 11, 1946), 31-32.

56. Dandridge interview.

57. *Chicago Tribune* (April 14, 1946) sec. II, F 1, 4.

58. Max Lanier, interview with William Marshall, June 26, 1987, Chandler Oral History Project.

59. Maglie interview.

60. Owen and Lanier interviews.

61. Zabala interview.

62. Owen interview.

63. Lanier interview.
64. Zabala interview.
65. Owen interview.
66. Ibid.
67. *Sporting News* (August 21, 1946), 2.
68. *Sporting News* (September 4, 1946), 2, and (August 21, 1946), 1.

Chapter 5. Murphy Money and More

1. Murphy also attended Harvard Law School for two years, but he earned his degree at Northeastern University.
2. *Time Magazine* (June 3, 1946), 3.
3. *Sporting News* (April 25, 1946), 1.
4. Ibid., 3.
5. Ibid.
6. *Louisville Courier-Journal* (May 5, 1946), 3.
7. Ibid.; *Sporting News* (May 2, 1946), 4.
8. *Sporting News* (June 5, 1946), 6.
9. *Pittsburgh Press* (May 16, 1946), 17.
10. *New York Times* (May 28, 1946), 28.
11. *Pittsburgh Press* (May 19, 1946), 18.
12. Ibid.
13. *Pittsburgh Press* (June 6, 1946), 26.
14. *New York Times* (June 6, 1946), 26L.
15. Ibid.
16. *Pittsburgh Press* (June 6, 1946), 6.
17. *New York Times* (June 6, 1946), 26L.
18. *Sporting News* (June 19, 1946), 4.
19. *Pittsburgh Press* (June 6, 1946), 6.
20. *Sporting News* (June 19, 1946), 4.
21. *Pittsburgh Press* (June 6, 1946), 1.
22. *Time Magazine* (June 3, 1946), 58.
23. *New York Times* (June 7, 1946), 23L.
24. Ibid.
25. Ibid.
26. Ibid.
27. A.B. "Happy" Chandler, interview with William Marshall, September 15, 1980, A.B. Chandler Oral History Project, Special Collections and Archives, Univ. of Kentucky Libraries (hereafter cited as Chandler Oral History Project).
28. Ibid.
29. *Sporting News* (June 19, 1946), 8.
30. Truett "Rip" Sewell, interview with William Marshall, April 23, 1980, Chandler Oral History Project.
31. Ibid.
32. *Sporting News* (June 19, 1946), 3.
33. Sewell interview.
34. *New York Times* (June 8, 1946), 24L.
35. *Sporting News* (June 19, 1946), 3.
36. Ibid., 4.

37. Al Lopez, interview with William Marshall, April 23, 1980, Chandler Oral History Project; Ralph Kiner, interview with William Marshall, September 26, 1979, Chandler Oral History Project.

38. *New York Times* (June 10, 1946), 27L. Players' organizations, such as the Guild, were not entirely new. In 1890, the Players Brotherhood, under the leadership of John Montgomery Ward, formed a Players League to combat a $2,500 minimum salary decree instituted by National League owners. Responding to issues not unlike those brought to the fore by Murphy, many players jumped to the new league. The resulting competition, commonly referred to as the Brotherhood War, ended in defeat for the players and left baseball financially devastated during the last decade of the nineteenth century. Had the Pirates voted affirmatively to strike, the work stoppage would have been only the second in major league history. The first strike occurred in 1912, when Detroit Tiger players struck to protest the ten-day suspension of Tiger star Ty Cobb as a result his fight with a heckler in the stands. Playing with a collection of semipro players and early-arriving fans, the Tigers lost a Saturday game 24-2 to the Philadelphia Athletics. Faced with $100 fines and a possible ban for life, the Tiger players returned after having made their point. A second players' organization, the Players Fraternity, grew out of the Cobb incident but died in 1917, soon after the collapse of the Federal League.

39. *Sporting News* (June 19, 1946), 12.

40. *New York Times* (June 7, 1946), 27L.

41. *Sporting News* (May 23, 1946), 1, 3.

42. *Sporting News* (June 19, 1946), 12, and (July 24, 1946), 10.

43. *Sporting News* (July 31, 1946), 3.

44. *New York Times* (July 20, 1946), 6L.

45. *Sporting News* (July 31, 1946), 3.

46. Ibid., 6.

47. Selected were the following players: Terry Moore and Marty Marion, Cardinals; Dixie Walker and Augie Galan, Dodgers; Phil Cavarretta and Billy Jurges, Cubs; Bill Lee and Billy Herman, Braves; Bucky Walters and Joe Beggs, Reds; Roy Hughes and Rollie Hemsley, Phillies; Hal Schumacher and Buddy Blattner, Giants; Rip Sewell and Lee Handley, Pirates; Pinky Higgins, Red Sox; Johnny Murphy and Tommy Henrich, Yankees; Hank Greenberg, Tigers; Buck Newsom, Senators; Mel Harder, Indians; Babe Dahlgren and Johnny Berardino, Browns; Joe Kuhel, White Sox; and Gene Desautels, Athletics.

48. *Sporting News* (July 31, 1946), 4, 6.

49. Stan Musial, interview with William Marshall, May 17, 1978, Chandler Oral History Project.

50. Martin Marion, interview with William Marshall, May 19, 1978, Chandler Oral History Project.

51. Ibid. See also Ellis Veech, "Mr. Shortstop Takes Charge," *Baseball Magazine* (February, 1951), 312.

52. Sewell interview; Robert Broeg, interview with William Marshall, May 16, 1978, Chandler Oral History Project.

53. *Sporting News* (July 31, 1946), 6.

54. This was in addition to room, meals, transportation, and laundry expense already borne by the clubs.

55. *Sporting News* (August 7, 1946), 5.

56. Mel Harder, interview with William Marshall, June 1, 1988, Chandler Oral History Project.

57. Ibid.; Marion interview.

58. *Sporting News* (August 14, 1946), 3.

59. Marion interview.

60. [Leland MacPhail, Sr.], "Report for Submission to National and American Leagues on 27 August 1946" (hereafter cited as the MacPhail Report), Chandler Papers, box 162.

61. Ibid., 2, 10.

62. Ibid., 12.

63. Ibid., 18-19.

64. Ibid., 4, 17.

65. According to testimony before the 1951 Celler Committee investigation of baseball, after MacPhail's report was reviewed by major-league representatives, the gray-covered reports were collected and destroyed. Only two copies escaped destruction: one in Will Harridge's office, which was to be copied and sent to the minor leagues, and Comissioner Chandler's copy, which ended up in the files of his Versailles office. The patchwork version, which purged MacPhail's offending sections, was also gathered up and destroyed after it was considered. See Celler Committee Report, U.S. Congress, House of Representatives, *Study of Monopoly Power: Organized Baseball* (Washington, D.C.: Government Printing Office, 1951), ser. 1, pt. 1, 515-16 (hereafter cited as Celler Report). A final version appears on pages 497-505 of the Celler Report.

66. *Sporting News* (September 4, 1946), 3.

67. Improvement for players that were reflected in the new uniform contract included (1) $500 for moving expenses if a player's contract was assigned to another team, (2) a broadened interpretation of player disability, (3) a requirement that owners must deliver contracts to players by February 1, and (4) elimination of the ten-day notice of release clause.

68. Celler Report, 1951, 503.

69. William O. DeWitt, interview with William Marshall, September 29, 1980, Chandler Oral History Project.

70. *Sporting News* (September 4, 1946), 1.

71. *Sporting News* (August 28, 1946), 6.

72. Lee Lowenfish and Tony Lupien, *The Imperfect Diamond: The Story of Baseball's Reserve System and the Men Who Fought to Change It* (New York: Stein and Day, 1980), 151.

73. Harder interview.

Chapter 6. 1946: Season of Tumult

1. *Sporting News* (August 16, 1945), 12.

2. *Sporting News* (April 25, 1946), 2.

3. Harold Kaese, "They're Digging a Pennant in Boston," *Saturday Evening Post* (June 28, 1947), 122.

4. *Sporting News* (November 8, 1945), 12.

5. "A Jolly Good Feller," *Baseball Magazine* (February 1946), 291.

6. Robert Feller, interview with William Marshall, July 3, 1979, A.B. Chandler Oral History Project, Special Collections and Archives, Univ. of Kentucky Libraries (hereafter cited as Chandler Oral History Project).

7. *Sporting News* (January 10, 1946), 12, and (February 14, 1946), 14.

8. *Sporting News* (February 14, 1946), 7.

9. Ted Williams, interview with William Marshall, March 17, 1988, Chandler Oral History Project.

10. Dan Daniel, "Old Spring Baseball Trouping Memories Revived by 1946 Experiences," *Baseball Magazine* (April 1946), 373-74.

11. *Sporting News* (February 14, 1946), 6.

12. *Sporting News* (February 7, 1946), 3, 7. The ten players were Hal Newhouser, Virgil Trucks, Dizzy Trout, Al Benton, Stubby Overmire, Bob Swift, Eddie Mayo, Skeeter Webb, Doc Cramer, and Roy Cullenbine.

13. *Sporting News* (March 7, 1946), 5.

14. Lee Lowenfish and Tony Lupien, *The Imperfect Diamond: The Story of Baseball's Reserve System and the Men Who Fought to Change It* (New York: Stein and Day), 132-34.

15. *Sporting News* (July 3, 1946), 8.

16. Hal Schumacher, interview with William Marshall, June 17, 1987, Chandler Oral History Project.

17. *Sporting News* (May 16, 1946), 3.

18. An agreement was created between the major and minor leagues covering bonus players in 1945. Players receiving a bonus of $6,000 or more to sign with a major-league team could be sent to a lower classification only for one year, after which time they must remain on a major-league team's roster. Teams who put bonus players on waivers lost both player and investment. For a history of the bonus rule, see Brent Kelley, *Baseball's Biggest Blunder: The Bonus Rule of 1953-1957* (Lanham, Md.: Scarecrow, 1997).

19. *Sporting News* (June 5, 1946), 4.

20. Stan Musial, interview with William Marshall, May 17, 1978, Chandler Oral History Project.

21. Max Lanier, interview with William Marshall, June 26, 1987, Chandler Oral History Project.

22. Harry Walker, interview with William Marshall, May 11, 1988, Chandler Oral History Project.

23. Albert "Red" Schoendienst, interview with William Marshall, n.d., Chandler Oral History Project.

24. Martin Marion, interview with William Marshall, May 19, 1978, Chandler Oral History Project; Musial interview; Walker interview.

25. Marion, Lanier, and Walker interviews.

26. Marion, Musial, and Lanier interviews.

27. Walker and Marion interviews.

28. Walker interview; *Sporting News* (June 26, 1946), 3.

29. Musial interview.

30. Robert Broeg, interview with William Marshall, May 16, 1978, Chandler Oral History Project.

31. John Drebinger, "The Playoff Series," *Baseball Magazine* (December 1946), 219.

32. Nolan Ryan now holds the single-season strikeout record with 383, which he achieved in 1973.

33. *Sporting News* (May 16, 1946), 3.

34. *Sporting News* (September 11, 1946), 2.

35. Ted Williams with John Underwood, *My Turn at Bat: The Story of My Life* (New York: Simon and Schuster, 1988), 113.

36. Walker and Schoendienst interviews.

37. Ralph Knight and Bob Broeg, "Country Keynotes the Cards," *Saturday Evening Post* (May 17, 1947), 174.

38. *Sporting News* (October 23, 1946), 8.

39. Schoendienst interview.

40. Walker interview.

41. Williams with Underwood, 113; *Sporting News* (October 23, 1946), 12.

42. *Sporting News* (October 16, 1946), 2.

43. Marion interview.

44. *Sporting News* (October 16, 1946), 2. In December 1946, the major leagues voted to give the money from World Series broadcasts to the pension plan and agreed that each club would contribute $250 toward the plan for each player who was willing to match the sum. The players also established a committee to iron out all of the plan's details.

45. J.G. Taylor Spink, *Official Baseball Guide, 1947* (St. Louis: The Sporting News, 1947), 138.

Chapter 7. Durocher Finishes Last

1. Leo Durocher, *Nice Guys Finish Last* (New York: Simon and Schuster, 1975), 46.

2. *Sporting News* (October 9, 1946), 2.

3. *Sporting News* (July 17, 1946), 9.

4. Ibid.

5. Pete Castiglione, interview with William Marshall, September 7, 1991, A.B. Chandler Oral History Project, Special Collections and Archives, Univ. of Kentucky Libraries (hereafter cited as Chandler Oral History Project).

6. Stan Musial, interview with William Marshall, May 17, 1978, Chandler Oral History Project.

7. Harold Parrott, *The Lords of Baseball* (New York: Praeger, 1976), 169.

8. Carl Erskine, interview with William Cooper, May 25, 1978, Chandler Oral History Project.

9. Durocher, 255.

10. *Sporting News* (September 18, 1946), 4.

11. *Sporting News* (July 17, 1946), 9, and (September 18, 1946), 3.

12. *Sporting News* (April 16, 1947), 5.

13. Ed Fitzgerald, "Leo Durocher: Man With Nine Lives," *Sport* (April, 1951), 28-29.

14. Red Smith, interview with William Marshall, November 13, 1979, Chandler Oral History Project.

15. Parrott, *The Lords of Baseball*, 155.

16. Red Barber, *1947-When All Hell Broke Loose in Baseball* (Garden City, N.Y.: Doubleday, 1982), 95-96; Charles Dressen to Branch Rickey, June 25, 1943, Branch Rickey Papers, Library of Congress, box 11 (hereafter cited as Branch Rickey Papers).

17. Lewis Yablonsky, *George Raft* (New York: McGraw-Hill, 1974), 178.

18. Dean Jennings, *We Only Kill Each Other* (Englewood Cliffs, N.J.: Prentice-Hall, 1967), 38-39.

19. Arthur Mann, *Baseball Confidential* (New York: David McKay, 1951), 38.

20. Ibid., 43-44.

21. Ibid., 45-46; A.B. Chandler interview with William Marshall, December 4, 1980, Chander Oral History Project.

22. Mann, *Baseball Confidential*, 46.

23. Chandler interview, December 4, 1980.

24. In *Nice Guys Finish Last* (pp. 244-45), Durocher tells of avoiding Connie Immerman and Memphis Engelberg in a Havana hotel and of his refusal to shake hands with Lucky Luciano.

25. Chandler interview, December 4, 1980.

26. Westbrook Pegler, "Fair Enough" (syndicated column), December 13, 1946, newspaper clipping in A.B. Chandler Papers, Special Collections and Archive, Univ. of Kentucky Libraries, box 576. See Mann, *Baseball Confidential*, 49-50; Barber, 101.

27. *New York Times* (February 1, 1945), 1-3.

28. *Sporting News* (December 25, 1946), 12.

29. *New York Times* (January 28, 1947), 1.

30. *Sporting News* (July 3, 1946), 24, and (September 4, 1946), 12.

31. The suspended players included Paul Fugit, Leonard Pecou, Alvin Kaiser, Don Vettoral, and W.C. Thomas. *Sporting News* (February 5, 1947), 9.

32. Ibid., 9-10.

33. *Sporting News* (December 25, 1946), 12.

34. *Sporting News* (February 26, 1947), 3.

35. *Sporting News* (February 12, 1947), 3, 12

36. Durocher, 227-31.

37. *Sporting News* (February 12, 1947), 10.

38. *Sporting News* (March 12, 1947), 8.

39. *Sporting News* (February 19, 1947), 5.

40. *New York Herald-Tribune* (March 4, 1947).

41. Mann, *Baseball Confidential*, 76-77; *New York Daily News* (March 11, 1947).

42. One plausible reason for the firing was MacPhail's insistence that Rickey send him several players after the Cardinals called up infielder Burgess Whitehead. The two clubs had an agreement that the parent club could not call up a player without MacPhail's approval. Don Warfield, *The Roaring Redhead* (South Bend, Ind.: Diamond, 1987), 31. Another rationale for his dismissal was his apparent extravagance. Rickey complained to Columbus manager Ray Blades that MacPhail had been spending more money than "we're making." Murray Polner, *Branch Rickey: A Biography* (New York: Signet, 1983), 101. Warfield argues this point. He noted that the Cardinals were upset with McPhail's lavish office in Columbus—an area that was paneled free by a grateful contractor who had earned a $50,000 construction bonus for early project completion and covered with oriental rugs obtained at a fire sale. Warfield pointed out that the Columbus Redbirds were the only American Association team to make a profit in 1932 and that they drew 279,000 more fans than their parent club, the Cardinals. Warfield, *The Roaring Redhead*, 31-36.

43. Lee MacPhail, interview with William Marshall, May 9, 1977, Chandler Oral History Project.

44. Barber, 46; Arthur Mann, "The Larry MacPhail Story," *Sport* (April, 1956), 70. MacPhail's biographer attributes MacPhail's departure to his own waning interest in the team and to his patriotic reaction to the onset of the war. Warfield, *The Roaring Redhead*, 143-44.

45. *Sporting News* (February 1, 1945), 8.

46. *Sporting News* (November 13, 1946), 2. Rickey decided to let Dressen go, even though he believed that he had a verbal commitment from him to remain with the Dodgers. Branch Rickey to Larry MacPhail, October 25, 1946, Branch Rickey Papers, box 128.

47. Memorandum H.P. [Harold Parrott] initialed by A.M. [Arthur Mann], Yankee Press Conference No. 5, 1946, Branch Rickey Papers, box 128.

48. *Brooklyn Eagle* (March 3, 1947); Durocher, 246-47.

49. *Sporting News* (March 19, 1947), 6.

50. Durocher, 238. Described as a "gambling czar" by author Noel Hynd, Engelberg, apparently through foul play, later suffered an inglorious end on a Brooklyn wharf. Noel Hynd, *The Giants of the Polo Grounds: The Glorious Times of Baseball's New York Giants* (New York: Doubleday, 1988), 384.

51. Polner, 138-39; Barber, 99; Mann, *Baseball Confidential*, 108; obituary of Arthur Mann, *New York Times* (October 25, 1967), 47.

52. *Sporting News* (March 26, 1947), 3.

53. *Sporting News* (April 23, 1947), 2.

54. *Sporting News* (March 26, 1947), 3.

55. Durocher, 252.

56. Mann, *Baseball Confidential*, 102. Mann's work provides the most detailed published account of the Durocher hearings.

57. Durocher, 254. According to Chandler, they shook hands. Albert B. Chandler with Vance Trimble, *Heroes, Plain Folks, and Skunks* (Chicago: Bonus Books, 1989), 216.

58. Mann, *Baseball Confidential*, 103-4.

59. Ibid., 110-13.

60. Ibid., 113-14.

61. *Sporting News* (April 9, 1947), 6.

62. Decision "In Re: MacPhail-Rickey-Durocher Controversy," April 9, 1947, A.B. Chandler Papers, "Decisions," box 162, Special Collections and Archives, Univ. of Kentucky Libraries. Parrott's fine was later rescinded.

63. Chandler interview, December 4, 1980.

64. Ibid.

65. Ibid.

66. Ibid.

67. *Sporting News* (April 16, 1947), 6, 8, and 10.

68. Ibid., 10.

69. Ibid.

70. *Sporting News* (April 23, 1947), 10.

71. *Sporting News* (May 7, 1947), 2.

72. Durocher, 257.

73. Walter "Red" Barber, interview with William Marshall, June 27, 1987, Chandler Oral History Project.

74. *Sporting News* (April 23, 1947), 4.

75. Lee MacPhail, interview with William Marshall, May 9, 1977, Chandler Oral History Project.

76. Memorandum of Conversation, Louisville, Kentucky, June 5, 1947, Branch Rickey Papers, box 78.

77. Durocher, 261.

78. Ernie Harwell, interview with William Marshall, June 2, 1988, Chandler Oral History Project. Shirley Povich, interview with William Marshall, March 29, 1976, Chandler Oral History Project.

79. William Veeck, interview with William Marshall, February 23, 1977, Chandler Oral History Project.

80. Frederic A. Johnson, interview with William Marshall, August 26, 1980, Chandler Oral History Project.

81. Ibid.

82. Barber, 132.

Chapter 8. Jackie Robinson's America

1. "Jim Crow," *Survey Graphic* (January 1947), 65.

2. Charles G. Bolte, "He Fought for Freedom," *Survey Graphic* (January 1947), 70.

3. *Sporting News* (November 1, 1945), 6.

4. Monte Irvin, interview with William Marshall, May 12, 1977, A.B. Chandler Oral History Project, Special Collections and Archives, Univ. of Kentucky Libraries (hereafter cited as Chandler Oral History Project).

5. Robert Peterson, *Only the Ball Is White* (New York: McGraw-Hill, 1984), 176.

6. John B. Holway, *Voices from the Great Black Baseball Leagues* (New York: Dodd, Mead, 1975), 324.

7. Murray Polner, *Branch Rickey: A Biography* (New York: Signet, 1983), 148-49.

8. William O. DeWitt, interview with William Marshall, September 29 and October 1, 1980, Chandler Oral History Project.

9. Polner, 150. Bill Veeck also told a story about attempting to buy the Philadelphia Phillies in 1943 from Gerry Nugent and being thwarted by Judge Landis because Veeck planned to stock the team with Negro League stars (William Veeck, interview with William Marshall, February 23, 1977, Chandler Oral History Project). The story has been discredited by three researchers (David Jordan, Larry Gerlach, and John Rossi) in "The Truth About Bill Veeck and the '43 Phillies," *The National Pastime: A Review of Baseball History* (spring 1998), 3-13.

10. Ibid., 146-47.

11. Harold Parrott, *The Lords of Baseball* (New York: Praeger, 1976), 187-88.

12. The Thomas story can be found in several sources: Carl T. Rowan and Jackie Robinson, *Wait Till Next Year* (New York: Random House, 1960), 105-6; Polner, 38-41; Jackie Robinson, as told to Alfred Duckett, *I Never Had It Made* (New York: G.P. Putnam's Sons, 1972), 38-39; Arnold Rampersad, *Jackie Robinson: A Biography* (New York: Alfred A. Knopf, 1997), 121-22; and Jules Tygiel, *Baseball's Great Experiment* (New York: Oxford Univ. Press, 1983), 51-52.

13. Tygiel, 55.

14. The Red Sox were attempting to get a Massachusetts Sunday curfew law repealed, and the chairman of the committee that controlled the bill would let it go to the floor of the commonwealth's legislature only if the team agreed to sponsor a tryout. Ed Linn, "Joe Cronin, the Irishman, Who Made His Own Luck," *Sport* (April 1956), 55.

15. Rowan and Robinson, 96-101.

16. Robinson and Duckett, 41.

17. Sam Jethroe, interview with William Marshall, May 23, 1981, Chandler Oral History Project.

18. Linn, 55.

19. *Sporting News* (April 12, 1945), 2.

20. Memorandum to Harry Walsh, November 29, 1947, Branch Rickey Papers, Library of Congress, box 80 (hereafter cited as Branch Rickey Papers). According to Rickey, Hall turned out to be a very poor executive who had no feel for promotional activities, public relations, or player procurement. The Brooklyn Dodgers ended up advancing the team more than $6,000. At the end of 1945, the United States League folded.

21. Effa Manley, interview with William Marshall, October 19, 1977, Chandler Oral History Project.

22. Peterson, *Only the Ball Is White*, 187.

23. *Sporting News* (May 24, 1945), 2.

24. Dan W. Dodson, "The Integration of Negroes in Baseball," *Journal of Educational Sociology*, October, 1954, 77-78.

25. Undated speech, Branch Rickey Papers, box 7.

26. Branch Rickey to Arthur Mann, Pittsburgh, Pa., May 3, 1958, Arthur Mann Papers, Library of Congress, box 2.

27. Arthur Mann, "The Negro and Baseball" (manuscript), Branch Rickey Papers, box 68. Written for publication before Robinson was signed, this was likely the first account of the Robinson/Rickey encounter.

28. Robinson and Duckett, *I Never Had It Made*, 43.

29. Ibid.

30. Mann, "The Negro and Baseball," 11.

31. Rowan and Robinson, 117.

32. Robinson and Duckett, *I Never Had It Made*, 46.

33. Branch Rickey, *The American Diamond* (New York: Simon and Schuster, 1965), 45-47; See also manuscript, Branch Rickey Papers, box 13.

34. Manley interview.

35. Irvin interview.

36. Branch Rickey to Arthur Mann, Chicago, Illinois, October 7, 1945. Branch Rickey Papers, box 68. The story of Branch Rickey's attempt to break the color line with several ballplayers at once was first reported by Jules Tygiel and John Thorn in "The Signing of Jackie Robinson: The Untold Story," *Sport* (June 1988), 65-70.

37. Ibid., 70.

38. *Sporting News* (November 29, 1945), 6.

39. *Sporting News* (October 4, 1945), 14.

40. Ibid. Lacey was quoted as saying, "I am reluctant to say that we haven't a single man in the ranks of colored baseball who could step into the major league uniform and disport himself after the fashion of a big leaguer. . . . There are those among our league players who might possibly excel in the matter of hitting or fielding or base-running. But for the most part, the fellows who could hold their own in more than one of these phases of the game are few and far between—perhaps nil."

41. Ibid.

42. Polner, 171.

43. *Kansas City Call* (October 5, 1945).

44. *New York Times* (October 24, 1945).

45. Thorn and Tygiel, 70.

46. *Sporting News* (November 1, 1945), 4.

47. Ibid., 6.

48. Ibid., 5-6.

49. Ibid., 12.

50. Ibid., 4.

51. Manley interview.

52. *Sporting News* (November 1, 1945), 4.

53. *Sporting News* (November 15, 1945), 17.

54. *Sporting News* (March 7, 1946), 8.

55. Tygiel, 103-4.

56. Unidentified Branch Rickey speech. Branch Rickey Papers, box 7.

57. *Sporting News* (April 11, 1946), 20.

58. *Pittsburgh Courier* (April 20, 1946).

59. Walter "Red" Barber, interview with William Marshall, June 27, 1987, Chandler Oral History Project.

60. Polner, 180.

61. *Sporting News* (October 9, 1946), 27.

62. Robinson and Duckett, 63.

63. Ibid., 64.

64. *Sporting News* (October 16, 1946), 18.

65. Roy Campanella, *It's Good to Be Alive* (New York: Signet, New American Library, 1974), 116.

66. Don Newcombe, interview with William Marshall, May 4, 1976, Chandler Oral History Project.

67. Campanella, 119.

68. MacPhail Report, Chandler Papers, box 162. Versions of the original and final reports are also located in U.S. Congress, House of Representatives, *Study of Monopoly Power: Organized Baseball* (Washington, D.C.: Government Printing Office, 1951), 474-88 (hereafter cited as Celler Report).

69. Tygiel, 83.

70. MacPhail Report, 18-20.

71. Both Rickey and Chandler stated that the owners voted 15-1 not to allow blacks to play major-league baseball during the 1947 season. There is a discrepancy between the two as to where and when such a vote took place. During his Wilberforce speech (delivered at Wilberforce University, February 17, 1948), Rickey first claimed that an actual 15-1 vote took place at the August 28, 1946, major-league sessions at the Blackstone Hotel in Chicago. See "Rickey Claims that 15 Clubs Voted to Bar Negroes from the Majors," *New York Times* (February 18, 1948), 37. Under attack by some of the owners, he altered his story a few days later, stating that the 15-1 vote approving the MacPhail Report was the action to which he had been referring. See "MacPhail Contradicts Rickey on Speeches," *New York Times* (February 21, 1948), 16L, and "Rickey Agrees that Club Owners Might Not Recall Anti-Negro Vote," *New York Times* (February 19, 1948), 31. A.B. Chandler insisted that the 15-1 vote took place at a meeting over which he presided, at the Waldorf Astoria Hotel in January 1947. See Chandler interview, September 22, 1980; Frank Dolson, *Lexington Leader* (August 2, 1982), B1; Roger Nesbitt, *Lexington Leader* (July 29, 1982), A1, 14; and Billy Reed, *Louisville Courier-Journal* (August 14, 1982), C1, -7. Baseball's winter meetings, however, did not take place in New York, but instead were held in Los Angeles, December 5-7, 1946. See the *New York Times* (December 2-8, 1946). It is unlikely (although possible) that the owners would meet in January just a few weeks later to discuss the Robinson issue, when they could have done so in Los Angeles. Indeed, the commissioner's own remarks, uttered in December 1946 and praising Robinson's potential as a major leaguer, suggest that the decision to bring Robinson up from the minor leagues had already been decided by Rickey and Chandler (see the *Pittsburgh Courier* [December 21, 1946]). It is also unlikely, as some writers have postulated, that the nation's sportswriters could have missed or ignored a special meeting on the Robinson issue (see Billy Reed, *Louisville Courier-Journal*, [August 14, 1982]). Even in the winter, baseball was America's favorite sports topic, especially in New York.

72. Celler Report, 496.

73. Chandler interview, September 22, 1980.

74. Ric Roberts, "Chandler's Views on Player Ban Sought," *Pittsburgh Courier* (May 5, 1945). See also Roberts, "Remarks on A.B. Chandler, Fifth Annual Negro Baseball League Players' Reunion, Ashland, Kentucky, June 22, 1982" (tape in Special Collections and Archives, Univ. of Kentucky Libraries).

75. J. Cullen Fentress, "Chandler and Wife Laud Jackie Robinson," *Pittsburgh Courier* (December 21, 1946).

76. Arthur Mann, "The Truth About the Jackie Robinson Case," *Saturday Evening Post* (May 20, 1950), 150, 152.

77. *Sporting News* (January 22, 1947), 16.

78. *Brooklyn Eagle* (March 17, 1947), 11.

79. Leo Durocher, *Nice Guys Finish Last* (New York: Simon and Schuster, 1975), 205; Polner, 193-94.

80. Rowan and Robinson, 176-177; Tygiel, 170-71; Mann, "Truth about Jackie Robinson," 152-53; Polner, 194-95; Robinson, 68-69; and Milton Gross, "The Emancipation of Jackie Robinson," *Sport* (October 1951), 83.

81. *Brooklyn Eagle* (March 22, 1947), 7.

82. *Sporting News* (March 12, 1947), 17.

83. Robinson and Duckett, 68.

84. *Sporting News* (January 8, 1947), 15.

85. *Pittsburgh Courier* (November 3, 1945).

86. Bob Feller, interview with William Marshall, July 3, 1978, Chandler Oral History Project. Robinson failed to hit Feller in six plate appearances, which included three strikeouts in a row in San Diego, when the pair faced each other on the 1946 barnstorming tour against Satchel Paige's All-Stars. Feller's remarks became a point of contention between the two men in later years—this was particularly unfortunate because it was Feller who organized several successful barnstorming trips between groups of white players and Satchel Paige's All-Stars. Although the motivating force behind these barnstorming tours was to provide extra economic benefits for the players and to give entertainment to people who rarely saw major-league baseball, they did serve to showcase the not inconsiderable talents of black players. See Bob Feller with Bill Gilbert, *Now Pitching, Bob Feller* (New York: Harper Perennial, 1991), 140-41.

87. Stan Musial, interview with William Marshall, May 17, 1978, Chandler Oral History Project.

88. *Brooklyn Eagle* (April 12, 1947), 6.

89. *Sporting News* (April 23, 1947), 3.

90. *Brooklyn Eagle* (April 21, 1947), 3.

91. *Brooklyn Eagle* (April 17, 1947), 20.

92. *Brooklyn Eagle* (April 21, 1947), 3.

93. Collie Small, "The Terrible-Tempered Mr. Chapman," *Saturday Evening Post* (April 5, 1947) 25, 152-53.

94. Robinson and Duckett, 71; Rowan and Robinson, 181.

95. Robinson and Duckett, 71.

96. Parrott, 192-93.

97. Ibid.

98. *Sporting News* (May 7, 1947), 6.

99. Robinson and Duckett, 76.

100. Parrott, 194-95.

101. *Sporting News* (May 21, 1947), 4.

102. Ibid.

103. Ford Frick, *Games, Asterisks, and People: Memoirs of a Lucky Fan* (New York: Crown, 1973), 97-98.

104. Robert Broeg, interview with William Marshall, May 16, 1978, Chandler Oral History Project.

105. Musial interview.

106. Harry Walker, interview with William Marshall, May 11, 1988, Chandler Oral History Project.

107. Martin Marion, interview with William Marshall, May 19, 1978, Chandler Oral History Project.

108. Gene Schoor, *The Pee Wee Reese Story* (New York: Julian Messner, 1956), 94-95.

109. Ibid., 95; Parrott, 198-99.

110. Arthur Mann, "Truth about Jackie Robinson," 154.

111. Several attempts were made to trade Walker during the 1947 season. Three days after he made his request, Rickey initiated a deal that would have sent him to Pittsburgh for $40,000 and Al Gionfriddo and Frank Kalin. At the eleventh hour, Rickey's insistence that either Wally Westlake or Ralph Kiner be substituted for Kalin torpedoed the arrangement. Rickey offered Walker, Carl Furillo, and Vic Lombardi to the Giants for Johnny Mize, but he was turned down. He then offered Walker to the Pirates again for pitcher Nick Strincevich and $40,000 but had to cancel the deal when Pete Reiser fractured his skull after crashing into an outfield wall. Finally, at the end of the season Rickey allowed the Pirates to claim Walker off the waiver list for $1.00. The usual $10,000 waiver price was added to Walker's salary in order that the Pirates could pay him $30,000 for 1948. The Pirates and Dodgers buried this transaction in a large multiplayer trade announced in November and December 1947, in order to spare Walker the ignominy of being claimed for a dollar and to hide a large cash exchange. The trade sent Walker, Ed Stevens, Stan Rojek, Vic Lombardi, Hal Gregg, and Monte Basgall to Pittsburgh for Gene Mauch, Elwin "Preacher" Roe, Billy Cox, Vic Barnhart, Jimmy Bloodworth, and $315,000. The deal proved to be one of the greatest ever made by Rickey. Ibid., 153-54; Arthur Mann to Leonard Koppett, June 8, 1953, Arthur Mann Papers, Library of Congress, box 1.

112. *Sporting News* (September 17, 1947), 3. Also quoted in Robinson, 80, and Rowan and Robinson, 194.

113. Willard Marshall, interview with William Marshall, September 13, 1985, Chandler Oral History Project.

114. Ralph Kiner, interview with William Marshall, September 26, 1979, Chandler Oral History Project.

115. William Veeck, interview with William Marshall, February 23, 1977, Chandler Oral History Project.

116. Manley interview.

117. *Sporting News* (July 16, 1947), 3-4.

118. Larry Doby, interview with William Marshall, November 15, 1979, Chandler Oral History Project.

119. *Sporting News* (July 16, 1947), 3.

120. Doby interview.

121. Lou Boudreau, interview with William Marshall, 1983, Chandler Oral History Project.

122. Joseph Thomas Moore, *Pride Against Prejudice* (New York: Praeger, 1988), 54.

123. Joseph Paparella, interview with William Marshall, March 16, 1988, Chandler Oral History Project.

124. James Hegan, interview with William Marshall, May 15, 1979, Chandler Oral History Project.

125. *Sporting News* (November 12, 1947), 10

126. *Sporting News* (July 16, 1947), 4.

127. DeWitt interview.

128. *Sporting News* (July 23, 1947), 8. Brown openly admitted that he subtracted five to seven years from his real age. Willard Brown, interview with William Marshall, June 22, 1982, Chandler Oral History Project.

129. Janet Bruce, *The Kansas City Monarchs: Champions of Black Baseball* (Lawrence: Univ. Press of Kansas), 137-40.

130. DeWitt interview.

131. Ibid.

132. Brown's salary with the Monarchs was $9,000, and he was paid only $5,000 to play with the Browns. Willard Brown interview.

133. DeWitt interview; *Sporting News* (November 12, 1947), 3.

134. DeWitt interview.

135. Brown interview.

136. *Sporting News* (November 12, 1947), 3.

137. Brown interview.

138. *Sporting News* (June 4, 1947), 11.

139. James Enright and Edgar Munzel, interview with William Marshall, February 24, 1977, Chandler Oral History Project.

140. *Sporting News* (September 17, 1947), 8.

141. *Sporting News* (December 31, 1947), 4.

142. Newcombe interview.

143. Jackie Robinson to A.B. Chandler, n.d. [Fall, 1956], Chandler Papers, box 314. For another view of Chandler's role in the Robinson affair, see Tygiel, 81-82.

Chapter 9. 1947: Season of Fury

1. *Sporting News* (October 1, 1947), 2.

2. Red Barber, *1947-When All Hell Broke Loose in Baseball* (Garden City, N.Y.: Doubleday, 1982), 140.

3. *Sporting News* (August 6, 1947), 1.

4. *Sporting News* (December 31, 1947), 8.

5. *Sporting News* (October 8, 1947), 11, and (December 31, 1947), 10.

6. *Sporting News* (November 26, 1947), 12.

7. Ibid., 1-2. The St. Louis Browns sent Vern Stephens and Jack Kramer to the Red Sox for Roy Partee, Ed Pellagrini, Pete Layden, Jim Wilson, Al Widmar, Joe Ostrowski, and $310,000 (November 17) and then sent Ellis Kinder and Billy Hitchcock to Boston for Jim Dreisewerd, Sam Dente, Bill Sommers, and $65,000 (November 18). On November 20, they sent Walt Judnich and Bob Muncrief to the Cleveland Indians for Bryan Stephens, Joe Stevens, Dick Kokos, and $25,000. Then, on December 9 they traded Johnny Berardino to Cleveland for George Metkovich and $50,000.

8. *Sporting News* (September 17, 1947), 11.

9. Ibid., 14.

10. *Sporting News* (October 8, 1947), 15.

11. *Sporting News* (September 24, 1947), 11-12, and (October 8, 1947), 8; Joe Page and Joe Trimble, "I Was Baseball's Bad Boy," *Saturday Evening Post* (May 22, 1948), 28, 145-47, 149.

12. Joe DiMaggio, *Lucky to Be a Yankee* (New York: Grosset and Dunlap, 1951), 135-36.

13. Ibid., 137.

14. *Sporting News* (September 24, 1947), 12.

15. *Sporting News* (March 5,1947), 3-4.

16. Hank Greenberg and Ira Berkow, *Hank Greenberg: The Story of My Life* (New York: Times Books, 1989), 181.

17. *Sporting News* (March 12, 1947), 12.

18. Greenberg and Berkow, 195.

19. *Sporting News* (April 30, 1947), 3.

20. The Cincinnati Reds tied the record in 1956, and the New York Yankees surpassed it in 1961, with 240. The previous record was established by the 1936 New York Yankees, at 182.

21. *Sporting News* (July 23, 1947), 3.

22. *Sporting News* (April 30, 1947), 5. The players included Mort Cooper, Red Barrett, Eddie Joost, Johnny Hopp, Tommy Nelson, Johnny Beazley, Danny Litwhiler, and Ken O'Dea.

23. Roscoe McGowen, "Branca, Boy Behemoth of the Brooks," *Baseball Magazine* (October 1947), 365.

24. *Sporting News* (June 11, 1947), 10.

25. Barber, 283-86.

26. *Sporting News* (September 10, 1947), 6.

27. *Sporting News* (October 1, 1947), 11.

28. *Sporting News* (September 17, 1947), 3.

29. Red Barber provides an excellent account of this game in his *1947—The Year All Hell Broke Loose in Baseball*, 314-29.

30. *Sporting News* (October 15, 1947), 9.

31. Ibid., 19; and (December 24, 1947), 2.

32. Ibid., 2.

33. Ibid, 1-2, 4.

34. Red Smith, "What Broke Up the Yankees?" *Saturday Evening Post* (March 29, 1947), 134.

35. *Sporting News* (October 22, 1947), 2.

36. *Sporting News* (November 5, 1947), 1-2, 4.

37. *Sporting News* (November 12, 1947), 5-6, 8.

38. *Sporting News* (October 8, 1947), 12.

39. Robert W. Creamer, *The Babe: The Legend Comes to Life* (New York: Simon and Schuster, 1974), 418.

40. *Sporting News* (February 12, 1947), 2.

41. *Sporting News* (March 5, 1947), 4.

42. *Sporting News* (April 30, 1947), 6.

43. *Sporting News* (November 5, 1947), 8.

Chapter 10. Miracle on Lake Erie

1. Bill Veeck with Ed Linn, *Veeck—as in Wreck* (New York: G.P. Putnam's Sons, 1962), 36.

2. Ibid., 52.

3. Ibid., 52-54; *Sporting News* (July 3, 1946), 8, and (July 10, 1946), 8; Dan Daniel, "32-Year-Old Bill Veeck, New Type of Major League Magnate," *Baseball Magazine* (September 1946), 331.

4. *Sporting News* (November 6, 1946), 11.

5. Bill Veeck with Gordon Cobbledick, "Baseball and Me: Am I Bad for Baseball?" *Sport* (May 1950), 62; Hal Lebovitz, interview with William Marshall, October 15, 1992, A.B. Chandler Oral History Project, Special Collections and Archives, Univ. of Kentucky Libraries (hereafter cited as Chandler Oral History Project).

6. Included in the group was one of William Veeck Sr.'s old friends, Phil Clarke of Chicago's City National Bank. Others included Lester Armour and Phil Swift of the meat-packing families, Arthur Allyn, Sr., an investment broker, Bob Goldstein of Universal-International Pictures, and comedian Bob Hope. Veeck, *Veeck—as in Wreck*, 85-96.

7. Ibid., 96.

8. Ibid., 102.

9. *Sporting News* (July 10, 1946), 8.

10. Dan Daniel, "Veeck," 332.

11. *Sporting News* (September 4, 1946), 9.

12. *Sporting News* (July 10, 1946), 36.

13. Ibid., 8.

14. Ibid.

15. *Sporting News* (July 3, 1946), 8.

16. *Sporting News* (July 10, 1946), 10.

17. *Sporting News* (July 31, 1946), 11.

18. *Sporting News* (August 14, 1946), 14.

19. Ibid., 13.

20. Veeck, *Veeck—as in Wreck*, 105

21. *Sporting News* (August 14, 1946), 14.

22. Veeck, *Veeck—as in Wreck*, 52.

23. Ibid., 105.

24. *Sporting News* (September 11, 1946), 5.

25. Veeck, *Veeck—as in Wreck*, 107

26. Bill Veeck with Gordon Cobbledick, "Baseball and Me: I Believed in Fireworks," *Sport* (April, 1950), 92.

27. Veeck, *Veeck—as in Wreck*, 107; *Sporting News* (September 11, 1946), 5.

28. Max Patkin, interview with William Marshall, August 5, 1984, Chandler Oral History Project.

29. Ibid.

30. Veeck, *Veeck—as in Wreck*, 105.

31. Veeck with Cobbledick, "Fireworks," 92.

32. Veeck, *Veeck—as in Wreck*, 105.

33. *Sporting News* (October 22, 1947), 4.

34. *Sporting News* (July 16, 1947), 11.

35. *Sporting News* (July 30, 1947), 14.

36. *Sporting News* (August 19, 1947), 9.

37. *Sporting News* (September 17, 1947), 10.

38. Ellis J. Veech, "Players' Days," *Baseball Magazine* (November 1947), 407; *Sporting News* (August 27, 1947), 4.

39. *Sporting News* (September 11, 1946), 10.

40. Veeck with Cobbledick, 92.

41. Patkin interview.

42. *Sporting News* (September 11, 1946), 10.

43. *Sporting News* (April 9, 1947), 8.

44. Hal Lebovitz, "Tribe Had City in Its Palm during Heat of Pennant Chase," *News-Herald* (Lake County, Ohio) (July 10, 1988), sec. B, "Happy 40th Anniversary" insert, 5.

45. Veeck, *Veeck—as in Wreck*, 144.

46. *Sporting News* (May 14, 1947), 1, and (June 18, 1947), 14.

47. *Sporting News* (June 18, 1947), 14.

48. Stanley Frank, "They're Just Wild about Boudreau," *Saturday Evening Post* (September 4, 1948), 91.

49. Ibid.

50. *Sporting News* (July 17, 1946), 12.

51. Veeck, *Veeck—as in Wreck*, 100-101.

52. Frank, 90.

53. Ibid.

54. *Sporting News* (October 15, 1947), 13.

55. Lou Boudreau, interview with William Marshall, 1983, Chandler Oral History Project.

56. Lebovitz interview.

57. Veeck, *Veeck—as in Wreck*, 153-55; *Sporting News* (November 12, 1947), 9. Veeck hired Bill Mckechnie, Muddy Ruel, and Mel Harder as coaches for the 1948 season.

58. *Sporting News* (January 28, 1948), 1.

59. Bob Feller, *Strikeout Story* (New York: A.S. Barnes, 1947), 257.

60. Veeck, *Veeck—as in Wreck*, 74-80, 144-45.

61. *Sporting News* (October 20, 1948), 4.

62. *Sporting News* (May 14, 1947), 14, (October 6, 1948), 23, and (October 13, 1948), 14.

63. *Sporting News* (December 3, 1947), 25.

64. Ned Garver, interview with William Marshall, June 3, 1988, Chandler Oral History Project.

65. *Sporting News* (March 10, 1948), 4.

66. *Sporting News* (March 3, 1948), 5.

67. Daniel, "Veeck," 331.

68. Lebovitz interview.

69. *Sporting News* (April 21, 1948), 7, and (May 5, 1948), 8.

70. *Sporting News* (May 5, 1948), 8.

71. Veeck, *Veeck—as in Wreck*, 125-26.

72. *Sporting News* (April 28, 1948), 11, and (May 5, 1948), 5.

73. Veeck, *Veeck—as in Wreck*, 157.

74. *Sporting News* (June 2, 1948), 2, 12.

75. Ibid.

76. Veeck, *Veeck—as in Wreck*, 157.

77. *Sporting News* (June 30, 1948), 7.

78. Ibid.

79. Veeck, *Veeck—as in Wreck*, 112-13; *Sporting News* (October 6, 1948), 23; Veeck with Cobbledick, "Fireworks," 92.

80. Veeck with Cobbledick, "Fireworks," 92.

81. Ibid., 93.

82. Ibid., 92; see also Veeck, *Veeck—as in Wreck*, 208-9.

83. Veeck with Cobbledick, "Am I Bad for Baseball?" 61.

Chapter 11. Ownership Has Its Privileges

1. Lights were installed at Wrigley Field in 1988.

2. American League teams that recorded losses were Boston (1945, 1947-48, and 1950), Philadelphia (1945 and 1950), and Washington (1949). National League teams included Boston (1945 and 1950), Brooklyn (1950), Chicago (1950), New York (1945, 1948, and 1950), Cincinnati (1945 and 1950), and Philadelphia (1945 and 1948). See Consolidated Profit and Loss Statements for American and National League Clubs, 1920-1950, U.S. Congress, House of Representatives, *Study of Monopoly Power: Organized Baseball* (Washington, D.C.: Government Printing Office, 1951), ser. 1, pt. 1, 1599-1600 (hereafter cited as Celler Report).

3. *Sporting News* (April 18, 1951), 8.

4. Mack was born and christened Cornelius McGillicuddy in East Brookfield, Massachusetts.

5. *Sporting News* (September 6, 1950), 5.

6. *Philadelphia Evening Bulletin* (February 9, 1956), G3.

7. Charlie Metro, interview with William Marshall, June 13, 1991, A.B. Chandler Oral History Project, Special Collections and Archives, Univ. of Kentucky Libraries (hereafter cited as Chandler Oral History Project).

8. *Sporting News* (June 15, 1949), 15.

9. *Sporting News* (November 1, 1950), 11.

10. Grantland Rice, "The Fifty Years of Connie Mack," *Sport* (June 1950), 31.

11. Metro interview.

12. *Sporting News* (September 6, 1950), 5.

13. Red Smith, interview with William Marshall, November 13, 1979, Chandler Oral History Project. Earle and Roy Mack sold the team to Arnold Johnson in 1954. Johnson moved them to Kansas City.

14. Clark Griffith, "Building a Winning Baseball Team," *Outing Magazine* (May 1913), 132; the parody was first made in 1909. See The Associated Press Biographical Service, "Clark Griffith—Sketch 3737," March 15, 1952, Hall of Fame file, National Baseball Library, Cooperstown, New York.

15. *New York Times* (October 28, 1955).

16. Ibid.

17. Cambria signed such players as Early Wynn, Walt Masterson, Mickey Vernon, Mickey Haeffner, Jake Powell, George Case, Reggie Otero, Thomas De La Cruz, Bobby Estalella, Mickey Guerra, Roberto Ortiz, and so on. *Sporting News* (January 18, 1945), 3.

18. Ibid.

19. J.G. Taylor Spink, *Official Baseball Guide*s for 1951 and 1952 (St. Louis: *The Sporting News*, 1951/52), 158 and 168, respectively.

20. David Voight, *From Postwar Expansion to the Electronic Age,* vol. 3 of *American Baseball* (University Park: Pennsylvania State Univ. Press, 1983), 80. The terms "old guard," gentleman sportsman, and "the capitalists," used to describe the owners, were first used by Voight.

21. Harry T. Paxton, "The White Sox Come Back from the Dead," *Saturday Evening Post* (March 11, 1950), 158.

22. *Sporting News* (June 15, 1949), 6.

23. *Sporting News* (July 12, 1950), 7.

24. Ed FitzGerald, "How They are Building a Winner in Chicago," *Sport* (April 1952), 46.

25. Jim Enright, ed. *Trade Him: 100 Years of Baseball's Greatest Deals* (Chicago: Follett, 1976), 258.

26. Mrs. Grace Comiskey, who died in 1956, willed control of the club to daughter Dorothy. After several years of family wrangling and court battles, the Comiskeys sold the team to Bill Veeck, in 1959.

27. Frank Graham, *The New York Giants* (New York: G.P. Putnam's Sons, 1952), 108.

28. Charles Alexander, *John McGraw* (New York: Viking, 1988), 210.

29. John Drebinger, "The House of Stoneham," *Baseball Magazine* (May 1945), 399.

30. Ibid., 400.

31. Graham, 222-23.

32. Bill Veeck with Ed Linn, *The Hustler's Handbook* (New York: Fireside, Simon and Schuster, 1989), 96.

33. *Sporting News* (July 24, 1976), 24.

34. *Chicago Sun-Times* (April 13, 1977), 44; *New York Times* (April 13, 1977).

35. Powel Crosley, Jr., "50 Jobs in 50 years," *American Magazine* (October 1948), 134.

36. Richard Miller and Gary L. Rhodes, "The Life and Times of the Old Cincinnati Ballparks," *Queen City Heritage* (Summer 1988), 33.

37. Transcribed "Interview with Mr. Powel Crosley, Jr., October 14, 1938," The Powel Crosley, Jr., Papers, Cincinnati Historical Society; Don Warfield, *The Roaring Redhead* (South Bend, Ind.: Diamond, 1987), 50-51.

38. Malcolm W. Bingay, "The Fan Who Bought the Ball Park," *Saturday Evening Post* (March 6, 1943), 84.

39. *New York Times* (January 18, 1952), L27.

40. *Sporting News* (July 24, 1976), 24.

41. *Sporting News* (October 1, 1947), 15.

42. Bingay, 84.

43. *Sporting News* (March 14, 1946), 14.

44. *New York Times* (April 13, 1977), D15.

45. *Sporting News* (October 27, 1948), 8.

46. *Sporting News* (September 26, 1951), 4.

47. *Sporting News* (August 14, 1946), 9.

48. *Sporting News* (June 21, 1950), 20.

49. *Sporting News* (June 13, 1951), 21, (April 6, 1949), 15, and (July 6, 1950), 3.

50. Harry T. Paxton, "It's Raining Dollars in Pittsburgh," *Saturday Evening Post* (May 8, 1948), 139.

51. *Sporting News* (May 31, 1945), 4, and (June 7, 1945), 7.

52. Paxton, 20.

53. Fred Lieb, *The Pittsburgh Pirates* (New York: G.P. Putnam's Sons, 1948), 289.

54. *Sporting News* (June 21, 1950), 20.

55. Kiner averaged 45.5 home runs per season between 1947 and 1950.

56. *Philadelphia Bulletin* (June 12, 1949), Y1; *Sporting News* (June 22, 1949), 15-16.

57. *Philadelphia Inquirer* (July 11, 1990), A4.

58. Frederic Lieb and Stan Baumgartner, *The Philadelphia Phillies* (New York: G.P. Putnam's Sons, 1953), 214.

59. *Sporting News* (January 31, 1946), 3.

60. *Sporting News* (February 11, 1948), 6.

61. Frank Yeutter, "The Squire of Kennett Square," *Baseball Magazine* (May 1948), 405.

62. *Sporting News* (August 9, 1950), 5.

63. *Sporting News* (October 6, 1948), 3.

64. *Sporting News* (August 2, 1950), 1.

65. *Sporting News* (March 1, 1950), 14. Harold Kaese, "They're Digging a Pennant in Boston," *Saturday Evening Post* (June 28, 1947), 122.

66. *Sporting News* (October 6, 1948), 3; Kaese, 122.

67. *Sporting News* (November 22, 1945), 10.

68. *Sporting News* (October 6, 1948), 3.

69. *Sporting News* (April 25, 1951), 1.

70. Elmer L. Irey, *The Tax Dodgers* (New York: Greenberg, 1948), 204-9. See also the *Boston Globe* (May 13, 1940), 13, (May 14, 1940), 12, and (May 15, 1940), 15.

71. Jerry Nason, "Braves Title Ground Dug in '46," *Baseball Digest* (November 1948), 23.

72. *Sporting News* (September 29, 1948), 1, and (August 2, 1950), 2.

73. Celler Report, 1617.

74. *Sporting News* (April 25, 1951), 1-2.

75. Veeck with Linn, *Hustler's Handbook*, 304.

76. Ed Fitzgerald, ed., *The Story of the Brooklyn Dodgers* (New York: Bantam, 1949), 173.

77. Ibid., 180.

78. *Sporting News* (June 1, 1949), 13.

79. *Sporting News* (December 3, 1947), 6, 8.

80. J. Roy Stockton, "Baseball's Amazing Amateur," *Saturday Evening Post* (May 27, 1950), 138, 140; *Sporting News* (December 28, 1949), 11.

81. Fred Saigh, interview with William Marshall, May 16, 1978, Chandler Oral History Project.

82. Ibid.

83. The Cardinals paid the Browns a $35,000 rental fee and the two clubs shared park maintenance, which amounted to about $130,000 in 1949. The Browns, who accounted for only 16 percent of the total attendance that year, argued that maintenance costs should be factored on a per capita basis.

84. William Mead, *Even the Browns: The Zany True Story of Baseball in the Early Forties* (Chicago: Contemporary Books, 1978), 56.

85. *Sporting News* (August 31, 1949), 3.

86. Ibid., 4.

87. *Sporting News* (December 22, 1948), 3.

88. *Sporting News* (June 27, 1951), 3, and (July 4, 1951), 1.

89. *Sporting News* (June 19, 1946), 13.

90. *Sporting News* (April 25, 1946), 6, and (April 18, 1951), 8.

91. *New York Times* (July 5, 1974).

92. Joe David Brown, "The Webb of Mystery," *Sports Illustrated* (February 29, 1960), 75; "Del Webb Story Told," undated newspaper clipping (ca. 1960s) from Del Webb biographical file, National Baseball Library, Cooperstown, New York.

93. Lewis Yablonsky, *George Raft* (New York: McGraw-Hill, 1974), 191-93; Dean Jennings, *We Only Kill Each Other: The Life and Bad Times of Bugsy Siegal* (Englewood Cliffs, N.J.: Prentice-Hall, 1967), 17; Ed Reid and Ovid DeMaris, *The Green Felt Jungle* (London: Cox and Wyman, 1965), 27.

94. *New York World Telegram and Sun* (October 10, 1964).

95. *Sporting News* (June 1, 1974).

96. *Sporting News* (June 1, 1974), and (February 1, 1945), 1-2.

97. *Sporting News* (February 1, 1945), 2.

98. Fitzgerald, *Brooklyn Dodgers*, i.

99. Robert Rice, "Profiles: Thoughts on Baseball," *New Yorker* (May 27, 1950), 40; *Sporting News* (May 4, 1949), 20.

100. Roscoe McGowen, "Vero Beach—Baseball Factory Deluxe," *Baseball Magazine* (March 1950), 328; *Sporting News* (May 4, 1949), 20.

101. Robert Smith, *Baseball* (New York: Simon and Schuster, 1970), 145.

102. Ed Fitzgerald, "Branch Rickey, Baseball Innovator," *Sport* (undated article in Rickey Papers, Library of Congress, ca. November 1961-March 1962), 63.

103. Smith interview.

104. Ibid.

105. Veeck with Linn, *Hustler's Handbook*, 121.

106. Fifty-seven of "The Game's '400'" players included in the *Sporting News*'s 1951 *Baseball Register* had Rickey ties.

107. Murray Polner, *Branch Rickey: A Biography* (New York: Signet, 1983), 214.

108. Polner, 214-15.

109. *Sporting News* (March 10, 1948), 6.

110. Only Fenway Park, Crosley Field, and Sportsman's Park had smaller seating capacities.

111. Donald A. Beach to Arthur Mann, October 17, 1949, Arthur Mann Papers, Library of Congress, box 1.

112. Rice, 36; Roger Kahn, *The Era: 1947-1957, When the Yankees, the Giants, and the Dodgers Ruled the World* (New York: Ticknor and Fields, 1993), 115 n.

113. Arthur Mann to Max Kase, October 25, 1957, Arthur Mann Papers, Library of Congress, box 2.

114. Kahn, 267. Each of the partners paid $346,666.66 for a quarter interest in the team in 1944. Mann to Kase, October 25, 1957, Arthur Mann Papers, Library of Congress, box 2.

115. Mann to Kase, October 25, 1957, Arthur Mann Papers, Library of Congress, box 2.

116. Red Smith, *To Absent Friends from Red Smith.* (New York: Atheneum, 1982), 376.

117. *Sporting News* (February 21, 1951), 9.

118. Ernie Harwell, interview with William Marshall, June 2, 1988, Chandler Oral History Project.

Chapter 12. 1948: Indian Summer

1. *Sporting News* (September 1, 1948), 8.

2. *Sporting News* (August 25, 1948 [special supplement]), 1.

3. *Sporting News* (September 1, 1948), 8.

4. Robert W. Creamer, *Babe: The Legend Comes to Life* (New York: Simon and Schuster, 1974), 22.

5. Dan Daniel, "Babe Ruth Greatest Player, Golden Figure in Golden Era," *Baseball Magazine* (October 1948), 363.

6. Waite Hoyt, *Babe Ruth as I Knew Him* (New York: Dell, 1948), 46.

7. *Sporting News* (June 23, 1948), 6.

8. *Sporting News* (August 25, 1948 [special supplement]), 1.

9. *Sporting News* (January 28, 1948), 8.

10. *Sporting News* (September 15, 1948), 2.

11. Danny Peary, *We Played the Game: 65 Players Remember Baseball's Greatest Era, 1947-1964* (New York: Hyperion, 1994), 63.

12. Willard Marshall, interview with William Marshall, September 13, 1985, A.B. Chandler Oral History Project, Special Collections and Archives, Univ. of Kentucky Libraries (hereafter cited as Chandler Oral History Project).

13. Murry Polner, *Branch Rickey: A Biography* (New York: Signet, New American Library, 1982), 219.

14. *Sporting News* (June 2, 1948), 4.

15. *Sporting News* (August 18, 1948), 12.

16. *Sporting News* (July 28, 1948), 2, 6.

17. *Sporting News* (June 16, 1948), 2.

18. Bob Broeg, *Stan Musial: "The Man's" Own Story as Told to Bob Broeg* (Garden City, N.Y.: Doubleday, 1964), 117-18.

19. Clifford Bloodgood, "A Few Batting and Pitching Highlights of 1948," *Baseball Magazine* (November 1948), 222.

20. *Sporting News* (March 17, 1948), 8.

21. *Sporting News* (August 25, 1948), 3.

22. Al Silverman, *Warren Spahn: Immortal Southpaw* (New York: Sport Magazine Library, Bartholomew House, 1961), 67.

23. *Sporting News* (September 22, 1948), 8.

24. *Sporting News* (September 29, 1948), 6.

25. Silverman attributes the phrases to the Boston writers, whereas Johnny Sain indicates that it came from Billy Southworth. See Silverman, 67, and Peary, 56.

26. *Sporting News* (August 18, 1948), 14.

27. Peary, 73.

28. *Sporting News* (May 26, 1948), 3.

29. Jack B. Moore, *Joe DiMaggio: Baseball's Yankee Clipper* (New York: Praeger, 1987), 67.

30. Richard Whittingham, ed., *1942-1951*, vol 2 of *The DiMaggio Albums*, (New York: G.P. Putnam's Sons, 1989), 531.

31. Lou Boudreau, interview with William Marshall, 1983, Chandler Oral History Project.

32. Ibid.

33. Michael Seidel, *Ted Williams: A Baseball Life* (Chicago: Contemporary Books, 1991), 196.

34. Mel Harder, interview with William Marshall, June 1, 1988, Chandler Oral History Project.

35. *Sporting News* (July 14, 1948), 8.

36. James Hegan, interview with William Marshall, May 15, 1979, Chandler Oral History Project.

37. *Sporting News* (August 25, 1948), 4.

38. *Sporting News* (September 1, 1948), 4.

39. LeRoy "Satchel" Paige, as told to Hal Lebovitz, *Pitchin' Man* (Cleveland: The Cleveland News, 1948), 61.

40. Bob Lemon, interview with William Marshall, May 15, 1979, Chandler Oral History Project.

41. *Sporting News* (May 19, 1948), 18.

42. Al Rosen, interview with William Marshall, May 15, 1979, Chandler Oral History Project.

43. *Sporting News* (May 5, 1948), 5, and (August 18, 1948), 18; and Ed Rumill, "Cleveland's 'Robbie' Masters Tough Breaks," *Baseball Magazine* (August 1948), 293-94.

44. *Sporting News* (January 14, 1948), 15, and (March 17, 1948), 18; and Veeck, *Veeck—as in Wreck*, 148.

45. Ed Fitzgerald, "Joe Gordon, the Acrobatic Flash," *Sport* (July 1949), 18.

46. *Sporting News* (October, 20, 1948), 12.

47. Ibid.

48. Stanley Frank, "They're Just Wild about Boudreau," *Saturday Evening Post* (September 4, 1948), 23.

49. *Sporting News* (May 12, 1948), 9

50. Hank Greenberg, *Hank Greenberg: The Story of My Life*, ed. Ira Berkow (New York: Times Books, 1989) 200.

51. *Sporting News* (January 12, 1949), 4.

52. Lou Boudreau with Russell Schneider, *Lou Boudreau: Covering All the Bases* (Champaign, Ill.: Sagamore Publishing, 1993), 118.

53. Bob Feller with Bill Gilbert, *Now Pitching, Bob Feller* (New York: Harper Perennial, 1991), 166-67; Boudreau interview; Boudreau with Schneider, *Lou Boudreau: Covering All*

the Bases, 130-31. Joe Williams, sports columnist of the *New York World-Telegram*, reported that "Umpire Bill Stewart broke down and confessed to me that he may have missed that pickoff play in the first game of the World Series but added that he was absolutely right on the other two, meaning when Dark was called safe at first in the second game and Boudreau was out at third in the fourth. Each decision provoked a rhubarb" (*Sporting News* [October 27, 1948], 26). Later, while on the banquet circuit, Stewart again denied that he made the wrong call on Masi (ibid. [November 3, 1948], 13).

54. Hal Lebovitz, "Tribe Had City in Its Palm during Heat of Pennant Chase," *Lake County (Ohio) News-Herald* (July 10, 1988), 7.

55. *Sporting News* (October 20, 1948), 17.

56. *Sporting News* (November 17, 1948), 17.

Chapter 13. Gardella's Folly

1. *Sporting News* (March 19, 1947), 2. "Organized baseball" is a contemporary term used to describe the government of Major League Baseball and the National Association of Professional Baseball Leagues.

2. *Sporting News* (March 5, 1947), 17.

3. *Sporting News* (April 2, 1947), 11

4. *Sporting News* (April 30, 1947), 34.

5. *Sporting News* (October 27, 1947), 18.

6. Ibid.

7. *Sporting News* (May 7, 1947), 24.

8. Ibid.

9. *Sporting News* (September 24, 1947), 37; Mickey Owen, interview with William Marshall, May 27, 1980, A.B. Chandler Oral History Project, Special Collections and Archives, Univ. of Kentucky Libraries (hereafter cited as Chandler Oral History Project).

10. U.S. Congress, House of Representatives, *Study of Monopoly Power: Organized Baseball* (Washington, D.C.: Government Printing Office, 1951), ser. 1, pt. 1, 1285-87 (hereafter cited as Celler Report).

11. Ibid., 222-23.

12. *Sporting News* (March 2, 1949), 10.

13. Danny Gardella, interview with William Marshall, August 27, 1980, Chandler Oral History Project; Frederic A. Johnson, interview with William Marshall, August 26, 1980, Chandler Oral History Project.

14. Frederic A. Johnson, "Baseball Law," *United States Law Review* 73:252-70.

15. See Lee Lowenfish and Tony Lupien, *The Imperfect Diamond: The Story of Baseball's Reserve System and the Men Who Fought to Change It* (New York: Stein and Day, 1980).

16. Johnson interview.

17. The firm of Willkie, Owen, Farr, Gallagher and Walton represented baseball at the time.

18. "Champerty" is an illegal sharing in the proceeds of a lawsuit by an outsider who promoted the suit.

19. Johnson interview.

20. *Sporting News* (November 6, 1946), 14.

21. Ibid.

22. *Sporting News* (December 18, 1946), 2.

23. *Sporting News* (February 19, 1947), 20.

24. *Sporting News* (January 29, 1947), 19. Lanier easily beat Martin 9-1.

25. *Sporting News* (March 5, 1947), 18; Max Lanier, interview with William Marshall, June 26, 1987, Chandler Oral History Project.

26. *Sporting News* (February 19, 1947), 20.

27. *Sporting News* (March 5, 1947), 7.

28. *Sporting News* (January 1, 1947), 22.

29. *Sporting News* (December 25, 1946), 18.

30. *Sporting News* (November 19, 1947), 6.

31. *Sporting News* (December 31, 1947), 22, (January 14, 1948), 19, and (February 25, 1948), 21.

32. *Sporting News* (April 14, 1948), 26.

33. *Sporting News* (November 5, 1947), 1-2.

34. *Sporting News* (January 28, 1948), 1-2, and (February 4, 1948), 2.

35. *Sporting News* (February 4, 1948), 1.

36. *Sporting News* (February 11, 1948), 1.

37. *Sporting News* (February 4, 1948), 2.

38. *Sporting News* (March 3, 1948), 1.

39. *Sporting News* (August 4, 1949), 36.

40. *Sporting News* (September 1, 1948), 37.

41. *Sporting News* (September 29, 1948), 30.

42. *Sporting News* (November 3, 1948), 20.

43. Sal Maglie, interview with William Marshall, May 25, 1981, Chandler Oral History Project.

44. Gardella interview.

45. Lanier interview

46. Stanley Frank, "How the Giants Found a Pitcher in the Doghouse," *Saturday Evening Post* (May 5, 1951), 153; Lanier interview.

47. Donald Honig, *A Donald Honig Reader* (New York: Simon and Schuster, 1988), 172.

48. *Gardella v. Chandler, et al.*, 172 F.2d 402, 98 (2d Cir. 1948). The full text of this decision can be found in the *Sporting News* (February 23, 1949), 10; see also the *New York Times* (February 10, 1949), 2 et passim.

49. *Sporting News* (February, 16, 1949), 3-4.

50. *New York Times* (February 11, 1949), 30.

51. *Sporting News* (February 23, 1949), 20.

52. *Sporting News* (February 16, 1949), 16.

53. *Sporting News* (February 23, 1949), 9.

54. *Sporting News* (February 16, 1949), 1, 4.

55. Chandler kept his promise. Today Owen receives two pensions: one from the commissioner's office, for his service between 1937 and 1945, and another from the players' pension plan, for his years between 1949 and 1952. Owen interview.

56. Owen interview; *Sporting News* (February 23, 1949), 20. The petition was signed by Klein, Lanier, Adams, Feldman, Franklin, Hausmann, Maglie, Olmo, Owen, Martin, and Zimmerman. See also the *New York Times* (Feb 10, 1949), 2 et passim.

57. *Sporting News* (February 23, 1949), 20.

58. Johnson interview.

59. *Sporting News* (March 9, 1949), 4.

60. Owen interview.

61. *Sporting News* (March 16, 1949), 2.

62. *Sporting News* (March 23, 1949), 3.

63. *Sporting News* (March 2, 1949), 18; Johnson interview.

64. *Sporting News* (April 6, 1949), 6.

65. *New York Times* (April 14, 1949), 33.

66. *Sporting News* (April 13, 1949), 8, and (April 27, 1949), 13.

67. Monteagudo, Reyes, and Hausmann were playing in the revamped Mexican League, while Olmo, Estalella, and Ortiz were in Venezuela. Klein and Carrasquel began the season in the Mexican League. Carrasquel jumped his contract, Klein obtained his release, and both joined the Quebec League, where Zabala, Maglie, Lanier, Martin, Gladu, Hayworth, Zimmerman, Feldman, and Gardella were already playing.

68. *Sporting News* (June 1, 1949), 32; Gardella interview.

69. *New York Times* (June 3, 1949), 32.

70. Ibid. (June 6, 1949), 24.

71. *Sporting News* (June 15, 1949), 11.

72. Ibid., 2.

73. Ibid., 12.

74. Gladu, Feldman, Zimmerman, Adams, Hayworth, and Monteagudo failed to appear in another major-league game. Hausmann, Reyes, Carrasquel, and Estalella made cameo appearances.

75. Adrian and Mary Zabala, interview with William Marshall, March 2, 1989, Chandler Oral History Project.

76. Maglie interview; Sal Maglie. "I'm the Luckiest Guy in Baseball," *Sport* (September 1951), 75.

77. *Sporting News* (June 22, 1949), 8, 14.

78. Lanier interview. At the time of the interview, Lanier had not received his pension benefits. The *Sporting News* (July 6, 1949, 9) reported that Lanier received his original $11,000 salary and a promise that he would get a raise if he did well. Lanier told Donald Honig that Saigh promised to double his salary and give him expense money if he could reach the team by July 4, 1949 (Honig, 173).

79. *Sporting News* (September 28, 1949), 1-2.

80. Johnson interview.

81. Fred Saigh, interview with William Marshall, May 16, 1978, Chandler Oral History Project.

82. Johnson interview.

83. Ibid.

84. *Sporting News* (September 28, 1949), 2.

85. *New York Times* (September 20, 1949), 39.

86. *New York Times* (September 21, 1949), L43.

87. Johnson interview.

88. Saigh interview.

89. Gardella interview.

90. Johnson interview.

91. Lowenfish and Lupien, 167.

92. A.B. "Happy" Chandler, interview with William Marshall, November 7, 1984, Chandler Oral History Project.

93. *Sporting News* (November 9, 1949), 1, (October 26, 1949), 10, and (October 19, 1949), 2.

94. *Toolson v. New York Yankees*, 346 US 356 (U.S. Supreme Court 1953).

95. *Radovich v. National Football League, et. al.* 352 US 445 (U.S. Supreme Court 1957). This decision established that all team sports except baseball were subject to antitrust laws unless Congress specifically exempted them. The decision left baseball with the only exemption.

96. Saigh interview.

97. *Sporting News* (June 28, 1950), 2, 4.

Chapter 14. A Stepchild in Peril, The Minors

1. Neil J. Sullivan, *The Minors* (New York: St. Martin's Press, 1991), 141, 136-37; *Sporting News* (February 12, 1947), 6. The Shaughnessey playoffs were adapted by ice-hockey teams from English soccer leagues, who called them "play downs." Hockey called them "playoffs" (*Sporting News* [March 21, 1946], 2).

2. *Sporting News* (June 5, 1946), 8, (April 11, 1946), 8, (July 28, 1948), 16, (April 18, 1946), 12, (June 5, 1946), 19, (November 5, 1947), 13, (November 10, 1948), 13, and (April 25, 1949), 24-25.

3. Sullivan, 235.

4. Francis Wallace, "Are the Major Leagues Strangling Baseball?," *Collier's Magazine* (March 10, 1951), 18.

5. David Voight, *From the Commissioners to Continental Expansion*, vol. 2 of *American Baseball* (College Park: Pennsylvania State Univ. Press, 1983), 296-97. Voight also points out that the G.I. Bill encouraged hundreds of would-be ballplayers to attend college and reduced baseball's huge 1946 talent pool. Compared with the uncertainty of a baseball career, college degrees provided better job opportunities. By the early 1950s, notes Voight, baseball organizations were offering large bonuses and scholarships to attract high school and college players to its ranks.

6. Sullivan, 235-36.

7. Ibid., 185.

8. *Sporting News* (September 25, 1946), 11.

9. *Sporting News* (January 17, 1946), 10.

10. U.S. Congress, House of Representatives, *Study of Monopoly Power: Organized Baseball* (Washington, D.C.: Government Printing Office, 1951), ser. 1, pt. 1, 359 (hereafter cited as Celler Report).

11. Willie Mays and Lou Sahadi, *Say Hey: The Autobiography of Willie Mays* (New York: Pocket Books, 1989), 57-58; *Sporting News* (June 27, 1951), 16.

12. Sullivan, 185.

13. *Sporting News* (May 2, 1946), 5.

14. *Sporting News* (November 3, 1948), 3-4.

15. *Sporting News* (November 10, 1948), 1, 6.

16. *Sporting News* (April 16, 1947), 15.

17. *Sporting News* (March 16, 1949), 4, (March 23, 1949), 10, and (July 12, 1949), 8.

18. *Sporting News* (July 21, 1948), 11.

19. *Sporting News* (February 23, 1949), 11.

20. *Sporting News* (March 19, 1947), 1, 4.

21. *Sporting News* (April 16, 1947), 14. In 1947, teams employed the following number of scouts: Cubs, 47; Cardinals, 33; Reds and Pirates, each 25; Red Sox, 23; Braves, 22; Giants, Yankees, and Indians, each 21; White Sox, 17; Dodgers, 16; Phillies, 15; Browns, 13; Tigers, 10; Athletics, 8; and Senators, 3.

22. *Sporting News* (February 26, 1947), 15.

23. Voight, 297.

24. John Drebinger, "Bonus Babies—$$$," *Baseball Magazine* (August 1951), 15.

25. *Sporting News* (November 24, 1948), 2.

26. Celler Report, 1951, 873. Factored into their figure were the salaries and expenses

of scouts, communications, various player salaries, bonuses, spring-training expenses, travel, and working agreement expenses.

27. *Sporting News* (January 19, 1949), 17.

28. *Sporting News* (August 4, 1948), 4.

29. *Sporting News* (November 3, 1948), 1, 8.

30. *Sporting News* (October 26, 1949), 4.

31. Senate Committee on Interstate and Foreign Commerce, Broadcasting and Televising Baseball Games, 83d Congress, 1st Session, 1953. See also Sullivan, 237.

32. Wallace, 18.

33. *Sporting News* (May 4, 1949), 26, (May 19, 1948), 1, 6, (June 2, 1948), 6, (November 24, 1948), 8, and (December 8, 1948), 6.

34. *Sporting News* (December 15, 1948), 2.

35. *Sporting News* (November 24, 1948), 8.

36. *Sporting News* (March 30, 1949), 32, (April 20, 1949), 26, and (May 4, 1949), 26.

37. *Sporting News* (May 11, 1949), 28, (June 8, 1949), 20, and (July 6, 1949), 21.

38. Wallace, 64-66.

39. *Sporting News* (November 2, 1949), 6.

40. Wallace, 65.

41. Ibid.

42. *Sporting News* (February 19, 1947), 18.

43. Kyle Crichton, "The Coast Demands Long Pants," *Collier's Magazine* (August 16, 1947), 16.

44. *Sporting News* (January 12, 1949), 17; *Baseball Digest* (November 1948), 65-70.

45. *Sporting News* (December 29, 1948), 18.

46. *Sporting News* (September 10, 1947), 4.

47. Sullivan, 219.

48. *Sporting News* (December 5, 1951), 2; Sullivan, 222.

49. Celler Report, 1612.

50. Testimony of Seymour Block, Celler Report, 582-84.

51. *Sporting News* (July 17, 1946), 14, and (August 28, 1946), 21. Lohrke seemed to lead a charmed life. When he was in Germany during World War II several men around him were killed. He survived a train wreck in 1944 without a scratch, and in 1945 he missed a military aircraft that took off without his unit and later crashed, killing all twenty-three persons aboard.

52. Testimony of Ross Horning, Celler Report, 377.

53. Carlton Brown, "Baseball's Dizziest Owner," *Saturday Evening Post* (August 9, 1947), 44.

54. Pete Castiglione, interview with William Marshall, September 7, 1991, A.B. Chandler Oral History Project, Special Collections and Archives, Univ. of Kentucky Libraries (hereafter cited as Chandler Oral History Project).

55. *Sporting News* (August 14, 1946), 30.

56. *Sporting News* (July 16, 1947), 28

57. *Sporting News* (August 3, 1949), 36.

58. *Sporting News* (August 27, 1947), 33.

59. Al Rosen, interview with William Marshall, May 15, 1979, Chandler Oral History Project; Franklin Lewis, "Bat Title for Rosen?" *Baseball Digest* (May 1951), 58.

60. *Sporting News* (May 18, 1949), 3; Edgar Williams, "Biggest Little Man in Baseball," *Saturday Evening Post* (July 1952), 25 et passim; Bobby Shantz and Ralph Bernstein, *The Story of Bobby Shantz* (Philadelphia: J.B. Lippincott, 1953), 83-84.

61. Al Widmar testimony, Celler Report, 543-51; *Sporting News* (February 1, 1950), 26, and (April 26, 1950), 7.

62. Lon Carter Barton, interviews with William Marshall, Chandler Oral History Project, March 27-28, May 23, 1991.

63. Barton interviews; Charles Metro, interview with William Marshall, June 13, 1991, Chandler Oral History Project; and Berry Craig, interview with William Marshall, May 23, 1991, Chandler Oral History Project.

64. Barton interviews.

65. Ibid.

66. *Sporting News* (July 16, 1947), 34.

67. Craig interview.

68. Barton interviews.

Chapter 15. 1949: Pinstripes Prevail

1. *Sporting News* (February 9, 1949), 5. Players in *The Stratton Story* included Peanuts Lowery, Gus Zernial, Gene Mauch, Clarence Maddern, Jess Dobernic, George Vico, Johnny Bero, Eddie Stewart, Al Zarilla, Gerry Priddy, and Jack Lohrke (*Sporting News* [May 11, 1949], 13).

2. James E. Odenkirk, *Plain Dealing: A Biography of Gordon Cobbledick* (Tempe, Ariz.: Spider-Naps, 1990), 1; Lou Boudreau with Russell Schneider, *Lou Boudreau: Covering All the Bases* (Champaign, Ill.: Sagamore Publishing, 1993), 144-45.

3. *Sporting News* (July 6, 1949), 29, (August 10, 1949), 18, and (June 29, 1949), 9.

4. *Sporting News* (March 16, 1949), 20.

5. *Sporting News* (June 1, 1949), 3, and (June 8, 1949), 11.

6. J.G. Taylor Spink, *Baseball Guide and Record Book, 1950* (St. Louis: The Sporting News, 1950), 89.

7. Edmund Lopat, interview with William Marshall, August 26, 1988, A.B. Chandler Oral History Project, Special Collections and Archives, Univ. of Kentucky Libraries (hereafter cited as Chandler Oral History Project).

8. *Sporting News* (March 9, 1949), 13.

9. *Sporting News* (April 27, 1949), 9.

10. *Sporting News* (April 20, 1949), 2.

11. Bobby Brown, interview with William Marshall, September 11, 1985, Chandler Oral History Project.

12. Gene Woodling, interview with William Marshall, December 11, 1992, Chandler Oral History Project.

13. Ibid.

14. *Sporting News* (August 24, 1949), 6.

15. Lopat interview; David Halberstam, *Summer of '49* (New York: William Morrow, 1989), 236-37.

16. *Sporting News* (October 12, 1949), 3.

17. Al Silverman, *Warren Spahn: Immortal Southpaw* (New York: Sport Magazine Library, Bartholomew House, 1961), 78.

18. Sain interview with Peary, in Danny Peary, *We Played the Game: 65 Players Remember Baseball's Greatest Era, 1947-1964* (New York: Hyperion, 1994), 86; *Sporting News* (December 28, 1949), 4.

19. *Sporting News* (August 31, 1949), 7.

20. *Sporting News* (April 27, 1949), 9.

21. Bob Hannegan, who sold the Cardinals to his partner Fred Saigh at the beginning of 1949, made the trade with Saigh's approval (*Sporting News* [February 9, 1949], 4, and [April 20, 1949], 5).

22. *Sporting News* (April 27, 1949), 28.

23. *Sporting News* (June 8, 1949), 20.

24. *Sporting News* (March 23, 1949), 2.

25. Jackie Robinson, *I Never Had It Made* (New York: G.P. Putnam's Sons, 1972), 92-93.

26. *Sporting News* (June 29, 1949), 7.

27. *Sporting News* (September 14, 1949), 8.

28. *Sporting News* (October 26, 1949), 3.

Chapter 16. "Who Were Those Guys?"

1. William H. Haines and Robert A Esser, "Case History of Ruth Steinhagen," *American Journal of Psychology* (April 1950), 737-39.

2. *Sporting News* (June 22, 1949), 2.

3. Haines and Esser, 741-42.

4. Ibid., 742.

5. Bob Brumby, "Can Eddie Waitkus Come Back?," *Sport* (April 1950), 83.

6. *Sporting News* (June 29, 1949), 9.

7. *Sporting News* (July 6, 1949), 14.

8. *Sporting News* (May 3, 1950), 3.

9. Brumby, 23.

10. Ross Morrow, "Ballplayers vs. Bobbysoxers!" *Sport* (September 1950), 98.

11. *Sporting News* (May 3, 1950), 3.

12. Ibid.; and Morrow, 16, 97.

13. *Sporting News* (July 30, 1947), 2.

14. Robert Brown, interview with William Marshall, September 11, 1985, A.B. Chandler Oral History Project, Special Collections and Archives, Univ. of Kentucky Libraries (cited hereafter as Chandler Oral History Project).

15. J.G. Taylor Spink, comp. *Baseball Register* (St. Louis: The Sporting News, 1951). Information was drawn from questionnaires filled out by the players themselves.

16. The states included Colorado, Delaware, Maine, Mississippi, Montana, Nevada, North Dakota, Vermont, and Wyoming.

17. Geoffrey Ward and Ken Burns argued that baseball as a small-town game is a myth and that it was largely derived in its present form out of innovations that first appeared in New York City. Geoffrey Ward and Ken Burns, *Baseball: An Illustrated History* (New York: Alfred A. Knopf, 1994), 4.

18. Players often listed two or more nationalities in their responses. The first nationality listed was the one that was counted.

19. George "Doc" Medich, who pitched for seven teams between 1972 and 1982, duplicated Brown's feat.

20. Brown interview.

21. Ibid.

22. *Sporting News* (February 26, 1947), 8.

23. Frank Baumholtz, interew with William Marshall, December 10, 1992, Chandler Oral History Project.

24. *Sporting News* (January 24, 1951), 10.

25. Fred Saigh, interview with William Marshall, May 16, 1978, Chandler Oral History Project.

26. Ned Garver, interview with William Marshall, June 3, 1988, Chandler Oral History Project.

27. Stan Musial, interview with William Marshall, May 17, 1978, Chandler Oral History Project.

28. Harry Walker, interview with William Marshall, May 11, 1988, Chandler Oral History Project

29. Ibid.

30. Edmund Lopat, interview with William Marshall, August 26, 1988, Chandler Oral History Project; and Vic Raschi in Dom Forker, *The Men of Autumn* (New York: Signet, New American Library, 1989), 30.

31. Donald Honig, *A Donald Honig Reader* (New York: Simon and Schuster, 1988), 385-86.

32. Al Rosen, interview with William Marshall, May 15, 1979, Chandler Oral History Project.

33. *Sporting News* (January 1, 1947), 12.

34. Scott Dereks, *The Value of a Dollar, 1860-1989* (Detroit: Gale Research, 1994); U.S. Department of Commerce, *Historical Statistics of the United States, Colonial Times to 1970*, Part I (Washington: U.S. Bureau of the Census, 1975), 175-76.

35. Peter Gammons, "1950 vs. 1990: A Tale of Two Eras," *Sports Illustrated* (April 16, 1990), 42-43.

36. Baumholtz interview.

37. *Sporting News* (February 9, 1950), 24.

38. Baumholtz interview.

39. Virgil Trucks, interview with William Marshall, May 11, 1988, Chandler Oral History Project.

40. *Sporting News* (December 8, 1948), 29.

41. *Sporting News* (January 7, 1948), 22, and (January 14, 1948), 15.

42. *Sporting News* (January 8, 1947), 20, and (February 19, 1947), 5.

43. *Sporting News* (February 4, 1948), 13

44. *Sporting News* (June 2, 1948), 10.

45. Willard Marshall, interview with William Marshall, September 13, 1985, Chandler Oral History Project.

46. Bobby Thomson, interview with William Marshall, September 13, 1985, Chandler Oral History Project.

47. Garver interview.

48. *Sporting News* (July 23, 1947), 13.

49. *Sporting News* (November 17, 1948), 8.

50. Ralph Kiner, interview with William Marshall, September 26, 1979, Chandler Oral History Project.

51. Bob Cain, interview with William Marshall, June 4, 1988, Chandler Oral History Project.

52. Little League baseball was initiated in 1939 in Williamsport, Pennsylvania. See Harold Seymour, *The People's Game* (New York: Oxford Univ. Press, 1990), 127-28.

53. *Sporting News* (November 12, 1947), 12. American Legion baseball was begun in 1927.

54. Andy Seminick, interview with William Marshall, March 2, 1989, Chandler Oral History Project.

55. Albert "Red" Schoendienst, interview with William Marshall, 1982, Chandler Oral History Project; Bob Broeg, "Red Loves to Take Chances," *Saturday Evening Post* (July 22, 1950), 96.

56. Bobby Shantz and Ralph Bernstein, *The Story of Bobby Shantz* (Philadelphia: J.B. Lippincott, 1953), 23-28.

57. *Sporting News* (October 3, 1951), 13.

58. *Sporting News* (September 12, 1951), 5.

59. Marshall interview.

60. Bob Lemon, interview with William Marshall, May 15, 1979, Chandler Oral History Project.

61. Kiner interview.

62. *Sporting News* (January 8, 1947), 3.

63. *Sporting News* (May 28, 1947), 1.

64. *Sporting News* (April 6, 1949), 4.

65. Cynthia Wilber, *For the Love of the Game: Baseball Memories from the Men Who Were There* (New York: William Morrow, 1992), 11.

66. *Sporting News* (June 18, 1947), 6

67. Violet A. Dickey, "I Married a Ballplayer," *Saturday Evening Post* (May 28, 1949), 34.

68. *Sporting News* (September 29, 1948), 2.

69. *Sporting News* (January 22, 1947), 2

70. *Sporting News* (February 22, 1950), 6.

71. *Sporting News* (November 19, 1947), 9.

72. *Sporting News* (October 13, 1948), 14, and (March 23, 1949), 28

73. Bob Broeg, *Stan Musial: "The Man's" Own Story as Told to Bob Broeg* (Garden City, N.Y.: Doubleday, 1964), 269.

74. *Sporting News* (November 15, 1945), 15, (January 14, 1948), 22, and (January 21, 1948), 22.

75. *Sporting News* (October 27, 1948), 19.

76. *Sporting News* (June 16, 1948), 12.

77. *Sporting News* (July 23, 1947), 11; Bill Veeck with Ed Linn, *Veeck—as in Wreck* (New York: G.P. Putnam's Sons, 1962), 115.

78. Ed Fitzgerald, ed., *The Story of the Brooklyn Dodgers* (New York: Bantam, 1949), 125.

79. Honig, 237-38.

80. Branch Rickey to Harold F. Reiser, January 20, 1945, Branch Rickey Papers, Library of Congress, box 78.

81. *Sporting News* (November 22, 1950), 11.

82. George Kell, interview with William Marshall, June 4, 1988, Chandler Oral History Project.

83. *Sporting News* (September 13, 1950), 6.

84. *Sporting News* (May 25, 1949), 13, (June 15, 1949), 7, and (August 24, 1949), 4.

85. *Sporting News* (June 27, 1951), 4.

86. *Sporting News* (April 7, 1948), 8.

87. *Sporting News* (April 20, 1949), 5.

88. *Sporting News* (December 22, 1948), 7.

89. *Sporting News* (March 8, 1950), 3

90. *Sporting News* (August 16, 1950), 11.

91. *Sporting News* (September 18, 1946), 2, and (July 6, 1949), 1.

92. *Sporting News* (March 28, 1951,) 6.

Chapter 17. The Great Triumvirate and Other Stars

1. Hank Greenberg, *Hank Greenberg: The Story of My Life,* ed. Ira Berkow (New York: Times Books, 1989), 176.

2. The incentives included (1) the construction of a "front porch" in left field only 340 feet from home plate, (2) the privilege of rooming by himself, (3) the ability to travel exclusively by air, (4) the promise that he would be given his unconditional release at the end of the season, and (5) a financial package that would earn him more than $100,000. Greenberg received a $40,000 salary from Pittsburgh to go along with the $75,000 he was getting from Detroit. Then, he purchased $74,000 worth of Pirates' stock and got the ballclub to agree to buy it back for $134,000. Thus, Greenberg paid a capital-gains tax on the $60,000 and income tax on the $40,000 (ibid., 179-81).

3. *Sporting News* (August 27, 1947), 5.

4. *Sporting News* (November 10, 1948), 20; Bob Broeg, *Stan Musial: "The Man's" Own Story as Told to Bob Broeg* (Garden City, N.Y.: Doubleday, 1964), 6-7.

5. Roy Campanella, *It's Good to Be Alive* (New York: Signet, New American Library, 1974), 33.

6. Ed Fitzgerald, "The Scooter that Carried the Yanks," *Sport* (January 1950), 28.

7. Ted Williams with John Underwood, *My Turn at Bat: The Story of My Life* (New York: Simon and Schuster, 1988), 29.

8. *Sporting News* (November 19, 1947), 7.

9. Jackie Robinson, as told to Alfred Duckett, *I Never Had It Made* (New York: G.P. Putnam's Sons, 1972), 16-17.

10. Bob Richelson. "Baseball's Vanishing American," *Sports Stars* (October 1950), 78.

11. *Sporting News* (December 1, 1948), 26.

12. Harry T. Paxton. "Everything Happens to Me," *Saturday Evening Post* (April 29, 1950), 117.

13. *Sporting News* (May 11, 1949), 14.

14. Tom Meany, "Hey DiMag! The Great Story of Two Brothers," *Sport* (April 1947), 62.

15. Bob Feller, *Strikeout Story* (New York: A.S. Barnes, 1947), 11-13.

16. Milton Gross, "Duke of the Dodgers," *Sport* (July 1951), 78.

17. Joe DiMaggio, *Lucky to Be a Yankee* (New York: Grosset and Dunlap, 1951), 47.

18. Ibid., 52.

19. Ed Linn, *Hitter: The Life and Turmoils of Ted Williams* (New York: Harcourt, Brace, 1993), 189-90.

20. Williams with Underwood, *My Turn at Bat*, 7.

21. Ibid., 37-39.

22. Broeg, *Stan Musial*, 22.

23. Bob Broeg, *The Superstars of Baseball: Their Lives, Their Loves, Their Laughs, Their Laments* (St. Louis: The Sporting News, 1971), 182.

24. *Sporting News* (May 16, 1946), 5.

25. Joe DiMaggio, *Lucky to Be a Yankee*, 196.

26. Maury Allen, *Where Have You Gone, Joe DiMaggio? The Story of America's Last Hero* (New York: E.P. Dutton, 1975), 46.

27. *Sporting News* (April 11, 1946), 10.

28. Tommy Henrich with Bill Gilbert, *Five O'Clock Lightning: Ruth, Gehrig, DiMaggio, Mantle and the Glory Years of the New York Yankees* (New York: Birch Lane Press, Carol Publishing Group, 1992), 114.

29. Ned Garver, interview with William Marshall, June 3, 1988, A.B. Chandler Oral History Project, Special Collections and Archives, Univ. of Kentucky Libraries (hereafter cited as Chandler Oral History Project).

30. Broeg, *The Superstars of Baseball*, 68.

31. Allen, 40.

32. *Sporting News* (March 3, 1948), 13.

33. *Sporting News* (August 20, 1947), 13.

34. *Sporting News* (July 14, 1948), 3.

35. Bob Broeg, *Stan Musial*, 250.

36. Ted Williams with John Underwood, *The Science of Hitting* (New York: Simon and Schuster, 1986), 37; Williams with Underwood, *My Turn at Bat*, 63.

37. *Sporting News* (June 2, 1948), 1.

38. Joseph Paparella, interview with William Marshall, March 16, 1988, Chandler Oral History Project.

39. Gene Woodling, interview with William Marshall, December 11, 1992, Chandler Oral History Project.

40. Williams with Underwood, *The Science of Hitting*, 34, 38-40.

41. *Sporting News* (July 14, 1948), 3.

42. *Sporting News* (January 24, 1946), 2.

43. *Sporting News* (April 14, 1948), 7.

44. Jimmy Powers, "Will Ted Williams Ever Hit .400 Again?," *Sport* (July 1950), 10.

45. Williams with Underwood, *My Turn at Bat*, 16.

46. Bob Cain, interview with William Marshall, June 4, 1988, Chandler Oral History Project.

47. Garver interview.

48. Virgil Trucks, interview with William Marshall, May 11, 1988, Chandler Oral History Project.

49. *Sporting News* (July 17, 1946), 4.

50. Mel Harder, interview with William Marshall, June 1, 1988, Chandler Oral History Project; Williams with Underwood, *My Turn at Bat*, 106-7.

51. Harder interview.

52. Lou Boudreau, interview with William Marshall, 1983, Chandler Oral History Project.

53. Lou Boudreau with Russell Schneider, *Lou Boudreau: Covering All the Bases* (Champaign, Ill.: Sagamore Publishing, 1993), 85.

54. *Sporting News* (October 16, 1946), 2.

55. Michael Seidel, *Ted Williams: A Baseball Life* (Chicago: Contemporary Books, 1991), 343.

56. Williams with Underwood, *The Science of Hitting*, 56.

57. Jack Sher, "The Stan Musial Nobody Knows," *Sport* (March 1949), 58; Biggie Garagnani as told to J. Roy Stockton, "My Partner Stan Musial," *Sport* (July 1950), 38.

58. *Sporting News* (June 15, 1949), 9, and (September 8, 1948), 17.

59. *Sporting News* (September 7, 1949), 3.

60. Mel Allen, "The Yankees Nobody Knows," *Sport* (February 1948), 86.

61. *Sporting News* (June 25, 1947), 14.

62. David Halberstam, *Summer of '49* (New York: William Morrow, 1989), 58, 55.

63. Roger Kahn, *The Era: 1947-1957, When the Yankees, the Giants, and the Dodgers Ruled the World* (New York: Ticknor and Fields, 1993), 211.

64. *Sporting News* (February 4, 1948), 13.

65. Allen, 97.

66. Tom Meany and Tommy Holmes, *Baseball's Best: The All-Time Major League Baseball Team* (New York: Franklin Watts, 1964), 198-99.

67. Halberstam, 57.

68. *Sporting News* (January 19, 1949), 9.

69. *Sporting News* (August 22, 1951), 5.

70. Linn, *Hitter*, 131. Linn provides a superb description of Egan (130-34), as does David Halberstam in *Summer of '49*, 164-68.

71. *Sporting News* (April 27, 1949), 4.

72. Williams with Underwood, *My Turn at Bat*, 125.

73. *Sporting News* (May 24, 1950), 6.

74. *Sporting News* (June 21, 1950), 9.

75. *Sporting News* (May 24, 1950), 6

76. *Sporting News* (August 8, 1951), 13.

77. Ted Williams, interview with William Marshall, March 17, 1988, Chandler Oral History Project.

78. *Sporting News* (March 31, 1948), 4.

79. *Sporting News* (June 14, 1945), 11.

80. Projected numbers for World War II, 1943-45 seasons, and for Korea, 1952-53 seasons, were obtained by taking the statistics compiled from the three seasons on each side of the missed years and using the average figures for the missed seasons.

81. In 1950, the Yankees' payroll was $651,605, and the Red Sox payroll was $561,482. U.S. Congress, House of Representatives, *Study of Monopoly Power: Organized Baseball* (Washington, D.C.: Government Printing Office, 1951), ser. 1, pt. 1, 1610.

82. *Sporting News* (March 30, 1949), 14, and (February 16, 1949), 5.

83. *Sporting News* (February 12, 1947), 6

84. Bob Feller, interview with William Marshall, July 3, 1978, Chandler Oral History Project.

85. Ibid.

86. Ibid.

87. Ibid.

88. Ed Fitzgerald, "Bob Feller Incorporated," *Sport* (June 1947), 60.

89. *Sporting News* (September 25, 1946), 9.

90. Bob Lemon, interview with William Marshall, May 15, 1979, Chandler Oral History Project.

91. Feller interview.

92. Fitzgerald, "Bob Feller Incorporated," 59-60; *Sporting News* (January 14, 1948), 21.

93. Feller interview.

94. *Sporting News* (August 13, 1947), 2.

95. Frank Graham, "Bob Feller's Greatest Victory," *Sport* (August 1951), 36.

96. *Sporting News* (December 29, 1948), 11.

97. Jules Tygiel, *Baseball's Great Experiment* (New York: Oxford Univ. Press, 1983), 202.

98. *Sporting News* (October 22, 1947), 18, (October 29, 1947), 12, (November 12, 1947), 22, (December 24, 1947), 4, (February 4, 1948), 13, and (February 11, 1948), 1.

99. Harvey Frommer, *Rickey and Robinson: The Men Who Broke Baseball's Color Barrier* (New York: MacMillan, 1982), 156-57.

100. *Sporting News* (October 6, 1948), 23, (July 27, 1949), 2, (August 24, 1949), 20, (May 3, 1950), 21, and (May 10, 1950), 21.

101. *Sporting News* (April 20, 1949), 30.

102. *Sporting News* (January 14, 1948), 20, and (February 7, 1951), 4.

103. *Sporting News* (March 14, 1951), 2.

104. *Sporting News* (September 10, 1947) (Lifebuoy Soap), 39; and (July 14, 1948) (Winthrop Shoes), 36.

105. Biggie Garagnani, "My Partner Stan Musial," *Sport* (July 1950), 36.

106. Kell interview.

107. *Sporting News* (November 5, 1947, 17.

108. Kiner interview; *Sporting News* (January 24, 1951), 18.

109. *Sporting News* (September 21, 1949), 13.

110. *Sporting News* (January 21, 1948), 12.

111. Al Stump, "What's Ahead for Kiner?" Baseball Digest (August 1950), 20.

112. Branch Rickey to John W. Galbreath, March 21, 1952, Branch Rickey Papers, Library of Congress, box 99.

113. The Cubs received Kiner, Howie Pollet, Joe Garagiola, and George Metkovich and sent Toby Atwell, Bob Schultz, Preston Ward, George Freese, Bob Addis, Gene Hermanski, and $150,000 to Pittsburgh.

114. Kiner interview.

Chapter 18. 1950: Year of the Whiz Kids

1. *Sporting News* (December 20, 1950), 4.

2. *Sporting News* (December 27, 1950), 7.

3. *Sporting News* (September 20, 1950), 9.

4. *Sporting News* (May 3, 1950), 9.

5. *Sporting News* (March 8, 1950), 8.

6. *Sporting News* (January 4, 1950), 8.

7. *Sporting News* (April 5, 1950), 7.

8. *Sporting News* (May 10, 1950), 10-11.

9. The A's also sent the Browns outfielders Ray Coleman and Ray Ippolito and infielders Frank Guistine and Billy DeMars.

10. *Sporting News* (September 6, 1950), 6, and (October 25, 1950), 3.

11. *Sporting News* (August, 30, 1950), 8.

12. Appling's record was subsequently broken by Larry Bowa (2,222), Ozzie Smith (2,573), Luis Aparicio (2,581), and by current player Cal Ripken, Jr.

13. *Sporting News* (February 22, 1950), 9.

14. *Sporting News* (September 20, 1950), 1.

15. Ed Linn, *Hitter: The Life and Turmoils of Ted Williams* (New York: Harcourt, Brace, 1993), 309.

16. Harold Kaese, "Billy Goodman Makes Good," *Sport* (October 1949), 52.

17. George Kell, interview with William Marshall, June 4, 1988, A.B. Chandler Oral History Project, Special Collections and Archives, Univ. of Kentucky Libraries (hereafter cited as Chandler Oral History Project).

18. *Sporting News* (May 4, 1949), 7.

19. Bobby Brown, interview with William Marshall, September 11, 1985, Chandler Oral History Project.

20. Curt Gowdy with John Powers, *Seasons To Remember: The Way It Was in American Sports, 1945-1960* (New York: HarperCollins, 1993), 72.

21. Edmund Lopat, interview with William Marshall, August 26, 1988, Chandler Oral History Project

22. Ibid.

23. Gene Woodling, interview with William Marshall, December 11, 1992, Chandler Oral History Project.

24. Dom Forker, *The Men of Autumn,* (New York: Signet, New American Library, 1989), 6.

25. In early 1947, when Berra was down because of a mild batting slump, DiMaggio corrected him for not running out to the outfield the following inning. See Tommy Henrich

with Bill Gilbert, *Five O'Clock Lightning: Ruth, Gehrig, DiMaggio, Mantle and the Glory Years of the New York Yankees* (New York: Birch Lane Press, Carol Publishing Group, 1992), 158. In another instance, witnessed by Eddie Lopat a year later, DiMaggio, who played both games of a double-header and "was totally out on his feet," chewed Berra out in the clubhouse for almost twenty minutes because he did not want to catch the second game of the twin bill. See Jack B. Moore, *Joe DiMaggio: Baseball's Yankee Clipper* (New York: Praeger, 1987), 66-67.

26. Woodling interview.

27. *Sporting News* (November 15, 1950), 3.

28. *Sporting News* (September 6, 1950), 3.

29. Joe Trimble, *Phil Rizzuto: A Biography of the Scooter* (New York: A.S. Barnes, 1951), 154-55; Phil Rizzuto and Tom Horton. *The October Twelve: Five Years of New York Yankee Glory, 1949-1953* (New York: Forge, 1994), 66.

30. Trimble, 152.

31. *Sporting News* (September 6, 1950), 9.

32. *Sporting News* (September 20, 1950), 9.

33. Bobby Brown interview.

34. *Sporting News* (May 3, 1950), 7.

35. *Sporting News* (July 26, 1950), 11.

36. Willard Marshall, interview with William Marshall, September 13, 1985, Chandler Oral History Project; Jethroe lost a line drive in the lights off the bat of Granny Hamner in Shibe Park in August, 1950. The ball hit him flush in the mouth, split his upper lip, and broke his upper plate." *Sporting News* (August 23, 1950, 9.

37. *Sporting News* (April 12, 1950, 14.

38. *Sporting News* (September, 13, 1950), 8.

39. *Sporting News* (March 8, 1950), 11.

40. Willard Marshall interview.

41. *Sporting News* (July 26, 1950), 11.

42. *Sporting News* (August 23, 1950), 1.

43. Others who preceded Hodges included Bobby Lowe (May 30, 1894), Ed Delahanty (July 13, 1896), Lou Gehrig (June 3, 1932), Chuck Klein (July 10, 1936), and Pat Seerey (July 18, 1948).

44. *Sporting News* (September 13, 1950), 13.

45. *Sporting News* (December 13, 1950), 2.

46. *Philadelphia Bulletin* (October 1, 1967), VB1.

47. Frederick G. Lieb and Stan Baumgartner, *The Philadelphia Phillies* (New York: Putnam, 1953), 214.

48. Kevin Kerrane, *Dollar Sign on the Muscle: The World of Baseball Scouting* (New York: Avon, 1984), 62-63, 259.

49. *Sporting News* (August 9, 1950), 5. Baumgartner's figure breaks down thusly: $800,000 for player bonuses, $900,000 for the purchase of player contracts, and $1.8 million for scouting and farm system.

50. *Sporting News* (June 29, 1949), 3.

51. Andy Seminick, interview with William Marshall, March 2, 1989, Chandler Oral History Project.

52. *Sporting News* (January 4, 1950), 11.

53. *Sporting News* (May 3, 1950), 8.

54. *Sporting News* (June 14, 1950), 4.

55. *Sporting News* (May 17, 1950), 6.

56. *Sporting News* (September 6, 1950), 6.

57. *Sporting News* (May 3, 1950), 8, and (July 26, 1950), 4.

58. *Sporting News* (November 15, 1950), 7.

59. Ford and Pepe, *Slick*, 77.

60. Richard Whittingham, ed., *1942-1951*, vol. 2 of *The DiMaggio Albums*, (New York: G.P. Putnam's Sons, 1989), 693.

Chapter 19. Chandler's Waterloo

1. Fred Saigh, interview with William Marshall, May 16, 1978, A.B. Chandler Oral History Project, Special Collections and Archives, Univ. of Kentucky Libraries (hereafter cited as Chandler Oral History Project).

2. *Sporting News* (December 27, 1950), 6. Frank Yeutter discovered the deliberations on Chandler when a bellboy in the lobby of Soreno Hotel mistook him for an owner and asked him whether he knew they were voting on Chandler. When he replied in the affirmative and attempted to assure the hotel employee that Chandler would make it easily, the bellboy replied, "The hell he will. I was just in the room delivering some more ice water and you should have heard the fracas that was going on. He hasn't a Chinaman's chance of being elected."

3. Ibid.

4. Walter "Red" Smith, *New York Herald-Tribune*, March 14, 1951; Red Smith, interview with William Marshall, November 13, 1979, Chandler Oral History Project; Stanley Woodward, *New York Herald-Tribune*, March 1951, in *Sporting News* clippings files; Gene Kessler, *Chicago Sun-Times*, 1947, in *Sporting News* clippings files; John Lardner, *Newsweek* (October 18, 1948), 87; Arthur Daley, *New York Times* (December 13, 1950), 55; and Gerry Hern, unidentified newspaper clipping dated December 13, 1950, in *Sporting News* files.

5. Smith interview.

6. Shirley Povich, interview with William Marshall, March 29, 1976, Chandler Oral History Project.

7. Walter "Red" Barber, interview with William Marshall, June 27, 1987, Chandler Oral History Project.

8. *New York Herald-Tribune*, March, 1951, clipping in *Sporting News* files.

9. William O. DeWitt, interview with William Marshall, October 1, 1980, Chandler Oral History Project.

10. Those who purportedly voted against the proposal included Fred Saigh, Horace Stoneham, Branch Rickey, Clark Griffith, and Connie Mack (Shirley Povich, "Happy Chandler Stumps for Reelection," *Sport* [July, 1950], 11, 84). Fred Saigh tells another story. In an interview with the author, he noted that his vote along with Webb, Perini, and Phil Wrigley were among the original five votes against Chandler (Saigh interview).

11. Saigh interview.

12. John P. Carmichael, *Boston Globe* (March 13, 1951), 46.

13. Confidential report re: Ownership of St. Louis Cardinals Fred M. Saigh, Jr. by Robert E. A. Boyle (compiled February 26-March 1, 1949), Chandler Papers, box 162.

14. Saigh interview.

15. *Sporting News* (June 14, 1950), 8.

16. *New York Mirror*, ca. 1951, undated clipping in the Chandler Papers, box 577.

17. The Yankees were forced to keep Dick Wakefield and to guarantee his $17,000 salary because the White Sox pulled out of a deal for him when he refused to report on time (Carmichael, 46).

18. Saigh interview.

19. A.B. "Happy" Chandler, interview with William Marshall, December 4, 1980, Chandler Oral History Project.

20. *Sporting News* (April 18, 1951), 8.

21. Hy Goldberg, "Sports in the News," *Newark Evening News* (1965), the Chandler Papers, box 584.

22. Harold Kaese, *Boston Globe*, undated, in *Sporting News* clippings files; Carmichael.

23. Carl Erskine, interview with William Cooper, May 25, 1978, Chandler Oral History Project.

24. *Philadelphia Evening Bulletin* (February 27, 1951), 52

25. *Boston Globe*, March 13, 1951, 46.

26. Saigh interview.

27. DeWitt interview, October 1, 1980.

28. Ibid.

29. *New York Times* (December 12, 1950), 48.

30. *Sporting News* (December 27, 1950), 3-4.

31. DeWitt interview, October 1, 1980.

32. Saigh interview.

33. *Sporting News* (December 20, 1950), 4; *New York Times* (December 13, 1950), 52.

34. *Sporting News* (August 16, 1950), 2.

35. *Sporting News* (November 29, 1950), 10, and (November 15, 1950), 2.

36. Chandler interview, November 7, 1984.

37. Povich interview.

38. *Sporting News* (December 20, 1950), 3.

39. *New York Times* (December 14, 1950), 14.

40. Saigh interview.

41. Undated clipping from *New York Daily Mirror*, ca. early 1951, Chandler Papers, box 577.

42. *Sporting News* (January 3, 1951), 4.

43. Gillette's gamble paid off handsomely. Thirty-seven of a possible forty-two World Series games were played during the next six years. The only lopsided Series during the period was the Giants' 4-0 sweep of the Indians in 1954.

44. *Sporting News* (August 16, 1950), 2.

45. *Sporting News* (January 24, 1951), 2.

46. *New York Times* (February 5, 1951), 25.

47. Clark Griffith to A.B. Chandler, January 22, 1951, Orlando, Florida, Chandler Papers, box 162.

48. Povich interview.

49. *Sporting News* (December 27, 1950), 11.

50. *Lexington Herald-Leader* (March 11, 1951), 18; *Sporting News* (March 7, 1951), 9.

51. *St. Louis Post-Dispatch* (March 11, 1951), 5d.

52. DeWitt interview, October 1, 1980.

53. William Veeck, interview with William Marshall, February 23, 1977, Chandler Oral History Project.

54. Roger Doulens to A.B. Chandler, February 22, 1951, n.p., Chandler Papers, box 162.

55. *Boston Globe* (March 13, 1951), 46.

56. See Boyle report, Chandler Papers, box 162.

57. *Lexington Herald* (March 10, 1951), 6.

58. Bill Cunningham, *Boston Herald*, undated newspaper clipping, ca. March 1951, Chandler Papers, box 577.

59. Roger Doulens to A.B. Chandler, February 19, 1951, Chandler Papers, box 162.

60. Roger Doulens to A.B. Chandler, February 22, 1951, n.p., Chandler Papers, box 162.

61. *Lexington Herald* (March 11, 1951), 18.

62. *St. Louis Post-Dispatch* (March 11, 1951), 5d.

63. *New York Times* (March 12, 1951), 23.

64. *Boston Globe* (March 13, 1951), 18 (1st ed.). William O. DeWitt maintained that Yawkey was anti-Chandler "all-the-way." DeWitt interview, October 1, 1980.

65. *St. Louis Post-Dispatch* (March 12, 1951), 4b.

66. *Boston Herald* (March 13, 1951), 18.

67. *Sporting News* (March 21, 1951), 5.

68. *St. Louis Post-Dispatch* (March 12, 1951), 4b.

69. *New York Times* (March 12, 1951), 28; *Boston Globe* (March 13, 1951), 18.

70. *Boston Globe* (March 14, 1951).

71. John Galbreath, interview with William Marshall, May 22, 1981, Chandler Oral History Project.

72. *Sporting News* (March 21, 1951), 5-6.

73. DeWitt interview, October 1, 1980.

74. *Sporting News* (March 21, 1951), 6.

75. *Boston Herald* (March 13, 1951), 18.

76. Statement by Congressman Emanuel Celler, May 18, 1951, Chandler Papers, box 162.

77. John Lord O'Brian to Albert B. Chandler, May 21, 1951, Chandler Papers, box 162.

78. *New York Times* (July 16, 1951), 16.

79. *Sporting News* (March 21, 1951), 6.

80. *Sporting News* (January 3, 1951), 12.

81. *Sporting News* (December 20, 1950), 4.

82. *Boston Globe* (March 13, 1951), 46.

83. *Boston Daily Record* (December 16, 1950), 41.

84. *St. Louis Post-Dispatch* (December 24, 1950), 3E.

85. Bowie Kuhn, interview with William Marshall, May 12, 1977, Chandler Oral History Project.

86. U.S. Congress, House of Representatives, *Study of Monopoly Power: Organized Baseball* (Washington, D.C.: Government Printing Office, 1951) ser. 1, pt. 1, 1616.

87. Chandler Papers, boxes 165-70.

88. *St. Louis Post-Dispatch* (March 20, 1951), 1B; *New York Times* (March 20, 1951), 37; *Sporting News* (March 28, 1951), 2.

89. *Sporting News* (December 27, 1950), 5.

90. David Voight, *From Postwar Expansion to the Electronic Age,* vol. 3 of *American Baseball* (University Park: Pennsylvania State Univ. Press, 1983), 95.

91. *Sporting News* (July 4, 1951), 10.

Chapter 20. 1951: The Shot Heard 'Round the World

1. *Sporting News* (May 30, 1951), 11. See also William Manchester, *American Caesar: Douglas MacArthur, 1880-1964* (Boston: Little, Brown, 1978), 666.

2. *Sporting News* (May 16, 1951), 1-2.

3. *Sporting News* (August 1, 1951), 1, 4, and (August 22, 1951), 9.

4. *Sporting News* (January 10, 1951), 7.

5. Ibid., 22.

6. *Sporting News* (June 20, 1951), 14.

7. Other pitchers to win twenty games with a last-place team since 1900 include Noodles Hahn, Reds (22-19, 1901), Scott Perry, A's (21-19, 1918), Howard Ehmke, Red Sox (20-17, 1923), Steve Carlton, Phillies (27-10, 1972), Nolan Ryan, Angels (22-16, 1974), and Phil Niekro, Braves (21-20, 1977).

8. Ned Garver, interview with William Marshall, June 3, 1988, A.B. Chandler Oral History Project, Special Collections and Archives, Univ. of Kentucky Libraries (hereafter cited as Chandler Oral History Project).

9. Bill Veeck with Ed Linn, *Veeck—as in Wreck* (New York: G.P. Putnam's Sons, 1962), 219.

10. Ibid., 12-13. Although Veeck was very aware of Thurber's story, he maintained that he was inspired more by the tales he heard as a child from the lips of Giants' manager John McGraw, a frequent guest at the Veeck home in Chicago. Veeck recalled that McGraw often talked about sending little Eddie Morrow to the plate. Morrow was a hunchback kept by the Giants as a good-luck charm.

11. Joseph Paparella, interview with William Marshall, March 16, 1988, Chandler Oral History Project.

12. Bob Cain, interview with William Marshall, June 4, 1988, Chandler Oral History Project.

13. *Sporting News* (August 29, 1951), 6-7.

14. Veeck, 222.

15. *Sporting News* (June 20, 1951), 3.

16. *Sporting News* (May 30, 1951), 11.

17. *Sporting News* (August 22, 1951), 7.

18. The first of Cy Young's three no-hitters occurred in the nineteenth century. Other pitchers with three or more career no-hitters include Larry Corcoran (3), Jim Maloney (3; he lost the first 1-0 after giving up two hits in the eleventh inning), Sandy Koufax (4), and Nolan Ryan (7).

19. Other switch-hitters in the major leagues at the time of Mantle's arrival included pitchers Steve Gromek, Hal Newhouser, Bob Chesnes, Russ Meyer, and Early Wynn, outfielders Dave Philley, Pete Reiser, and Sam Jethroe, and infielder Red Schoendienst.

20. Mickey Mantle with Herb Gluck, *The Mick* (Garden City, N.Y.: Doubleday, 1985), 48.

21. *Sporting News* (April 25, 1951), 4.

22. *Sporting News* (April 4, 1951), 3

23. *Sporting News* (July 25, 1951), 12.

24. Peter Golenback, *Dynasty: The New York Yankees, 1949-1964,* (Englewood Cliffs, N.J.: Prentice-Hall, 1975), 68.

25. Billy Martin and Peter Golenback, *Number 1* (New York: Dell, 1980), 159.

26. Maury Allen, *Where Have You Gone, Joe DiMaggio? The Story of America's Last Hero* (New York: E.P. Dutton, 1975), 163.

27. *Sporting News* (August 22, 1951), 5.

28. Golenback, *Dynasty*, 67.

29. Murray Polner, *Branch Rickey: A Biography* (New York: Signet, 1983), 226.

30. Jack O'Brien, "The Man Who Beat the Yankees," *Esquire Magazine* (May 1954), 115.

31. To go along with ex-Cardinals Murry Dickson and Rocky Nelson, the Pirates acquired Howie Pollet, Joe Garagiola, Dick Cole, Ted Wilks, and Bill Howerton from Cardinals for Cliff Chambers and Wally Westlake on June 15, 1951. Ex-Dodgers included Monty Basgall and Pete Reiser.

32. Pete Castiglione, interview with William Marshall, September 7, 1991, Chandler Oral History Project.

33. *Sporting News* (March 28, 1951), 4.

34. Ibid., 9.

35. *Sporting News* (May 23, 1951), 2.

36. *Sporting News* (May 16, 1951), 11.

37. Bobby Thomson, interview with William Marshall, September 13, 1985, Chandler Oral History Project.

38. Peter Golenback, *Bums: An Oral History of the Brooklyn Dodgers* (New York: Pocket Books, 1986), 284.

39. *Sporting News* (May 9, 1951), 4.

40. *Sporting News* (June 27, 1951), 1; Harvey Rosenfeld, *The Great Chase: The Dodgers-Giants Pennant Race of 1951* (Jefferson, N.C.: McFarland, 1992), 23.

41. Bobby Thomson with Lee Heiman and Bill Gutman, *"The Giants Win the Pennant! The Giants Win the Pennant!" The Amazing 1951 National League Season and the Home Run That Won It All* (New York: Zebra Books, 1991), 130.

42. *Sporting News* (June 27, 1951), 9.

43. Thomson, Heiman, and Gutman, 147-48.

44. *Sporting News* (October 10, 1951), 6.

45. *Sporting News* (September 5, 1951), 3.

46. Willie Mays and Charles Bernstein, *Willie Mays: My Life in and out of Baseball* (New York: E.P. Dutton, 1966), 29.

47. Willie Mays with Lou Sahadi, *Say Hey: The Autobiography of Willie Mays* (New York: Pocket Books, 1989), 57.

48. *Sporting News* (September 19, 1951), 4.

49. Rosenfeld, 28.

50. Others accomplishing the feat before Mueller included Cap Anson, 1884, Ty Cobb, 1925, Tony Lazzeri, 1936, and Ralph Kiner, twice in 1947.

51. *Sporting News* (September 5, 1951), 4.

52. Ibid., 5.

53. *Sporting News* (September 19, 1951), 7.

54. Ernie Harwell, interview with William Marshall, June 2, 1988, Chandler Oral History Project.

55. Thomson interview.

56. Golenback, *Bums*, 295-96.

57. Bob Costas, in Bob Edwards, *Fridays with Red: A Radio Friendship* (New York: Simon and Schuster, 1993), 114.

58. Frank Graham, *The New York Giants* (New York: G.P. Putnam's Sons, 1952), 306.

59. Thomas Kiernan, *The Miracle at Coogan's Bluff* (New York: Thomas Y. Crowell, 1975). Cartoonist Willard Mullin, of the *New York World-Telegram and Sun,* coined the home run "the Little Miracle of Coogan's Bluff." Graham, 306.

60. Ray Robinson, *The Home Run Heard 'Round the World: The Dramatic Story of the 1951 Giants-Dodgers Pennant Race* (New York: Harper-Collins, 1991), 230

61. Rosenfeld, 259.

62. Dave Anderson, ed., *The Red Smith Reader* (New York: Random House, 1982), 120.

63. Others who accomplished the feat included Elmer Smith (1920), Tony Lazzeri (1936), Mike Cuellar (1970), Dave McNally (1970), Ron Cey (1977), Dusty Baker (1977), Don Baylor (1982), and Lonnie Smith (1992).

Chapter 21. Baseball Then and Now

1. Tom Callahan, "A Commissioner on Deck," *Time Magazine* (March 12, 1984), 58.

2. *Sporting News* (November 28, 1951), 4.

3. University of Virginia law professor E. Gerald White noted that, "In retrospect, the inaction of both the Supreme Court and Congress may appear stunning. Not only was Organized Baseball undeniably an enterprise in interstate commerce, other 'entertainment' industries, such as the motion picture industry, had been held to come within the antitrust laws" (E. Gerald White, *Creating the National Pastime: Baseball Transforms Itself, 1903-1953* [Princeton, N.J.: Princeton Univ. Press, 1996], 299).

4. *Sporting News* (October 24, 1951), 2.

5. Calvin Griffith moved the original franchise to Minnesota for the 1961 season, and the expansion Senators were moved to Texas in 1972.

6. Red Smith, "Has Baseball Forgotten the Fan?" *Saturday Evening Post* (October 4, 1947), 169.

7. David Voight, *From Postwar Expansion to the Electronic Age,* vol. 3 of *American Baseball* (University Park: Pennsylvania State Univ. Press, 1983), xvii.

8. Grantland Rice, "Is Baseball Afraid of Television?" *Sport* (April, 1951), 90.

9. Ibid.

10. Roger Kahn, *The Era 1947-1957: When the Yankees, the Giants, and the Dodgers Ruled the World* (New York: Ticknor and Fields, 1993), 286.

11. In 1949 under Rule 1 (d), Commissioner Chandler bowed to the will of the Justice Department and eliminated most broadcasting restrictions on major-league games in minor-league areas.

12. Neil J. Sullivan, *The Minors* (New York: St. Martin's Press, 1991), 240-41.

13. Ralph Kiner, interview with William Marshall, September 26, 1979, A.B. Chandler Oral History Project, Special Collections and Archives, Univ. of Kentucky Libraries (hereafter cited as Chandler Oral History Project).

14. Peter Gammons, "1950 vs. 1990: A Tale of Two Eras," *Sports Illustrated* (April 16, 1990), 28.

15. In 1951 players stole 866 bases. Players on the same franchises stole 1,641 in 1995. Statistics drawn from J.C. Taylor, compiler, *Baseball Guide and Record Book* (St. Louis: Charles C. Spink and Son, 1952 and *Baseball America's 1996 Almanac* (Durham, N.C.: Baseball America, 1995).

16. Gene Woodling, interview with William Marshall, December 11, 1992, Chandler Oral History Project.

17. Charlie Metro, interview with William Marshall, June 13, 1991, Chandler Oral History Project.

18. Joseph Paparella, interview with William Marshall, March 16, 1988, Chandler Oral History Project.

19. Robert Brown, interview with William Marshall, September 11, 1985, Chandler Oral History Project.

20. George Kell, interview with William Marshall, June 4, 1988, Chandler Oral History Project.

21. Willard Marshall, interview with William Marshall, September 13, 1985, Chandler Oral History Project.

22. Frank Baumholtz, intervew with William Marshall, December 10, 1992, Chandler Oral History Project.

23. Woodling interview.

24. Brown interview.

25. Pete Castiglione, interview with William Marshall, September 7, 1991, Chandler Oral History Project.

26. Paparella interview.

27. Ernie Harwell, interview with William Marshall, June 2, 1988, Chandler Oral History Project.

28. Baumholtz interview.

29. Kell interview.

30. Harry Walker, interview with William Marshall, May 11, 1988, Chandler Oral History Project.

31. Hal Schumacher, interview with William Marshall, June 17, 1987, Chandler Oral History Project.

32. Walker interview.

33. Paparella interview.

34. Baumholtz interview.

35. Paparella and Woodling interviews.

36. Woodling interview.

37. Al Lopez, interview with William Marshall, April 23, 1980, Chandler Oral History Project.

38. Hitters in 1951 struck out only 11 percent of the time, while those in 1995 struck out 18 percent of the time. The ratios of walks to at bats were strikingly similar (.093187 in 1995 to .095778 in 1951). Statistics drawn from *Baseball Guide and Record Book, 1952*, and *Baseball America 1996 Almanac*.

39. Ibid. Hitters in 1951 connected for a home run 2.2 percent of the time, while in 1995 they did so 3 percent of the time.

40. Paparella interview.

41. Baseball was played with an ersatz baseball during World War II because of a yarn shortage. The owners experimented with a livelier ball in 1969 but quickly abandoned that effort. See George Will, *Men at Work: The Craft of Baseball* (New York: Harper Perennial, 1991), 104, 106.

42. Virgil Trucks, interview with William Marshall, May 11, 1988, Chandler Oral History Project.

43. Barney McCosky, interview with William Marshall, March 16, 1988, Chandler Oral History Project.

44. Lopez interview

45. Harwell interview.

46. Harder interview.

47. Bob Cain, interview with William Marshall, June 4, 1988, Chandler Oral History Project.

48. Garver interview.

49. *The Diamond* (November 1993), 28.

50. Marshall interview.

51. Baumholtz interview.

52. McCosky interview.

53. Cain interview.

54. The issues during those stoppages were pensions (March 13-April 13, 1972), arbitration (February 8-25, 1980), free agency (February 25-March 17, 1980), free-agent compensation (April 1-9, 1980, and June 12-August 10, 1981), salary cap/arbitration (August 6-7, 1985, and February 15-March 18, 1990), and salary cap (August 11, 1994-May 1, 1995). See *Baseball Weekly* (August 17-23, 1994), 4-5.

55. *Image: The Magazine of the San Francisco Examiner* (April 11, 1993), 11. When Bonds left Pittsburgh, "he was subject to such belittling headlines as 'Bonds offered golden egg, asks Pirates for the goose' and 'Business advice for Bucs: Junk Bonds" (14).

56. During 1993, seats from Ebbets Field or the Polo Grounds sold for more than $2,000, and a San Francisco auction, where a Ted Williams 1955 home jersey sold for $93,500 and Joe DiMaggio's 1939 home jersey brought $132,000, realized $1.5 million for 135 items (*USA Today Baseball Weekly* [September 22-28, 1993], 18).

57. *Washington Post Magazine* (January 29, 1995), 16.

58. *Baseball America's 1996 Almanac*, 6.

59. Red Smith, "Has Baseball Forgotten the Fan?" *Saturday Evening Post* (October 4, 1947), 24-25

60. *USA Today Baseball Weekly* (August 17-23, 1994), 6.

61. This is based on a survey conducted periodically since 1990 by Leisure Trends Group, a firm affiliated with the Gallup Poll. *Lexington Herald-Leader* (June 25, 1996), B5.

62. *USA Today Baseball Weekly* (April 17-23, 1996), 21; *Lexington Herald-Leader* (May 10, 1996), C4.

63. *St. Louis Post-Dispatch* (May 15, 1994), F1. Figure includes parking, concessions, souvenirs, program, and tickets. See Shannon Dortch, "The Future of Baseball," *American Demographics* (April 1996), 22-28, 57.

Sources

Along with the more than eighty oral history interviews listed in the preface, general primary source materials crucial to a study of the Pivotal Era include the Branch Rickey Papers, Arthur Mann Papers, and Emanuel Celler Papers, all at the Library of Congress, and the A.B. Chandler Papers at the University of Kentucky. Contemporary periodicals and newspapers of importance to the period are the *Sporting News, Baseball Magazine, Baseball Digest, Sport Magazine, Collier's,* the *Saturday Evening Post,* and the *New York Times.* Contemporary season summaries and statistical information is also provided by two other *Sporting News* publications, the *Official Baseball Guide* and the *Baseball Register* (1945-52). Current statistical resources of course include Rick Wolff, ed., *The Baseball Encyclopedia* (9th ed., 1993), and John Thorn and Pete Palmer, eds., *Total Baseball* (4th ed., 1995).

General baseball works that provide significant interpretations of the period are Robert Smith, *Baseball* (1970), Charles Alexander, *Our Game: An American Baseball History* (1991), Benjamin Rader, *Baseball: A History of America's Game* (1994), G. Edward White, *Creating the National Pastime: Baseball Transforms Itself, 1903-1953* (1996), and David Voight's monumental work *American Baseball* (3 vols.; 1966-83). Two other important works also encompass years within the Pivotal Era's time period: Roger Kahn, *The Era 1947-1957: When the Yankees, the Giants, and the Dodgers Ruled the World* (1993), and J. Ron Oakley *Baseball's Last Golden Age, 1946-1960: The National Pastime in a Time of Glory and Change* (1994).

Baseball's World War II period is well represented in baseball literature by Bill Gilbert, *They Also Served: Baseball and the Homefront, 1941-1945* (1992), Richard Goldstein, *Spartan Seasons: How Baseball Survived World War II* (1980), and William B. Meade, *Even the Browns* (1978). The latter was later expanded, with the addition of a conclusion by Harold Rosenthal, to produce *The 10 Worst Years of Baseball* (1982).

The 1946 season is covered in Frederick Turner, *When the Boys Came Back: Baseball and 1946* (1996). Topics that await full monographic treatment include Robert Murphy's attempt to unionize the Pittsburgh Pirates and the Mexican League raids. Murphy and the American Baseball Guild and the Danny Gardella story are included in Lee Lowenfish and Tony Lupien, *The Imperfect Diamond: The Story of Baseball's Reserve System and the Men Who Fought to Change It* (1980), and the best piece on the Mexican League raids is Frank Graham, Jr.'s "The Great Mexican War," in *Sports Illustrated* (September 19, 1966). John Phillips' insightful seventy-nine page work, *The Mexican-Jumping Beans: The Story of the Baseball War of 1946* (1947), furnishes new details about the league, while Alan M. Klein, *Baseball on the Border: A Tale of Two Laredos* (1997), provides a good historical background on Mexican baseball. A Mexican vantage point is provided in Jorge Pasquel's biography Teodulo M. Agundis, *El Verdadero Jorge Pasquel: Ensayo Biographico Sobre un Caracter* (1957). Issues involving the reserve clause are located in testimony found in the 1951 Celler House Judiciary Committee Hearings (1952).

The tumultuous 1947 season is excitingly described by Red Barber in *1947: When All Hell Broke Loose in Baseball* (1982). The most detailed account of Leo Durocher's 1947 suspension from baseball is found in Arthur Mann, *Baseball Confidential* (1952). Other insights are provided by Harold Parrott, *The Lords of Baseball* (1976), Leo Durocher with Ed Linn, *Nice Guys Finish Last* (1975), and Gerald Eskenazi, *The Lip: A Biography of Leo Durocher* (1993).

The breaking of the color barrier and the Jackie Robinson saga has deservedly received more attention than any other event during the Pivotal Era. Foremost is Jules Tygiel's landmark work, *Baseball's Great Experiment: Jackie Robinson and His Legacy* (1983). Background material on Robinson and the Negro Leagues can be gleaned from Robert Peterson's pioneering book *Only the Ball was White* (1970), Janet Bruce, *The Kansas City Monarchs: Champions of Black Baseball* (1985), John Holway, *Voices From the Great Black Baseball Leagues* (1976), Effa Manley and Leon H. Hardwick, *Negro Baseball . . . Before Integration* (1976), Donn Rogosin, *Invisible Men: Life in Baseball's Negro Leagues* (1983), Dick Clark and Larry Lester, eds., *The Negro Leagues Book* (1994), and James A. Riley, *The Biographical Encyclopedia of the Negro Baseball Leagues* (1994).

Jackie and Rachel Robinson's own stories are covered in Jackie Robinson and Wendell Smith, *Jackie Robinson: My Own Story* (1948), Jackie Robinson and Carl T. Rowan, *Wait Till Next Year* (1960), Jackie Robinson and Alfred Duckett, *I Never Had It Made* (1972), Rachel Robinson and Lee Daniels, *Jackie Robinson: An Intimate Portrait* (1996), and Arnold Rampersad, *Jackie Robinson: A Biography* (1997). Other important works on Robinson include Arthur Mann, *The Jackie Robinson Story* (1950), David Falkner, *Great Time Coming: The Life of Jackie Robinson from Baseball to Birmingham* (1995), and

Harvey Frommer, *Rickey and Robinson* (1982). Biographical accounts of other significant black major-league pioneers include Roy Campanella, *It's Good to Be Alive* (1959), Joseph T. Moore, *Pride Against Prejudice: The Biography of Larry Doby* (1988), Monte Irvin and James Riley, *Nice Guys Finish First* (1996), Willie Mays and Charles Einstein, *My Life in and out of Baseball* (1966), Willie Mays and Lou Sahadi, *Say Hey: The Biography of Willie Mays* (1988), Hank Aaron and Lonnie Wheeler, *I Had a Hammer: The Hank Aaron Story* (1991), LeRoy "Satchel" Paige and Hal Lebowitz, *Pitchin' Man* (1948), LeRoy "Satchel" Paige and David Lipman, *Maybe I'll Pitch Forever* (1993), and Mark Ribowsky, *Don't Look Back: Satchel Paige in the Shadows of Baseball* (1994).

Full-fledged accounts of the 1948 season have only recently appeared with the publication of David Kaiser, *Epic Season: The 1948 American League Pennant Race* (1998) and Russell Schneider, *The Boys of the Summer of '48* (1998). Bill Veeck and Ed Linn, *Veeck as in Wreck* (1962), also provides delightful vignettes of the season. The great pennant race in 1949 between the New York Yankees and Boston Red Sox is beaufifully told by David Halberstam, in *Summer of '49* (1989), and the 1950 season is chronicled by C. Paul Rogers and Robin Roberts in *The Whiz Kids and the 1950 Pennant* (1996). The 1951 season, which was capped in the National League by Bobby Thomson's dramatic playoff game home run, has a literary genre of its own. Included in this group are Thomas Kiernan, *Miracle at Coogan's Bluff* (1975), Bobby Thomson with Lee Heiman and Bill Gutman, *"The Giants Win the Pennant! The Giants Win the Pennant!"* (1991), Harvey Rosenfeld, *The Great Chase: The Dodgers-Giants Pennant Race of 1951* (1992), and Ray Robinson, *The Home Run Heard 'Round the World: The Dramatic Story of the 1951 Giants-Dodgers Pennant Race* (1991).

While a plethora of works on the minor leagues is beginning to appear, the area still remains wide open for scholarship. Significant books include Robert Obojski, *Bush League: A History of Minor League Baseball* (1975), Neil J. Sullivan, *The Minors: The Struggles and Triumphs of Baseball's Poor Relations* (1991), Bill O'Neal, *The Texas League* (1987) and *The Pacific Coast League* (1990), Paul J. Zingg and Mark D. Medeiros, *Runs, Hits, and an Era: The Pacific Coast League, 1903-1958* (1994), and Kevin Kerrane, *Dollar Sign on the Muscle: The World of Baseball Scouting* (1984). The testimony of Seymour Block and Ross Horning in the Celler Hearings (1951) is also enlightening.

A number of player histories have employed oral history interviews to supply a rich vein of information on major-league players during the period, including Donald Honig, *A Donald Honig Reader* (1988), Roger

Kahn, *The Boys of Summer* (1972), Peter Golenback, *Dynasty: The New York Yankees, 1949-1964* (1975), and *Bums: An Oral History of the Brooklyn Dodgers* (1984), Dom Forker, *The Men of Autumn: An Oral History of the 1949-1953 World Champion New York Yankees* (1989), Phil Rizzuto with Tom Horton, *The October Twelve* (1994), Cynthia Wilber, *For the Love of the Game: Baseball Memories from the Men Who Were There* (1992), David Craft and Tom Owens, *Redbirds Revisited: Great Memories and Stories from St. Louis Cardinals* (1990), and Danny Peary, *We Played the Game: 65 Players Remember Baseball's Greatest Era, 1947-1964* (1994).

Individual player biographies also abound with the "Great Triumvirate," Joe DiMaggio, Stan Musial, and Ted Williams receiving the most attention. Works sanctioned by DiMaggio include Joe DiMaggio with Tom Meany, *Lucky to be a Yankee* (1951), and Richard Whittingham, ed., *The DiMaggio Albums* (2 vols., 1989). Other insightful books are Maury Allen, *Where Have You Gone Joe DiMaggio? The Story of America's Last Hero* (1975), George DeGregorio, *Joe DiMaggio: An Informal Biography* (1981), Joseph Durso, *DiMaggio: The Last American Knight* (1995), and Jack B. Moore, *Baseball's Yankee Clipper* (1986). Stan Musial's story is told by Bob Broeg in *Stan Musial: "The Man's" Own Story* (1964), and *The Man, Stan: Musial, Then . . . and Now . . .* (1977), and Jerry Lansche, *Stan the Man Musial: Born to Be a Ballplayer* (1994). Ted Williams is well represented by three excellent works: Ted Williams and John Underwood, *My Turn at Bat: The Story of My Life* (1988), Michael Seidel, *Ted Williams: A Baseball Life* (1991), and Ed Linn, *Hitter: The Life and Turmoils of Ted Williams* (1993). Other significant player biographies include Rex Barney and Norman Macht, *Rex Barney's Thank Youuuu* (1993), Lou Boudreau with Russell Schneider, *Lou Boudreau: Covering All the Bases* (1993), Bob Feller, *Strikeout Story* (1947), Bob Feller and Bill Gilbert, *Now Pitching, Bob Feller* (1990), Whitey Ford and Phil Pepe, *Slick: My Life in and Around Baseball* (1987), Hank Greenberg and Ira Berkow, *Hank Greenberg: The Story of My Life* (1989), Tommy Henrich and Bill Gilbert, *Five O'Clock Lightning* (1992), Kirby Higbe and Martin Quigley, *The High Hard One* (1967), Ralph Kiner and Joe Gergen, *Kiner's Korner* (1987), Mickey Mantle, *The Quality of Courage* (1964), Mickey Mantle with Herb Gluck, *The Mick* (1985), Billy Martin and Peter Golenback, *Number 1* (1980), David M. Jordan, *A Tiger in His Time: Hal Newhouser and the Burden of Wartime Baseball* (1990), Joe Trimble, *Phil Rizzuto: A Biography of the Scooter* (1951), Duke Snider and Bill Gilbert, *The Duke of Flatbush* (1988), and Al Silverman, *Warren Spahn: Immortal Southpaw* (1961).

Other nonplaying participants also shed light on the Pivotal Era. Max Patkin's antics as a baseball entertainer are explored in Max Patkin and

Stan Hochman, *The Clown Prince of Baseball* (1994). The umpires are represented by Larry Gerlach's fine oral history, *The Men in Blue* (1980), and biographies by Babe Pinelli, *Mr. Ump* (1953), and Jocko Conlan and Robert Creamer, *Jocko* (1967). Broadcasters are the subject of Curt Smith's encyclopedic work, *Voices of the Game* (1987). Important works by individual broadcasters include Mel Allen and Ed FitzGerald, *You Can't Beat the Hours* (1965), Red Barber, *The Broadcasters* (1970), Red Barber with Robert Creamer, *Rhubarb in the Catbird Seat* (1968), Harry Caray and Bob Verdi, *Holy Cow* (1989), Curt Gowdy and John Powers, *Seasons to Remember: The Way It Was in American Sports, 1945-1960* (1993), Russ Hodges, *My Giants* (1963), and three books by Ernie Harwell, *Tuned to Baseball* (1985), *Ernie Harwell's Diamond Gems* (1991), and *The Babe Signed My Shoe* (1994).

   Although books by or on sportswriters are not common, several of note include Bob Broeg, *Memories of a Hall of Fame Sportswriter* (1995), Ira Berkow, *Red: A Biography of Red Smith* (1986), Earl Lawson, *Cincinnati Seasons: My 34 Years with the Reds* (1987), Fred Lieb, *Baseball as I Have Known It* (1977), and James Oldenkirk, *Plain Dealing: A Biography of Gordon Cobbledick* (1990). Works on or authored by baseball executives are also in short supply. Foremost are two biographies of Branch Rickey: Arthur Mann, *Branch Rickey: American in Action* (1957), and Murry Polner, *Branch Rickey: A Biography* (1982). Rickey's New York rival, Larry MacPhail, is the subject of Don Warfield, *The Roaring Redhead: Larry MacPhail—Baseball's Great Innovator* (1987), and baseball iconoclast Bill Veeck produced two humorous accounts of his fascinating career, in Bill Veeck and Ed Linn, *Veeck as in Wreck* (1962), and Bill Veeck with Ed Linn, *The Hustler's Handbook* (1965).

   To understand baseball's government, the rise of the commissioner–ship, and the tenor of its first twenty years, readers should see J.G. Taylor Spink, *Judge Landis and Twenty-Five Years of Baseball* (1974), David Pietrusza, *Judge and Jury: The Life and Times of Judge Kenesaw Mountain Landis* (1998), Richard C. Crespo, *Baseball: America's Diamond Mind, 1919-1941* (1981), and Harold Seymour, *Baseball, the Golden Age* (1971). Publications on baseball's second commissioner, A.B. "Happy" Chandler, appear in two *Sports Illustrated* articles, A.B. Chandler with John Underwood, "How I Jumped from Clean Politics into Dirty Baseball" (April 26, 1971), and "Gunned Down by the Heavies," (May 3, 1971). Another article, "A.B. Chandler as Baseball Commissioner: An Overview," by William Marshall, is found in *The Register of the Kentucky Historical Society* (Autumn 1984). Chandler's autobiography, Happy Chandler with Vance Trimble, *Heroes, Plain Folks, and Skunks: The Life and Times of Happy Chandler*, appeared in 1989. The most insightful picture of baseball immediately following

Chandler's tenure is contained in James Edward Miller's *The Baseball Business: Pursuing Pennants and Profits in Baltimore* (1990). Subsequent biographies of commissioners—particularly Ford C. Frick, *Games, Asterisks and People* (1973), and Bowie Kuhn, *Hardball: The Education of a Baseball Commissioner* (1987), also shed light on the Pivotal Era.

Finally, comparisons between the Pivotal Era and today's game offer endless discussion during long winter months. Former San Diego Padre (Pacific Coast League) owner Bill Starr argues for the "old" game in *Clearing the Bases* (1989), while respected baseball commentator Peter Gammons provides a more balanced approach in his clever *Sports Illustrated* piece "1950 vs. 1990: A Tale of Two Eras (April, 16, 1990).

Index